THE *A* TO *Z* OF
SUPERHERO MOVIES
FROM ABAR TO ZSAZSA VIA THE MCU

THE A TO Z OF
SUPERHERO MOVIES

FROM ABAR TO ZSAZSA VIA THE MCU

ROB HILL

PUBLISHING

For Stanley and Daisybelle

Published by Hunter Eve Publishing
Editor: Emma Hill
Cover design: Ben Turner
Designer: Eliza George
Production manager: Glenn Williams

First published in Great Britain in 2019
by Hunter Eve Publishing Limited,
17 Hedgeway, Guildford, Surrey, GU2 7RB

A CIP catalogue record for this title is
available from the British Library.

ISBN: 978-1-5272-4484-9

Printed and bound in The Netherlands

Contents

INTRODUCTION

Welcome to *The A-Z of Superhero Movies*, the most comprehensive exploration of the subject ever undertaken. Featuring around 2,000 blockbusters, mockbusters, foreign curiosities, hidden wonders, forgotten disasters and brazen ripoffs, the objective is to provide an entertaining and, crucially, *accessible* guide to a genre dominated, but certainly not limited, by the ubiquitous comic book movie. Beyond Hollywood's meddling billionaires and otherworldy deities lie an abundance of less familiar but equally well seasoned heroic archetypes, including Filipino transvestites, Italian rogues, Mexican wrestlers, Hindu deities and Turkish degenerates. Through these characters we can trace the surprising history of cultural attitudes to race, gender and sexuality, as well as our evolving fantasy of rightiousness. Perhaps we can even come to understand why there need to be four Inspector Gadget movies.

Reader's Manual

The main section of this book consists of over 1,000 entries, most featuring major credits, a brief synopsis, capsule review and star rating. When an entry is not reviewed and rated it's either due to a lack of availability (many older foreign movies are considered lost) or because it's a re-edited version of another entry (usually a serial cut down to feature-length). Star ratings range from one (run away) to five (shut up and take my money). Where possible and sensible I've used English language US release titles (with original foreign and prominent alternative titles below). Sequels are cited at the end of entries only when nomenclature renders their existance less than obvious. Entries in the main section are alphabetised using the word-at-a-time arrangement, which means *Superman* follows *Super Soul Brother* (in this sense and no other).

Around 1,000 further entries can be found in the Grouped Franchises section. When a particular series is missing so many titles that it makes more sense to discuss the actual property than the individual movies, it ends up here. More importantly, Grouped Franchises is also home to repetitive and impossibly extensive collections such as the 1960s Italian 'peplum' subgenre, Japanese tokusatsu properties such as Kamen Rider (there are dozens of them and they're all the same), and classic series featuring fringe superheroes such as Tarzan.

Towards the back of the book you'll find a small selection of statistics, suggestions and lists, including a complete catalogue of every superhero movie identified in this book.

For reasons of practicality terms such as 'hero' and 'superhero' are not applied gender specifically.

___

What is a superhero?

A good place to start when trying to approximate a universal definition is Stan Lee's observation that, "a superhero is a person who does heroic deeds and has the ability to do them in a way that a normal person couldn't." As elegant as that rationale is, we need to be flexible with it, and ultimately the *feel* of a character is as important as any exacting criteria. Luke Skywalker is not a superhero despite conforming to virtually all conceivable definitions. Batman is despite having no superpowers.

Adding to the problem of definition are the perspectives of different cultures and eras. Although Hollywood has rendered American comic book superheroes internationally ubiquitous, Mexico has traditionally had its luchadors, Japan its henshin heroes and Turkey its sado-masochistic misogynists (seriously Turkey, what's with your superheroes?). Most societies have their colourful, mythic protectors, but the combination of characteristics they employ varies, often in unexpected and interesting ways.

In curating the entries in this book I've been guided by a predictable criteria, but with contentious characters the line has to be drawn somewhere, and I'm sure it will often be in the wrong place for those with strong views on the subject. Some entries don't quite fit but deserve to be in the conversation, others might qualify on grounds of legacy or association, but, ultimately, the answer to questions such as "why Zorro but not Robin Hood?" or "why this robot/animal but not that one" must be "because I said so." There are good reasons, and I could spend a whole chapter torturously explaining them, but the world needs that about as much as it needs four Inspector Gadget movies.

___

What is a movie?

This is somewhat easier to answer. To be eligible a 'movie' must be at least one hour in length and have gained some form of distribution (these criteria eliminate the plethora of TV shows, horrifying fan films and Mighty Mouse cartoons that would otherwise swamp these pages). Entries may be drawn from animations, silents, serials, TV specials, pilots, unlicensed adaptations and even multi-episode narrative arcs (when subsequently edited and released as a stand alone movie). Ineligible are documentaries, motion comics and pornography. This is a book for fans of all ages and I have no intention of exposing children to the impropriety of motion comics.

Abar, the First Black Superman
★★★

1977, USA
Director: Frank Packard
Cast: J. Walter Smith, Tobar Mayo, Roxie Young

On moving to an 'exclusive' neighbourhood, African-American scientist Dr. Ken Kinkade (Smith) and his family are greeted with hostility by its universally white residents. But Kinkade is not the mild-mannered geneticist he appears, and his experimental elixir will turn radical activist Abar (Mayo) into the First Black Superman.

Often bracketed with the era's blaxploitation B-movies, this first legitimate outing for an African-American superhero gives us an angrier, more intelligent protagonist than the conspicuously cool urban ego-trips of *Shaft* and *Super Fly*. As Public Enemy to their Kanye West, Abar's social commentary is rough, uncompromising and pervasive. There's some ropey acting and the technical standard is poor, but the zeal director Frank Packard brings to his full-frontal assault on American inequality compensates.

ABCs of Superheroes: see *League of Superheroes*

The Adventures of Buckaroo Banzai Across the 8th Dimension ★★★★

1984, USA
Director: W.D. Richter
Cast: Peter Weller, John Lithgow, Ellen Barkin

Supernaturally gifted Buckaroo Banzai (Weller) must prevent an invasion from the eighth dimension.

'Proto-revisionist pseudo superhero movie' is as good a label as any for this infamously unclassifiable comedic adventure. Banzai excels to genius level in various fields (brain surgeon, rock musician, jet-car engineer), but it's his preternatural physical abilities, awesome crime-fighting club the Hong Kong Cavaliers, and psychotic nemesis Dr. Emilio Lizardo (Lithgow) that make him feel like a superhero. Indefinably subversive fun.

The Adventures of Captain Africa, Mighty Jungle Avenger! ★★

1955, USA
Director: Spencer G. Bennet.
Cast: John Hart, Rick Vallin, Ben Welden

Captain Africa (Hart), masked jungle lord, teams up with a roguish hunter and a US government official to defend a fictional African nation from a counterfeit caliph.

Filmed as a sequel to 1943's *The Phantom* and then reworked when that character's commercial rights reverted to the previous owner, *Captain Africa* proved to be the last superhero serial made in Hollywood. It's also among the most boring and poorly made, with its abrupt episodes a brew of stock footage, mismatched re-shoots necessitated by the rights issue, and low-grade original material. However, the outdoor locales create a sense of space lacking in its more studio-bound siblings.

The Adventures of Captain Marvel ★★★

1941, USA
Directors: John English, William Witney
Cast: Tom Tyler, Frank Coghlan Jr., William 'Billy' Benedict

Scientists raiding antiquities in Siam stumble on a set of magical lenses and steal them, thus angering their supernatural protector The Scorpion (Gerald Mohr). Fortunately a wizard deems Billy Batson (Coughlan Jr.), the youngest member of the scientists' party, worthy to protect innocents from some sort of curse, and bestows on him the superpowers of Captain Marvel (who has subsequently become known as Shazam).

With supervillains today expected to do more than just sound foreign, this enjoyable serial is a morally confusing affair. The ostensible baddie just wants to recover a dangerous device from the people who stole it. Our heroes, on the other hand, are marauding imperialist thieves. Eventually a world-conquering motivation is developed, but it seems like an afterthought. Captain Marvel himself is unremarkable and enjoys surprisingly little screen time but the main characters, all broad-stroked stereotypes, play well within an episodic structure that keeps itself nice and busy.

The Adventures of Captain Zoom in Outer Space ★★

1995, USA
Director: Max Tash
Cast: Daniel Riordan, Liz Vassey, Ron Perlman

With the corrupt forces of Vestron about to seize control of the planet Pangea, a young boy somehow summons fictional superhero Captain Zoom (Riordan) to help save the day.

Scrappy comedy that flits between mocking and homaging classic superhero serials. Some of the gags land but the sexual humour is dumb and, in a movie that looks like an episode of *The Mighty morphin' Power Rangers*, incongruous.

The Adventures of El Frenetico and Go Girl ★★

1993, USA
Director: Pat Bishow
Cast: Charles Pellegrino, Frances Lee, Jon Sanborne

Drunk, overweight and over the hill luchador-cum-superhero El Frenetico (Pellegrino) and his sidekick Go-Girl (Lee) battle a cake-pushing psychopath.

One of the better amateur spoofs of the era, but still an amateur spoof. Shot 4x3 on video in dark rooms, it couldn't look any cheaper at first glance. But the camera is handled well enough, the editing is vaguely passable and the central performances are likeable. El Frenetico himself is somewhat reminiscent of The Toxic Avenger in the way his slovenly appearance contrasts amusingly with his eloquent nature.

The Adventures of Hercules ★★

aka Le avventure dell'incredibile Ercole, 1985, Italy/USA,
Director: Luigi Cozzi
Cast: Lou Ferrigno, Milly Carlucci, Sonia Viviani

Zeus (Claudio Cassinelli) tasks Hercules (Ferrigno) with recovering seven magical MacGuffins from Earth before he loses control of the universe.

Sequel to 1983's Hercules and, like that movie, a nonsensical peplum update with more than its share of 1960s visual effects. And baby oil. It's swamped by excessive exposition determined to explain every aspect of a convoluted mythology, while also filling in gaps in the screenplay. Ferrigno doesn't face off with a bear, as he does in the previous movie, but at one point he does have to fight electricity.

The Adventures of Iron Pussy ★★

aka Hua jai tor ra nong, 2003, Thailand
Directors: Michael Shaowanasai, Apichatpong Weerasethakul
Cast: Siriyakorn Pukkavesh, Michael Shaowana-sai, Krissada Sukosol

A transvestite superhero and spy challenges a drug smuggler.

This spoof of 1970s Thai action movies is a fun side project for Thai master filmmaker Apichatpong 'Joe' Weerasethakul (here co-directing with performance artist and actor Michael Shaowanasai). Strangeness abounds with anachronistic music, nods to silent cinema, European arthouse and all sorts of quirkiness. There is craft and much originality, but it's buried beneath some impenetrable colloquial curiosities and abysmal production quality. A curiosity but one with narrow appeal.

Abar, the First Black Superman

THE FIRST BLACK SUPERMAN!

THE FIRST BLACK SCIENCE FICTION FILM!

The Adventures of Sharkboy and Lavagirl 3-D ★

2005, USA
Director: Robert Rodriguez
Cast: Cayden Boyd, Taylor Dooley, Taylor Lautner

A boy raised by sharks and a girl from a volcano call on their 12-year-old inventor to save his own dream world from the sinister Mr. Electric (Lopez).

More baffling than *Inception* and more distressing than *Cannibal Holocaust*, *The Adventures of Sharkboy and Lavagirl* seems to exist in order to give parents sleepless nights. Everything about it is horrible. The dialogue bends over backwards to make room for dreary puns and, despite a free reign (if not an obligation), to create the most outlandish settings and environments imaginable, it all looks like the background to a 1990s platform game.

Adventures of the American Rabbit
★

1986, USA
Directors: Nobutaka Nishizawa, Fred Wolf
Cast: Bob Arbogast, Pat Fraley, Barry Gordon

Born to maddeningly virtuous parents, Rob the Rabbit (Gordon) soon sprouts wheels, prompting a local wizard to dose us with mythology. After becoming a nightclub pianist (obviously) Rob does battle with a gang of biker foxes.

Pre-school drivel made more disagreeable by its tedious moralising. The animation is bland and the voices will have you dreaming of bunnycide before the end of the first act. The jingoistic title and US flag 'costume' (technically the rabbit just changes colour) go unexplained. I should have been stricter on animal superhero eligibility.

Æon Flux ★★

2005, USA
Director: Karyn Kusama
Cast: Charlize Theron, Frances McDormand, Sophie Okonedo

In the year 2415 humankind has been decimated by a relentless virus. One city remains, its five million inhabitants largely freed from life's more laborious duties by advances in technology. The Monicans, an underground resistance against the ruling regime, still aren't satisfied

When this blockbuster adaptation of MTV's shapeless exercise in style was announced, the world reacted with ambivalence. But on release audiences developed an opinion and decided en masse they weren't going to see it. While it's easy to appreciate why, *Æon Flux* isn't quite as bad as its reputation suggests. There are no memorable moments, interesting performances, original ideas, or any other worthy qualities, and in fact it washes over you like air. But it looks fine and isn't quite as dumb as you might expect (finale not withstanding).

Agent Beetle ★

2012, Canada
Director: Brett Kelly
Cast: Emanuelle Carriere, Phil Dukarsky, Christine Emes

Dan Garrett (Lavigne), an undercover cop who developed superpowers after being subjected to an experimental medical procedure, must battle Widow (Emes), a femme fatale with mutated pheromones.

It used to be simple: Hollywood made blockbusters and The Asylum ripped them off. But now there's Tom Cat Films, and that means Western society needs to take a look at itself. Mockbusters (low-budget imitations designed to capitalise on a blockbuster's success) are nothing new, but never have they been made to Tom Cat's standards. *Agent Beetle*, like most of their movies, is shot largely in a Canadian industrial unit with curtains for sets and less for costumes. Nevertheless it does stand out from its worst-of-the-worst brethren thanks to an anomalous preoccupation with sexual exploitation (these things are usually about as sexually charged as Uncle Ben).

Agimat, Anting-anting Ni Lolo ★★

2002, Philippines
Director: Augusto Salvador
Cast: Ramon Revilla, Bong Revilla Jr., Jolo Revilla

Ajooba

A young boy is given a magical amulet by his grandfather and, after learning how to wield its power, teams up with his adult self to battle an evil queen.

The last of Ramon Revilla's roughly 5,000 *anting-anting* movies sees the former heartthrob finally move into the wise old sage role. Otherwise it's business as usual, with Revilla snr.'s son Bong and grandson Jolo in the other key roles. There's no real attempt to attract a younger audience, which might have been sensible given the teenage lead and coming-of-age themes, but there's some unexpected visual variety and dynamism. Plus Ramon snr. wears a ridiculous wig.

Aian gâru: see *Iron Girl*

Ajin Parts 1-3: see Grouped Franchises

Ajin: Demi-Human ★★★★

aka *Ajin*, 2017, Japan
Director: Katsuyuki Motohiro
Cast: Takeru Satoh, Minami Hamabe, Gamon Sakurai

Medical student Kei Nagai (Satoh) discovers he is one of only a handful of Ajin, immortal beings able to summon powerful inner spirits to do battle on their behalf. Although preferring to live in peace, he is recruited to help the government prevent a devestating nerve gas attack by unhinged ex-military man Ajin Sato (Sakurai).

Highlander meets *X-Men* in this live-action adaptation of the Gamon Sakurai manga series. It follows a collection of OVA's and a TV show, which itself was adapted into a trilogy of features (see Grouped Franchises) and perhaps explains why the story has been reorganised a little. Some fans didn't approve, but this is a good movie. We skip quite a lot of the backstory and get straight down to the action, which makes excellent use of the Ajins' regenerative abilities. The plot progresses logically and with regular explosions of stylish violence, while Sakurai steals the show as the enigmatic Sato. It lacks detail, and Nagai could have been better developed, but if you want a more nuanced take on the story there's always the anime. This thing's job is to be a big shiny actioner, and it does it well.

Ajooba ★★★★

1991, India
Directors: Shashi Kapoor, Gennadiy Vasilev
Cast: Amitabh Bachchan, Dimple Kapadia, Rishi Kapoor

A devil-worshipping Vazir (Puri) murders the Sultan of Baharistan (Shammi Kapoor) in a power grab, leaving his infant son to drown in the sea. The child grows up to avenge his father as fearsome folk hero Ajooba (Bachchan).

Based on Arabian mythology, influenced by Western folk heroes, conceived with creative input from the Soviet Union and executed in the traditional Bollywood style, *Ajooba* is a multicultural joy. Bachchan, arguably the most popular film star of all time and unquestionably among the most charismatic, is perfectly cast in the lead. With so much drama and colour, any less magnetic an actor risks being overshadowed (presumably that's why Puri overcooks his performance to such an amusing extent). The song and dance sequences aren't the most polished, and there are more dolphins than one might reasonably expect from a movie set in Afghanistan, but *Ajooba's* simple joys are to be cherished.

Alag: He Is Different... He Is Alone... ★★

aka *Different*, 2006, India
Director: Ashu Trikha
Cast: Akshay Kapoor, Dia Mirza, Yatin Karyekar

Having spent his whole life hidden in a basement, telekinetic teen Tejas (Kapoor) is forced into a reform school for troubled boys after the death of his father. Defending himself from bullies one day, Tejas reveals his amazing abilities and is soon abducted by scientist Dr. Dyer (Tom Alter).

This Indian stab at a cerebral superhero is great to look at and scores points for a handful of enjoyable songs (not to mention one of the best moustaches ever caught on camera). But it's overly melodramatic even for Bollywood, too drawn out, and lumbered with an unconvincing romance.

Alamid: Ang alamat ★★★

1998, Philippines
Director: Dan Alvaro
Cast: Lito Lapid, Dan Alvaro, Bernard Bonnin

As the superhero torch is passed from one 'Alamid' (quasi-official supernatural folk hero) to another, an unusually brutal and ambitious gang emerges from Manilla's criminal underworld.

The tone is darker than that of most Pinoy superhero movies. Gloomy music, morose characters and a nihilistic air see to that. It's edgier too, with Alamid essentially a brutal, gun-wielding version of Michael Keaton's Batman (numerous costumes and scenarios are borrowed from Tim Burton's films). It's an interesting change of pace but the lack of English subtitles might limit appreciation.

Algol - Tragödie der Macht: see *Power*

Alien Arsenal ★

aka *Teenage Alien Avengers*, 1999, USA
Director: David DeCoteau
Cast: Josh Hammond, Danielle Hoover, Michele Nordin

Two teenage losers find a hoard of alien weaponry in their high school basement (while in 'manual labour' class, whatever that is).

Attempt at a standard issue teen fantasy. As a result of notorious low-budget hack David DeCoteau's (*Creepozoids*, *Sorority Babes in the Slimeball Bowl-O-Rama*) presence at the helm, this one is worse than most. The pieces are all in play: angry bullies, nerdy comic book fans, menacing aliens, etc. But nobody has bothered forming them into a pleasing shape.

All Superheroes Must Die ★★★

2011, USA
Director: Jason Trost
Cast: Jason Trost, Lucas Till, James Remar

The estranged members of a superhero team are forced to play the sick games of a criminal mastermind while working through their personal issues.

Concentrating on the characterisation and dynamics of these former colleagues is an interesting idea, but why Trost chose to pursue it in a movie he pitched as *Saw* meets *The Running Man* is unclear. Luckily he gets that the spandexy introspection needs to be undercut with something, but going for gore over humour is a tonal blindside for an audience lead by the setup to expect comedy. An interesting last act twist edges it into worthwhile territory.

All Superheroes Must Die 2: The Last Superhero ★★★

2016, USA
Director: Jason Trost
Cast: Tallay Wickham, Jason Trost, Sean Whalen

Faux documentary investigating a mystery surrounding Charge/John Ford (Trost), the first film's lead character.

Rather than directly addressing the events of the previous movie this inventive sequel builds a mythology around it, expanding its universe exponentially. The structure drip-feeds us revelations before turning our expectations on their heads, just as the best true crime documentaries might. Ultimately a more intelligent and interesting film than its predecessor.

All-Star Superman ★★

2011, USA
Director: Sam Liu
Cast: James Denton, Christina Hendricks, Anthony LaPaglia

Lex Luthor (LaPaglia) hatches a scheme to trick Superman (Denton) into flying too close to the sun, then teams up with Solaris (Robin Atkin Downes) to finish him off. An unrelated Kryptonian assault on Earth is the focus of the second half.

With detours involving Atlas (Steve Blum), Samson (John DiMaggio), an alien invasion and a spell wooing Lois Lane (Hendricks), *All-Star Superman* lacks a core narrative and feels padded. But it isn't just about fighting and has some interesting things to say about power and responsibility.

Allegiance of Powers ★

2016, USA
Director: Michael Crum
Cast: Joshua Winch, Ariah Davis, Justin Armstrong

Two supertribes wage war over the future of a superbeing.

Seemingly inspired in equal measure by the DCEU, mumblecore and a desire to induce epilepsy in its audience, *Allegiance of Powers* is apparently a movie. We can assume this because if it was the result of a first year VFX student splicing his showreel with home video footage (which is what it most resembles) then the sound would be better.

Almighty Thor ★

2011, USA
Director: Christopher Ray
Cast: Cody Deal, Richard Grieco, Patricia Velasquez

A deranged Loki (Grieco) murders both Odin (Kevin Nash) and his eldest son Baldir (Jess Allen) in pursuit of Thor's (Deal) hammer. Thor and cohort Jarnsaxa (Velasquez) flee to Earth, where they wander around some of L.A.'s most convenient complimentary filming locations.

Not one of The Asylum's best mockbusters, which must be words of warning to anyone. Deal looks like he got lost on the way to a *High School Musical* audition, while Grieco wouldn't seem less committed if he hadn't turned up at all. It's a strikingly ugly movie that uses two equally clumsy colour grades: a rusty brown for Asgard and a sea of flat, desaturated grey for Earth.

Alter Egos ★★★

2012, USA
Director: Jordan Galland
Cast: Kris Lemche, Brooke Nevin, Joey Kern

Brendan, aka ice-making superhero Fridge (Lemche), is not having a good time of it. There are no supervillains left to battle, his state funding has been cut, and he's increasingly jealous of the relationship his alter ego enjoys with girlfriend Emily (Christine Evangelista).

Patchy but quite funny rumination on how superheroes could, if they existed, be as full of insecurities and existential doubts as the rest of us. Galland succeeds in creating a cohesive, distinctive environment on what is clearly a small budget, and in the second half shakes off the pacing issues that are *Alter Ego's* most significant fault.

Alyas Batman at Robin

1965, Philippines
Director: Paquito Toledo
Cast: Bob Soler, Lou Salvador Jr., Nova Villa

There aren't many rules when it comes to Filipino genre cinema but, sadly, one of the most prevalent clearly states movies made in the 1960s will probably be lost. We must forever wonder what a pre-Adam West Filipino Batman would be like.

Alyas Batman en Robin ★★★★

1991, Philippines
Director: Tony Y. Reyes
Cast: Keempee de Leon, Joey de Leon, Rene Requiestas

Arch criminal Tiyo Paeng (Tiyo Panchito) is released from prison and immediately adopts the persona of The Penguin for a string of robberies. Luckily, goody-goody college kid Kevin (K. de Leon) and his big brother Kuya (J. de Leon) want to play too, so Batman and Robin face off against The Penguin once more.

This lunatic comedy from prolific Filipino filmmaker Tony Y. Reyes defies all critical appraisal. Unusually for one of these rare Pinoy genre movies, *Alyas Batman en Robin* is available with English subtitles, but don't expect them to be much help: words can never explain why we see Batman, Wonder Woman and a Spider-Man dwarf hula dancing with The Joker. Although a spiritual descendent of the 1966 *Batman* TV series, it ceratinly can't compete in terms of quality (or legitimacy).

Alyas Hunyango ★★

1992, Philippines
Directors: Dante Pangilinan and Emer Labra
Cast: Bernard Bonnin, Donita Rose, Monsour Del Rosario

A mysterious supernatural martial artist in a green jumpsuit sorts out a criminal gang.

With no English language options and a picture so dark it's hard to make out what's happening, *Alyas Hunyango* isn't an ideal viewing experience. There's consolation in the occasional explosions of weird; like when a bad guy is electrocuted and turns into stainless steel for some reason, and the visual effects are endearingly silly.

Alyas Palos: see Grouped Franchises and *Palos*

Alyas Phantom

1966, Philippines
Director: Paquito Toledo
Cast: Bob Soler, Rebecca, Lou Salvador Jr.

Bob Soler, star of the lost 1965 Batman movie and several lost Captain Barbell movies, stars as an unlicensed version of the Phantom. This film is... lost.

The Amazing Bulk ★

2012, USA
Director: Lewis Schoenbrun
Cast: Terence Lording, Shevaun Kastl,
Randal Malone

Have you seen *The Incredible Hulk*? It's that
but purple and rubbish.

The closest thing the execrable Tom Cat
Films has had to a breakout hit, *The Amazing
Bulk* could be the worst movie they, and
perhaps the filmmaking community as a
whole, have ever released. Say what you
will about *Agent Beetle*, at least it's sincere.
This thing is so bad it must be going for
ironic appeal, its tongue wedged in its giant
purple cheek. It's the only explanation for
a CGI beast that wouldn't pass muster as
pre-vis on a proper movie. 'Running' scenes
see actors bounce up and down on the spot
in front of a green screen. They didn't even
bother with a treadmill.

Unlicensed oddity *Alyas Batman en Robin*

The Amazing Spider-Man ★★

1977, USA
Director: E.W. Swackhamer
Cast: Nicholas Hammond, David White,
Michael Pataki

Photographer Peter Parker (Hammond) is
bitten by a radioactive spider. Meanwhile a
terrorist holds New York to ransom with a
mind control device.

Pilot serving as origin story, stand-alone
adventure and dire warning for anyone
tempted to check out the brief series that
followed. Columbia somehow squeezed
three feature-length movies from its 14
episodes (the other two being *Spider-Man
Strikes Back* and *Spider-Man: The Dragon's
Challenge*), releasing them all in European
theatres within months of each other. This
is the weakest of the three. Hammond is
too wet, too old and far too boring to play
Spidey, and there's a near complete lack of
action. The funky jazz score is about the
only highlight. (Followed by *Spider-Man
Strikes Back*.)

The Amazing Spider-Man ★★

2012, USA
Director: Marc Webb
Cast: Andrew Garfield, Emma Stone, Rhys Ifans

When his parents disappear, six-year-old
Peter Parker (Garfield) is sent to live with
his Aunt May (Field) and Uncle Ben (Martin
Sheen). Years later, after being bitten by a
genetically modified spider, Parker becomes
web-slinging superhero Spider-Man.

With this reboot hitting screens within just
five years of Sam Raimi rounding out his
Spider-Man trilogy, it's strange more wasn't
done to distinguish it from the earlier series.
Not only does it retread much of the now
over-familiar origin story, it also hits largely
the same emotional and narrative beats.
Garfield isn't a natural fit for Parker and

lacks the presence we expect from a hero. Worse, he makes Parker smug, which might work for billionaires and demigods but not your friendly neighbourhood Spider-Man. Denis Leary adds some weight to the cast as an irascible cop, and Ifans is memorably far-out as The Lizard.

The Amazing Spider-Man 2 ★★
2014, USA
Director: Marc Webb
Cast: Andrew Garfield, Emma Stone, Jamie Foxx

As Peter Parker (Garfield) faces up to the difficult promise he made to Gwen Stacy's (Stone) father, submissive Oscorp engineer Max Dillon (Foxx) becomes New York's latest mega-malefactor.

Two years on and Garfield still seems out of his depth, Stone has become tedious, and neither of the first film's best characters (Denis Leary's Captain Stacy and Rhys Ifans' The Lizard) are alive enough to return. Not much to get excited about, then. To be fair to the cast, the screenplay is the bigger problem here. New big, bad Electro (Foxx) is fatally underwritten, and even during the finale it isn't clear what his objectives are. Harry Osborn (Dane DeHann), son of Oscorp founder Norman (Chris Cooper), hangs about in the background commited to being inexplicably bitter at Spider-Man. DeHann is an interesting, enigmatic actor, and focusing on his descent into madness and Green Goblinery could have lead to something interesting. Instead it's treated as a casual sequel tease.

American Hero ★★★★
2015, USA
Director: Nick Love
Cast: Stephen Dorff, Eddie Griffin, Bill Billions

Melvin (Dorff), a loser with unexplained telekinetic powers, bums aimlessly around LA smoking weed and boozing with his buddy Lucille (Griffin). Eventually a near-death experience encourages him to use his abilities for good.

Don't assume from the synopsis that this is just a formulaic slice of feel-good banality. Shot vérité style on the streets of Louisiana, *American Hero* is primarily a character study of an almost willfully self-destructive father with good intentions and bad habits (who just happens to have superpowers). We're offered no easy answers and are left unsure what Melvin's future has in store for him. Dorff and Griffin are excellent.

American Rescue Squad ★★★★
2015, USA
Director: Elliot Diviney
Cast: Tony D. Czech, Douglas Sidney, KariAnn Christensen

Superhero The Taxpayer (Jimmy Keebs) is captured by terrorists, creating panic and confusion within local government. Can Mr. Average, Richard Randolph (Czech), orchestrate a rescue?

What does the US do in a crisis when it can't turn to The Taxpayer? That's the none-too-subtle question at the heart of *American Rescue Squad*, a movie so on the nose it could be a sequel to *Team America: World Police*. Apparently forgotten heroes including Personal Responsibility (Anjel White) and Common Sense (Roger Wayne), 'who haven't been active since the Reagan administration', are the answer to society's problems. Whether you see it as edgily satirical, profoundly offensive or just plain idiotic will depend on your sense of humour and, potentially, political beliefs. And that's *American Rescue Squad's* biggest flaw. It's basically *South Park* with the benign content stripped out, which makes it less accessible and more tiresome. Not everything works, not by a long shot, but there's real wit and imagination here if you can stomach it. It's also a musical.

Americano ★★

aka *El Americano 3D*, *El Americano: The Movie*, *Cuco's Big Adventure*, 2016, Mexico/USA
Directors: Ricardo Arnaiz, Mike Kunkel, Raul Garcia
Cast: Edward James Olmos, Rico Rodriguez, Cheech Marin

When his parents' circus is taken over by bad birds, Anthropomorphic parrot Cuco (Rodriguez) travels to Hollywood hoping to enlist the help of a fictional superhero.

Pueblan production company Animex's go at a Pixar-style movie was derided by critics (the few who saw it; there aren't enough scores on rottentomatoes.com to form a consensus) and fell flat at the box office (it didn't even get a full US release), but it isn't completely without merit. Well made and boasting some top voice talent, its greatest asset perhaps lies in the way it reflects different (i.e. non-US) cultural archetypes. The screenplay's lack of originality will make it a chore for many adults but shouldn't bother kids.

Anak ng kidlat

1959, Philippines
Director: Mario Barri
Cast: Cecilia Lopez, Cesar Ramirez, Lillian Leonardo

After being struck by lightning a woman gives birth to an invulnerable flying child. One of many Filipino superhero movies in which the protagonist receives their power via a strike of magic 'kidlat'. Others include *Babaeng Isputnik*, *Babaing Kidlat*, *Kapitan Inggo*, *Kapitan Kidlat*, *Pepeng Kuryente* and *Volta*. Considered lost.

Angel Wars: The Messengers ★★

2009, USA
Director: Jason Brian Adams
Cast: Justin Moran, Nancy Johnson, John Daniels

New recruits to the Guardian Force find themselves in the heat of battle sooner than expected.

The last in a string of four Christian-themed CG superhero adventures falling under the '*Angel Wars*' banner (the others are shorts). The religious angle is played down to such an extent it's hardly noticeable, meaning superhero Eli (Moran), comedy relief Que (Ruth Nika) and friends are generic enough to appeal to all audiences. In theory.

Another WolfCop ★★★

2017, Canada
Director: Lowell Dean
Cast: Leo Fafard, Amy Matysio, Yannick Bisson

Shortly after the events of *WolfCop*, dodgy businessman Sydney Swallows (Bisson) arrives in Woodhaven with a scheme to regenerate the town. At the same time there's an increase in what might be called peculiar activity.

Another WolfCop feels thinner than the first film and the screenplay isn't as tight, but it's still thoroughly entertaining and frequently laugh-out-loud funny. Lycan police officer Lou Garou (Fafard) and chief of police Tina (Matysio) must contend with a supernatural hockey team and penis monsters, which is a hard setup to get wrong.

Ant-Man ★★★★

2015, USA
Director: Peyton Reed
Cast: Paul Rudd, Evangeline Lilly, Michael Douglas

Scientist Dr. Hank Pym (Douglas) discovers his former protege Darren Cross (Corey Stoll) is about to replicate his extraordinary, and extraordinarily dangerous, shrinking technology. Pym and daughter Hope (Lilly) recruit morally upright burglar Scott Lang (Rudd) to help save the day.

For those left bewildered by the epic scope of MCU movies, *Ant-Man* offers something on an appropriately smaller scale. It shares the same formula-conforming approach (not to mention blinding colour palette) as its big brothers, but feels less like being shouted at in a toy shop. And the sarcastic banter these Marvel films are prone to doesn't seem forced when it comes from Rudd, who has natural timing and a gift for deadpan delivery.

Ant-Man and the Wasp ★★★★

2018, USA
Director: Peyton Reed
Cast: Paul Rudd, Evangeline Lilly,
Michael Douglas

Despite being sentenced to house arrest for his role in the events of *Captain America: Civil War*, Scott Lang, aka Ant-Man (Rudd), is compelled to help Hank Pym (Douglas) rescue his wife from the quantum realm. Meanwhile Ava Starr (Hannah John-Kamen), a young woman with 'quantum instability', will die without access to Pym's lab.

It seems odd to criticise an MCU movie for its small stakes, but *Ant-Man and the Wasp* is built around an objective it's hard to care about. Hank Pym isn't a particularly sympathetic character, and we've never met his wife, so why should we care whether he rescues her or not? Added to that, rescuing Mrs. Pym (Pfeiffer) means dooming Ava Starr (for unknown reasons). It feels like the audience is being asked to back the wrong horse. And why has the always engaging Evangeline Lilly's Hope Van Dyne been given nothing to do? Despite these issues it's a lot of fun.

Antboy ★★★

2013, Denmark
Director: Ask Hasselbalch
Cast: Oscar Dietz, Amalie Kruse Jensen,
Samuel Ting Graf

When 12-year-old Pelle Nøhrmann (Dietz) is bitten by an ant carrying an experimental serum, he develops superpowers and soon makes a nemesis of portly adult evildoer The Flea (Nicolas Bro).

Although the title seems to risk infringing on Marvel's Ant-Man copyright, *Antboy* is actually more of a Spider-Man reimagining. Young Pelle's life, full of bullying, confusion and unrequited love, closely mirrors Peter Parker's, as do the powers he develops. Unlike Spider-Man there's little about the character that will interest adults, although he's slick and colourful enough that kids of the right age will probably like him. A European sensibility delivers some amusing moments you wouldn't see in an American kids' movie (acidic pee strong enough to destroys urinals, anyone?) (Followed by *Antboy: Revenge of the Red Fury*.)

Antboy 3 ★★

2016, Denmark
Director: Ask Hasselbalch
Cast: Oscar Dietz, Samuel Ting Graf,
Amalie Kruse Jensen

In his third and final adventure, Antboy (Dietz) must prevent a villainous CEO from taking over the world, while also dealing with old enemy The Flea (Nicolas Bro) and the apparent betrayal of a friend.

Gone is the moon-faced youngling of the first films. Instead we find a strapping, husky-voiced Dietz who, as Antboy, is now looking to overcome larger scale villainy. But with the hero having lost the charms of adolescence without yet developing the intensity of a young adult, this is probably one for hardcore fans of the series only.

Antboy: Revenge of the Red Fury ★★★

aka *Antboy: Den Røde Furies hævn*, 2014, Denmark

Director: Ask Hasselbalch
Cast: Oscar Dietz, Amalie Kruse Jensen, Samuel Ting Graf

Antboy (Dietz) faces his most dangerous adversary yet: a spurned teenage girl.

Doubling down on the social politics of school life turns out to be the right move by Hasselbalch and series writer Anders Olholm. By developing a plot from the everyday jealousies and insecurities of our now teen protagonists, this first sequel to 2012's *Antboy* somehow feels more organic and less forced. (Followed by *Antboy 3*.)

Aquaman ★★★★
2018, USA
Director: James Wan
Cast: Jason Momoa, Amber Heard, Willem Dafoe

Hercules must claim Excalibur, a mythical trident guarded by Merdusa, in order to prevent Loki starting a war between the Gungans and the Naboo. Or something.

How can a franchise fumble Batman and Superman but nail Aquaman? The former are heavyweight characters with scope, depth and built-in audiences. The latter is a trivial cartoon with nowhere to go. At least that was conventional wisdom. While *Aquaman* can't quite match the previous year's *Wonder Woman* for dramatic weight, it amounts to more than the collection of scenes-from-other-movies it could be. Although I'm not sure how. Things get off on the right foot with the origin story folded into the main plot: Aquaman must complete Hercules-style tasks in order to become sea-king and stop bad things, and it's his execution of these tasks that constitutes most of the movie. Happily we don't have to reconfigure from origin story to story story somewhere around the middle. The visual effects and action set pieces are impressive, and Momoa is good if unspectacular. But none of that really explains how such a ridiculous movie can be so entertaining.

Arahan ★★★★
aka *Arahan jangpung daejakjeon*, 2004, South Korea
Director: Seung-wan Ryoo
Cast: Seung-bum Ryoo, So-yi Yoon, Sung-Ki Ahn

Astro Boy (1964 version)

Five ageing Tao masters help clumsy cop Sang-hwan (Ryoo) unlock his ch'i and foster superpowers. With help from the beautiful Wi-jin (Yoon), they must stop megalomaniac Heuk-woon (Jung) taking over the world.

Genuinely funny and thoroughly enjoyable spiritual take on life as a superhero. Ryoo shares great chemistry with Yoon, and his bumbling admiration for her is an amusing contrast to her cynical contempt for him.

Argoman the Fantastic Superman ★★★

aka *The Incredible Paris Incident; The Fantastic Argoman; Come rubare la corona d'Inghilterra*,
1967, Italy
Director: Sergio Grieco
Cast: Roger Browne, Dominique Boschero, Eduardo Fajardo

St Edward's Crown, the centrepiece of the Crown Jewels of the United Kingdom, has been stolen by arch Eurovillain Jenabell (Boschero). Roger Browne's Sir Reginald Hunter (or maybe Hoover, depending on the version you're watching), an inexplicably superpowered English aristocrat, is the only man with the requisite skills to retrieve it. Little do the authorities know Hunter is also infamous cat burglar Argoman.

Typically stylish Italian nonsense boasting spectacular James Bond-meets-Power Rangers sets and a 'hero' who appears as morally reprehensible as the villain. Though frequently labelled a comedy it actually takes itself seriously, but that doesn't mean it isn't funny.

Armstong ★★

2017, USA
Directors: Kerry Carlock, Nicholas Lund-Ulrich
Cast: Vicky Jeudy, Shawn Parsons, Jason Antoon

During the course of a night shift, Rookie EMT Lauren (Jeudy) becomes embroiled

in a mechanically enhanced superhero's attempt to stop a doomsday cult destroying the world.

After an inspired decision to have the story unfold from Lauren's perspective instead of more obvious protagonist Armstrong's, Carlock and Lund-Ulrich seem to run out of ideas. What looks like being a fresh twist on the post-modern superhero movie soon descends into a forgettable blend of shaky-cam cinematography and sequel baiting.

Ashes of CHIKARA ★

2014, USA
Director: Ian Vaflor
Cast: Icarus, Fire Ant, Scott Parker

Various wrestlers adopt random quests in the wake of their championship's demise.

Constructed from a series of web shorts released under the banner '*Ashes*', this lumpy mess of a movie offers the wrestlers of the defunct CHIKARA series (which I'm just going to call the American lucha libra) a multimedia platform on which to do their stuff. That 'stuff' is unwatchable questing.

Asterix: see Grouped Franchises and *Asterix & Obelix*

Astro Boy ★★

1962, Japan
Director: Unknown
Cast: Unknown

World leaders are being assassinated, and Astro Boy is in prison for a crime he didn't commit. Whatever can be done?

With no entry in any online database, and no credits on the DVD-R, it's hard to gather any information about the movie that marks Astro Boy's feature-length debut. We know it was formed of three episodes from the

1950s live-action TV series but, beyond that, the Japanese language-only bootleg is about all there is to go on. From watching it we can infer money was in short supply. Even nondescript corridors (always popular shooting locations in cheap movies) seem to be painted on walls. We also learn that a plastic wig can make an otherwise angelic child look like a serial killer. For anything more we must await an official release.

Astro Boy ★★★

aka *Tetsuwan Atom: Uchû no yûsha*, *Mighty Atom*, *The Brave in Space*, 1964, Japan
Director: Yositake Suzuki, Eiichi Yamamoto
Cast: Mari Shimizu, Hisashi Yokomori, Hisashi Katsuta

After replacing his deceased son with an automaton named Atom (Shimizu), leading roboticist Dr. Tenma (Yokomori) turns on his creation and sells it to the circus. Adventures are then had.

Another cut-and-shut, with this one using episodes from the 1963 animated *Astro Boy* TV series. The black-and-white animation is basic and will either seem charming or primitive to audiences (I adore it). The plot sticks reasonably close to Osamu Tezuka's manga but there are some dull spells.

Astro Boy ★★★

2009, Hong Kong
Director: David Bowers
Cast: Freddie Highmore, Nicolas Cage, Kristen Bell

When his son Toby (Highmore) dies in an accident, Dr. Tenma (Cage) recreates him in artificial form. For various convoluted reasons their city is then threatened with destruction, and the robot child forced on a dangerous adventure.

Seemingly Westernised in an attempt to make Astro Boy more palatable beyond his native Japan, the unique tone of what is a fairly twisted tale has been watered down too far. There are still some nice ideas among the debris of The Surface (the post-apocalyptic wasteland that's home to the planet's less fortunate residents), including a coliseum converted to host robot fights. And no kids' movie starting with the death of a 13-year-old can be all bad.

Athisayan ★★

2007, India,
Director: Vinayan
Cast: Master Devadas, Jackie Shroff, Kavya Madhavan

Bullied orphan Devan (Devadas) drinks an invisibility elixir, then takes advantage of its effects by avenging himself on those who wronged him. Eventually he grows to enormous size.

Those drawn to Athisayan by the image of an angry 50-foot child on the posters will be disappointed. Most of the movie involves incomprehensible drama dealing with a reporter, her boyfriend and corrupt officials, with the massive child not making an appearance until close to the two hour mark. It's a long, hard slog. This is a Keralan production in the Malayalam language, and there was obviously little money, not that it seems to have affected anyone's ambition. We get the usual song and dance routines, large scale action sequences, multiple plot strands and an entirely CG mega-Devan. It's all a bit rubbish, though.

Atlas ★★

1961, USA
Director: Roger Corman
Cast: Michael Forest, Frank Wolff, Barboura Morris

A standoff ensues when Proximates the tyrant (Wolff) lays siege to the city of Thenos. King Telektos (Andre Filippides) persuades Proximates to settle the deadlock by electing champions who will fight to the death. Proximates tricks the supernaturally strong Atlas (Forest) to fight on his behalf.

Pseudo-biblical epic from Roger Corman done in the vein of the era's Italian peplum movies. Wolff's cheerfully camp villain lends proceedings some fire, but Forest dampens it down with negative charisma. A lack of action is the nail in the coffin, but at least we learn where the name Atlas comes from: "When I was three days old I pulled my father's beard. In a fit of mischief he called me Atlas." So, that explains that.

Atom Man vs. Superman ★★★

1950, USA
Director: Spencer Gordon Bennet
Cast: Kirk Alyn, Noel Neill, Lyle Talbot

Lex Luthor (Talbot) has rebranded himself Atom Man and developed a teleportation machine he's using to wreak havoc on the city of Metropolis. Can Superman (Alyn) save the day?

The second Superman serial sticks with the cast from the first while adding Lyle Talbot's Lex Luthor to the mix. A welcome inclusion, he's suitably sinister and makes the stakes seem higher, but Kirk Alyn's Superman remains the least charismatic performer on screen (the cartoon stand-in used for flying scenes is more interesting). Superior special effects and an apparently bigger budget help up the ante.

Atom Nine Adventures ★★★

2007, USA
Director: Christopher Farley
Cast: Christopher Farley, Paul Meade, Jennifer Ferguson

Astrophysicist Dr. Adam Gaines (Farley) is rendered superhuman by a metal spacebug. It's lucky for us, because someone has to

stop Gremlo Flugg (Colin Armstrong) using his doom machine to smash the moon into the Earth.

This inexpertly made sci-fi adventure avoids the usual pitfalls of such low-budget fare by refusing to accept it is low-budget. Farley (who not only stars and directs but also writes, produces, edits and even created the visual effects) seems to have nurtured the script, thought about the editing and sunk serious time into the CGI. The result is no masterpiece, but novice and zero-budget filmmakers could do worse than look to Farley for inspiration.

Atomic Rulers ★★

aka *Attack of the Flying Saucers; Atomic Rulers of the World*, 1965, Japan
Directors: Koreyoshi Akasaka, Teruo Ishii
Cast: Ken Utsui, Sachihiro Ohsawa, Junko Ikeuchi

Leaders from the Emerald Planet despatch Starman (Utsui) to help prevent Magolian invaders conquering Earth with hypnosis.

At least that's what Opening Voiceover Man informs us. *Atomic Rulers* is actually about gangsters, orphans and the vague hunt for a nuclear MacGuffin. But you can never quite relate what's happening on screen to either plot. The movie isn't without charm (Starman successfully shields people from a point blank nuclear blast with his cape) but boredom sets in early. (Followed by *Invaders from Space*.)

Attack from Space ★★

aka *Super Giant Vs the Satellites*, 1965, Japan
Director: Koreyoshi Akasaka, Teruo Ishii
Cast: Ken Utsui, Utako Mitsuya, Sachihiro Ohsawa

Yet again the Council of the Emerald Planet sends Starman (Utsui) to protect we poor Earthlings from alien invaders. This time it's the pesky Sufferians.

Each of the four Starman movies (the others being *Atomic Rulers, Invaders from Space* and *Evil Brain from Outer Space*) were cobbled together by US distributor Medallion Films from a 9-part Japanese TV series known in the West as *Super Giant*. As a result they're largely indistinguishable, and about equally incoherent in their attempt to address fears relating to atomic weapons, a theme that's handled with the subtlety of a mushroom cloud. (Followed by the aforementioned *Evil Brain from Outer Space*.)

Attack of the Super Monsters ★★

1982, Japan
Directors: Toru Sotoyama, Tom Wyner
Cast: Tom Wyner, Dan Woren, Robin Levenson

Dinosaurs from the past set out to destroy us, and only Gemini Force, led by cyborg siblings Jim (Woren) and Gem (Levenson), can stop them.

Welcome to one of the oddest and most repetitive 'movies' ever released. Originally a 1977 Japanese TV show entitled *Dinosaur War Izenborg*, in 1982 the first few episodes were spliced together, dubbed into English and released as *Attack of the Super Monsters*. Nothing too unusual about that; what's odd is the original show, which is a mixture of regular live-action, miniature photography, suitmation, cel animation and stop motion. The opening sequence alone features a suitmation dinosaur speaking (really) to 2D animated dogs comped against a live-action background. The effect is indescribable, but words like 'insane' and 'bewildering' would be involved if it wasn't.

August in the Water ★★★

aka *Mizu no naka no hachigatsu*, 1995, Japan
Director: Gakuryû Ishii
Cast: Rena Komine, Shinsuke Aoki, Reiko Matsuo

After a series of meteorite strikes, a high school diving champ evolves superpowers.

Other than that setup, nothing about *August in the Water* is predictable. It might best be described as a more existential take on *The X-Files*, with its detached style and surreal edges better suited to the arthouse than the multiplex. Contrasts (fast and slow edits, busy and empty frames, quiet and noisy scenes, etc.) begin to define an unusually potent atmosphere that will either irritate or captivate depending on taste.

Autâman: see *Outer Man*

Avenger X ★★

aka *Mister X*, 1967, Italy/Spain
Director: Piero Vivarelli
Cast: Pier Paolo Capponi, Gaia Germani, Armando Calvo

Falsely implicated in a murder, suave English golf pro and retired gentleman thief Mister X (Capponi) is drawn into a drug smuggler's evil scheme as he desperately attempts to clear his name.

These Italian fumetti neri movies can be hit or miss. As a character, Mister X is extremely unlikeable and, thanks to a plot built almost entirely on his endless master-of-disguise shenanigans, doesn't really do much of interest (even the finale is just a conversation followed by a judo chop). I call this one a miss despite some incredible promotional artwork.

The Avengers ★★★★★

aka *Avengers Assemble*, 2012, USA
Director: Joss Whedon
Cast: Robert Downey Jr., Chris Evans, Tom Hiddleston

With help from an alien army, sociopathic Asgardian demigod Loki (Hiddleston) plans to make Earth his personal fiefdom. Iron Man (Downey Jnr.) and the gang are all that stand in his way.

This shouldn't work. It's basically the origin story for a team whose members have just starred in their own origin stories. Who wants to see that? Everyone, apparently, because this became the most financially successful superhero film (worldwide, until *Infinity War* trumped it in 2018 and *Endgame* the following year). Looking back, it's odd to think of the concern fans had over wrangling so many characters into a single coherent narrative (around four times as many have been featured in subsequent films). The script is key in that regard. Dialogue seldom does just one thing and is instead carefully calibrated to develop both character and plot simultaneously. With no word wasted, an impressive density and feel of quality develops. The leads, who can be pious, smug or one-dimensional in their own rights, play off each other brilliantly, and the plot is kept simple enough that it doesn't complicate matters. The first *Iron Man* movie may be credited as the foundation on which this Marvel Cinematic Universe was built. But, really, this was the key movie. After a couple of average instalments it was *The Avengers* that had to instil fresh confidence, shift things up a gear and prove a big ensemble cast would work. (Followed by *Avengers: Age of Ultron*.)

Avenger X, aka *Mister X*

features. A lack of top tier characters, not to mention action, might have been forgiven if the Punisher's monotone gloominess didn't put such a dampener on everything.

Avengers Confidential: Black Widow & Punisher ★★

2014, USA
Director: Kenichi Shimizu
Cast: Jennifer Carpenter, Brian Bloom, John Eric Bentley

The Punisher (Bloom) teams up with Black Widow (Carpenter) to discover how SHIELD technology is being used to create an army of genetically enhanced soldiers.

With 'Avengers' in the title fans might be disappointed to discover they aren't really in the movie. It creates a sense Marvel are short-changing us in favour of building an interconnected universe for their animated

Avengers Grimm ★★

2015, USA
Director: Jeremy M. Inman
Cast: Casper Van Dien, Lauren Parkinson, Lou Ferrigno

Rumpelstiltskin (Van Dien) forces Snow White (Parkinson) to open a portal to Earth, where the dastardly degenerate takes over Los Angeles. Years later, a gaggle of fairytale heroines arrive to help Snow return order.

An interesting idea is compromised by a lack of care, not to mention a tiny budget and some spectacularly bad acting. It might have made sense to go all-out for comedy (Cinderella mocking Red Riding Hood in a valley girl accent could have been willfully rather than inadvertantly funny). But this is a mockbuster so there's a recipe to follow, despite nobody telling Caspar Van Dien. It's bad, but there are worse ideas than combining elements from fairytales, *Game of Thrones* and superhero lore.

Avengers Grimm: Time Wars ★★

2018, USA
Director: Maximilian Elfeldt
Cast: Lauren Parkinson, Elizabeth Eileen, Marah Fairclough

Magda (Maya), the queen of Atlantis, follows Prince Charming (Marcel) to modern-day Los Angeles, where the so-called Looking Glass Agency has been established in order to protect mankind from magical beings.

More of the same from The Asylum. There's a little bit more humour, which is welcome, and less Snow White (Parkinson) and the princesses, which is also welcome. All in all it's slightly more enjoyable (or slightly less unenjoyable), but there are only so many times you can hear the word 'mermen' and keep a straight face.

Avengers of Justice: Farce Wars ★

2018, USA
Director: Jarret Tarnol
Cast: Ramsey Anderson, Justin Carmouche, Justin Castor

With damage caused by Earth's overzealous superheroes having plunged the entire planet into 'Super Recession' and bankrupted our greatest hero, SuperBat (Steve Rannazzisi), intergalactic villain Emperor Purple Guy (John D. Hickman) decides the time is right to steal the sun.

As the title suggests, this comedy spoofs Marvel, DC and *Star Wars* with equally indiscriminate laziness. Less spoofed than shamelessly ripped-off is *The Incredibles*.

The setup sees a former superhero couple forced into early retirement, which suits her but frustrates him, and it isn't long before they get back in the swing of things to face a supervillain threatening the world. Much hilarity does not ensue.

Avengers: Age of Ultron ★★★★

2012, USA
Director: Joss Whedon
Cast: Robert Downey Jr., Chris Evans, Mark Ruffalo

Tony Stark (Downey Jr.) develops an artificial intelligence, Ultron (Spader), to protect us from potential alien threats. It goes nuts.

This second Avengers movie feels like a stopgap. Having introduced the characters and developed their dynamics by drawing them together to overcome an alien invasion, the team was primed for The Big Mission: Thanos. Instead we get a generic adventure. It's understandable Marvel wanted to extract more value from the franchise before bringing it to a head, but this all seems a bit routine. Whether or not that's a bad thing will depend on your views of the MCU's more ersatz entries. I love the schlock, others may not. Speaking of which, James Spader's villain more than meets the high performance standard set in the first film, leaving fellow newcomers Elizabeth Olsen and Aaron Taylor-Johnson to struggle by comparison. Elsewhere characterisation remains exceptional. (Followed by *Avengers: Infinity War*.)

Avengers: Endgame ★★★★★

2019, USA
Directors: Anthony Russo, Joe Russo
Cast: Robert Downey Jr., Chris Evans, Mark Ruffalo

Five years after Thanos snapped his fingers and magicked away half of all life in the universe, Ant-Man (Paul Rudd) tumbles out of an old van with an improbable scheme to make things right.

Audiences with a low tolerance for plot holes may have abandoned the Avengers series by now, but if not they're in for a rough ride: this monumental conclusion to *Avengers: Infinity War* doesn't make a jot of sense. Let's get that out of the way first, because there's so much good stuff here. *Endgame's* ample runtime is largely the result of a profusion of tightly focused character scenes. The writers understand we will experience the emotional fallout of Thanos' genocide through the loss felt by those who remain, and the first half of the screenplay has pathos woven into its fabric. Tony Stark (Downey Jr.) has walked away, but other surviving Avengers maintain a forlorn attempt to continue with their past lives, each attempting to kid the others it's working. Once hope finally emerges from the anguish (in a form that cleverly allows us to nostalgically revisit earlier events in the franchise) the pace and tone pick up, but we're left with the poignant heft of the early scenes. It adds immeasurably to the stakes. With everything lined up just so, finding the right resolution must have been a big challenge. Simply bringing everyone back would have been as unsatisfying as leaving them dead, but the weight of history demands sacrifice. The solution is perfect... plot holes aside.

Avengers: Infinity War ★★★★★

2018, USA
Directors: Anthony Russo, Joe Russo
Cast: Robert Downey Jr., Chris Hemsworth, Mark Ruffalo

Thanos (Brolin), the most feared warlord in the galaxy, attempts to unite the mythical Infinity Stones in order to use their power to wipe out half of all life in the universe. A smug billionaire, an angry demigod and a few scientific abnormalities are all that stand in his way.

And so the end, or at least the beginning of the end, is upon us. With over twenty superheroes to wrestle into the plot, *Infinity War* is wisely broken down into a handful of interconnected strands. Thus Dr. Strange (Benedict Cumberbatch), Iron Man (Downey Jr.) and Spider-Man (Holland) are teamed up for one mission, Rocket (Bradley Cooper), Thor (Hemsworth) and Groot (Vin Diesel) for another, and so on. The structure that results is inevitably episodic, but it creates clarity, streamlining each objective. To both hamper and aid our heroes the script is laced with lazy contrivances and it can feel a little flawed as a result. But the stakes are so well established, the characters so well defined and our engagement at such a high level by this point, that the film is no less riveting and heartrending for its occasionally wonky logic. (Followed by *Avengers: Endgame*.)

Avenging Force: The Scarab ★

2010, Canada
Director: Brett Kelly
Cast: Jennifer Barnes, Matthew Champ, Mark Courneyea

A secret military agency tasks a gaggle of superheroes with retrieving a magical rock before the evil Sphinx (Haucke) gets his hands on it.

It seems almost unfair on the letter 'A' that this chapter must be home to three Tom Cat movies. This one is the shortest and therefore the best (if you cut the padded credits it's barely an hour). Apparently there was no money to dress the villain's lair with black curtains this time, so we just have to accept the battle for mankind's future was fought in a mattress storage warehouse.

Awara Abdulla ★★

1963, India
Director: Tara Harish
Cast: Dara Singh, Chandrashekhar

Raised incognito for his own protection, the scion of a noble family grows up to be a defender of the vulnerable.

With the frankly enormous Dara Singh in the lead, *Awara Abdulla's* aping of luchador and peplum movies seems fitting. More incongruous are the attempts to pass the goliath off as an Indian Zorro, something his poor horse can't have been happy about. If you enjoy hysterical melodrama or watching Singh slowly wrestle bad guys, you're in luck. For the rest of us there's little on offer.

Ang Babaeng Isputnik

1963, Philippines
Director: Efren Reyes
Cast: Nida Blanca, Tony Ferrer, Jess Lapid

This first *Babaeng Isputnik* (*Rocket Woman*) movie starred Nida Blanca as a flying alien do-gooder. She returned later in the year to do battle with the ubiquitous Darna in *Sputnik vs. Darna*. Unavailable on home formats, but there's a reasonable chance it isn't completely lost.

Babaing Kidlat

1964, Philippines
Director: Tony Cayado
Cast: Liza Moreno, Dolphy, Apeng Daldal

Another female Pinoy superhero, another victim of the Pinoy film industry's apparent determination to demolish its cinematic heritage. This one was born with the power of flight after her mother was struck by lightning during childbirth (the title loosely translates to *Lightning Lady*). Considered lost, as is 1974 remake *Gemma: Babaing Kidlat*.

Bak bin sing gwan: see *Sixty Million Dollar Man*

Baji ★★★

2015, India
Director: Nikhil Mahajan
Cast: Shreyas Talpade, Amruta Khanvilkar, Jitendra Joshi

Residents of a village built on a stash of buried gold are threatened by miscreants when the treasure is discovered. Will Baji (Talpade), their once-forgotten supernatural protector, be able to save them?

The first Marathi language superhero movie has the air of a mythic folk tale, but as far as I can see Baji is a recent concoction. His

Lewis Wilson as Batman & Douglas Croft as Robin in the duo's first screen adventure, 1943's *Batman*

status as a multi-generational local guardian marks him out as a kind of Indian version of the Phantom, although he's better fleshed out thanks to his prominent public persona being given plenty of everyday issues to contend with. The movie itself features top performances, a more serious tone than we might expect from neighbouring Bollywood, beautiful scenery and slick camera trickery.

Bajrang Bali

1956, India
Director: Manibhai Vyas
Cast: Mahipal, Chandrashekhar, Ramayan Tiwari

This early take on the Hindu legend seems to be lost, but there is also evidence it's just unavailable on home formats.

Bajrangbali ★★

1976, India
Director: Chandrakant
Cast: Biswajeet, Dara Singh, Moushumi Chatterjee

The heroic doings of Hindi deity and Rama devotee Hanuman (Singh).

This stagey production of Hanuman's life story boasts more than its fair share of unintentional humour. The visual effects, occasional animal costumes and make-up (Singh's face is slathered in prosthetics to achieve the requisite Hanuman look) seem absurd, while action scenes are played out with comic awkwardness. In terms of the content it's utterly bewildering, perhaps because I'm not versed in the mythology, but it's all the more interesting a cultural experience as a result.

'Bangla RoboCop': see *Shoktir Lorai*

'Bangla Superman': see *Superman* (year unknown, Bengal)

Barb Wire ★★★

1996, USA
Director: David Hogan
Cast: Pamela Anderson, Amir AboulEla, Adriana Alexander

In a future USA ravaged by war, bounty hunter Barb Wire (Anderson) runs a sleazy bar in Steel Harbor, the only remaining free city. Things get complicated when she finds herself in the middle of a resistance plot to topple the government.

Think of this as Russ Meyer's *Casablanca*. The screenplay features some genuinely interesting scheming and gives a handful of characters logical trajectories dictated by actual events. This is not what I expected; occasionally it's like a real movie. But only occasionally, because most of the runtime is spent fetishising Anderson, whose job is to not *quite* burst out of whatever PVC bondage gear she's been sewn into for the scene at hand. Anderson is an odd performer and more in the mould of an old school muse such as Brigitte Bardot, Anita Ekberg or even Marilyn Monroe than she is a real thespian. Bothering about her bad acting is pointless. This is just a big, daft B-movie, so see her as a big, daft B-movie queen.

Barbarella ★★★★

1968, USA
Director: Roger Vadim
Cast: Jane Fonda, John Phillip Law, Anita Pallenberg

An agent of the Republic of Earth crosses the galaxy in search of a missing scientist.

The action and effects look every bit their 50+ years of age and the flimsy plot is more episodic than a web series cut-and-shut. But the soundtrack, sets, poiltical idealism and sheer nerve of the campery are all consistently, fabulously jaw dropping.

Barbie in Princess Power ★

2015, USA
Director: Ezekiel Norton
Cast: Kelly Sheridan, Britt Irvin, Michael Kopsa

A magical butterfly gives a princess with dead eyes superpowers.

And those who look upon the eyes of Barbie shall tremble, for in their depths lies naught but true sorrow.

Bat-man contra los hombres de estrella negra: see Black Star and the Golden Bat

Batman ★★

1943, USA
Director: Lambert Hillyer
Cast: Lewis Wilson, Douglas Croft, J. Carrol Naish

Something rum is afoot in Gotham's Little Tokyo, where criminal mastermind Prince Daka (Naish) is brainwashing scientists. What can Batman (Wilson) and his nimble sidekick Robin (Croft) do to help?

Batman's first appearance on film could have been more auspicious. There's a rule of thumb with serials that says Superman good, Batman bad, but in reality it's a little more nuanced than that. In its own right this isn't awful; it's a little talky and Batman could certainly do with being more effective in combat, but it's basically sound... apart from the racism. The US was at war with Japan at the time of production and it shows. At one point Voiceover Man informs us that "a wise government has rounded up the shifty-eyed Japs..." and, needless to say, the Japanese who appear on screen are presented as offensive caricatures. So, while this may be a seminal superhero adventure, it's more interesting as wartime propaganda. (Followed by 1949's *Batman and Robin*.)

Batman ★★★★★

1989, USA
Director: Tim Burton
Cast: Michael Keaton, Jack Nicholson, Kim Basinger

A neophyte Batman (Keaton) faces his first big challenge when The Joker (Nicholson) threatens Gotham with a deadly chemical.

A film with much to answer for. Although Richard Donner broadened the appeal of the superhero movie with his classic 1979 take on Superman, it inspired little more than a string of increasingly awful sequels and spinoffs. It's Tim Burton's *Batman* that changed everything, sewing the seeds that have given rise to the army of conflicted, costumed crusaders who now decimate the box office each summer. Why did it happen? Because Burton made him cool as hell. The impact of ditching the puritanical image of superhero-ing can't be underestimated. By drawing inspiration from Batman's modern, edgy comic book persona rather than the underpants-over-tights sanctimonious prig of previous eras, Burton and Keaton created a character not only more easily relatable (thanks to his flaws and doubts), but one who seemed achingly, aspirationally cool.

For me it still juggles those tricky comic book tones better than any other superhero film. (Followed by *Batman Returns*.)

Batman & Mr. Freeze: SubZero ★★★

1998, USA
Director: Boyd Kirkland
Cast: Kevin Conroy, Michael Ansara, Loren Lester

In an attempt to save his comatose wife, mad scientist Mr. Freeze (Ansara) kidnaps Barbara Gordon, aka Batgirl (Mary Kay Bergman), causing Batman (Conroy) and Robin (Lester) to spring into action.

With the previous year's live-action *Batman & Robin* mauled by critics, fans and even its own stars, it seems strange this animated adventure should look to it for inspiration. It covers much of the same ground as Joel Schumacher's offering, but with a gothic

The stunning *Batman Ninja*

sensibility. Danny Elfman's theme music and the shadowy visuals combine nicely with the pre-WWII fashions and Art Deco architecture, while Robin is less annoying than in other animated outings.

Batman & Robin ★★

1997, USA
Director: Joel Schumacher
Cast: Arnold Schwarzenegger, George Clooney, Chris O'Donnell

Physisict Dr. Victor Fries, aka raving lunatic pun machine Mr. Freeze (Schwarzenegger), attempts to destroy Gotham with an ice ray. Batman & Robin attempt to stop him destroying Gotham with an ice ray.

In the right mood *Batman & Robin* is a so-bad-it's-good masterpiece. In the wrong mood it may cause mental derangement and bleeding from the eyes, brain and soul.

Batman and Harley Quinn ★★

2017, USA
Director: Sam Liu
Cast: Kevin Conroy, Melissa Rauch, Paget Brewster

Batman (Conroy) and Nightwing (Loren Lester) team up with Harley Quinn (Rauch) to foil Poison Ivy's (Brewster) plot to turn mankind into plants.

Poorly written, cynically contrived and horribly misjudged; we're well into the realms of tasteless male wish fulfilment here. Female objectification has been an unfortunate component of these DC Universe Animated Original Movies from the start, but this one takes it too far.

Batman and Robin ★★

1949, USA
Director: Spencer Gordon Bennet
Cast: Robert Lowery, John Duncan, Jane Adams

Gotham City is subject to a crimewave, and a scientist's latest MacGuffin will only aid the villainous Wizard (Leonard Penn).

A change of cast ties in with a less hoary approach in this followup to the original 1943 serial. There's a much stronger female lead in Jane Adams' Vicki Vale, too, but a less engaging narrative balances things out.

Batman Begins ★★★★★
2005, USA
Director: Christopher Nolan
Cast: Christian Bale, Michael Caine, Katie Holmes

Fifteen years after his parents were killed by a hoodlum, Bruce Wayne (Bale) determines to understand the criminal subculture by throwing himself into it. Emerging as a lean and brutal weapon in the war on crime, he returns home to Gotham City to tackle mob boss Carmine Falcone (Tom Wilkinson). But little does he know trouble has followed close on his heels.

Generally speaking, the more expansive a superhero's origin story the more established the superhero, but the less satisfying their movie's narrative. Meaty origin stories can lead to a disconnected structure and rushed second half. One great success of Nolan's *Dark Knight* series is to deliver an exhaustive origin story that's independently engaging, and informs the plot all the way to its end. In fact it's almost as if the whole movie is the trilogy's origin story, but that isn't the backhanded compliment it may sound like. *Batman Begins* is constantly building. There's an irresistible momentum leading us to the finale. As a film it's less ambitious than its sequel, *The Dark Knight*, whose thematic, allegorical and character elements are so confidently, and consciously, bombastic. But it's also less flawed. There are certainly examples of the plot holes and contrivances that plague the subsequent films, but these are fewer in number and less egregious in

nature. The story is fundamentally sound, something you can't say about the sequels, and that makes it easier to enjoy Nolan's achievement. On a side note it's interesting how much *Batman Begins* harks back to the character's origins in Zorro. It isn't just superficial stuff (cave lair accessed via a waterfall, etc.) it includes crucial narrative and character elements. Like Zorro, Bruce Wayne travels in order to learn his warrior trade, then returns to the town in which he grew up and is considered a scion. There he adopts the public persona of an obnoxious playboy as cover for his crepuscular duties. There seems little doubt Nolan went back to the source for inspiration. (Followed by *The Dark Knight*.)

Batman Beyond: Return of the Joker ★★★★
2000, USA
Director: Curt Geda
Cast: Will Friedle, Mark Hamill, Kevin Conroy

The Joker (Hamill) is back, and he's brought an army of henchmen, henchwomen and henchbeasts with him. Batman (Friedle) is forced into action to put a stop to the chaos reigning over Gotham.

With Bruce Wayne occupying the Alfred role in support of new Batman Terry McGinnis (Friedle), this violent direct-to-video animated movie keeps one foot in the past and one in the future, much like its direct predecessor *Batman Beyond: The Movie*. Hamill remains the highlight as The Joker, but the script is among the best of any animated superhero movie and would have made for an intriguing live-action *Dark Knight* adventure.

Batman Beyond: The Movie ★★★★
1999, USA
Directors: Curt Geda, Butch Lukic, Dan Riba, Yukio Suzuki
Cast: Will Friedle, Kevin Conroy, Teri Garr

An ageing Bruce Wayne (Conroy) hangs up his cape after suffering a heart attack on a case. Twenty years later he reluctantly trains teenage rogue Terry McGinnis (Friedle) in the art of caped crusading.

Among the first animated DC movies to feel as if it was inspired by the comics and made for their fans. The animation is dynamic, the themes dark and Batman himself downbeat. Although technically a cut-and-shut based on the animated series, it feels cinematic in its scope and really zeroes in on character detail. (Followed by *Batman Beyond: Return of the Joker*.)

Batman Dracula

1964, USA
Director: Andy Warhol
Cast: Gregory Battcock, David Bourdon, Tally Brown

This is, or was, an experimental film made by Andy Warhol in his original New York 'Factory'. It's considered lost (although clips can be seen, just about, on YouTube). And, yes, it really did star a man called Battcock. He was an art critic and friend of Warhol.

Batman Fights Dracula

1967, Philippines
Director: Leody M. Diaz
Cast: Jing Abalos, Dante Rivero, Vivian Lorrain

Frustrated by Batman's (Abalos) continued disruption of his smuggling business, Dr. Zorba (D'Salva) decides to resurrect Dracula and pitch the two against each other. We know *Batman Fights Dracula* proved a star-making turn for prolific Filipino actor Jing Abalos, and that it was an early outing for director Leody M. Diaz, who would go on to make *The Bionic Boy*. But unfortunately even clips and trailers are apparently lost to time. That means we can only guess at what a Filipino Batman v Dracula movie might have looked like.

Batman Forever ★★★

1995, USA
Director: Joel Schumacher
Cast: Val Kilmer, Tommy Lee Jones, Jim Carrey

Disgruntled and unhinged, The Riddler (Carrey) teams up with Two-Face (Jones) in order to unmask Batman (Kilmer).

With the horror of *Batman & Robin* casting such a shadow over Joel Schumacher's tenure at the helm of this series, it's easy to forget *Batman Forever* isn't quite as silly. At least not all the time. There are various stylistic hangovers from the first two films, which means Tim Burton's gothic imagery grapples gracelessly with Schumacher's high contrast neon colour schemes. It's a similar dynamic with the characters: Jones and Carrey take their cues from the 1966 TV series while Kilmer's Bruce Wayne is inspired by the brooding, introspective take Michael Keaton introduced in 1989 (Kilmer is quite incredibly awful, by the way). As schizophrenic as the movie is, it's surprisingly entertaining. Just don't expect to take anything seriously. (Followed by 1997's *Batman & Robin*.)

Batman Ninja ★★★★

2018, USA/Japan
Director: Junpei Mizusaki
Cast (American version): Roger Craig Smith, Tony Hale, Grey Griffin

Batman (Yamadera/Smith) and a handful of enemies and allies are subjected to time displacement and find themselves in feudal era Japan.

With just the sort of far-out premise these movies should be delivering, and absolutely gorgeous animation to boot, *Batman Ninja* attempts to shake up the moribund world of animated superhero movies. It's a shame the (admittedly problematic) freewheeling narrative and unique style didn't appeal to fans (the movie has a 41% audience score on Rotten Tomatoes, so maybe you should ignore me on this one) because DC could be less inclined to take risks like this in the future. It's a long way from perfect, but still stunning.

Batman Returns ★★★★

1992, USA
Director: Tim Burton
Cast: Michael Keaton, Danny DeVito, Michelle Pfeiffer

The Penguin (DeVito), Catwoman (Pfeiffer) and devious businessman Max Schreck (Walken) play their parts in a plan to take control of Gotham and avenge numerous perceived injustices. Both Bruce Wayne (Keaton) and Batman become targets of their ire.

After the commercial success of 1989's *Batman*, director Tim Burton was afforded greater creative control over this follow-up and, predictably, delivered a film so wilfully, awkwardly uncommercial that the studio decided Joel Schumacher must henceforth be forced on us out of spite. The incredible imagery we're treated to here is among the most unique and eerie ever to feature in a major studio blockbuster, and DeVito's Penguin is surely as unsettling a villain as PG-13 audiences have ever had to contend with. It's no surprise box office takings were down on those of the first film. (Followed by *Batman Forever*.)

The Batman Superman Movie: World's Finest ★★★

1997, USA
Director: Toshihiko Masuda
Cast: Tim Daly, Dana Delany, Kevin Conroy

Lex Luthor (Clancy Brown) hires the Joker (Mark Hamill) to kill Superman (Daly), who must reluctantly work with Batman (Daly again) in order to save himself.

Constructed from three episodes of the 1996 *Superman* TV series (which explains why the focus remains on Kal at the cost of Bruce), this elementally animated old-school feature suffers from clunky dialogue and a weak plot. There is plenty of charm, though, and the family-friendly tone leaves it accessible to all ages.

Batman Unlimited: Animal Instincts ★★

2015, USA
Director: Butch Lukic
Cast: Roger Craig Smith, Chris Diamantopoulos, Will Friedle

Batman (Smith) defends Gotham from a plague of robot animals.

Enthusiastic tie-in with the Mattel toy line. The animation is bright and friendly while the central conceit (animal-themed DC villains banding together to cause trouble) is hokey fun. It's nice not to be taking things too seriously. (Followed by *Batman Unlimited: Monster Mayhem*.)

Batman Unlimited: Mechs vs. Mutants ★★

2015, USA
Director: Curt Geda
Cast: Roger Craig Smith, Oded Fehr, Lucien Dodge

Mr. Freeze (Fehr) mutates Killer Croc (John DiMaggio) and Bane (Carlos Alazraqui) into giant monsters, leaving Batman (Smith) and friends to save Gotham from destruction.

Third and final Batman Unlimited animated movie. At the end of the day each of these things are pretty much the same, they just have different themes, so if you've seen the previous two (and you're a grown-up) the formula will seem tired. We've done animals and monsters so now it's the turn of... well, despite the title the theme seems to be 'everyone who was left'. It's neither better nor worse for it.

Batman Unlimited: Monster Mayhem ★★

2015, USA
Director: Butch Lukic
Cast: Troy Baker, Eric Bauza, Steve Blum

The Joker (Baker) teams up with Scarecrow (Brian T. Delaney), Solomon Grundy (Fred Tatasciore), Clayface (Dave B. Mitchell) and Silver Banshee (Kari Whurer) in a scheme to release a devastating computer virus and compromise all Gotham's crucial technology.

The Halloween setting makes for a colourful backdrop to a humorous adventure; two aspects which help us ignore the fact this is just a re-tread based on a toyline. (Followed by *Batman Unlimited: Mechs vs. Mutants.*)

Batman v Superman: Dawn of Justice ★★

2016, USA
Director: Zack Snyder
Cast: Ben Affleck, Henry Cavill, Amy Adams

After witnessing the destruction caused by Superman (Cavill) and Zod (Michael Shannon) during the epic finale to *Man of Steel*, Bruce Wayne (Affleck) resolves to rid Earth of what he sees as the menace of Kal-El. Lex Luthor (Jesse Eisenberg) comes up with the same bright idea.

Cynics might say *Batman v Superman* is just three hours of buff men frowning, but we mustn't devalue the frowning done by Gal Gadot. Fans concerned that *Man of Steel* could have derailed the DCEU even as it pulled out of the station will not appreciate this train wreck of a sequel. Motivations are nonsensical, with people responding to situations in ways that create drama rather than believability, lending a Kafkaesque surreality to the character interactions. It's

horribly ugly to look at – the desaturated palette complimented by oddly depthless cinematography reminiscent of early 2000s digital. And the Superman-as-Christ analogy is too stupid for words. Once again the cast is too good for this. (Followed by 2017's *Justice League*.)

The Batman vs. Dracula ★★★★

2005, USA
Directors: Michael Goguen
Cast: Rino Romano, Peter Stormare, Tara Strong

After escaping Arkham Asylum, the Penguin (Tom Kenny) inadvertently resuscitates a dormant Dracula (Stormare), leaving Batman (Romano) to deal with the consequences.

Believe it or not, this is at least the third Batman movie to pitch the caped crusader against the king of vampires (in the mid 1960s Andy Warhol's *Batman Dracula* was followed by Philippine B-movie *Batman Fights Dracula*, but both are now considered lost). Based on the 2004 animated series *Batman*, there are some surprisingly scary visuals mixed into the childish aesthetic. The artists went all out to give Dracula and his zombie-like minions a genuinely alarming appearance, and their pasty-faced lunging at the camera seems like strong stuff in an unrated movie. While it's far from the best animated Batman adventure, the left-field villain and aforementioned spookiness make it well worthwhile.

Batman vs. Robin ★★★★

2015, USA
Director: Jay Oliva
Cast: Jason O'Mara, Stuart Allan, Kevin Conroy

With new Robin, Damian Wayne (Allan), resisting Batman's (O'Mara) authority, a wedge is driven between the crimefighters. Meanwhile, the mysterious Court of Owls has risen from the shadows to become a significant threat to Gotham.

Sort-of sequel to *Son of Batman*. Once you get over how obnoxious Robin is there's some good stuff here. The DC Universe Animated Original Movies series doesn't always know what to do with the freedom afforded by its older audience; usually these movies just feature more sexualised female characters and violence. But this one boasts proper themes of belonging and identity, and at least one sequence that's genuinely scary (Robin being rushed by children in freaky doll masks).

Batman vs. Teenage Mutant Ninja Turtles ★★★

2019, USA
Director: Jake Castorena
Cast: Troy Baker, Andrew Kishino, Cas Anvar

The Turtles follow the Shredder (Kishino) to Gotham, where he's up to no good with Ra's al Ghul (Anvar) and some ooze. Batman (Baker) takes charge.

Visually the Turtles are disappointingly featureless, but the fan service mandated by the title is well delivered. Judicious use of the ooze means we're treated to weird animal/supervillain chimeras, and even a brief but brilliant bat-Batman. The action is good with an early Batman/Shredder fight particularly engrossing.

Batman vs. Two-Face ★★★

2017, USA
Director: Rick Morales
Cast: Adam West, Burt Ward, William Shatner

Doused with evil in a botched experiment, District Attorney Harvey Dent becomes the deranged supervillain Two-Face (Shatner, thank you superhero movie gods). Batman (West) and Robin (Ward) must put a stop to the ensuing crimewave.

After *Batman: Return of the Caped Crusaders* this is the second animated throwback to the 1960s TV series. Rather than sticking to the reality defined by that show, it's all a little more cartoony this time. The script, scenario and characterisation are looser and less well defined. It still works and is certainly entertaining, but it isn't the little oasis of perfection *Return of the Caped Crusaders* is.

Batman: Assault on Arkham ★★★

2014, USA
Director: Jay Oliva, Ethan Spaulding
Cast: Kevin Conroy, Neal McDonough, Hynden Walch

Batman (Conroy) tears Gotham apart in search of a bomb planted by the Joker (Troy Baker). Meanwhile, the Suicide Squad break into Arkham Asylum to retrieve data stolen by the Riddler (Matthew Gray Gubler).

It's not unusual for animated superhero movies to be distracted with trying to look cool, but *Assault on Arkham* seems to think of little else. The opening titles are straight out of a Guy Ritchie movie and the Suicide Squad is painted as a schizophrenic teenage boy's fantasy. Self-conscious or not, it's still a good little movie. Harley Quinn (Walch) has a more significant role than Batman and proves bags of fun, while CCH Pounder is great as Amanda Waller. Best of all is the heist movie format, which gives us the proper structure animated movies often ignore in favour of shapeless fight scenes.

Batman: Bad Blood ★★

2016, USA
Director: Jay Oliva
Cast: Jason O'Mara, Yvonne Strahovski, Stuart Allan

Robin (Allan) and Nightwing (Sean Maher) hold the fort while Batwoman (Strahovski) investigates the mysterious disappearance of Batman (O'Mara).

There are good character dynamics and an intriguing story, but this is the 24th entry in the DC Universe Animated Original Movies series and with nothing new on the table it just seems boring. Robin is still a loathsome brat, Nightwing a still a dull irrelevance and Batman is still a judgemental drag (when he's in it, which isn't much). And if I have to see one more flashback to Bruce Wayne's parents being murdered in an alley…!

Batman: Gotham by Gaslight ★★

2018, USA
Director: Sam Liu
Cast: Bruce Greenwood, Jennifer Carpenter, Chris Cox

A Victorian era Batman (Greenwood) battles Jack the Ripper.

Pseudo-Steampunk 'Elseworlds' tale that isn't as original as it thinks it is. There's a misguided attempt to touch on feminist themes which, within the DCAU, is a bit like the Joker lecturing us on fair play. The different setting and nod to progressive ideas barely amount to a new coat of paint, and underneath whatever thin veneer it amounts to there's a familiarly flimsy plot full of trivial characters.

Batman: Gotham Knight ★★★

2008, USA
Directors: Yasuhiro Aoki, Futoshi Higashide, Toshiyuki Kubooka, Hiroshi Morioka, Jong-Sik Nam, Shôjirô Nishimi, Yûichirô Hayashi
Cast: Kevin Conroy, Jason Marsden, Scott Menville

A series of adventures sketching some key events of Batman's (Conroy) early career.

Numerous Japanese animation styles and techniques are employed in this visually stunning and hugely ambitious anthology movie. More abstract in its narratives and lead by aesthetic considerations, it won't be to everyone's tastes and is riddled with issues. But there are moments of genius in Gotham Knight.

Batman: Mask of the Phantasm ★★★★

1993, USA
Directors: Eric Radomski, Bruce Timm
Cast: Kevin Conroy, Dana Delany, Hart Bochner

An aggressive vigilante has put Gotham's criminals on the run and Batman (Conroy) under suspicion.

Theatrically released spinoff from the 1992 series and the first proper animated Batman movie. Worrying pretentions are revealed early as we open on Art Deco styling and choral music, but it soon gives way to child-friendly animation and amusing, sharply written characters. Batman gets a chance to exercise his detective skills, and ghosts from the past emerge to add an emotional dimension to a strong narrative.

Batman: Mystery of the Batwoman ★★

2003, USA
Directors: Curt Geda
Cast: Kevin Conroy, Kimberly Brooks, Kelly Ripa

In addition to The Penguin (David Ogden Stiers) and Rupert Thorne (John Vernon), who are smuggling guns, Batman (Conroy) and Robin (Eli Marienthal) must contend with an inscrutable female masked avenger.

Based on The New Batman Adventures and within the continuity of Batman: Mask of the Phantasm and Batman & Mr. Freeze: SubZero (in spite of the different animation style). It's a bit lightweight compared to the Batman Beyond titles of the previous few years, and isn't nearly as engaging. That could just be down to the writing, though, which seems to position the movie for a younger audience and relies on too many coincidences. The charmless animation doesn't help.

Batman: Return of the Caped Crusaders ★★★★

2016, USA
Director: Rick Morales
Cast: Adam West, Burt Ward, Julie Newmar

Batman (West) duplicates himself after being exposed to Catwoman's (Newmar) 'batnip' formula and turning bad.

Almost perfectly judged extension to the original Adam West TV series. By adding around 10% more self-awareness the tone is updated from 60s camp to modern kitsch without sacrificing anything important. Sets, props and character designs are lovingly recreated in crisply rendered widescreen, while the dialogue and scenarios could have come from an un-produced original script. We can forgive a few moments of excess creeping in from the modern DCAU (the Dynamic Duo never fought with such ferocity and their foe's seldom resided in space stations).

Batman: The Dark Knight Returns, Parts 1 & 2 ★★★★

2013, USA
Director: Jay Oliva
Cast: Peter Weller, Ariel Winter, David Selby

With Batman (Weller) retired and old ally Commissioner Gordon (Selby) about to join him, a gang known as The Mutants has turned Gotham into a war zone.

Faithful animated adaptation of the 1986 comic book mini-series. This is probably as close as a mainstream animated superhero movie can get to being an epic masterpiece. Human nature is explored through Batman's attempt to deny his true self, murky political realities are behind the president's decision to have Superman (Mark Valley) put a stop

to Batman's vigilantism, and everything is framed by diplomatic tensions between the USA and the Soviet Union.

Batman: The Killing Joke ★★

2016, USA
Director: Sam Liu
Cast: Kevin Conroy, Mark Hamill, Tara Strong

After escaping from Arkham, The Joker (Hamill) goes after Commissioner Gordon (Ray Wise) and his daughter Barbara, aka Batgirl (Strong). A typically moody Batman (Conroy) investigates.

Based on Alan Moore's influential graphic novel of the same name (Christopher Nolan and Tim Burton each cite it as an influence on their Batmen), this ambitious animated film maintains Moore's adult tone. Hamill and Conroy are at their best but the script renders key characters one-dimensional, takes some pretty silly turns and offers us an horrendously trite Batgirl.

Batman: The Movie ★★★★★

1966, USA
Director: Leslie H. Martinson
Cast: Adam West, Burt Ward, Lee Meriwether

A roll call of supervillains team up to hold the world ransom with a dehydration formula. Batman (West) and Robin (Ward) take care of business.

With the 1966 Batman TV series proving an immediate hit for the ABC network, rights holders 20th Century Fox greenlit the feature film they had turned down earlier in the year, and managed to rush it into theatres between the show's first and second seasons. Like the series, *Batman: The Movie* bounds gleefully across the line into parody, but it also takes satirical swipes at some of the era's more appealing targets, presenting the US president as a publicity-seeking phony, and the 'United World' organisation (read United Nations) as an ineffectual bureaucracy. The approach of the TV show remains the movie's template, however, which is perfectly illustrated by a scene in which Robin's cry of "holy sardine" alerts Batman to the shark attached to his leg (it's ok, they have their Shark Repellent Bat Spray). A more purely joyous superhero movie does not exist.

Batman: Under the Red Hood
★★★★

2010, USA
Director: Brandon Vietti
Cast: Bruce Greenwood, Jensen Ackles, John DiMaggio

A brutal new crimefighter known as The Red Hood (Ackles) is terrorising Gotham's criminals. Ever morally upstanding, Batman (Greenwood) won't accept such violence and calls on the assistance of old friends, and older foes, to bring him down.

Hugely successful and profoundly dark (it opens with the second Robin apparently being tortured to death, which certainly got me onboard), *Batman: Under the Red Hood* takes some cues from the usual live action Batventures, but remains its own animal. The central mystery is engrossing and nudges our hero towards introspective territory animated superhero movies don't like to mess with. (FYI it's extremely unsuitable for young children.)

Batman: Year One ★★★★

2011, USA
Directors: Sam Liu, Lauren Montgomery
Cast: Bryan Cranston, Ben McKenzie, Eliza Dushku

As Bruce Wayne (McKenzie) returns home after 12 years abroad, idealistic cop Jim Gordon (Cranston) is transferred to Gotham P.D. The city's corrupt police force are happy about neither turn of events.

Numerous attempts have been made to adapt Frank Miller's *Year One* comic book arc for the screen, with Joss Whedon and Darren Aronofsky nearly managing to get their respective projects off the ground. While it's influenced numerous other films, this animated feature is the only formal adaptation. With a film noir approach it focuses as much on Jim Gordon as Batman, and the young detective proves just as capable of dealing with Gotham's scum.

BATMoN vs MAJURo ★★

2016, Marshall Islands
Directors: Jack Niedenthal, Ben Debrum Wakefield
Cast: Ben Debrum Wakefield, Karen Earnshaw, Arelong Simon

An elderly Catwoman (Earnshaw) steals the Batcopter and hides it on the Marshall Islands. A distinctly podgy Batmon/Batman (Wakefield) flies in to find it and remind her who's boss. While visiting he faces numerous wacky challenges.

Where do fan films end and zero budget movies begin? Looking like a cross between a Tom Cat mockbuster and a Wakaliwood take on the DC Universe, *BATMoN vs MAJURo* (Majuro being the capital of the Marshall Islands, a string of volcanic atolls in the Pacific) is as sloppy as a movie can be. What it lacks in technical expertise it doesn't quite make up for in enthusiasm, but my goodness it tries, and that makes criticism a tricky proposition. So let's simply say it's a unique and (just about) worthwhile experience. Tracking down a copy might prove tricky, though, or maybe you caught it at the Guam International Film Festival back in 2017?

Battle of the Planets: The Movie
★★★

2005, USA/Japan
Cast: Casey Kasem, Keye Luke, Ronnie Schell

The pernicious Zoltar (Luke) steals Earth's gold and intends to smuggle it to his home planet of Spectra. Teenage superhero team G-Force try to stop him.

Cut-and-shut made of episodes from the 1970s TV series, which was an English dubbed version of Japanese anime show *Gatchaman*. *Battle of the Planets: The Movie* was a peculiar and somewhat belated go at relaunching the franchise using original footage. Nothing substantial has changed: one of the minor characters is voiced by a different actor and the theme tune has been remixed; otherwise the only additions are shots of violence previously culled when the show was Westernised for US TV. If you liked *Battle of the Planets* you'll probably like this. Trivia fans may note the villainous Zoltar is played by Keye Luke, who returns to the world of superhero movies 65 years after originating the role of Kato on screen in 1940's *The Green Hornet*.

The Batwoman ★★

aka *La mujer murcielago*, 1968, Mexico
Director: René Cardona
Cast: Maura Monti, Roberto Cañedo, Héctor Godoy

Batwoman (Monti), wealthy socialite and champion wrestler (this is a Mexican movie after all), travels to Acapulco to help solve a spate of mysterious murders.

With Batwoman's costume consisting of a tiny bikini, and the mad scientist behind the murders attempting to create a 'fish-man' using wrestler's spinal fluid, this is not the most serious Batmovie, official or otherwise (unsurprisingly it sits in the latter camp). In fact it's a standard low-budget ripoff with little sign of director René Cardona Snr.'s early promise (he was the first to make a Spanish language film in the USA and won numerous awards during his early career. Needless to say he also made a number of luchador movies).

Batman: The Movie

Batwoman and Robin

1972, Philippines
Director: Jun Aristorenas
Cast: Robin Aristorenas, Virginia Aristorenas, Sofia Moran

At least the second unlicensed Batwoman movie after Mexico's 1968 attempt. Lost.

Batwoman and Robin Meet the Queen of the Vampires

1972, Philippines
Director: Tony Cayado
Cast: Robin Aristorenas, Virginia Aristorenas, Angelina Ortiz

A Hammer horror vibe appears to have been adopted for this sequel to the above, which is also considered lost.

The Beastmaster ★★★★

1982, USA
Director: Don Coscarelli
Cast: Marc Singer, Tanya Roberts, Rip Torn

A prince raised in anonymity discovers he can communicate with animals. As an adult he seeks vengeance for the murder of his adoptive family.

Developed contemporaneously with the better known *Conan the Barbarian* it took until *The Beastmaster's* TV and home video release for it to find much of an audience. There's no denying it's poorly written (the main villain is ultimately killed by a ferret almost as an afterthought), and the cast is nowhere near the standard of its more illustrious Hyborean cousin. But it's also less mean-spirited and boasts a surprisingly sensitive and amiable hero.

Beastmaster 2: Through the Portal of Time ★★★

1991, USA

Director: Sylvio Tabet
Cast: Marc Singer, Kari Wuhrer, Sarah Douglas

Heinous warlord Arklon (Wings Hauser) has used 'unholy magic' to enslave the people of Arok. Dar, aka The Beastmaster (Singer), leads the resistance.

Belated sequel built on the questionable idea of depositing its inter-dimensional barbarian protagonist into contemporary California. Singer is responsible for half the movie's appeal, while the campier tone takes credit for the rest. Whether that camp is a hangover from filmmaker Jim Wynorski's early, and controversial, involvement in the writing process isn't clear, but it feels like the work of the B-movie legend. Wings Hauser delivers an absurd performance as the villain and Sarah Douglas chews the scenery as sinister enchantress Lyranna. A kitsch favourite among B-movie fans.

Beastmaster III: The Eye of Braxus ★★

1996, USA
Director: Gabrielle Beaumont
Cast: Marc Singer, Tony Todd, Keith Coulouris

Dar The Beastmaster (Singer) learns of a tyrannical Sorcerer's plan to gain ultimate power by stealing a magical amulet from King Tal (Casper Van Dien).

Bad writing and contrivances help make this final instalment in the series the shoddiest. Van Dien is comically miscast as a barbarian king, and even a tired looking Singer can't muster much by way of charm. There's still some tongue-in-cheek fun to be had, but it's not on the level of the second film.

Behind the Mask ★★

aka *The Shadow Behind the Mask*, 1946, USA
Directors: Phil Karlson, William Beaudine
Cast: Kane Richmond, Barbara Read, George Chandler

Suave detective Lamont Cranston, aka The Shadow (Richmond), investigates a nightclub owner who may, or may not, have set him up for the murder of blackmailing reporter Jeff Mann (James Cardwell).

Second in a series of three disposable Shadow quickies. It's full of bad takes and dumb jokes (hey cops, maybe the man-shaped bed sheet running away from you is the guy you're chasing and not a ghost), and never gets off the ground. (Followed by *The Missing Lady*.)

Behind the Mask of Zorro ★
aka *El Zorro cabalga otra vez, Oath of Zorro*, 1965, Spain/Italy
Director: Ricardo Blasco
Cast: Tony Russel, María José Alfonso, Roberto Paoletti

Zorro (Russel) battles corruption. Vaguely.

Russel's Zorro isn't afforded a particularly auspicious introduction: after looming off in the distance for a spell, he turns tail and frantically runs from the baddies. Imagine Tyrone Power or Douglas Fairbanks debuting like that. A strange affair follows. The movie seems to forget Zorro can appear on screen and, despite him being the main subject of conversation, he only pops up a couple of times for brief (apparently unrehearsed) sword fights. Eventually he just blends his way into what purports to be a finale, but it remains easy to forget he's there. Most of the runtime is spent with Wild West men going round in circles rambling about this, that or Zorro, which creates the effect of being trapped on a wagon train full of badly dubbed Spaniards.

Behold the Raven ★
2004, USA
Directors: J.A. Tripp, J.L. Pollack
Cast: Bobby Browning, Janet Lynn, April Billingsley

High schooler Tommy Taylor (Browning) is The Raven, a motorcycling superhero who must stand up to the supernatural forces of criminal organisation SERPENT.

More fan film than mockbuster, this obvious passion project just about qualifies as a real movie due to somehow gaining a DVD release. Afficianados of lo-fi filmmaking (or bewildering colour grades) might find something to enjoy. I didn't.

Ben 10: Alien Swarm ★
2009, USA
Director: Alex Winter
Cast: Ryan Kelley, Alyssa Diaz, Nathan Keyes

Weird insect-like computer chips attempt an invasion, which leaves Ben (Kelley), or his babysitter, to work with a frenemy in an attempt to stop them.

Five years after Ben 10's disastrous live-action debut in *Race Against Time*, Cartoon Network decided to have another stab at the property. Sadly it's even worse. For some inexplicable reason Ben has been rebooted as a 23-year-old mallrat doing dodgy deals in an abandoned warehouse. Presumably this fits with his then current TV persona, but that doesn't mean it works.

Ben 10: Destroy All Aliens ★★
2012, USA
Director: Victor Cook
Cast: Tara Strong, Meagan Moore, Paul Eiding

A terrifying alien bounty hunter seems bent on murdering Ben (Strong), whose Omnitrix is malfunctioning.

The final Ben 10 feature film, *Destroy All Aliens*, is a 3D animated adventure which slots into the timeline after the far superior *Secret of the Omnitrix*. Although popular among fans it lacks broad appeal and the fight scenes are partiuclarly wearing.

Hitoshi Matsumoto, or a CG rendering of him, in
Big Man Japan aka *Dai-Nihonjin*

Ben 10: Race Against Time ★

2007, USA
Director: Alex Winter
Cast: Graham Phillips, Christien Anholt,
Haley Ramm

An ancient alien known as Eon (Anhalt)
plans to open a time rift that will destroy
Ben's (Phillips) home town.

Disappointing live-action debut for Ben
Tennyson and co. While I'm not overly
familiar with the TV series, fan criticism
of this adaptation seems driven by the
characters deviating too much from their
animated counterparts. I'm happy simply
to call it out as a terrible movie. It's badly
written, badly acted, full of incoherent
and excessive action and fails to nail the
tokusatsu tone it aims for.

Ben 10: Secret of the Omnitrix
★★★★

2007, USA
Directors: Sebastian Montes, Scooter Tidwell
Cast: Tara Strong, Meagan Moore, Paul Eiding

Ben (Strong) must find the creator of his
Omnitrix before it completes a countdown
and destroys the universe.

The best of the Ben 10 movies is a fast,
fun and surprisingly witty 2D computer
animation similar in style to the original
series (to which it's the official conclusion,
although it stands alone just fine). There's
well handled antagonism between Ben and
his cousin Gwen (Moore), and guest starring
alien robot Tetrax (Dave Fennoy) has some
wonderfully dry one-liners. A diamond
among the stones of this franchise.

Bertong Ipu-Ipo

1969, Philippines
Director: Artemio Marquez
Cast: Roberto Gonzalez, Jessica, Danny Rojo

Ipo-ipo (aka Ipu-Ipo), created in 1947
by Lib Abrena and Oscar del Rosario, is
widely seen as the first Filipino comic book
superhero. Powered by the whirlwind
from which he takes his name, this is the
character's only known movie adaptation
and is believed lost.

Bhavesh Joshi Superhero ★★★

2018, India
Director: Vikramaditya Motwane
Cast: Harshvardhan Kapoor, Priyanshu Painyuli, Ashish Verma

After three friends start a YouTube channel aimed at exposing Mumbai's corruption, one of them, Bhavesh (Painyuli), turns up dead. The others investigate.

There's a point early on in *Bhavesh Joshi Superhero* when one of the protagonists identifies his little gang of moral crusaders as being similar to the Justice League, but emphatically NOT like the Avengers. With Bollywood superhero movies traditionally a blur of primary colours and jaunty singing, it's hard not to see the scene as an allegory. This is a determinedly downbeat film. There are no songs, much of it is shot at night, the colour has been washed out and there's a relentless sense of doom pervading almost everything. It may not be *Requiem for a Dream*, but nor is it escapist fantasy. Quite good though.

Bianong Bulag ★★

aka *One-Eyed Terror of Cavite*, 1977, Philippines
Director: Jose Yandoc
Cast: Ramon Revilla, Charito Solis, Armida Siguion-Reyna

Bibiano Angeles (Revilla) returns to his home town and discovers the bullies who blinded him in one eye are now involved in shady doings. A magical amulet gives him the power to fight back, at least when not being a bit of a scumbag himself.

An unselfconscious performance from Revilla almost distinguishes this anting-anting 'Pinoy folksploitation' movie from dozens of similar examples. His nervous stammer is a surprise, as is the comically over-the-top make-up job on the eye, which is shot like a Universal monster. There's a

great opening title sequence, but ultimately it's just one of many similar movies.

Big Hero 6 ★★★★★

2014, USA
Directors: Don Hall, Chris Williams
Cast: Ryan Potter, Scott Adsit, Jamie Chung

In order to investigate the death of his brother, child prodigy Hiro (Potter) forms a superhero group from a disparate group of oddball students. Inflatable healthcare robot Baymax (Adsit) proves to be their most important member.

The setting (San Fransokyo) is, as the name suggests, some sort of alternate universe amalgamation of Tokyo and San Francisco, with similarly symbiotic diversity reflected in the characters. Rather than feeling like a casual sop to whichever culture was chosen to (co-)host Disney's latest extravaganza, it seems like a unique and carefully conceived new world. There's a surprising amount of emotional heavy lifting on display (one of many signs Disney may have looked to Studio Ghibli for inspiration), and a pair of heroes so engaging that the poignance of the finale lingers long after the credits roll.

Big Man Japan ★★★★

aka *Dai-Nihonjin*, 2007, Japan
Director: Hitoshi Matsumoto
Cast: Hitoshi Matsumoto, Riki Takeuchi, Ua

Outwardly average Tokyo citizen Masaru Daisatô (Matsumoto) is in fact a kyodei hero able to grow to 30 metres in height when Japan needs defending from kaiju.

Shot as a mockumentary, *Big Man Japan* presents our hero as a slightly dishevelled and apparently disillusioned everyman. His forebears, each of whom performed the same role as supernatural protector of Japan, were all lauded as champions, but an ungrateful populace is no longer impressed by heroic exploits. That seems to have lead to a crisis of confidence in Daisatô. There's much comedy (and social commentary) to be mined from the scenario. This is a wonderful movie: intelligent, imaginative and unique.

Binibining Tsuper-Man ★★★

1987, Philippines
Director: Ben Feleo
Cast: Roderick Paulate, Miguel Rodriguez, Panchito

Gay jeepney driver Rogelio (Paulate) is bullied by his colleagues and undermined by a father who believes he can be 'cured' of homosexuality. Until, that is, the queen of a distant planet grants him superpowers so he can fight the devil.

As a broad comedy that derives much humour from its star's cartoonish campery, it's questionable to what extent *Binibining Tsuper-Man* can lay claim to progressive sensibilities, but I'm giving it the benefit of the doubt. Rogelio is a sympathetic character who has the last laugh, and it seems like the movie's motivation is sound. There are plenty of absurd costumes and terrible visual effects to laugh at, and the pace doesn't let up.

Biokids ★★★

1990, Philippines
Director: Bebong Osorio
Cast: Dick Israel, Ai-Ai de las Alas, Bembol Roco

A mad scientist gives a bunch of children henshin hero costumes and motorcycles so they can fight thugs.

Apparently this is an in-joke made for Pinoy Super Sentai fans. *Bioman*, the 8th iteration of Toei's Super Sentai meta-series, was so popular in the Philippines that enterprising producer Tony Gloria thought it might be fun to spoof the formula, only with small

children replacing the adults. He was about half right. The endless fight scenes break off every now and then for fart jokes and general weirdness, but it's the air of anarchy that stays with you. So bad it's good.

The Bionic Boy ★★★

aka *Trionic Warrior, Superboy*, 1977, Philippines/Hong Kong
Director: Leody M. Diaz
Cast: Johnson Yap, Joe Sison, Chito Guerrero

Maimed when his parents are murdered by gangsters, young Johnson 'Sonny' Lee (Yap) is given various bionic limbs, organs and other accoutrements, becoming an Interpol superagent in the process.

Lee loses his legs, arms, hearing, sight, half his internal organs and suffers such severe brain damage the doctors summise that, in the unlikely event of his survival, he'll be left a 'vegetable'. This is not the knockabout romp suggested by the poster, but once you get over the shock it's kind of fun. The premise is taken seriously, it's nicely shot, there's some great jazz on the soundtrack and a top-drawer wacky villain.

The Bionic Boy II ★★

aka *The Return of the Bionic Boy, Dynamite Johnson, Dinamit Johnson*, 1979, Philippines/Hong Kong
Director: Bobby A. Suarez
Cast: Johnson Yap, Marrie Lee, Ken Metcalfe

Sonny Lee (Yap) is back, and this time he has help from Cleopatra Wong (Lee) as he fights Nazis armed with robot dragons.

Acting as a sequel to both *The Bionic Boy* and 1978's *Cleopatra Wong*, *The Return of the Bionic Boy* never quite lives up to its premise. The dragons are excellent but appear only briefly, leaving us abandoned in a quarry for much of the movie. A strong finale is too little too late.

Bionic Ever After? ★★

aka *Bionic Breakdown*, 1994, USA
Director: Steve Stafford
Cast: Lindsay Wagner, Lee Majors,
Richard Anderson

While Jamie Sommers' (Wagner) bionics
are sabotaged by a shadowy villain, Steve
Austin (Majors) attempts to rescue an old
friend from a terrorist siege.

Having tried and failed to launch a spinoff
with Austin's son in the fourth movie, and
Sommers' protege in the fifth, this sixth
and final Six Million Dollar Man TV movie
doubles down on the soap opera that is its
original stars' personal lives, and abandons
all attempts to extend the franchise. As
usual the action is limited to occasional
interjections from a plot that never seems
to be the point of anything. But the big
surprise of these later *6MDM* movies is
Jamie Sommers, who, as played by the
excellent Lindsay Wagner, is among the
strongest female superheroes. She's at least
the equal of Austin in every way, drives the
plot just as much, gets more dialogue and
even enjoys top billing.

Bionic Showdown: The Six Million Dollar Man and the Bionic Woman ★★★

1989, USA
Director: Alan J. Levi
Cast: Lindsay Wagner, Lee Majors,
Richard Anderson

The World Unity Games are threatened by
an unidentified bionic agent, which leaves
Steve Austin (Majors) under suspicion.

Again we get a heavy dose of melodrama
thanks to more unnecessary bionic-ising
(this time the subject is a young Sandra
Bullock), but at least it's in service of the
plot. There's a cold war feel to everything,
with lots of double agents and secret
schemes, although that might suggest it's
more exciting than it is. Steve and Jamie
are less prominent, as if they're overseeing
the passing of the torch to Bullock's Kate,
which would be more than welcome if she
wasn't so wet. (Followed *Bionic Ever After?*)

Black Cougar ★

2002, USA
Director: Silvio DiSalvatore
Cast: Lenny DiSalvatore, Tom Delaney,
Lil Sil DiSalvatore

A criminal gang is kidnapping children and
selling them into slavery, so an old man
kits out his adopted son with homemade
superhero gear and, voila: Black Cougar.

This is more like a community initiative
on stranger danger than an actual film.

The Bionic Boy II, aka *Dinamit Johnson*

Full of non-actors, cardboard props and dialogue like 'I just gave you the power of a ventriloquist', *Black Cougar* is beyond incompetent. Unlike the sloppy offerings from production companies such as Tom Cat (see the next entry) its intentions seem admirable, but it's still bad.

The Black Knight Returns ★

2009, USA
Director: Juan Avilez
Cast: Adam Salandra, Win De Lugo, Cheryl Texiera

Evan Grail (Salandra), the scion of an ancient crimefighting dynasty, becomes costumed vigilante the Black Knight just in time to save the world from a deadly virus.

The lighting blows out every white surface in the frame, we can see the pattern of the OSB board through the grey paint that's meant to make it look like steel, walls are made of paper (not even cardboard) and the same ornaments feature in multiple locations. Business as usual for Tom Cat.

Black Lightning ★★

aka *Chernaya Molniya*, 2009, Russia
Directors: Dmitriy Kiselev, Aleksandr Voytinskiy
Cast: Grigoriy Dobrygin, Ekaterina Vilkova, Viktor Verzhbitskiy

Schoolboy Dmitry Maykov (Dobrygin) inadvertently acquires a flying car. When he fails to save a dying man who turns out to be his father, he learns the hard way that, with great power, comes great, etc.

There's nothing new in this derivative Herbie meets Spider-Man adventure. The bad guy wants a MacGuffin, the good guy has the MacGuffin but doesn't realise it, so the bad guy tries to get the MacGuffin. That's about it, apart from the strangely depressing Russian humour filling in the gaps. Not so much bad as pointless.

Black Mask ★★★★

aka *Hak hap*, 1996, Hong Kong
Director: Daniel Lee
Cast: Jet Li, Ching Wan Lau, Karen Mok

Apparently pacifist librarian Tsui Chik (Li) is actually the survivor of an abandoned supersoldier project. When he learns his former colleagues are taking over Hong Kong's underworld he dons a mask and attempts to stop them.

Plentiful (and quite brutal) kung fu scenes underpin the appeal of this enjoyably silly martial arts romp. Li is exceptional and Yuen Woo-Ping's choreography stunning (it proved a significant influence on The Wachowskis and their concept for the fight scenes in *The Matrix*). The only real drawback is a tendency to accompany the action with inexplicable bursts of hip hop.

Black Mask 2: City of Masks ★★

aka *Hak hap 2*, 2002, Hong Kong/USA
Director: Hark Tsui
Cast: Andy On, Tobin Bell, Jon Polito

Black Mask (On) must prevent a gang of genetically enhanced wrestlers setting off a bomb that will mutate human DNA. (How many genetically enhanced wrestlers does one genre need?)

More of a techno noir sci-fi thriller than a superhero or martial arts movie like its predecessor, *Black Mask 2: City of Masks* also bears significant Western influence. Shot in English and featuring numerous US actors (we lose Jet Li but gain... Traci Lords), it's calibrated for an international audience. Unfortunately it isn't very good. The fight scenes are drab, which is a let down after the first film, and the story incoherent.

The Black Ninja ★

2003, USA

Director: Clayton Prince
Cast: Clayton Prince, Carla Brothers, Nicky DeMatteo

Maliq Ali (Prince) is a charismatic defence attorney by day, and a crimefighting ninja vigilante by night.

Part-time actor/full-time narcissist Clayton Prince wrote, directed and starred in this spectacularly inept cult ego-trip. Shot on domestic-grade video, it mashes Chinese and Japanese cultural clichés (Prince seems not to recognise the difference) and martial arts disciplines into the concept for Marvel's *Daredevil*. Unsubtlely. Banal R&B drowns out the echoey voices whenever the awful theme tune isn't playing, and the fight scenes are as bad as any I've seen.

Black Panther ★★★★

2018, USA
Director: Ryan Coogler
Cast: Chadwick Boseman, Michael B. Jordan, Lupita Nyong'o

The fictional African nation of Wakanda, seemingly poor and isolationist but in reality rich and isolationist, faces a trying time. The king is dead, his successor has doubts, and an usurper seeks to turn tradition on its head. That's a lot of problems for a fledgling superhero to deal with.

In the run up to its release, conversation surrounding *Black Panther* dealt mainly with the race of its cast and director. While it's by no means the first 'black superhero movie', it is the first American studio example to draw so comprehensively on African culture. The score, the costumes, the sets and more reflect a keen intent to soak the Marvel formula in Alkebu-lan personality. The film's extraordinary box office haul (it's the second most successful superhero movie released in the US, after only *Avengers: Endgame*) suggests audiences were wondering why it took so long. Although subject to the same CGI waves that risk drowning most Marvel movies, the scale is quite sensible. The villain isn't an alien monster; he's a disillusioned outsider. The stakes don't pit mankind against obliteration; they risk civil uprising. And the hero isn't an invincible ego-monster; he's a fallible leader with the weight of a nation on his shoulders. Of all the microcosms housed by an increasingly crowded MCU, Wakanda is among the best.

Black Scorpion ★★

1995, USA
Director: Jonathan Winfrey
Cast: Joan Severance, Garrett Morris, Bruce Abbott

After being suspended from duty and then frustrated by the slow-turning wheels of justice, detective Darcy Walker (Severance) assumes the identity of costumed vigilante The Black Scorpion. Aided by car thief and reluctant assistant Argyle (Morris), she defends Angel City from The Breathtaker, a maniac with mechanical superlungs.

Created by B-movie legend Roger Corman and screenwriter Craig J. Nevius (the man responsible for penning Corman's infamous unreleased take on The Fantastic Four), *Black Scorpion* premiered on the Showtime TV network just as *Batman Forever* hit the big screen. The timing was no coincidence. While this subsidiary superhero may have been a cash-in on Warner's successful bat-franchise (it goes for a similar balance of elements), it just about proves its worth thanks to a committed performance from Severance and some gloriously silly tonal shifts. Just don't try to take it any more seriously than a superhero invented by Roger Corman should be taken.

Black Scorpion II: Aftershock ★★★

1996, USA
Director: Jonathan Winfrey
Cast: Joan Severance, Whip Hubley, Matt Roe

Joan Severance as the title character in
Black Scorpion.

Black Scorpion Returns ★

2001, USA
Director: Gwyneth Gibby
Cast: Michelle Lintel, Guy Boyd, Martin Kove

Det. Darcy Walker (Lintel), faces a dilemma when her new partner becomes obsessed with bringing her alter ego, Black Scorpion, to justice. Even worse, a deranged cyborg and a superpowered eco-terrorist are up to no good on her beat.

In 2001, the Sci-Fi Channel rebooted Roger Corman's perennially underdressed vigilante for a TV series, and it's from the first two episodes of that short-lived show that this straight-to-video cut-and-shut is derived. Like *Black Scorpion II: Aftershock* it finds its tone by channeling *Batman '66*, and brings back the dafter villains from the previous movies. That means there's plenty of kitsch fun on offer. Lintel is a letdown, though, her flat monotone and lack of presence sucking the life out of everything.

Black Scorpion: Sting of the Black Scorpion ★★

2002, USA
Directors: Gwynethh Gibby, Stanley Yung, Tim Andrew
Cast: Michelle Lintel, Frank Gorshin, Martin Kove

Det. Darcy Walker (Lintel), faces a dilemma when her new partner becomes obsessed with bringing her alter ego, Black Scorpion, to justice. Even worse, a deranged cyborg and a superpowered eco-terrorist are up to no good on her beat... if this sounds like the last movie, there's a good reason.

Cut-and-shut of the 2001 Black Scorpion TV series that re-treads much of the same ground covered by its predecessor, *Black Scorpion Returns*. Both use the show's first episode as a launching point, but where the earlier 'movie' covers two adventures

Darcy slips back into the PVC to face off against a crooked mayor, psychotic seismic specialist and a villain known as Gangster Prankster (Jackson).

Although produced by the same creative team, this sequel to 1995's *Black Scorpion* is some way off the limp imitation of 1990s Batman its predecessor was. Instead it's a limp imitation of the 1960s Batman TV show which, it transpires, is actually a slight improvement. If the first movie occasionally splashed us from the camp shallows, this one drags us into the depths and pins us beneath the waves.

fairly comprehensively, this one strips most of the highlights from three and stitches them together. This means there's a lot of crossover, which is useful because it's all quite confusing. Key characters are removed entirely, along with any background and exposition they may have been involved in. So we're not told how Black Scorpion got her transforming car and lightning gun, why she does what she does or who the guy helping her is. The insanity of it all helps.

Black Star and the Golden Bat ★

1979, South Korea
Director: Heon-myeong Han
Cast: Unknown

The villainous Black Star is constructing a weapon of mass destruction, so a bunch of children ask Golden Bat to stop him.

Unintelligible animation featuring a very unlicensed bright yellow Batman. He's kept off screen most of the time, almost as if the producers hoped DC wouldn't notice, which leaves us with the kids. The movie itself is stylistically similar to Japanese TV animation of the day and has little to offer.

Blackbelt Avengers

1969, Philippines
Director: Armando Garces
Cast: Tony Ferrer, Antonio Ganiela, Amando Diaz

Tony Ferrer's nunchaku-wielding masked hero leads a three-man superteam in the fight for justice. Presumably inspired by Bruce Lee's sudden success. This movie is generally believed lost.

Blade ★★★★★

1998, USA
Director: Stephen Norrington
Cast: Wesley Snipes, N'Bushe Wright, Stephen Dorff

Blade (Snipes), a half-human, half-vampire vigilante tries to stop a renegade vampire lord taking over the world.

The level of cheese is incredible and the writing is atrocious, but somehow *Blade* works despite such apparent deficiencies. This is a film that doesn't care how obvious the cliché or ridiculous the contrivance, it commits to everything and expects the audience to do likewise. We've seen time and again this is the only approach if you're taking things seriously. Dumb as a bag of hammers *and* essential viewing.

Blade II ★★★★

2002, USA
Director: Guillermo del Toro
Cast: Wesley Snipes, Kris Kristofferson, Ron Perlman

Blade (Snipes) rescues and cures sidekick Whistler (Kristofferson), then teams up with Eurovampires to defeat a mutant.

An unconvincing premise (that Blade would so willingly aid his enemies makes no sense) is typical of this sequel's shortcomings, what with its tendency to create bothersome inconsistencies that don't need to be. Not that it spoils much. We plough on through the nonsense, and the non-plot, with such bluster and verve that complications are soon forgotten. The action is plentiful and updated with a little post-*Matrix* camera swoopery, while Blade's penchant for slicing and dicing the bad guys is afforded lots of gory close-ups and lingering slo-mo. A bit of well-handled schlock never did anyone any harm. (Followed by *Blade: Trinity*.)

Blade of the Phantom Master ★★★

aka *Shin angyo onshi*, 2004, Japan/South Korea
Director: Joji Shimura
Cast: Kang-ho Song, Jung-jae Lee, Young-chang Song

Munsu (Song, in the original Japanese), one of the last ahmeng osas (officially appointed supernatural guardians against oppression) wanders the wasteland of a broken society known as Jushin, seeking the man who killed its former king.

Based largely on South Korean legend and very reminiscent of Buronson and Tetsuo Hara's *Fist of the North Star*, *Blade of the Phantom Master's* mythology is quite rich and interesting. Unfortunately the animation is a letdown, along with the English dub.

Blade: House of Chthon ★★

2006, USA

Director: Peter O'Fallon

Cast: Jill Wagner, Sticky Fingaz, Neil Jackson

Returning from service, army Sergeant Krista Starr (Wagner) finds her brother has been murdered by vampire cult the House of Chthon. Teaming up with half-vampire Blade (Fingaz), she goes after them.

Surprisingly gory and uncompromised TV pilot that lead to a brief series. Blade has less dialogue and influence on the plot than in the Snipes movies, effectively leaving Starr as our protagonist (it's her origin story, not his). Fortunately Wagner is great in the role, although she has some scenes stolen by Randy Quaid cameoing as a paranoid eccentric. It must have been a stretch. The action is good, the tone severe and, although there's a fair amount of character stuff to squeeze in, everything keeps moving at a good pace.

Blade: Trinity ★★

2004, USA

Director: David S. Goyer

Cast: Wesley Snipes, Jessica Biel, Ryan Reynolds

Blade (Snipes) teams with The Nightstalkers (Biel and Reynolds) when Dracula (Dominic Purcell) hits town.

Once you get beyond the confusion of Deadpool providing the opening voiceover (Reynolds' take on Hannibal King is pretty much identical to his 'Merc with a Mouth', making this movie's ironic, fourth wall breaking narration indistinguishable from *Deadpool's*) we get into what's essentially noisy fan service. The requisite flashy action scenes wash over us, we grieve the (now traditional) death of Whistler, endure Blade's awkward comedy asides (they've never worked) and then witness a big fight with the Most Dangerous Vampire Ever. Again. It's not bad, just a little pointless. Adding Reynolds and Biel to the cast was a good idea in theory, but little is done to give them space and they can't quite establish their credentials on these terms.

Blankman ★★

1994, USA

Director: Mike Binder

Cast: Damon Wayans, David Alan Grier, Robin Givens

When his beloved aunt is killed by thugs, genius inventor Kevin Walker (Grier) applies his talents to a crimefighting getup to be used, for some reason, by his idiot brother Darryl (Wayans).

With developmental disorders and deadly gang violence played for easy laughs, there is some awkward humour on display in *Blankman*. Even worse, Damon Wayans' eponymous hero takes childish mugging to unheralded lows, proving spectacularly irritating in the process. On the brighter side, Grier is both funny and convincing as long-suffering brother David, and some of the quieter gags (i.e. the ones Wayans has nothing to do with) land.

Blind Fury ★★★

1989, USA

Director: Phillip Noyce

Cast: Rutger Hauer, Terry O'Quinn, Brandon Call

Blind Vietnam vet and expert swordsman Nick Parker (Hauer) comes to the aid of an old friend threatened by mobsters, and winds up helping a young mother.

Blind Fury doesn't always feel like a proper superhero movie but it warrants mention both as a remake of the excellent *Zatoichi Challenged*, and because its protagonist is more altruistic and supernaturally able than most superheroes. Hauer is unusually droll in one of his best star vehicles, an action movie that's so 1980s you won't believe Carl Weathers isn't in it.

Blood: The Last Vampire ★★★
aka *Rasuto buraddo*, 2009, Japan
Director: Chris Nahon
Cast: Ji-hyun Jun, Allison Miller, Liam Cunningham

In an ancient war between vampires and humans, a halfbreed named Saya battles evil for a mysterious agency.

There is good use of great songs, some very entertaining gore and violence, and the plot drip-feeds us pieces of the puzzle at a pace that holds our interest. The film's biggest challenge is finding a new way through the overly familiar subject matter. To an extent it succeeds, thanks partly to featuring an unusual mix of Western and Japanese characters (the movie takes place during the Vietnam War on a US Air Base), although fans of Japanese genre cinema aren't going to find much new here.

BloodRayne ★★
2005, Germany/USA
Director: Uwe Boll
Cast: Kristanna Loken, Michael Madsen, Michelle Rodriguez

In 19th-century Europe, a partly-human vampire (yes, another one) escapes from a freak show to avenge her mother's murder.

If you made a list of actors not suited to playing 19th-century Europeans, Michelle Rodriguez and Michael Madsen might come near its top. Everything they say is funny (Mr. Blonde mumbling "Sebastian" in a cod English accent never gets tired). Obviously this is basically *Blade*. Our protagonist, Rayne (Loken), is a unique hybrid who has sided with humans, regardless of their antipathy to her, and uses her powers to kill vampires. The biggest difference is it's rubbish. Infamously incompetent filmmaker Uwe Boll has overseen a slapdash mess of a movie. Handed a reasonable budget for once, he chose to spend it on 'name' actors rather than the production, which means everything looks cheap and nobody wants to be there. That it's better than its sequels is staggering.

BloodRayne II: Deliverance ★
2007, Canada/Germany
Director: Uwe Boll
Cast: Natassia Malthe, Zack Ward, Michael Paré

Dhampir paladin (don't ask) Rayne (Malthe) tackles Billy the Kid (Ward) and his band of vampire outlaws.

Bobo Cop

53

From 18th-century Europe we head to the Wild West of the 19th century for a sequel nobody wanted (the first movie grossed $3.6m worldwide from a $25m budget). None of the leading cast have returned, and that's an unexpected problem. While Kristanna Loken wasn't great as Rayne, she was better than Malthe, and without Ben Kinglsey's ham and Michael Madsen's accent there's little to laugh at. For some reason Boll strikes a more serious tone, as if we're actually meant to care, but without the camp factor this is a significantly more boring film.

BloodRayne: The Third Reich ★

2011, USA/Canada/Germany
Director: Uwe Boll
Cast: Natassia Malthe, Brendan Fletcher, Michael Paré

Rayne (Malthe) has found her way back to Europe at the outbreak of WWII, where she teams up with the resistance to stop Hitler (Boris Bakal) taking over the world.

Few filmmakers are less suited to material dealing with Nazi atrocities than Uwe Boll. Michael Bay would be more sensitive. Boll maintains the miserable tone he established in the second of these ridiculous things, which leads to something extraordinary: nostalgia for the first. Clint Howard's Nazi scientist is the only highlight.

Bloody Mallory ★★

2002, France
Director: Julien Magnat
Cast: Olivia Bonamy, Adrià Collado, Jeffrey Ribier

In what seems to be an alternate reality (in which everyone is badly dubbed), an ostensibly female superhero team lead by 'anti-paranormal commando' Mallory (Bonamy) specialises in battling demons and ghosts. Who you gonna call when the pope is kidnapped by a fallen angel?

Elements lifted from film noir, video games, fairytales, gothic horror, superhero lore and Sam Raimi movies are all thrown at the screen, with the patchy results suggesting a filmmaker inclined to stylistic bravery if not formal coherence. There's weird imagery and schlock aplenty to keep things somewhat interesting, but don't expect anything to make sense, and beware of a slow descent into deliberate comedy.

Blubberella ★

2011, Germany/Canada
Director: Uwe Boll
Cast: Lindsay Hollister, Michael Paré, Brendan Fletcher

An obese semi-vampire battles Nazis in WWII. I'm afraid you read that right.

For a filmmaker to release two unrelated vampire movies in the same year suggests a lack of imagination. For both to revolve around half-vampire women fighting Nazis suggests something more, but I don't know what. This is typical grotesque idiocy from hack provocateur Uwe Boll, who plays a sitcom Hitler in what I wish was the least tasteful segment of the movie.

Blue Demon series: see Grouped Franchises and Luchador Movies

Bobo Cop ★★

1988, Philippines
Director: Tony Y. Reyes
Cast: Joey Marquez, Alice Dixson, Matet De Leon

A roboticist cyborgs a badly injured cop. Hijinks nearly follow.

Slow to get going and prone to the twin horrors of fast-motion farce and children singing, Bobo Cop's apparent cult status in the Philippines isn't likely to translate to the West. If it was the *RoboCop* spoof it purports to be things might be different, but it's more a genre-blending, all-purpose comedy. On the plus side we get to see a bionic bonehead lasering zombies to the score from *Rambo III*, so it has something going for it.

Boboiboy: The Movie ★★★

2016, Malaysia
Director: Nizam Razak
Cast: Nur Fathiah Diaz, Anas Abdul Aziz, Mohd Fathi Diaz

Intergalactic pirates kidnap Ochabot (M.F. Diaz) to aid their search for the Sphere of Power, so Boboiboy (N.F. Diaz) and his friends set out to rescue him.

Based on a kids' TV series about a boy given superpowers by a peculiar robot, this debut CGI feature from Razak proved a box-office hit in its native Malaysia. Cues have clearly been taken from Pixar and although the animation is not up to their high standard, neither does it seem primitive. Everything is bright and dynamic, the characters are well developed and there's just about enough adult humour to call it a family movie even if it clearly plays best to young children.

Boku no Hero Academia the Movie: see *My Hero Academia: Two Heroes*

The Bold Caballero ★★★

aka *The Bold Cavalier*, 1936, USA
Director: Wells Root
Cast: Robert Livingston, Heather Angel, Sig Ruman

Zorro (Livingston) is framed for murder by Commandante Sebastian Golle (Ruman).

The first colour superhero movie. Action scenes are decent, female lead Heather Angel is very good and the dialogue is

exceptional ("I have no use for men who smell of perfume!"). It has dated very well, but Zorro is played too effeminately and there's more than a little clunk to some of the technical aspects.

Bomb Squad ★★

2011, USA
Director: Nick Chamberlin
Cast: Craig Beeman, Keagan Karnes, Erin Kupay

One morning four siblings wake up with superpowers. Could it be connected to the mysterious past of the family's incarcerated patriarch? If so, why is mother behaving so strangely?

Zero budget and messy, *Bomb Squad* has much in common with the worst digital mockbusters. Even so, a fairly interesting plot unfolds. It's full of holes and idiocy, but is cryptic enough to hold the interest and help everything feel like a passion project rather than an exercise in exploitation.

Boy Putik ★★

1979, Philippines
Director: Jose Yandoc
Cast: Marlon Bautista, Rosanna Ortiz, Ramon Revilla

When his father is killed by bandits, a man aided by a magical amulet seeks vengeance.

We're told by the IMDb that Revilla stars as Nardong Putik, but when it comes to movies this obscure it's wise to treat what few online scraps of info can be found with caution. It actually stars Marlon Bautista as Putik's son, a teenager who ends up fighting villains with the help of mud-based superpowers (Putik Sr. was a real-life gangster whose nickname translates as 'Muddy Leonard' and was derived from his alleged habit of hiding from the authorities in muddy puddles). Revilla does appear but only briefly. These movies aren't the most accessible, and without Revilla's charisma anchoring everything this one descends into dreary melodrama.

Boy Wonder ★★★★
2010, USA
Director: Michael Morrissey
Cast: Caleb Steinmeyer, Zulay Henao, Bill Sage

Having witnessed his mother's murder as a young child, teenager Sean (Steinmeyer) becomes a vigilante. Investigating the circumstances around the brutal incident that shaped his life, he makes a startling discovery. Or maybe he doesn't.

First-rate psychological thriller that draws you straight in and doesn't let up. There's a powerfully depressing atmosphere brought about by downbeat characters, desaturated colours and, of course, the material itself. Some of the plot elements are a bit hokey and it's debatable how realistic this world is, assuming that even matters.

Bratz: Super Babyz ★
2007, USA
Director: David Mucci Fassett
Cast: Britt McKillip, Britt Irvin, Dorla Bell

The Bratz develop superpowers.

Think of the worst thing there is. Unless it's *Barbie: Princess of Power* or Adam Sandler's in it, trust me, this is worse.

BraveStarr: The Movie ★★★★
aka *BraveStarr: The Legend*, 1988, USA
Director: Tom Tataranowicz
Cast: Charlie Adler, Susan Blu, Pat Fraley

When a valuable ore is discovered on the remote planet of New Texas, it attracts an army of prospectors and outlaws. Galactic Marshal Barry BraveStarr (Fraley), a Native American with several animal-inspired superpowers, is despatched in an attempt to keep the peace.

Unusually for an origin story based on an animated TV series, *BraveStarr: The Movie* was produced after the show's brief run and works as a cohesive standalone movie (rather than a mess of re-edited episodes). It's good, too. The frontier setting is a great idea and affords even familiar scenarios an interesting twist, while the allegorical elements give New Texas a compelling depth. Care and thought has gone into the mythology and characters, with their intricate backstories often interwoven and used to inform current events. (He might not really be called Barry.)

Bride of the Incredible Hulk ★★★
aka *Married*, 1978, USA
Director: Kenneth Johnson
Cast: Bill Bixby, Mariette Hartley, Lou Ferrigno

Banner (Bixby) travels to Honolulu seeking a cure for his Hulkism, but winds up falling in love with the terminally ill Dr. Carolyn Fields (Hartley), the expert whose help he so badly needs.

Hartley is very good and shares some great chemistry with Bixby, who, having shot a whole series of the TV show by this stage, is well bedded-in as Banner. It's fortunate because most of the movie is just the two scientists doing science, which leads to an abundance of trippy hypnosis sessions and weird dreams. (Followed by *The Incredible Hulk Returns*.)

Brightburn ★★★★
2019, USA
Director: David Yarovesky
Stars: Elizabeth Banks, David Denman, Jackson A. Dunn

What if Superman was a psycho? Ma and Pa Kent score themselves a wrong'un.

The Superman origin story has been hijacked numerous times, but never has it been so gleefully or horrifically subverted. This is a brilliant idea for a movie, but *Brightburn* is far from perfect. The association between psycho-supe Brandon's (Dunn) metaphysical awakening and the onset of puberty is a variation on a hoary old trope and goes nowhere, while the emotional and narrative beats are predictable. Dunn is memorably creepy, though, and Elizabeth Banks a stand out as Brandon's confused and desperate mother.

Brittle Glory ★★

aka *The Continued Adventures of Reptile Man*, 1997, USA
Director: Stewart Schill
Cast: Tony Curtis, Arye Gross, Ally Walker

Jack Steele (Curtis), a has-been actor known for 1960s TV show *Reptile Man*, hires Lewis Rosen (Gross) to play sidekick Tadpole in public appearances. They bond, they learn, they vanquish demons, etc.

It's easy to see how *Brittle Glory* happened. Faded stars love roles like this; it's a chance to have some fun and show they're in on the joke, while any success can introduce them to new audiences and reinvigorate a career. And for a first-time director like Schill (then, as now, a successful TV editor) a 'name' star validates their movie and can help attract funding and distribution. Sadly *Brittle Glory* is not a success (sad because it's the kind of movie you want to like): shot on the cheap, tonally awkward, full of jokes that aren't funny and insights that aren't insightful. With more work on the script and a star who's a pleasure to watch it might have worked, but it seems slapdash and Curtis is no fun.

Bruce Lee Against Superman ★★

aka *Meng long zheng dong, Superdragon vs. Superman*, 1975, Hong Kong

BraveStarr: The Movie

Director: Chia Chun Wu
Cast: Bruce Li, Fei Lung, Lu Wen Lu

Kato (Li) is tasked with rescuing a scientist kidnapped by villains. After calling on his old friend the Green Hornet for help, the bad guys recruit Superman.

Like *Dragon and the Green Hornet*, this is a confused mash-up of Brucesploitation and vigilante shenanigans with *The Green Hornet* name slapped on (thanks to Bruce Lee, the 1960s TV show was extremely popular in Hong Kong). People appear out of nowhere, fights start for no reason, Li plays two characters without explanation, and nothing makes sense. However, we do learn that Superman, who is apparently a mercenary and can be hired for "cash, girls and a truckload of booze" in this universe, can be defeated with a knife to the genitals. And Lex Luthor went all the way into space to find kryptonite.

Buck Rogers ★★★

1939, USA
Directors: Ford Beebe, Saul A. Goodkind
Cast: Buster Crabbe, Constance Moore,
Jackie Moran

After crashing a dirigible in the Arctic, Buck
Rogers (Crabbe) and sidekick Buddy (Moran)
fall into suspended animation. Awakening
500 years in the future, they find Earth is
ruled by a twisted master criminal.

Moore is average at best as the female lead
and Warde's Kane fatally underwritten. But
Crabbe couldn't put a foot wrong if he tried,
with this sort of material, and Moran brings
new meaning to the word perky (he makes
Burt Ward's Robin seem emo). Effects and
action are good.

Buck Rogers

1977, USA
Directors: Ford Beebe, Saul A. Goodkind
Cast: Buster Crabbe, Constance Moore,
Jackie Moran

Feature-length edit of the previous entry.
We may wonder why a 1939 serial was
re-packaged for audiences almost forty
years after release. For the answer look to
its advertising slogan: "*Star Wars* owes it all
to *Buck Rogers*."

Buck Rogers in the 25th Century
★★★

1979, USA
Director: Daniel Haller
Cast: Gil Gerard, Erin Gray, Pamela Hensley

NASA spaceship captain Buck Rogers
(Gerrard) is flung into deep space, finally
returning to Earth's orbit 500 years later to
find a world on the brink of alien invasion.

Far saucier than memory suggests, this
Feature-length pilot for the TV series was
greenlit in the wake of *Star Wars* and aimed
squarely at the same audience. There's
fun to be had, but it's hamstrung by a flat
narrative and uninteresting leading man.
It's surprisingly interesting as a reflection
of the era's politics, though. Paranoia and
distrust of 'the other' are driving factors
in the plot and retain some degree of
relevance today.

Buffy the Vampire Slayer ★★★

1992, USA
Director: Fran Rubel Kuzui
Cast: Kristy Swanson, Donald Sutherland,
Paul Reubens

Spoilt teen Buffy Summers (Swanson)
is chosen to become her generation's
defender against the hordes of hell.

Presumably someone saw *Beverly Hills
90210* and thought it would be a good idea
to add vampires. It goes without saying they
were right, at least in principle, but stodgy
execution prevents Buffy's debut meeting
its potential either as the smart comedy it
aims to be, or the teen soap the subsequent
TV show would become. Having said that
there's nothing terrible about it. Kristy
Swanson does her best with the script and
the rest of the actors are fine. There are a
handful of laugh-out-loud moments and it
could appeal to younger girls who might
turn their noses up at more traditional
superhero movies.

Buffy the Vampire Slayer: Welcome
to the Hellmouth ★★★★

1996, USA
Directors: Charles Martin Smith, Joss Whedon
Cast: Sarah Michelle Gellar, Nicholas Brendon,
Alyson Hannigan

Teenage vampire slayer Buffy Summers
(Gellar) starts life at a high school built over
the gates to hell. A powerful demon wants
them open.

Dissatisfied with the direction the studio chose for his *Buffy* movie script (which was filmed as a broad comedy, see previous entry), writer Joss Whedon eventually realised his own vision for the character when the WB TV Network approached him to create a series. The cast and script are first-rate, while the blend of humour, horror and real life issues (most of which revolve around what people are wearing) engages and entertains to such an extent you hardly notice how poorly staged the action is.

Indie slacker comedy shot on a shoestring and predictably rough. It could be forgiven if it were funnier, but the gags are terrible and the writing in general reflects a lack of maturity and insight. What Joey Lauren Adams is doing in this is a mystery.

Bulletproof Monk ★★★

2003, USA
Director: Paul Hunter
Cast: Yun-Fat Chow, Seann William Scott, Jaime King

A nameless, supernatural Tibetan monk trains his unlikely American successor in defending an ancient scroll from Nazis.

As affable as it is predictable, Bulletproof Monk arrived in the middle of Hollywood's attempt to transform Yun-Fat Chow into a domestic action star (by pretending he was Jackie Chan, which he was not). Miscasting aside, he does have some chemistry with Scott, who's surprisingly entertaining as cocky pickpocket and kung fu movie afficianado Kar. There's nothing here you won't have seen dozens of times before, but the fight choreography is good and it's officially impossible to dislike a movie starring Yun-Fat Chow.

Bunny Whipped ★

2007, USA
Director: Rafael Riera
Cast: Joey Lauren Adams, Esteban Powell, Laz Alonso

A jilted loser suffering a minor breakdown adopts the persona of a masked superhero to fight evil. It isn't long before he's caught up in the murder of a rap mogul. Sigh.

Capitan Basilico ★★

2008, Italy
Director: Massimo Morini
Cast: Davide Ageno, Ale, Massimo Bosso

Superhero Capitan Basilico (Bosso) is framed for the theft of various monuments by a jealous ex-girlfriend.

Crowdfunded oddity from Northern Italy. While the central gag (Basilico is a short, overweight man in his 50s) runs its course quite quickly, the passion of the filmmakers shines through, maintaining our good will. The simple jokes work best, but a little more polish and planning would have been appreciated. (And I'm not convinced the producers licensed image rights to Darth Vader, Lara Croft, Batman and the various other superheroes and pop culture figures appearing in the movie.)

Capitan Basilico 2 - I Fantastici 4+4

2011, Italy
Director: Massimo Morini
Cast: Davide Ageno, Mariangela Argentino, Maurizio Baggetta

Sequel to the above. Unavailable at the time of writing.

Captain America ★★

aka *Return of Captain America*, 1944, USA
Directors: Elmer Clifton, John English
Cast: Dick Purcell, Lorna Gray, Lionel Atwill

D.A. Grant Gardner, aka Captain America (Dick Purcell), tries to prevent a disgruntled scientist known as The Scarab from getting hold of a thermo-dynamic vibrator.

Republic's last superhero serial and the first live-action outing for a Marvel character, not that you'd recognise him. Instead of being the perfect supersoldier, he's a short, pudgy guy with a receding hairline and no abilities (as per Capitan Basilico). If you want to spend four hours watching men in hats point guns at each other, knock yourself out, but don't expect much more.

Captain America ★

1979, USA
Director: Rod Holcomb
Cast: Reb Brown, Len Birman, Heather Menzies-Urich

An origin story in which a contemporary Steve Rogers (Brown) wants to bum around at the beach but is forced to become a superhero after being maimed.

The first of a brace of Captain America TV movies (the other being *Captain America: Death Too Soon*) graced with Reb Brown's excruciating vapidity. Anyone still awake when Cap' finally breaks cover after 50 minutes of melodrama will be treated to a budget Evel Kneivel. Having wilfully discarded the character's historical context, and inadvertently failed to realise his other essential characteristics, the filmmakers have left us with a dull man in a motorcycle helmet. (Followed by *Captain America II: Death Too Soon*.)

Captain America ★★

1990, USA
Director: Albert Pyun
Cast: Matt Salinger, Ronny Cox, Ned Beatty

Unable to serve in WWII on grounds of ill-health, enthusiastic would-be enlistee Steve Rogers (Salinger) volunteers for an experimental procedure that could make him a supersoldier.

As with Captain America's earlier outings in 1979, B-movie stalwart Albert Pyun's 1990 effort is limited by its TV budget. But unlike those facile bores this movie doesn't let such things get in the way of its ambition. We get everything we want from a Captain

America movie: supersoldier experiments, WWII/polio backstory, proper costume, missile trip to the arctic, etc. We even get a prosthetically enhanced Red Skull to battle in the finale. None of it works and everything looks like crap, but the ambition and adherence to the mythology counts for at least one additional star.

Captain America II: Death Too Soon ★★

1979, USA
Director: Ivan Nagy
Cast: Reb Brown, Connie Sellecca, Len Birman

Captain America (Brown) returns to thwart reviled revolutionary Miguel (Christopher Lee), who plans to poison a large chunk of the American populace with an ageing drug.

The second of Brown's Captain America TV movies represents a slight step up in bearability thanks to a lack of origin story, a more Bond-like plot, and Christopher Lee. It's still dull, though.

Captain America: Civil War ★★★★

2016, USA
Directors: Anthony Russo, Joe Russo
Cast: Chris Evans, Robert Downey Jr., Scarlett Johansson

With numerous recent operations resulting in civilian casualties, the Avengers are pressed to sign a UN accord revoking their freedom to act unilaterally. This creates two factions among the group; one, lead by Tony Stark (Downey Jr.), willing to comply, and the other, lead by Captain America (Evans), determined to resist.

There's a scene around half an hour into this third Captain America MCU entry in which various Avengers discuss their reasons for adopting one side or the other in the upcoming Superhero World Championships. It's very well written and each argument sounds plausible, but it's still impossible to believe these characters would resort to potentially deadly combat for any reason, let alone disagreement over a perfectly reasonable administrative expectation. It demonstrates how hard this conceit is to establish if excellent characters with an excellent script can't make it sound convincing. Cleverly, additional adversarial motivation is provided by Bucky Barnes (Sebastien Stan), who comes between Cap' and Stark when he's framed for a deadly bombing. The problem is it doesn't justify the numerous other characters deciding to risk everything for... something. However valid that gripe might be on one level, it doesn't really alter the fact this is a hugely enjoyable movie. The action is top notch and tends to work on a much smaller and more personal scale than usual. Black Panther and Spider-Man also prove superb additions to the lineup.

Captain America: The First Avenger ★★★★

2011, USA
Director: Joe Johnston
Cast: Chris Evans, Hugo Weaving, Hayley Atwell

Too sickly and weak to serve his country in WWII, Steve Rogers (Evans) volunteers for an experimental procedure that could land him on the front line.

As early attempts to put Captain America on screen demonstrate, there are many ways to get things wrong. He's a decidedly lo-fi superhero with roots in the harsh reality of war, not an Asgardian demigod or eccentric tech genius. The fantastical lends itself less readily to his world than it does to others, and his attributes lie in the unglamorous realms of decency and fair play. Rogers' transformation and the villainous Red Skull (Weaving) are just two inherently silly elements we have to take completely seriously if we're going to buy into the movie. Plausability is established

early with some great scenes in Brooklyn (some of the best ever filmed for the MCU) featuring a CG de-enhanced Rogers, and a focus on character over action. A sensible script and unflashy visual style help keep all the balls in the air until the finale, which comes as a significant letdown. Throughout it all Jonhston makes excellent use of his biggest asset: leading man Chris Evans. He nails Cap's down-home charm and quiet rightiousness in a way that transforms the character from jingoistic banality to mythic saviour. (Followed by *Captain America: The Winter Soldier*.)

Captain America: The Winter Soldier ★★★★★

2014, USA
Directors: Anthony Russo, Joe Russo
Cast: Chris Evans, Samuel L. Jackson, Scarlett Johansson

SHIELD has been compromised and Nick Fury (Jackson) forced underground. Not knowing who to trust, Captain America (Evans) investigates a mystery reaching back to his inception.

The MCU's second stand-alone Captain America movie sees the franchise at its peak. We're getting to know characters more intimately and mining their potential before the inevitable staleness sets in. Cracks in the relationship between Rogers and the authorites are starting to show, which serves a dual purpose as texture for this film and setup for the next. Hitherto underused characters such as Black Widow (Johansson) and Nick Fury get to stretch their legs in some of the most impressive action scenes the franchise has delivered. Even the frustratingly rote climax can't diminish one of the best films of its kind. (Followed by *Captain America: Civil War*.)

Captain Barbell: see Grouped Franchises

Captain Battle: Legacy War ★

2013, USA
Director: David Palmieri
Cast: Cuyle Carvin, Andrew J McGuinness, Marlene Mc'Cohen

A soldier injured in Northern Iraq is saved by an experimental serum that leaves him with unexpected superpowers. Back in the US he finds Nazis have invaded his home town. Big mistake on their part.

Creators and publishers beware: let your character fall into the public domain and Tom Cat might make a movie about them. The most shameless production company in the business plumbs new depths with their particularly crass use of Nazi iconography *and* lazy Islamic stereotypes. It's almost worth seeing one of these things in order to understand how bad they are. Almost.

Captain Berlin versus Hitler ★★★

2009, Germany
Director: Jörg Buttgereit
Cast: Adolfo Assor, Jürg Plüss, Sandra Steffl

With Hitler's brain alive but langushing in a jar, doctors decide the blood of Dracula will somehow restore him to full health. Superhero Captain Berlin must step in to prevent the resurrection of his nemesis.

Filmed version of controversial German dramatist Jörg Buttgereit's stage play of the same name. Those familiar with Buttgereit's best-known work, 1987's twisted body horror film *Nekromantik*, will find little that's familiar in this absurdist comedy. Having said that, all the performances are over-the-top, as are the visual effects (added as a nod to the contention this is a real movie), dialogue and everything else. It's hit and miss at best, but this is the kind of movie you watch to see how far the premise can be pushed. If you want considered probing of the themes in play, go elsewhere.

Captain Eager and the Mark of Voth ★★

2008, UK
Director: Simon Davison
Cast: James Vaughan, Tamsin Greig, Steve Clark

Legendary space hero Captain Ted Eager (Vaughan) is drawn out of retirement to face an inscrutable enemy.

Similar in style and tone to the B-movie spoofs of US filmmaker Larry Blamire, this British homage to Buck Rogersesque kitsch is an acquired taste. Visually it's reminiscent of strangely saturated green screen jamborees like *Sky Captain and the World of Tomorrow* or Mamoru Oshii's *Avalon*, with influences including comic strips and what looks like late-era *Red Dwarf*. There's a lot of Captain America in the way our hero struggles to find his place in a world that's moved on from his own time, but a promising mystery is obfuscated by dubious writing, and too many of the gags fall flat.

Captain Karate: Katulong Ng Batas

1965, Philippines
Director: George Rowe
Cast: Bernard Bonnin, Max Alvarado, Bessie Barredo

This movie is considered lost.

Captain Marvel ★★★★

2019, USA
Directors: Anna Boden, Ryan Fleck
Cast: Brie Larson, Samuel L. Jackson, Ben Mendelsohn

Air Force test pilot Captain Carol Danvers (Larson) absorbs the power of an exploding alien energy source, and soon learns she's developed unique superpowers as a result. Having lost her memory, Danvers is adopted and trained by the Kree, a warrior race embroiled in a feud with the shapeshifting

Skrulls. Eventually landing back on Earth, Danvers and Nick Fury (Jackson) begin piecing her memory back together.

We're thrown into the trippy stuff too soon, before we have a character to latch on to and lead us through the different realities, dreams and general confusion. When we get to Earth some excellent scenes between Danvers and Fury announce that the film is willing to settle down, and it's here we finally get to know our hero at least a little. Interestingly, she has avoided even casual sexualisation and been given a personality uncompromised by gender expectations (so much so she makes 2017's Wonder Woman look like a tool of patriarchal chauvinism). It's debatable whether this has ever been done before in an American superhero film. The 1990s setting is presented well, with fun but heavy-handed elements such as a cameo from Blockbuster Video balanced out with character detail (Danvers has such

era-specific characteristics it can be like watching Janeane Garofalo at times). Structurally questionable, but a reasonably fresh take on the superhero protagonist.

Captain Philippines at Boy Pinoy: see *Captain Barbell* in Grouped Franchises

---

Captain Scarlet vs. the Mysterons ★★★

1980, UK
Directors: Brian Burgess, Robert Lynn, Ken Turner
Cast: Francis Matthews, Ed Bishop, Donald Gray

After dying in a car crash, agent of Spectrum Captain Scarlet (Matthews) is recreated as an indestructable superman by invading aliens The Mysterons.

Cut-and-shut pulled from the 1967 British supermarionation TV series created by Gerry and Sylvia Anderson. It's strong stuff for a kids show thanks to a few intensely dramatic sequences, a bit of blood and the unsettling, unseen villains (represented only by a haunting, inhumanly dispassionate voice). The sets, vehicles and characters are fantastic in concept and detail, anticpating 1970s sci-fi cinema styles. The plot is a bit of a mess but let's be generous and say it's just down to having been conceived as a series of episodes. (Followed by *Revenge of the Mysterons from Mars*.)

Captain Underpants: The First Epic Movie ★★★

2017, USA
Director: David Soren
Cast: Kevin Hart, Thomas Middleditch, Ed Helms

Goodhearted tearaways George (Hart) and Harold (Middleditch) hypnotise their principal into believing he's the comic book superhero Captain Underpants.

Casshern

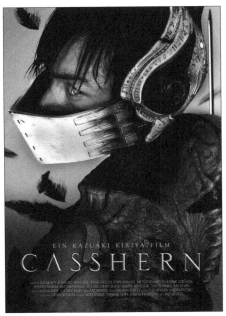

Captain Underpants peddles a digestible anti-authoritarian philosophy that will help kids blow off steam without fostering any genuinely anarchic tendencies. As a parent/authority figure (seriously) that means I have no business evaluating it, but my kids love it.

Captain Video: Master of the Stratosphere ★★
1951, USA
Directors: Spencer Gordon Bennet, Wallace Grissell
Cast: Judd Holdren, Larry Stewart, George Eldredge

Crime-fighting team The Video Rangers must stop the evil dictator of planet Atoma invading Earth.

Based on 1949 TV series *Captain Video and His Video Rangers*, this cheap and quite shabby serial may have been a favourite of *Star Wars'* George Lucas, but it's hard to see why today. It's densely packed with action and drama, but the writing is poor and the overall effect boring. The Ranger's insistence on wearing motorcycle helmets at all times, even when sitting at desks in their HQ, at least becomes comical.

Captain Z and the Terror of Leviathan ★
2014, USA
Director: Steve Rudzinski
Cast: Zoltan Zilai, Madison Siple, Steve Rudzinski

Captain Z (Zilai) attempts to stop baddies releasing the ultimate evil.

At one point a character complains "this is not some after-school special". They're right; the production values aren't good enough. The audio seems to have been recorded by broken camera mics and the performances suggest rehearsals for a gag skit being put together by a bunch of drunks. Among the worst things.

Casshern ★★★★
2004, Japan
Director: Kazuaki Kiriya
Cast: Yûsuke Iseya, Kumiko Asô, Akira Terao

With the earth poisoned and humanity exhausted by 50 years of war, a genetic experiment unleashes an army of mutants that threaten to finish us off. Only the invulnerable avenger Casshern (Iseya) stands in their way.

Visually extraordinary, narratively baffling and thematically ambitious hypnagogic lunacy. *Casshern* is more a series of ultra-stylised set pieces than a movie, and as such is beyond appraisal or criticism. It simply exists: make of it what you will.

Casus Kiran (- 7 canli adam): see *Spy Smasher(: Man of 7 Lives)*

Catalina: A New Kind of Superhero ★★
2009, UK
Director: Kenneth D. Barker
Cast: Nathan Lubbock-Smith, Anthony James Berowne, Cleone Cassidy

Obnoxious solicitor Ben (Lubbock-Smith) finds himself wrapped up in an intergalctic armageddon sort of thing when he ingests a space orb.

The opening text pitches us priests, ancient prophecies, a mythic savior, Meta-weapons, things called Zenadan, Kiros and Thrixium, and "planetary biological destruction", all in the space of 30 bewildering seconds. This is a movie of fascinating awfulness. Much of it is a light-hearted character study of our transvestite lead Ben, aka Catalina, but there are chunks of serious sci-fi B-movie and an enormous, pointless mythology, too. It might be amateurish nonsense, but there are some wonderfully absurd moments, a clear passion behind the camera and some lovely DIY effects.

Catman in Lethal Track ★★★

aka *U.S. Catman: Lethal Track*, 1990, Hong Kong
Director: Godfrey Ho
Cast: Jonathan Isgar, Howard Anderson, Johanna Brownstein

A delivery driver scratched by a radioactive cat gains superpowers.

Godfrey Ho's contribution to world cinema is both extensive and wretched. Over the course of a 50-year career he's racked up over 100 directing credits, most making use of his signature technique; a process which involves splicing action footage (usually featuring ninjas) into pre-existing foreign dramas, and releasing the resulting mess as a new movie. *Catman in Lethal Track* is a fairly typical example (albeit without ninjas), and it's about as incoherent as you'd imagine. It's probably much funnier, though. Catman and his buddy have been subjected to a particularly hilarious dub that features cartoonishly butch voices saying things like "watch your mouth, s**thead, or I'll put you over my knee and spank your bottom".

Catman: Boxer's Blow ★★★

aka *U.S. Catman 2: Boxer Blow*, 1993, Hong Kong
Director: Godfrey Ho
Cast: Jonathan Isgar, Glen Anderson, Howard Anderson

Catman (Isgar) is back, and this time he must prevent the bad guys blowing up the world with a nuclear bomb.

It's more of the same in this sequel, so strap yourselves in for the traditional Godfrey Ho blizzard of badly dubbed fighting. As with the other Catman adventure, the secondary movie is Thai in origin, and once again it doesn't intersect with Ho's new footage at any point. It really can't be stressed enough how unintentionally amusing these two movies are. Speaking of which...

Catwoman ★★★

2004, USA
Director: Pitof
Cast: Halle Berry, Sharon Stone, Benjamin Bratt

Graphic designer Patience Phillips (Berry) returns from the dead to avenge her murder as Catwoman. Evil cosmetics executive Laurel Hedare (Stone) should be worried.

It's funny before the movie even starts. The titles show artistic depictions of great events before casually zooming in on a cat in the corner as if it's some sort of omnipotent deity overseeing human history. Then we're beaten about the head with everything we need to know about everything. Emerging from an expository daze after a few short scenes, it's apparent we have all the information we need to correctly predict the entire movie. Don't turn it off though, it's hilarious.

Chakra: The Invincible: see Grouped Franchises

Chameleons ★★★

1989, USA
Director: Glen A. Larson
Cast: Crystal Bernard, Marcus Gilbert, Stewart Granger

Unbalanced heiress Shelly Carr (Bernard) discovers her grandfather Jason (Granger) was a superhero, and that his apparently natural death was in fact murder. As various relatives blather, Shelly investigates with the help of Jason's sidekick Ryan (Gilbert), aka The Paraclete of Justice.

Doolally pilot featuring a campy death cult that runs the city, an absurd superhero who plays it straight and a protagonist who's *literally* insane. If *Chameleons* had been commissioned it would have been one of the most unlikely TV shows of the era (but at least we may have found out why it's called Chameleons). The deadpan absurdity of the infrequent humour is unlikely to appeal to everyone, and tonally it's all over the place, but this wacky mess is a barrel of fun all the same.

Chandu on the Magic Island

1935, USA
Director: Ray Taylor
Cast: Bela Lugosi, Maria Alba, Clara Kimball Young

I guess this is most accurately described as a feature-length edit of the second half of the 1934 serial *The Return of Chandu*, the first half of which was released as a separate feature-length edit (this movie's prequel), also in 1934, also under the title *The Return of Chandu*, and is a sequel not to a serial, but to the 1932 B-movie *Chandu the Magician*. But you already knew that.

Chandu the Magician ★★★

1932, USA
Directors: William Cameron Menzies, Marcel Varnel
Cast: Edmund Lowe, Irene Ware, Bela Lugosi

After three years in India studying with the yogis, American adventurer Frank Chandler (Lowe) masters their magic and heads off to thwart world evil as the wizard Chandu.

Based on the 1932 *Chandu* radio series so loved by a ten-year-old Stan Lee (Doctor Strange was heavily influenced by it), this enjoyable B-movie is usually overlooked in conversations about early cinematic superheroes. That's particularly odd as he was probably the first to boast actual

superpowers (he can mesmerise, teleport, disguise himself, etc.) For fans unwilling to accept the likes of Zorro or Judex as proper superheroes, Chandu is probably the first to appear on screen. Lowe is a bit dull in the lead but Lugosi, in one of his first post-*Dracula* performances, is an appropriately menacing miscreant. There are also some great sets (probably left over from a bigger studio production). (Followed by *The Return of Chandhu*).

Cheng fung hap: see *Dragon and the Green Hornet*

Chôjin Locke: see *Locke the Superman*

The Chosen One: Legend of the Raven ★

1998, USA
Director: Lawrence Lanoff
Cast: Carmen Electra , Conrad Bachmann, Tim Bagley

When her sister is murdered, McKenna Ray (Electra) returns home to take over the family business of being a folk hero.

Softcore smut-monger Lawrence Lanoff squeezed out this zero-budget catastrophe between *Playboy* videos. Going by the result he shouldn't have bothered. Carmen Electra plays former marine and current Native American (erm...) supernatural hero, The Raven, and brings all the authenticity you'd expect to the role. A laughably pretentious voiceover perseveres throughout and might make sense of what's happening on screen, but it's too dull to hold our attention.

Chronicle ★★★★

2012, USA
Director: Josh Trank
Cast: Dane DeHaan, Alex Russell, Michael B. Jordan

Three teenagers gain superpowers from an unexplained crystal. The most troubled among them, Andrew (DeHaan), struggles to come to terms with his new abilities and becomes dangerously withdrawn.

At a glance *Chronicle* looks like a remake of 2002's *The Source*, but it adds at least two significant elements to the mix: a found footage premise of questionable merit, and, more importantly, quality filmmaking. This is a well written, well acted and well shot movie. DeHann exhibits that magnetic film star quality even if the world hasn't yet admitted it, while Jordan has unsurprisingly gone on to great things. Trank achieves a realistic tone (perhaps with a little help from the found footage angle, I may begrudgingly admit) that features exhilirating immediacy and relatability.

Cicak-man ★★★
2006, Malaysia
Director: Yusry Abd Halim
Cast: Saiful Apek, Fasha Sandha, Aznil Hj Nawawi

When research scientist Hairi (Apek) drinks from a cup containing a lizard infected with an experimental virus, he inherits some of its abilities. Soon afterwards he learns his boss is an insane supervillain.

Inspired to some extent by Sam Raimi's *Spider-Man* films, Cicak-man (literally 'lizard-man') is a wacky comedy with an interesting visual style. Humour often fails to translate from one culture to another, and that can be the case here (Apek's mugging is boring), but the absurdity of everything should raise the occasional smile at the very least.

Cicak-man 2: Planet Hitam ★★★
2008, Malaysia
Director: Yusry Abd Halim
Cast: Saiful Apek, Fasha Sandha, Aznil Hj Nawawi

Cicak-man's (Apek) nemesis Professor Klon (Nawawi) arrives back in Metrofulus with a plan to control the world's water supply.

A despondent Cicak-man, returns to duty in this tonally identical sequel to Yusry Abd Halim's 2006 domestic hit. Apparently violent death is no obstacle to a character's reappearance if they're popular enough, so not only does Cicak's best friend Danny (Yusry Abdul Halim) make a comeback (sort of) from the dead, we also get resurrected versions of Klon's twin henchmen (sort of). For most of the movie the main antagonist is a new character, hired assassin Rrama (Tamara Bleszynski), but elsewhere little has changed and things are as bonkers as ever.

Cicak Man 3 ★★
aka *Cicakman3*, 2015, Malaysia
Directors: Ghaz Abu Bakar, Yusry Abd Halim
Cast: Zizan Razak, Lisa Surihani, Fizz Fairuz

With Cicik Man (Razak) missing in action, a new superhero assumes responsibility for the city of Metrofulus.

Less humorous final movie in the series. What charm there was has left the building, and the predictable plot (it's painfully clear that Superbro will turn out to be the villain, don't even see it as a spoiler) only makes everything more of a slog.

Code Name: Dynastud ★★
2018, USA
Director: Richard Griffin
Cast: Derek Laurendeau, Anthony Gaudette, Bruce Church

In the future the USA is a right-wing police state in which homosexuality is punishable by death. Prior to presidential elections, a jingoistic nominee attempts to capture gay superhero Dynastud (Gaudette) and the escaped convict Bart (Laurendeau).

If movies like the relatively benign *Surge of Power* represent the gentle end of the gay superhero cinema spectrum (there is such a thing), *Code Name: Dynastud's* vehemently uncompromising approach places it firmly at the opposite extreme. This is a movie for people who like their satire more frenzied axe attack than surgical incision. Nothing wrong with that, and at times it's absolutely hilarious (Bruce Church in particular is quite brilliant), but it suffers horribly with every budget-related issue you can imagine. It should also be pointed out this is not a film for the sensitive or feint of heart!

Colossus (Italian series): see Grouped Franchises and Peplum Movies

---

Come rubare la corona d'Inghilterra: see *Argoman the Fantastic Superman*

Comic Book: The Movie ★★★★
2004, USA
Director: Mark Hamill
Cast: Mark Hamill, Donna D'Errico, Billy West

A documentary crew follows comic book expert Don Swann (Hamill) as he tries to prevent Hollywood reinventing his favourite superhero at the same time as shamelessly ingratiating himself into both the film and comic industries.

The obvious creative inspiration here is the mockumentary work of Christopher Guest, and there are moments that match the likes of his *Best in Show, Waiting for Guffman* et al. Hamill is brilliant on camera and knows exactly what he's doing off it. It's hard to make talking heads like Stan Lee and Kevin Smith both sincere and funny, and it's harder to string them together with the staged footage, faux clips and voiceover into something that remains consistently entertaining at feature length. Hamill does it with aplomb. This is an underrated gem.

Commando Cody: Sky Marshal of the Universe ★★
1952, USA
Directors: Harry Keller, Franklin Adreon, Fred C. Brannon
Cast: Judd Holdren, Aline Towne, Gregory Gaye

Commando Cody (Holdren) goes up against the King of Venus, who is somehow in cahoots with Earth gangsters.

The second Cody serial and fourth of the so-called 'Rocket Man' series (each of which seems to feature aliens trying to destroy or take over Earth with the help of gangsters, only to be foiled by a scientist with a rocket pack). On the whole it's better than *Zombies of the Stratosphere* and *Radar Men from the Moon* thanks to fewer clumsy cliffhangers and a better lead in Holdren. But it's not up to the standard of *King of the Rocket Men*, although it could have been if it had tried to do something new.

Chronicle

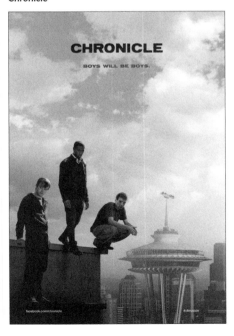

Computer Superman ★★

aka *Yod Manut Computer, Thai Six Million Dollar Man*, 1977, Thailand
Director: Sompote Sands
Cast: Duangcheewan Komolsen, Lor Tok(?)

Magical lightning leads to a boy being born with a tail. As an adult his girlfriend cuts it off, so a mad professor makes him bionic. It's one of those.

Presumably retitled *Computer Superman* after the Christopher Reeve movie became a hit, this is actually a comedy take on *The Six Million Dollar Man* US TV series. The humour is broader than a broad thing and illicits few laughs, while the action is non-existent. *6MDM* references are limited to ripping off the show's theme tune and shots of our hero (whose name I don't know, thanks to a lack of both English subtitles and credits, but I think is played by Lor Tok) running in slow motion. The plot ends up being about he and three friends – one with enormous ears, one with enormous hands and one with radioactive nasal mucus – saving their village from opium smugglers.

Conan the Barbarian ★★★★★

1982, USA
Director: John Milius
Cast: Arnold Schwarzenegger, Sandahl Bergman, James Earl Jones

A Cimmerian orphan raised a slave escapes to avenge the murder of his parents.

From the opening theme, which drifts over the titles as angel song snatched from a heavenly breeze, to a jubilant denouement in which our hero reconciles his fate with that of his tormentor, *Conan the Barbarian* is a model of restraint and good taste. Schwarzenegger offers a fragile performance imbued with integrity. The script is Swiftian in its wit, Shakespearian in its scope and breathtakingly nuanced, while John Milius'

direction is like a reticent whisper cajoling us toward an indelible truth. Watch it, you'll see. (Followed by *Conan the Destroyer*.)

Conan the Barbarian ★★

2011, USA
Director: Marcus Nispel
Cast: Jason Momoa, Ron Perlman, Rose McGowan

Barbarian boy sees father murdered, grows up to be vengeful warrior.

The lengthy opening voiceover conjures a mythic backstory befitting a superhero-era Conan film. Then he's born, on a battlefield, at the very moment of his mother's death, and into the bloody hands of his savage father amid a whirlwind of clichés. Sadly this ridiculous scene is the highlight. As a remake, *Conan the Barbarian* suffers from a lack of star power, a nasty attitude to women and the sense it's all been done before and better.

Conan the Destroyer ★★★

1984, USA
Director: Richard Fleischer
Cast: Arnold Schwarzenegger, Olivia d'Abo, Wilt Chamberlain

Conan (Schwarzenegger) and friends escort a princess on a quest to find a magical key.

The original Conan film has a wonderful sense of order. The screenplay is excellent, successfully navigating a series of unlikely scenarios while taking care to build a world that's consistent and detailed. There's none of that in the sequel. We're just thrown into a generic plot full of generic characters. What's worse, a studio mandated PG rating leads to a dearth of ultra violence and an excess of compromise (Conan was born to behead snake-gods, not babysit teenage brats). And snappy one-liners belong in these movies as much as Jason Momoa.

Conan: The Heart of the Elephant
★★
1997, USA
Director: Gérard Hameline
Cast: Ralf Moeller, Danny Woodburn, Robert McRay

The wizard king Hissah Zul (Jeremy Kemp) learns of Conan (Moeller), the fearsome warrior who will one day take his thrown. Zul pre-empts the inevitable by kidnapping his impending nemesis.

If *Conan the Destroyer's* PG rating left it a little anaemic, imagine what television's constraints do for the franchise. This pilot/feature-length season opener for the rightly forgotten Conan TV series features no death and a talking elephant, which is about all you need to know.

The Condor ★★
2007, USA
Director: Steven E. Gordon
Cast: Wilmer Valderrama, Maria Conchita Alonso, Kathleen Barr

All skateboarding teen Tony (Valderrama) wants to do is be a skateboarding teen, but when his parents are murdered and his skateboarding legs are broken, he uses bio tech to become superhero The Condor.

Stan Lee pulled 'Hispanic boy', 'bionic aids' and 'rich orphan' out of his hat for this one, then seems to have gone on holiday. But even direct-to-DVD irrelevancies deserve a little love. The animation, characters and plot are all stock, while the excessive and mildly creepy sexualisation of magazine publisher Valeria (Mary Elizabeth McGlynn) is out of place.

Condorman ★
1981, UK/USA
Director: Charles Jarrott

Cast: Michael Crawford, Oliver Reed, Barbara Carrera

A clumsy comic book artist is called upon to help a Soviet agent defect to the West.

This powerfully unamusing misfire attempts to spoof James Bond-style spy movies and superhero conventions, but doesn't seem to understand how either works (I'm not sure the writers are even familiar with the latter – at one point we're told Superman lives in New York). It's comprehensively terrible, but the effects, script and Michael Crawford deserve particular censure. Sporting a silly accent and unable to shake off his Frank Spencer sitcom character, Crawford kills every scene in which he appears (despite being a talented actor). Proof, if it were needed, of the importance of casting.

Constantine ★★★
2005, USA
Director: Francis Lawrence
Cast: Keanu Reeves, Rachel Weisz, Djimon Hounsou

John Constantine (Reeves), a cynical occult detective who seeks salvation by exorcising demons, helps policewoman Angela Dodson (Weisz) investigate her sister's suicide.

Although visually impressive and at times exciting, *Constantine*'s insistence that we take its inherently silly concept seriously starts to grate after a while. Reeves is Reeves, make of that what you will. But be warned he's playing a character written to be duller and flatter than even he would normally go for.

Constantine City of Demons: The Movie ★★★
2018, USA
Director: Doug Murphy
Cast: Matt Ryan, Laura Bailey, Robin Atkin Downes

John Constantine (Ryan) helps an old friend whose daughter is languishing in a demon-induced coma.

The plot and execution are more filmic than most modern animated movies, so much so that the interesting screenplay could have made a tidy little live-action movie. Some of the accents take a little getting used to (Constantine is supposed to be Scouse but there's at least as much of Ryan's native Welsh seeping through) and the desaturated colour scheme leaves everything looking a bit dull.

Cornman: American Vegetable Hero ★

2001, USA
Director: Barak Epstein
Cast: Mike Wiebe, Melissa R. Bacelar, Adam Lockhart

Dr. Hoe (Wiebe) wants to control all the corn in the world, but Cornman (Lockhart) won't stand for Dr. Hoe controlling all the corn in the world. That's the plot.

Barak Epstein might have made his buddies laugh outlining this idea, but as a 70-minute movie it's a trial (and not just because of the unrelenting punk music). A lower than lo-fi aesthetic doesn't need to be a terminal problem, but this is so rough you have to wonder if anyone cared.

Cosplay Fetish Battle Drones ★

aka *Struggled Reagans*, 2013, USA
Director: Gregg Golding
Cast: Kawal Arora, Aleksey Calvin, Mark Edwards

A group of people with a shared tumour form a superhero team.

Surreal scenes of nonsense are cut with non-actors running around a wood dressed as Power Rangers. I have no idea who this is for, why it was made or how it gained distribution. A genuine contender for worst live-action superhero movie.

The Crimson Bat: see Grouped Franchises

Brandon Lee as Eric Draven in *The Crow*

Cross ★

2011, USA
Director: Patrick Durham
Cast: Brian Austin Green, Michael Clarke Duncan, Vinnie Jones

Amulets, birthrights, responsibilities, blah.

From the 'let's spend the budget on cameos' school of filmmaking comes a movie so bad both Vinnie Jones and Danny Trejo are in it. It's angry, noisy, ugly and shot largely in car parks. (Followed by *Cross Wars*.)

Cross Wars ★

2017, USA
Director: Patrick Durham
Cast: Brian Austin Green, Vinnie Jones, Danny Trejo

Callan (Green) is back, and up to his old blah.

Oh God there's another one. And it's just the same. Absolutely worthless, unless you feel an urge to mark the precise moment Tom Sizemore ceased being an actor.

The Crow ★★★★★

1994, USA
Director: Alex Proyas
Cast: Brandon Lee, Michael Wincott, Rochelle Davis

On Halloween eve, a year after he and his fiancée were brutally murdered, Eric Draven (Lee) returns from the grave to avenge their deaths and play electric guitar.

Perfectly conceived and executed, *The Crow* was something of a watershed film when it was released in 1994. Five years earlier, Tim Burton's *Batman* had proved the multiplex crowd was ready for a sombre superhero, but there was no guarantee a relatively unknown and thoroughly uncompromising property like this could find an audience.

That it did is thanks in no small part to its star. Lee is the personification of tragedy and his every moment on screen bristles with emotional resonance. It's not just that we project real sentiment onto him (as a result of his tragic death on set), the film's masterstroke lies in teaming him with street kid Sarah (Davis). If the real victims in death are those who are left behind, who better to leave behind than a child in order to trigger sympathy and draw us in? The death of a young couple is sad. The death of a young couple idolised as de facto parents by an abandoned child is devastating. (Followed by *The Crow: City of Angels*.)

The Crow: City of Angels ★★

1996, USA
Director: Tim Pope
Cast: Vincent Perez, Mia Kirshner, Richard Brooks

The Crow resurrects Ashe Corven (Perez), a father murdered alongside his young son.

The one significant change to the original film's formula (thanks to Miramax it's more of a remake than a sequel) is the relationship of the victim to their avenger – son rather than girlfriend. But The Crow's hero, Eric Draven (Brandon Lee) was a tragic and romantic figure, and because *City of Angels* automatically copies its predecessor where possible, so is Corven. That makes things a bit weird. It's a small complaint in some ways, but indicative of a movie that's lazy and disdainful of its audience. (Followed by *The Crow: Salvation*.)

The Crow: Salvation ★★

2000, USA
Director: Bharat Nalluri
Cast: Eric Mabius, Kirsten Dunst, William Atherton

Alex Corvis (Mabius) is resurrected to catch a murderer for whom he took the fall.

Although still confined to a perpetually dark and damp industrial cityscape populated exclusively by scumbags, there are attempts to distinguish this third film in the series from the first two. Rather than avenging the death of an innocent at the hands of a drug lord's underlings, we're avenging the death of an innocent at the hands of corrupt cops. That counts as revelatory after *City of Angels*. Unfortunately, it's still rubbish. (Followed by *The Crow: Wicked Prayer*, although it's best to pretend otherwise.)

The Crow: Wicked Prayer ★

2005, USA
Director: Lance Mungia
Cast: Yuji Okumoto, Marcus Chong, Tito Ortiz

A bad guy kills a less bad guy, who is then resurrected to kill bad guys.

Based on Norman Partridge's 2000 novel of the same name, the fourth Crow movie scales new depths as it shifts its setting to an Aztec reservation, and its focus to the most unlikeable characters imaginable. A vaguely ecclesiastical note is struck with a murderous biker gang presented as the Four Horsemen of the Apocalypse, and pointless characters like Danny Trejo's priest, but there's no obvious reason why. Cheap, ugly and extremely boring. I'd argue there's no greater decrease in quality and value over the course of a film series.

Cucuo's Big Adventure: see *Americano*

Cutie Honey: Live Action ★★

aka *Kyûtî Hanî*, 2004, Japan
Director: Hideaki Anno
Cast: Eriko Satô, Mikako Ichikawa, Jun Murakami

Cutie Honey (Satô), the vigilante alter-ego of office drone Honey Kisaragi, must avenge the death of her father and rescue her uncle.

Nausea-inducing blizzard of flashing lights, grating music and squealing. The tone is absurd, mixing Power Rangers kitsch with anime excess. The sequel teased at the conclusion never materialised, although there is a 2016 reboot.

Cutie Honey: Tears ★★

2016, Japan
Director: Takeshi Asai
Cast: Keita Arai, Hina Fukatsu, Ren Imai

In cyberpunk near-future Japan, the ruling elite live in towers high above the poverty stricken masses below. After creating a lifelike 'female' android, Cutie Honey (Nishiuchi), genius inventor Dr. Kisaragi (Kouichi Iwaki) sends her to the surface to start a revolution.

This much darker second live-action Cutie Honey movie seems to take its stylistic cues from *Ghost in the Shell* rather than a blender full of Skittles, as its predecessor did. In fact what little remains of the source material is so indistinct there's no obvious reason for retaining the title, other than its commercial value. There are some lovely dystopian visuals and the technical elements are impressive, but it never quite comes alive.

Cyber-C.H.I.C. ★

1990, USA
Directors: Ed Hansen, Jeffrey Mandel
Cast: Kathy Shower, Jennifer Daly, Burt Ward

A crazed supervillain has hidden nuclear bombs around the country. Luckily Prof. Von Colon's (Kip King) latest creation, a cybernetic crime fighter in the form of a Playboy playmate, is on the case.

It's unclear whether the protagonist of this fiasco is a robot or a cyborg (the script can't decide), but the character and plot are pure superhero. Unfortunately. If they weren't I wouldn't have had to watch this ridiculous thing. What looks like being a typical action B-movie is in fact a comedy that spoofs the news media and local politics. The plot makes literally no sense, with pimps, drug lords, armed robbers and a biker gang all somehow inveigling themselves into the narrative, along with various public officials and newsmen, few of whose motivations or relevance are ever declared.

Cyber Desesperado: see *8 Man After*

Dai-Nihonjin: see *Big Man Japan*

Daleks' Invasion Earth 2150 A.D.
★★★
1966, UK
Director: Gordon Flemyng
Cast: Peter Cushing, Bernard Cribbins,
Ray Brooks

In the future, Daleks have taken control of
Earth and only Doctor Who (Cushing) can
put things right.

Second theatrical outing for the timelord
after *Dr. Who and the Daleks*. Although
scheduling conflicts mean Bernard Cribbins
replaces Roy Castle as comic relief, this
feels much like a re-tread of the other film
thanks to its familiar plot. Even so, in many
ways it's the better of Cushing's brace of
Whovies. The production design and visual
effects are stronger, the Daleks a bit more
menacing and the tone slightly darker.

Danger: Diabolik: see Grouped Franchises
and Diabolik Super-Kriminals

Daredevil ★★★
2003, USA
Director: Mark Steven Johnson
Cast: Ben Affleck, Jennifer Garner, Colin Farrell

Crusading attorney Matt Murdock (Affleck)
moonlights as superhero Daredevil, despite
having been blinded as a child.

Clichéd and formulaic superantics with a
character of dubious cinematic suitability.
The film seems to be inspired by Burton's
Batman (it's astonishing how often that
sentence can be used when writing about
superheroes), but such a stylised aesthetic
requires commitment from the filmmakers
and, ideally, a more enigmatic protagonist
who seems at home in the shadows.

Dark Avenger ★★

1990, USA
Director: Guy Magar
Cast: Leigh Lawson, Maggie Han,
Robert Vaughn

Former judge Paul Cain (Lawson) fakes his own death before reinventing himself as a masked avenger.

Rejected CBS feature pilot that borrows heavily from *Darkman* and others. The mask makes *The Dark Avenger* himself look like the Phantom of the Opera, and his endlessly wisecracking techy sidekick is so New Yoik she says stuff like "the microwave activity out there is gettin' me jammed up the wazzoo!"

The Dark Knight ★★★★★

2008, USA
Director: Christopher Nolan
Cast: Christian Bale, Heath Ledger,
Aaron Eckhart

Now established as Gotham's premier protector, Batman (Bale) faces his greatest challenge yet: an anarchic clown in league with the city's crime lords.

Over a decade since release, and in spite of the best efforts of Tony Stark and co, *The Dark Knight* remains perhaps the most lauded of all superhero films, but it's far from perfect. Nolan plays it fast and loose with the internal logic, allows too many plot holes and indulges a social ideology that, denied the necessary space to develop, seems simplistic and trite. That's the devil's advocate stuff, though, because this is an extraordinary movie, perhaps the closest the genre has to a masterpiece. Christian Bale's Batman radiates a complicated depth, and when his selfless commitment to the betterment of his city ("I'm whatever Gotham needs me to be") reaches its almost nihilistic peak in the closing scenes, we buy his motivation without question. Ledger's appearance as the Joker was perhaps the biggest talking point on release, but not only because of his tragic death months earlier. It's an incredible performance, with the time and effort devoted to conceiving it palpable. Visually the film is stunning, but not in the manner of a CGI spectacular. Cinematographer Wally Pfister doubled down on the gritty aesthetic toyed with in predecessor *Batman Begins*, and, inspired by nighttime hikes around Chicago, conjured a hyperreal style that's almost hypnotic. It's the director's movie, though, and proves beyond doubt that Nolan is one of the finest craftsmen working in mainstream cinema today.

The Dark Knight Rises ★★★★

2012, USA
Director: Christopher Nolan
Cast: Christian Bale, Tom Hardy,
Anne Hathaway

Eight years after the events of *The Dark Knight*, with his knees shot, spirit broken and legacy tainted, Batman/Bruce Wayne (Bale) has withdrawn from the world. But after a visit from curious cat burglar Selina Kyle (Anne Hathaway), and the appearance of masked malevolence Bane (Hardy), our hero is forced out of retirement.

As with the previous film, it doesn't do to look too closely at the plot machinations of this final instalment in Christopher Nolan's trilogy. Better to stick with the stuff that works, and there's plenty of it. As before, the stakes here are rational. There's no advanced alien race trying to take over the world; just a nutter with a bomb who wants to destroy a city. How much you can get behind the film might depend on how much you can get behind that nutter; Bane proved to be an acquired taste for audiences. Having to follow Heath Ledger's much-adored Joker as the chief antagonist should have been a no-win situation for

The Dark Knight

Tom Hardy, and Bane's necessarily muffled tones might seem like a handicap too far. But the peculiarly stifled annunciation the actor developed draws us in brilliantly and, combined with Hardy's presence, renders a character who is little more than a well-trained thug a truly memorable villain.

The Darkest Minds ★★★

2018, USA
Director: Jennifer Yuh Nelson
Cast: Amandla Stenberg, Mandy Moore, Bradley Whitford

When 98% of the world's children suddenly die, the remaining 2% start exibiting strange abilities and are promptly locked up by their rattled parents. Six years later, a powerful young girl escapes into a broken world full of confusing factions.

We're expected to believe some fairly silly things and there's much that's familiar, but perhaps these are problems for an older audience rather than this movie's YA target demographic (I appreciate that sounds like a cop out). Lumps of Romero's *Dead* series, Arthur C. Clarke's *Childhood's End*, *Children of Men*, *The Hunger Games*, *X-Men* and all sorts of similarly themed social apocalypse sci-fi are churned together into a well paced, well acted and quite affecting movie. Free from the violence and machismo inherent to the genre, this is a good option for those not typically attracted to superheroes, or who are looking for something a bit more mature and thoughtful (but not *too* mature and thoughtful). It's noteworthy that this is a mainstream American superhero film starring one non-white woman (which is unusual) and directed by another non-white woman (which is unprecedented).

Darkman ★★★

1990, USA
Director: Sam Raimi
Cast: Liam Neeson, Frances McDormand,
Larry Drake

Peyton Westlake (Neeson), a scientist who
has developed an unstable synthetic skin
formula, is terribly burnt and left for dead
by crime lord Robert Durant (Drake).

There are some pleasing foreign elements
(many lifted from classic Universal horror
films), but this is very much a Sam Raimi
joint, in spite of studio and even personal
attempts to make it otherwise. The style
goes for a slightly camp industrial gothic,
and Raimi's ideosyncracies, familiar from his
earlier low-budget work, abound. It's quite
flawed, but there's more good than bad.

Darkman II: The Return of Durant ★★

1995, USA
Director: Bradford May
Srarring: Arnold Vosloo, Larry Drake,
Renee O'Connor

Darkman (Vosloo, taking over from Liam
Neeson) continues to perfect his synthetic
skin while Durant (Drake), who has somehow
returned from the dead, builds a laser gun.

Although R rated, the jaunty tone of this
sequel is similar to that of 1990s TV movies
such as *Black Scorpion* and *Justice League
of America*. In a pleasingly hokey turn of
events, Darkman now lives in a sewer and
uses a secret underground railway allowing
him to travel around the city (things get so
broad we're treated to a *Silence of the Lambs*
spoof that would be more at home in *Scary
Movie*). Everything works fine for the most
part. The first half is spent on Darkman's
search for magic skin and Durant's pursuit
of a property he needs, the second half
on the conflict resulting from the two

narratives intersecting. A lack of action
means it may not be for everyone.

Darkman III: Die Darkman Die ★★

1993, USA
Director: Bradford May
Cast: Jeff Fahey, Arnold Vosloo,
Darlanne Fluegel

Darkman (Vosloo) goes to war with a drug
dealer marketing a new steroid derived
from our hero's own altered adrenaline.

Filmed concurrently with the first sequel
and largely indistinguishable in most ways.
The loss of Larry Drake as crime boss
Durant is offset by Jeff Fahey's fabulously
hammy turn as new big bad Peter Rooker.
The movie tries to expand the parameters
of the character a little with one eye clearly
on further instalments in the series, and
to that end Darkman's superstrength and
invulnerability are emphasised, while the
plot revolves around his desire to feel pain
again (these elements are hardly mentioned
in the previous movies). It's all kind of fine.

Darna: see Grouped Franchises

DC Super Hero Girls: see Grouped
Franchises

The Dead One ★

aka *El Muerto*, 2007, USA
Director: Brian Cox
Cast: Wilmer Valderrama, Angie Cepeda,
Joel David Moore

A year after Diego de la Muerte (Valderrama)
is sacrificed to Aztec gods, he is returned to
Earth to fulfil a prophecy.

Landing somewhere between *The Crow* fan
fiction and a best-forgotten episode of *The
X-Files*, *The Dead One* never establishes its

own identity. With no misdeeds preceding de la Muerte's demise, and no apparent reason for his sacrifice, it isn't clear why he's been resurrected or what he's supposed to be doing. Michael Parks appears as a local sheriff and is by far the best thing in a very poor movie.

Deadly Ray from Mars

1966, USA
Director: Ford Beebe, Frederick Stephani, Robert Hill
Cast: Buster Crabbe, Jean Rogers, Charles Middleton

Feature-length edit of 1938's *Flash Gordon's Trip to Mars*.

Deadpool ★★★★★

2016, USA
Director: Tim Miller
Cast: Ryan Reynolds, Morena Baccarin, T.J. Miller

Wisecracking mercenary Wade Wilson (Reynolds) is subjected to an experimental biological procedure that renders him both effectively immortal and horribly scarred. After adopting the alter ego Deadpool he hunts down, and messily murders, those responsible for his ordeal.

The arrival of *Deadpool* might have marked the end of the current comic book movie cycle. We can debate whether it's quite as clever as it wants to be but, regardless, Reynolds' passion project laid bare the gimmicks and bombastic tendencies of the modern superhero blockbuster, flensing the formula with a katana. Relentless in-jokes and deconstruction work to deny the genre its mystery after decades of refinement leaves proto-self-aware posturers like Tony Stark looking old-school. Whether you love him or hate him, Deadpool is a thing now, and it's not just Wolverine who has to learn to live with it.

Deadpool 2 ★★★★

2018, USA
Director: David Leitch
Cast: Ryan Reynolds, Josh Brolin, Morena Baccarin

Deadpool (Reynolds) plays the reluctant role model to confused 14-year-old mutant Russell Collins, aka Firefist (Julian Dennison). Ultimately, that involves battling the time-travelling cyborg Cable (Brolin), but also forming his own superhero team.

After a bold decision to kill off love interest Vanessa (Baccarin) in the pre-title sequence, the tone shifts wildly and we're bludgeoned with familiarly ironic pop culture references until other things happen, things that aren't explained for ages. The contrivances required to get us to the halfway point are extensive, and the plot is full of holes. But complaining about any of this stuff in a Deadpool movie is like complaining about Aquaman being wet.

Deadwood Dick ★★★

1940, USA
Director: James W. Horne
Cast: Donald Douglas, Lorna Gray, Harry Harvey

Dick Stanley (Douglas), mild-mannered newspaper editor, is actually Deadwood Dick, masked hero, and only he can prevent an enigmatic bandit known as the Skull (Forrest Taylor) from sabotaging Dakota's chanches of achieving statehood.

Despite the dull premise (which will sound familiar to Zorro fans) this is a fairly spritely serial with some fun performances. Like the Lone Ranger's John Reid, Stanley is an intellectual pacifist only persuaded into action when people close to him are murdered. We miss Tonto, but otherwise this is at least as good as the Lone Ranger serials and, if anything, benefits from a more natural narrative flow.

Death Note ★★★★

aka *Desu nôto*, *Death Note: The First Name*,
2006, Japan
Director: Shûsuke Kaneko
Cast: Tatsuya Fujiwara, Ken'ichi Matsuyama,
Asaka Seto

Pitch: write a person's name in a magical
notebook, that person dies.

We meet our prospective protagonist, Light
Yagami (Fujiwara), as he sees a newsflash
detailing a hostage situation. The culprit is
named, Yagami emotionlessly transcribes
that name into his apparently ordinary
notebook, the culprit dies on the spot and
the hostages are saved. The public credit
Kira, a supernatural folk hero they deem
to be responsible for a spate of recent
'miracles'. This is the rawest of superhero
movies; it's impossible to strip the formula
back any further. Various details enhance
the core concept, in particular the debate
surrounding the legitimacy of Yagami/Kira's
actions. Yagami is a law student, an expert
disillusioned with poor justice, which adds
an extra dimension to his role as Judge Judy
and executioner. The notebook's demonic
former owner and an enigmatic detective
each force his hand in unexpected and
interesting ways, before a cliffhanger blows
the story wide open, setting up what is
the second half of the movie more than a
sequel (*Death Note: The Last Name*).

Death Note ★★★

2017, USA
Director: Adam Wingard
Cast: Nat Wolff, Lakeith Stanfield,
Margaret Qualley

When teenager Light Turner (Wolff) finds an
enchanted notebook with the power to kill
anyone whose name is added to its pages,
he sees an apparently consequence-free
means of righting the world's wrongs. Not
so simple.

This Hollywood remake does a good job
of exploring the ramifications of ultimate
vigilante power. The detached, impersonal
nature of the method of killing shields our
hero from the responsibility associated
with it, so not only are his actions more
uncompromising than those of the typical
superhero, he doesn't have to face their
consequences (or even apply any effort to
achieving them: he casually selects targets
from 'most wanted' lists as if internet
shopping). We might expect Turner to
learn a moral lesson about the ills of this
kind of frontier justice but, intriguingly, the
movie doesn't judge him for what he does.
No innocents are mistakenly targeted and
he never really abuses his power. Tension
grows from his need to evade capture by
the authorities, and complications caused
by lunatic girlfriend Mia (Qualley), as in
the original. There are plot holes, a slight
tendency toward a YA aesthetic and the
characterisation can be uneven, but *Death
Note* is never less than interesting.

Death Note: Light Up the New World ★★★

aka *Death Note - Desu nôto: Light Up the New
World*, 2016, Japan
Director: Shinsuke Sato
Cast: Masahiro Higashide, Sosuke Ikematsu,
Masaki Suda

Ten years after the events of the first films
(2006's *Death Note* and *Death Note: The
Last Name*), six new notebooks appear on
Earth, leading to the creation of an Interpol
team tasked with recovering them. A cyber
terrorist sets out to do the same.

Virtually a soft reboot but technically a
sequel, *Light Up the New World* is a huge
step forward in terms of cinematography
and CGI, but can't match its predecessors
for real depth and originality. L (Kenichi
Matsuyama) is dead, but Ryuzaki (Sôsuke
Ikematsu), his successor as superdetective,
has the same DNA (long story), which

just seems like an excuse to revisit the character's entertaining eccentricities. A similar cat-and-mouse situation ensues, all of which is indicative of a movie that's different... but the same.

Death Note: The Last Name ★★★★

2006, Japan
Director: Shûsuke Kaneko
Cast: Tatsuya Fujiwara, Erika Toda, Ken'ichi Matsuyama

Yagami (Fujiwara) tries to avoid entrapment by weird genius L (Matsuyama), as Mira (Toda) takes over the Death Note killings.

The second half of the *Death Note* story sees the thoughtful Yagami and slightly unhinged Mira, who has also come into posession of a notebook, struggling to find their own just paths while dealing with L, who manages to be a thorn in their side despite being unable to figure out what the hell's going on. The mythology continues to expand, relationships evolve in fascinating ways and the role of the media becomes ever more crucial (in rather unexpected ways). No other superhero series addresses the nature of right and wrong as effectively or interestingly as these films. (Followed by *Death Note: Light up the World*.)

The Death of Superman ★★★

2018, USA
Directors: Jake Castorena, Sam Liu
Cast: Jerry O'Connell, Rebecca Romijn, Rainn Wilson

An alien kills another alien.

How do you know when someone in an animated Superman movie is doomed? When they say "I'm not worried because Superman will rescue me" three times in two minutes. Lex Luthor (Wilson) is manipulative, Lois (Romijn) is frustrated by Clark's secrecy, and the Justice League

sit around a big table taking the piss out of Batman (Jason O'Mara). In other words, everything is as it should be in the world of DC animation.

The Death of the Incredible Hulk ★★

1990, USA
Director: Bill Bixby
Cast: Bill Bixby, Lou Ferrigno, Elizabeth Gracen

David Banner (Bixby) is closer than ever to finding a cure for his affliction, but efforts are complicated by a nefarious spy network out to steal his work.

A return to the sciencey narratives of the earlier Hulk TV movies leaves Big Green's final outing feeling like he's going home to die. That death is an anticlimax (he just falls), but it came at the right time. Bixby is looking old and it's hard to take a green bodybuilder seriously in the age of Tim Burton's *Batman*. Although the ratings were poor it's not a bad effort.

The Deathless Devil ★★★★

aka *Yilmayan seytan*, 1973, Turkey
Director: Yilmaz Atadeniz
Cast: Mine Mutlu, Kunt Tulgar, Erol Tas

A Mr. Yilmaz (Muzaffer Tema) reveals to his adopted son Tekin (Tulgar) that the boy's real father was legendary superhero The Copperhead, and that he must take on his mantle. Meanwhile, the malevolent Dr. Seytan (Tas) will stop at nothing to steal Prof. Dogan's (Yalin Tolga) new invention.

Ham-fisted (and presumably unlicensed) remake of 1940 serial *The Mysterious Doctor Satan*. Even by the standards of Turksploitation this thing's ridiculous, but it starts to make sense if you imagine the crew were all drunk. It's the only way to explain the wild crash-zooms, arbitrary editing and narrative non sequiturs. Tulgar was more director than actor (he made *The Return of Superman* and *Tarzan the Mighty Man*, among others) and lacks charisma, but it doesn't matter. This is among the most entertaining movies of its kind.

Defendor ★★★★

2009, Canada/USA
Director: Peter Stebbings
Cast: Woody Harrelson, Sandra Oh, Kat Dennings

Delusional vigilante Arthur Poppington (Harrelson) searches among the detritus of a crime-ridden city for self-proclaimed nemesis Captain Industry.

Like its better-known companion piece, the following year's *Super*, *Defendor* follows a character who's essentially dealing with an unspecified mental disorder by acting out a superhero fantasy (coincidentally Ellen Page, who plays *Super's* confidente/sidekick, was at one time signed on for a similar role in this). Both are good films but *Defendor* is the more uncompromising of the two; there's less humour, the hero is harder to read and there's a universal refusal to conform to genre archetypes.

Demir Yumruk: Devler geliyor: see *Iron Fist: The Giants Are Coming*

Democrazy ★

2005, USA
Director: Michael Legge
Cast: Robin Gabrielli, Diane Mela, John Shanahan

Terrorist group the All-Crazy Network (ugh) attacks the great nation of Martika, forcing a handful of superheroes to come together in defence of their country.

Michael Legge, writer, director and, in the role of President Douche, one of the chief

forgetters-of-lines (even when reading directly from a script held in his hand he gets it wrong) may have an audience for his uniquely dumb zero-budget comedies. I have decided I am not part of it.

Demolition Man ★★★★★

1993, USA
Director: Marco Brambilla
Cast: Sylvester Stallone, Wesley Snipes, Sandra Bullock

L.A. action cop John Spartan (Stallone) is sentenced to cryogenic suspension for a crime he didn't commit. Thawed out 36 years in the future (where his now unique skill set effectively makes him a superhero) in order to recapture his nemesis Simon Phoenix (Snipes), Spartan finds he's a colourful barbarian in the quasi-fascist beigeness of 2032.

Newspaper ad for *The Death of the Incredible Hulk*

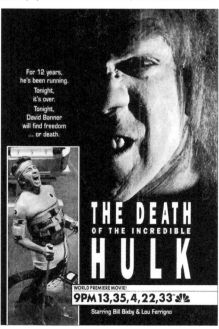

The concept is fantastic despite being spectacularly silly (it's just 22 years since the beginning of social reforms, yet only one elderly man remembers what the world used to be like), and the execution is perfect. It's not obvious who's in on the joke and who isn't, but Stallone and co. deliver gloriously direct performances.

The Demolitionist ★★★★
1995, USA/Canada
Director: Robert Kurtzman
Cast: Nicole Eggert, Bruce Abbott, Susan Tyrrell

Killed in the line of duty, Detective Alicia Lloyd (Eggert) is resurrected as a supercop.

For a while nothing makes sense, then *RoboCop* happens but it's like a big, stupid fever dream. The movie starts in a German Expressionist style before turning into a cop show on the way to a weird spell of sadomasochistic psychodrama. For some reason we spend 20 minutes locked in a room with a miserable Nicole Eggert learning about dead people's feelings. But once we're done there it's all Dutch angles and dumb action. This is a brilliantly good bad movie, and worth seeing for Richard Grieco's villain alone.

Denjin Zabôgâ: see *Karate-Robo Zaborgar*

Descendant of the Sun ★★★★
aka *Ri jie*, *Yat gip*, 1983, Hong Kong
Director: Yuen Chor
Cast: Tung-Shing Yee, Cherie Chung, Fei Ai

A baby made of the sun falls to Earth in a glacier and is taught to use his powers by a rock spirit. He then faces an infanticidal cult leader and a supernatural nemesis hatched from an egg.

It may not sound like it but this is basically Hong Kong's answer to 1979's *Superman*.

The legendary Shaw Brothers lift whole scenes from Richard Donner's classic, but also mimic the score and recreate the Clark/Lois/Superman romantic dynamic surprisingly accurately. There are plenty of fantastical fight scenes slathered in endearingly lo-fi visual effects.

Destination Saturn
1939, USA
Directors: Ford Beebe, Saul A. Goodkind
Cast: Buster Crabbe, Constance Moore, Jackie Moran

Feature-length re-edit of the 1939 serial *Buck Rogers*.

Desu nôto: see *Death Note*

Devilman ★★
aka *Debiruman*, 2004, Japan
Director: Hiroyuki Nasu
Cast: Hisato Izaki, Yûsuke Izaki, Ayana Sakai

When a portal to hell is opened, invading demons merge with humans as a means to survive. After becoming host to such a demon, seemingly ordinary teenager Akira Fudô (Izaki) finds he is pure-hearted enough to withstand its influence, and even able to harness its power.

With the original *Devilman/Debiruman* manga spawning numerous sequels, anime series, novels and OVAs it was inevitable a live-action movie would find its way to the screen one day. It's just a shame it isn't very good. Anyone new to the franchise will struggle to understand what's going on, the bleak music and dour mood is depressing, the extensive CG effects are poor and the cast seemingly uninterested.

Different: see *Alag: He Is Different.... He Is Alone...*

Doc Savage: The Man of Bronze
★★★★

1975, USA
Director: Michael Anderson
Cast: Ron Ely, Paul Gleason, William Lucking

Adventurer Doc Savage (Ely) investigates his father's disappearance with the aid of his 'Brain Trust' aka The Fabulous Five.

Second-tier pulp hero Doc Savage was created by Henry Ralston and John Nanovic in 1933 as a reaction to the Shadow, one of the hottest literary properties of the day. He starred in his own magazine series and radio show during the 30s and 40s before being resurrected in novel form prior to this spectacular one-off big screen outing. I haven't read the source stories, but, as played by Ely, the venerable detective, inventor, scientist, physician, explorer, musician and adventurer has his tongue wedged so firmly in his cheek Adam West would think he's overdoing it. Rocking a tone similar to 1980's *Flash Gordon* (but with special effects straight out of 1936's *Flash Gordon*), this is about as much fun as you can have with a superhero movie. It looks smashing, the plot doesn't stop for breath and Ely is magnificent. If you like your superheroes camp, you need this in your life.

Doctor Mordrid ★★★

1992, USA
Directors: Albert Band, Charles Band
Cast: Jeffrey Combs, Yvette Nipar, Jay Acovone

An unidentified god sends space-wizard Mordrid (Combs) to Earth so he can await the arrival of his evil stepbrother Kabal (Thompson), who has pledged to destroy mankind and something or other.

Apparently Full Moon Entertainment had planned to make a *Doctor Strange* movie only for the rights to lapse on the eve of production. Being a resourceful bunch it seems they decided to just film the script under a different name. True or not, it is distinctly Strangesque. There are alternate dimensions, mystifying monsters, gods, prophecies, magic and even stop-motion dinosaurs; all of which are rendered with the brightly-coloured incoherence of a kids' TV movie. Combs looks great in his day-glo wizard jammies and tiny cape.

Doctor Satan's Robot

1966, USA
Directors: John English, William Witney
Cast: Eduardo Ciannelli, Robert Wilcox, William Newell

Feature-length edit of the 1940 Republic serial *Mysterious Doctor Satan*. Among the best (and certainly the best titled) of a slew of serial re-edits released by Republic Pictures as part of a syndicated TV package in 1966.

Doctor Strange ★★★

2016, USA
Director: Scott Derrickson
Cast: Benedict Cumberbatch, Chiwetel Ejiofor, Rachel McAdams

When arrogant surgeon Doctor Stephen Strange (Cumberbatch) sustains irreparable nerve damage in a car accident, he spirals into a despondent oblivion. On discovering a secretive cult he persuades its leader to teach him magic, and soon gets into a rumble with her former students.

The film struggles to overcome Strange's fundamental flaws and he remains too cerebral and unlikeable throughout. We're treated to technically impressive visual effects but, at this point, there's nothing exciting about that even when they're inventive, and these are not. It's hardly a failure but there's a sense the B-team were assigned to this one.

Doctor Strange: The Sorcerer Supreme ★★

aka *Doctor Strange*, 2007, USA
Directors: Patrick Archibald, Jay Oliva, Dick Sebast, Frank Paur
Cast: Bryce Johnson, Paul Nakauchi, Kevin Michael Richardson

Neurosurgeon Stephen Strange (Johnson) becomes Earth's magical defender as The Sorcerer Supreme.

Another Marvel animated movie left largely redundant by the MCU freight train. The secondary plot (bad wizard makes Earth children into fire-breathing zombies) differs from that of the 2016 live-action movie, but most of the focus is on the origin story, and that plays out in pretty much the same way. It's a little more grown-up than these movies tend to be, but it's hard to see the point now.

Doctor Who: see Grouped Franchises. See also Dr. Who.

Doctor Who ★★★

1996, UK
Director: Geoffrey Sax
Cast: Paul McGann, Eric Roberts, Daphne Ashbrook

The Doctor (McGann) tries to prevent The Master (Roberts) creating a black hole that will destroy the earth.

McGann is perfectly good as the eighth incarnation of the Time Lord, although his eccentricities seem a little forced at times.

Doc Savage

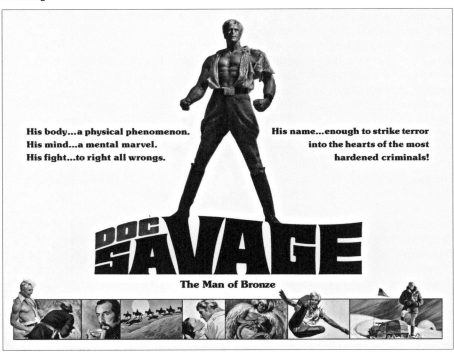

Roberts brings some Hollywood to the role of the villain and the production values allow for some reasonable CGI effects. All are welcome, but they work to make the movie feel more like nondescript TV than *Doctor Who*.

Dollman ★★★★
1991, USA
Director: Albert Pyun
Cast: Tim Thomerson, Jackie Earle Haley, Kamala Lopez

Hard boiled intergalactic cop Brick Bardo (Thomerson) crash-lands on Earth, where he finds he's one sixth the size of its human residents. That doesn't stop him cleaning up the South Bronx, which is subject to terrible gang violence.

Dollman poses a very important question: what if Dirty Harry was thirteen inches tall? (Spoiler: it turns out it wouldn't have made much difference.) Unfortunately, Dollman doesn't really use his size to his advantage or do anything clever with space knowledge, which renders him nothing more than an autonomous laser gun (although said hand cannon is so absurdly over-powered that it proves excellent fun). Nevertheless there's a reason this is a cult favourite. The script is witty, the cast are great and the direction is the most assured of B-movie stalwart Albert Pyun's career.

Dollman vs Demonic Toys ★★★
1993, USA
Director: Charles Band
Cast: Tim Thomerson, Tracy Scoggins, Mel Behr

Dollman (Thomerson) hooks up with Ginger (Behr), a former nurse shrunk to his size by aliens, and then heads off to face a gang of, well, demonic toys.

Charles Band rolls three sequels into one movie by revisiting his Dollman, Demonic Toys and Bad Channels properties all at the same time. Unsurprisingly, we're taken to some pretty weird places, but characters mix well and Band makes better use of Dollman's size than Pyun did in the first film, which opens up all sorts of plot and gag opportunities (simply providing him with a companion of the same stature doubles the character's potential). Perhaps it's missing a little of the first movie's raw genre appeal, though. There's something about its structure that isn't quite as neat.

Don Q Son of Zorro ★★
1925, USA
Director: Donald Crisp
Cast: Douglas Fairbanks, Mary Astor, Jack McDonald

Don Cesar de Vega (Fairbanks), eldest son of Zorro and, confusingly, also called Zorro, is framed for murder while in Madrid. He must find a way to win the girl and prove his innocence. Apparently in that order.

Unlike his father, Don Cesar seems to be more lover than fighter and does precious little defending of the vulnerable in this sequel to 1920's *The Mark of Zorro*. The romantic angle is ramped up and more consideration is given to the class system aspect (the setting has shifted from the US to Europe after all), though there's still room for plenty of swordplay. However, it seems hollow without a more moralistic motivation, and it's difficult to care about the characters, most of whom are either spoilt or evil.

Dong fang san xia: see *The Heroic Trio*

Dr. Strange ★★★
1978, USA
Director: Philip DeGuere Jr.
Cast: Peter Hooten, Clyde Kusatsu, Jessica Walter

An unidentified demon sends space-witch Morgan LeFay (Walter) to Earth so she can kill Lindmer (Mills), a wizard who protects mankind from evil and must train his replacement as Sorcerer Supreme if Earth is to survive.

With hindsight, there's no way this staid TV pilot was going to work. The characters are too ambiguous, the mythology too vague, and the screenplay far too slow and wordy. What's more, Strange doesn't don the outfit or take centre stage until the confusing finale. It is oddly appealing, though. Walter and Mills are exceptional actors and, while the pacing may be a problem for some viewers, it will be a relief for others.

Dr. Syn, Alias the Scarecrow ★★★★

1963, UK
Director: James Neilson
Cast: Patrick McGoohan, George Cole, Tony Britton

Country parson Dr. Christopher Syn (McGoohan) secretly leads a charitable smuggling operation as masked alter ego The Scarecrow.

While Superman takes care of Metropolis and Spider-Man New York, The Scarecrow's more modest beat covers Romney Marsh on the Kent/East Sussex border of England's rural Southeast. Created in 1915 by author Russell Thorndike, our hero is hard to pin down: he uses fear to keep his followers in line, flagrantly flouts what seem to be quite reasonable laws and routinely risks his life for a community that doesn't seem to need him. In the ambiguity of his motives and self-aggrandising of his methods he's reminiscent of anarchic revolutionary V (or vice versa), while his morally dubious nature brings to mind Italian fumetti neri heroes. The movie, though, is a lesson in succinct, efficient storytelling and reminiscent of British folk horror films such as 1968's Witchfinder General.

Dr. Who and the Daleks ★★★

1965, UK
Director: Gordon Flemyng
Cast: Peter Cushing, Roy Castle, Jennie Linden

The Doctor (Cushing) and his assorted companions find themselves out of place and time on a planet being subjugated by the Daleks.

This first of two feature films based on the TV series covers events from the Dalek's eponymously titled debut serial of two years previous. The mythology diverges considerably, though, with this Doctor a benevolent human inventor rather than a cantankerous Gallifreyan Time Lord, but tonally there's little change; what we get is essentially a better produced, bigger budgeted version of the Doctor's (here Dr.) small screen adventure. (Followed by Daleks' Invasion Earth 2150 A.D.)

Dragon and the Green Hornet ★★★

aka Qing feng xia, Green Hornet, 1994, Hong Kong
Director: Ching-Ying Lam
Cast: Kar Lok Chin, Esther Kwan, Rongguang Yu

A reporter and a cop with something to prove each attempt to unmask the Green Hornet while he's busy dealing with a master criminal.

I'm not sure anyone involved in this movie knew what they were meant to be ripping off. The Green Hornet connection makes it Brucesploitation but, confusingly, there seem to be two substitute Bruce Lees: one playing the Green Hornet and one playing Dragon, who is presumably the sidekick, although that name is not mentioned in the version I saw. Instead, he's called Alfred and uses a boomerang as a weapon. So we've elements from the Green Hornet, Batman and also the Flash/Suicide Squad (Captain Boomerang), but they're all used differently.

(Director Ching-Ying Lam was better known as an actor and starred in 1985 classic *Mr. Vampire*. Before that he was a close friend of Bruce Lee.)

Dragon Ball (Z): see Grouped Franchises

Dredd ★★★★

2012, USA
Director: Pete Travis
Cast: Karl Urban, Olivia Thirlby, Lena Headey

In the near future, 800 million people live in Mega City One, a vast and violent slum policed by 'Judges' licensed to execute criminals on sight. While assessing a new recruit, the infamous Judge Dredd (Urban) is trapped inside a hostile tower block by ruthless drug kingpin Mama (Headey).

The screenplay is nearly perfect. We learn everything we need to know via a series of clever and entertaining opening sequences, and once we're inside the high-rise that's home to most of the movie, action flows organically from the scenario and leads us to a logical conclusion. Urban excels as Dredd, capturing his relentlessness and weary menace (without ever removing the helmet). There are minor failings for us to pick at if so inclined, but this is one of the best modern films of its type.

Drive Angry ★★

2011, USA
Director: Patrick Lussier
Cast: Nicolas Cage, Amber Heard, William Fichtner

After stealing Satan's gun and escaping hell, deceased criminal John Milton (Cage) searches for the cult leader responsible for his daughter's death.

Violent, explicit and very silly supernatural revenge trash. Cage's approach to *Drive Angry* can be summed up by a scene in which he becomes physically intimate with a waitress without setting down his drink or taking his shades off: he couldn't care less. The same can't be said for Lussier, who crams the movie with set pieces, scenery-chewing and heavy metal.

Drona: see *The Legend of Drona*

The Dynamic Scooby-Doo Affair ★★★★

aka *Scooby-Doo Meets Batman*, 1972, USA
Directors: Joseph Barbera, William Hanna
Cast: Don Messick, Casey Kasem, Frank Welker

Scooby (Messick) and the gang stumble on a counterfeiting ring being investigated by Batman (Olan Soulé) and Robin (Kasem).

Among the first episodes of *The New Scooby-Doo Movies*, which was the second series in the franchise (probably not crucial information, but's it's worth pointing out it pre-dates Scrappy-Doo). Sadly we aren't treated to Adam West and Burt Ward voice work, but you wouldn't know it and they're certainly here in spirit. It's marvellous.

Dynamite Johnson: see *The Return of the Bionic Boy*

The Eagle ★★

1925, USA
Director: Clarence Brown
Cast: Rudolph Valentino, Vilma Bánky, Louise Dresser

Vladimir Dubrovsky (Valentino), a soldier in the Russian army, brings doom upon his family by spurning the advances of the matronly Czarina (Dresser). Donning mask and cape, he becomes The Eagle and sets out for revenge.

Taking the role of The Eagle in an attempt to move away from the romantic characters then defining his screen persona, Valentino plays against type as a (supposedly) rough and ready military sort. However this went down at the time, today the combination of insipid score, clichéd script and peacock star leave *The Eagle* feeling about as rough and ready as *Barbie in Princess Power*. Not a bad movie but a dreadful *action* movie.

Earth vs the Spider ★★

2001, USA
Director: Scott Ziehl
Cast: Dan Aykroyd, Devon Gummersall, Amelia Heinle

Laboratory security guard Quentin Kramer (Gummersall) injects himself with arachnid blood, gains superpowers, goes nuts.

Strange mix of superhero antics, psycho thriller chills, and even body horror. Ziehl fails to manage the shifting moods, which creates awkward unpredictability that's only exacerbated by the uneven lead performance. The screenplay introduces and then fails to resolve various subplots, all the while expecting us to buy endless nonsensical machinations.

Eiga: minna! Esupâ da yo!: see *Everyone is Psychic*

8 Man ★★

aka *Eitoman - Subete no sabishii yoru no tame ni*, *8 Man – For All Lonely Nights*, 1992, Japan
Director: Yasuhiro Horiuchi
Cast: Kai Shishido, Etsushi Takahashi, Sachiko Ayase

Yokoda (Shishido), a detective all but killed in the line of duty, is transformed into a cyborg supercop. Problems arise when he begins to remember his past.

If you have ever wondered what *RoboCop* would look like without the existentialism and satire, here you go. Otherwise *8 Man* serves no obvious purpose, despite the promising tech noir aesthetic and unusally functional English language dub.

8 Man After ★★★

1993, Japan
Directors: Sumiyoshi Furakawa, Yoriyasu Kogawa
Cast: Mari Devon, Steve Bulen, Mike Reynolds

Hosted by private detective Hazama Itsuru (Bullen), 8 Man sets out to clean up a city degenerating into chaos.

Unrelated to the live-action movie of the previous year, this anime version of the cyborg/android/ghosted shell hero is more effective. Conceived as an OVA series, it's since been released as a stand-alone movie without suffering structural side effects. Describing it in the same generic manner with which it goes about its business; this is a solid-to-good manga adaptation with plenty of action and violence. It does feel derivative of other properties (*Astro Boy*, *Ghost in the Shell*), though.

The Eight Rangers ★★★

aka *Eito renjâ*, *Eight Ranger*, 2012, Japan
Director: Yukihiko Tsutsumi
Cast: Becky, Noriyuki Higashiyama, Wataru Ichinose

Seven flawed teenagers must unite under the tutelage of a legendary henshin hero, and save the decaying Eight City from a criminal organisation lead by the malignant Dark Kuruseido (Higashiyama).

Starring Japanese pop group Kanjani Eight, and based on skits performed during their live shows, *Eight Rangers* is an easygoing Super Sentai spoof and (just for a change) meditation on the importance of working as a team. Each member has clearly defined attributes that not only distinguish them but can also be a source of power, a great idea that suddenly seems questionable when we meet the alcoholic member of the squad. Undue levity is also applied to themes including child trafficking, which adds to the impression Kanjani Eight could be massacred by demons without it upsetting the maniacally positive tone.

Eight Ranger 2 ★★

aka *Eito renjâ 2*, 2014, Japan,
Director: Yukihiko Tsutsumi
Cast: Maho Hashimoto, Atsuko Maeda, Ryûhei Maruyama

With crime in Eight City a distant memory thanks to the Rangers, the team is on the verge of splitting up. Until, that is, a familiar face emerges as a new enemy.

If ever there was a one-shot idea it was the previous *Eight Rangers* movie. The arc was neat and impossible to repeat, while its parodic nature had a clear shelf life. In this sequel the choice of villain (which shouldn't be spoiled) is inspired and goes some way to justifying its existance, but a predictable decision to re-tread the 'learning the value of teamwork' stuff is a problem. Ultimately fans won't care, they seem to lap up anything Kanjani Eight spill.

Eitoman - Subete no sabishii yoru no tame ni: see *8 Man*

Esupai, aka *ESPY*

Wheelchair-bound billionaire Marcus Roach (Eirik) and his goons go after a college kid with the world's worst mother and the secret to a superhero serum.

Electra's central conceit (that superpowers can be passed on via unprotected sex) is more than trashy enough in its own right, but where director Julian Grant takes it is unforgivably obnoxious. In order for this book to remain accessible to people of all ages and sensibilities I won't go into it. Nor will I use language that might adequately explain how much I hated this thing.

Electra Woman and Dyna Girl
★★★★

2016, USA
Cast: Grace Helbig, Hannah Hart, Christopher Coutts

A small time superhero team is picked up by a major agency and propelled to stardom, causing problems in the duo's relationship.

The narrative is aimless but production values are decent for a web series and the well developed script is peppered with a few exceptional gags. Helbig is a revelation as Electra Woman, the well-meaning but flawed everywoman protagonist. There's an authenticity and emotional intelligence to her performance that elevates this already enjoyable comedy enormously.

El man, el superhéroe nacional ★

2009, Colombia,
Director: Harold Trompetero
Cast: Bernardo García, Aida Bossa, Fernando Solórzano

Taxi driver Felipe de Las Aguas (García) uses his faith in Christ to fight crime as a costumed vigilante.

Considering the financial limitations, *El Man* looks ok thanks to a pleasing colour palette. Otherwise... let's move on. Actually, let's not. I've just seen what's next.

Electra ★
1996, USA
Director: Julian Grant
Cast: Shannon Tweed, Joe Tabb, Sten Eirik

Electrika kasi, eh!
1977, Philippines
Director: Danilo Cabreira
Cast: Trixia Gomez, Chanda Romero, Celia Rodriguez

Surreal, female-driven, lost (which explains a large number of Pinoy superhero movies).

Elektra ★★
2005, USA

Director: Rob Bowman
Cast: Jennifer Garner, Will Yun Lee, Goran Visnjic

An elite assassin with an attitude problem develops a heart.

It feels like there were two movies made and this is the compromise edit that ruins both. The grand mythology explained at the start (all ancient wars, supernatural legends and good vs evil) has nothing to do with what follows: woman protects girl and girl's father from baddies. Girl is some sort of kung fu prodigy but it's just window dressing. Half film noir, half *Wonder Woman*.

Elf-Man ★★

2012, USA
Director: Ethan Wiley
Cast: Jason 'Wee Man' Acuña, Jeffrey Combs, Mackenzie Astin

When their father is kidnapped two siblings face a miserable Christmas alone with their grandmother. Luckily Santa (Jack Hoke) strands a pushy elf (Acuna) with the family so they can all learn something or other.

One of those unbearable Christmas movies full of bright colours, sensible sweaters, soppy children, and cartoon sound effects. This is what *Home Alone* would have been like if Hallmark had made it. Acuna is no actor and struggles to bring much to the role, even after adopting his superhero persona. Highly missable.

Elias Paniki: see *The Mysterious World of Elias Paniki*

Enteng Kabisote 10 and the Abangers ★

2016, Philippines
Directors: Tony Y. Reyes, Marlon Rivera
Cast: Vic Sotto, Jeffrey Quizon, Oyo Boy Sotto

A man living with a fairy is given a powered suit to help defeat a duck-themed villain.

The tenth entry in a film series derived from 1980s Pinoy sitcom *Okay Ka, Fairy Ko!* seems, unsurprisingly, rather tired and lazy. Sotto's character, the eponymous Enteng, had been struggling to retain his sanity in a *Bewitched*-style domestic farce for nearly 30 years before someone decided to throw superheroes into the mix, and it seems like too little too late. Local critics savaged the movie and I see no reason to dissent.

Esupai ★★★★

aka *ESPY*, 1974, Japan
Director: Jun Fukuda
Cast: Hiroshi Fujioka, Kaoru Yumi, Maso Kusakari

Racecar driving telepath Jirou (Kusakari) is recruited into ESPY, a secret government organisation tackling a plot to destroy the planet by assassinating world leaders.

Esupai's stylised cinematography and soundscapes lend an almost abstract air and incredible intensity to the telepathic conflicts (echoes of which are found in David Cronenberg's 1981 genre favourite *Scanners*). At times it threatens to lose itself but inevitably delivers a stylish action scene or burst of plot development just in time.

Everyone Is Psychic!, the Movie ★★

aka *Eiga: minna! Esupâ da yo!*, *The Virgin Psychics*, 2015, Japan
Director: Sion Sono
Cast: Mika Akizuki, Tokio Emoto, Motoki Fukami

After a mysterious light illuminates the night sky above a typical Japanese town, some residents develop mental powers.

Sexually-charged comedy based on the manga (and TV series) *Minna! ESPer Dayo!* If Benny Hill was reincarnated as a Japanese author it would explain everything. The plot ends up being about disgraced researchers trying to save everyone from psychics, but it hardly matters. It's just an endless sequence of saucy absurdities involving horny boys and knicker-flashing girls.

Evil Brain from Outer Space ★★

aka Super Giant 7, 8 and 9, 1965, Japan
Director: Ichirô Miyagawa
Cast: Ken Utsui, Junko Ikeuchi, Minoru Takada

Starman (Utsui) defends Earth from a fanged monster leading a fascist army.

Another instalment in the Starman movie series adapted from Japanese TV show *Super Giant*. It's hard to tell which is which (the others being *Attack from Space*, *Atomic Rulers* and *Invaders from Space*) because they all follow an identical structure, but we can call *Evil Brain from Outer Space* the one with the silly villain. As with the others, watching this thing is a tightrope walk balancing ironic amusement and boredom.

Exo-Man ★★

1977, USA
Director: Richard Irving
Cast: David Ackroyd, Anne Schedeen, A Martinez

When a failed assassination on professor Dr. Nicholas Conrad (Ackroyd) leaves the physicist paralysed, he uses a MacGuffin to build a crimefighting suit of armour.

Try to imagine Tony Stark as a depressed lecturer with an Iron Man suit that looks like it was built to protect 1950s Japanese astronauts from gamma rays. Plodding and dated, this pilot is notable only for featuring a protagonist who becomes less heroic as his superhero alter ego.

Extranghero ★★

1997, Philippines
Director: Ben Feleo
Cast: Andrew E., Michelle Aldana, Jorge Estregan

Two rivals for the affections of a beautiful woman are each hit by meteorites and left with superpowers. While one, Botong (E.), uses his newfound abilities for good, the other, Ivan (Estregan), takes the path of evil.

Extranghero lacks focus and takes too long to get going, but its amiable slapstick gags and inherent daftness just about make it worthwhile. The highlight is Ivan, at least once he becomes a cartoon evildoer. Estregan has a whale of a time chewing the scenery and ensures there isn't a dull moment as long as he's on screen.

Fantabulous Inc. ★★

aka *La donna, il sesso e il superuomo*, 1967, Italy
Director: Sergio Spina
Cast: Richard Harrison, Adolfo Celi, Judi West

Cynical spy chief Karl Maria van Beethoven (Celi) and his hand-less crazed scientist Professor Krohne (Gustavo D'Arpe) subject the unwilling Richard Werner (Harrison) to a process of superfication, then try to pimp him out to the UN as an invincible soldier.

Low budget sci-fi Bond movie with a sex obsession. Richard Harrison is... Richard Harrison (in other words wooden and frequently shirtless), although it's nice to see him in a comedy for a change. The silly sets and costumes are a giggle, but *Fantabulous Inc.'s* camp appeal is limited.

Fantastic 4: Rise of the Silver Surfer ★★

2007, USA
Director: Tim Story
Cast: Ioan Gruffudd, Jessica Alba, Chris Evans

On the eve of Reed Richards' aka Mr. Fantastic (Gruffud) marriage to Susan Storm aka Invisible Woman (Alba), a curious alien arrives on Earth with cataclysmic plans.

At one point Storm gets in a strop when Richards is *momentarily* distracted from planning their wedding by needing to save the world. More recent mainstream superhero movies may not be paragons of progressiveness, but at least they have mostly moved beyond such lazy and sexist dramatic cliché. Largely. As a result, it's hard to know where this sequel to Story's 2005 *F4* movie fits in. It doesn't benefit from the practical stakes and simple charms of pre-CGI comic book adventures, but nor is it dazzling, ambitious, witty or exciting, as superhero movies need to be in a world that includes Nolan's Batman series and the MCU. It's just some stuff that happens.

The Fantastic Four ★★

1994, USA
Director: Oley Sassone
Cast: Alex Hyde-White, Jay Underwood, Rebecca Staab

Four astronauts develop superpowers after being exposed to cosmic rays. On returning home they use them to battle a former colleague with a dangerous plan.

Interred after a predictably catastrophic screening for Marvel executives (allegedly they paid off the German rights holder to keep it on the shelf), this low-budget Roger Corman calamity isn't quite as awful as its history, and all indications, suggest. The effects are laughable, nothing seems quite finished and Underwood's performance as Johnny Storm is indescribable; but the plot makes sense, relationships are believable, motivations are clear and it feels like the cast were having fun. It's not a good movie, don't get me wrong, but it's arguably better than the 2015 reboot and certainly much more enjoyable.

Fantastic Four ★★★

2005, USA
Director: Tim Story
Cast: Ioan Gruffudd, Michael Chiklis, Chris Evans

Five scientists, in space to investigate the human genome, gain superpowers after being exposed to cosmic radiation.

The most enjoyable of the *Fantastic Four* movies, which isn't saying much. There's a breakneck pace, sense of humour, some agreeable performances (and some terrible ones, to be fair) and decent visual effects. Most importantly it's unashamedly cheesy, which seems a good way to go when your protagonist's superpower is the ability to stretch himself. (followed by *Fantastic 4: Rise of the Silver Surfer*.)

Fantastic Four ★

2015, USA
Director: Josh Trank
Cast: Miles Teller, Kate Mara, Michael B. Jordan

After teleporting into another dimension, four friends find they have superpowers.

A pretentious, poorly-cast, boring and thoroughly miserable mess. Compare it to any previous *Fantastic Four* effort for a lesson in why failed attempts at serious superhero movies are so much worse than failed attempts at silly superhero movies.

Fantastic Man ★★★

2003, Philippines
Director: Tony Y. Reyes
Cast: Vic Sotto, Ara Mina, Michael V.

Butter-fingered lab assistant Fredo (Sotto) inadvertently absorbs the power from an alien orb, somehow becoming superhero Fantastic Man in the process. He must use his new abilities to combat girlfriend Helen (Mina), who has turned into a demon.

One of an impressive 39 collaborations between prolific director Reyes and comedy star Sotto, *Fantastic Man* is in the same vein as the duo's other superhero spoofs *Kabayo Kids* and *Lastikman*. The lack of subtitles is a problem during the first half, with the wordy screenplay light on physical humour and the performances too flat to reveal much nuance. But once the origin story is dealt with the action picks up and some amusing visual effects take centre stage.

Fantômas: see Grouped Franchises

Faust: Love of the Damned ★★★

2000, Spain
Director: Brian Yuzna
Cast: Mark Frost, Isabel Brook, Jennifer Rope

When his girlfriend is murdered by thugs, artist John Jaspers (Mark Frost) makes a deal with the Devil for vengeance on the people who killed his girlfriend.

Avant-garde avenging and metaphysical horror are the order of the day. Told in flashback from our protagonist's padded cell, *Faust* is a very odd film. Its cacophany of screaming, stabbing sounds and heavy metal accompanies nightmarish imagery edited to within an inch of our lives. This is probably terrible but it's also engrossing and almost completely unique.

Fearless Frank ★★

1967, USA
Director: Philip Kaufman
Cast: Monique van Vooren, Jon Voight, Joan Darling

Country boy Frank (Voight) arrives in the big city to make his mark, and is promptly killed by gangsters. Brought back to life by a scientist, he finds he has superpowers.

Sophomore directorial effort from Philip Kaufman, who would go on to pen *Raiders of the Lost Ark* and direct *The Right Stuff*. It's so freewheeling and surreal it could only have been made in the 1960s. The humour is a strange mix of the absurd and the vaguely satirical, and keeps bringing to mind a diverse array of other movies (including *The Jerk*, *Putney Swope*, 1966 *Batman* and *The Ninth Configuration*. Not to mention Troma). Most of it fails, but there's always a nagging sense you're not getting it.

Fehérlófia: see *Son of the White Mare*

Fei Ying: see *Silver Hawk*

Fenomenal and the Treasure of Tutankamen ★★

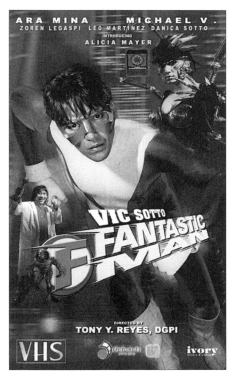

Original VHS sleeve for *Fantastic Man*

aka *Fenomenal e il tesoro di Tutankamen*, 1968, Italy
Director: Ruggero Deodato
Cast: Mauro Parenti, Lucretia Love, Gordon Mitchell

Masked crimefighter Fenomenal (Parenti) attempts to scupper a scheme to steal Egyptian relics.

Italian superhero nonsense that seems embarrassed by its protagonist, who hardly appears on screen during the movie's first half. When he does show up he's just a typical fumetti neri style black-clad figure accompanied by cool music. Among the more boring examples of these colourful late-1960s superhero-inspired James Bond knock-offs.

Fight! Batman, Fight!

1973, Philippines
Director: Romeo N. Galang
Cast: Victor Wood, Lotis Key, Rod Navarro

A red-caped Batman does battle with The Joker and Catwoman in this unlicensed Pinoy adventure. Considered lost.

Firebreather ★★

2010, USA
Director: Peter Chung
Cast: Tia Texada, Jesse Head, Dante Basco

The new kid in school struggles with fitting in and being half-dragon.

Based on the comic from Phil Hester and Andy Kuhn, this CGI animated movie from Cartoon Network features dynamic action scenes and reasonably interesting character designs, but fails to bring anything new to the 'disaffected teen' archetype.

Firestarter ★★

1984, USA
Director: Mark L. Lester
Cast: Drew Barrymore, David Keith, Freddie Jones

Telepathic parents spawn a pyrokinetic child and are pursued by government agents.

Director Mark L. Lester adds little to a novel Stephen King seems to have written on autopilot. There are some greats among the cast but they spend the movie either hamming it up or looking embarrassed. The practical special effects are a blast, though.

Fist of the North Star ★★★★

aka *Hokuto no Ken*, 1986, Japan
Director: Toyoo Ashida
Cast: Akira Kamiya, Yuriko Yamamoto, Kenji Utsumi

In post-apocalyptic Japan, Fist of the North Star, Ken (Kamiya), is bested in combat by Fist of the South Star, Shin (Toshi Furukawa), losing girlfriend Yuri (Yamamoto) in the process. After recovering, Ken wanders the wasteland helping the vulnerable and seeking vengeance.

Anime adaptation of the revered manga. There are some great ideas conveyed via near-abstract visuals, even if the animation itself is slightly dated. Little time is wasted on exposition and we're left to figure out much of the backstory ourselves, but plot isn't the point. This is all about violence and style, and there's plenty of both.

Fist of the North Star ★★

1995, USA
Director: Tony Randel
Cast: Gary Daniels, Malcolm McDowell, Costas Mandylor

In the aftermath of World War III, Kenshiro (Daniels), a gifted martial artist with certain supernatural abilities, defends survivors from the barbaric Crossmen.

Compared to the stripped back simplicity of the anime, this live-action take on *FotNS* is a latticework of flashbacks, voiceovers, subplots and other superfluousness. And instead of a distinctive wasteland as the backdrop we get the generically grungy post-apocalypse world of dozens of other Hollywood movies (and hundreds of Pinoy ones). The cast is an eclectic bunch and features British kickboxer Gary Daniels, firebrand renaissance man Melvin Van Peebles, B-movie legend Clint Howard and MTV host Downtown Julie Brown (you might notice a lack of actors with any Asian heritage in that lineup). When considered independently, this is an uninspiring and forgettable waste. But as an adaptation of existing work it's even more disappointing. Still, it's significantly better than Korea's *Legend of Fist of the North Star*.

Fist of the North Star Legends & Sagas: see Grouped Franchises. See also *Legend of Fist of the North Star*

The Flash ★★★

1990, USA
Director: Robert Iscove
Cast: John Wesley Shipp, Amanda Pays, Alex Désert

A police chemist develops the power of superspeed after the science he's holding is struck by lightning.

Belated live-action debut for DC's nimble hero. Shipp is bland in the lead but the general standard across the board is a little higher than the average 1990s superhero TV movie, though the villains are a letdown. For a supposedly terrifying biker gang they seem a little too preoccupied with high school hijinks (like throwing paint bombs at a police station) rather than doing anything that's actually menacing.

The Flash II: Revenge of the Trickster ★★★

1991, USA
Director: Danny Bilson
Cast: John Wesley Shipp, Amanda Pays, Alex Désert

Barry Allen, aka the Flash (Shipp), is caught up in the criminal schemes of an insane magician known as The Trickster (Hamill).

With the cast slimmed down and the Flash already origin storied, this second of three movies feels less cluttered and works more like the TV show from which it's derived. Unfortunately, Shipp is still flat and his endless romantic schmoozing never works. Mark Hamill, on the other hand, is right at home playing an absurdly over-the-top pantomime villain, and channels most of *Batman* '66's bad guys at some stage.

Flash III: Deadly Nightshade ★★★

1992, USA
Director: Bruce Bilson
Cast: John Wesley Shipp, Amanda Pays, Alex Désert

When supercriminal The Ghost (Anthony Starke), a remnant from Central City's past, awakens from cryo-sleep, the Flash (Shipp) teams up with aged superhero Nightshade (Jason Bernard) to take him down. Matters become complicated when a Nightshade imposter introduces himself into the mix.

The last and perhaps most entertaining of these TV movies thanks to a streamlined narrative (although Mark Hamill is missed). It's also the least filmic, with the two TV episodes it's formed from having little to do with each other. For comic fans it's basically porn, thanks to a brace of superheroes and a triptych of supervillains all vying to be the most preposterous thing in the movie.

Flash Gordon ★★★★

1936, USA
Directors: Frederick Stephani, Ray Taylor
Cast: Buster Crabbe, Jean Rogers, Charles Middleton

Flash Gordon (Crabbe), Dale Arden (Rogers) and Dr. Zarkoff (Frank Shannon) take a rocket ship to Planet Mongo.

When a model rocket crash-lands in a terrarium (aka Mongo), startling its iguana (aka terrifying space monsters) inhabitants we aren't exactly thrust into a magical world of wonder, but we are reassured the next four hours will be fun. The problem with serials is they go on forever and repeat themselves every 20 minutes. *Flash Gordon* serials are more entertaining than most thanks to their exotic sets, colourful characters and special effects. They also boast the best villain in Ming the Merciless (Middleton), a hammy tyrant who looks like a cross between Fu Manchu and Satan. We get appearances from Shark Men and Lion Men, races excised from the 1980 movie, and, most importantly, Buster Crabbe, the most charismatic genre star of the day (Followed by *Flash Gordon's Trip to Mars*.)

Flash Gordon ★★★★★

1980, USA
Director: Mike Hodges
Cast: Sam J. Jones, Melody Anderson, Max von Sydow

Star football player 'Flash' Gordon (Jones) and travel agent Dale Arden (Anderson) find themselves aboard the rocket ship of Dr. Hans Zarkov (Topol) and headed for the planet Mongo, where the three must topple vindictive dictator Ming the Merciless (von Sydow) in order to save the Earth.

Cultural cornerstone, exercise in kitsch, arthouse classic, experimental masterpiece, abominable farce... Mike Hodges' take on

Flashman

Flash Gordon is bound to be at least one of those things to anyone who's seen it. What's easy to forget is how beautiful it is. Mongo's atmosphere, all primary colours and swirling fluids, looks stunning; the props and costumes mix retro with chintz in the most gloriously camp manner; and the elaborate production designs demonstrate an originality and creative imagination that puts most fantasy movies to shame.

Flash Gordon Conquers the Universe ★★★

1940, USA
Directors: Ford Beebe, Ray Taylor
Cast: Buster Crabbe, Carol Hughes, Charles Middleton

Ming's (Middleton) latest scheme involves seeding Earth's atmosphere with poison. Flash (Crabbe) and friends head to Mongo to enlist the help of Prince Barin (Roland Drew) in saving mankind.

Flash's serials have never lacked pace, and this third and final one is breakneck. The first ten minutes alone cover the exposition that gets us up to speed on purple dust (apparently victims can be identified by a small purple dot on their forehead, which works well in a serial devoid of close-ups and colour), establishes around a dozen characters and then sees Flash and Zarkov skirmish with an enemy spaceship, travel to Mongo, meet up with Barin, form some sort of alliance with the Ice Kingdom, concoct a plan and then infiltrate Ming's palace. Ten minutes! In broader terms, we all know what to expect at this point: cyclical adventuring, cliffhangers and stiff performances.

Flash Gordon's Trip to Mars ★★★

1938, USA
Director: Ford Beebe, Frederick Stephani, Robert Hill
Cast: Buster Crabbe, Jean Rogers, Charles Middleton

Ming is holed up on Mars using a science ray to rob Nitron from Earth's atmosphere. Flash Gordon (Crabbe) isn't going to stand for that, so he heads to Mars with Zarkov (Frank Shannon), love interest Dale Arden (Rogers) and comedy relief Happy Hapgood (Donald Kerr). Yes, the comic relief guy is called Happy Hapgood.

It's a less naive Flash taking a trip to Mars than the one who visited Mongo a couple of years earlier, but Buster Crabbe still plays him so all's well. Richard Alexander returns as Prince Barin too, even though he lives in another galaxy (apparently he's on Mars looking for help protecting Earth, but it might have made sense to tell us we were in danger in the first place). Essentially the gang rolls from one little fiefdom to the next, alternately being imprisoned by and befriending each, all of which allows plenty of opportunity for Flash to be heroic and for Dale to faint. (Followed by *Flash Gordon Conquers the Universe*).

Flash Gordon: The Greatest Adventure of All ★★★★

1982, USA
Director: Unknown
Cast: Robert Ridgely, Diane Pershing, Bob Holt

Flash (Ridgely) heads to Mongo and battles Ming (Vic Perrin).

While Dino De Laurentis was plugging away at the live-action Flash Gordon movie that would ultimately reach screens in 1980, the popularity of *Star Wars* also encouraged animation house Filmation to take a stab at the proto-superhero. Although the result wouldn't be released until three years after its completion, it's surprisingly good. Maniacally faithful to the original narrative, and pitched to appeal to all ages, it's a mature, inventive but grounded adventure. On a side note, viewers of a certain age might notice some familiar characters and settings. Filmation were responsible for the

1980s *He-man* TV show and many of its environments and character designs were recycled from this movie.

Flash Gordon's Battle in Space ★★

aka *Baytekin - fezada çarpisanlar*, 1967, Turkey
Director: Sinasi Özonuk
Cast: Hasan Demirtag, Derya Tanyeli, Sevgi Can

Aliens in need of help kidnap Flash Gordon (Demirtag) from Earth, where he seems to be in jail.

Flash Gordon first appeared in Turkish comics in 1935 and proved an instant hit, making an unlicensed domestic feature such as this inevitable. The cape, costume and plot (as much of it as can be discerned without subtitles) place this Gordon at the superhero end of the character spectrum, which is lucky because he faces some of his toughest opponents (it's hard to say which is scarier; the men in sacks waving their arms about or the killer muppets). Fortunately he ditches the conical bra halfway through.

Flashman ★★

1967, Italy
Director: Mino Loy
Cast: Paolo Gozlino, Claudie Lange, Ivano Staccioli

Lord Alex Burman, aka superhero Flashman (Gozlino), pursues The Kid (Staccioli) to mainland Europe, where he can't prevent an assassination.

Not to be confused with George MacDonal Fraser's Flashman, or any of the other far superior fictional heroes who share the name, this particular Flashman is the lazy creation of screenwriter Ernesto Gastaldi. He's essentially Batman but without a sense of purpose, unless you consider sleazing over pretty women a purpose. There are some hilarious visual effects (an invisibility device is central to the plot, so there's lots of stuff hanging from fishing wire, and at one point a miniature Flashman uses what looks like a handkerchief for a parachute) and great music, but the central character is so unlikeable it's impossible to engage.

Fly Me to the Moon ★★

1988, Philippines
Director: Mike Relon Makiling
Cast: Tito Sotto, Vic Sotto, Joey de Leon

Pinoy comedy troupe Tito, Vic and Joey are tricked into travelling to the moon, where they encounter Superman and battle aliens.

Fly Me to the Moon toys with superhero elements but it's here due to the extended cameo from an unofficial Superman (the boys hit him with their spaceship, which somehow leaves him naked). Highlights include the soundtrack, which features a version of the eponymous song with lyrics in Tagalog, and the blatant theft of some prominent themes from 1978's *Superman* and *E.T.: The Extra Terrestrial*. The first hour is dull but the lightsaber duals and laser battles of the finale are marvellously awful.

A Flying Jatt ★★

2016, India
Director: Remo D'Souza
Cast: Tiger Shroff, Jacqueline Fernandez, Nathan Jones

Martial arts instructor Aman Dhillon (Shroff) receives superpowers from a magical tree when he saves it from a cynical industrialist.

There's a strong and effective ecological theme (while the goody acquires his powers from nature, the baddy gets his from toxic waste) and some animated sequences to break things up. But the romance feels tacked on, events towards the conclusion are too contrived and the fight scenes lack the usual Bollywood pizzazz.

The Flying Mr. B ★★★

aka *Gui ma fei ren*, 1985, Hong Kong
Director: Jing Wong
Cast: Kenny Bee, Cherie Chung, Jing Wong

School soccer coach Mr. Shi (Bee) becomes a superhero after taking a pill developed by a colleague seeking a cure for obesity.

Family comedy from Hong Kong's fabled Shaw Brothers. The humour is decidedly slapstick and the surreal interludes might not appeal to adults, but if you can find a dubbed version small children will adore it.

Franklyn ★★

2008, UK
Director: Gerald McMorrow
Cast: Eva Green, Ryan Phillippe, Sam Riley

In contemporary London, a suicidal artist, a lovelorn jiltee and a desperate father endure various states of misery. Meanwhile, in the dystopian future of Meanwhile City, a masked hero named Preest (Phillippe) searches for his nemesis.

Franklyn never quite reconciles its pair of narratives; the sci-fi is just too tonally different to the kitchen sink stuff. Eva Green is great as the London artist, but it's the neo-noir future that's the more interesting place to be. Similar in look to Alex Proyas' *Dark City*, it's a place in which religious zealotry has become the norm, and only Preest seems to object.

Freedom Fighters: The Ray ★★★

2018, USA
Director: Ethan Spaulding
Cast: Russell Tovey, Jason Mitchell, Melissa Benoist

On Earth X, evil nazi versions of several DC superheroes do evil nazi stuff. On Earth Normal, Ray Terrill (Tovey) turns superhero.

This web series cut-and-shut mixes visual styles to great effect. Striking fascist imagery with an anime flavour and more traditional US animation each look good and work well. The structure is fine at feature length and an openly gay protagonist allows for some unusual character beats and emotional dynamics.

Frozen ★★★★

2013, USA
Directors: Chris Buck, Jennifer Lee
Staring: Kristen Bell, Idina Menzel, Jonathan Groff

Born with the unwanted and dangerous ability to create ice, Princess Elsa chooses to live in isolation for what she believes is the good of her people.

While I'm not entirely in favour of classing *Frozen* as a superhero movie, there are enough opposing views that it requires a mention. So: mentioned.

Full Eclipse ★★

1993, USA
Director: Anthony Hickox
Cast: Mario Van Peebles, Patsy Kensit, Bruce Payne

LA cop Max Dire (Van Peebles) is recruited into an unofficial vigilante wing of the force, but soon finds his new mentor may not be what he seems.

It's hard to dance around the key revelation here, but it happens early enough in the movie that it isn't much of a spoiler, so... they're all werewolves. Amusingly *Full Eclipse* takes itself entirely seriously (unlike the superior *WolfCop*), which is a brave, if foolish, move. The cast do what they can and it isn't a complete catastrophe, but if the only laugh-out-loud moments in a film about werewolf cops are unintentional, it's fair to say we're not dealing with a classic.

Full Metal Yakuza ★★★

aka *Full Metal gokudô*, 1997, Japan
Director: Takashi Miike
Cast: Tsuyoshi Ujiki, Tomorô Taguchi, Takeshi Caesar

Neophyte yakuza Kensuke Hagane (Ujiki) is rendered into a bionic avenger after a failed assassination attempt on his boss.

Full Metal Yakuza is almost cinema vérité in its casualness and early leisurely pace, which only serves to make the gruesome body horror a greater surprise when it kicks off. Director Takashi Miike seems to be having fun (he couldn't be more at home than with a decapitated, wire-sprouting head arguing with a mad scientist). Not as full-on as some of his later movies, but it's still not one for the faint of heart.

Fullmetal Alchemist ★★★★

aka *Hagane no renkinjutsushi*, 2017, Japan
Director: Fumihiko Sori
Cast: Ryôsuke Yamada, Tsubasa Honda, Dean Fujioka

Two young brothers suffer horrendous physical consequences when they try to resurrect their recently deceased mother with magic. Subsequently they dedicate themselves to finding the Philosopher's Stone, which may enable them to lead normal lives once more.

Visually this live-action manga adaptation is stunning. The period setting is faithfully recreated and the snazzy visual effects are elaborate and plentiful, as they need to be in a movie like this. The screenplay is good but, if there is a problem, it could perhaps have stripped out a couple of strands in order to get the runtime down.

Fullmetal Alchemist: Conqueror of Shambala ★★★★★

aka *Gekijô-ban hagane no renkinjutsushi: Shanbara wo yuku mono*, 2005, Japan
Director: Seiji Mizushima
Cast: Vic Mignogna, Aaron Dismuke, Jason Liebrecht

Edward Elric (Mignogna), a gifted alchemist from a magical dimension, is trapped in a version of our 1930s Europe in which his powers don't work. After discovering a plot by Nazis to invade his homeworld, Ed must save it by solving a series of mysteries.

This first *Fullmetal Alchemist* movie is a bewildering experience for those who are unfamiliar with the 2003 anime series it concludes. An immense backstory we know nothing about feeds into every aspect of a plot involving multiple character iterations and realities. It's all so ambitious and well executed there's plenty to enjoy even if you can't grasp 100% of what's happening. The visuals in particular are stunning, which seems to be a hallmark of the franchise: scenes of an industrial pre-war Europe are rendered via flat, sepia tones and melancholy vibe; while the more fantastical sequences pop with saturated primary colours and dynamic movement.

was with *Conqueror of Shambala*, some prior knowledge is assumed. Unlike that 2005 movie, this one feels like an extended episode of its antecedent TV show. We're off on a tangent here accompanying Ed and Al on an adventure that feels fairly random. It's well done, though. A little more generic than its theatrical predecessor, and perhaps skewed younger (although that could just be the English dub performances), it's an interesting and well-balanced story that makes good use of its characters.

Fullmetal Alchemist: The Sacred Star of Milos ★★★★

aka *Hagane no renkinjutsushi: Mirosu no seinaru hoshi*, 2011, Japan
Director: Kazuya Murata
Cast: Vic Mignogna, Maxey Whitehead, Alexis Tipton

In a world of magic, state alchemist Edward Elric (Mignogna) and his brother Alphonse (Whitehead) pursue an escaped criminal into a dangerous dimension.

Each of the three (unrelated) *Fullmetal Alchemist* films present different versions of its universe and, unusually, tell different stories. This one is an offshoot of the 2009 *Brotherhood* anime series and, just as it

G.I. Joe: see Grouped Franchises

Gacchaman: see *Gatchaman*

Gadis Bionik ★★
aka *The Bionic Woman*, 1982, Indonesia
Director: Ali Shahab
Cast: Eva Arnaz, Don Nasco, Jaja Mihardja

After escaping jail, Kontet (Nasco) maims Rita (Arnaz), one of the police officers responsible for capturing him. In order to save her life she's given bionic limbs.

With the Warkop comedy troupe deciding not to return for this sequel to *Manusia enam juta dolar*, Eva Arnaz steps up to a central role she seems more than comfy with. A female protagonist is a welcome change and the entertainingly colourful villains are good value, but this is even scrappier than the first movie and has no better ideas for exploiting the conceit.

Gagamba: see Grouped Franchises

Gagamboy ★★★
2004, Philippines
Director: Erik Matti
Cast: Vhong Navarro, Jay Manalo, Aubrey Miles

Rival ice-cream vendors gain superpowers after eating radioactive bugs, and their competition for the affections of a local beauty soon get out of hand.

Although clearly influenced by Spider-Man, *Gagamboy* has its own sense of humour and personality. The narrative is a simplistic 'good guy prevails over bad guy' story arc, but it's executed with enough invention to keep things interesting. There's a fast pace and clever use of music, but it might all come off too childish for some audiences.

Gandarrapiddo! The Revenger Squad ★★

2017, Philippines
Director: Joyce Bernal
Cast: Vice Ganda, Daniel Padilla, Pia Wurtzbach

A group of misfits form a superhero squad to protect the world from Mino (Ejay Falcon), a supervillain manipulating followers from his prison inside a mirror.

Following in the psychedelic footsteps of gender-bending Pinoy extravaganzas like *Sheman: Mistress of the Universe* and *Zsa Zsa Zaturnnah*, this nutty comedy fails badly at the jokes and worse at the commentary on social media, something it seems unduly preoccupied by. Essentially 90 minutes of people squealing.

Garo: see Grouped Franchises

Garuda Superhero ★★

2016, Indonesia
Director: X.Jo
Cast: Rizal Idrus, Slamet Rahardjo, Agus Kuncoro

A defence system intended to protect Earth from asteroids is hijacked by terrorist Durja King (Rahardjo). Wealthy playboy Bara, aka Garuda Superhero (Idrus), steps in.

Allegedly the first Indonesian movie to make widespread use of computer graphics, *Garuda Superhero* floods the screen with so much ropey CGI it looks like a stylistic experiment along the lines of *Sky Captain and the World of Tomorrow*. Adding to a surreal vibe is the (presumably unofficial) English language dub, apparently recorded by a couple of buddies in their living room. Inspiration comes from Batman, the MCU, G.I. Joe and, surprisingly, horror sequel *Jason X* but, as a result of its peculiarities, it remains very much its own thing. Exactly what that thing is remains debatable.

Gatchaman ★★★

aka *Gacchaman*, 2013, Japan
Director: Tôya Satô
Cast: Tôri Matsuzaka, Ryôhei Suzuki, Gô Ayano

In the year 2050 Earth has been conquered by alien invaders known as Galactors. Our last line of defence is five teenagers able to channel the power of magic crystals.

Impressive looking tokusatsu version of the anime (see below). There's little point expecting logic from such a property (half of all humans are dead but the remaining populace seem quite chipper about it). It's enough that the narrative is comparatively straightforward and the frivolous wackiness of shows such as the *Super Sentai* series is kept in check. If you were/are a *Gatchaman/Battle of the Planets* fan it's an undeniable buzz to see these seminal and visually striking characters rendered in live-action.

Gatchaman the Movie ★★★

aka *Kagaku ninja tai Gatchaman, Science Ninja Team Gatchaman*, 1978, Japan
Director: Hisayuki Toriumi
Cast: Katsuji Mori, Isao Sasaki, Kazuko Sugiyama

Galactor's Leader X (Nobuo Tanaka) intends to decimate Earth. The Science Ninja Team move in.

Feature-length movie using material from the 1972 Japanese anime series *Kajaku Ninjatai Gatchaman* (aka *Science Ninja Team Gatchaman*), which was dubbed into English and shown in the West as *Battle of the Planets*. Unlike the US movie belatedly scraped together from the same footage in 2002, this one is hugely melodramatic. Some members of the team are given a bit of backstory and they spend plenty of time in their civvies interacting and generally winding each other up, which makes them more interesting characters. There's also more of an atmosphere, and it feels less like random episodes of the TV show have been nailed together (although that's not to say it's exactly coherent). I'm not sure any of this is worth losing Casey Kasem's voice performance for, though.

Gegege no Kitarô: see *Kitaro*

Gekijô-ban hagane no renkinjutsushi: Shanbara wo yuku mono: see *Fullmetal Alchemist the Movie: Conqueror of Shamballa*

Gekijouban Tiger & Bunny: see *Tiger & Bunny*

Gekko Kamen: see Grouped Franchises and *Moonlight Mask*

Gemma: Babaing Kidlat

1974, Philippines
Director: Danny Holmsen
Cast: Ricky Belmonte, Ramil Rodriguez, Rudy Fernandez

Although much of the picture remains for this 1974 remake, the entire audio track is lost. Therefore this movie is unreleased on home formats.

Gen¹³ ★★

2000, USA
Director: Kevin Altieri
Cast: Alicia Witt, John de Lancie, Elizabeth Daily

College student Caitlin Fairchild (Witt) is transformed into a supersoldier as part of a controversial military programme.

This attempt at an adult-oriented animation fails thanks largely to oddly childish dialogue and characterisation. A commercial rights curiosity has left it hard to obtain in the US, but nobody's missing out.

Generation X ★★★

1996, USA
Director: Jack Sholder
Cast: Matt Frewer, Finola Hughes, Jeremy Ratchford

Teenage mutants at The Xavier School for Gifted Students are drawn into the evil scheme of a mad scientist who can enter people's dreams.

X-Men meets *Saved by the Bell*, replete with all the horrors that implies. We cover much of the same ground Brian Singer's more successful X-movie would tread in 2000, with the attempted oppression and widespread fear of mutants a backdrop to the wicked exploitation of their abilities. Unfortunately, Frewer is a lightweight and irritating villain, while none of the youthful supermutants capture the imagination. Interestingly the location used for Prof X's school, Hatley Castle in British Columbia, fulfilled the same role in *X2* (2003) and subsequent entries in the series.

Gatchaman (2013 version)

Ghost of Zorro ★

1949, USA
Director: Fred C. Brannon
Cast: Clayton Moore, Pamela Blake, Roy Barcroft

A descendant of Zorro battles an outlaw who is attempting to prevent expansion of the telegraph.

As in all but the second (*Zorro Rides Again*, aka the good one) of Republic's five Zorro serials, our hero doesn't even make an appearance. The grandson this time is a distinctly non-Hispanic engineer by the name of Ken (Moore, who would become a TV superstar later in the year playing the Lone Ranger on ABC's hugely popular series). Republic gave Don Diego de la Vega a grandson named Ken, and he's the weakest protagonist in the series. This comprehensive disappointment at least answers the question of whether a serial can feature so much stock footage and repetition it actually ceases to function as drama. (Yes, it can.)

Ghost of Zorro

1959, USA
Director: Fred C. Brannon
Cast: Clayton Moore, Pamela Blake, Roy Barcroft

Feature-length edit of the 1949 serial of the same name. It was adapted for TV in order to piggyback on the success of Disney's then current *Zorro* TV series.

Ghost Rider ★★

2007, USA
Director: Mark Steven Johnson
Cast: Nicolas Cage, Eva Mendes, Sam Elliott

Tricked in a deal with the Devil (Fonda), motorcycle stunt rider Johnny Blaze (Cage) must find and kill Blackheart (Wes Bentley), a rogue demon determined to claim Earth for himself.

If there's an applicable cliché *Ghost Rider* neglects to exploit, I can't think what it is. The lack of originality and imagination scupper any chance the movie has of rising above its teenage emo's idea of a setup, and laziness seems to pervade everything from the dialogue to the effects.

Ghost Rider: Spirit of Vengeance ★★

2011, USA
Director: Mark Neveldine, Brian Taylor
Cast: Nicolas Cage, Ciarán Hinds, Idris Elba

Johnny Blaze (Cage) is living as a recluse in Eastern Europe when he's asked to protect an enigmatic child in exchange for the lifting of his curse.

Everything is different enough to qualify this sort-of sequel as more of a reboot. It's gothic and scuzzy where the first movie is cheesy and shiny, and almost everything has been reset. Unfortunately, bad silly is more fun than bad moody. And there's less Nic Cage too, thanks to a more cluttered plot and the entirely-CGI-all-the-time Ghost Rider. It isn't very good, but Cage was born to play this character.

Giant and Jumborg Ace: see *Jumborg Ace & Giant*

Glass ★★★

2019, USA
Director: M. Night Shyamalan
Cast: James McAvoy, Bruce Willis, Samuel L. Jackson

Three potential superpeople with knotty pasts are examined by a psychiatrist.

The conclusion to Shyamalan's Eastrail 177 Trilogy (following *Unbreakable* and *Split*) takes a surreal turn. Everything is so off-key it must be deliberate, but the contrivances, coincidences and absurdities necessary to get us to the conclusion render it all a bit meaningless. Silly as it is there's also plenty to like. McAvoy is brilliant, just as he was in *Split*, and no matter how silly things get there are interesting ideas and some tense, well-executed highlights.

God of Thunder ★
2015, USA
Director: Thomas Shapiro
Cast: Max Aria, Jacqui Holland, Preston Hillier

Thor comes to Earth and hangs out in places that don't require filming permits.

Anyone planning to watch over 1,000 superhero movies should beware of three particularly troublesome categories (not to mention origin story fatigue). First, serials go on forever and repeat themselves constantly. Second, there are a hell of a lot of animated superhero movies and most of them are rubbish. Third, you'd better get used to demigods who happen to be in the public domain. With the popularity of the MCU, Thor has replaced Hercules as the go-to 'free' hero, and he stars in a handful of mockbusters that are among the worst movies you're ever likely to see. This one isn't as bad as *Thunderstorm: The Return of Thor*, but it's not far off.

Godzilla vs Megalon ★★★
aka *Gojira tai Megaro*, 1973, Japan
Director: Jun Fukuda
Cast: Katsuhiko Sasaki, Hiroyuki Kawase, Yutaka Hayashi

Concerned by the effects of Japan's nuclear weapons tests, the underwater kingdom of Seatopia send Megalon and Gigan to attack Tokyo. Scientist Goro Ibuki (Sasaki) sends in Jet Jaguar, who teams up with Godzilla to defend Japan.

Derided by fans for being at the sillier end of the Gojira movie spectrum (what do you want from a giant nuclear lizard movie?), this 13th film in the series was originally conceived as a Jet Jaguar solo vehicle and wasn't intended to feature the king of the monsters at all. Jaguar is the reason for the movie's presence here, with the Kyodai favourite making his only feature-film appearance (and stealing every scene on his way to saving the day). Presumably inspired by Ultraman, the plan was to set up the size-changing robot for his own franchise, but it seems dwindling box office returns for Showa period kaiju movies put the kibosh on that plan (although I wouldn't be surprised if it was actually the insufferable child who worms his way into every scene).

The Golden Bat: see Grouped Franchises

The Golden Blaze ★★★★
2005, USA
Director: Bryon E. Carson
Cast: Blair Underwood, Michael Clarke Duncan, Sanaa Lathan

The fathers of a bullied 12-year-old and his schoolyard tormentor each develop superpowers, and take the family feud to a new dimension.

The Flash animation fails a great cast and a surprisingly good script that manages to build emotional depth into believable characters. There's also a disappointing tendency to play it safe with some overly familiar archetypes (I'm through with 'real world' superhero movies featuring a comic store owning acquaintance advising the protagonist), but this unusual mishmash survives its contrasting quality levels to become if not quite essential, then at least useful. An immense amount of heart went into this thing.

Gojira tai Megaro: see *Godzilla vs. Megalon*

Goldface, the Fantastic Superman ★★

aka *Goldface il fantastico Superman*, 1967,
Italy/Spain
Director: Bitto Albertini
Cast: Espartaco Santoni, Evi Marandi,
Attilio Severini

Genius scientist and champion wrestler Dr.
Vilar, aka Goldface (Santoni), is drawn into a
convoluted insurance and kidnapping scam
perpetrated by The Cobra (Hugo Pimentel).

There's a bit of everything in *Goldface, the
Fantastic Superman*. Our lead incorporates
elements of Bruce Banner, Argoman, El
Santo, and Tony Stark, while inexplicably
borrowing Mandrake the Magician's African
sidekick Lothar (Mario Brito). The movie's
Italian heritage comes through in some
stylish cinematography, fantastic music
and Vilar's relentless womanising (why are
all Italian movie superheroes obsessive

The Golden Blaze

philanders?), but it's pretty standard fare
despite some decent set pieces.

Goliath (1960s Italian series): see Grouped
Franchises and Peplum Movies

Gothic Lolita Battle Bear ★★★

aka *Nuigurumâ Z*, 2013, Japan
Director: Noboru Iguchi
Cast: Shôko Nakagawa, Jiji Bû, Norman England

An alien disguised as a pink teddy bear
gives an insane woman superpowers, then
tells her to protect a girl from zombies.

It's hard to identify the most bewildering
aspect of *Gothic Lolita Battle Bear*, but it's
probably between the narrative incoherence
and a peculiar determination to use every
Adobe After Effects plug-in on the market.
You'll know whether you'll like it from the
trailer; this sort of over-amped tokusatsu
madness either appeals or doesn't, whether
it's any good or not seems beside the point.
For what it's worth, the bear is funny and
Nakagawa makes for a charming lead.

The Great Adventure of Zorro ★★★

aka *La gran aventura del Zorro*, 1976, Mexico
Director: Raúl de Anda Jr.
Cast: Rodolfo de Anda, Helena Rojo,
Pedro Armendáriz Jr.

Don Diego returns home to California and
learns of the horrors commited by the
military in his absence. With the addition of
mask and rapier, he becomes Zorro.

Scrappy take on the Zorro origin story that
benefits from better than typical music and
action scenes. We also get a good idea of
the impact the villains' behaviour has on
the community (there's a strange thread
running through the majority of Zorro
movies that sees their peasant victims
sidelined by a tendency to *tell* us what the

bad guys have done rather than *show* us). Zorro's is the most frequently told origin story in superhero cinema, and this is a solid if not exactly revolutionary take on it.

The Great Shu Ra Ra Boom ★★★
aka *Idainaru, Shurarabon*, 2014, Japan
Director: Yutaka Mizuochi
Cast: Shihori Kanjiya, Kyoko Fukada, Masaki Okada

An ancient feud between two noble (and superpowered) Japanese families is brought to a head on the shores of Lake Biwa.

Based on the bestseller by Manabu Makibe, *The Great Shu Ra Ra Boom* offers a great insight into Japanese social conventions and, in a way, folk mythology. Equal parts fantasy, drama and comedy, it's well acted and looks beautiful. A little less time could have been spent spoon-feeding us details about the rival clans' powers, but that's hardly a fatal flaw.

The Green Hornet ★★★
1940, USA
Directors: Ford Beebe, Ray Taylor
Cast: Gordon Jones, Keye Luke, Wade Boteler

Aided by his faithful sidekick Kato (Luke), wealthy publisher Britt Reid (Jones) uncovers a series of rackets as masked crimefighter The Green Hornet.

This first of The Hornet's screen outings came just four years after his creation for radio by Fran Striker and George W. Trendle (who were also responsible for The Lone Ranger). It's dated better than the typical serial thanks to strong lead performances from Jones and Luke, and a clever structure that keeps things interesting. In having our hero investigate a series of crimes (which are ultimately tied together), the narrative is naturally episodic and therefore a good fit for the serial format. Kato could have done

with more screen time but, on the whole, this is one of the better Earthbound serials. (Followed by sequel *The Green Hornet Strikes Again*.)

The Green Hornet ★★★
1974, USA
Directors: William Beaudine, Norman Foster, E. Darrell Hallenbeck
Cast: Bruce Lee, Van Williams, Wende Wagner

Adventures lifted from the 1966 TV series.

Less a movie than a clip show: things kick off halfway through a scene and no plot ever emerges. Instead, Britt Reid (Williams) talks on the phone for a bit before picking up Kato (Lee) and rushing to a fight. The whole process is repeated over and over, with occasional cameos from weirdos and space aliens.

The Green Hornet
1990, USA
Director: Ford Beebe
Cast: Gordon Jones, Keye Luke, Wade Boteler

Feature-length edit of 1939 serial *The Green Hornet*. Strangely, it only includes material from its second half, suggesting there must once have been a companion piece.

The Green Hornet (1994): see *Dragon and the Green Hornet*

The Green Hornet ★★★
2011, USA
Director: Michel Gondry
Cast: Seth Rogen, Jay Chou, Christoph Waltz

Spoilt party-boy Britt Reid (Rogen) becomes a superhero just for the buzz. Together with tech genius, kung fu master and barista extraordinaire Kato (Chou), he sets about ridding Los Angeles of crime.

As comedy substitutes for Van Williams and Bruce Lee, Rogen and Chou are fine. They share decent chemistry and don't annoy. The idea is good, too, basically *Batman: The Comedy*. The problem lies in the flat script, which fails to provide either belly laughs or direction, preferring instead to indulge the central duo and tick boxes. In Cameron Diaz's Female Character we have one of the most underwritten parts ever given to an A-list acress.

The Green Hornet Movie Edition

2011, USA
Director: Ford Beebe
Cast: Gordon Jones, Keye Luke, Wade Boteler

Another feature-length edit of 1939 serial *The Green Hornet*. I don't know what it is about the Green Hornet, but he's probably been subject to more cut-and-shuts than any other superhero. This version was released to coincide with the 2011 reboot.

The Green Hornet Strikes Again! ★★★

1941, USA
Directors: Ford Beebe, John Rawlins
Cast: Warren Hull, Keye Luke, Wade Boteler

A crime syndicate threatens Los Angles and has installed a mole at The Sentinel. Britt (Hull) and Kato (Luke) kick back in Hawaii.

The second Green Hornet serial (following 1940's *The Green Hornet*) is pretty much a re-run of the first, only with a little foreign colour and a new Britt Reid in Warren Hull. Anne Nagel is given more to do as his no-nonsense secretary Lenore, but Kato remains marginalised, at least compared to later adaptations. The structure remains a distinct asset.

Green Lantern ★★★

2011, USA

Director: Martin Campbell
Cast: Ryan Reynolds, Blake Lively, Peter Sarsgaard

Unbeknown to mankind, immortal aliens have harnessed the power of emerald energy, and use it to operate a universe-wide peacekeeping corps of superheroes. Hotdog fighter pilot Hal Jordan (Reynolds) is the latest recruit.

Maligned by critics and met with near universal disdain from fans, *Green Lantern* feels cobbled together from old ideas and superfluous to requirements. But it's not *that* bad. The lead actors are good, there's a decent female character in love interest Carol Ferris (Lively), the narrative zips along humorously, and the hokey mythology and visuals are good fun as long as you don't mind your superheroes silly.

Green Lantern: First Flight ★★★

2009, USA
Director: Lauren Montgomery
Cast: Christopher Meloni, Victor Garber, Tricia Helfer

Test pilot Hal Jordan (Meloni) is recruited into an intergalactic police force known as The Green Lantern Corps, and he's just in time to rumble a plot by one of its most decorated members.

With the origin story over and done with inside five minutes, *First Flight* will win fans from the outset. The Green Lantern himself is underdeveloped and unremarkable, but the plot is reasonably well executed if hardly original.

Green Lantern: Emerald Knights ★★

2011, USA
Directors: Christopher Berkeley, Jay Oliva, Lauren Montgomery
Cast: Nathan Fillion, Jason Isaacs, Elisabeth Moss

Hal Jordan (Fillion) recounts various stories illuminating the history of the Lanterns.

The anthology format is unsatisfying and risks alienating viewers with no interest in the minutiae of the franchise's mythology. Top voice talent helps and the segmented structure at least dictates some diversity in the characters and situations.

Griff the Invisible ★★

2010, Australia
Director: Leon Ford
Cast: Ryan Kwanten, Maeve Dermody, Marshall Napier

Awkward, bullied and alienated by his own peculiarities, office worker Griff (Kwanten) spends his evenings fighting crime. His life changes when he meets Melody (Dermody), a similarly delusional lost soul.

A drier than dry comedy touching on well-worn themes of social estrangement. It takes the personality-disorder-as-comical-quirk route but does nothing with it, which can make for uncomfortable viewing (Griff and Melody are not just unconventional kooks, they're seriously mentally ill, and that should probably be addressed at some point). It's ok, but this isn't among the best of a fistful of similar films released around the time (perhaps look instead to *Defendor*, *Special* or *Super*).

Groove Squad ★

2002, USA
Director: Patrick A. Ventura
Cast: Jennifer Love Hewitt, Stefanie Abramson, Kathleen Barr

Three schoolgirls develop superpowers when a mad scientist accidentally zaps them with magic electricity.

There are a handful of these shrill animated atrocities aimed at young girls, and they tend to be just as overtly sexist as anything else the superhero genre has to offer. The Groove Squad spend most of the movie obsessing over boys, their appearances and an impending cheerleading competition, presumably because they're girls and that's what girls do. There are lazy stabs at self-awareness, but it's hard to see how this might empower anyone. Nevermind. The animation is so bad and the characters so hateful young girls probably wouldn't sit through it anyway.

Guardians ★★

aka *Zashchitniki*, 2017, Russia
Director: Sarik Andreasyan
Cast: Anton Pampushnyy, Sanjar Madi, Sebastien Sisak

A rogue cyborg scientist invades Moscow as a first step in his plan to control all the world's electrical devices. The authorities reactivate a cold war superhero team in order to stop him.

Russian stab at an *Avengers*-style superhero extravaganza (the villain is just *Iron Man 2's* Ivan Vanko). A lot of effort has gone into the sets and CG effects, the cinematography is top notch and at first glance *Guardians* could pass for a Hollywood release. But the closer you look, the more the cracks show. There's a complete lack of originality, which means even the stuff that works is blandly derivative. None of the stars has any charisma, the clumsy score can't stop attracting attention to itself and the earnestness becomes exhausting.

Guardians of the Galaxy ★★★★★

2014, USA
Director: James Gunn
Cast: Chris Pratt, Zoe Saldana, Bradley Cooper

A fresh batch of colourful Marvel characters learn the importance of teamwork as they try to stop a warlord taking over the galaxy.

Mark Hamill as Max Reed in *The Guyver*

Marvel took something of a risk branching out into the realms of space opera when they did. The MCU was coming into its own as a cash cow and conventional wisdom might have suggested they keep milking it. The weird franchise with the blue alien, sentient tree and talking raccoon would normally be kept in the back pocket, ready to use in a last gasp attempt to re-interest audiences once they start tailing off. Ever confident in his concept for an enormous shared universe, Marvel Studios head honcho Kevin Feige ploughed on with these oddballs. Not only are they fairly out there, back in 2014 they were unfamiliar to filmgoers. They were also, essentially, baddies: thieves, bounty hunters, killers and mercenaries. Thanks to clever casting and a script drenched in well calibrated gags, they become antiheroes. It's that outsider quality that makes them so complimentary to the Avengers. The likes of Iron Man, Captain America and Thor are kings among men and idolised for their abilities. The Guardians, on the other hand, are scrappy survivors in a universe that couldn't care less about them.

Guardians of the Galaxy Vol. 2
★★★★

2017, USA
Director: James Gunn
Cast: Chris Pratt, Zoe Saldana, Dave Bautista

Peter Quill's (Pratt) father turns up with paternal urges and claims of divinity. At the same time surrogate father Yondu (Michael Rooker) is betrayed by his crew.

It's hard to argue with filmmaking this good. But to play Devil's advocate, maybe it's all too easy. Great little scenes like the alien Yondu taking out a horde of space pirates with his magic chopstick started writing themselves as soon as James Gunn defined this universe. Revisiting it, things almost seem too rich. Every line is so on-the-nose we experience these characters almost as pastiche. They bounce off each other more than they talk. It's fantastic fun but there's no real depth. Once again the screenplay shines a bright light on Quill, but it still doesn't illuminate much that seems authentic. No matter, with the plot stuff kept to a minimum it's all about enjoying the wacky nonsense that comes of having a *Star Trek* villain pulling the strings. There are interjections from the aforementioned Yondu, Nebula (Karen Gillan) and even the outside world (including a cameo from Sylvester Stallone), but much of the movie is spent on the hypnotically odd planet that is Quill's father. It's not exactly a change of pace, Marvel-wise, but it is at least a picturesque detour.

Guardians of the Lost Code ★

aka *Brijes 3D*, 2010, Mexico
Director: Benito Fernández
Cast: José Luis Orozco, José A. Toledano, Miguel Calderón

In our ancient history, human children lived in symbiotic partnership with spirit animals known as Brije, the two beings combining into a single warrior form when the child came of age. As mankind turned increasingly to science, this magical rite of passage was forgotten, allowing the forces of darkness to muster. Today, three children are chosen by the Brije to enact a prophecy that will establish a new alliance between humans and Brije, and defeat the evil threatening us.

If you somehow manage to plough through the film's lengthy opening exposition dump outlining an incomprehenisble mythology (that could be the longest synopsis in this book), maybe you'll find something worthy here, but I didn't. The animation is a poor blend of 2D and 3D, the characters are dull and the writing is too reliant on other properties (there's a lot of Pokemon, *His Dark Materials*, Tolkien's Middle Earth, etc.).

Gui ma fei ren: see *The Flying Mr. B*

Gummi T: see *Ivan the Incredible*

Gundala Putra Lightning ★★

aka *Gundala Putra Petir*, *Gundala, Son of Thunder*, 1981, Indonesia
Director: Lilik Sudjio
Cast: Teddy Purba, WD Mochtar, Anna Tairas

After being struck by lightning, genius scientist Ir. Sancaka (Purba) is adopted by Emperor Kronz of the Lightning Kingdom and bestowed with superpowers and funky theme music. He uses them to battle drug dealing nemesis Ghazul (Mochtar).

Inspired by the Flash (whose abilities and costume are distinctly similar), Gundala is a popular Indonesian superhero introduced by Hasmi comics in 1969. The movie is a low-budget take on his barking mad origin story, with space scenes that seem lifted from an early-80s music video and visual effects that wish they could say the same. It's unlikely to make much sense (unless you speak Indonesian, and even then I wouldn't take it for granted), but the TV movie vibe and general absurdity make it a reasonably pleasant diversion.

The Guyver ★★★★

aka *Mutronics*, 1991, USA/Japan
Directors: Screaming Mad George, Steve Wang
Starring: Jack Armstrong, Vivian Wu, Mark Hamill

Superhuman Zoanoids are attempting to take over the world and only the wearer of The Guyver, a semi-organic supersuit, stands in their way.

Unable to decide whether to be a colourful kids adventure or adult-themed sci-fi noir, *The Guyver* attempts both and ends up a tonally confused oddity. But it's a tonally confused oddity full of good stuff. The bad guys are entertainingly over-the-top as they stomp around a screenplay that zips along nicely, and Mark Hamill is huge fun as a stressed-out CIA agent. Plus any movie that can smuggle legitimate body horror into theatres under a PG-13 cloak must be doing something right.

Guyver: Dark Hero ★★★

1994, USA
Director: Steve Wang
Cast: David Hayter, Kathy Christopherson, Bruno Patrick

After receiving an alien bio-armour implant, Sean Barker (Hayter) seeks to discover its origin, which brings him face-to-face with an old enemy.

Ropey sets and flat lighting make this sequel feel like a TV show, and there's not a lot of action. It also rips off clunking great lumps of other movies with a *Close Encounters of the Third Kind* 'reference' that's shameless. But it's all well within the parameters of a naff B-movie, and ultimately it isn't time wasted if you like this sort of thing.

Hagane no renkinjutsushi: see *Fullmetal Alchemist*

Hak hap (2): see *Black Mask (2)*

Hariken Porimâ: see *Hurricane Polymar*

Hamara Hero Shaktimaan ★★★
2013, Indian,
Director: Dinkar Jani
Cast: Mukesh Khanna, Vaishnavi Mahant,
Kitu Gidwani

Having energised his seven chakras and attained supernatural powers through advanced yoga, newspaper photographer Pandit Gangadhar Vidhyadhar Mayadhar Omkarnath Shastri (Khanna) has become a superhero. Lucky for us, because a crazy bird-man is up to no good.

Despite being based on 1997 Indian TV series *Shaktimaan*, little information is available on this TV movie follow-up (there seem to be no fan reviews or entries in online databases). It is real, though, and also fairly mad. The performances are oddly childish and there's an abundance of low-quality visual effects, with much of the movie shot on green screen. It's more tokusatsu than Bollywood, which is fine, and the fast pace, exuberant performances and general absurdity work well.

Hancock ★★★
2008, USA
Director: Peter Berg
Cast: Will Smith, Charlize Theron,
Jason Bateman

After befriending a P.R. specialist, alcoholic amnesiac superhero Hancock (Smith) begins sorting his life out, which leads to various unexpected twists and turns.

There's a sense *Hancock* was supposed to be darker. True or not, once a star like Will Smith signs on everyone involved expects a blockbuster, and blockbusters don't have alcoholic misanthropes in the lead. So we get a sanitised drunken oaf and a lot of life lessons. Incredibly, this is the most financially successful stand-alone superhero movie ever released, with a worldwide gross (fully adjusted for inflation) of $788,000,000. It was a bigger hit than *Iron Man*!

Hanuman and the Five Riders: see Grouped Franchises and Kamen Rider

---

Hardcore Henry ★★★★
2015, Russia/USA
Director: Ilya Naishuller
Cast: Sharlto Copley, Tim Roth, Haley Bennett

A man wakes up in a medical facility with no memory. After being fitted with bionic limbs he's thrust into a world of violence, confusion and lies.

High concept, first-person perspective action thriller, much like a cross between watching *Memento* and playing *Half-Life 2*. There are some jaw-dropping moments and while the visual gimmick can be exhausting it's well exploited, allowing for a relentless, unedited stream of action so immediate it occasionally feels like live theatre. Also, Sharlto Copley has the most fun any actor has ever had on screen.

The Haunted World of El Superbeasto ★★
2009, USA
Director: Rob Zombie
Cast: Joe Alaskey, Ken Foree, Sheri M. Zombie

Occasional superhero El Superbeasto (Tom Papa) investigates seedy goings on. After opening with a monochrome scene homaging Universal's classic monster era,

it's doubly disappointing when this cartoon degenerates into a sub-*Fritz the Cat* exercise in sleazy titillation.

He-Man and She-Ra: The Secret of the Sword ★★★★
1985, USA
Directors: Ed Friedman, Lou Kachivas, Marsh Lamore, Bill Reed, Gwen Wetzler
Cast: John Erwin, Melendy Britt, George DiCenzor

The Sorceress (Linda Gary) sends Prince Adam (Erwin) on a mission to Etheria.

The opening episodes of *She-Ra: Princess of Power* edited into a feature-length film. Producers apparently wanted a 'He-Man for girls' and that's what they got: there's a flying unicorn instead of a green tiger, a useless witch instead of a useless wizard and a Hordak (DiCenzo) instead of a Skeletor (Alan Oppenheimer), but otherwise it really is just 'He-Man for girls'. There's the same music, same backgrounds, same sound effects, same voice actors and the same penchant for homoeroticism.

He-Man and the Masters of the Universe: The Beginning ★★★
2002, USA
Director: Gary Hartle
Cast: Cam Clarke, Lisa Ann Beley, Brian Dobson

On the planet Eternia, Captain Randor (Michael Donovan) traps the pestiferous Keldor (Dobson) and his followers behind a magical wall. Years later, Randor is king and Keldor (now called Skeletor) escapes in search of revenge. Randor's son Adam (Clarke) accepts his calling and becomes the supernatural defender of his people.

Although some anime influence has crept into the designs, and certainly the kinetic action sequences, characters and dynamics remain largely unchanged in this He-Man reboot (so much so that its only purpose seems to be to amp up the violence and ditch the moralising). We're dealt a pretty standard origin story that fails to explain why the Sorceress (Nicole Oliver) gifts the callow and clumsy Adam superpowers rather than the superior-in-every-way Teela (Beley), and from there the plot is thinner than we might expect from the original show. Hartle and co. have done a decent job, though, particularly given the extent to which this idea seemed set up to fail.

Hectic Knife ★★★

2016, USA
Director: Greg DeLiso
Cast: Peter Litvin, Georgia Kate Haege, J.J. Brine

Downtrodden vigilante Hectic Knife (Litvin) must raise his game if he's to overcome the supervillain known as Piggly Doctor (Brine).

Even by Troma standards this is a rumpled wreck of a movie. Shot in black-and-white, allegedly as a homage to Stanley Kubrick (?), *Hectic Knife* is nonstop dumb jokes, dumb gore and dumb weirdness. How it works is anyone's guess, but it does.

Hellboy ★★★★

2004, USA
Director: Guillermo del Toro
Cast: Ron Perlman, Doug Jones, Selma Blair

A demon conjured by Nazis is raised under the watchful eye of a paranormal expert, ultimately becoming superhero Hellboy (Perlman). He and the secret government bureau to which he belongs must defend mankind from Grigori Rasputin (Karel Roden) and his black magic.

Dimensional portals, Russian wizards, space whales, mechanical Nazis... somehow the smorgasbord of random absurdities that is *Hellboy's* opening sequence coalesces into a heartfelt story about a stone-fisted demon.

The combination of visual ideosyncracies, character detail, physical humour, general weirdness and so on is judged perfectly by del Toro, and is reasonably similar in tone to that of Sam Raimi's Spider-Man series (it isn't exactly tongue-in-cheek, but nor does it take its protagonist entirely seriously). The cast seem to be having fun and it's infectious, which helps us through a few bumps in the road – such as the underwritten supporting characters and a strangely claustrophobic air. (Followed by *Hellboy II: The Golden Army*.)

Hellboy ★★

2019, USA
Director: Neil Marshall
Cast: David Harbour, Milla Jovovich, Ian McShane

He-Man and She-Ra: The Secret of the Sword

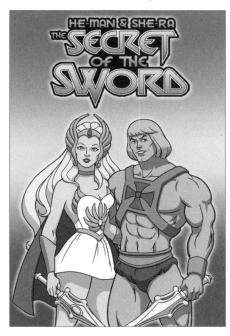

119

Hellboy (Harbour) travels to England where he fights giants and Milla Jovovich.

Harbour faced a near-impossible task in escaping the shadow of fan favourite Ron Perlman as Hellboy, but he does ok. Neil Marshall helps by taking a very different approach to Guillermo del Toro, depositing Big Red in some sort of semi-Arthurian Britain, and opening up new avenues in the process. It might have worked but there's no originality or style, and the screenplay is too thin (it would have been perfect for a lightweight animated adventure).

Hellboy II: The Golden Army ★★★★
2008, USA
Director: Guillermo del Toro
Cast: Ron Perlman, Selma Blair, Doug Jones

Disgruntled Elf prince Nuada (Luke Goss) breaks the truce between humans and magical beings by attempting to unleash an ancient army of supernatural warriors upon mankind. Hellboy (Perlman) puts his domestic issues to one side and tries to stop him.

Beautiful stylistic flourishes are the order of the day in *Hellboy II*. It's one of the most uniquely imaginative studio superhero movies ever made, with a handful of ideas, characters and scenes so brilliantly weird you wonder how they were smuggled past the suits. Practical effects take precedent but, even when it's CG, everything in the densely-packed frame has a tactile quality.

Hellboy Animated: Blood and Iron ★★★
2007, USA
Directors: Victor Cook, Tad Stones
Cast: Ron Perlman, Selma Blair, John Hurt

Hellboy's Bureau for Paranormal Research investigates the possible re-emergence of an ancient vampire.

Having missed out on the first animated *Hellboy* movie, John Hurt turns up in this sequel to voice Professor Bruttenholm, the character he originated in the 2004 live-action film. (That means John Merrick has appeared in a superhero cartoon.) It's a good thing because Bruttenholm is an interesting character and effectively acts as the lead here. Like its predecessor, *Sword of Storms*, *Blood and Iron*, it features a strong plot and solid animation while going even darker in tone.

Hellboy Animated: Sword of Storms ★★★
2006, USA
Directors: Phil Weinstein, Tad Stones
Cast: Ron Perlman, Selma Blair, Doug Jones

After travelling to Japan to investigate a strange disappearance, Hellboy (Perlman) is drawn into a supernatural underworld where he must battle a demonic monster.

First of two animated adventures slotted in between Guillermo del Toro's live-action movies. Unusually, the cast of those movies has been convinced to voice their cartoon counterparts which, combined with del Toro's presence as the 'creative producer' (whatever that means), afford's a degree of visual and thematic harmony across all four features. The animation is unremarkable but the plot is top notch. (Followed by *Hellboy Animated: Blood and Iron*.)

Henchmen ★★★
2018, Canada
Director: Adam Wood
Cast: Thomas Middleditch, James Marsden, Rosario Dawson

Hank (Marsden), a disillusioned freelance Henchman, is assigned to mentor Lester (Middleditch), an enthusiastic new recruit. Together they decide to foil supervillain Baron Blackout's (Alfred Molina) latest plot.

A neat idea and a decent cast are slightly let down by an uneven script and noticeably out-of-date animation.

Hercules

1953, Philippines
Director: Unknown
Cast: Cesar Ramirez, Gloria Romero

This movie is believed lost.

Hercules (1960s Italian series): see Grouped Franchises and Peplum Movies

Hercules ★★★

1964, India
Director: Shriram
Cast: Dara Singh, Mumtaz, Habib

On a mission to restore the throne to its true heir, Hercules (Singh) fights monsters, seeks MacGuffins and wrestles Hungarians.

Only available (as far as I know) as a low-resolution VCD pulled from Indian TV, this cheerfully pied nonsense offers a predictable blend of songs, melodrama and eccentricity. Singh was born to play Hercules (even if he does so dressed as Tarzan for some reason), and embraces the madness with glee.

Hercules ★

1983, Italy/USA
Director: Luigi Cozzi
Cast: Lou Ferrigno, Brad Harris, Sybil Danning

Created from energy, Hercules (Ferrigno) must save his girlfriend and prevent an evil wizard from conquering Earth with robots.

Farcical catastrophe from Italian hack Luigi Cozzi (the man who made infamous *Star Wars* ripoff *Starcrash*). The special effects would be better suited to 1970s television, some shots are out of focus and it's horribly

Arnold Schwarzenegger as the title character in *Hercules in New York*

edited, dubbed, scripted and acted. There are inadvertent laughs (Hercules throws a bear into space), but this isn't worth seeing. (Followed by *The Adventures of Hercules*.)

Hercules ★★★★

1997, USA,
Directors: Ron Clements, John Musker
Cast: Tate Donovan, Susan Egan, James Woods

Deprived of his status as an immortal god by crazy Uncle Hades (Woods), Hercules (Donovan) must earn his place on Mount Olympus by proving his worth among the mortals of Earth.

Disney take some liberties with the classic story, with the most obvious change being to identify Hercules' mother as Zeus' wife Hera rather than human woman Alcmene, with whom Zeus was unfaithful. I suppose that's convenient if you don't want to deal with issues such as infidelity in a kids' film, but it means we lose a fundamental aspect that's important to the mythology. It's indicative of a movie that feels like the last gasp for 'classic Disney'. Despite computer-aided animation, their *Hercules* could have been released in the 1950s. That's not a criticism, it's one of the best Mouse House offerings of the era. But don't expect cutting-edge social attitudes or self-awareness.

Hercules ★★

1997, USA
Director: Diane Eskenazi
Cast: Mary Kay Bergman, Cam Clarke,
Jeannie Elias

Hercules (Clarke) is tricked into tackling his twelve tasks by Hera (Bergman).

Mockbuster from now defunct production company Golden Films, who were also responsible for low-budget animated takes on *The Little Mermaid*, *Beauty and the Beast*, *Aladdin*, *Pinocchio*, *Jungle Book*, *Sleeping Beauty* and *Cinderella*. If you spot a common theme there, so did Disney, who sued. Like the Italian clone from the following year, this is rushed, messy and unsatisfying, but at least features proper voice actors.

Hercules ★

1998, Italy
Director: Peter Choi
Cast: Unknown

Hercules' descendent tells the story of his illustrious ancestor.

The second of two feature-length animated movies hoping to associate themselves with Disney's 1997 blockbuster *Hercules* (there are two more that don't quite reach feature length). The animation is almost reasonable... and that's about as positive as I can be. If the voice work doesn't drive you mad then the score will.

Hercules ★★

2014, USA, 98,
Director: Brett Ratner
Cast: Dwayne Johnson, John Hurt, Ian McShane

A band of mercenaries lead by a man who may be Hercules (Johnson) accepts an offer to defend a king or lord from another king or lord (the film isn't clear on the details).

An experimental exercise in obfuscation. We have no idea who Hercules is fighting for, against or why. There's no exposition; just scenes with goodies who turn out to be baddies, and baddies who turn out to be goodies (in a twist so obvious it isn't a spoiler, and probably isn't even a twist). Obviously, The Rock is brilliant, and Ratner and his writers try to do something a little different with the character by muddying the water on whether he's actually the eponymous demigod. Nevertheless it's a weak screenplay poorly executed.

Hercules and Xena – The Animated Movie: The Battle for Mount Olympus ★★

1998, USA
Director: Lynne Naylor
Cast: Kevin Sorbo, Lucy Lawless, Michael Hurst

Hera (Joy Watson) unleashes The Titans, so Hercules (Sorbo) and Xena (Lawless) team up to save The Gods of Olympus.

Visually distinct lightweight animated adventure that's too hectic and too loaded with humour. It helps to have a working knowledge of the TV shows from which it's derived (*Hercules: The Legendary Journeys* and *Xena: Warrior Princess*).

Hercules in New York ★★

1970, USA
Director: Arthur Allan Seidelman
Cast: Arnold Stang, Arnold Schwarzenegger, Deborah Loomis

Hercules (Schwarzenegger) moves to New York and struggles to fit in.

Shabby but memorable comedy marking Schwarzenegger's debut as a thespian. Originally dubbed when producers felt his accent would be unintelligible, the great man's unique vocal contribution has since been restored. Comedic actor Stang hams

Anita Mui as Wonder Woman in *The Heroic Trio*

it up to such an extent as a New York cab driver that Arnold may be the stronger (no pun intended) of the two leads. A truly awful movie that lands none of its gags, it's still worthwhile as a curisoity.

Hercules Reborn ★★

2014, USA
Director: Nick Lyon
Cast: John Hennigan, Christian Oliver, Marcus Shirock

A disgraced Hercules (Hennigan) helps Arius (Oliver) rescue his kidnapped bride from an usurping General.

Released just two weeks after the Dwayne Johnson blockbuster, *Hercules Reborn* is a typically pointless offering from mockbuster specialists The Asylum. There are a couple of reasonable actors involved, but on the whole we're dealing with unlikely accents conveying rudimentary dialogue. A lack of money limits the locations and action, but there are much worse examples of this sort of thing.

Hercules Recycled ★★★

1994, USA
Director: Richard Bickerton
Cast: Greg Alt, Richard Bickerton, Craig Kitchens

Late-1950s peplum 'classics' *Hercules* and *Hercules Unchained* are re-edited and re-dubbed into a makeshift comedy about the search for an energy formula.

More slapdash than previous examples of this process such as Woody Allen's *What's Up Tiger Lilly* and the excellent serial spoof *J-Men Forever*, the raw material used here at least offers plenty of potential. There's something inherently amusing about oiled-up musclemen in loincloths taking things too seriously, and it doesn't require much effort to cut through the stern pomposity. Tricky to get hold of but well worth a look.

Hercules Recycled 2.0 ★★★

2014, USA
Directors: Cole & Sean
Cast: Greg Alt, Richard Bickerton, Craig Kitchens

More 'gay panic' fun with re-edited Italian peplum movies.

I guess this is *Hercules Recycled* recycled. From the sons of the men responsible for the first movie comes this remake/sequel that ups the ante with a plethora of green screened visual elements clumsily comped into the frame. Sometimes less is more. It's still surprisingly funny, though.

Hercules: The Legendary Journeys: see Grouped Franchises

Hercules: Zero to Hero ★★★
1999, USA
Director: Bob Kline
Cast: Tate Donovan, Diedrich Bader, Barbara Barrie

The childhood adventures of (Disney's version of) Hercules (Donovan).

Portmanteau (aka cut-and-shut) sequel to Disney's 1997 animated film *Hercules*. The three stories are episodes of the 1998 TV series, and have been glued together with weak connecting scenes involving Hercules reminiscing to wife Meg (Susan Egan). It is what it is: a bonus for devotees of the first film, an irrelevance to the rest of us.

Hero at Large ★★
1980, USA
Director: Martin Davidson
Cast: John Ritter, Anne Archer, Bert Convy

After foiling a robbery while dressed as the superhero Captain Avenger, struggling actor Steve Nichols (Ritter) decides to give vigilantism a go.

Romantic comedy with a superhero twist. Ritter makes for an amiable leading man, and the late-1970s New York aesthetic is great. But the hackneyed script sits there

being predictable until everyone outstays their welcome.

Hero Tomorrow ★★★
2007, USA
Director: Ted Sikora
Cast: Perren Hedderson, Jocelyn Wrzosek, Bryan Jalovec

Struggling comic writer David (Hedderson) adopts the persona of his latest character, to the dismay of girlfriend Robyn (Wrzosek).

Since the advent of cheap digital cameras we've seen many zero-budget revisionist superhero comedies from aspiring young filmmakers. The vast majority are terrible; full of almost inaudible in-jokes and any pasty-faced buddies the creators could cajole into being actors for the day. Ted Sikora's surreal directorial debut doesn't manage to sidestep all the pitfalls inherent to these things, but it's a clear step above the typical example. The script is funny, almost as if it was written for general consumption rather than the guys at the local comic shop, and Wrzosek's deadpan performance is kind of great.

The Heroic Trio ★★★★
aka *Dong fang san xia*, 1993, Hong Kong
Director: Johnnie To
Cast: Michelle Yeoh, Anita Mui, Maggie Cheung

Three gifted women: an assassin, a masked crimefighter and a troubled kung fu master (mistress?) attempt to work together and stop a supernatural evildoer's unusually appalling plot.

Perfectly realised kung fu adventure with exceptional fight scenes and cast. Hong Kong genre cinema likes to present us with morally complicated heroes and clearly defined villains; so our protagonists are a mess of ambiguous, paradoxical lost souls while the antagonist steals babies and is called Evil Master. A less welcome habit of these films is to toss devestating emotional curveballs at us, and *The Heroic Trio* has a couple of doozies it doesn't really earn. But they're the only dud notes, and this a seriously enjoyable movie.

Heroic Trio 2: Executioners ★★★★
aka *Executioners*, 1993, Hong Kong
Directors: Siu-Tung Ching, Johnnie To
Cast: Maggie Cheung, Michelle Yeoh, Anita Mui

In the years following a 'nuclear event' our society has collapsed and water is the only commodity of value. Wonder Woman (Mui) is now retired with a daughter, Thief Catcher (Cheung) is bounty hunting, and Invisible Girl (Yeoh) is tutoring a deformed and reformed former henchman. They must reunite when a rebel leader is assassinated amid a convoluted power grab.

We're in a post-apocalyptic world now? The two *Heroic Trio* movies came out just a few months apart, could nobody pick a concept? The setup might be different but the girls haven't changed. Their chemistry is as fantastic as ever and they all remain well-developed, multi-dimensional characters in their own rights, despite a busier plot and more villains to steal the focus. There are perhaps fewer big action set pieces, and the superhero aspect has been toned down, but this is still a top-notch sci-fi/kung fu movie.

Hi-Yo Silver
1940, USA
Directors: John English, William Witney
Cast: Chief Thundercloud, Lynne Roberts, Stanley Andrews

Feature-length edit of Republic's 1938 serial *The Lone Ranger*.

Hokuto no Ken: see *Fist of the North Star*

Holy Musical B@tman! ★★★
2012, USA
Directors: Matt Lang, Nick Lang
Cast: Joe Walker, Brian Holden, Nick Lang

Filmed stage musical which sees Batman (Walker) teams up with Robin (Lang), avoid Superman (Holden) and face famous foes.

Musical theatre troupe StarKid's tribute to characters they seem to love is a mixed bag. With a live audience this must be a blast; the songs aren't bad and the gags are consistently amusing, even if there are few laugh-out-loud moments. But it wasn't made for the screen and the amateurish video production is painful.

Honeymoon Travels Pvt. Ltd. ★★★
2007, India
Director: Reema Kagti
Cast: Ranvir Shorey, Dia Mirza, Abhay Deol

Six newlywed couples honeymoon together on a tour bus.

Anthology comedy in which a husband and wife are, unknown to each other, both superheroes. That's about as sophisticated as things get, but there's nothing wrong with that. Overlong but amusing enough if you're down with Indian romantic comedy.

Hound ★★
2017, UK
Director: Simba Masaku
Cast: Jimm Stark, Simba Masaku, Neal Ward

When his beloved Staffordshire Bull Terrier is shot dead by gangster Raj Singh Dhillon (Masaku), drunk loner Andy (Stark) adopts the alter-ego Hound and dedicates himself to fighting crime.

London-set thriller with its fair share of style and violence. It's not exactly polished, though, and some of the accents may prove tricky for non-British viewers, but Hound is a reasonably effective and surprisingly visceral revenge thriller.

Howard the Duck ★
1986, USA
Director: Willard Huyck
Cast: Lea Thompson, Jeffrey Jones, Tim Robbins

A humanoid duck is accidentally beamed to Earth, where he thwarts an alien invasion.

No thank you.

Huhulihin si Tiagong Akyat ★★★
aka *Tiagong Akyat, Santiago Ronquillo*, 1973, Philippines,
Director: Armando A. Herrera
Cast: Ramon Revilla, Liza Lorena, Robert Jawoski

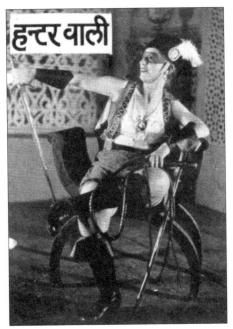

Fearless Nadia as the title character in *Hunterwali*

A man framed for murder tackles bad guys with the aid of a magical amulet.

Notorious Pinoy bandit Santiago Ronquillo (Revilla) is reimagined as a superpowered, wrongly convicted Robin Hood figure (the title translates to 'Arrest Tiagong Akyat' in reference to Ronquillo's nickname). It seems like an attempt to capitalise on the wildly successful *Nardong Putik* of the previous year, and amounts to a straight remake of the movie that returned Ramon Revilla to the top of the Filipino film industry tree. In spite of the derivative roots it's none too shabby, with Revilla making the most of an atypically multi-dimensional character and delivering a strong performance.

Hulk ★★
2003, USA
Director: Ang Lee
Cast: Eric Bana, Jennifer Connelly, Sam Elliott

When an accident triggers a genetic abnormality, scientist Bruce Banner (Bana) becomes the Hulk. Helped by colleague Betty Ross (Connelly), he begins piecing together the clues and memories that may explain his extraordinary condition.

By developing the plot directly from the origin story, *Hulk* sidesteps the traditionally awkward balancing act between the two elements. Unfortunately, it also leads to a convoluted narrative involving flashbacks to both Bruce and Betty's childhoods, all in service of a mystery that never seems particularly interesting. The solemn tone is at odds with cartoonish presentation that includes daft CGI, wacky scene transitions and attempts to mimic comic book panel presentation. There's some good acting and a few interesting moments, but this is disappointing given the director's pedigree.

Hulk vs. ★★
aka *Hulk vs. Thor and Wolverine*, 2009, USA

Directors: Sam Liu, Frank Paur
Cast: Fred Tatasciore, Matthew Wolf, Bryce Johnson

A brace of short adventures featuring The Incredible Hulk (Tatasciore). First Loki summons Bruce Banner (Bryce Johnson) to Asgard in an attempt to kill Thor (Wolf), then Wolverine (Steve Blum) falls into the hands of Weapon X as he tries to prevent The Hulk entering Canada.

Slight, child-oriented animated frolics. The first story is entirely redundant at this point. The MCU has since given us the Hulk vs. Thor melee fans wanted to see in *Thor: Ragnarok*, and an animated Bruce Banner struggling with his inner monster doesn't compare to the live-action equivalent. The second story is a bit more interesting but still covers little new ground. The eventual Wolverine/Hulk face-off results in a no-score-draw when it's interrupted, and Wolverine's forced return to the Weapon X program will just make you want to watch *X2* instead, which isn't such a bad idea. Some fun Deadpool nonsense will please fans of the Merc with a Mouth.

Hulk: Where Monster's Dwell ★★
2016, USA
Director: Mitch Schauer
Cast: Fred Tatasciore, Liam O'Brien, Jesse Burch

The Hulk (Tatasciore) and Doctor Strange (O'Brien) try to stop dreams coming to life or something.

Badly written, meandering and confusing animated adventure with a Halloween theme. Monsters fight for 75 minutes. And that's about it.

Hunterwali ★★
aka *The Princess and the Hunter*, 1935, India
Director: Homi Wadia
Cast: Fearless Nadia, Sharifa, Gulsham

An heroic princess disguises herself with mask and cape in order to fight for the downtrodden as Hunterwali (Nadia, aka Mary Evans).

Early Indian spin on Zorro with a female protagonist. Being Indian it adds rather more melodrama and dancing than the aforementioned folk hero was known for. Unfortunately, it's something of a bust, with technical limitations rendering it hard to watch and the main character's motivations and objectives bafflingly convoluted and contradictory.

Hunterwali Ki Beti
aka *Daughter of Hunterwali*, 1943, India
Director: Batuk Bhatt
Cast: Fearless Nadia, John Cavas, Shyamsunder

Extremely obscure sequel to *Hunterwali*. Based on an extended excerpt it looks like more of the same, but the complete movie appears to be lost.

Hurricane Hansa
1937, India
Director: R.N. Vaidya
Cast: Fearless Nadia, Husn Banu, Sardar Mansur

Coincidentally this is another Indian folk hero adventure starring Fearless Nadia. Here she plays a woman avenging injustices done to her family. There is surviving audio of some songs but I've found no sign the film was ever released on home formats. The term 'Hurricane' is derived from the Hindi word Harijan, meaning untouchable. As with Nadia's *Hunterwali* films, *Hurricane Hansa* is/was apparently bursting with the stunts the actress was famous for.

Hurricane Polymar ★★★
aka *Hariken Porimâ*, 2017, Japan
Director: Koichi Sakamoto
Cast: Junpei Mizobata, Yûki Yamada, Mikie Hara

Takashi Yoroi (Mizobata), a detective with an 'artificial polymer transforming power suit', goes up against similarly well-equipped bad guys.

Shiny live-action update of the 1974 anime series. It's more humorous than the typical Henshin tokusatsu, while the fight scenes and visuals are perhaps more interesting, but overall this is standard issue. A 1996 anime OVA also exists.

Hwasango: see *Volcano High*

Hydrozagadka ★★
1971, Poland
Director: Andrzej Kondratiuk
Cast: Józef Nowak, Zdzisław Maklakiewicz

A mad scientist has stolen Warsaw's water, and police don't know where to look for it. Enter Polish superhero As (Nowak).

From behind the Iron Curtain comes this surreal comedy, supposedly intended as a spoof on the capitalist values of American superhero comics. Interpreted by domestic audiences as a satire on Polish life, it's safe to say it missed the target. Either way, it remains a prominent cult film in Poland, and in some circles is considered to be among the nation's best. Unfortunately, its sense of humour, which relies on intricate wordplay and Polish idioms, doesn't translate. As (Ace in English) also looks more like Father Ted than any superhero should.

I Was a Teenage Superhero Sidekick

2013, USA
Director: J. Hanna
Cast: Barrett Mitchell, Emily Sandifer, Milena Mortati

Dispirited sidekick Kid Dynamic (Mitchell) quits the superhero game and goes into therapy. Unavailable on home formats at the time of writing.

I-Man ★★★

1986, USA
Director: Corey Allen
Cast: Scott Bakula, Ellen Bry, Joey Cramer

Cab driver Jeffrey Wilder (Bakula) is made indestructable when he's exposed to a gas retrieved from an alien atmosphere. It isn't long before the government sends him on a mission to save Northern California from an industrialist with a radioactive time bomb.

The tired cliché of the down-to-earth guy refusing to believe in the wacky science that's happened to him is pushed to the extreme in *I-Man*. Even as bullets bounce off him, explosions fail to harm him and his appendix grows back, Wilder sticks to his line: "I'm a cab driver, that's all. And I need to go find my dog." Bakula and the script are dreadful, although both generate a lot of inadvertent laughs. Part of the *Magical World of Disney* anthology series.

iBoy ★★★★

2017, UK
Director: Adam Randall
Cast: Bill Milner, Maisie Williams, Miranda Richardson

When pieces of a mobile phone become lodged in schoolboy Tom Harvey's (Milner) brain after a gang shooting, he develops supernatural abilities and sets out to rid his neighbourhood of drug dealers.

An interesting idea is left underdeveloped, either by lack of ambition or determination to keep the focus narrow. Either way it's all profoundly dour. They're the negatives, but there are more positives, and chief among them is the cast. We already knew Miranda Richardson was special, and if we needed any more evidence in order to say the same of Maisie Williams (we didn't) then it's here in spades. Milner is also strong and Rory Kinnear makes for a fabulous villain.

Ichi ★★★

2008, Japan
Director: Fumihiko Sori
Cast: Haruka Ayase, Shidô Nakamura, Yôsuke Kubozuka

Ichi (Ayase), the former pupil of legendary blind swordsman Zatoichi, searches for her master. Also blind, she becomes embroiled in a feud with the yakuza after coming to the aid of an oppressed townsfolk.

Serviceable if overly arty gender swapping Zatoichi update. Ayase is a subtly intense central figure and a good fit for the tone, which is quiet and glum. Perhaps a little slow and long, it's still essential viewing for fans. However, anyone new to the character would be wise to avoid it in favour of the original Shintaro Katsu Zatoichi films of the 1970s, or the superb 2003 update from Takeshi Kitano.

Idainaru, Shurarabon: see *The Great Shu Ra Ra Boom*

The Illusionauts ★

aka *Los ilusionautas, Fantastic Force*, 2012, Peru
Director: Eduardo Schuldt
Cast: Christopher Collet, Sarah Michelle Gellar, Christopher Lloyd

Nefarious types at the top of French government remove several key characters from the fictional works of Jules Verne, leaving four exceptional children to enter the stories and fix the conceptual damage.

Someone should have thought about the conceptual damage this horrible thing may do to children attempting to make sense of it. There are two points of interest. First, the way characters can be cyphers for the different sides of an individual's personality, which presages Pixar's *Inside Out* by several years. Second, there's some extremely brutal satirising of former French president Nicolas Sarkozy and wife Carla Bruni. Even so, if you have a desire to see an animated Peruvian superhero movie set in Paris, I'd suggest waiting for the next one.

In Your Face: see *Abar, the First Black Superman*

The Incredible Hulk ★★★

1977, USA
Director: Kenneth Johnson
Cast: Bill Bixby, Lou Ferrigno, Susan Sullivan

Hoping to unlock the mysterious secret of superstrength, a scientist grieving for his wife exposes himself to high levels of gamma radiation. It turns him into a big green anger monster.

More sophisticated (and adult-oriented) than comparable Marvel TV movies of the era such as *Captain America* or *Dr. Strange*, this straight-faced pilot is heavy on pseudo-science and light on action, which seems a good place to start. Bixby is excellent as Banner, the desperate scientist looking for meaning in his work. (Followed by *The Return of the Incredible Hulk*.)

The Incredible Hulk ★★

2008, USA
Director: Louis Leterrier
Cast: Edward Norton, Liv Tyler, Tim Roth

Alone and on the run, Dr. Bruce Banner (Norton) seeks a cure for his Hulkism. But when the military create a new monster, Banner must make peace with his alter ego.

How Edward Norton fell out of the MCU isn't clear. He claims he jumped, Marvel say he was pushed, but what's obvious is this version of Banner would never have worked in the long-term. The thought of this guy bantering with Thor or being cajoled by Tony Stark is laughable. The fact it doesn't sit right in the MCU doesn't make it a bad movie, but it's hard to call it a good one.

The Incredible Hulk Returns ★★
1988, USA
Director: Nicholas Corea
Cast: Bill Bixby, Lou Ferrigno, Jack Colvin

Two years since David Banner's (Bixby) last 'episode', he's drawn into a bizarre mystery surrounding the discovery of Thor's (Eric Kramer) tomb.

Six years after the cancellation of the TV series, this first of three reunion movies strikes a sillier tone. What stands out today is just how similar this movie's Thor is to Chris Hemsworth's. The costume is naff and Kramer's performance poor, but the fish-out-of-water stuff produces many of the same scenes and moments we're familiar with from the MCU, and the character assumes the same amiably pompous comic relief duties he performs there. (Followed by *The Trial of The Incredible Hulk*.)

The Incredible Hulk: Death in the Family:
see *Return of the Incredible Hulk*

The Incredibles ★★★★★
2004, USA
Director: Brad Bird
Cast: Craig T. Nelson, Samuel L. Jackson, Holly Hunter

With superheroes outlawed, the Parr family are forced to conceal their powers and lead normal lives. Nostalgic for past glories, patriarch Bob (Nelson) is more than happy to get back in the game when the opportunity arises.

The characters, writing, animation, acting, score... in fact everything, are simply perfect. There's little else to say. A superhero movie for those who don't like superhero movies, *and* for those who do.

Incredibles 2 ★★★★
2018, USA
Director: Brad Bird
Cast: Craig T. Nelson, Holly Hunter, Sarah Vowell

Mr. Incredible (Nelson) is forced to stay home and look after the kids as Elastigirl

Infra-Man

131

(Hunter) spearheads a campaign to re-legalise superheroes.

The early scenes are very well written, as you'd expect from Pixar, and everything works perfectly in isolation. But for quite some time there's no indication who the villain is or what the stakes will be. And when the ball does start rolling it's kind of obvious which way it's going to go. There's also a tendency to repeat the best gags and scenes, not only from the first movie but from this one too (how many laughs can be squeezed from Jack-Jack doing something unexpected?). But these are minor niggles that only stand out in comparison to the masterpiece that is the first movie, they're not significant failings.

Infra-Man ★★★★

aka *Super Inframan*, *Zhong guo chao ren*, 1975, Hong Kong
Director: Shan Hua
Cast: Danny Lee, Terry Liu, Hsieh Wang

A demonic princess awakens after millions of years and decides to take over Earth.

Although among the best-known examples in the West of the Japanese kyodai hero subgenre, *Infra-man* is in fact a Chinese creation (based on Japanese kyodai such as Ultraman and Kamen Rider). Generally considered the first Chinese superhero movie (a smattering of oddities pre-date it), *Infra-Man* is the definition of dumb fun. Full of dodgy special effects, silly costumes and exuberant kung fu, it's a camp treat for those with a penchant for weirdness, and a good induction for children open to new kinds of superhero.

Inhumans ★★

aka *Marvel's Inhumans*, *Inhumans: The First Chapter*, *Behold... The Inhumans*, 2017, USA
Director: Roel Reiné
Cast: Anson Mount, Serinda Swan, Ken Leung

In a secret moonbase, a superhuman race look for things to argue about.

Feature debut for the MCU-adhering TV show. For the uninitiated, Inhumans are a bit like X-Men's mutants, only with a well-defined caste system, established monarchy and no sense of humour. There seems to be a *Game of Thrones* influence with the narrative following various factions battling for the hot seat, but the characters are all underdeveloped and predictable.

Insae Daeng (Mitr Chaibancha series): see Grouped Franchises and The Red Eagle. For the 2010 Thai film of the same name see *Red Eagle*.

Inseparable ★★★

aka *Xing ying bu li*, 2011, China
Director: Dayyan Eng
Cast: Kevin Spacey, Daniel Wu, Beibi Gong

A suicidal young man is given new purpose when an otherworldly neighbour convinces him to take on a superhero alter ego.

Apparently the first Chinese film to feature a Hollywood star (Kevin Spacey plays the neighbour), renowned filmmaker Dayyan Eng uses *Inseparable's* superhero elements as a means to comment on corruption. It's a surreal movie and we never feel entirely at ease with the relationship between its leads, or indeed where the plot might be taking us. That could be down to the odd mix of comedy, drama, fantasy and satire that, when it works, proves quite potent. Unfortunately, it doesn't work as often as it needs to. Still interesting, though.

Inspector Gadget ★

1999, USA
Director: David Kellogg
Cast: Matthew Broderick, Rupert Everett, Joely Fisher

When John Brown (Broderick), an energetic but incompetent security guard, is horribly maimed in the line of duty, he's rebuilt as a bionic defender of justice.

Apparently embarrassed by its own origins, this live-action assault on the meaning of fun ditches most of what made the original cartoon work. Gadget's affable pomposity is replaced with an uncomfortably childlike puritanism, the memorable Doctor Claw is replaced with generic Euro-villain Scolex (Everett), and the roles of secret saviours Penny and Brain are performed by a talking hip hop car. The weirdest deviation from source? Gadget isn't even a policeman! I hope there isn't an obscure sequel.

Inspector Gadget 2 ★
2003, USA
Director: Alex Zamm
Cast: French Stewart, Elaine Hendrix, Tony Martin

Claw (Martin), Inspector Gadget's (Stewart) arch nemesis, escapes from prison in order to plot a raid on the US Federal Reserve. Meanwhile, Gadget feels threatened by an updated model.

The tone of this obscure sequel has shifted all the way to Saturday morning television, and production values have been adjusted accordingly. It's unspeakably horrendous. But, unlike the first live-action movie, it's at least aimed at the children who might conceivably enjoy it, rather than nostalgic parents. That means it's more like the original series, so Claw is a faceless gauntlet, Brain and Penny save the day, etc.

Inspector Gadget's Biggest Caper Caper Ever ★
2005, Canada/USA
Director: Ezekiel Norton
Cast: Maurice LaMarche, Bernie Mac, Jim Byrnes

Claw (Brian Drummond) escapes from prison and steals a pterodactyl.

CGI feature blending the worst aspects of the live-action movies and animated series. It's hard to explain how depressing this is. The alleged humans behind it choose to ditch the TV show's fantastic theme tune but bring back the movies' despicable hip hop car, which tells us all we need to know about the decision-making process used here. Aggressively horrendous.

Inspector Gadget's Last Case: Claw's Revenge ★
2002, Canada/USA
Director: Michael Maliani
Cast: Maurice LaMarche, Bettina Bush, Jim Byrnes

A scientist creates a transformation formula for Dr. Claw (Brian Drummond), but Gadget (LaMarche) is on the case.

Pointless re-jig that positions Gadget for a younger audience (which makes the double entendres disconcerting) and employs the same animation style as the *Gadget and the Gadgetinis* TV show. Audiences will have to contend with a staggering realisation: this contemptible idiocy is the best of the four Inspector Gadget movies.

Instant Heroes ★★★
aka *Jagoan Instan*
2016, Indonesia
Director: Fajar Bustomi
Cast: Kemal Palevi, Kevin Julio, Anisa Rahma

Bumi (Palevi), teenage nephew to former superhero Om Gun (Ded Yusuf), is recruited into the family business after being injected with a special serum. As alter ego Earth, Bumi has superstrength and is capable of flight, two abilities he will need in his battle with Romeo (Julio), a crime lord intent on acquiring Bumi's serum.

Indonesian comedy with good production values and an accessible sense of humour. Although tonally different, not to mention much tamer, there's a surprising amount of *Kick-Ass* in the costumes, characters and situations. Further cues have been taken from Hollywood, not least in the excellent cinematography, though it's at the expense of some indigenous personality.

International Crime ★★★

1938, USA
Director: Charles Lamont
Cast: Rod La Rocque, Astrid Allwyn, Thomas E. Jackson

Radio announcer Lamont Cranston (La Rocque) plays the role of the Shadow on his nightly crime broadcasts (think celebrity gossip mixed with a weather forecast, only on the subject of crime). When someone convinces him to publicise a fake robbery he's drawn into a murder investigation.

With the Shadow debuting in 1930 as a (fictional) narrator of radio thrillers, this 1939 quickie develops him in an unusually meta direction. Predictably confined to a couple of small sets and shot on a measly budget, it's a solid enough mystery that relies entirely on the charisma of its lead actor. La Rocque is in every scene and must have 80 percent of the dialogue, so it's fortunate he's good. It's his second outing in the role after *The Shadow Strikes*.

Invaders from Space ★★

1965, Japan
Directors: Koreyoshi Akasaka, Teruo Ishii, Akira Mitsuwa
Cast: Ken Utsui, Minako Yamada, Junko Ikeuchi

Superhero Starman (Utsui) faces off against the Salamander Men from planet Kulimon.

The second cut-and-shut film derived from Japanese series *Super Giant*. It's *exactly* the same as the first (*Atomic Rulers*). (Followed by *Attack from Space*.)

Invasion of the Neptune Men ★★

aka *Uchu Kaisoku-sen*, 1961, Japan
Director: Kôji Ohta
Cast: Shin'ichi Chiba, Ryûko Minakami, Mitsue Komiya

Astronomer Tachibana (Chiba) is secretly Space Chief, a superhero with a flying car. When Earth is invaded his twelve-year-old friends spring into action.

Released in the US in 1964, this dubbed version of 1961's *Uchu Kaisoku-sen* gained cult status after featuring on the movie-spoofing comedy series *Mystery Science Theatre 3000*. It's a typical-for-the-time spaceman tokusatsu, which means it's much like watching early *Doctor Who* but without the doctor. Space Chief turns up only occasionally, so we're effectively left with the companion and some rogue kids for most of the movie. And that scuppers that!

The Invincible Iron Man ★★★

2007, USA
Directors: Patrick Archibald, Jay Oliva, Frank Paur
Cast: Marc Worden, Gwendoline Yeo, Fred Tatasciore

Tony Stark (Worden) incurs the wrath of the Jade Dragons, a secretive order dedicated to preventing the return of an ancient evil known as the Mandarin.

Released just a year before the MCU's live-action *Iron Man* origin story, this animated version employs several similar narrative components but incorporates them into a fundamentally different story. There are notably fewer fight scenes than animated superhero adventures tend to feature, which gives the plot a welcome opportunity to progress naturally instead of having to bend over backwards every five minutes to justify more fisticuffs. And the voice acting is nicely low-key thanks to a lack of grandstanding celebrities among the cast.

The Invincible Six Million Dollar Man ★

aka *Billion Dollar Kid*, 1977, South Korea
Director: Si-Hyeon Kim
Cast: John Kelley Justus, Hie So, Ki-Ju Kim

When the top secret plans for an advanced weapon are stolen by Korean criminals, The Invincible Six Million Dollar Man (Justus) is called in to retrieve them.

Little more than an unofficial retread of the original pilot movie for *The Six Million Dollar Man*, which is a particularly dull story. As such, this is pretty much worthless beyond showcasing some excellent 1970s fashions.

The Invisible Avenger ★★★

aka *Tômei ningen*, 1954, Japan
Director: Motoyoshi Oda
Cast: Seizaburô Kawazu, Miki Sanjô, Minoru Takada

A man rendered invisible via vile military experimentation attempts to live a quiet life, but is ultimately compelled to help a blind orphan and a fearful showgirl, each of whom have been wronged by gangsters.

Sentimentality is laid on pretty thick in *The Invisible Avenger*, but despite its bathetic indulgences this quiet little melodrama is really worthwhile. The standard approach to invisible men movies is to have the protagonist go crazy and run about the place shrieking and killing. Nanjo (Kawazu), however, is a gentle, caring soul struggling to come to terms with what, to him, is a terrible affliction. Our sympathy is only compounded by his appearance, when he does appear, as a clown. The painted face is a clever idea allowing him to get out and

about and function within the story, while also emphasising his mournful pathos.

Invisible Avenger ★★★

1958, USA
Directors: James Wong Howe, Ben Parker, John Sledge
Cast: Richard Derr, Mark Daniels, Helen Westcott

Lamont Cranston, aka the Shadow (Derr), heads to New Orleans to investigate the disappearance of an old friend.

Tidy little B-movie conceived as a TV pilot before being adapted for the big screen. As a result, it feels much like the Falcon and Saint series of the early 1940s, which is no bad thing. The mystery is intriguing enough and the New Orleans setting allows for plenty of jazz (and middle-aged white men talking jive with a sometimes shocking lack of self-awareness).

Isputnik vs. Darna

The Invisible Boy ★★★★

aka *Il ragazzo invisibile*, 2014, Italy
Director: Gabriele Salvatores
Cast: Ludovico Girardello, Valeria Golino,
Fabrizio Bentivoglio

After buying a strange superhero costume
from a Chinese junk shop, 13-year-old
Michele Senzi (Girardello) finds it has the
power to make him invisible. But is there
more to the magical ensemble than a single
bullied schoolboy can handle?

Intelligent, original, funny and sensitive tale
of alienation in the shape of a revisionist
superhero movie. As a child actor Girardello
is exceptional. The role demands everything
from soul-searching depth to dry humour
and he pulls off whatever's thrown at him.
Some of the credit for that must go to
Salvatores who, based on the standard
across the numerous young performers,
must have a gift. When the mystery finally
starts to unfold around the halfway mark
it's compelling and surprising.

The Invisible Boy: Second ★★★ Generation

aka *Il ragazzo invisibile: Seconda generazione*,
2018, Italy
Director: Gabriele Salvatores
Cast: Ludovico Girardello, Kseniya Rappoport,
Galatéa Bellugi

Michele (Girardello) unites with his sister
Natasha (Bellugi) and biologicial mother
Yelena (Rappoport) in order to rescue
his father from a Russian oligarch known
for kidnapping 'specials' (superpowered
humans). Once again, things may be more
complicated than they seem.

While the first movie largely kept within
Michele's narrow world, this sequel opens
things up, essentially becoming a less fighty
X-Men. Michele's mother is a Magneto
figure: intelligent and rational, but blinded

by her righteous militancy. It puts Michele
in a difficult position. The performances
remain strong and it's to the movie's credit
that it develops rather than re-treads the
same ground as its predecessor, but it feels
less unique and doesn't work quite as well.

The Invisible Man vs. the Human Fly ★★★

aka *Tômei ningen to hae otoko*, 1957, Japan
Director: Mitsuo Murayama
Cast: Ryûji Shinagawa, Yoshirô Kitahara,
Junko Kanô

A series of improbable murders has Tokyo's
police force baffled. They need someone to
wander in front of an invisibility ray.

Loose sequel to 1949's *Invisible Man
Appears* which, like that film's inspiration,
Universal's 1933 classic *The Invisible Man*, is
not a superhero movie. It takes a long time
to get going, but once it does we're into a
world of corrupt industrialists, crazy science
and latent resentment. The Human Fly is
the villain's henchman, hooked on the drug
that makes him tiny and suggestible. The
Invisible Man exists pretty much just for the
hell of it. Even when it's boring it's strangely
satisfying in a methodical sort of way.

Invisible: The Chronicles of Benjamin Knight ★★

1993, USA
Director: Jack Ersgard
Cast: Brian Cousins, Jennifer Nash, Michael
Della Femina

Direct sequel to *Mandroid* in which Wade
(Cousins) and Zanna (Nash) try to cure
Knight's (Della Femina) problems with
invisibility. The previous film's villain, Drago
(Curt Lowens), is still up to no good.

Drago's motivation and objectives are not
clear and there's no real order to anything,
things just happen for... reasons. Mandroid

spends most of the movie on the sidelines and Knight doesn't really step up, so we're left with Wade and Zanna flirting and doing experiments. The finale is an anticlimax and a teased third instalment never happened.

Iron Claw the Pirate ★★★

aka *Demir pençe*, *Korsan Adam*, 1969, Turkey
Director: Çetin Inanç
Cast: Demir Karahan, Nebahat Çehre, Yildirim Gencer

The villainous Fantomas (Gencer) makes some vague threats against the citizens of Istanbul, in particular the heroic vigilante Iron Claw (Karahan), who sets out to kill his nemesis once and for all.

Action-packed unofficial Fantomas movie with no reference to pirates. But there's everything else you'd expect from this sort of thing. Opening credits written on cardboard are intercut with a woman doing a striptease, then black-masked villain and black-masked hero each swear vengeance on the other for reasons to which we're not privy. Iron Claw then rides around on a motorcycle shooting baddies.

Iron Fist: The Giants Are Coming ★★

aka *Demir Yumruk*, *Black Superman*, 1970, Turkey
Director: Tunç Basaran
Cast: Enver Özer, Feri Cansel, Süleyman Turan

An army of supervillains that includes Fu Manchu and a disabled transvestite seeking uranium, all run into Black Superman (Özer), so called because of the colour of his outfit, needless to say.

Great music and cartoonish bad guys are about all this unmemorable B-movie has going for it. Its personality can be summed up by a sequence in which our hero's girlfriend catches him with another woman, but is immediately talked into taking her

place in the still-warm bed. May or may not be a sequel to *Iron Claw the Pirate*.

Iron Girl ★

aka *Aian gâru*, 2012, Japan
Director: Masatoshi Nagamine
Cast: Kirara Asuka, Rina Akiyama, Mickey Koga

In an undefined post-apocalypse world, the peaceful Just must defend themselves from violent aggressors the Crazy Dogs. At least they have help from Iron Girl (Asuka), a beautiful woman with a bionic suit.

Every now and then there's a nod to the extremely thin plot, but this is pretty much pure exploitation. The filmmakers go for high-intensity fight scenes, but they're so badly choreographed, executed and shot they come off as silly. A botched attempt at flashy editing only compounds the problem, and there's none of the visual invention we might expect from a Japanese genre movie. (It's nothing to do with the Iron Man franchise and doesn't even crib from it.)

Iron Man ★★★★★

2008, USA
Director: Jon Favreau
Cast: Robert Downey Jr., Gwyneth Paltrow, Terrence Howard

Kidnapped by terrorists, narcissistic arms-dealing drunk Tony Stark (Downey Jr.) is forced to build a missile. He surreptitiously makes something more interesting instead.

The MCU kicked off in style with this origin story-heavy primer that, hard as it is to believe today, marks most of the world's introduction to the character. While some of the MCU's hallmarks, both good and bad, are certainly present (well-developed script, disappointing finale, tension-popping humour), it's surprisingly untypical of what the series would become. The pace is quite slow and the focus narrow, while stakes are kept under control and CGI is generally used sparingly.

Iron Man 2 ★★★

2010, USA
Director: Jon Favreau
Cast: Robert Downey Jr., Mickey Rourke, Gwyneth Paltrow

Having somehow achieved complete world peace, Tony Stark (Downey Jr.) is under fire from all sides: his own technology is poisoning him, the US government want to take away his suits and a crazy physicist with a grudge is out to get him.

When it was released in 2010, audiences and critics were in agreement that *Iron Man 2* was disappointing, but revisiting the movie eight years later it stands up quite well. With the MCU formula homologating subsequent instalments in the franchise, the uneven narrative and imperfections give it a bit of personality without causing much harm. In other words, it's not as good as *Iron Man 3*, but it is more distinct. In part that's due to Rourke, who's not your typical Marvel Big Bad. His vengeful genius Ivan Vanko is horribly underused, but Rourke's charisma makes him memorable.

Iron Man 3 ★★★★★

2013, USA
Director: Shane Black
Cast: Robert Downey Jr., Guy Pearce, Gwyneth Paltrow

A troubled Tony Stark (Downey Jr.) must contend with an enigmatic terrorist and a fire-breathing lunatic.

The dialogue is some of the best in the franchise, the action scenes are top notch and the whole is engaging from start to finish. With Downey Jr.'s characterisation blending so well with Shane Black's script, it seems a good time to acknowledge

what Marvel has done with Tony Stark. Superhero movies tend not to delve too deeply into their protagonist's psyche, and in modern Hollywood it's not often a character is given this much time and space to evolve. When it has been done (perhaps Christian Bale's Batman or Hugh Jackman's Wolverine), it's been with lots of heavy writing and drama. Stark is basically a comedy character, but one with immense depth. This film takes advantage of that better than any other he features in.

Iron Man & Captain America: Heroes United ★★

2014, USA
Directors: Eric Radomski, Leo Riley
Cast: Adrian Pasdar, Roger Craig Smith, Fred Tatasciore

Iron Man (Pasdar) must rescue Captain America (Smith) from The Red Skull (Liam O'Brien) before he uses Cap's blood to create a superarmy.

Sort-of sequel to 2011's live-action *Captain America: The First Avenger,* and from the same stable as the dreary *Iron Man & Hulk: Heroes United.* It features stock dialogue, bland performances, basic animation and a non-plot plot.

Iron Man & Hulk: Heroes United ★★

2013, USA
Directors: Eric Radomski, Leo Riley
Cast: Adrian Pasdar, Fred Tatasciore, Dee Bradley Baker

HYDRA's scheme to highjack the Hulk's (Tatasciore) gamma-based superstrength releases an electrical being determined to destroy Earth.

Aimed at the young ones. Remarkable for its interesting (if ugly) combination of 2D and 3D animation techniques.

Iron Man: Rise of Technovore ★★

2013, USA
Director: Hiroshi Hamazaki
Cast: Norman Reedus, Matthew Mercer,
Eric Bauza

Iron Man (Mercer) is framed for a disaster by vengeful genius Ezekiel Stane (Bauza).

Nicely animated but underwritten, clichéd and humourless. Stark teams up with The Punisher (Reedus) and goes toe-to-toe with both Black Widow (Clare Grant) and Hawkeye (Troy Barker) before eventually battling the insane son of former mentor Obediah Stane.

The Iron Superman ★★★

aka *Tie chao ren, Super Robot Mach Baron: The Movie*, 1974, Japan/China,
Directors: Ting Hung Kuo, Koichi Takano
Cast: Lin Lin Li, Paul Chun, Stephan Yip

A team of highly-trained operatives use a robot to defend Earth from a wizard.

Cut together from episodes of the 1974 Japanese tokusatsu TV series *Super Robot Mach Baron*, *The Iron Superman* replaces footage of the original cast with material featuring Hong Kong actors. Although a little wilder than most, this is fairly standard stuff for the kyodai subgenre, with a team of perky youngsters becoming one with various mech in order to battle a crazy-haired wizard (with help from a cop on a hot-air balloon motorcycle).

Isputnik vs. Darna

1963, Philippines
Director: Natoy B. Catindig
Cast: Nida Blanca, Liza Moreno, Tony Ferrer

Nida Blanca's Isputnik faces off against Liza Moreno's Darna. In Hollywood terms that's like Wonder Woman going toe-to-toe with Captain Marvel, so it's a shame it's unavailable, if not lost. (See Grouped Franchises for more Darna.)

It's a Bird... It's a Plane... It's Superman! ★

1975, USA
Director: Jack Regas
Cast: David Wilson, Lesley Ann Warren, Kenneth Mars

A mad scientist wants to destroy the world because he hasn't won the Nobel Prize.

Superman stage production. The songs aren't great and the production is a mess, but the biggest problem is that it's designed for a live audience and filmed without one. Gags and crescendos are greeted with silence rather than laughter and applause, leaving the performers stranded and killing the atmosphere. The Batman musical, *Holy Musical B@tman!*, can't convey the buzz of of its live audience but at least it has one.

Ivan the Incredible ★

aka *Gummi T*, 2012, Denmark
Director: Michael Hegner
Cast: Thure Lindhardt, Nicolaj Kopernikus, Signe Egholm Olsen

Ivan Olsen (Lindhardt), a schoolboy lacking confidence and struggling with bullies, drinks a gypsy's potion that grants him powers.

There's something about Ivan's features that suggest an ongoing existential crisis. It's unnerving. In fact all the character designs in this bottom-drawer CG fiasco are similarly distressing. It's meant to be a message movie, but what the message is or why we should care is never made clear.

J-Men Forever ★★★★

1979, USA
Director: Richard Patterson
Cast: Peter Bergman, Phil Proctor, M.G. Kelly

Shapeshifting nogoodnik the Lightning Bug (Kelly) schemes to destroy humanity with rock 'n' roll and marijuana. Luckily for us, the J-Men are on duty.

An amalgamation of scenes from early superhero serials cut together and re-dubbed for comic effect. The disjointed nature makes it feel like a sketch show as much as a movie, but that doesn't stop it being hugely funny. This film should be sought out immediately and by everyone.

J.O.E. and the Colonel ★★

1985, USA
Director: Ron Satlof
Cast: Terence Knox, Gary Kasper, Aimee Eccles

The Mobius group genetically engineers the perfect human, intending to use him to explore mountains and the sea (come again?). After demonstrating independence during a test, the government decide J.O.E. (Kasper) should be killed off. With the aid of sympathetic scientist Dr. Rourke (Knox) he escapes to become an altruistic mercenary.

Nobody cares about establishing anything. We fly through a voiceover explaining the scientific background to the project, the creation of the boy, his maturing, his escape from Mobius (it sounds exciting, maybe we could have seen it), and the inauguration of a one-man A-Team. As a TV pilot this stuff is supposed to be the meat and potatoes – it's how you establish the setup and characters. Instead, we're talked at for 10 minutes and then a couple of episodes happen. The concept: naive superman does covert stuff with tech genius buddy while evading the government, might have worked. But it's boring and the performances are flat.

Jai Karnataka ★★★

1989, India
Director: Dwarakish
Cast: Ambarish Rajani, Jr Narasimharaju, Mukhyamantri Chandru

The kindly foster father to an abundance of orphans finds himself battling a Bond villain after accidentally becoming invisible.

With no English subtitles and absolutely no information online, this likeable comedy is something of a mystery. Rajani mugs, waves his arms and dashes about like a loon while an hilariously over-the-top villain cackles maniacally in his lair. It's nuts, and great fun until our hero's favourite child is horribly murdered. Images of her little bandaged head periodically flash up on screen for the rest of the movie. Just a warning. (It seems to be a remake or 1987's *Mr. India*.)

James Batman ★★★

1966, Philippines
Director: Artemio Marquez
Cast: Dolphy, Shirley Moreno, Boy Alano

The CLAW organisation demands Asia and Europe be placed under the control of the Red Army, and their citizens be taught hatred of America. James Batman (Dolphy) is given the case.

On the off-chance we need reminding this is a mashup of James Bond and Batman, the movie steals both theme tunes within the first 20 minutes. But rather than a straight up zero-budget knock-off, this is a comedic zero-budget knock-off, and it's actually quite funny. Dolphy spent several decades as the undisputed king of Filipino comedy, and the well-timed slapstick of *James Batman* fits his talents well. Whether casually drying his hands on Robin's cape, or attempting to avoid the more arduous aspects of his job, this Pinoy Batman is genuinely funny, albeit very unlicensed.

Jagoan Instan: see *Instant Heroes*

Jay and Silent Bob's Super Groovy Cartoon Movie ★★★

2013, USA,
Director: Steve Stark
Cast: Jason Mewes, Kevin Smith, Eliza Dushku

After winning the lottery, Jay (Mewes) and Bob (Smith) decide to become superheroes Bluntman and Chronic.

The superhero references, swearing and sex jokes come thick and fast in this profoundly silly, occasionally hilarious Rorschach test of a movie. Some audiences will see comedy genius, some childish idiocy, some the end of civilisation as we know it. Each opinion has at least some merit.

Jesus Christ Vampire Hunter ★★

2001, Canada
Director: Lee Demarbre
Cast: Phil Caracas, Murielle Varhelyi, Maria Moulton

Jesus is called in to see off a vampire threat in Ottawa.

The grimy, lo-fi 70s vibe is convincing and those involved really seem to care about what they're doing. But the joke wears thin pretty quickly and within 20 minutes it has become an ordeal.

Jing wu feng yun: Chen Zhen: see *Legend of the Fist: The Return of Chen Zhen*

Jinzô ningen Hakaidâ: see *Roboman Hakaider*

Joaquin Bordado ★★★

1988, Philippines

Unlicensed Pinoy spoof *James Batman*

is a rough diamond and tragic hero using his superpowers to defeat either crime, witches or both.

John Carter ★★

2012, USA
Director: Andrew Stanton
Cast: Taylor Kitsch, Lynn Collins, Willem Dafoe

Civil War soldier John Carter (Kitsch) finds himself on Mars, a planet enduring an all-too-familiar conflict. Able to perform incredible physical feats for some reason, Carter becomes a central figure in the struggles of an oppressed Martian race.

As a low-key B-movie with fewer visual effects shots and more originality, this could have been good. Kitsch is an interesting actor, but he's lost in an overblown movie that doesn't do its source material justice.

Director: Carlo J. Caparas
Cast: Ramon Revilla, Tanya Gomez, Janice Jurado

After killing the men he deems responsible for his son's death (or injury, the boy seems to be alive again at the end of the movie), Joaquin Bordado is imprisoned with a mysterious elderly man who covers his new cellmate's body with magical animal tattoos. Upon release, Bordado goes after the local crime syndicate.

Directed by the source comic's original author, this late-career heroic outing for Revilla harks back to the amulet movies that returned him to prominence in the 1970s. He's still a formidable leading man, although the movie itself is hard to follow without English subtitles, particularly in the rushed first act and finale involving a mud monster. We can assume from the catalogue of similar Revilla vehicles (*Nardong Putik, Huhulihin si Tiagong Akyat, Kapitan Inggo, Tonyong Bayawak, Pepeng Agimat, Pepeng Kuryente*, etc.) that our man

Johnny Joker

1973, Philippines
Director: Jun Aristorenas
Cast: Jun Aristorenas, Robin Aristorenas, Virginia Aristorenas

Unofficial Batman movie without Batman. Based on surviving promotional material it did feature Batwoman, 'Spider-Web', Catwoman, Lastikman and Robin, though. Sadly it's considered lost.

Jonah Hex ★★

2010, USA
Director: Jimmy Hayward
Cast: Josh Brolin, Megan Fox, John Malkovich

A resurrected bounty hunter is given the chance to avenge his family's death and save a nascent United States from another civil war.

Hugely forgettable waste of an intriguing idea and top-drawer talent (aside from the headliners, Michaels Fassbender and Shannon appear in supporting roles). Brolin looks the part and gives good sneer, but there's no way to conceal the disinterest permeating the cast. Megan Fox allegedly considers this her worst film, but I wouldn't go quite that far (she's worked with Michael Bay five times).

Jossy's ★★
aka *Joshīzu*, 2014, Japan
Director: Yūichi Fukuda
Cast: Mirei Kiritani, Mina Fujii, Mitsuki Takahata

Five ordinary young women are brought together to battle a dangerous monster (on the grounds they're all named after colours!).

The girls wear colour-coded costumes, the monster is a man in a rubber suit and the battle takes place in a quarry; *Jossy's* couldn't be more *Super Sentai* if a US TV company bought the rights, changed the names and inserted their own footage. It's funny at times, but there's some tedious repetition and a lack of interesting sets or locations.

Judex ★★★
1916, France
Director: Louis Feuillade
Cast: René Cresté, Musidora, René Poyen

Judex (Cresté), the cryptic moral crusader, kidnaps corrupt banker Favraux (Louis Leubasto) in an attempt to make him pay for his crimes. Meanwhile a sinister gang have their own plans for the wealthy crook.

Heeding the criticism levelled at him for glamorising the immoral Fantômas in the villain's 1913 screen debut, filmmaker Louis Feuillade set about devising a protagonist combining ethically sound sensibilities with a similarly roguish technique. The result was this labyrinthine and hugely

successful silent serial. The complexity of the plot and sheer scale of the production are unusual for the time (it was completed in 1914 but went unreleased for two years due to the war) and give it a strangely modern feel, relatively speaking. It's easier to enjoy than one might expect, and less repetitive than the Hollywood serials that would follow a couple of decades later. It's worth noting this is possibly the earliest release with a viable claim to being the first ever superhero movie: Judex is unusually committed to justice, uses an alter ego with an identifiable costume, is a master of disguise and operates out of a cave-based lair. Although he's seeking revenge in this serial, the 1917 sequel saw him segway into altruistic vigilantism. (Followed by *Judex's New Mission*.)

Judex ★★★★★
1963, France
Director: Georges Franju
Cast: Channing Pollock, Francine Bergé, Edith Scob

Judex (Pollack) threatens a corrupt banker with death if he doesn't make amends by repaying those he's swindled.

This streamlined remake of the 1916 serial is the fourth and most recent *Judex* film. It consciously harks back to the character's silent cinema roots with stylised inter-titles, stunning black-and-white cinematography and a period setting. Extremely well made, it benefits from superb performances, a beautiful score from Maurice Jarre and some unforgettable costumes: although worn in only one scene, Judex's bird mask is among the most haunting superhero accessories on film.

Judex 34
1934, France
Director: Maurice Champreux
Cast: René Ferté, Louise Lagrange, Paule Andral

Remake of the 1916 serial. Unavailable at the time of writing.

Judex's New Mission

aka *La nouvelle mission de Judex*, *The New Mission of Judex*, 1917, France
Director: Louis Feuillade
Cast: René Cresté, Marcel Lévesque, Yvette Andréyor

Sequel serial in which Judex must prevent a secret society from stealing a dangerous device. Unavailable at the time of writing.

Judge Dredd ★★

1995, USA
Director: Danny Cannon
Cast: Sylvester Stallone, Armand Assante, Rob Schneider

It's 2139 and society has withdrawn from the 'Cursed Earth' into giant megacities policed by Judges: agents of the state who are licensed to execute criminals on the spot. The most feared such judge is Dredd (Stallone), and he's been framed for murder.

Botched blockbuster that fundamentally fails to 'get' its protagonist. Dredd isn't a complicated character to write; you just need to remember he doesn't compromise, doesn't wink at the audience and doesn't take his helmet off. So it's disappointing to find he does all three constantly, although you'll probably be too busy dreaming up ways to murder Rob Schneider to care.

Jumborg Ace & Giant ★★

aka *Giant and Jumbo A*, *Janbōgu Ēsu to Jaianto*, *Yak Wat Jaeng phop Chambo E*, *Mars Men*, 1974, Thailand
Director: Tojo Shohei or Sompote Sands (maybe)
Cast: Unknown

Kaiju are destroying Thailand, so Jumborg Ace and Giant are sent in to save the day.

Delirious Thai tokusatsu featuring Ultraman knock-off Jumborg Ace and lively Buddhist idol, Giant. The whole movie is one long fight between various kaiju and kyodai heroes (constantly accompanied by the same four bars of theme music) and is quite incredible. Aside from the relentless action, the Thai influence (it's a joint production between Japan's Tsuburaya and Thailand's Chaiyo) seems to mandate more comedy and a complete lack of plot. In small doses the effect is comic, but sustained exposure may cause distress.

Jumper ★★

2008, USA
Director: Doug Liman
Cast: Hayden Christensen, Samuel L. Jackson, Jamie Bell

Fanatical religious extremists hunt 'jumpers', individuals able to teleport at will.

Boring characters, an uninvolving narrative and lazy execution leave *Jumper* plunging past mediocrity on its way down towards disappointing irrelevance.

Jungle Jim: see Grouped Franchises

The Junior Defenders ★★★★

2007, USA
Director: Keith Spiegel
Cast: Ally Sheedy, Brian O'Halloran, Justin Henry

Norman Nields (Fred Hazelton), a psychotic uberfan of 1970's superhero show *Junior Defenders*, kidnaps its former stars in order to have them make more episodes.

The documentary/vérité style is what makes this work. It creates an immediacy and some valuable comic opportunities, but most importantly it sidesteps some of the biggest issues these zero-budget genre movies suffer from: poor sound, lighting and camerawork. Faux documentaries (or whatever this is) are allowed to have poor sound, lighting and camerawork. There's some superficial commentary on fandom and the fickle nature of the entertainment industry but, really, this thing just wants to make us laugh. It does well.

Justice League ★★★
2017, USA
Director: Zack Snyder
Cast: Ben Affleck, Gal Gadot, Jason Momoa

With Superman (Cavill) dead, mankind is vulnerable, and the psychotic Steppenwolf (Hinds) is first to take advantage. Batman (Affleck) and Wonder Woman (Gadot) set out to build a team of superheroes to defend the planet, but Superman has left some big boots to fill.

And so the DCEU freight train shudders to a halt at another foggy station, and unloads a fresh delivery of existential scowls. Zack Snyder remains the driving force in spite of being absent from parts of the shoot, but at least stand-in Joss Wheedon has done away with most of the incongruous shaky-cam cinematography and allowed a small amount of colour to creep in among the shiny greys, dull greys and other greys. It makes a big difference, but we miss Cavill's Superman. Aquaman might have filled the void (in the movie's biggest surprise, Jason Momoa is fine and the character believable), but he's given nothing to do.

Justice League Dark ★★
2017, USA
Director: Jay Oliva
Cast: Rosario Dawson, Camilla Luddington, Matt Ryan

Batman (Jason O'Mara) seeks answers to a mystery from occult detective John Constantine (Ryan). Along with others of his kind, Constantine forms a transmundane equivalent to the Justice League.

Luring some of DC's lesser-known characters out of the shadows is an

Judex (1963 version)

overdue and welcome move. Unfortunately, executives weren't convinced the likes of Constantine, Deadman (Nicholas Turturro) and friends could carry a movie alone, so Batman is placed at the centre of an already crowded ensemble cast, with the rest of the Justice League showing up too. And that's the story of the movie: every time it seems like something brave and original is going to happen, it doesn't.

Justice League of America ★★
1997, USA
Directors: Félix Enríquez Alcalá, Lewis Teague
Cast: Matthew Settle, Kimberly Oja, John Kassir

Green Lantern (Settle), Fire (Micelle Hurd), the Flash (Kenny Johnston), Atom (Kassir) and sometimes Ice (Oja) protect New Metro City from a crazed scientist who can control the weather.

Conceptually confused failed pilot aimed at a young audience. Our superheroes are four exaggerated stereotypes living together in a trendy apartment, and for some reason we regularly cut to documentary-inspired interview footage of them talking about their day. It's as if someone put the Power Rangers on *MTV's Real World*. They're pretty ineffectual for the most part – the biggest rescue of the first hour being a cat stuck in a storm drain – and there's no sense we're headed anywhere specific. Instead, we just watch the cast meander about dealing with everyday problems. At least when the finale comes it's suitably stupid.

Justice League vs. Teen Titans ★★
2016, USA
Director: Sam Liu
Cast: Rosario Dawson, Christopher Gorham, Shemar Moore

When the Justice League are possessed by a demonic spirit, the Teen Titans go to hell in search of answers.

Origin story of sorts, with the permanently sullen Robin (Stuart Allan) begrudgingly joining the Teen Titans at Batman's (Jason O'Mara) insistence. Raven (Taissa Farmiga) is the central figure in a thin plot with too many irritating characters.

Justice League vs the Fatal Five ★★★
2019, USA
Director: Sam Liu
Cast: Elyes Gabel, Diane Guerrero, Kevin Conroy

Sixty percent of the Fatal Five travel back from the 31st century to todayish in search of rookie Green Lantern, Jessica Cruz (Guerrero). Star Boy (Gable) of The Legion of Super-Heroes tags along and teams up with The Justice League to stop a prison break.

A proper plot (there's a lot to keep track of) is executed in a serviceable fashion, albeit with some dull characters at its forefront. An attempt to address anxiety related psychological disorders is interesting and well thought out, while Jessica Cruz's origin story is worthwhile if a little self-consciously woke. Very solid.

Justice League: Crisis on Two Earths ★★
2010, USA
Directors: Sam Liu, Lauren Montgomery
Cast: William Baldwin, Mark Harmon, Chris Noth

A kindly Lex Luthor (Noth) appeals to the Justice League for help battling their evil counterparts from a backwards dimension.

Ultimately, the concept is too familiar and isn't taken anywhere particularly interesting. There are opportunities for fun but too many go unexploited, and the weak script allows an overabundance of characters to bog everything down.

Justice League: Doom ★★★

2012, USA
Director: Lauren Montgomery
Cast: Kevin Conroy, Tim Daly, Phil Morris

After gaining access to Batman's (Conroy) computer system, Vandal Savage (Morris) steals contingency plans highlighting each Justice League member's weakness. With even Superman (Daly) in danger, Batman leads the attempt to stop his friends being wiped-out by supervillains.

A neat idea is well realised and brims with just the sort of uncynical fan service these animated movies should be dishing up. It's light without being shallow, and extremely tightly written. Not the most sophisticated thing in the world, but who cares.

Justice League: Gods and Monsters ★★

2015, USA
Director: Sam Liu
Cast: Benjamin Bratt, Michael C. Hall, Tamara Taylor

In an alternate reality, very different versions of Superman (Bratt), Batman (Hall) and Wonder Woman (Taylor) are framed for murder and become government targets.

Hello to bloodsucking Batman, nihilistic Wonder Woman and bearded Superman, not to mention silly dialogue ("upon your egg I bestow my eminence" announces Zod, while combining his DNA with an embryo). The Justice League's motivation is never explained: they seem to have nothing but contempt for mankind, and the feeling is mutual, so why are they breaking their necks being superheroes? That anomaly is typical of what feels like an undercooked concept. It's as if a brainstorming writer pitched the idea of edgy takes on these characters, only for nobody to develop it any further.

Justice League: The Flashpoint Paradox ★★★

2013, USA
Director: Jay Oliva
Cast: Justin Chambers, C. Thomas Howell, Michael B. Jordan

After an encounter with Professor Eobard Thorne (Howell), The Flash (Chambers) goes back in time and inadvertently creates a reality in which The Justice League never came together.

A good idea is fleshed out with some imaginative role reversals. Superman (Sam Daly) is an imprisoned weakling, Aquaman (Cary Elwes) is at war with the Amazons, Bruce Wayne's father Thomas (Kevin McKidd) is a disillusioned, alcoholic Batman, etc. It leads to the sort of freedom that allows us to see Wonder Woman (Vanessa Marshall) murder Captain Thunder (Steve Blum). It's best not to think about causality (the writers didn't), but that's easy enough when there's always something going on.

Justice League: The New Frontier ★★

2008, USA
Director: Dave Bullock
Cast: David Boreanaz, Miguel Ferrer, Neil Patrick Harris

In the 1950s a supernatural alien threat brings together Green Lantern (Boreanaz), Martian Manhunter (Ferrer), The Flash (Harris) and others, who form a superhero team known as the Justice League.

Mature themes (it references the rape of civilian women during the Korean war and is set against the backdrop of McCarthyism) are married to functional animation in this first animated *Justice League* movie. Plenty of time is devoted to the plot and the voice cast is good, but there's an irritating worthiness and a confused tone.

Justice League: Throne of Atlantis ★★

2015, USA
Director: Ethan Spaulding
Cast: Matt Lanter, Sam Witwer, Sean Astin

Blaming mankind for the death of his father, Atlantean prince Orm (Witwer) invades Metropolis just as his half-brother Arthur Curry (Lanter) becomes Aquaman.

No matter how dull Aquaman's origin story might be, at least there are no billionaire orphans, bullied teenagers or mad scientists. Unfortunately, it's not just the origin story that's dull, though. I fully understand not everyone 'gets' Arthur Curry (presumably due to his Merman schtick, which does seem pretty hokey) but the filmmakers do themselves no favours by introducing him getting into a humourless fist-fight due to his liberating a live lobster from a Chinese restaurant. That's simply not a scene that should be played straight.

Justice League: War ★★★

2014, USA
Director: Jay Oliva
Cast: Sean Astin, Zach Callison, Christopher Gorham

When monstrous alien Darkseid (Steve Blum) attacks Earth, a disparate group of superheroes and crimefighters form the Justice League in order to defend mankind.

In typical animated superhero fashion, the Justice League origin story is told in their fifth adventure of the DC Universe Animated Original Movies series. It's done well enough and without sacrificing any of the relentless action audiences have come to expect. In fact there may be too much action: lose concentration for just a moment and by the time you work out who's fighting who they'll be fighting someone else.

Jumborg Ace & Giant **aka... all kinds of things**

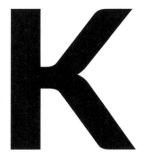

The Kabayo Kids ★★

1990, Philippines
Director: Tony Y. Reyes
Cast: Tito Sotto, Vic Sotto, Joey de Leon

A trio of idiots become henshin heroes and tackle a crime syndicate.

Between the three of them, comedy troupe Tito, Vic & Joey, have appeared in at least a dozen superhero movies, so it's no great surprise they decided to fold some of the genre's archetypes into this slapstick tale of crime and brightly-coloured leotards. Unusually, they choose to spoof Japanese tokusatsu, particularly the Kamen Rider franchise, with the boys throwing henshin hero shapes on their motorcyles. It's fun at times but there's too much plot and not enough action, gags or silliness.

Kagaku ninja tai Gatchaman: *see* *Gatchaman: The Movie*

Kalimán, el hombre increíble ★★

aka *Kalimán, the Incredible Man*, 1972, Mexico
Director: Alberto Mariscal
Cast: Jeff Cooper, Nino Del Arco,
Susana Dosamantes

While searching for evidence of aliens in Egypt, Kalimán (Cooper), a brown-skinned, blonde-haired, turban-wearing superhero, becomes embroiled in a scheme to rob a Pharaoh's tomb.

Once one of the most popular superheroes in Latin America, thanks to a successful 1960s radio series and comic, Kalimán (the name is derived from the goddess Kali) wanders the earth protecting the weak and dispensing justice. This is the first of two live-action movies based on his adventures. It seems talky and dated now, but features numerous foreign actors and a crew who cared, so it's well-made compared to other

Mexican movies of the era. An interesting artefact rather than essential viewing.

Kalimán en el siniestro mundo de Humanón ★★★

aka *Kalimán in the Sinister World of Humanón*, 1976, Mexico
Director: Alberto Mariscal
Cast: Jeff Cooper, Milton Rodríguez, Lenka Erdo

In the jungles of South America a mad scientist is attempting to create the master race. Who can stop him? Kalimán. Maybe.

Jauntier and sillier sequel to *Kalimán, el hombre increíble*. Everything is ramped up to 11 and much the better for it. Rodríguez is particularly good as the villain Humanón (a lunatic in a black and red KKK outfit, sunglasses and giant medallion) who keeps live human heads in jars. Cooper still sports blackface, though, which makes a mockery of the movie's anti-racism elements.

Kamen Rider(s): see Grouped Franchises

Kanthaswamy ★★★

2009, India
Director: Susi Ganesan
Cast: Vikram, Shriya Saran, Prabhu

A policeman who spends his spare time fighting crime and corruption as cockerel-like superhero Kanthaswamy (Vikram) is targeted by the vengeful daughter of a crippled reprobate.

Michael Caine advised us to "be calm on the surface, but always paddling like the dickens underneath". Kanthaswamy flips the philosophy. Seldom has so much action yielded so little in the way of practical results in a movie. At one point a single punch requires 13 edits, five sound effects, three pieces of music and two sets! Even basic conversations are shot as if they're

on fire. It's exhausting but great fun (for the first couple of hours at least – it's way too long). The vibrant song and dance routines are built around the fantastic Shriya Saran.

Kapitan Inggo ★★★

1984, Philippines
Director: Jose Yandoc
Cast: Ramon Revilla, Marissa Delgado, Susan Valdez-LeGoff

A dying man gives Domingo Alejandro Santiago, aka community official Kapitan Inggo (Revilla), an amulet able to attract lightning and provide superstrength.

Although Kapitan Inggo opens with an announcement in English, it proves nothing more than a tease and we're soon plunged into another subtitle-free Tagalog folk hero adventure. This one goes all out with the folksploitation stuff, presenting Inggo as an almost messianic figure and amping up the propaganda aspect. He seems to have been a real-life anti-Communist firebrand, although this movie interpretation has obviously been sugarcoated.

Kapitan Kidlat

1981, Philippines
Director:Emmanuel H. Borlaza
Cast: Carlo Gabriel, Rio Locsin, Elizabeth Oropesa

Inspired by Leonardo P. Abutin's 1950 radio series *Kapitan Kidlat* (Captain Lightning). This movie is assumed lost.

Kapoww!! ★

2010, Malaysia
Director: Azizi Chunk
Cast: Zizan Razak, Ngasrizal Ngasri, Lisa Surihani

An everyman superhero'd by lightning moves to the city to become an arrogant vigilante. Will he learn his lesson before the spiteful Alikazambo (Ngasri) murders his family? Will we care either way?

Predictably plotted, poorly-made comedy determined to pay homage to its comic book roots. It might have been wise to spend a little more money on microphones and tripods and a little less on silly effects.

Karate-Robo Zaborgar ★★★

aka *Denjin Zabôgâ*, 2011, Japan
Director: Noboru Iguchi
Cast: Itsuji Itao, Asami, Akira Emoto

Karate student Yutaka Daimon (Itao) sees his scientist father murdered by the Sigma organisation and vows to take revenge. Fortunately, his pops bequeathed him the perfect tool for the job: a motorcycle that transforms into a karate-fighting robot!

Somewhat bloody tongue-in-cheek homage to the tokusatsu classics of the 1970s and 1980s. A relentless and surreal series of melees sees our heroes do battle with all sorts of weird machines and creatures, with everything undercut by filmmaker Noboru Iguchi's apparently profound fear of women. Cyborg bikini babes kidnap businessmen, breasts turn into monsters (in Iguchi's *Mutant Girls Squad* they sprout swords), and the finale sees a 200-ft robot woman exploding people's heads with her giant cellphone. It's completely insane.

Kataude mashin gâru: see *The Machine Girl*

Kdo chce zabít Jessii?: see *Who Wants to Kill Jessie?*

Kenny Begins ★★★

2009, Sweden
Directors: Mats Lindberg, Carl Åstrand
Cast: Johan Rheborg, Bill Skarsgård, Carla Abrahamsen

Apprentice superhero Kenny Starfighter (Rheborg) must team up with an ordinary Joe to prevent a magical crystal falling into the hands of evil alien Rutger Oversmart (Jan Mybrand).

Kenny Begins is an (apparently inferior) spinoff from popular Swedish TV comedy *Kenny Starfighter*, but without knowing the show I can only judge the movie on its own terms, and it's quite funny. Some of the humour is similar in style (though not standard) to that of ZAZ productions like *Airplane* and *Naked Gun*, if somewhat less relentless. Rheborg does a good amiable idiot, however co-star Bill Skarsgård (who features here in his first significant role but has since gone on to become a Hollywood star as Pennywise in the recent *It* films and Zeitgeist in *Deadpool 2*) is surprisingly forgettable by comparison.

Nicolas Cage as Big Daddy in *Kick-Ass*

Kiara the Brave ★

aka *Super K*, 2011, India
Directors: Vijay S. Bhanushali, Smita Maroo
Cast: Steve Rassin, Michael Yeager,
Anthony Lawson

The jealous brother of Dreamzone's King
Maximus (Marc Matney) creates a superhero
child to help him conquer the throne, but
things don't go according to plan.

With elements borrowed from *Astro Boy*
and a US marketing campaign pushing
claimed similarities to Pixar's *Brave*, it's no
surprise this Indian CG animation offers us
nothing groundbreaking. What is a surprise
is how awful it is. The CGI has a textureless,
contrast-less quality that literally induces
nausea, and the actual animation is dire.

Kibakichi ★★★★

aka *Werewolf Warrior*, *Kibakichi: Bakko-yokaiden*,
2004, Japan
Director: Tomo'o Haraguchi
Cast: Ryûji Harada, Nozomi Andô,
Tatsuo Higashida

Kibakichi (Harada), a vagrant who happens
to be a part-wolf master swordsman, stops
off in a town populated by monsters.

The wandering ronin arriving at a village
in need of his help is a time-honoured
chanbara narrative trope, but this movie
applies a pair of twists that leave it feeling
anything but traditional. Aside from our
protagonist turning out to be a werewolf,
he also comes down on the side of the
monsters. We might reasonably expect it
to be them preying on the local humans,
but in fact it's the reverse. Unfortunately
this promising concept is compromised by
a stodgy screenplay that spends too long
on moody close-ups and dramatic dialogue.
With more dynamism this could have been
a classic. What action there is involves an
inordinate amount of blood and violence.

Kibakichi 2 ★★★

aka *Kibakichi: Bakko-yokaiden 2*, 2004, Japan
Directors: Tomo'o Haraguchi, Daiji Hattori
Cast: Ryûji Harada, Miki Tanaka,
Masakatsu Funaki

The wandering samurai/werewolf helps
residents of a village intimidated into
subservience by a murderous swordsman.

Cheaper and less fun than the first movie,
Kibakichi 2 is still worth seeing if only for
the insane werewolf mating ritual/dance
scene. We get fewer actors slathered in
prosthetics and fur, less fighting, but just
as many moody scenes of nothing much.
Flawed but still interesting.

Kick-Ass ★★★★

2010, USA
Director: Matthew Vaughn
Cast: Aaron Taylor-Johnson, Nicolas Cage,
Chloë Grace Moretz

A teenager decides to become a superhero,
but finds it more difficult than expected.

Hugely violent exercise in bad taste full of
gory murders, swearing and unnecessary
brutality. It's great! Cage and Moretz steal
the show as Big Daddy and Hit Girl, whose
vendetta against crime boss Frank D'Amico
(Mark Strong) is the closest this thing has to
a... heart? Like *Kingsman*, which comes from
the same creative team, there's a curious
emotional detachment to everything.

Kick-Ass 2 ★★★★

2013, USA
Director: Jeff Wadlow
Cast: Aaron Taylor-Johnson, Chloë Grace
Moretz, Christopher Mintz-Plasse

It's three years since the events of the first
film and Dave Lizewski (Taylor-Johnson) is
bored with retirement. Determined to get

back in the crimefighting game, he forms a superhero team. Meanwhile, Mindy Macready, aka Hit Girl (Moretz), struggles to adapt to an ordinary life.

There's less of a focal point this time as various unconnected narratives are able to wander as far as the final act before converging. And with the once unexpected ultraviolence no longer a surprise, *Kick-Ass 2* is robbed of one of its predecessor's best assets. There's still a lot to like, particularly Chloe Moretz. Her performance as a now teenage Hit Girl moves the character beyond the novelty act she was in the first film and gives us someone to root for.

Kid Krrish ★

2013, India
Director: Sooraj M.K.
Cast: Unknown

11-year-old Kid Krrish uses superpowers given to him by aliens to battle the heinous Dr. Para, who has some scheme or other.

Presumably produced to capitalise on the enormous success of Bollywood superhero franchise Krrish, this first of four almost anonymously produced TV movies relies on Flash-style animation and, to a greater extent, audience apathy. There are worse things in the world, but at least they tend to have English subtitles.

Kid Krrish 2: Mission Bhutan ★

2014, India
Director: Indra Narayan Datta
Cast: Unknown

Kid Krrish and his friends battle Dr. Para for a MacGuffin and some scrolls.

More of the same. Seriously, go and watch one of these things on YouTube and then try to think of something worth saying about it.

Kid Krrish 3: Mystery in Mongolia ★

2014, India
Director: Deepak Nair
Cast: Unknown

Thanks to alien interference Dr. Para is now a cyborg, and Kid Krrish must prevent him destroying a Mongolian village.

Please make it stop.

Kid Krrish 4: Shakalaka Africa ★

2015, India
Director: Deepak Naidu
Cast: Unknown

Aliens want to destroy Earth, but Kid Krrish is on hand. Plus robot dinosaurs.

I don't think I'm the target audience.

Kidlat... Ngayon!

1953, Philippines
Director: Oscar del Rosario
Cast: Armando Goyena, Evelyn Villar, Milagros Naval

Shazam-inspired Pinoy superhero who was gifted superpowers by Zeus and began life on radio. This movie is believed lost.

Kikaider: The Ultimate Human Robot ★★★

aka *Kikaidâ Reboot*, 2014, Japan
Director: Ten Shimoyama
Cast: Jingi Irie, Kazushige Nagashima, Aimi Satsukawa

An android protects its creator's children from a government agency charged with developing military robots.

Starting life as a TV series in 1972, the Kikaider franchise has quietly percolated away ever since, occasionally throwing up new shows, OVAs and spinoffs. This latest adaptation is slick, fast paced and bursting with the sort of camera-swirling, speed ramping mayhem films of this era love. It's fairly exciting stuff and features a strong performance from Irie as the titular hero who, crucially, develops a believable bond with his human wards.

Kiliç Aslan: see *Lion Man*

Kilink: see Grouped Franchises and Diabolik Super-Kriminals

Kill Order ★★

2017, Canada
Director: James Mark
Cast: Chris Mark, Jessica Clement,
Denis Akiyama

Krrish 3

A teenager tormented by violent visions discovers he was a test subject in a project to create superheroes, and was involved in drawing energy from other dimensions.

Reasonably compelling energetic martial arts movie. The action scenes are shot in closeup shakycam and although we get glimpses of Chris Mark's impressive fight skills, in cinematic terms they're largely wasted by poor (filmmaking) technique. Unfortunately, he's not so strong an actor as he is a martial artist, and director James Mark (the star's brother) doesn't seem able to do much with him in the dramatic stuff. But the movie's target audience will perhaps forgive such failings in a trade-off with the relentless action.

Killing vs. Mandrake: see *Mandrake vs. Killing*

King of the Rocket Men ★★★

1949, USA
Director: Fred C. Brannon
Cast: Tristram Coffin, Mae Clarke,
Don Haggerty

Scientist Jeff King (Coffin) dons the Rocket Man suit to hunt down a traitor to Science Associates, a collective of leading physicists with which he is involved.

King of the Rocket Men eventually gives in to the blanket of repetitive uniformity that smothers most serials, but it puts up a good fight. There's an unusual physicality to the action scenes and the flying stuff is spookily convincing. Neither shatters your suspension of disbelief or raises an ironic smile. There's also a surprisingly bleak ending, less deliberate humour and silliness than you'd expect, and with its relatively truncated length (it's only three minutes longer than *The Dark Knight Rises*) it's a good choice for modern audiences. Fans of *The Rocketeer* should certainly think about checking it out. Three similar Republic serials followed: *Radar Men from the Moon*, *Zombies of the Stratosphere* and *Commando Cody: Sky Marshal*. Although the hero of each wears the same Rocket Man costume featured here, they are not intended to be the same character.

Kingsman: The Golden Circle
★★★★
2017, UK/USA
Director: Matthew Vaughn
Cast: Taron Egerton, Colin Firth, Mark Strong

Loopy drug lord Poppy Adams (Julianne Moore) razes the Kingsman organisation, murdering all its members except Eggsy (Egerton) and Merlin (Strong). In a last ditch bid for help, they appeal to a previously unknown sister organisation in the USA.

More exaggerated super-Bondery from the team who brought us the first film. Despite seismic surface changes brought about by our base of operations shifting from London to Kentucky, there's nothing here to match the breathtaking originality of the first film. As a result, it feels like we're treading water (it's a similar story with *Kick-Ass* and its sequel, which originated from the same creative stable). This is a series that needs to constantly evolve its inventiveness if its to be more than passing entertainment. Then again, the first movie wasn't really any more than passing entertainment. Damn entertaining entertainment, though.

Kingsman: The Secret Service
★★★★
2014, UK/USA
Director: Matthew Vaughn
Cast: Colin Firth, Taron Egerton, Samuel L. Jackson

Eggsy (Egerton), a teenage cockney wide boy, is recruited into a secret intelligence agency and must help prevent a billionaire techno-terrorist's scheme to wipe out undesirables by blowing up their heads.

Based on the 2012 graphic novel by Mark Millar and Dave Gibbons, *Kingsman* marries classic narrative archetype 'the monomyth' (a naive hero is whisked into a magical world in which they learn, grow and ultimately save the day - see *Star Wars*, *The Wizard of Oz*, *The Lord of the Rings*, etc.), to a self-consciously cool style and strangely dispassionate tone. The result is simultaneously familiar and unique. We've seen plenty of refined, upper-crust superspies before; Eggsy not so much. Harry Palmer, Michael Caine's working-class response to James Bond, was an Eton toff compared to Eggsy. The class commentary is interesting, but the character is great because he's convincing, not because he's blue collar. Where *Kingsman* works, and works brilliantly, is in the superficial realm: the action setpieces are among the most inventive and well edited of their kind; the performances from Egerton, Firth and Jackson are extremely good fun; the script is perfectly paced and balanced; and there's a cocky spirit of creativity that makes this one of the most stimulating, if utterly empty, comic book adaptations so far. (Followed by *Kingsman: The Golden Circle*.)

Kiss Meets the Phantom of the Park
★
1978, USA
Director: Gordon Hessler
Cast: Peter Criss, Ace Frehley, Gene Simmons

While performing at an amusement park, rock brand KISS uncover mad scientist Abner Devereaux's (Zerbe) evil scheme to recreate them in robot form. Fortunately, KISS have superpowers for some reason.

At some point, presumably in one of many discussions about how to further monetise the commercial juggernaut that is KISS, a human said "let's make a movie where they all play superheroes and fight robot versions of themselves". Then other human beings agreed. Why this happened is anyone's guess, but it did, and we all have to deal with the consequences.

Kitaro ★★

aka *Gegege no Kitarô*, 2007, Japan,
Director: Katsuhide Motoki
Cast: Eiji Wentz, Mao Inoue, Rena Tanaka

An orphan keeps the peace between humankind and the world of monsters.

Based on an early 20th-century Japanese folk tale, *Kitaro* is like a Japanese *Blade* for children. He's half human, half yokai monster, and dedicated to keeping mankind safe from the latter. This low-budget live-action feature, which looks to have been shot on early standard definition digital cameras (or even some sort of analogue system) is reminiscent of much older Kids TV shows such as the BBC's *The Lion, the Witch and the Wardrobe*, what with its dodgy yokai costumes and cheap sets. It's unlikely to hold much appeal for adults and the subtitles may rule out non-Japanese speaking kids too, regardless of the fact it's so culturally specific you really need background knowledge of the mythology. It's not very good either.

Kitaro and the Millennium Curse ★

aka *Gegege no Kitarô: Sennen noroi uta*,
2008, Japan
Director: Katsuhide Motoki
Cast: Eiji Wentz, Kii Kitano, Rena Tanaka

Kitaro must solve a series of mysterious disappearances while facing a threat from the past.

Another cheap after-school adventure for the half-monster Kitaro and his friends. At some stage of post-production the wrong colour settings have been applied (it's as if an incorrect lookup table was used for a shift in colour space, if you happen to be techy and interested) and everything looks horrible. Having already established the only audience for these things is Japanese-speaking children of low expectations, I wonder how many viewers have noticed.

Kitaro's Graveyard Gang

2009, Japan/USA
Director: William Winckler
Cast: Caleb Pearson, Jason Barker,
G. Larry Butler

Kitaro must stop an evil wizard becoming monster king in this third instalment in the franchise. Unavailable at the time of writing. For which I'm grateful.

Kizil Maske: see *The Red Mask*

Koi... Mil Gaya ★★

2003, India
Director: Rakesh Roshan
Cast: Rekha, Hrithik Roshan, Preity Zinta

Rohit Mehra (Roshan), a boy with a development disorder resulting from an accident suffered by his pregnant mother, receives superpowers from an alien.

This first instalment in the Krrish franchise is less of a superhero movie than its two sequels, choosing to spend more time on characters and relationships than vigilante action. Rohit's learning difficulties make him an unusual protagonist and it's hard to imagine how the character might be received by modern audiences. (Followed by *Krrish*.)

Krrish ★★★★

2006, India
Director: Rakesh Roshan
Cast: Rekha, Hrithik Roshan, Priyanka Chopra

Child prodigy Krishna Mehra (Roshan) is raised in near isolation by a grandmother determined to keep his incredible mental and physical abilities secret.

Follow-up to 2003's *Koi... Mil Gaya*, in which the focus shifts to the son of that movie's protagonist. Conceived as a blockbuster, no expense was spared in its production. There's a dynamism and opulence to it all that, even by Bollywood standards, seems exuberant. A circus-based song and dance sequence that morphs into an action scene is particularly impressive, and the sheer joy exhibited by Roshan throughout the movie is infectious. (Followed by *Krrish 3*, surprisingly.)

Krrish 2: see *Krrish 3*

Krrish 3 ★★★

2013, India
Director: Rakesh Roshan
Cast: Hrithik Roshan, Vivek Oberoi, Priyanka Chopra

Now living happily with wife Priya (Chopra) and the father he thought was dead, Krrish (Roshan) struggles to juggle superhero duties with his day job. He soon finds he has bigger problems when mad scientist Kaal (Oberoi) puts humanity at risk with a scheme to get rich with a deadly virus.

Confusingly there is no *Krrish 2*. *Koi... Mil Gaya* is the first in the series and was followed by the more successful direct sequel *Krrish*. Producers chose to stick with the latter nomenclature for this third film (it's the same scenario that saw *First Blood* followed by *Rambo* and then *Rambo III*, if that helps anyone). The same mix of science fiction, humour and action seen in the previous film is employed in this one, but isn't quite as successful thanks to a less satisfying (and more convoluted) plot. Kaal and his mutant powers do at least present

a challenge to the superhuman Krrish this time, although there's never any real sense of danger. But these movies aren't about believable stakes, they're about fun, and on that score it delivers, particularly in the elaborate finale.

Kryptonite ★★

aka *Kryptonita*, 2015, Argentina
Director: Nicanor Loreti
Cast: Diego Velázquez, Juan Palomino, Susana Varela

The Justice League are reimagined as gritty vigilantes working the mean streets of an Argentian slum.

It's rare to stumble on a film within the superhero movie genre that's this original (I'm fairly sure Wonder Woman has never been realised as a despondent transvestite before), and it's a great shame more wasn't done with the premise. Presumably budget was the main handicap. Most of our time is spent in a hospital with our antiheroes mumbling to each other, and there's virtually no action. That makes *Kryptonite* a specialist product; one for hardcore fans only. But within those confines it's an interesting way to spend 80 minutes.

Kyûtî Hanî: see *Cutie Honey*

The Last Airbender ★

2010, USA
Director: M. Night Shyamalan
Cast: Noah Ringer, Nicola Peltz,
Jackson Rathbone

Aang (Ringer), a gifted bender (it doesn't deserve an explanation), must prevent the Fire Nation conquering the Water Tribes.

Boring, derivative, poorly acted, poorly written and deeply stupid waste of time.

Lastik Man

1965 or 1968, Philippines
Director: Richard Abelardo
Cast: Von Serna, Lyn D'Amour, Bella Flores

An alien with stretching powers is stranded on Earth and becomes a superhero. Created in 1964 by Mars Ravelo, Lastik Man was a popular Filipino superhero in the 60s, and then again in the late 90s. This first screen incarnation is considered lost.

Lastikman ★★★

2003, Philippines
Director: Tony Y. Reyes
Cast: Vic Sotto, Donita Rose, Michael V.

When a meteorite strikes a nearby rubber tree, Hilario (Sotto) develops the ability to drastically stretch his body. As an adult physics professor he uses his power to help people, but a feud between his students soon becomes a serious distraction.

Although inspired by The Fantastic Four's Reed Richards/Mister Fantastic, Lastikman lacks his inspiration's confidence and smooth demeanour, which often works to amusing effect when juxtaposed with his abilities. The movie makes the most of its comic tone and works well enough, but the biggest laughs will probably be inspired by the ropey CGI.

Lastikman ★★★

2004, Philippines
Director: Mac Alejandre
Cast: Mark Bautista, Sarah Geronimo, Cherie Gil

Adrian Rosales (Bautista) is bestowed with superpowers just in time to fight monsters.

This second *Lastikman* film in the space of two years feels a little more thought through, as if it's aimed at an audience rather than being blindly rendered onto the screen. Again it's comedic, perhaps even more so than the 2003 film, but the humour is better integrated and of a more consistent nature. The CGI stretch effects are also (slightly) more successful. On the down side the cartoonish tone will prove divisive with adult audiences. (How the Vic Sotto offering ended up the more serious of the two is beyond me.)

El Latigo: see *The Whip*

Lazer Team ★★★

2015, USA,
Director: Matt Hullum
Cast: Burnie Burns, Gavin Free, Michael Jones

A dim-witted sheriff and three degenerates become the accidental recipients of bionic enhancements gifted to mankind by aliens.

First feature film from Austin-based media company and comedy collective Rooster Teeth. Character detail builds on a promising idea but only goes so far. The pedestrian execution and abundance of clichés make *Lazer Team* easily forgettable even if there are some good laughs.

Lazer Team 2 ★★★

2018, USA
Directors: Daniel Fabelo, Matt Hullum
Cast: Burnie Burns, Gavin Free, Michael Jones

Disbanded and disillusioned, Lazer Team must pull themselves together in order to save Woody (Free) from another dimension.

Similarly prosaic sequel that retreads the 'discordant group must learn to work together' schtick of the first movie. It feels a little more rounded out with the addition of 'science girl' Maggie (Nichole Bloom), and there's a brief flirtation with satire, but it's nothing that will convert the unbeliever.

The League of Extraordinary Gentlemen ★★★

2003, USA
Director: Stephen Norrington
Cast: Sean Connery, Stuart Townsend, Peta Wilson

In an alternate late 19th century in which fictional literary figures are real, a band of heroes lead by Allan Quatermain (Connery) must work together to prevent a world war.

Pilloried by critics and thoroughly ignored by audiences, among the many crimes for which *The League of Extraordinary Gentlemen* stood accused on its 2003 release is being overblown, predictable and too crowded with characters. It was ahead of its time, in other words. Years later, none of those issues are likely to occur to cinemagoers well used to excess, but more importantly it really isn't that bad. The characters are fantastic, the plot skips along at the perfect pace and there's plenty of spectacle. It's really stupid, don't get me wrong, and it makes no sense at all. But then nor does *The Dark Knight* and that's considered a masterpiece. Besides, anyone expecting rational storytelling from a movie in which Captain Nemo (Naseeruddin Shah) hangs out with Dorian Gray (Stuart Townsend) has only themselves to blame.

League of Superheroes ★

aka *ABCs of Superheroes*, 2015, Germany

Directors: Jens Holzheuer, Oliver Tietgen
Cast: Bai Ling, Uwe Boll, Lloyd Kaufman

A series of short stories, each dealing with a different superhero.

The diverse segments inevitably vary in quality, with the worst being unforgivably wretched and the best merely terrible. The objective seems to be to offend as many people as possible with gore, nudity and bodily functions. It would have been fun to sit in on the casting process, though: "hack provocateur with no experience in front of the camera? You're in!"

The Legend of Drona ★★

aka *Drona*, 2008, India
Director: Goldie Behl
Cast: Jayshree Arora, Veer Arya,
Abhishek Bachchan

An orphan learns his dad was a superhero, and that he's one too.

Occasionally visually stunning but ultimately empty and pretentious failed blockbuster. Star Abhishek Bachchan (who, as the son of Amitabh Bachchan and Jaya Bhaduri, is Bollywood royalty) does his best but seems to have inherited little of either parent's innate magnetism.

Legend of Fist of the North Star ★

1993, South Korea
Director: Unknown
Cast: Unknown

Various magical martial artists fight each other in a junkyard.

All but indistinguishable from an amateur fan film, this obscure, apparently unofficial live-action South Korean version of the popular manga is 76 minutes of bad wigs and guttural whining. There are no English subtitles on the version I saw, but the plot

appears faithful, although it can be hard to see through the murky visuals.

The Legend of Hercules ★★

2014, USA
Director: Renny Harlin
Cast: Kellan Lutz, Gaia Weiss, Scott Adkins

Hercules (Lutz) learns of his fate to restore peace in ancient Greece, and must decide whether to follow it.

There was a time in the 1990s when Renny Harlin was an A-list director, having made popular blockbusters including *Die Hard 2*, *Cliffhanger* and *The Long Kiss Goodnight*. But here he is two decades later knocking out what amounts to a Hercules mockbuster starring one of the brothers from *Twilight*. Strangely, it doesn't seem like a Hercules movie at all, perhaps because the aesthetic is so distractingly similar to that of Zack Snyder's *300*. Like *300* it's full of speed ramping, has been colour-graded to within an inch of its life and is largely populated by sweaty, bearded men talking about destiny. As a PG-13 family movie it doesn't have *300's* edge, so there doesn't seem to be much point.

Legend of the Fist: The Return of Chen Zhen ★★★★

aka *Jing wu feng yun: Chen Zhen*, 2010,
Hong Kong
Director: Wai-Keung Lau
Cast: Donnie Yen, Alex Ahlstrom, Qi Shu

In 1940s Shanghai, suave WWII veteran Chen Zhen (Yen) becomes a masked paladin in order to obfuscate a Japanese invasion.

Wrapped in the tensions of the day, this loosely-related sequel to 1994's *Fist of Legend*, which itself was a remake of Bruce Lee's 1972 classic *Fist of Fury*, is a very different animal to either predecessor. For one thing, neither of them was a superhero movie. For another, the period detail here is gorgeous. No expense seems to have been spared recreating the era-appropriate sets and costumes, and they're lit and shot beautifully. There's proper acting too, with characters wrestling over complicated issues of personal responsibility. This is not your typical kung fu movie; it's at least as much an historical drama, although that wasn't seen as an excuse to cut corners on the action. Zhen adopts the now traditional Chinese superhero garb of peaked cap and domino mask for some spectacular and superbly staged fight scenes. (Inspired by the chauffeur's costume worn by Bruce Lee's Kato in the 1960s *Green Hornet* TV series, in Hong Kong the ensemble has become as synonymous with superheroes as capes and spandex are in the West).

Legend of the Fist: The Return of Chen Zhen

The Legend of the Lone Ranger (1952): see *The Lone Ranger* (1949)

The Legend of the Lone Ranger ★

1981, USA
Director: William A. Fraker
Cast: Klinton Spilsbury, Michael Horse, Christopher Lloyd

An extended origin story in which city lawyer John Reid (Spilsbury) becomes the Lone Ranger and rescues the president of the United States from outlaw Butch Cavendish (Lloyd).

How not to reboot a franchise. Producer and rights owner Jack Wrather replaced the brisk, focused adventures of his TV series with this confused and sloppy calamity. It has an uncanny knack of focusing on the least interesting aspects of the mythology, so we spend 35 minutes messing about before getting to the deadly ambush that conceives our hero, a further 23 before he dons the mask, and from there a full half an hour before he does anything of interest or consequence. It's exceptionally boring.

Mired in bad publicity (exacerbated by a petty legal dispute with Clayton Moore, the former Ranger and firm fan favourite), the movie was a box-office and critical disaster. Spilsbury never acted again.

The Legend of Zorro ★★★★

2005, USA
Director: Martin Campbell
Cast: Antonio Banderas, Catherine Zeta-Jones, Rufus Sewell

Ten years after the events of the previous movie, 1998 reboot *The Mask of Zorro*, California is in the process of joining the United States. Under pressure from love interest Elena (Zeta-Jones) to hang up his cape, Zorro (Banderas) must ride again to prevent a scheme to tear the nation apart.

Without Anthony Hopkins' credibility, and his dignified Don as a counterpoint, *The Legend of Zorro* risks collapsing under the weight of its own preposterousness. This is a movie so daft that Zorro's horse lives in a straw-strewn stable lit by hundreds of naked candles. Presumably it knows not to move, because the slightest swish of its tale would burn the place to the ground. There's also a lot of intentional silliness and Banderas mugs too much at times, although Zeta-Jones benefits from being given more to do. Despite these issues, and the fact it makes no sense, it's raucous good fun.

Legends of the Superheroes ★★★★

1979, USA
Directors: Bill Carruthers, Chris Darley
Cast: Ed McMahon, Adam West, Burt Ward

Television special involving numerous DC heroes horsing around and performing skits for a live audience.

A bizarre, fabulously cheesy monument to simpler times. Pre-recorded sketches break up the on-stage antics, which generally involve the superheroes being roasted by their arch-nemeses. MCing in character as Batman, Adam West single-handedly makes

this curious relic enjoyable. Say what you will of his prowess as a thespian, the man certainly commits.

LEGO DC: see Grouped Franchises

The Lego Batman Movie ★★★★

2017, USA
Director: Chris McKay
Cast: Will Arnett, Michael Cera, Rosario Dawson

Batman's (Arnett) scheme to relegate The Joker (Zach Galifianakis) to the Phantom Zone backfires when a cross-franchise gang of robots, monsters and supervillains is unleashed on Gotham.

Arnett's Batman is an amusing spoof but only just gets away with carrying his own movie. He's really more comic relief than protagonist. But this shallow and insecure version of the character is fundamentally funny, as are numerous jokes poking fun at his previous iterations. We never reach the multi-layered comedy heights of *The Lego Movie*, but any modern kids' film

The cast of NBC special *Legends of the Superheroes*

that references 1985 martial arts schlock masterpiece *Gymkata* deserves respect, awards and all the love.

The Lego Movie ★★★★★

2014, USA
Directors: Phil Lord, Christopher Miller
Cast: Chris Pratt, Will Ferrell, Elizabeth Banks

Construction worker Emmet Brickowski (Pratt) embarks on a quest to prevent the tyrannical Lord Business glueing the LEGO universe together.

Not really a superhero movie, but most of DC's big guns pop up for at least a cameo, so this delightful computer-animated family comedy deserves a mention. Will Arnett's Dark Knight-spoofing performance as Batman is the highlight.

The Lego Movie 2: The Second Part ★★★★

2019, USA
Director: Mike Mitchell
Cast: Chris Pratt, Elizabeth Banks, Will Arnett

Five years after the annihilation of the Kragle and a Duplo invasion, Bricksburg is a post-apocalyptic wasteland. Batman (Arnett) and Lucy (Banks) are kidnapped by Duplo queen Watevra Wa'Nabi (Tiffany Haddish), leaving Master Builder Emmet (Pratt) with a lot of master building to do.

The structure and emotional beats mirror those of a *Toy Story* movie, but the manic pacing, profusion of characters, humour and emotional distance (these are hardly relatable characters) make it difficult to engage in the way we need to for things to work as intended. And there's far too much plot for a movie in which quick-fire gags relentlessly charge at you from every direction. Fortunately, it's very funny, and that probably makes the conceptual flaws largely irrelevant.

The Lego Ninjago Movie ★★★

2017, USA/Denmark
Directors: Charlie Bean, Paul Fisher, Bob Logan
Cast: Jackie Chan, Dave Franco, Justin Theroux

A teen superhero team defends Ninjago City from evil Lord Garmadon (Theroux).

The familiar Lego movie formula (estranged fathers, irreverent humour, learning about feeeelings) is either getting tired or wasn't applied with the usual ingenuity. *The Lego Ninjago Movie* isn't bad, but nor is it in any way original or essential.

Leonard Part 6 ★★

1987, USA
Director: Paul Weiland
Cast: Bill Cosby, Tom Courtenay, Joe Don Baker

Former secret agent Leonard Parker (Cosby) is forced out of retirement to battle a bad guy able to control animals.

Leonard Part 6 starts with a barking trout biting a man in the trunks and then goes downhill fast. Cosby looks embarrassed, as if he's constantly shrinking away from the camera. He doesn't commit to being either super-Bond or Drebin light, leaving it unclear how his idiocy results in success. What's worse, he may not even qualify as a superhero, despite boasting what, by any definition, should be called superpowers. But I sat through this thing and it needs to have been for a reason.

LeSeurdmin ★★★

2017, USA
Director: Nicholas de Fina
Cast: Patrick Serrano, Rasheeda Moore, Brett Mannes

A disillusioned misanthrope accidentally becomes a lizard-themed superhero after getting drunk in an old Halloween costume.

This obscure animated comedy won't be for everybody. It's inept, childish and frequently in very bad taste. But there's a unique and consistent voice to the writing and at least as many laugh-out-loud moments as can be found in the typical mainstream comedy.

Lightspeed ★★

2006, USA
Director: Don E. FauntLeRoy
Cast: Jason Connery, Nicole Eggert, Daniel Goddard

Mutant malefactor The Python (Goddard) botches the assassination of Daniel Leight (Connery), but subjects the government agent to special radiation that leaves him able to move at incredible speed.

A hero in spandex tries to conceal his true identity, a villain in a cape seeks a MacGuffin. Then they fight. The End. Despite starring a former *Baywatch* babe, being directed by the man responsible for *Anaconda 3* and produced for the Sci-Fi Channel, somehow this isn't very good. It's a mystery.

Limitless ★★★

2011, USA
Director: Neil Burger
Cast: Bradley Cooper, Anna Friel, Abbie Cornish

A writer begins taking an experimental drug that expands human brain functions.

It's tough to call this a superhero movie, but like a handful of high-profile mainstream releases from around this time it belongs in the conversation. Cooper is great, De Niro is De Niro and the visual style, which is dominated by two contrasting grades, is extremely easy on the eye. Unfortunately, the script is naff and predictable.

Lik wong: see *Riki-Oh: The Story of Ricky*

Lion Man ★★★

aka *Kiliç Aslan, sword and the Claw, Aslan Adam*, 1975, Turkey
Director: Natuch Baitan
Starring: Cüneyt Arkin, Bahar Erdeniz, Charles Garret

Lion Man (Arkin), a man raised by lions (what else?), is destined to lead a rebellion against the tyrannical Kumandan Antuan (Yildirim Gencer), ruler of an unidentified medieval fiefdom. A convoluted backstory creates conflict.

A perfect role for Cüneyt Arkin (think Errol Flynn crossed with Michael Madsen), one of Turkey's most popular and prolific stars. All he has to do is look cool, keep quiet and jump about clawing at baddies. Random chunks of Dumas, Shakespeare, Kipling and Monty Python (seemingly) are thrown into the pot, but fail to coalesce into anything sensible. And I'm sure all the voices were done by the same actor. It's fun regardless, or more likely *because*, of those issues.

Lionman II: The Witchqueen ★★

aka *Lion Man 2*, 1979, Turkey
Director: Mehmet Aslan
Cast: Fevzi Mengen, Eris Akman, Necdet Kökes

Dissatisfied with life on the throne, Lion Man (or Lionman, as he's now called), goes back to the forest. In his absence many bad things happen.

Once the first act has been dealt with, this sequel essentially re-treads the battle-for-the-throne narrative of the previous movie, only with a smaller budget and, fatally, no Cüneyt Arkin.

Little Hercules in 3-D ★

2009, USA
Director: Mohamed Khashoggi
Cast: Elliott Gould, Robin Givens, Diane Venora

A 12-year-old Hercules (Richard Sandrak) sneaks away from Mount Olympus to live in Los Angeles and learn about being human.

There are numerous disconcerting aspects to this movie. Hulk Hogan's disembodied appearance in a toilet bowl is one, but the most peculiar is the way a freakishly musclebound child 'excites' a middle-aged woman. This is a dreadful thing that ends up being about Hercules competing for his school in various sporting events. The drama is supposed to stem from the audience not knowing whether he'll win, but the fact he's a demigod rather spoils the tension.

Little Superman ★★

2014, India
Director: Vinayan
Cast: Master Deny, Baby Nayanthara, Ansiba Hassan

12-year-old Willy (Deny) falls through an open manhole and into a primordial realm in which he's saved from dinosaurs by a mysterious superhero. On waking up back in his own world, Willy discovers he has inherited superpowers himself.

Little Superman emits the kind of vibe we get from pre-schooler TV shows. Set in a cosy little town full of bright colours and friendly, happy people, it comes as a shock when Willy's father is brutally murdered right in front of him. Things remain jovial as Willy tracks down the killers and either drowns them or feeds them to wild animals. Tonally it's a bit odd. The effects are poor by modern standards and a particularly dumb last act revelation is unforgivable.

Locke the Superman ★★★★

aka *Chôjin Locke, Star Warrior, Star Warrior 2, Locke the Superpower*, 1984, Japan
Director: Hiroshi Fukutomi
Cast: Keiichi Nanba, Keiko Han, Taeko Nakanishi

Industrialist Lady Kahn (Nakanishi) has been training an army of psychics, known as 'ESPers', in a bid to overthrow the human race. Locke (Nanba), a 100-year-old child and unusually powerful ESPer, accepts the government's call for help.

Based on the Witch Era arc of the popular, publisher-hopping manga *Chôjin Locke*, this first and only proper movie outing for the immortal psychic is an ambitious mix of action, pseudo-philosophy and grand themes. Locke is a reluctant hero drawn into a war against his own kind, a war that raises questions surrounding issues the X-Men franchise is best known for tackling: what makes us human, and how do we react to those we see as less human than ourselves? As anime *Locke* works in a more abstract manner than the X-movies, and although it doesn't scale the heights of similarly themed masterpieces such as *Ghost in the Shell*, it is a solid precursor to such movies and well worth 120 minutes of your time. (I saw the 2012 Discotek DVD release, which is apparently a faithful transfer of *Chôjin Locke*. There are other releases featuring different dubs and cuts of the film.)

Logan ★★★★★

2017, USA
Director: James Mangold
Cast: Hugh Jackman, Patrick Stewart, Dafne Keen

Years after the introduction of genetically engineered plants has all but stripped the world's few remaining mutants of their powers, Logan (Jackman) and Professor X (Stewart), find themselves on the fringes of society and sliding into ill health. But when a shady science experiment gets out of hand, they're both drawn back into the superhero business for one last mission.

It says a lot for Logan/Wolverine's standing in the world of popular entertainment that this R rated, action-light, emotionally taxing character study was deemed viable by a Hollywood studio. That it became one of the two most commercially successful films in the series (depending on the vagaraies of budget and inflation) is staggering. Jackman is better than he's ever been and Stewart will bring a tear to the eye of anyone with an investment in Prof X.

The Lone Ranger ★★★

1938, USA
Directors: John English, William Witney
Cast: Silver King the Horse, Lynne Roberts, Chief Thundercloud

After escaping the massacre of his posse, a Texas Ranger fakes his death and adopts masked alter ego the Lone Ranger to tackle the outlaws responsible.

Locke the Superman aka *Chôjin Locke*

The Lone Ranger made his screen debut in this Republic serial, but it's hardly the confident declaration of intent we might expect. Due to Republic's predilection for unmasking main characters in the final act, *Scooby Doo*-style, we don't actually know who our protagonist is until a few seconds from the end. Something similar is done in *The Masked Marvel*, but it doesn't suit the Lone Ranger, who should be a more charismatic presence than a full face mask and dubbed voice allows. What's more, none of the potential Rangers ever utter his "Hi-Yo Silver, away!" catchphrase (radio Ranger Brace Beemer's recitation is heard instead). Aside from these unfortunate creative decisions the standard is a little better than average for a serial. (Followed by *The Lone Ranger Rides Again*.)

The Lone Ranger ★★★★

aka *Enter the Lone Ranger*, 1949, USA
Director: George B. Seitz Jr.
Cast: Clayton Moore, Jay Silverheels, Silver

The solitary survivor of an ambush on a detachment of Texas Rangers fakes his death in order to pursue villains incognito as the Lone Ranger. He's aided in his endeavour by sidekick Tonto (Silverheels) and horse Silver (Silver).

Pilot for the hugely successful TV series. There's a pleasing simplicity to everything and we always know what's going on; who's firing at whom, from where and why. A determined voiceover streamlines scene transitions and the writers seem to have a sixth sense for what needs to be included and what doesn't. The meticulousness and efficiency with which it all comes together is striking. (In 1952 a TV movie edited from the same material aired. Titled *The Legend of the Lone Ranger*, it was designed to get latecomers to the show up to speed on the Ranger's origin story. Although a longer runtime is listed, the version I saw is identical to this pilot.)

The Lone Ranger ★★★★

1956, USA
Director: Stuart Heisler
Cast: Clayton Moore, Jay Silverheels, Lyle Betger

Illegal mining on Native American land is in danger of triggering a war. The Lone Ranger (Moore) and Tonto (Silverheels), intervene.

Surprisingly nuanced and complicated story detailing the social and political challenges of the day. Produced by Jack Wrather, who had recently picked up the rights to the TV series, it effectively relaunches the show with the same cast and crew. Despite this it feels reasonably fresh thanks to location shooting and colour cinematography. With Moore and Silverheels so comfortable in their roles, and a well-polished script devoid of fat, this is a much better movie than it may seem on paper. (Followed by *The Lone Ranger and the Lost City of Gold*).

The Lone Ranger ★★

2003, USA
Director: Jack Bender
Cast: Chad Michael Murray, Nathaniel Arcand, Anita Brown

A law student sees his brother killed by outlaws and dons a mask to avenge him.

Someone spilled *Beverly Hills 90210* in my Lone Ranger. This slick TV pilot was clearly an attempt to attract America's modern mall kids to the franchise (the Lone Ranger looks like Brad Pitt and Tonto does kung fu). Drenched in hair gel, Gen X clichés and electric guitar, it's a concept that might be pitched as a gag in a Hollywood satire.

The Lone Ranger ★★

2013, USA
Director: Gore Verbinski
Cast: Johnny Depp, Armie Hammer, William Fichtner

An elderly Tonto (Depp) recounts a version of the Lone Ranger's (Hammer) origin story in which our hero was an idiot, Silver drives the plot, and Tonto was Johnny Depp with a bird on his head.

The Lone Ranger in name only. Going the comedy route apparently means making him an oaf, and his background is fleshed out into a demeaning coincidence initiated by a magical but idiotic horse. The Ranger is then relegated to passenger status for much of the movie, with Tonto's push to the fore an additional ignominy. Depp, who is the first non-native North American to play the character (odd when you think about how progessive Hollywood is supposed to be today), is notoriously good/awful/hilarious/racist depending on factors we'll probably make our minds up about in advance. It starts out ok with a decent train-based set piece, but soon falls prey to the predictably bloated extravaganza mandated by a screenplay that's too long, too contrived, too confused, and inexplicably dumps 20 minutes of horror movie in our laps around the halfway mark.

The Lone Ranger and the Lost City of Gold ★★★★

1958, USA
Director: Lesley Selander
Cast: Clayton Moore, Jay Silverheels, Douglas Kennedy

The deaths of three Native Americans who each carried pieces of a silver medallion leads to a mystery involving much treasure.

Second (or third counting the pilot) movie spinoff from the 1949 TV series. Once again we deal with some serious themes, in particular the lot of the Native American during the era of expansion into the West. And once again we get a solid screenplay well balanced with action, intrigue and melodrama. Moore and Silverheels remain exceptional as the Ranger and Tonto.

Logan

produced) allows all of this to happen on bigger sets and with better actors. Once believed lost, a battered print was found and restored by archivists Serial Squadron.

Lord Hanuman: see *Bajrangbali* (1976)

The Lost Planet ★
1953, USA
Director: Spencer Gordon Bennet
Cast: Judd Holdren, Vivian Mason, Michael Fox

Alien scientist Dr. Grood (Fox) attempts to conquer the earth, but doesn't count on resourceful reporter Rex Barrow (Holdren) and his friends.

This sequel to *Captain Video: Master of the Stratosphere* in all but name is renouned as among the worst serials ever made, *but* at least boasts an unhinged, scenery-chewing performance from Michael Fox.

The Lone Ranger Rides Again ★★★
1939, USA
Directors: John English, William Witney
Cast: Robert Livingston, Chief Thundercloud, Silver Chief

Homesteaders attempting to settle in New Mexico are being murdered by crooked rancher Bart Dolan (Ralph Dunn) and his Black Raiders. The Lone Ranger (Livingston) comes to their aid.

The second Lone Ranger serial features a more routine structure than the first. With our hero's identity known to the audience from the start (in the original it was kept secret until the last episode), we avoid the tricky compromises resulting from needing to conceal it. And with altruistic motivation this time, the character is established as a more traditional superhero. A good budget (this is among the most expensive serials

Lost Planet Airmen
1951, USA
Director: Fred C. Brannon
Cast: Tristram Coffin, Mae Clarke, Don Haggerty

Feature-length re-edit of 1949 serial *King of the Rocket Men*. Due to the time and patience hoovered up by the typical serial, these abridged adventures can make sense. That may sound like heresy to some, but unless you're going to watch one episode each week, as originally intended, most serials become fatally repetitive. But with *King of the Rocket Men* being quite short and rather good, and this edit featuring a less satisfying conclusion, it's well worth commiting to the original.

Lucy ★★★★
2014, France
Director: Luc Besson

Cast: Scarlett Johansson, Morgan Freeman, Min-sik Choi

When a bag of synthetic baby hormones bursts in her stomach, unwilling drug mule Lucy (Johansson) harnesses an array of mental and physical abilities that mankind has hitherto been unable to access. But it comes at a cost.

Crank meets *Star Trek* via *Ghost in the Shell* with some *Run Lola Run* thrown in for good measure. Studded with excursions into too-literal symbolism and weiged down with pseudo-science babble, the movie constantly threatens to blow it. Due to it not standing still long enough for us to notice how silly things are getting, it doesn't.

M.A.N.T.I.S. ★★★

1994, USA
Director: Eric Laneuville
Cast: Carl Lumbly, Bobby Hosea, Gina Torres

A reporter and his coroner wife investigate a teched-up vigilante against a backdrop of tension and gang violence.

TV pilot with a lot to say about civic issues and institutional racism. It's a unique movie both in its presentation of the superhero (who has little impact on the plot and isn't identified until the last act) and how blunt it is. Much time is spent establishing the hypocrisies within both political and social systems, particularly how white politicians manipulate black gangbangers for their own ends. It's one of very few superhero movies to feature not only a black protagonist but a black supporting cast, director and, most unusually of all, perspective. (By the way, M.A.N.T.I.S. stands for Mechanically Augmented Neuro Transmitter Interception System. In case it's important one day.)

Machete ★★★★

2010, USA
Directors: Ethan Maniquis, Robert Rodriguez
Cast: Danny Trejo, Michelle Rodriguez, Jessica Alba

A former *Federale* known only as Machete (Trejo) drifts into Texas where he's double-crossed in a scheme to manipulate political opinion. A rampage ensues.

One part hero exaltation, one part surreal satire, one part deliriously self-indulgent homage to exploitation cinema, *Machete* wallows in its own mythic fantasies and invites audiences to do the same. It follows much the same stylistic M.O. as *Grindhouse*, Rodriguez and Quentin Tarantino's 2007 experiment in self-awareness that featured the spoof *Machete* trailer from which this movie was spawned (after much lobbying from Trejo). It's an enormous amount of fun if that aesthetic works for you. Things go off the rails in the second act, but with characters like Robert De Niro's right-wing politician, Jeff Fahey's drug kingpin and Steven Seagal's Steven Seagal, it remains entertaining when wandering aimlessly.

Machete Kills ★★★★

2013, USA
Director: Robert Rodriguez
Cast: Danny Trejo, Demián Bichir, Mel Gibson

The US president recruits Mexican secret agent Machete (Trejo) to track down and kill an arms dealer threatening the world with destruction.

The stupid is cranked up even higher in this sequel to 2010's *Machete*. The plot is looser and the cameos feel more contrived (a shapeshifting assassin cycles through celebs as if checking off items on a 'to do' list), but the absurdist joys of the original are back in spades. Gibson's star power makes his cartoon villain Voz a real treat, but if he ever rehabilitates his career film historians will have a baffling time trying to figure out why this crops up on his CV. But the movie belongs to Demián Bichir, a psychopath with a split personality and all the best lines. Sadly, the much teased third instalment of the franchise, *Machete Kills Again... In Space* has yet to materialise.

The Machine Girl ★★★

aka *Kataude mashin gâru*, 2008, Japan
Director: Noboru Iguchi
Cast: Minase Yashiro, Asami, Nobuhiro Nishihara

Pushed well beyond breaking point by the ambivalence of those denying her brother's murder, high school girl Miki Sugihara (Asami), who just happens to boast a fully automatic right arm, seeks revenge and does vigilante stuff.

Splatter punk, ero guro, new Japanese gore... whatever these ultra-violent, tasteless explosions are called this is certainly one of them. Blades swing, limbs fly and blood spurts in a maniacal orgy of revenge. It's not quite as crazy as the similarly themed *Mutant Girls Squad*, or *Full Metal Yakuza*, and it lacks the truly memorable characters the genre tends to produce, but it's fun enough and there's an English dub that's sporadically hilarious.

Maciste series: see Grouped Franchises and Peplum Movies

Magico: The Messenger of the Gods ★★★

aka *Mágico, el enviado de los dioses*, 1990, Mexico
Director: Ángel Rodríguez Vázquez
Cast: Mágico, Roberto Cañedo, Ana Luisa Peluffo

An apparently alien superhero clad in pink is charged by gods with protecting Earth from cosplayers.

This attempt to make a star of lucha libra wrestler Mágico is about as bad as a movie can be; let's get that out of the way first. The cameraman is so reluctant to move the camera that he lets characters walk out of shot before begrudgingly trailing after them, and in a stroke of genius someone decided to keep the original audio track despite the whole thing being ADR'ed. That means the on-set and studio-dubbed dialogue play simultaneously. Not only does it create a disorienting echo effect, but we also get to hear instructions and line prompts shouted out by the director. It's very funny. That makes it worthwhile and earns it an extra star. One day it might be vital to know that a luchador in full-body spandex looks just like an obese Power Ranger, which is something mankind may never have discovered without this film.

The Machine Girl aka *Kataude mashin gâru*

After various improbable things happen to people we don't know, *Man of Steel* settles into an hour of shaky-cam footage relaying the existential angst of our protagonist (nice one, fun superhero movie!), before some plot finally limps out of the muddy cinematography. Sadly, it's immediately consumed by CGI. Hating on DC films has become so ubiquitous it feels like bullying, but there are some good things here. Adams is fine, if underwritten, as Lois Lane, making an often unsympathetic archetype (largely humourless, pushy career woman) engaging and believable without softening her through flippancy. But by far the most successful aspect is Cavill's performance as the eponymous Kryptonian. Yes, he spends too much time furrowing his brow, but we can blame director Zack Snyder for that. What Cavill does so well is imbue Superman/Clark Kent/Kal-El with a suitably otherworldly immaculacy.

Major Tayfun

aka *Binbasi Tayfun*, 1968, Turkey
Director: Tolgay Ziyal
Cast: Nihat Ziyalan, Sezer Güvenirgil, Erol Tas

Major Tayfun is a combination Captain America/KiLliNK ripoff and is believed lost.

Man of Steel ★★★

2013, USA
Director: Zack Snyder
Cast: Henry Cavill, Amy Adams,
Michael Shannon

As the planet Krypton dies, Kal-El (Cavill), its first naturally born son for generations, is dispatched to expected safety on Earth. Three decades later, the leaders of a failed Kryptonian coup arrive looking to colonise our planet with genetic codes written into Kal's DNA.

The Man With the Power

1977, USA
Director: Nicholas Sgarro
Cast: Bob Neill, Tim O'Connor, Vic Morrow

While saving a turtle from a freight train, school teacher Eric Smith discovers he has telekinetic powers. It transpires his father was an alien and he begins moonlighting as a government agent. The world seems to have been denied this failed pilot on home formats, and I'm not happy about it.

Man-Thing ★★

2005, Australia
Director: Brett Leonard
Cast: Jack Thompson, Matthew Le Nevez, Steve Bastoni

After a strange swamp monster apparently replaces all the residents of a Louisiana town with Australians, it starts killing them off as a means of defending the bayous from a ruthless oil tycoon.

Allegedly this thing had a $30m budget, but about a tenth of it is visible on screen. Despite featuring a small cast and limited effects there was apparently no money to shoot in Louisiana, and so production took place in Australia. Unfortunately, the bayous and local culture are integral to every aspect of the movie, and it's obvious we're not seeing the real thing. Worse, all the actors are Australian and few even attempt an appropriate accent. It's unlikely this would have been worthwhile even if we could buy into its reality. Although proficiently made on a technical level it never manages to build a head of steam, perhaps because we don't really know why all these people are being killed. All we see, particularly the ecology porn, points to Man-Thing being a simple protector of his environment. So when a 'nexus of all realities'(?!) is thrown into the mix it demands an explanation we never get.

Manborg ★★
2011, Canada
Director: Steven Kostanski
Cast: Matthew Kennedy, Adam Brooks, Meredith Sweeney

The armies of hell have conquered Earth, but three humans and a cyborg have a plan.

Self-consciously ironic gorefest that might make you laugh a couple of times before boring you senseless. That's pretty much a guarantee. It looks like the cut scenes from a noughties video game and serves less purpose. Retro exercises in wink-wink-smuggery seldom work at feature length (there are many more hobos with shotguns than there are turbo kids).

Mandrake
1979, USA
Director: Harry Falk
Cast: Anthony Herrera, Simone Griffeth, Ji-Tu Cumbuka

Pilot for a potential NBC series that never was. It's hard to tell if it was ever released on home video, but there's no sign of it now. Going on the original promotional material there seem to have been some fantastic perms involved.

Mandrake the Magician ★★
1939, USA
Directors: Norman Deming, Sam Nelson
Cast: Warren Hull, Al Kikume, Doris Weston

Mandrake (Hull) and Lothar (Kikume) try to prevent mad scientist The Wasp (Edward Earle) from stealing a radium MacGuffin.

Mediocre serial that turns its hero into a generic detective. The only remarkable aspect is Kikume's presence as Lothar, an African prince and sidekick to Mandrake. Kikume's Hawaiian heritage (producers Columbia either weren't brave enough to cast a black actor or none were deemed suitable) makes him Hollywood's first non-white, superpowered superhero.

Mandrake vs. Killing ★★
aka Sihirbazlar Krali Mandrake Killing'in pesinde, 1967, Turkey
Director: Oksal Pekmezoglu
Cast: Güven Erte, Mine Mutlu, Sadettin Düzgün

Suave magician Mandrake (Erte) and his sidekick Lothar (Düzgün) cross swords with master criminal Killing/Kilink/KiLiNK (Mustafa Dik. Yes, that's his real name).

Stylish (the first scene is a masterpiece), ramshackle (the rest seems to have been edited at random), sexist (this is a Turkish genre movie from the 1960s) and racist (Düzgün plays Lothar in blackface!) in vaguely equal measure. The striking monochrome cinematography, degenerate characters and scuzzy tone are typical of Turksploitation, but 1968's Spy Smasher is a better example of this subgenre.

Mandroid ★★

1993, USA
Director: Jack Ersgard
Cast: Brian Cousins, Jane Caldwell, Michael Della Femina

Two scientists create a robot powered by mushrooms, then fall out over whether or not it should be evil.

You'd think that having decided to make a movie about a robot, someone might give it something to do. Instead, Mandroid just performs tasks any ordinary human could, only via an inconvenient and unreliable remote-control system. We're given no reason why the technology, the robot (or the movie) need to exist. (Followed by *Invisible: The Chronicles of Benjamin Knight*.)

Mantera ★★

2012, Malaysia
Directors: Aliyar Ali Kutty, Miza Mohamad
Cast: Tomok Shah Indrawan, Kamaliya, Mikhail Dorozhkin

Bullied high schooler Azman (Indrawan) is the chosen one in a battle between the Alliance of Light and Dark Legion.

Poor attempt to mix a traditional superhero narrative with a Transformers film (Azman has a motorcycle that can transform into bio-armour via the medium of cheap CGI). A bit like *The Guyver* if Michael Bay had made it on a budget.

Manusia enam juta dollar ★★

aka *Humans 6,000,000 Dollars*, 1981, Indonesia
Director: Ali Shahab
Cast: Wahyu Sardono, Kasino Hadiwibowo, Indrojoyo Kusumonegoro

Mown down and crippled by a fleet of tuk-tuks, police officer Dono (Sardono) is given experimental bionic limbs and, along with his incompetent colleagues, sent to rescue a nightclub singer kidnapped by a dastardly crime boss.

Starring popular Indonesian comedy troupe Warkop, this spoof of *The Six Million Dollar Man* struggles to marry theme and humour. Although the boys are known for slapstick there's relatively little on display, and the bionic aspect is never properly exploited. Dedicating early to a Bond spoof might have helped, it's pretty much what we end up with anyway. (Followed by *Gadis Bionik*.)

The Mark of Zorro ★★★★

1920, USA
Director: Fred Niblo
Cast: Douglas Fairbanks, Marguerite De La Motte, Robert McKim

In California at the turn of the 19th century, an apparently foppish aristocrat protects the vulnerable from crime and corruption.

Created by author Johnston McCulley for his 1919 novel *The Curse of Capistrano*, Zorro has perhaps informed the superhero paradigm more than any other fictional character. Batman is particularly derivative, with elements including the servant-as-confidante and cave-as-secret-sanctum lifted from the swashbuckling caballero. But in the most striking similarity (apart from the near identical setup) is both characters' adoption of the callow playboy archetype as their public persona. The influence isn't limited to Batman. Tony Stark's impish arrogance is pure Zorro, and the Superman/Lois Lane/Clark Kent 'alter ego love triangle' was played out in Spanish California years before the *Man of Steel* grappled with such emotional complexities in *Metropolis*. Whether Zorro is the first superhero is debatable (the archetype evolved gradually rather than springing to life), but there's a strong argument to be made for *The Mark of Zorro* being the first superhero movie. It draws together most of the key elements, except formalised superpowers, although our protagonist's invincibility with a rapier is a superpower in all but name. It's good, too. For those who simply don't like silent movies it's unlikely to be revelatory, but it's as exciting an example of the era's cinema as any. Douglas Fairbanks is spectacular in the lead, the impressive physicality he brings to the role setting a new standard in action movies. There's also a strong sense of romance to deepen the themes and broaden the appeal. There are many valid alternatives for the title of first superhero movie, but for me it's probably this.

The Mark of Zorro ★★★★★
1940, USA
Director: Rouben Mamoulian
Cast: Tyrone Power, Linda Darnell, Basil Rathbone

After a spell at Madrid's military academy, Don Diego Vega (Power) returns home to Spanish California to find his people under the kosh of a brutal magistrate, and his father marginalised by corrupt officials.

Loose remake of the 1920 silent. Incredibly, this is the only sound superhero 'A picture' made in Hollywood prior to *Superman* in 1978 (that's assuming you consider Zorro a superhero). There were of course B-movies (though surprisingly few), serials and TV shows, but they were largely cheap fodder aimed at kids. This was something new; a beautifully crafted demonstration from a film industry at the peak of its powers. Among many standouts now is the pace. The famous swordfight between Zorro and Rathbone's evil Captain Pasquale remains outstanding (an exceptional fencer in real life, Rathbone required no stunt double), but nimble direction helps make the rest of the densely-packed screenplay fly past. It's fitting the first proper Hollywood superhero movie should have been remade as the first *great* Hollywood superhero movie.

The Mark of Zorro ★★★
1974, USA
Director: Don McDougall
Cast: Frank Langella, Ricardo Montalban, Gilbert Roland

Tyrone Power as Zorro and Basil Rathbone as Pasquale in *The Mark of Zorro* (1940 version)

Don Diego (Langella) arrives in California to find his people exploited.

A backdoor pilot for a potential TV series. This take diligently recreates scenes from the 1940 film, and uses the same music, dialogue and often even the same blocking. Unfortunately, that only serves to highlight its comparative deficiencies. As a TV movie in its own right it's an enjoyable lark, but as a remake of a classic it falls well short of its inspiration. The cast are good though, with Langella a decent Zorro and Montalban an inspired choice for the villainous Esteban.

Mark of Zorro ★★

aka *Ah sì? E io lo dico a Zzzzorro!*, *They Call Him Zorro*, 1975, Italy/Spain
Director: Franco Lo Cascio
Cast: George Hilton, Lionel Stander, Charo López

Injured in action, Zorro (Hilton) hands his cape and mask to an incompetent lookalike.

If Zorro's mask renders him unrecognisable, why does his double need to be a lookalike? The answer, it seems, is to allow for all sorts of painfully obvious japery. Impressive period detail adds little to a repetitive live-action cartoon that's far too light on laughs for a comedy.

The Mark of Zorro

aka *La marque de Zorro Gartner*, 1975, France
Directors: Marius Lesoeur, Jesús Franco, Alain Payet
Cast: Clint Douglas, Monica Swinn, Jean-Pierre Bouyxou

Confusingly, this is one of two films titled *The Mark of Zorro* released in 1975. It was unavailable at the time of writing.

Mars Attacks the World

1938, USA

Directors: Ford Beebe, Robert F. Hill
Cast: Buster Crabbe, Jean Rogers, Charles Middleton

Feature-length edit of the the 1938 serial *Flash Gordon's Trip to Mars*. It was rushed into theatres to capitalise on the popularity of the Mercury Theatre Group's infamous *War of the Worlds* radio dramatisation.

Marvel Rising: Secret Warriors ★★

2018, USA
Directors: Alfred Gimeno, Eric Radomski
Cast: Dee Bradley Baker, Chloe Bennet, Kathreen Khavari

A gaggle of teen superheroes, each with distinct personality quirks, must learn to work together as a team in order to etc.

Marvel's attempt to launch a series of animated movies based on some of their newer and less well known characters gets off to a rocky start with *Secret Warriors*. The prime objective seems to have been to demonstrate progressive values, and with Kathreen Khavari starring as Pakistani Muslim Ms. Marvel, and Cierra Ramirez featuring as Latino lesbian Miss America, it does at least manage that much. Could have worked better as a TV series.

Marvel Super Hero Adventures: Frost Fight! ★

2015, USA
Director: Mitch Schauer
Cast: Mick Wingert, Matthew Mercer, Travis Willingham

The Avengers must defend Santa Claus (Steve Blum) from Loki (Troy Baker) and the Frost Giant Ymir (Fred Tatasciore).

Sloppy animated Christmas movie for kids. The character designs and voice work are inspired by the live action MCU and mark a concerted effort to piggyback its success.

Effort should have gone on the poor script instead. Lame visual gags (Hulk gets thrown through a tailor's window and comes out looking confused in a shirt and top hat) and the addition of Reptil (Anthony Del Rio), a child who can turn into a dinosaur, further scupper any chances of even teens finding anything to enjoy.

The Mask ★★★★★

1994, USA
Director: Chuck Russell
Cast: Jim Carrey, Cameron Diaz, Peter Riegert

Timid bank clerk Stanley Ipkiss (Carrey) comes into possession of a magical mask that transforms him into an unhinged lunatic able to defy physics.

Rambunctious mayhem is the order of the day; which is unsurprising for a character once described by its writers as a blend of Tex Avery and the Terminator. Conceived by Mike Richardson in the early 1980s, Big Head, as he was then known, has been toned down a bit for this family movie, and developed into a more benign, if still anarchic, figure. It's a great role for Carrey, who gurns, flaps, squeals and writhes his way through the alter ego scenes, but also brings pathos to Ipkiss in human form.

Mask Man ★

2017, India,
Director: Parijat Saurabh
Starring: Unknown & uncredited

A teenager uncovers his father's secret past, and a scientist is kidnapped by aliens. What will link these events? Don't ask.

The only online evidence of *Mask Man's* existence is a short article about it being selected to play at the Cannes Animation Day in 2016. It's hard to correlate the franchise-starting worldwide hit described by the movie's producers with what I've just

endured. The animation is inferior to that of the Dire Straits' Money for Nothing music video, which was made over three decades before. The dialogue sounds like it's been run through Google Translate at least twice, and the vocal performances suggest actors speaking phonetic English. There are weird visual glitches, the score occasionally drops out and at times everything freezes for a couple of frames. It's a lot like unfinished pre-viz. There are computer animated superhero movies that amount to a more subjectively unpleasant experience (*Bratz: Super Babyz* comes to mind, or that hellish Barbie thing), but I don't think there's one so objectively badly made (unless I've said the same thing in another review).

The Mask of Zorro ★★★★

1998, USA
Director: Martin Campbell
Cast: Antonio Banderas, Anthony Hopkins, Catherine Zeta-Jones

Twenty years after Don Diego de la Vega, aka Zorro (Hopkins), is imprisoned by the corrupt governor responsible for his wife's death, he escapes to find his long-lost daughter and train a replacement.

Zorro gets the Hollywood treatment in this bloated but entertaining popcorn romp. By focusing on de la Vega's successor, rather than the Don himself, Campbell frees the movie up to follow its own path. One of the biggest deviations is in the new Zorro's status. By re-branding the character as a common hoodlum of fairly modest talents, he's given far more of an arc and becomes somewhat relatable. There's also a strong dual revenge story which raises the stakes in a way that makes sense in films like this.

Masked Devil ★★★

aka *Maskeli Seytan*, 1970, Turkey
Director: Yilmaz Atadeniz
Cast: Irfan Atasoy, Feri Cansel, Necati Er

Masked Devil aka Maskeli Seytan

When smuggled gold goes missing en route from Istanbul to London, the mafia, a corrupt archaeologist, and masked vigilante Maskeli Seytan (Atasoy) all seek answers.

Even by Turkish B-movie standards the opening to *Maskeli Seytan* seems a bit excessive. As maniacal music shouts at us, the images cut violently between a car crashing, a helicopter exploding, a woman showering, a bomb going off, an exotic dancer and a knife murder. And that's just the first 60 seconds. Eventually it settles down into a fairly standard Turksploitation action movie. Most of our time is spent watching Seytan flail at bad guys in half choreographed fight scenes, before blatting around Istanbul with a saucy sidekick on the back of his motorcycle.

The Masked Marvel ★★★
1943, USA
Director: Spencer Gordon Bennet
Starring: William Forrest, Louise Currie, Johnny Arthur

The Masked Marvel (Steele) combats Japanese secret agent and saboteur Mura Sakima (Arthur), who is intent on disrupting America's war effort.

Unusual in that the identity of the villain is known from the start while the (disguised) hero remains nameless until the finale, *The Masked Marvel* is one of Republic's better serials and a good pairing with the previous year's *Spy Smasher* (while Marvel takes care of Japanese spies on American soil, Smasher does the same with their Nazi equivalents). Arthur's characterisation as the Japanese villain would make Mickey Rooney squirm (with hindsight he's perhaps the most un-PC actor of his era, as a straight white man who specialised in East asian villains and comically camp homosexuals).

Masters of the Universe ★★★
1987, USA
Director: Gary Goddard
Cast: Dolph Lundgren, Meg Foster, Billy Barty

He-Man (Lundgren), champion of Eternia, is pursued to Earth by Skeletor (Langella).

With no dual identity for its hero, no Battle Cat, no Orko and an Earth-like Eternia, *Masters of the Universe* is a dramatically different property to its cartoon forebear. Maybe that's why it proved such a disaster at the box office, although that could be down to being so awful. Regardless, it isn't possible to dislike it if you're my age.

The Matrix ★★★★★
1999, USA
Directors: The Wachowskis
Cast: Keanu Reeves, Laurence Fishburne, Carrie-Anne Moss

A computer hacker learns the world is just an artificial construct created by machines.

Monomyth + Yuen Woo-Ping x sunglasses.

The Matrix Reloaded ★★★

2003, USA
Directors: The Wachowskis
Cast: Keanu Reeves, Laurence Fishburne,
Carrie-Anne Moss

Neo (Reeves), Morpheus (Fishburne) and
Trinity (Moss) follow clues they hope will
lead them to the Source, and a means to
defeat the machines enslaving mankind.

I didn't know it was possible to be bored
and tense at the same time. The party piece
bullet time and martial arts salvos appear
painfully slow these days, and are inevitably
swallowed up by an abyss of unconvincing
CGI. This is a curious and cerebral film for
a tentpole blockbuster, though, no matter
how wonky its... everything (Neo and co.
look ridiculous and nothing makes sense).
The big problem is how to follow up the
monomyth. Neo is basically a god, so you
have to put him in his place for there to be
any conflict and therefore drama. How the
Wachowskis do that is somehow subversive
at the same time as clichéd. It's also at the
expense of offering satisfaction, because
(spoilers) we're kind of being told it's all for
nothing. Determinism is both a theme and a
fundamental problem. But this is effectively
the second act of the story, it should end
on a downer and leave it up to the the third
film to make things right. Uh-oh.

The Matrix Revolutions ★★

2003, USA
Directors: The Wachowskis
Cast: Keanu Reeves, Laurence Fishburne,
Carrie-Anne Moss

Thousands of Sentinels attack Zion while
ethereal transcendental cyber-messiah
Thomas A. Anderson (Reeves) quests for
the machine city.

Neo drops out of the narrative for lengthy
periods, abandoning us to Zion. Populated

by people we hardly know and subjected
to endless waves of identical CG attackers,
it's an extremely boring place. It's confusing
too. Nobody there even seems to be aware
of the real threat (Hugo Weaving's rogue
Agent Smith), so it's hard to invest in their
peril. Although it's harder to invest in Neo.
Reeves' performance is so spaced-out he's
impossible to relate to. A disappointing
conclusion delivers a neat bow that isn't
earned and a sense there was no point to
any of it.

Max Steel ★★

2016, USA
Director: Stewart Hendler
Cast: Ben Winchell, Josh Brener, Maria Bello

Having lost his genius father, Max McGrath
(Winchell) discovers his body can generate
huge amounts of power. In order to contain
it he bonds with an alien lifeform.
Based on a 1990s Mattel toy line and about
half as profound. Andy Garcia and Maria
Bello are wasted in what must be among
the most unoriginal and unnecessary films
of its kind. The effects are decent and it
might appeal to kids, but you'll forget about
it within moments of the end roller rolling.

Mega Mindy: see Grouped Franchises

Megamind ★★★★

2010, USA
Director: Tom McGrath
Cast: Will Ferrell, Jonah Hill, Brad Pitt

Having finally prevailed over superhero
Metro Man (Pitt), alien reprobate Megamind
(Ferrell) finds life without a nemesis dull, so
he decides to create a worthy adversary.

Even if it does become predictable, for a
while it seems like anything could happen
in *Megamind*. Essentially that's because we
identify and sympathise with the villain, not

the hero. Of course he doesn't stay bad for long, which is disappointing, but there are great voice performances and gags.

Mekura no Oichi: see *The Crimson Bat*

Men in Black ★★★★★
1997, USA
Director: Barry Sonnenfeld
Cast: Tommy Lee Jones, Will Smith, Linda Fiorentino

New York cop James Edwards (Smith) is recruited by Agent K (Jones) into a secret quasi-governmental agency responsible for policing all aliens on Earth.

Although perhaps not seen as superheroes, the Men in Black have secret identities, figurative costumes and alien technology, which places them at least as close to the superhero paradigm as Tony Stark. Smith and Jones' fantastic chemistry is well served by a screenplay that's tight, dedicated to driving things forward and extremely funny.

Men in Black II ★★
2002, USA
Director: Barry Sonnenfeld
Cast: Tommy Lee Jones, Will Smith, Rip Torn

When the MiB HQ is taken over by an angry alien in search of The Light of Zartha, agent Jay (Smith) must find some way to recover the now retired agent Kay's (Jones) memories of an episode of interstellar peacekeeping deep in his past.

Given the great strength of the first film is the dynamic between its two leads, why would this sequel choose to keep them apart for much of its runtime? It also suffers from a poorly communicated plot, a tin ear for dialogue, underwritten peripheral characters and inexplicably weak computer generated effects.

Men in Black 3 ★★★★
2012, USA,
Director: Barry Sonnenfeld
Satrring: Will Smith, Tommy Lee Jones, Josh Brolin

An alien with a vendetta against agent K (Jones) escapes prison and goes back in time seeking revenge.

For the first half hour *Men in Black 3* is worryingly reminiscent of the series' second instalment, but once we jump back in history things get on track. Brolin is an excellent stand-in for Jones, Smith conjures the old charm and the inventive plot skips along a treat.

Men in Black: International ★★★
2019, USA
Director: F. Gary Gray
Starring: Chris Hemsworth, Tessa Thompson, Kumail Nanjiani

Rookie agent Molly wright (Thompson) is assigned to MiB's London branch, where a mole appears to be facilitating an alien invasion of Earth.

Hemsworth and Thompson enjoy some (sadly not all) of the chemistry they shared in *Thor: Ragnarok*, and this fourth Men in Black movie (effectively a reboot) is at least a reminder of this franchise's ultimate potential. Unfortunately, both script and direction are woefully uninspired, while every shot, gag and playful exchange seem staged (which of course they are, but they shouldn't *seem* to be). A Rotten Tomatoes critic's score of just 22% seems harsh, though. There's nothing heinous going on here, it's all just a bit too banal.

Men of Action Meet Women of Dracula
aka *Acrobat Masters*, 1969, Philippines

Director: Artemio Marquez
Cast: Dante Varona, Eddie Torrente, Ruben Obligacion

Acrobats do battle with Dracula and his vampire horde. This movie is assumed lost. Given that title and the synopsis it seems unbearably cruel.

Meng long zheng dong: see *Bruce Lee Against Superman*

Mercury Man ★★★

aka *Ma noot lhek lai*, 2006, Thailand
Director: Bhandit Thongdee
Cast: Wasan Khantaau, Anon Saisangcharn, Jinvipa Kheawkunya

Chan (Khantaau), a firefighter granted superpowers after being stabbed with an amulet, must prevent terrorist Osama bin Ali (Saisangcharn) destroying America.

The fight choreography is *Mercury Man's* greatest asset in more ways than one. It's exceptionally good but, more importantly, when characters aren't fighting they're usually doing something boring (Chan does a lot of soul searching, training and general pondering). Once he's suited up he looks good and the old-school 'rescuing citizens from peril' stuff is highly entertaining.

Metal Hero Series: see Grouped Franchises

Metal Man ★

2008, USA
Director: Ron Karkoska
Cast: Reggie Bannister, Samuel Nathan Hoffmire, P. David Miller

A college kid testing a professor's supersuit somehow becomes fused to it, and must defend himself from an evil scientist bent on acquiring the secret technology.

Sound the alarm, it's a Tom Cat movie. This is their first superhero mockbuster and although it was released the same week *Iron Man* hit stores, the plot is unrelated – not only to *Iron Man* but also to the basic concepts of dramatic structure adhered to by most authors since Greek playwright Aeschylus laid them out 2,000 years ago. If I had a gun to my head I might admit this is among the least offensive Tom Cats, but it's still worse than every superhero movie made by every production company that isn't Tom Cat. And I remind you there are four Inspector Gadget movies.

The Meteor Man ★★

1993, USA
Director: Robert Townsend
Cast: Robert Townsend, Marla Gibbs, Eddie Griffin

A mild-mannered teacher struck by lightning transforms into a superhero.

The first of two superhero movies starring, written and directed by comedian Robert Townsend (the unrelated but equally family-friendly *Up, Up and Away* followed seven years later). On this occasion he takes a scattershot approach to the script, throwing everything imaginable at the screen to see what sticks. It's not an entirely successful approach but his lack of screen presence is the bigger issue, with endless superstar cameos (Bill Cosby, Don Cheadle, Luther Vandross, most rappers) only serving to highlight a lack of charisma. In spite of all that, it's a strangely charming movie with a social conscience to be applauded. It also features a scenery-chewing James Earl Jones in a succession of absurd wigs, and that alone makes it worth seeing.

Ang Mga lawin

1963, Philippines
Director: Artemio Marquez
Cast: Bernard Bonin, Robert Campos, Von Serna

Adapted from the previous year's *Espesyal Komiks* series. This movie is believed lost.

The Middle Finger ★★

2016, Ireland
Director: Séamus Hanly
Cast: Séamus Hanly, Casey Jones, Simon Mulholland

Dennis (Hanly), an 18-year-old repeating his final year of school, is chosen by aliens to fight evil.

I guess I'm calling this an Irish mumblecore superhero spoof. It looks dated with all its empty streets, 90s styles and old-school mobile phones. Whether or not that's a deliberate decision I'm not sure. The subtle humour is hit-and-miss but grows on you despite a lack of likeable characters.

Mighty Man

1978, South Africa
Director: Percival Rubens
Starring: Unknown

This movie is considered lost. Very little information is available on what was billed as the 'African Superman'. Aside from the uniqueness of being a properly produced, released and distributed Zulu language superhero film, it's possibly the first in any language other than English to feature a black superhero in the lead role. Potentially the most important missing superhero film.

Mighty Morphin' Power Rangers: see Grouped Franchises and Power Rangers for cut-and-shuts derived from the TV series. See also *Turbo: A Power Rangers Movie* (1997) and *Power Rangers* (2017). Or don't.

Mighty Morphin Power Rangers: The Movie ★★

1995, USA

Director: Bryan Spicer
Cast: Karan Ashley, Johnny Yong Bosch, Steve Cardenas

The tyrannical Ivan Ooze (Paul Freeman) escapes imprisonment and disables Zordon (Nicholas Bell), depriving the Rangers of their powers. Their only chance to save Earth requires them to travel to a distant planet and prove themselves in combat.

This first American theatrical outing for the mystifyingly popular Power Rangers (based on Toei's Super Sentai) is much like the TV show: the Rangers are dull, the monsters are stupid, the action is basic, the narrative is nonsensical and the overall effect is nausea-inducing. Apart from that it's fine. (Followed by *Turbo: A Power Rangers Movie*.)

Mighty Mouse in the Great Space Chase ★★★

1982, USA
Directors: Ed Friedman, Lou Kachivas, Marsh Lamore, Gwen Wetzler, Kay Wright, Lou Zukor
Cast: Alan Oppenheimer, Diane Pershing

Pernicious space cat Harry the Heartless (Oppenheimer) kidnaps Pearl Pureheart (Pershing), who summons Mighty Mouse (also Oppenheimer) to save her. Over and over again.

With this feature-length 'movie' no more than a shoddily edited collection of *Mighty Mouse* shorts (explaining why it credits six directors but only two actors, which must be a first), the narrative borders on the surreal. It's so repetitive you may as well dip in and out at leisure – you'd be unlikely to miss anything that won't come round again. But it is worth at least a look. The extent to which characters, environments, scenarios (and everything else) are drawn from classic serials is striking, and it's interesting to see where those elements can be taken when animation eliminates practical and budgetary constraints.

Mighty Rock

1969, Philippines
Director: Nilo Saez
Cast: Jing Abalos, Lourdes Medel, Lucita Soriano

A wheelchair-bound boy is bitten by one of his pet ants and develops superpowers. He uses them to pursue the gang who killed his love interest's brother. This movie is believed lost.

Mil Máscaras series: see Grouped Franchises and Luchador Movies

Minerva

1960, Philippines
Director: B.F. Ongpauco
Cast: Celia Fuentes, Jess Medina, Doris Estrella

This movie is believed lost.

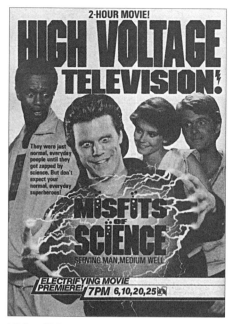

Misfits of Science

Minty: The Assassin ★

2009, USA
Director: Eugene Baldovino
Cast: Elina Madison, Anthony Ray Parker, Chip Joslin

Powered by chocolate and trained to be the world's greatest assassin, Minty (Madison) finds herself battling numerous colourful supervillains as she attempts to rescue her mentor, Big Boss (Parker).

Shot in empty offices by a cinematographer with no spacial awareness and who can't hold his hands still, *Minty the Assassin* would probably be unwatchable even without all the jokes.

Mirageman ★

2007, Chile/USA
Director: Ernesto Díaz Espinoza
Cast: Marko Zaror, María Elena Swett, Ariel Mateluna

A nightclub bouncer obsessed with physical fitness and kung fu becomes a superhero after rescuing a kidnapped news reporter.

Amateurish debacle so badly lit and shot it's hard to tell what's happening. It tries to do too many things (love story, media satire, social commentary...) instead of sticking with what it might have been good at (fighting).

Mirrorman Reflex ★★

2006, Japan
Director: Kazuya Konaka
Cast: Ryô Karato, Miku Ishida, Nobuyuki Ishida

After dying in battle, Japanese soldier Akira Kageyama (Karato) is resurrected, becoming a 'mirror demon', a supernatural agent who can grow to an enormous size. He uses his new abilities to defend the Manifest Realm from spirits.

Culled from a DVD based attempt to reboot the popular 1970s tokusatsu TV show, this re-edited feature-length adventure returns to that series' dark origins whilst shedding its characters and mythology. With demons, spirits and Japanese folklore featuring over classic monsters, *Mirrorman Reflex* is skewed for an older audience than most kyodai hero properties, and only benefits as a result. Nevertheless, it suffers with the same narrative jerkiness fans will be familiar with from similar TV show cut-and-shuts.

Misfits of Science ★★★★

1985, USA
Director: James D. Parriott
Cast: Dean Paul Martin, Kevin Peter Hall, Mark Thomas Miller

An arms manufacturer unveils its latest weapon of mass destruction, and only an eccentric team of scientists, oddballs and genetic anomalies have the power to... prevent... something?

Marvellous, if largely nonsensical, feature-length pilot for the short-lived TV series. Although alledgely inspired by *Ghostbusters*, it's more akin to *Scooby Doo*. We spend a little too long setting things up (then again it is a pilot), but once we're moving the pace is breakneck, and the finale, in which lens filters and editing are coordinated with an intense soundtrack, is unforgettable.

The Missing Lady ★★★

1946, USA
Director: Phil Karlson
Cast: Kane Richmond, Barbara Read, George Chandler

The Shadow (Richmond) investigates the murder of an antique dealer and theft of a jade statue.

With underworld heavies in jazz clubs and the Shadow being blamed for murder, this final movie in the brief Kane Richmond series feels just like its predecessor, *Behind the Mask*. Fortunately, it's a little better. The plot is intriguing enough to keep us plugged in, Richmond is nicely settled in the role and the comic relief is well handled.

Missy and the Maxinator ★

2009, USA
Director: D.J. Lynch
Cast: Kevin Winters, Colleen Lynch, Neal Shea

An orphaned high schooler realises he's developing superpowers, and that his teachers are murdering his classmates.

Horribly acted, incompetently written and frequently out of focus derivative drivel. The responsibility has to lie at the feet of director D.J. Lynch (also the only credited writer), who was moonlighting from his job as a sound mixer on animated TV shows like *Teenage Mutant Ninja Turtles*. The kids are non-actors and can't be blamed for whatever it is they're doing.

Mister Freedom: see *Mr. Freedom*

Mister X: see *Avenger X*

Mizu no naka no hachigatsu: see *August in the Water*

Model by Day ★★

1994, USA
Director: Christian Duguay
Cast: Famke Janssen, Stephen Shellen, Clark Johnson

After her roommate is carjacked, a fashion model turns superhero. Before long she's juggling Chinese assassins, lookalikes and Russian gangsters, all while exacting brutal vengeance for minor slights.

Model by Day is every bit as improbable as it sounds. The paper-thin plot is slipped in between incessant montages full of pouting wannabes, exposed flesh and soft rock. The overall effect is like an R rated cross between *Black Scorpion* and *Miami Vice*. A pre-James Bond Famke Janssen is way too good for this silliness and knows it.

Monarch of the Moon ★★

2005, USA
Director: Richard Lowry
Cast: Blane Wheatley, Monica Himmel, Brent Moss

America's greatest champion, bee-themed superhero The Yellow Jacket (Wheatley), must destroy a doomsday ray created by moon Nazis.

Attempt to spoof the perky optimism of early serials. It's enthusiastic and there are some laughs, but it feels like an in-joke that got out of hand more than it does a real movie made with audiences in mind. See *J-Men Forever* instead.

Moonlight Mask: see Grouped Franchises

Moron 5.2: The Transformation ★★

2014, Philippines
Director: Wenn V. Deramas
Cast: Luis Manzano, Billy Crawford, Marvin Agustin

Five idiots are electrocuted by an airport runway landing light they mistake for an alien artefact. Assuming it has given them superpowers (that they inexplicably fail to test), the cohorts become crimefighters.

This sequel to 2012's *Moron 5 and the Crying Lady* reunites the team and re-treads much of the same ground, which means our heroes misunderstand things for an hour and a half while their antagonist Beckie

(John Lapus) does everything she/he can to ruin their lives. It's all very amiable and there are moments so camp it's impossible not to smile, but, as can sometimes be the case with Pinoy comedy, the sense of humour is perhaps a little inaccessible for Western audiences.

Mosaic ★★

2007, USA
Director: Roy Allen Smith
Cast: Anna Paquin, Kirby Morrow, Cam Clarke

A young actress gains powers from an ancient rune, and uses them to prevent a sorcerer taking over the world.

Part of the Stan Lee Presents direct-to-DVD animated series. Expect lazily written, poorly executed generic superhero antics.

A Mosquito-Man ★★★

aka *Sucker*, 2013, USA
Director: Michael Manasseri
Cast: Michael Manasseri, Kimberley Kates, Jordan Trovillion

Having been used as a test subject by ethically challenged scientists, loser Jim Crawley (Manasseri) finds he has powers.

Schlocky comedy that borrows from Spider-Man, *The Fly*, *Sin City*, Troma and just about everything else. The visual style is too busy but the script and performances are fine. Comes together well for a low-budget indie.

The Mounties Are Coming: see *The Vigilante's Are Coming*

The Movie Extra: see *Superhero Man*

Mr. and Mrs. Incredible ★★★★

aka *San kei hap*, *Incredibly Ever After*, 2011, China

Director: Vincent Kok
Cast: Louis Koo, Sandra Ng, Zhang Wen

Retired husband-and-wife superheroes Huan, aka Gazer Warrior (Koo), and Red, aka Aroma Warrior (Ng), spend their days reminiscing and chatting with neighbours. But the peace can't last and a gangster's attempt to seize control of their village forces them back into costume.

Where could these filmmakers possibly have gotten the idea for a movie about an 'incredible' married superhero team dealing with the monotony of retirement? To be fair, it's easy to put Pixar's masterpiece out of your mind once things get going – there are no practical similarities. This is a much quieter and more thoughtful movie reliant on subtle character touches and deadpan humour. That won't be for everyone, but action fans will love the third act and it's all extremely beautiful.

Mr. Freedom ★★★
1968, France
Director: William Klein
Cast: John Abbey, Delphine Seyrig, Donald Pleasence

Jingoistic ultra-patriot Mr. Freedom (Abbey) leaves the USA for France, where he must prevent a communist invasion. Greeted less than enthusiastically by the locals, he makes the decision to destroy the country instead of helping it.

Surreal and unusually vicious satire on US foreign policy that works like a dry run for *Team America: World Police*. After a strong start, *Mr. Freedom* soon degenerates into a slapdash barrage of barbs that, although perhaps even more pertinent today than they were 50 years ago, aren't clever enough to earn the film's condescending tone. It's frustrating because the chutzpah on display is staggering and the ultimate point one that's worth making.

Mr. India ★★★★
1987, India
Director: Shekhar Kapur
Cast: Anil Kapoor, Sridevi, Amrish Puri

Compassionate optimist Arun (Kapoor) struggles to make ends meet providing a ramshackle home to dozens of orphans. After borrowing his dead father's invisibility device, Arun attracts the attention of crime boss Mogambo (Puri).

A cross between *Annie*, *Chitty Chitty Bang Bang* and James Bond, *Mr. India* has been a Bollywood family staple for over three decades. There's a lightness of touch, a joyous sense of humour and the songs are as uplifting as they come. Puri plays it wonderfully over-the-top and is a definite highlight, but it's Kapoor who holds things together. Apparently he wasn't among the first choices for the role, but it's impossible to imagine anyone else as the caring Arun.

Mr. Superinvisible ★★
aka *L'inafferrabile invincibile Mr. Invisibile*, 1970, Italy
Director: Antonio Margheriti
Cast: Dean Jones, Philippe Leroy, Gastone Moschin

A scientist is rendered invisible by an elixir sent to him by an Indian colleague. Wacky japes follow, whether or not we really want them to.

Who'd have thought the director of *Yor, the Hunter from the Future* would have skeletons like this in his closet? *Mr. Superinvisible* is a blatant attempt to duplicate the Disney formula behind high-concept fantastical family fare such as *The Love Bug* and *The Computer Wore Tennis Shoes*. While it's a reasonable enough idea and manages to drum up the desired vibe, flat direction, a weak script and awkward dubbing leave it mired in sub-B-movie territory.

Mr. X ★

2015, India
Director: Vikram Bhatt
Cast: Emraan Hashmi, Amyra Dastur, Tanmay Bhat

An elite anti-terrorist agent gains the power of invisibility when he's nearly murdered by a corrupt policeman.

Humourless and too tense revenge fantasy with no redeeming features. The script is stupid, visual effects hopeless, songs boring and there's so little joy to the thing it sucks the life out of you.

Mugamoodi ★★

2012, India
Director: Myshkin
Cast: Jiiva, Narain, Nassar

In an attempt to impress the object of his affection (the disinterested daughter of a local police chief), struggling martial arts devotee Anandan (Jiiva) puts his fight skills to use as a vigilante. It isn't long before crime boss Anguchamy (Narain) tires of the aggravation it's causing him and frames Anandan for murder.

Essentially a love letter to kung fu cinema and in particular Bruce Lee, *Mugamoodi* boasts superb fight choreography, but it doesn't do as well with the screenplay and characterisation. It's generally claimed to be the first Kollywood (the name given to the Tamil filmmaking community based in Chennai) superhero movie, but I think that credit goes to 2009's *Kanthaswamy*.

Mujeok 600manbul: see *The Invincible Six-Million Dollar Man*

Mysterious Doctor Satan

Mutant Girls Squad ★★★

aka *Sentô shôjo: Chi no tekkamen densetsu*,
2010, Japan
Directors: Noboru Iguchi, Yoshihiro Nishimura,
Tak Sakaguchi
Cast: Tak Sakaguchi, Asami, Naoto Takenaka

Outsider Rin (Sugimoto) discovers she is
an Elder, one of a despised race of ancient
superbeings. Pursued by death squads, she
is taken in by a militant group of her fellow
Elders and taught to harness her powers.

If David Cronenberg went out of his mind
on meth and made a superhero movie,
this is what it might look like. There are all
sorts of problems (buying into a supporting
character who can extend a full-size chain
saw from her butt is not the least of them),
but it's stylish, funny and even touching.
Occasionally. Sort of.

My Hero Academia the Movie
★★★★

aka *Boku no Hero Academia the Movie*, *My Hero
Academia: The Two Heroes*, 2018, Japan
Director: Kenji Nagasaki
Cast: Justin Briner, Christopher Sabat, Ray Chase

Recently graduated from superhero school,
Izuku Midoriya (Briner) accompanies the
indomitable All Might (Sabat) to a social
event on an isolated island, but soon finds
himself needing to help save its inhabitants
from the evil Wolfram (Keith Silverstein).

Coming between the third and fourth
seasons of the *My Hero Academia* anime
series, this first movie for the franchise is
confusing, at least at first. Reading up on
the backstory it becomes apparent we're
in a world in which 80 percent of the
population boasts a 'quirk' (special power),
and that Midoriya shares a particularly
potent quirk with the patriarchal All
Might. Whatever. While there's probably
much that will be missed by newbies,

there's enough good stuff that it doesn't
matter. *The Dragon Ball* meets *Die Hard*
narrative flies by in a flurry of exciting
set pieces and hyperbole. The appealing
animation, thoughtful scenarios, challenging
characters, universal themes and more
mean there's much in common with the
Fullmetal Alchemist anime films.

My Super Ex-Girlfriend ★★★

2006, USA
Director: Ivan Reitman
Cast: Uma Thurman, Luke Wilson, Anna Faris

When project manager Matthew Saunders
(Wilson) dumps his superhero girlfriend
Jenny Johnson, aka G-Girl (Thurman), she
uses her powers to make his life a misery.

Predictable mainstream Hollywood action
comedy that fits with the likes of *Hancock*
and *Sky High* as a great idea compromised
by sacrifices made to mass consumption.
Thurman is very good as a neurotic mess
and Faris, who can do no wrong even with
material shoddier than this, has funny
bones. So with Reitman's direction and
Wilson's everyman seeming too bland, the
men really let the women down on this one.

Mysterious Doctor Satan ★★★

1940, USA
Directors: John English, William Witney
Cast: Eduardo Ciannelli, Robert Wilcox,
William Newell

Rich orphan Bob Wayne (Wilcox) learns
his long-deceased father was actually the
masked superhero known as Copperhead.
When his guardian is murdered by heinous
genius Doctor Satan (Ciannelli), who is
building a robot army, Wayne adopts the
Copperhead persona and tries to stop him.

With the plot revolving around a wealthy
orphan and animal-themed crimefighter
named B. Wayne, it may not be a surprise

to learn the screenplay was originally intended as a vehicle for Superman (what?). A couple of unusual features lift it above the average. First, the villain is excellent. Whether deliberate or not he's reminiscent of Ernest Thesiger's Doctor Pretorius from *Bride of Frankenstein*, and he gets way more screen time than is typical for a mere serial antagonist. Second, we're always on the move. There are the usual scenes of men talking earnestly in smart hats and boring offices, but there's also a greater variety of locations than we're used to.

The Mysterious World of Elias Paniki ★★★

aka *Ang mahiwagang daigdig ni Elias Paniki*, 1989, Philippines
Director: Carlo J. Caparas
Cast: Ramon Revilla, Maria Isabel Lopez, Atong Redillas

Vampire hunter Elias the Bat (Revilla) plies his trade.

Among the final anting-anting movies of Ramon Revilla before a move into politics curtailed his magical amulet adventures (they would pick up again after he left office). This one has a more supernatural bent than most, and also more of an edge: it's a big surprise to see our hero beating a vampire to death with a hammer in the opening scene. The various ghosts, giant skeletons and werewolves are absurd and make it more fun than most similar movies.

Mystery Men ★★★

1999, USA
Director: Kinka Usher
Cast: Ben Stiller, Janeane Garofalo, William H. Macy

Having cleaned up Champion City's streets, superhero Captain Amazing (Greg Kenner) finds his popularity on the wain. In need of a high-profile challenge he schemes to have supervillain Casanova Frankenstein (Geoffrey Rush) released from prison, but is immediately captured by him. An inept team of wannabes step up to the plate.

Commercials director Kinka Usher tries to distance *Mystery Men* from the Hollywood mainstream with some bold camerawork and left-field characters. Hank Azaria's Blue Raja (special power: fork throwing) and Janeane Garofalo's Bowler (so called because she's armed with a supernatural bowling ball containing her father's skull) are highlights, but although it's funny it's never quite as funny as the sum of its parts should be.

Nardong Putik

aka *Kilabot ng Cavite*, 1972, Philippines
Director: Tony Cayado
Cast: Ramon Revilla, Max Alvarado,
Gloria Romero

Biopic of notorious criminal and self-styled folk hero Leonardo Manicio, better known as Nardong Putik, who credited his magical amulet for giving him superpowers. Sadly unavailable (or possibly even lost, opinion is divided), the movie played an important role in the history of Philippine cinema for two reasons. First, it revitalised the career of former star and future senator Ramon Revilla when it proved a surprise hit. Second, it became the template for the numerous anting-anting movies that would follow. Many starred Revilla as either a simple farmer or criminal anti-hero gifted superpowers in the face of injustice.

Nardong Putik Version II

aka *Kilabot ng Cavite Version II*,
1984, Philippines
Director: Jose Yandoc
Cast: Ramon Revilla, Julie Fortich,
Marilou Bendigo

Like the original 1972 film, it's hard to say if this remake still exists. The (presumably unofficial) DVD release I saw is actually a different Revilla film, 1979's *Tonyong Bayawak*, while the version on YouTube is the similar *Boy Putik*, also from 1979, also starring Revilla. Given how similar these anting-anting movies are it's easy to see where the confusion comes in.

Nausicaä of the Valley of the Wind
★★★★★

aka *Kaze no tani no Naushika*, *Nausicaa*,
1984, Japan
Director: Hayao Miyazaki
Cast: Sumi Shimamoto, Mahito Tsujimura,
Hisako Kyôda

In a post-apocalyptic feudal future, a young princess fulfils a prophecy to become the saviour of her people.

Sublime pre-Ghibli anime from Hayao Miyazaki. Environmentalism, the Japanese master's great passion, is the central theme, and a more potent clarion call for action can hardly be imagined. The animation is stunning, of course, and the overall effect breathtaking. Avoid hacked-up attempts at Americanisation such as 1985's *Warriors of the Wind*, a heavily edited and criminally inept English language version of the film. There is a perfectly good vaguely recent dub (featuring Alison Lohman and Patrick Stewart) for those who might be averse to subtitles, but go with the original Japanese for the optimum experience.

The New Mission of Judex: see *Judex's New Mission*

The New Original Wonder Woman: see *Wonder Woman* (1975)

Next Avengers: Heroes of Tomorrow ★★★

2008, USA
Directors: Jay Oliva, Gary Hartle
Cast: Tom Kane, Noah Crawford, Brenna O'Brien

With most of the Avengers now long dead, their (remarkably similar in appearance and temperament) children have been raised in secrecy by Tony Stark (Kane), and must now face the villain responsible for their parents' demise: Ultron (also Kane).

This animated movie is hazy on stuff like why the African defender of Wakanda has an American accent, but let's gloss over that. Fans of the original characters will probably hate this emasculated gimmick, but it's made for young children and they have every chance of enjoying it.

Nick Fury: Agent of Shield ★★★★

1998, USA
Director: Rod Hardy
Cast: David Hasselhoff, Lisa Rinna, Sandra Hess

Former SHIELD director Nick Fury (Hoff) is pulled out of retirement to save the world from a deadly virus wielded by Andrea Von Strucker, aka Viper (Hess).

Stan Lee once claimed Hoffman's portrayal of Fury was definitive, which may explain why the former Knight Rider expected to reprise the role in the MCU. *Avengers* director Joss Whedon quipped of casting Hasselhoff, "He wasn't available, so we got Sam (L. Jackson)". Implied criticism of Hasselhoff's performance didn't just come from Whedon, and apparently Jackson himself chipped in with, "I watched David Hasselhoff... and decided I was not going to do any of that". But what these two titans of the superhero landscape fail to appreciate is the sheer joy of watching Hasselhoff respond to someone who believed him dead by saying "I was, but now I'm better!" This movie is hilarious.

Night is Day: The Movie ★

2012, UK
Director: Fraser Coull
Cast: Chris Somerville, Kirsty Anderson, Steven McEwan

An ordinary man with extraordinary powers tries to prevent a witch demon destroying the world. In Glasgow.

Some shots are out of focus and a similarly low standard pervades all other disciplines. Everyone is overly stern, with lighthearted moments so rare and deadpan as to hardly count, although we can possibly put that down to the Scottish sense of humour. I don't think we can say the same for the absurd witch demon. It's as if Rita Repulsa invaded the set of *Taggart*.

David Hasselhoff as the title character in
Nick Fury: Agent of Shield

technically it exists in the same universe as *Manimal*, so it's got that going for it.

Northstar ★

1986, USA
Director: Peter Levin
Cast: Greg Evigan, Deborah Wakeham, Mitchell Ryan

Zapped by sunlight on a spacewalk, Major Jack North (Evigan) returns to Earth with incredible solar-powered superpowers.

It's no surprise this pilot wasn't picked up. Between the angry, arrogant jerk of a lead character, the poorly written story and the weak technical elements, *Northstar* manages to be awful in almost every way.

La nouvelle, mission de Judex: see *Judex's New Mission*

NightMan ★★

1997, Canada/USA
Directors: Nick Daniel, Mark Jones, Glen A. Larson
Cast: Matt McColm, Earl Holliman, Derek Webster

Rock saxophonist Johnny Domino (McColm) is tuned into the evil frequency when he's struck by lightning in a cable car accident (yup, that's your setup). He then battles weapons thieves with his many gadgets.

Shot on low-quality video, lumbered with actors who are winging it, inaudible sound and apparently temporary special effects, *NightMan* plays out like a taped rehearsal, which only serves to make the inherently silly concept seem even sillier. Matt McColm (a model turned stuntman turned actor turned stuntman again) is atrocious as Man/ Domino; just a hulking slab of handsome constantly on the brink of forgetting his next line. There's a certain retro charm and

Oath of Zorro: see *Behind the Mask of Zorro*

Officer Downe ★★★★

2016, USA
Director: Shawn Crahan
Cast: Kim Coates, Tyler Ross, Meadow Williams

In a surreal alternate Los Angeles ravaged by sleaze and crime, a naive rookie cop is assigned to back up the immortal Officer Terry Downe (Coates).

Coates' portrayal brings to mind Maniac Cop before any established superhero, while the specific combination of extreme violence, gore and black humour feels Japanese. It's probably not wise to linger too long on the morality (or objective quality) of *Officer Downe*, but if you like self-aware, stylised genre movies, or just want to see a gun-wielding nun's head explode, here you go. Those of a sensitive disposition don't need to go near this thing.

Ōgon batto: see Grouped Franchises

The Oily Maniac ★★★

aka *You gui zi*, 1976, Hong Kong
Director: Meng Hua Ho
Cast: Danny Lee, Ping Chen, Lily Li

Unable to protect the woman he loves from gangsters, crippled lawyer Shen Yuan (Lee) performs a magic ritual to turn himself into an avenging oil monster.

A vague motivation sees our ostensible hero flit around between protecting and murdering people, while the screenplay spends so long on irrelevant diversions it's easy to forget about the main plot. There's some imagination and a pleasing B-movie style to everything that makes it enjoyable. Although billed as horror its only adult content is a touch of sleaze.

Ophelia Learns to Swim ★★★★

2000, USA

Director: Jürgen Vsych

Cast: Julia Lee, Lauren Birkell, Camille Langfield

Stereotypical valley girl Ophelia (Lee) is drawn into a world of female superheroes when she breaks a witch's broom.

Lo-fi comedy mixing broad humour with social satire. This is probably not something that should be recommended to teen boys looking forward to *Venom 2*, but it's well written, intelligent, funny and worth your time. Just be aware it's *very* lo-fi.

Orgazmo ★★

1997, USA

Director: Trey Parker

Cast: Trey Parker, Dian Bachar, Robyn Lynne Raab

An uncomplicated Mormon becomes a kind of superhero when his fiancée is kidnapped by an angry pornographer.

Reaching screens around the same time as *South Park*, writer-director Trey Parker's better-known comedic property, *Orgazmo* is a satirical farce that takes aim at several familiar targets including Mormonism and Hollywood hypocrisy. It's nowhere near as sharp as Parker's later work with Matt Stone, but has its moments.

Orishas: The Hidden Pantheon ★

2016, Canada

Director: Yann Kieffoloh Jr.

Cast: Arielle Evora, Janice Choma, Milan Ewing

A disparate group of people discover they have superpowers, then sit around in rooms looking moody.

Inspired by aspects of the Yoruba religion (which has its home in modern-day Nigeria) dealing with spirits in human form, the idea of an African-Canadian perspective on an unfamiliar mythology may sound exciting. Unfortunately, the performances are weak even before you take into account the line stumbles (in the age of digital cameras this is inexcusable: do the take again!) and the technical aspects worse. If you can't coherently shoot two people talking....

Outer Man ★★

aka *Autâman*, 2015, Japan

Director: Minoru Kawasaki

Cast: Yasuhisa Furuhara, Gero, Gen Ichikawa

Hilarity abounds when an alien invader is mistaken for a popular TV superhero.

Obscure tokusatsu spoof in which kyodei heroes squash model buildings and shout at each other. Completely incomprehensible, I suspect not only because I couldn't find a version with English subtitles.

P.U.N.K.S. ★★

1999, USA
Director: Sean McNamara
Cast: Tim Redwine, Kenneth A. Brown,
Patrick Renna

Unscrupulous industrialist Edward Crow
(Henry Winkler) develops a mechanical
suit that gives its wearer powers such as
superhuman strength, but it's stolen by
school kids.

Achingly 90s family techno-adventure in
which our misfit heroes contrive to thwart
the villain's nefarious plans in increasingly
cartoonish ways. It's not as obnoxious as it
could be but, other than nostalgia junkies,
it's hard to see who the audience might be.

Painkiller Jane ★

2005, USA
Director: Sanford Bookstaver
Cast: Emmanuelle Vaugier, Eric Dane,
Richard Roundtree

After being exposed to a deadly bioweapon
created by her own side, Army Captain Jane
Browning (Vaugier) develops superpowers
that render her hyper sensitive and near
immortal. She will need her new abilities to
evade a secretive element within the army
hoping to conceal their involvement in the
illegal project.

Based on a comic book character created
by Jimmy Palmiotti and Joe Quesada,
Painkiller Jane has somehow found her
way to the bargain basement end of the
superhero movie spectrum. Cheap looking
even for the Sci-Fi Channel, this low-budget
TV movie served as a kind of precursor to
the TV series that followed (although it's
not directly related). It's a dull and formulaic
affair almost completely devoid of action,
and if disinterest could manifest itself into
a physical form, it would look like Richard
Roundtree in this movie.

Palos series: see Grouped Franchises

Panji Tengkorak ★★★

aka *Pandji Skull*, 1971, Indonesia
Director: A. Harris
Cast: Deddy Sutomo, Shan Kuang Ling Fung, Maruli Sitompul

Masked vigilante Panji Tengkorak (Sutomo) helps two sisters get revenge on the gang who killed their master.

Based on the popular Indonesian silat comic published in 1968, this first *Panji Tengkorak* adaptation (a belated sequel followed in 1983 and a reboot is claimed to be in the works) isn't the easiest movie to follow without subtitles. The minimalist plot, an imposter Tengkorak and the array of near identical looking actresses in key roles see to that. But an abundance of well-staged fight scenes (shot by an unidentified Hong Kong production company) make it worth a look for fans of this kind of thing.

Panji Tengkorak vs Jaka Umbaran ★★★★

1983, Indonesia
Director: M. Sharieffudin
Cast: Deddy Sutomo, Teddy Purba, Siska Widowati

A group of supernaturally capable female martial artists fight people. Sometimes Panji Tengkorak (Sutomo) or Jaka Umbaran (Purba) fight people. Then they all fight each other.

A wealth of wacky characters with *Street Fighter*-style special moves and powers wander around a wasteland with no obvious objective. Erratic editing and an impressive commitment to the camera's zoom function ensure the fights remain as incoherent and absurd as the plot. In keeping with the previous movie, *Panji Tengkorak*, the titular

hero doesn't spend much time on screen, but the unidentified ladies are more than entertaining enough. So bad it's great!

Paper Man ★★★

2009, USA
Directors: Kieran Mulroney, Michele Mulroney
Cast: Jeff Daniels, Emma Stone, Ryan Reynolds

An author suffering from a compulsive disorder moves to the wilderness and forms an unlikely friendship with a troubled teen. Also, his imaginary best friend is a superhero.

Quirky comedy that probably shouldn't be here (because the superhero isn't real), but fills a gap so... It's ultimately a lightweight look at relationships and the difficulties involved in hitting middle age. What makes it worthwhile are the performances from all three leads, with Daniels and Stone sharing exceptional chemistry and Reynolds doing his eminently enjoyable superhero schtick.

Paradox ★★★★

2010, Canada
Director: Brenton Spencer
Cast: Kevin Sorbo, Steph Song, Christopher Judge

In a parallel world in which technology is derived from magic rather than science, hardboiled detective Sean Nault (Sorbo) investigates a murder carried out with an alien device that shouldn't exist and can't be explained: a gun.

Lying somewhere between hidden gem and bizarre miscalculation is this mad adaptation of Christos N. Gage's comic series. It's a fantastic idea: instead of forensic science and coroners, there are crime scene spells and necromancers. Science is treated with the same sort of weary scepticism we might reserve for magic or Uwe Boll movies, and even simple medical procedures are unheard of. As a superhero Nault is unique in that his power is to have no powers. But he gets science in the same way Dr. Strange gets magic, and in this world that gives him an edge. There's a surreal, timeless air thanks to some strong world building that includes (apparently serious) assertions that Churchill defended Britain with Excalibur during WWII and that Kofi Annan is a leading wizard. This is badly made nonsense by any standard. But it's such ridiculous, unexpected and imaginative nonsense it defies reasonable attempts to dislike it.

Intriguing TV movie *Paradox*.

Pepeng Agimat ★★

aka *Pepeng Agimat...Sa Daigdig ng Kababalaghan*, 1973, Philippines
Director: Tony Canyado
Cast: Ramon Revilla, Gloria Romero, Rose Gil

An everyman farmer gifted special powers must save his community from demons.

Among the best known of Revilla's anting-anting magical amulet movies, in which he plays some sort of folk hero deriving superpowers from said object. Here he portrays Pepe, a rancher who must use his newfound abilities to overcome ghosts, monsters and various other spirit threats. As ever with these old Pinoy movies, the lack of English subtitles and terrible picture quality (my copy of the movie is so dark I didn't immediately realise a 'baby' thrown violently to the ground is actually a goblin) act as a barrier to plot details, but they can do nothing to neutralise Revilla's charisma.

Pepeng Agimat ★★

1999, Philippines
Director: Felix E. Dalay
Cast: Ramon 'Bong' Revilla Jr., Dennis Padilla, Princess Punzalan

Demons trying to take over our world must first defeat Sgt. Jose Ronquillo (Revilla), who becomes folk superhero Pepeng Agimat with the aid of a magical amulet.

Although quite unlike the 1973 Ramon Revilla movie of the same name (on which it's based) this supernatural thriller does at least feel like a modern take on the Pinoy film industry's anting-anting phenomenon. Having Ramon's son Bong in the lead is also a nice link back to the subgenre his father effectively owned (a link that was neatly extended when Jolo, son of Bong and grandson of Ramon, starred in a 2009 TV adaptation). There's an air of *Big Trouble in Little China* about this version, even if it does take itself too seriously. The make-up, visual effects and sets are all reminiscent of John Carpenter's classic, and Bong's sincere idea of a macho hero is pretty much the same as Kurt Russell's ironic impression of one. It's not the best of these movies but it is among the most accessible for Western audiences (both stylistically and literally; you can actually get hold of this one).

Pepeng Kuryente ★★

1988, Philippines
Director: Jose Yandoc
Cast: Ramon Revilla, Ramon 'Bong' Revilla jnr., Dante Rivero

Released from a spell in prison earned by avenging the murder of his parents, Pepe (Revillas jnr. and later snr.) is struck by lightning and left with superpowers.

Typical tough guy vehicle for Revilla snr. Pepeng's powers are inconsistent and much of the time he favours a machine gun even though he seems to boast electricity and fire-based projectiles. The numerous fight scenes are poorly choreographed and all attempts to add dramatic weight via pathos fail. (Incidentally, Revilla jnr., who is better known by his nickname Bong, followed his father into politics and in 2016 was tipped to make a run for president alongside the nephew of Imelda Marcos, who happens to be nicknamed Bongbong, on a Bongbong/Bong ticket. This is not a joke.)

Peril from the Planet Mongo

1966, USA
Director: Ford Beebe, Ray Taylor
Cast: Buster Crabbe, Carol Hughes, Charles Middleton

Feature-length edit of the second half of 1940 serial *Flash Gordon Conquers the Universe*. The first half was adapted under the title *Purple Death from Outer Space*.

The Phantom ★★

1943, USA
Director: B. Reeves Eason
Starring: Tom Tyler, Jeanne Bates, Ernie Adams

Seeing the ageing Phantom (Sam Flint) as an obstacle in his search for the Lost City of Zoloz, Doctor Max Bremmer (Kenneth MacDonald) has the fabled protector of Africa poisoned. As his last act, the dying Phantom summons son Geoffrey (Tyler) to take over the family business.

Columbia really doubled down on the arrogance inherent to the character in this first and only official Phantom serial. It's insulting enough that Africa's protector is a white American, here he's also cited as the leader of all the continent's 'natives' and has single-handedly taught them to live in peace. Also the 'African tribesmen' are white actors in black face. Popular at the time it's hard to see the appeal now, and not only for the reasons just mentioned. It feels like a cheap stage play and Tyler isn't leading man material.

The Phantom ★★

1996, USA/Australia
Director: Simon Wincer
Cast: Billy Zane, Kristy Swanson, Treat Williams

When crime lord Xander Drax (Williams) acquires two of the three magical skulls he needs to achieve ultimate power, only the Phantom (Zane) can stop him getting hold of the forth.

Inconsistencies and coincidences abound and I have an image of the editor banging his head on a Steenbeck screen frustrated at the lack of connecting tissue he has to work with. Time and space work differently in *The Phantom* and allow characters to pop up in places they can't possibly be. It's brainless enough to be funny, much like the performances and dialogue.

Phantom 2040 ★★★

1994, USA
Directors: Vincent Bassols, Michael Kaweski
Cast: Scott Valentine, Margot Kidder, J.D. Hall

Environmentalist Kit Walker (Valentine) becomes the Phantom and battles robots in a futuristic New York.

The Phantom's mythology and costume remain but everything else is modernised in this straight-to-video cut-and-shut (constructed from the first five episodes of a short-lived animated TV series of the same name). Although some of the voice work is dull it's surprisingly good, once you get past the incongruous setting. A subterranean jungle is a great idea, the animation is classy and the villain (a cross between Lady Macbeth and *Futurama's* Mom), is unusual and successful.

Phantom Boy ★★★★

2015, France
Directors: Jean-Loup Felicioli, Alain Gagnol
Cast: Edouard Baer, Jean-Pierre Marielle, Audrey Tautou

An 11-year-old boy able to transcend his physical form helps an injured detective prevent a cyber attack on Paris.

Gracefully animated dreamlike tale that may be too leisurely for young audiences. The unusual visuals and gentle tone won't necessarily appeal to parents, either, but for those who are willing and able to get onto *Phantom Boy's* wavelength it will prove touching and rewarding. Don't expect an earth-shattering plot.

Phantom Lady

1974, Philippines
Director: Leonardo L. Garcia
Cast: Vilma Santos, Nick Romano, Paquito Diaz

A magical mask returns a blind woman's sight, leading her to become a vigilante. This movie is believed lost.

Phantom Rancher ★★

1940, USA
Director: Harry L. Fraser
Cast: Ken Maynard, Dorothy Short, Harry Harvey

The Portuguese Falcon aka *Capitão Falcão*

Masked hero Ken Mitchell (Maynard) comes to the aid of bullied ranchers.

Another superhero called Ken? I suppose this one isn't really a superhero; he's adept in a scuffle but nothing special. However, the disguise, altruistic heroism and the fact he's essentially the Lone Ranger tilt portly Ken into eligibility. (Besides, the ability to wear a hat as enormous as this is a kind of superpower.) Everything is simple and rudimentary – this thing isn't going to light any fires, but it's an entertaining enough B-movie in the old-school mould with lots of investigating and double-crossing.

The Photon Effect ★

2010, USA
Director: Dan Poole
Writer: Dan Poole
Cast: Dan Poole, Derek Minter, Brian Razzino

Two engineers receive superpowers in an accident. One becomes good, the other bad.

Some movies only exist to allow a talentless egotist to pretend he's a superhero. There is a limit to how much of a person's life can be spent watching such movies. *The Photon Effect* pushed me beyond that limit.

Pizza Man ★

2011, USA
Director: Joe Eckardt
Cast: Frankie Muniz, Dallas Page, Amber Borycki

A pizza delivery boy ends up a superhero after an encounter with an experimental unsquashable tomato.

Someone at Rock On! Films heard that pitch and thought it was a winner. *Pizza Man* is aimed at children, but that's no excuse. If a child made it through the first half hour of old men in offices and Frankie Muniz being blandly morose, they'd be rewarded with an hour of old men in offices and Frankie Muniz being blandly determined. Ugh.

Planet Hulk ★★★

2010, USA
Director: Director: Sam Liu
Cast: Rick D. Wasserman, Lisa Ann Beley, Mark Hildreth

The Hulk crashes on a remote planet and is forced to compete as a gladiator.

John Carter of Mars meets *Spartacus* in an animated movie that could almost be a prequel to *Thor: Ragnorak*. It's not the most accessible Marvel adventure if you aren't an avid fan of the comics, but it's better in every way than *Hulk vs*, and our hero is given real depth (somehow).

Planet Outlaws

1953, USA

Directors: Ford Beebe, Saul A. Goodkind
Cast: Buster Crabbe, Constance Moore, Jackie Moran

Re-edit of 1939 serial *Buck Rogers*.

Popeye ★★

1980, USA
Director: Robert Altman
Cast: Robin Williams, Shelley Duvall, Ray Walston

Popeye the sailor man (Williams) arrives in the seaside town of Sweethaven in search of his missing father.

Revisionism seems to have struck *Popeye* in recent years, with some critics coming to the conclusion it may have been judged too harshly on its initial release. It wasn't. The Sweethaven set is marvellous (forty years after construction on the island of Malta it remains a popular tourist attraction) and some of the music is good, but as a film it just doesn't work. Altman constantly mixes realism with wackiness, leaving us grasping for a concept to latch on to.

The Portuguese Falcon ★★★★

aka *Captain Falcon*, *Capitão Falcão*,
2015, Portugal
Director: João Leitão
Cast: Gonçalo Waddington, David Chan Cordeiro, José Pinto

In 1960s Portugal, under the regime of the fascist Estado Novo, ultra-nationalist superhero Captain Falcon (Waddington) battles perceived threats from communism, socialism and heresy.

This may be satire but it's broad enough to qualify as farce too, and it consistently spoofs the superhero genre (everything from 1966's TV Batman to tokusatsu). All things considered it had better be funny, then. Whether or not you find it to be will depend on how you like your satire: probing and precise or brash and brutal. This is very much the latter.

The Posthuman Project ★
2014, USA
Director: Kyle William Roberts
Cast: Kyle Whalen, Collin Place, Lindsay Sawyer

Teenager Denny Burke (Whalen) becomes an unwitting guinea pig in a trial scheme to imbue ordinary people with superpowers. He must decide whether to... zzzzzzzz...

Nothing about *The Posthuman Project* rings true or draws you in. I don't care what 'zero energy' is, what happened to Denny's father or whether he'll choose to be a superhero, a college kid or a lion tamer, just as long as I don't have to watch him in a sequel.

Power ★★★
aka *Algol - Tragödie der Macht*, 1920, Germany
Director: Hans Werckmeister
Cast: Emil Jannings, John Gottowt, Hans Adalbert Schlettow

Miner Robert Herne (Jannings) is given a source of unlimited energy by a visiting alien, and is ultimately corrupted by the power it affords him.

A twist on Germany's Faust legend. This expressionist drama doesn't fit the criteria for a superhero movie, but it does work as an interesting counterpoint to the genre. The origin story is essentially the same as Black Panther's (and others). But where the *Black Panther* film demonstrates a society that has benefited from generations of benevolent rule, *Power* shows what can happen when the recipient of ultimate power loses his way because of it. It's kind of a revisionist superhero movie made before there were superhero movies to revise. It works fine as a simple morality tale, but I'm not sure it amounts to more.

Power Rangers: see Grouped Franchises, *Mighty Morphin' Power Rangers: The Movie* and *Turbo: A Power Rangers Movie*

Power Rangers ★★
aka *Saban's Power Rangers*, 2017, USA,
Director: Dean Israelite
Cast: Dacre Montgomery, Naomi Scott, RJ Cyler

Teens become superheroes when they discover a spaceship and its A.I. inhabitant.

An adult tone is about the only surprise this reboot has to offer. That and a lack of Power Rangers, I suppose. The childish themes remain, but now we get gloomy handheld cinematography and mutilated corpses floating in a lake.

The Powerpuff Girls Movie ★★★
2002, USA
Director: Craig McCracken
Cast: Cathy Cavadini, Tara Strong, Elizabeth Daily

Professor Utonium (Tom Kane) creates three girls from sugar, spice, all things nice and chemical X, which inadvertently gives them superpowers.

We hit a surprising number of classic origin story beats in this prequel to the popular Cartoon Network show. The girls must learn to be responsible with their powers whilst struggling to find their places in a society that sees them as different. It's not the most insightful character study, but still. As with a show like *Spongebob* there's an irreverence that broadens the appeal, but it only goes so far.

Pretty Cure: see Grouped Franchises

Prey of the Jaguar ★★
1996, USA

Director: David DeCoteau
Cast: Maxwell Caulfield, Trevor Goddard, Linda Blair

A former government agent sees his family murdered by the master criminal he thought he'd knobbled for good. After making himself a costume and learning kung fu, he sets out for revenge.

Cheesy, low-budget schlock. Caulfield and Goddard compete to be the most awful actor in the movie, only for Linda Blair to swoop in and snatch the honour away when they weren't looking. The camera constantly tilts from one side to the other, presumably looking for the worst Dutch angle for each new shot.

Prince of Space ★★
aka *Yûsei ôji*, 1962, Japan
Director: Eijirô Wakabayashi

Cast: Tatsuo Umemiya, Hiroko Mine, Takashi Kanda

Chicken men from the planet Krankor attempt to invade Earth but are (gradually) repelled by a peculiar alien called Prince of Space (Umemiya).

The original *Yûsei ôji* is a two part, two hour tokusatsu released theatrically in Japan in 1959, while this English dubbed re-edit runs to 85 minutes and followed in 1962. I'd like to say that missing 35 minutes explains why it's so silly, but it seems unlikely. We follow proceedings from the perspective of two children who inexplicably enjoy free access to Earth's rocket base, an experimental fuel laboratory, the local police, media and the Prince of Space himself. Neither alien goodies nor baddies seem interested in communicating with or kidnapping anyone until the second half of the movie. The dub takes itself seriously but can't help being ludicrous, and the plot eschews all narrative conventions in favour of random nonsense.

The Princess and the Hunter: see *Hunterwali*

Princess of Mars ★★
2009, USA
Director: Mark Atkins
Cast: Antonio Sabato Jr., Traci Lords, Matt Lasky

US Army sniper John Carter (Sabato Jr.) is teleported to a Mars where he becomes involved in a civil war between alien races.

The Asylum's take on the first novel of Edgar Rice Burroughs' popular Barsoom (aka John Carter of Mars) series. The limited resources present all kinds of problems for such a fantastical property. The Martian Tharks are supposed to be double torso'd, four armed, 15-ft tall warriors; not men in rubber masks. And instead of the grand CGI battles of Disney's *John Carter of Mars*, the

The Pumaman

blockbuster that would follow in 2012, we get a handful of dodgy matte paintings and a lot of desert.

Psychic Kusuo ★★

aka *Saiki Kusuo no sai-nan*, 2017, Japan
Director: Yûichi Fukuda
Cast: Kento Yamazaki, Kanna Hashimoto, Hirofumi Arai, Hideyuki Kasahara

Born with an array of psychic powers, Saiki Kusuo (Yamazaki) chooses to dedicate his life to mediocrity in the hope of going unnoticed at school.

Adapted from the manga and anime series, *Psychic Kusuo* is a meandering, plot-less exercise in character creation. A succession of weird friends, neighbours and other associates inadvertently complicate Kusuo's life in various ways. That's it, really.

Psychokinesis ★★★★

aka *Yeom-lyeok*, 2018, South Korea
Director: Sang-ho Yeon
Cast: Seung-ryong Ryu, Eun-kyung Shim, Jung-min Park

An irresponsible security guard attains telekinetic powers after drinking spring water polluted by a meteorite, and uses them to defend his estranged daughter from gangs and the construction company responsible for her mother's death.

Part misery porn, part whimsical fantasy, *Psychokinesis* offers an odd mix but it works. Shim is totally convincing as the daughter, Roo-mi; her expressive face able to convey unusually convincing grief. Ryu, as her oaf of a father Seok-heon, is responsible for most of the humour, which is generally derived from his near constant state of bewilderment. Once the downbeat stuff is done with, *Psychokinesis* develops into the sort of feel-good crowdpleaser that deserves to find a large audience.

Puella Magi Madoka Magica: The Movie Part 1: Beginnings ★★★★

aka *Gekijōban Mahō Shōjo Madoka Magika (Zenpen): Hajimari no Monogatari*, 2012, Japan
Directors: Yukihiro Miyamoto, Akiyuki Shinbo
Cast: Aoi Yûki, Chiwa Saitô, Eri Kitamura

School girl Madoka Kaname (Yûki) is given the opportunity to become a Magical Girl. In exchange for being granted any wish she will join a secret league who defend the living from witches responsible for all the world's suffering.

Spruced-up version of the 2011 TV series and the first entry in a trilogy. It's visually impressive and makes great use of music, while the scenarios are abstract and quite imaginative. This is not a good place to start for those intrigued by the Magical Girl anime genre, though. While it's more interesting than a property like Sailor Moon it bends too many conventions to be typical.

Puella Magi Madoka Magica: The Movie Part 2: Eternal ★★★★

aka *Gekijōban Mahō Shōjo Madoka Magika (Kōhen): Eien no Monogatari*, 2012, Japan
Directors: Yukihiro Miyamoto, Akiyuki Shinbo
Cast: Aoi Yûki, Chiwa Saitô, Eri Kitamura

The truth behind the girls' transformations into magical beings is revealed as their battle with the forces of darkness evolves.

More of the same. There's a bleakness and sophistication to the storytelling. It's hardly David Lynch, but compared to its subgenre brethren it's twisted.

Puella Magi Madoka Magica: The Movie Part III: Rebellion ★★★★

aka *Gekijōban Mahō Shōjo Madoka Magika (Shinpen): Hangyaku no Monogatari*, 2013, Japan
Directors: Yukihiro Miyamoto, Akiyuki Shinbo
Cast: Aoi Yûki, Chiwa Saitô, Eri Kitamura

Memory and reality crumble as we fall even deeper down the rabbit hole.

The third and final movie in the franchise ups the ante on the inventive visuals and in the process stakes its claim for being the most beautiful anime produced so far. The textures and stylistic contrasts are breathtaking. For those unversed in the Magical Girl genre the plot to this series was probably rendered impenetrable by the last movie, but, if not, this one should do it. There are alternate realities, soul gems, demons, a psychological labyrinth and more bewildering schemes than you can shake a wand at.

The Pumaman ★★★★
aka *L'uomo puma*, 1980, Italy
Director: Alberto De Martino
Cast: Walter George Alton, Donald Pleasence, Miguel Ángel Fuentes

Paleontologist Tony Farms (Alton) learns of his fate as a supernatural Aztec demigod.

Utterly bonkers and extremely funny Italian (English language) attempt to mop up some of the *Superman* audience. Of *Pumaman*'s two main stars Walter George Alton never acted again and Donald Pleasance branded it the worst film he ever appeared in. It's essential viewing for those with a fondness for ironic entertainment and one of the very best 'good bad' superhero movies. If that's not you, don't touch it with a ten-foot clown pole.

The Punisher ★★
1989, USA
Director: Mark Goldblatt
Cast: Dolph Lundgren, Louis Gossett Jr., Jeroen Krabbé

When his family is killed by the mob, Det. Frank Castle (Lundgren) transforms into a ruthless vigilante. His plans for revenge are complicated when the Yakuza attempt to take over the mafia's business, and kidnap its chief's children.

'Bad guy kills family, Punisher works his way through crime syndicate, kills bad guy.' That's what a Punisher movie is. It isn't 'Punisher rescues bus load of bad guys' children.' Lundgren gives one of his best performances and the 1980s action aesthetic is great, which just makes this even more of a missed opportunity.

The Punisher ★★★★
2004, USA
Director: Jonathan Hensleigh
Cast: Thomas Jane, John Travolta, Rebecca Romijn

When FBI agent Frank Castle (Jane) kills the son of Mob boss Howard Saint (Travolta), he retaliates by murdering Castle's family, and the two men find themselves competing to be the bloodiest avenger.

Marvel's morally questionable vindicator of violence finally gets the movie he deserves with this uncompromising revenge thriller. It's not perfect (there are all sorts of plot holes), but it is entertaining thanks to an abundance of action, brutality and John Travolta. It's a real treat to have someone with Travolta's panache filling the typically generic villain role in a movie like this. There's strong support from Will Patton as Saint's sadistic enforcer, and it's an established fact that every film featuring Roy Scheider is worth seeing.

Punisher: War Zone ★★★
2008, USA
Director: Lexi Alexander
Cast: Ray Stevenson, Dominic West, Julie Benz

After accidentally killing an FBI agent and inciting a crime lord to supervillainy, Frank Castle, aka the Punisher (Stevenson), is hunted by both sides of the law while trying to protect a woman and her child.

Reboot that dispenses with the origin story and catches up with Castle right as he could be about to retire the Punisher persona. It feels more like a superhero movie than the previous instalment in the franchise (he faces wackier villains, lives in abandoned tunnels, etc.), but that's not to say it has been sanitised and there's some surprisingly strong gore. Stevenson delivers a low-key performance and handles both Castle's emotional torment and physical aptitude reasonably well.

Punjab Mail

1936 or 1939, India
Director: Homi Wadia
Cast: Fearless Nadia, Unknown

Fearless Nadia dons a mask and takes revenge. As with most of this star's films, *Punjab Mail* is lost, which is a great shame. Nadia appeared in a string of folk hero/ vigilante films in the 1930s and 1940s, carving out a niche as a superhero before any of Bollywood's men did the same.

Purple Death from Outer Space

1966, USA
Director: Ford Beebe, Ray Taylor
Cast: Buster Crabbe, Carol Hughes, Charles Middleton

Feature-length edit of the 1940 Universal serial *Flash Gordon Conquers the Universe*. Unusually, the original serial is split in half, meaning you'll have to find a copy of the same year's *Peril from the Planet Mongo* to see whether Flash and co are successful in preventing Ming wiping out mankind with poisonous dust (spoiler: they are). The fact nobody created a new title card to reflect the new title (it sticks with '*Flash Gordon Conquers the Universe*') isn't an encouraging start, but it's actually a lot of fun.

Push ★★

2009, USA
Director: Paul McGuigan
Cast: Chris Evans, Camilla Belle, Dakota Fanning

A government agency known as Division is experimenting on superhumans in an attempt to create a supernatural army. Telekinetic lowlife Nick Gant (Evans) and 13-year-old Cassie Holmes (Fanning), a 'Watcher' able to see into the future, are forced to work together to find a young woman able to implant thoughts into people's minds.

Jumped-up episode of *The X-Files* with slick visuals, strong performances and perhaps even an interesting story somewhere, under all the convoluted exposition. For a movie that involves so much bending of reality it's fitting that we can never quite grasp what's going on, or why we should care.

Pussy Cat

1969, Philippines
Director: Jose Miranda Cruz
Cast: Divina Valencia, Bernard Belleza, Johnny Delgado

An exotic dancer moonlights as a secret agent. This movie is believed lost.

Ra.One ★★

2011, India
Director: Anubhav Sinha
Cast: Shah Rukh Khan, Arjun Rampal,
Kareena Kapoor

Shekhar (Khan), an Indian computer game designer working in London, creates a supposedly invincible villain to impress his gamer son, Prateek (Armaan Verma). But when the boy easily defeats it, the sprites take on physical form and escape the game in search of Prateek.

After several minutes of 'partner' logos and disclaimers a movie remembers to happen, and my goodness it's techy. Cold blue light, stainless steel, holographic projections, and Hindi dialogue peppered with English buzzwords like 'cyber' and 'virtual'. Early on it goes mainly for humour, but the only laughs come from a running joke about Westerners thinking all Chinese are Jackie Chan. As things progress we get bogged down in the melodrama of Shekhar's death and his virtual self turning up and needing to learn how to love his family and so on. Under the right circumstances it's still just about worth it, but *Tron* this is not.

Radar Men from the Moon ★★

1952, USA
Director: Fred C. Brannon
Cast: George Wallace, Aline Towne,
Roy Barcroft

Commando Cody (Wallace) takes his rocket ship to the moon to investigate the source of deadly atomic rays. There he finds the moon's dictator, planning an invasion.

The first of two Commando Cody serials (and not a sequel to *King of the Rocket Men*, as is often supposed. The costume was simply recycled.) Cody is essentially a combination of Zarkov and Flash Gordon: an accomplished scientist who has identified unusual phenomena as an alien threat to Earth *and* the square-jawed Jock who can do something about it. That's the extent of his characterisation, but it's more than anyone else gets. There's little here for a modern audience, but it's easy to see why kids (including a young George Lucas) so enjoyed it at the time.

Real Heroes

Rafathar ★★
2017, Indonesia
Director: Bounty Umbara
Cast: Verdi Solaiman, Rafathar Malik Ahmad, Raffi Ahmad

Thieves hired to kidnap a toddler find the child has superpowers.

Rafathar's IMDb user rating of 1.5/10 puts it in an elite category alongside some of the worst movies ever made. In superhero terms we're talking Tom Cat atrocities like *The Incredible Bulk*. It's bad, but it's nothing like Tom Cat bad (very little is), which makes me feel a bit defensive. With bumbling burglars trying to get the better of a much smarter child, there are inevitable *Home Alone* overtones, and a few sequences are even reminiscent of *Raizing Arizona*. That's not to say it's as good as either, it isn't (*Baby Geniuses 2: Superbabies* also came to mind), but it can raise a smile. Put a small child in front of slapstick morons chasing a toddler who's up to shenanigans and they will be entertained. Fact.

Il ragazzo invisibile: see *The Invisible Boy*

Rama Superman Indonesia ★★★
1974, Indonesia
Director: Frans Totok Ars
Cast: Boy Shahlani, Yenny Rachman, August Melasz

Good-natured orphan Andi (Shahlani) is given a magic necklace that turns him into a superhero when kissed. He uses his new powers to rescue schoolgirl Lia (Rachman), whose professor father has been kidnapped by villains.

There's no filmmaking acuity on display here. Characters we're meant to be looking at are positioned outside the frame, shots of cars driving are favoured over exposition, and scenes appear to lurch from one to the next when the editor tires of them as opposed to when a natural conclusion has been reached. So bad it's good.

Rat Pfink a Boo Boo ★
1966, USA
Director: Ray Dennis Steckler
Cast: Carolyn Brandt, Ron Haydock, Titus Moede

Pop star Lonnie Lord (Haydock) receives a call from kidnappers demanding $50,000 for the safe return of his girlfriend Cee Cee (Brandt), which leads him to transform into his crime-fighting alter ego Rat Pfink.

Lo-fi oddity that starts as a straight crime thriller but turns into a spoof of the 1966 Batman TV series at the halfway mark. Incredibly, Steckler and Haydock (who also wrote the screenplay) saw the show during filming and simply decided to start spoofing it. The technique is horrendous, but if you enjoyed Steckler's equally bonkers, but significantly more successful, *The Incredibly Strange Creatures Who Stopped Living and Became Mixed-Up Zombies!?* (1964), there's a chance this won't make you ill.

Rat-Man – Il segreto del supereroe ★★

2007, Italy
Director: Massimo Montigiani
Cast: Andrea Ward, Oliviero Dinelli, Saverio Maria Indrio

In the City Without a Name, an incompetent rodent superhero has a series of adventures.

Batman parody that also takes inspiration from Mickey Mouse, Star Wars and Pixar. It's based on the Panini comic created by Leonardo Ortolani and adapted into a TV show in 2006. The animation is basic and ugly, the scenarios obvious.

Real Heroes ★★★★

2014, USA
Director: Keith Hartman
Cast: Hunter Smit, Keila Hamilton, Melissa Jobe

A disparate group of minor superheroes are picked to appear on a reality TV show.

Although superficially reminiscent of Craig Mazin's 2000 comedy *The Specials*, *Real Heroes* is actually a unique proposition: *Big Brother* with superheroes. And it works, too, despite a microscopic budget and the spoofed formula seeming a little dated. Characters are carefully designed and share excellent chemistry, the script is full of great ideas and everything is tied together with

a lightness of touch some A-list filmmakers could learn from.

The Red Eagle (Mitr Chaibancha series): see Grouped Franchises and The Red Eagle

Red Eagle ★★

aka *Insee dang*, 2010, Thailand
Director: Wisit Sasanatieng
Cast: Ananda Everingham, Yarinda Boonnak, Wannasing Prasertkul

With crime and corruption at an all-time high, former special forces hardcase Rome Rittikrai (Everingham) reinvents himself as the heroic Red Eagle.

A much darker and more brooding version of the character than was portrayed in the original films, director Sasanatieng (best known in the West for 2000's fascinating *Tears of the Black Tiger*) is influenced by Christopher Nolan's then current Batman series. Like the earlier movies it proved a domestic hit, but its slow pace, clunky moralising and questionable acting make it something of a chore.

The Red Mask ★★

aka *Kizil Maske*, 1968, Turkey
Director: Çetin Inanç
Cast: Irfan Atasoy, Sezer Güvenirgil, Suzan Avci

A vigilante known as Kizil Maske, aka The Red Mask (Atasoy), must stop crime lord Al Kapon (Yildirim Gencer) from acquiring a mad professor's secret formula for rapid plant growth.

One of a pair of 1968 Turkish superhero movies titled *Kizil Maske* (the name the Phantom goes by in Turkey). All the action ended up in this one. With its star power and director credibility (Atasoy and Inanç have each produced some extraordinary B-movies), this automatically feels like the more senior of the two. There's some entertaining nonsense early on with a scene that looks like a result of the KKK and SPECTRE double-booking the same conference centre, but it soon settles down into flat action scenes intercut with men in hats talking.

The Red Mask ★★
aka Kizil Maske, 1968, Turkey
Director: Tolgay Ziyal
Cast: Ismet Erten, Nebahat Çehre, Süheyl Egriboz

Kizil Maske (Erten), Turkey's take on the Phantom, is hired to retrieve something from baddies. Beyond that it's hard to tell.

The presumed minor *Kizil Maske* (see prior entry) sticks closer to the original concept for the Phantom than does its namesake, with the setting, costume and character matching Lee Falk's original creation pretty closely. Unfortunately, that probably makes this the more blatant and egregious infringement of copyright.

Red Sonja ★★★
1985, USA
Director: Richard Fleischer
Cast: Arnold Schwarzenegger, Brigitte Nielsen, Sandahl Bergman

A warrior woman blessed with supernatural powers by an Irish Goddess feuds with a mad Queen trying to conquer the world.

With the commercial success of *Conan the Barbarian* heralding a slew of imitations, it was inevitable the big man's Marvel stablemate and associate adventurer Red Sonja would find her way to the big screen. Except she sort of hasn't. Although this was conceived as a *Conan* spinoff by Dino de Laurentis, producer of the Schwarzenegger movies, rights issues forced him to abandon the Marvel characters and officially credit the character to Robert E. Howard, the author who created Conan. That means this film's Hyborian barbarian Red Sonja is not based on the Hyborean barbarian Red Sonja, but on the 16th-century soldier Red Sonya. Whatever. The movie itself is similar to *Conan the Destroyer*. There may be less blood, sorcery and weird deities, but it's effectively the same plot: we follow an Amazonian, a barbarian (Schwarzenegger as Definitely Not Conan – that would be infringing copyright), a royal child and their bodyguard on a PG-13 mission to retreive a supernatural MacGuffin before the loopy queen kills them all.

Reign of the Supermen ★★★
2019, USA
Director: Sam Liu
Cast: Jerry O'Connell, Rebecca Romijn, Rainn Wilson

With Superman (O'Connell) dead, four imposters create a mystery in Metropolis.

Sequel to the previous year's *The Death of Superman*. The setup allows for some fun characters to take the limelight in Kal-El's absence, and the straggly-haired unkempt Superman Prime is a lark when he does finally resurrect.

Rendel: Dark Vengeance ★★★
aka *Rendel*, 2017, Finland
Director: Jesse Haaja
Cast: Kristofer Gummerus, Rami Rusinen, Renne Korppila

The mysterious Rendel (Gummerus) seeks vengeance in the criminal underbelly of the fictionalised Finnish town of Mikkeli.

Finland's first superhero film. There wasn't much money to go round but it looks good. The filmmakers have access to proper equipment and know how to use it (not that they shouldn't, but I take nothing for granted at this point), it has been colour graded and some thought has gone into the lighting and editing. For some reason the English dub has been provided by some amateurs inspired by 1980s anime, but I'll put that down to the US distributor rather than the filmmakers. It feels a bit generic (a few identifiably Finnish touches would have been nice), but this is a decent movie.

Resident Evil ★★★

2002, USA
Director: Paul W.S. Anderson
Cast: Milla Jovovich, Michelle Rodriguez, Ryan McCluskey

Waking up with no memory of who she is, Alice (Jovovich), a security operative for the sinister Umbrella Corporation, joins a special forces team as they investigate a

The Return of the Six Million Dollar Man and the Bionic Woman

WITH AMERICA ON THE BRINK OF DESTRUCTION ...
THEY CHANGED THEIR MINDS ABOUT EARLY RETIREMENT!

THE RETURN OF THE
SIX MILLION
DOLLAR MAN
AND THE
BIONIC WOMAN

Starring LEE MAJORS and LINDSAY WAGNER in the roles they made famous!

9PM° 4;13;22,33;35 NBC

WORLD PREMIERE MOVIE! *TELECAST IN STEREO

NBC-TV ad in the May 16-22, 1987 issue of TV Guide Mag. (Toledo-Lima Edition)   vintagetoledotv.squarespace.com/

viral outbreak in a subterranean research facility. As her memories slowly return, Alice realises there's more going on than she realised.

This first film based on the *Resident Evil* video game franchise is no masterpiece, but it is an efficient and entertaining little sci-fi actioner with some pleasingly gory horror leanings. The memory loss conceit is its greatest strength, allowing us to be drip-fed revelations as they occur to Alice, a process which builds tension and adds to the mystery. Technically she doesn't gain superhuman abilities until the first sequel, *Resident Evil: Apocalypse*, but there's no point omitting the best entry in the series. (Followed by *Resident Evil: Apocalypse*.)

Resident Evil: Afterlife ★★★

2010, USA
Director: Paul W.S. Anderson
Cast: Milla Jovovich, Ali Larter, Wentworth Miller

Alice (Jovovich) hooks up with a group of survivors in Los Angeles, eventually finding her way to an Umbrella cargo ship where all manner of crazy transpires.

The Mad Max post-apocalypse desert of film three has been replaced by an urban setting for film four, with most of the action taking place in a prison. Alice supposedly loses her superpowers in the first act but clearly draws on them again, particularly in a finale so bonkers it makes the whole thing worthwhile. There are a couple of character returnees but they could be anyone, and Alice's characterisation remains limited to 'resilient woman with face'. (Followed by *Resident Evil: Retribution*.)

Resident Evil: Apocalypse ★

2004, USA
Director: Alexander Witt
Cast: Milla Jovovich, Sienna Guillory, Eric Mabius

After being subjected to an experimental form of the zombie-inducing T virus, Alice (Jovovich) finds she has superpowers. They come in useful as she attempts to rescue a handful of survivors from the walking dead, and escape Raccoon City.

Among several serious problems inherent to this first *Resident Evil* sequel, one of the dumbest is the character inconsistency. Alice and STARS superagent Jill Valentine (Guillory) repeatedly forget which of them is supposed to be the emotionless badass and which the humanitarian, while comedy relief L.J. (Mike Epps) is so unpredictably written he appears to have a personality disorder. It's unfathomable and inexcusable how bad this film is. The villains have no obvious agenda, the non-plot is stretched well beyond breaking point and there isn't a single relatable character. (Followed by *Resident Evil: Extinction*.)

Resident Evil: Extinction ★★
2007, USA
Director: Russell Mulcahy
Cast: Milla Jovovich, Ali Larter, Oded Fehr

As the Umbrella Corporation experiments on clones of Alice (Jovovich), the real thing joins a convoy of survivors searching for a safe zone free of zombies.

Although perhaps a slight improvement on the second film, this third instalment in the series struggles with just as many issues. The protagonists and antagonists interact only briefly, so most of our time is spent cutting between their (unrelated) storylines, neither of which convey much by way of stakes. There's no sense the convoy knows where it's going or is passionate about getting there, and the Umbrella Corporation is once again fatally under-represented and under-explained. We're three movies in and still don't know who's in charge or what they're trying to achieve. (Followed by *Resident Evil: Afterlife*.)

Resident Evil: Retribution ★★
2012, USA
Director: Paul W.S. Anderson
Cast: Milla Jovovich, Sienna Guillory, Michelle Rodriguez

Albert Wesker (Shawn Roberts), previously the head of the Umbrella Corporation (not that we were ever told), arranges for Alice to escape the demonic Red Queen (Megan Charpentier), Umbrella's child A.I. and new overlord, in order to take part in mankind's last stand.

One of the main problems with this series is the constant chopping and changing. Each movie features a different kind of post-apocalypse earth, different zombies, different technology, different Umbrella Corporation, and, thanks to the incessant cloning, even different versions of familiar characters. There's no building on what's happened before and the first job of each new story seems to be to irradicate any hangovers from the last. It makes for a shallow and frustrating experience. This fifth entry in the series is perhaps the most shallow and frustrating of all, despite being more entertaining than the second and third. It's lazier too. Alice's escape should have been dealt with in the first half hour but it takes up the whole movie, meaning there's effectively no plot progression until the last five minutes (not that it matters, the conclusion is made redundant by the next movie anyway). (Followed by *Resident Evil: The Final Chapter*.)

Resident Evil: The Final Chapter ★★
2016, USA
Director: Paul W.S. Anderson
Cast: Milla Jovovich, Iain Glen, Ali Larter

Alice (Jovovich) returns to the Hive, the underground lab of the first movie, in search of an antidote to world poisoning or some similar nonsense.

History is rewritten once more but what the hell, at this point the series would be messing with its continuity by introducing continuity. Movie six finally delves into a little of Umbrella's history and objectives, contradicting all sorts of past events in the process and telling us nothing that makes sense. Alice is served with fresh sets of evil clones, enhanced zombies and ambiguous allies, but it's impossible to care.

Retik, the Moon Menace

1966, USA
Director: Fred C. Brannon
Cast: George Wallace, Aline Towne, Roy Barcroft

Feature-length edit of 1952 Captain Cody serial *Radar Men From the Moon*.

The Return of Captain Invincible
★★

1983, Australia
Director: Philippe Mora
Cast: Alan Arkin, Christopher Lee, Kate Fitzpatrick

Having retired from duty in the wake of a HUAC-style witch-hunt, Captain Invincible (Arkin) is called back into service when the villainous Mister Midnight (Lee) steals a superweapon. Unfortunately, a number of years spent off radar have left him a steaming drunk.

Arkin is well suited to playing a disillusioned superhero, Christopher Lee can do villains in his sleep and the concept has potential. On the other hand, the supporting cast are dire and nobody seems to commit to the song and dance numbers (oh yes, this is also a musical. And Lee sings), which are uniformly dreary.

The Return of Chandu ★★

1934, USA

Director: Ray Taylor
Cast: Bela Lugosi, Maria Alba, Clara Kimball Young

Frank Chandler, aka Chandu the Magician (Lugosi), protects an Egyptian princess from a black magic cult.

Unusually, this serial is effectively, if not technically, a sequel to *Chandu the Magician*, the 1932 B-movie starring Edmund Lowe as the eponymous supernatural yogi. Equally unusually, it replaces Lowe with Bela Lugosi, who played the first film's villain. Lugosi does well as the mystical Chandu but he's too cold and distant for Chandler. Maybe Lowe's blandness had its virtues after all. (And, not that it matters much, but Lugosi's thick Hungarian accent doesn't make a lot of sense on a character clearly established as American.) Apparently *The Return of Chandu* was concieved with feature-length edits in mind, meaning it was written so that key scenes could be lifted out and easily compiled into B-movies. It doesn't make a noticeable difference and we suffer with a fairly typical amount of the dreaded repetition inherent to serials. This is not as entertaining as *Chandu the Magician* but the character is interesting and should be noted as a very early example of a genuine superhero: Chandu acts altruistically, has two identities and proper supernatural powers (he teleports into his first scene).

The Return of Chandu

1934, USA
Director: Ray Taylor
Cast: Bela Lugosi, Maria Alba, Lucien Priva

Feature-length edit concocted from the first half of the serial of the same name. An edit of the second half, effectively this movie's sequel, was released the following year as *Chandu on the Magic Island*. As a result of the unusual approach taken to structuring the original serial (see previous entry) it's slicker than similar cut-and-shuts.

The Return of Mr. Superman ★★

1960, India
Director: Manmohan Sabir
Cast: P. Jairaj, Sheila Ramani, Naazi

Kal-el (Jairaj) arrives from Krypton and is taken in by a kindly farmer. After growing to adulthood he tackles some villainy.

Two unconnected Superman ripoffs were released in India in 1960, with this one considered the poor relation to director Mohammed Hussain's more sensibly titled *Superman*. Confusingly, Paidi Jairaj plays the Man of Steel in both movies, and only a last-minute legal intervention stopped them sharing the same title. (In a moment of surreal comic genius, the producers of the other ripoff sued the producers of this one for copyright infringement.) It's extremely cheaply made, with the 'city' locations looking suspiciously similar to the rural farming country featured at the beginning of the movie, and the components of Superman's costume apparently chosen at random. There are song and (sort of) dance numbers, but no English dub or subtitles.

The Return of Superman ★★

aka *Süpermen Dönüyor*, 1979, Turkey
Director: Kunt Tulgar
Cast: Tayfun Demir, Güngör Bayrak, Yildirim Gencer

A man learns he is a superpowered alien and faces off against a criminal gang with a weapon that can kill him.

Attention Hollywood: this film's origin story takes less than nine minutes. In most other regards you probably have the edge. This typical Turkish travesty lifts lumps of plot, score and characterisation from Richard Donner's 1978 box-office hit while adding nothing of its own, unless you count the Christmas tree that inexplicably doubles as Krypton. But it can amuse. The effects are

funny, the performances incomprehensible and the editing downright dangerous.

The Return of Swamp Thing ★★

1989, USA
Director: Jim Wynorski
Cast: Dick Durock, Heather Locklear, Louis Jourdan

Abby Arcane (Locklear), stepdaughter of the previous movie's villain Dr. Anton Arcane (Jourdan), ventures into the swamps in search of an explanation for her mother's mysterious death.

Despite dying in 1982's *Swamp Thing*, Dr. Arcane is back and he's created dozens of genetically engineered man-beasts. The tone is much campier this time, which might have worked if not for the fumbled direction. Wynorski is usually strong with this sort of material but too many elements fail to gel.

The Return of the Incredible Hulk ★★★

aka *The Incredible Hulk: Death in the Family*, 1977, USA
Director: Alan J. Levi
Cast: Bill Bixby, Jack Colvin, Lou Ferrigno

Now on the run, Dr. David Banner (Bixby) starts investigating his condition, but is sidetracked when he stumbles onto a murder plot.

(Not to be confused with *The Incredible Hulk Returns*, another TV movie starring Bixby and Ferrigno.) Second pilot that ended up being re-edited and aired in syndication as two episodes of the first series. Having no need to cover the origin story this is a more satisfying shape than the first Hulk TV movie, although it doesn't yet feel polished. We do get to watch Lou Ferrigno fight a bear, though. If you're getting déjà vu perhaps you read the entry on 1983's

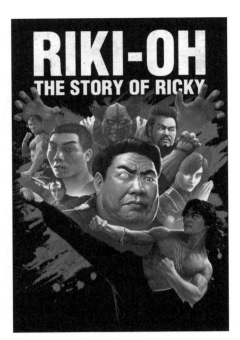

Riki-Oh: The Story of Riki/Ricky, aka Lik Wong

listen to an elderly Lee Majors complain about having feelings. Much has happened to Austin since the end of the original show, and the writers are determined all of it should have some bearing (so much so the plot involving Fortress is hardly mentioned and has no influence on anything until the final 20 minutes). Wagner is very good, as always, everyone knows what they're doing and the weight of history adds some depth.

Return to the Batcave: The Misadventures of Adam and Burt ★★★

2003, USA
Director: Paul A. Kaufman
Cast: Adam West, Burt Ward, Jack Brewer

When the Batmobile is stolen Adam West and Burt Ward reunite, this time out of costume, to try and track it down. We're also treated to a reconstruction of the making of the 1966 Batman TV series.

The narrative involving West and Ward plays out like a cross between an episode of their original show and a corporate video that got out of hand. It has the series' Dutch angles and wacky characters, but looks more like a 1990s car promo. It's an odd mix with the straight docudrama of the reconstruction segments and creates an effect similar to flicking channels. Weak as the end result is, it's kind of adorable, too. Fans of the original show will raise a smile.

Revenge of the Mysterons from Mars ★★

1981, UK
Directors: Brian Burgess, Robert Lyn, Ken Turner
Cast: Francis Matthews, Ed Bishop, Donald Gray

Spectrum engage in various goings on relating to the Mysteron base on the moon.

Thanks to minimal re-editing neither of the two Captain Scarlet cut-and-shuts (pulled

Hercules, in which Ferrigno also fights a bear. (Followed by *The Bride of the Incredible Hulk*, in which nobody fights a bear.)

The Return of the Six-Million-Dollar Man and the Bionic Woman ★★★

1987, USA
Director: Ray Austin
Cast: Lee Majors, Lindsay Wagner, Tom Schanley

Steve Austin (Majors) is reluctantly forced out of retirement by a threat from Fortress, a deadly criminal organisation from his past. Meanwhile, his son Michael (Schanley) and old flame Jaime, aka the Bionic Woman (Wagner), arrive on the scene carrying plenty of emotional baggage.

The first of three reunion TV movies (the others being *Bionic Showdown* and *Bionic Ever After*). For most of the first hour we from the 1967 series) are particularly satisfactory, but this one suffers from an even more schizophrenic structure than the previous year's *Captain Scarlet vs. the Mysterons*. Scarlet himself still seems to be voiced by Cary Grant, so it has that going for it, but you have to do more than glue episodes together for a cut-and-shut to work. However, the core material is strong enough to make the original series seem appealing, and that was the ultimate aim of these movies so... job done.

Ri jie: see *Descendant of the Sun*

Riki-Oh: The Story of Riki ★★★★

aka *Lik wong*
1991, Hong Kong
Director: Ngai Choi Lam
Cast: Siu-Wong Fan, Mei Sheng Fan, Ka-Kui Ho

Jailed for manslaughter, the supernaturally strong Riki-Oh (Fan) finds himself helping the vulnerable in a prison rife with violence and corruption.

Spectacularly gory and thoroughly insane kung fu black comedy. The ultra violence essentially makes it a live-action anime (one scene sees a villain commit seppuku before pulling out his own intestines to use as a garrotte), but in other respects it's a pretty formulaic prison movie. Riki's unwavering decency sees him become a hero to the abused inmates, and nemesis to a crooked warden, leaving us in little doubt how things will end. Siu-Wong Fan is excellent in the fight scenes.

Rise of the Black Bat ★

2012, Canada
Director: Brett Kelly
Cast: Jody Haucke, Richard Groen, Dixie Collins

A weirdo able to see in the dark pursues the crime lord who blinded him. (Yes, I know.)

What's the worst superhero movie of all time? If you're mentally cycling through titles such as *Batman v Superman*, *Spawn* and *Catwoman* then consider yourself lucky, because it means you haven't seen any of Tom Cat's leavings. The bargain basement US production company has excreted a number of reprehensible 'mockbusters' on the doormat of popular culture, and this is among the worst of them. Unworthy of the ink.

Rise of the Guardians ★★

2012, USA
Director: Peter Ramsey
Cast: Chris Pine, Alec Baldwin, Isla Fisher

Santa Claus (Baldwin), the Tooth Fairy (Fisher) and various other magical beings recruit Jack Frost (Pine) to stop the evil Pitch (Jude Law) enveloping the world in complete darkness.

Based on author and illustrator William Joyce's *The Guardians of Childhood* series, this CGI animated kids' movie benefits from some interesting ideas (like the rivalry between Santa and Hugh Jackman's Easter Bunny), but they're spread too thin. The script hasn't seen the sort of rigorous refinement Pixar might have subjected it to, and the animation falls well short of the gold standard.

RoboCop ★★★★★

1987, USA
Director: Paul Verhoeven
Cast: Peter Weller, Nancy Allen, Dan O'Herlihy

In a dystopian near-future, the Detroit police force field a cyborg cop.

There's so much going on here. Beyond the famously direct satire (of 1980s capitalism, the media, authoritarianism, privatisation...), which remains uncompromising and effective, everything from the nature of the human soul to the caste system in industry is contemplated. Meanwhile, the rock-solid story keeps building. There isn't a wasted frame and each scene serves to further the plot, deepen our understanding of the world and/or develop character. *RoboCop* is a lesson in how to work the medium.

RoboCop ★★

2014, USA
Director: José Padilha
Cast: Joel Kinnaman, Gary Oldman, Michael Keaton

After being blown up by criminals, Detroit police officer Alex Murphy (Kinnaman) is cyborged by a sinister multinational before being returned to duty. It isn't long before his computer software starts interfering with his cerebral hardware.

Miserable remake that fumbles the themes of the original and lays on the melodrama incomprehensibly thick. Padilha documents every moment of Murphy's anguish as if he revels in the suffering, which makes for a relentlessly gloomy movie (we really don't need on-screen analytics describing how emotionally distressed RoboCop's son is). In terms of similarities to the original there's corporate corruption and TV propaganda blather, but it's run-of-the-mill stuff with none of the edge previous director Paul Verhoeven gave us. There are some bizarre choices, too; why make Murphy a cynical and practically rogue cop rather than an idealistic new arrival? It robs the movie of impact and the audience of the one potentially likeable character.

RoboCop 2 ★★★

1990, USA
Director: Irvin Kershner
Cast: Peter Weller, John Glover, Mario Machado

OCP experiment with robotic law enforcers as a dangerous new drug ravages Detroit.

Although vastly inferior to the first film, *RoboCop 2* at least maintains its satirical absurdities (often it goes even further). For a while, anyway. The promisingly acerbic first act gives way to too much silliness and too much child star. But it's still in another league to the *RoboCops* that would follow, and it retains Peter Weller in the lead.

Robocop 3 ★

1993, USA
Director: Fred Dekker
Cast: Robert John Burke, Nancy Allen, Mario Machado

RoboCop (Burke) helps a community driven out of their homes by OCP's determination to create a modern city where Old Detroit once stood.

Oh boy. The violence is toned right down, the free-will angle is heightened, absolutely nothing makes sense, and RoboCop says things like "I hope you're insured" after smashing stuff up. This is a terrible movie.

RoboCop: The Future of Law Enforcement ★★

aka *RoboCop 4*, 1994, Canada
Director: Paul Lynch
Cast: Richard Eden, Yvette Nipar, Blu Mankuma

OCP science nutcase Dr. Cray Z. Mollardo (Cliff De Young, rocking one of the best character names ever) takes control of the mega-corporation's HQ using an unstable A.I. Only RoboCop (Eden) can save the day.

After licensing the TV rights from Orion Pictures, Canadian production company Skyvision re-tooled and relaunched the franchise for a younger audience with this feature-length pilot. Bizarrely they keep the dark satire which, in a kids' show, is either subversive genius or inadvertent nihilism. And it *is* a kids' show. Robo can't shoot anyone, the cast has been infiltrated by 10-year-olds, and a straight-laced cop describes a nice car as "a happenin' piece of road iron". I'm not sure Skyvision saw RoboCop the same way I do.

Roboman Hakaider ★★★

aka *Jinzô ningen Hakaidâ, Mechanical Violator Hakaider*, 1995, Japan
Director: Keita Amemiya
Cast: Yûji Kishimoto, Mai Hosho, Jiro Okamoto

After decades spent dormant, bad robot Hakaider (Okamoto) returns to life with no memory of his true self. After making his way to Jesus Town, a faux utopian oasis amid the wreckage of civilisation, he finds himself fighting on the side of good.

Kikaider spinoff in which that franchise's villain becomes the hero, while the hero is omitted entirely. It's surprisingly wacky with striking, often surreal imagery seemingly influenced by Shin'ya Tsukamoto's *Tetsuo*, Richard Stanley's *Hardware* and maybe even George Lucas' *THX 1138*. Well worthwhile but the English language dub ruins it – go for the subtitled version if you can.

Robot Ninja ★

1989, USA
Director: J.R. Bookwalter
Cast: Michael Todd, Bogdan Pecic, Maria Markovic

Comic book artist Leonard Miller (Todd) is inspired to become a costumed vigilante after witnessing a violent crime. With the help of scientist friend Doctor Goodknight (Pecic), he brings his latest character to life.

Micro-budget vigilante movie with few redeeming features. Those familiar with the work of low-budget schlockmeister J.R. Bookwalter (*Galaxy of the Dinosaurs, Zombie Cop*) may have guessed *Robot Ninja* features no robots or ninjas. Those who aren't, count yourselves lucky.

Rocco, ang batang bato ★★★

aka *Stone Boy, Boy God*, 1982, Philippines
Director: J. Erastheo Navoa
Cast: Niño Muhlach, Jimi Melendez, Cecille Castillo

11-year-old orphan Rocco (Muhlach) learns he's an immortal superhuman who must rescue his dead parents from their exile in 'the land of the small people'. He also does battle with a scientist who has been turning people into ape-men, vampires and so on.

Demented children's fantasy likely to turn a typical juvenile into an emotional wreck. Aside from the monsters, patricide and twitching corpses, its approach to narrative risks leaving modern minors questioning the nature of reality. For adults with a sense of the ridiculous there's much to enjoy.

Rocket Ship

1936, USA
Directors: Ford Beebe, Robert F. Hill
Cast: Buster Crabbe, Jean Rogers, Charles Middleton

Feature-length edit of 1936 serial *Flash Gordon*. *Spaceship to the Unknown*, a second edit of the same serial, appeared in 1966.

The Rocketeer ★★★★

aka *The Adventures of the Rocketeer*, 1991, USA
Director: Joe Johnston
Cast: Billy Campbell, Jennifer Connelly, Alan Arkin

Ace pilot Cliff Secord (Campbell) battles Nazis with his top-secret rocket pack.

More or less an updated Commando Cody serial dressed up as a would-be blockbuster. A lovely screenplay, beautiful Art Deco designs and more charm than one movie should contain help *The Rocketeer* soar to lofty, if not particularly original, heights.

Rocky Jones, Space Ranger: see Grouped Franchises

Rudraksh ★★

2004, India
Director: Mani Shankar
Cast: Sanjay Dutt, Bipasha Basu, Sunil Shetty

Reflecting the epic poem 'Ramayana', two supernaturally gifted men (one a good-hearted follower of Lord Hanuman, the other an evil disciple of the demon Ravan) battle over a magical MacGuffin and the future of mankind.

Rudraksh is so full of interesting ideas (that plot outline is the tip of the iceberg) it makes the poor execution frustrating. Steeped in Indian mythology, blessed with narration from the incomparable Amitabh

The Rocketeer

Bachchan, and seemingly given a free reign to be weird, it's certainly not a complete loss. But most of the cast are dreadful, the action sequences are worse, and the songs feel synthetic and poorly integrated.

Running Delilah ★★

1993, USA
Director: Richard Franklin
Cast: Kim Cattrall, Billy Zane, François Guétary

A government agent killed in the line of duty is transformed into a superbeing with drugs, bionics and elbow grease.

For a while things hold together fine in this *Six Million Dollar Man* update, the pilot for an un-produced series. While Cattrall is undercover it's only silly, but once she's turned into a cyborg the wheels come off. There's no consistency to her behaviour and actions – one moment she's horrified about being a head on a robot, the next she's laughing about being able to beat people up. There's some muddled feminist commentary, and lots of toing and froing over the ethics of turning a woman into a monster without her consent (apparently it's ok), but none of it convinces.

Sailor Moon (series): see Grouped Franchises

Sakima and the Masked Marvel

1966, USA, 100m
Director: Spencer Gordon Bennet
Starring: William Forrest, Louise Currie, Johnny Arthur

Feature-length edit of 1943 serial *The Masked Marvel*.

Salvage Mice ★★

aka *Sarubêji maisu*, 2011, Japan
Director: Ryuta Tasaki
Cast: Mitsuki Tanimura, Julia Nagano, Yûki Satô

Two women – one supernaturally strong, the other an ethical thief – team up for justice when the latter is betrayed.

Poor production values can't conceal the film's heart, dynamism and quality karate.

Samson (1960s Italian series): see Grouped Franchises and Peplum Movies

Samson ★★★

1964, India
Director: Nanabhai Bhatt
Cast: Dara Singh, Ameeta, Feroz Khan

Palace intrigue and romantic capers draw Samson (Singh) from the jungle, where he was quite happy living with his elephants.

Fast-paced, stuffed with songs, fighting and women obsessed with Samson, this Indian peplum movie indulges in more dancing and heightened drama than its Italian cousins, but at a glance looks similar thanks to all the oiled-up wrestlers and sandals. Singh is brilliant, even treating us to a ridiculous curly wig, while Mumtaz and Ameeta make for enchanting female leads.

Samson ★★

2018, USA/South Africa
Directors: Bruce Macdonald, Gabriel Sabloff
Cast: Taylor James, Billy Zane, Lindsay Wagner

Hebrew strongman Samson (James) leads a revolt against Philistine conquerors.

An historical epic from Pure Flix, the US producer of Christian-themed media. The apostolic elements are pronounced but, unlike better known Pure Flix movies such as *God's Not Dead*, Samson is accessible to people of all or no faiths. At first it seems much like an Asylum mockbuster, but the script and performances are superior and the objective more sincere.

San kei hap lui: see *Mr. and Mrs. Incredible*

El Santo (series): see Grouped Franchises and Luchador Movies

Satan's Satellites

1958, USA
Director: Fred C. Brannon
Cast: Judd Holdren, Aline Towne, Wilson Wood

The first of two feature-length edits of 1952 serial *Zombies of the Stratosphere*.

Satanik (series): see Grouped Franchises and Diabolik Super-Kriminals

Scooby-Doo & Batman: The Brave and the Bold ★★

2018, USA
Director: Jake Castorena
Cast: Frank Welker, Diedrich Bader, Matthew Lillard

Batman (Bader) recruits Mystery Inc. into his Mystery Analysts of Gotham organisation

and together they attempt to solve the only outstanding case on the books.

While the previous Scooby/Batman duet (*The Dynamic Scooby-Doo Affair*) employed the caped crusader's 1960s version, this updated adventure goes with a modern take. Due to being a Batman adventure featuring Scooby Doo (rather than the other way round, as before), numerous DC heroes and villains cameo, and it's they who provide most of the entertainment. There's plenty of fan service with Shaggy, Daphne and the rest dressing up as various former sidekicks (remember Ace the Bat-Hound?), but it's a shadow of the earlier movie.

Scooby Doo! Mask of the Blue Falcon ★★

2012, USA
Director: Michael Goguen
Cast: Frank Welker, Mindy Cohn, Grey Griffin

Unexplained shenanigans surround the release of a new film based on comic book superhero The Blue Falcon.

If a character trait was subtlely suggested in the original Scooby Doo TV series it's amplified tenfold here, which means Fred is pretentious, Daphne is an airhead and Velma constantly nags Shaggy and Scooby. Frank Welker is the only original voice actor among the cast, and in addition to reprising his role as Fred he takes over Scooby duties from the departed Don Messick. In terms of what's on screen all the components are here, but it's too ironic. Innocence is lost when Scooby gets depressed after a video of him falling into gunge gets 42 million hits on the internet.

Scott Pilgrim vs. the World ★★★★

2010, USA
Director: Edgar Wright
Cast: Michael Cera, Mary Elizabeth Winstead, Kieran Culkin

Toronto loser Scott Pilgrim (Cera) learns he must face girlfriend Ramona Flowers' (Winstead) seven evil exes in combat for the right to keep dating her.

The film relies heavily on Wright's visual invention, with Pilgrim's stylised clashes using every technical trick in the book to demonstrate a variety of superpowers and video game special moves. At least that's the superficial takeaway. But the director also gets the best from his sizeable cast, something that can be overlooked with all the fireworks. Cera and Winstead have never been better, and the exes amount to a cavalcade of entertaining eccentrics.

Sen Aydinlatirsin Geceyi: see *Thou Gild'st the Even*

Sentai: see Grouped Franchises and Super Sentai

Sentô shôjo: Chi no tekkamen densetsu: see *Mutant Girls Squad*

Sgt. Kabukiman N.Y.P.D. ★★★
1990, USA
Directors: Michael Herz, Lloyd Kaufman
Cast: Rick Gianasi, Susan Byun, Bill Weeden

An incompetent New York cop accidentally ingests the spirit of a Japanese superhero, becoming mythic crimefighter Kabukiman.

Gianasi is a bad actor but at least he suits this kind of broad comedy, unlike Byun, who seems to have taken the view she's in a real film. Kabukiman himself is funnier than The Toxic Avenger, Troma's principal superhero, but remains an acquired taste.

The Shadow ★★★
1940, USA

Director: James W. Horne
Cast: Victor Jory, Veda Ann Borg, Roger Moore

Eminent scientist Lamont Cranston (Jay) adopts alter ego the Shadow in his feud with invisible master criminal The Black Tiger (voiced by Richard Cramer).

From a theatrical perspective an invisible antagonist is one of the worst ideas a writer could have. There's the odd shot of a silhouette but for most of this nearly five hour serial The Black Tiger is represented by an unmoving tiger's head slowly exhaling smoke. Needless to say it leads to some dramatic limitations. But Jory is good as Lamont and there's a more adult, noir feel to things than most serials go for.

The Shadow ★★★
1994, USA
Director: Russell Mulcahy
Cast: Alec Baldwin, John Lone, Penelope Ann Miller

The Shadow (Baldwin) – millionaire playboy by day, masked do-gooder by night – must defeat arch nemesis Shiwan Khan (Lone).

Inadvertently humorous attempt to mop up some leftover *Batman* (1989) dollars, which is ironic given how derivative Batman is of the Shadow. The property had been floating around Hollywood for some time before *Highlander* director Russell Mulcahy finally gained some traction for a take that's best described as camp fun. Baldwin's innate self-importance fits the role well and the movie's glossy 1930s look is a welcome change from the overly dismal or overly saturated environments that tend to host these movies nowadays.

The Shadow Returns ★★★
1946, USA
Directors: Phil Rosen, William Beaudine
Cast: Kane Richmond, Barbara Read, Tom Dugan

Lamont Cranston (Richmond), the nephew of police commissioner J.R. West (Pierre Watkin), moonlights as super-sophisticated crimefighter the Shadow in order to help his uncle's boys solve a murder.

With the 1937 *Shadow* radio show (which originally featured Orson Welles in the lead) still popular after the war, a series of three films was developed by B-movie specialists Monogram Pictures. *The Shadow Returns* is the first and probably the best of them. Although stagy and cheap it's an effective mystery, if perhaps not quite up to the standard of similar B-series like *The Falcon*. Richmond is inoffensive enough, but Read (as Cranston's fiancée Margo Lane) grates. (Followed by *Behind the Mask*.)

The Shadow Strikes ★★★
1937, USA
Director: Lynn Shores
Cast: Rod La Rocque, Agnes Anderson, James Blakeley

The Shadow (La Rocque), winds up at the centre of a murder investigation when he's forced to impersonate a lawyer and is drawn into a complicated series of crimes.

La Rocque's Shadow has no powers to speak of and hardly wears the costume, so it's a stretch to call him a superhero in the classic mould. Ultimately, this movie, and its sort-of-sequel *International Crime*, are here thanks to their DNA. It's a bit stilted and the production feels like it was rushed, although no more so than you'd expect for a B-movie of the time. Crucially there's a decent little story; and it benefits from the best of the Shadows in La Rocque, whose easy charm and urbane wit make him a cross between William Powell and George Sanders.

Shadowman ★★★
aka *Nuits Rouges*, 1974, France

Director: Georges Franju
Cast: Gayle Hunnicutt, Jacques Champreux, Josephine Chaplin

The Man Without a Face (Champreux), is pursued by a cadre of interested parties as he hunts the treasure of the Knights Templar.

Formulaic Eurocrime thriller full of spies, cat burglars and unconvincing disguises. Shadowman himself takes a back seat for much of the movie as we hang out with the good guys on his trail. It's all a bit of a mess, perhaps thanks to a poor (but frequently amusing) English dub, but it looks good and there's always something happening.

Shahenshah ★★★★
1988, India
Director: Tinnu Anand
Cast: Amitabh Bachchan, Rohini Hattangadi, Supriya Pathak

Police officer Vijay Srivastava (Bachchan) accepts bribes in order to fund his second career as cyborg vigilante Shahenshah.

Chosen by Bachchan as his comeback film after a spell in politics, this epic tale of morality shifts awkwardly between its comedic and serious scenes but otherwise works very well. The crime thriller aspect is superior to most contemporary efforts and the song and dance routines are strong. But it's all about the immense charisma of Bachchan (as ever), who's superb both as clumsy clown Vijay and the supercool superhero Shahenshah.

Shapeshifter ★★
1999, Canada/Romania
Director: Philippe Browning
Cast: Paul Nolan, Bill MacDonald, Catherine Blythe

Bad guys chasing plutonium kidnap the secret-agent parents of teenager Alex (Paul

Nolan), who decides to investigate their disappearance in Romania. There he meets a shaman who gives him the ability to morph into animals.

Indescribably odd and inexplicably sincere stab at *Manimal Jr.* meets *The X-Files*. It's low budget, ineptly made and full of off-key performances suggesting inexpert direction. Plot threads appear and disappear leaving crucial issues unexplained or unresolved, and the end product feeling incomplete. It's so bad it becomes strangely entertaining. Alex crosses the globe, rescues his parents (then rescues their souls; long story), learns how to turn into animals, is shrunk into a jar, defies the CIA, makes a nemesis of a cyberwitch, stops terrorists blowing up the planet, befriends a magical gypsy, saves the universe, is revealed to be the messiah of a dwarf cult and gets tutored in wizarding by the 3D projection of a time-travelling A.I. living in a glass harmonica. There's a lot going on.

Sin City

Shazam! ★★★★

2019, USA
Director: David F. Sandberg
Cast: Zachary Levi, Mark Strong, Asher Angel

A wizard scouring the world for a worthy successor is outwitted by failed former contender Thaddeus Sivana (Strong), and forced to consolodate all his power in the first available recipient – troubled orphan Billy Batson (Angel), who gains the ability to transform into superhero Shazam! (Levi).

Levi and Angel should have swapped notes on how they were going to approach 14-year-old Billy Batson, because their two versions are impossible to reconcile. Angel plays him as a monosyllabic, confused cynic, whereas as Levi plays him as Tom Hanks in *Big*. It's a strange ball to drop and quite distracting, but about the only real problem here. Interestingly, Batson's foundling status is treated as more than

just an emotional device – it's crucial to who he is and drives a compelling subplot. The humour is well judged and there's a breakout performance from Jack Dylan Grazer, who's excellent as Batson's foster brother Freddie. But the real highlight is the screenplay. It's the sort of thing Steven Spielberg would have gone for in the 1980s, and as long you don't mind a cheesy formula it's just about perfect.

Sheena ★★

1984, USA
Director: John Guillermin
Cast: Tanya Roberts, Ted Wass, Donovan Scott

A girl lost in the African jungle is raised by a witch to protect her adopted people.

Dumb Tarzan-is-woman adventure movie. What a shame the first female character to be given her own comic book title has been so poorly represented on film. The camera's relentless focus on Tanya Roberts' half-naked torso leaves the rest of the cast looking awkward, as if they don't know whether they're supposed to be there and where they're supposed to look. The plot is an afterthought.

Sheman: Mistress of the Universe ★★

1988, Philippines
Director: Tony Y. Reyes
Cast: Joey de Leon, Panchito, Ruffa Gutierrez

Camp wizard Gay Skull (Joonee Gamboa) bestows superpowers on blacksmith Pando (de Leon), which transforms him into trans superhero Sheman.

A whole book could be written on the Pinoy approach to gender and sexual orientation in genre movies, but this probably isn't the time to get into it. *Sheman* is described by its prolific director as a spoof on popular Filipino comic, cartoon and film character Ang Panday (an heroic blacksmith who forges a magical knife from a meteor), and, of course, *He-Man and the Masters of the Universe*. But while it borrows some elements from the former, only character names and a few sneakily requisitioned frames come from the latter, with Reyes more interested in poking affectionate fun at classic anting-anting folk hero movies. In that regard it's perfectly pleasant, but so specific as to be of questionable interest to most audiences.

Shin angyo onshi: see *Blade of the Phantom Master*

Shiva Ka Insaaf ★★

1985, India
Director: Raj N. Sippy
Cast: Jackie Shroff, Poonam Dhillon, Vinod Mehra

A boy is raised by three supernatural men who train him to become a great warrior. When he comes of age he's given a mask, cape and trident, and sent out into the world to avenge the death of his father.

Although half played for laughs, most of the humour in *INDIA'S FIRST 3-D MOVIE* (as the poster shouts at us) is generated inadvertently by the wonky camerawork and performances. Bollywood warmth makes it tolerable.

Shoktir Lorai ★★★★

aka *Bangla RoboCop*, Year Unknown, Bangladesh
Director: Unknown
Cast: Danny Sidak, Munmun

Left for dead by the gangsters who killed his daughter, Dr. Johan Buchi (Sidak) is injected with a special serum that not only saves his life but renders him superhuman. With the addition of some RoboCop-esque armour, he's ready to fight crime.

Bengali genre quickie that 'borrows' music from *Superman*, footage from *RoboCop* and inspiration from Looney Tunes. Obviously it's awful and features no dub or subtitles, but there's an enormous amount of comedy value to the cardboard costume, cartoonish villains (one of whom seems to be an evil Wonder Woman) and Robo-dancing.

Sidekick ★★★

2005, Canada
Director: Blake Van de Graaf
Cast: David Ingram, Perry Mucci, Mackenzie Lush

Comic fan Norman Neale (Mucci) tries to persuade a colleague to use his newfound telekinetic powers to be a superhero.

Everything looks and sounds horrible and Mucci is out of his depth in the de facto lead role. Nevertheless there's something redeeming in what feels like Van de Graaf's heartfelt sincerity. Some movies just seem like the result of hard work by people who care, and that can go a long way when they aren't very good.

SideKicked ★
2016, USA
Directors: Johnathan Proenza, Steven Perez
Cast: Dave Noel, David Ausem, Christi Berlane

Enthusiastic but largely useless sidekick Boy Nova (Noel) has his nose put out of joint when he's passed over for promotion to superhero.

Obscure comedy that desperately needed some expert technical input. Microphones are routinely blown out, the image is eye-wateringly oversaturated and the postscript is misspelt.

Sign Gene ★★★★
2017, USA
Director: Emilio Insolera
Cast: Emilio Insolera, Benjamin Bahan, Hiroshi Vava

A gene mutation causing superpowers affects a small number of the world's deaf, and a sinister organisation seeks to wipe them out.

Sign Gene is so awash with themes relating to deafness and sound it's tempting to see it as a film made specifically for the hard of hearing but, ironically, the incredible audio mix is among its greatest assets. As is the case with the imagery, it's abstract and inventive – although not as inventive as the central conceit. The superpower inherent to the mutated gene manifests itself through sign language, and anything that can be signed can be brought into existence – signing 'gun' arms your index finger, and so on. An idea that good would be worth a punt even if it wasn't well executed.

The Sign of Zorro ★★★
1958, USA
Directors: Lewis R. Foster, Norman Foster
Cast: Guy Williams, Henry Calvin, Gene Sheldon

Don Diego de la Vega (Williams), scion of an influential family of Spanish origin, is called home to California when a corrupt official appoints himself local overlord.

In 1957 Disney debuted its successful *Zorro* TV series starring former model (and future *Lost in Space* star) Guy Williams. This movie was constructed from its first eight episodes arc, and uses exactly half its footage. There's a little resultant choppiness but on the whole it's not too noticeable. Williams is good and they do more with his frustration at having to play the foppish coward than in most versions of the story. There's more of his mute sidekick Bernardo (Sheldon) too, who adds a new dimension. Nothing is outstanding, but there's an indefinably pleasant air to it all; a TV cosiness that makes it seem familiar even if you haven't seen it before. (A second cut-and-shut followed in *Zorro, the Avenger*.)

Sihirbazlar Krali Mandrake Killing'in pesinde: see *Mandrake vs. Killing*

Silver Hawk ★★★
aka Fei Ying, 2004, Hong Kong
Director: Jingle Ma
Cast: Michelle Yeoh, Kôichi Iwaki, Brandon Chang

Wealthy socialite Lulu Wong (Yeoh) uses her alter ego Silver Hawk to investigate kidnappings in some way related to an A.I. computer chip.

Middling sci-fi kung fu movie set largely in an alternate Hong Kong. Michelle Yeoh is fantastic, of course, but the fight scenes are a little too reliant on obvious wire work

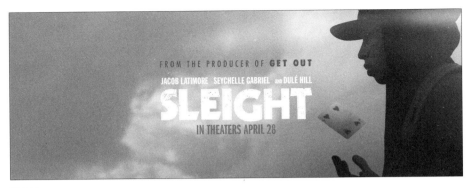

Sleight

and chaotic editing, while the sincerity of the melodramatic character stuff doesn't survive the dub.

Sin City ★★★★★
2005, USA
Director: Frank Miller, Robert Rodriguez, Quentin Tarantino
Cast: Bruce Willis, Mickey Rourke, Jessica Alba

Tales from the urban sprawl of doomed obsessives and degenerate wretches that is Basin City.

Sin City thunders along such a tightrope of excess it's easy to become preoccupied with wondering when it will fall. Hartigan (Willis) is more hardboiled than a Fabergé egg, Marv (Rourke) looks like Hellboy's Dad and Frodo gets eaten alive by dogs. All in obstinately stylised monochrome. It takes a deft touch to shuffle this stuff across the screen in such a way that we're able to suspend our disbelief, yet somehow that's what happens.

Sin City: A Dame to Kill For ★★★
2014, USA
Directors: Frank Miller, Robert Rodriguez
Cast: Mickey Rourke, Jessica Alba, Josh Brolin

The further adventures of Marv (Rourke), Nancy (Alba), Hartigan (Bruce Willis) and Sin City's highest lowlifes.

More of the same only not quite. Movies like this have to earn the colourful little bows that seem to tie up every story, and Rodriguez and Miller don't manage it quite so well in this sequel. Everything seems a little familiar, too. Mickey Rourke's Marv is back, but, like all Sin City's residents he's so one-dimensional there's not much more you can do with him, so he basically just performs an abbreviated version of his role in the first movie. It's still entertaining, and Eva Green is perfect as femme fatale Ava.

Sinister Squad ★
2016, USA
Director: Jeremy M. Inman
Cast: Johnny Rey Diaz, Christina Licciardi, Lindsay Sawyer

With Death himself (Nick Principe) on the rampage, Alice (Licciardi) puts together a superhero team.

As a blatant *Suicide Squad* mockbuster, the assumption might be that *Sinister Squad* follows the usual M.O. and copies its near namesake lock, stock and barrel. But the odd thing is how much more similar this dire effort is to The Asylum's earlier *Avengers Grimm* films. They share the same characters, setup, humour, and comprehensive lack of regard for audiences. This one is harder to like, though.

The Six Million Dollar Man ★★

1973, USA
Director: Richard Irving
Cast: Lee Majors, Martin Balsam, Darren McGavin

Astronaut and Air Force pilot Steve Austin (Majors) is horrendously injured testing an experimental plane. Luckily for him a government project aiming to create the world's first bionic secret agent is on the lookout for a candidate.

Going by this feature-length *Six Million Dollar Man* TV pilot, it's a miracle the series made it to air. The origin story runs well past the one-hour mark, leaving the action, such as it is, compressed into a brief and rudimentary single sequence. The dynamic between patient, doctor and their cynical government overlord is by far the strongest element, so it's strange it was reworked for the subsequent series. (Followed by *The Six Million Dollar Man: Wine, Women and War*.)

The Six Million Dollar Man: The Solid Gold Kidnapping ★★★

1973, USA
Director: Russ Mayberry
Cast: Lee Majors, Richard Anderson, Alan Oppenheimer

A naughty cabal is kidnapping international statesmen for ransom. When an American politician is abducted, Steve Austin (Majors) investigates, helped by a doctor sporting implanted memories.

With the formula now established there's time for a little thematic indulgence, and

we get some philosophising on the nature of humanity. It's secondary to the plot, which is almost as Bond-like as that of the previous movie (*The Six Million Dollar Man: Wine, Women and War*) with a casino, suave euro-criminals and a femme fatale contessa all featuring prominently. Again Steve's abilities are barely utilised, and again there's a huge amount of both reused and stock footage. (Followed by *The Return of the Six Million Dollar Man and the Bionic Woman*.)

The Six Million Dollar Man: Wine, Women and War ★★★

1973, USA
Director: Russ Mayberry
Cast: Lee Majors, Richard Anderson, Alan Oppenheimer

Steve Austin (Majors) investigates an arms dealer offering a US submarine for sale.

A retooling of the concept sees this second *6MDM* pilot present its hero as an American James Bond. Russian spies, underground lairs, Monte Carlo casinos, exotic villains and Bond alumni have all been shipped in from Pinewood to complete the effect (and Britt Eckland appears just a year before her breakout as a Bond girl in *The Man With the Golden Gun*.) The promising dynamic of the first film is lost, with two key roles recast unfavourably and tension between the characters largely written out, and there's still surprisingly little action. But writers at least deemed a plot necessary this time, and they did a great job with the double entendres: "In Russia we say all American men are soft" observes a villain. "We rise to the occasion" retorts Austin. Bond indeed. (Followed by *The Six Million Dollar Man: The Solid Gold Kidnapping*.)

Sixty Million Dollar Man ★★★

aka *Bak bin sing gwan*, 1995, Hong Kong
Directors: Jing Wong, Wai Man Yip
Cast: Stephen Chow, Gigi Leung, Man-Tat Ng

Blown up by gangsters, obnoxious playboy Lee Chak Sing (Chow) is the recipient of bionic implants that inexplicably allow him to transform into everyday items including a rice cooker and a toothpaste tube.

Bizarre early Stephen Chow (*Shaolin Soccer*, *Kung Fu Hustle*) comedy vehicle. Innovative (for the time) visual effects cleverly exploit Chow's gift for comedy, but the order of the day here is surreal madness. The film opens with a cover of Barry Manilow's 'Copacabana', and then spends a few scenes spoofing *Pulp Fiction* before Sing turns into a toilet and argues with a woman trying to defecate into his 'mouth'. I'm not sure how well these elements blend together, but it's fun trying to figure it out.

Sky High ★★★★

2005, USA
Director: Mike Mitchell
Cast: Kurt Russell, Kelly Preston, Michael Angarano

Young Will Stronghold (Angarano) fears he will disappoint his parents, superheroes Jetstream (Preston) and The Commander (Russell), by failing to develop superpowers of his own.

If *Sky High* sounds familiar you may once have caught 2000's *Up, Up and Away* on the Disney Channel. The setups are identical, although this is a rather more polished product. Kurt Russell is the main draw and steals every scene he's in, but only because he doesn't share any with cameoing cult favourite Bruce Campbell, who's hilarious as the acerbic Coach Boomer. Angarano isn't quite so good in the lead but few superhero movies have the potential to appeal to such a broad audience. The age range this thing caters to is literally boundless.

Sleight ★★★★

2016, USA

Director: J.D. Dillard
Cast: Jacob Latimore, Seychelle Gabriel, Storm Reid

Bo (Latimore), a street magician with a homemade bionic implant, tries to raise enough money to provide his sister with a better life. Unfortunately for them both, that means running afoul of ruthless drug dealer Angelo (Dulé Hill).

Blumhouse Productions, the company behind *Sleight*, achieved huge commercial success with the *Insidious* and *Paranormal Activity* horror franchises before applying their magic to more sophisticated genre fare like *Whiplash* and *Get Out*. *Sleight* isn't as successful as those illustrious awards magnets, it lacks that last ounce of nuance and ambition, but it doesn't embarass them. The central idea (tech genius Bo has installed an electromagnet in his arm in order to manipulate metal as part of his routine) is communicated realistically, as is everything else. Relationships between Bo and his sister Tina (Reid) and love interest Holly (Gabriel) aren't handled perfectly (the first is underdeveloped and the second verging on cheesy) yet seem believable thanks to good performances and direction.

Sogni mostruosamente proibiti ★★

1982, Italy
Director: Neri Parenti
Cast: Paolo Villaggio, Janet Agren, Alessandro Haber

Comic book writer and imaginary superhero Paolo Villaggio (himself) is drawn into a web of intrigue by a beautiful woman.

A year after the embarssment that was *Condorman*, here's the same movie only in Italian. The viewer's first task is to accept a grey-haired 60-year-old suit as a comic book writer, but it seems that's all part of the joke. As is everything else: the gags are relentless, which is fine, but also of the old-man-locked-outside-in-his-underwear variety, which is not. It soon starts to grate and the superhero element falls away.

Somebody's Hero ★★★

2011, USA
Director: Darin Beckstead
Cast: Christopher Gorham, Susan Misner, Arthur J. Nascarella

An accountant dressed as Superhero Man becomes an accidental vigilante.

This somewhat hackneyed message movie runs the risk of being written off as a soppy banality. We've seen this sort of thing too often (man stuck in boring job finds new inspiration through helping needy child), and *Somebody's Hero* does little to develop the idea. It's better than the average, though, and the right crowd should find something to like in the light romantic comedy. But the right crowd probably isn't reading a book about superhero movies.

Son of Batman ★★★

2014, USA
Director: Ethan Spaulding
Cast: Jason O'Mara, Stuart Allan, Thomas Gibson

When the League of Assassins is wiped out by former member Slade Wilson, aka Deathstroke (Gibson), Talia al Ghul (Morena Baccarin) sends her son to live with his biological father, Bruce Wayne (O'Mara).

The stuff with the child, Damian (Allan), is handled reasonably well. His arrogance is appropriate in this context (as opposed to irritating, as it will become in subsequent movies), and the dynamic between him and Batman allows for some new angles on the character. Folded into the narrative is a lightweight mystery involving Deathstroke trying to manufacture flying assassins, but it isn't developed beyond a justification for perfunctory fight scenes.

Son of Hercules

aka *Sons of Hercules*, 1964, India
Director: Sultan
Cast: Bipin Gupta, Kamran, Leela Kumari

It's tempting to assume this movie is lost but it seems more likely it has never been released on home formats (or is at least long out of print). Not to be confused with various Italian Peplum movies (see Grouped Franchises) released in 1964 and employing some variation of 'Son of Hercules' as alternate titles.

Son of the Mask ★

2005, USA
Director: Lawrence Guterman
Cast: Jamie Kennedy, Traylor Howard, Alan Cumming

Aspiring cartoonist Tim Avery (Kennedy) is a man so he doesn't want a baby. His wife Tonya (Howard) is a woman so she does want a baby. Then they have a baby.

Yes, that's what it's called. It's quite good, too

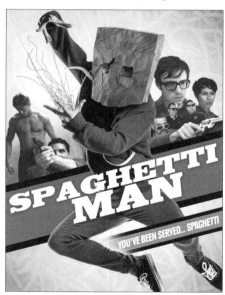

Sequel that positions the franchise within the remit of Norse mythology, and the audience within the seventh circle of hell.

Son of the White Mare ★★★★★
aka *Fehérlófia*, 1981, Hungary
Director: Marcell Jankovics
Cast: György Cserhalmi, Vera Pap, Gyula Szabó

The superhuman son of an exiled Goddess sets out to destroy the dragons who have taken over Earth.

Stunning animation derived from Hunnic fables. Visually it's unique, abstract and profoundly beautiful, while the story deals in mythic allegory. More like a haunting, half-remembered dream than a film, and impossible to describe accurately.

Son of Zorro ★★
1947, USA
Directors: Spencer Gordon Bennet, Fred C. Brannon
Cast: George Turner, Peggy Stewart, Roy Barcroft

Corrupt officials have taken over California, leaving Zorro's grandson, Jeffrey Stewart (Turner), to save the day.

A slight return to form after disappointing sequel, *Zorro's Black Whip*. It's a tad slow and clunky, and deviates so far from the original Zorro concept that the protagonist should probably have been established as a new character, as in the previous entry. But it's well enough written and played to be entertaining. (Fourth in the series of serials, it was followed by *Ghost of Zorro*.)

The Source ★★
aka *The Surge*, 2002, USA
Director: Steve Taylor
Cast: Mathew Scollon, Melissa Reneé Martin, Edward DeRuiter

Four teenage outcasts discover a rock that gives them superpowers. After settling some scores, events take a dark turn.

Handled with greater wit and intelligence the idea behind *The Source* might prove interesting (in fact it did, in Josh Trank's *Chronicle*), but as it stands this is a joyless and directionless waste of time. All four leads are fundamentally unconvincing, and the decision to sway and rotate the camera in every other scene can only be a passive aggressive act of audience defiance.

Space Sheriff: Grouped Franchises and Metal Hero Series

Space Soldiers Conquer the Universe
1972, USA
Directors: Ford Beebe, Ray Taylor
Cast: Buster Crabbe, Carol Hughes, Charles Middleton

Feature-length cut of *Flash Gordon Conquers the Universe*. It was created for the 16mm home movie market.

Space Warriors 2000 ★★
1985, Japan/Thailand
Directors: Marc Smith, Sompote Sands
Cast: Bob Sessions, Nicholas Curror, Sarah Taunton

A young boy is given an Ultraman toy that comes alive and whisks him away to a distant galaxy.

As if tokusatsu movies weren't bewildering enough already, this one is the result of a Thai production company cutting together a bunch of Japanese Ultraman TV shows on the quiet (and in the dark, apparently). Sold to US networks in the mid 80s, legal action from Ultraman's commercial rights owner, Tsuburaya Productions, meant it was only aired a handful of times. Unsurprisingly, it's a scrappy affair. Even the specially filmed (I think) intro doesn't cut between shots coherently, and it's a different aspect ratio to the rest of the footage (the image is slightly stretched instead of very stretched). Once we head off into space to meet the Galaxy Council, narrative anarchy renders it impossible to follow. Perhaps worth seeing as a curio but best imbibed in small doses. (See Grouped Franchises and Ultraman for official entries in the franchise .)

Spaceship to the Unknown

1966, USA
Directors: Frederick Stephani, Ray Taylor
Cast: Buster Crabbe, Jean Rogers, Charles Middleton

Second feature-length edit of the 1936 Flash Gordon serial of the same name. (The first was *Rocket Ship*.)

Spaghettiman ★★★★

2016, USA
Director: Mark Potts
Cast: Benjamin Crutcher, Winston Carter, Brand Rackley

A brazen layabout gains superpowers from spaghetti re-heated in a broken microwave.

Low-budget indie comedy that's initially determined to be disliked but soon relents. To be fair it's probably down to the viewer needing to slip onto the movie's bizarre wavelength, but if you manage it there's a lot to enjoy. The performances are sketchy but the script can be laugh-out-loud funny, daft as it is.

Sparks ★★

2013, USA
Directors: Todd Burrows, Christopher Folino
Cast: Chase Williamson, Ashley Bell, Clancy Brown

Idealistic wannabe superhero Ian Sparks (Williamson) teams up with Lady Heavenly (Bell) in order to battle arch criminal Matania (William Katt). Things don't go well.

The usual elements are borrowed from the usual superheroes and mixed into a period noir that seems to be going for the tone of *Watchmen* or Frank Miller's *The Spirit*. The generic archetypes and stylised aesthetic make for uncomfortable bedfellows and set *Sparks* up to fall between two stools; it's neither fun as a superhero story nor striking as an exercise in style.

Spawn ★★

1997, USA
Director: Mark A.Z. Dippé
Cast: Michael Jai White, John Leguizamo, Martin Sheen

Betrayed and murdered while on a covert mission, black ops badass Al Simmons (White) is offered a Faustian pact by the demonic Malebolgia (Frank Welker).

Often cited as the first American superhero movie with a black protagonist (it isn't), this much derided missed opportunity is lacking focus and sense. Michael Jai White is good, but the early promise of a bonkers opening is soon scuppered by clumsy direction. The writing is no better, and some of the visual effects deserve particular censure.

Spawn (animated series): see *Todd McFarlane's Spawn*

Special ★★★★

2006, USA
Directors: Hal Haberman, Jeremy Passmore
Cast: Michael Rapaport, Josh Peck, Ian Bohen

After taking part in a clinical trial, parking enforcement officer Les Franken (Rapaport) may or may not develop superpowers.

There are a lot of these movies: frugal but well-made US Indies with a high concept, revisionist intentions, melancholic tone and slightly faded sort-of-star in the lead. This is a good one. Imagine *Jacob's Ladder* meets *Kick-Ass*, if you can. Are we watching a man have a mental breakdown, a man suffering side effects from an experimental drug, or a man who has accessed his extraordinary physical and mental potential? It's very difficult material to handle and you might not bet on two unknowns pulling it off, but there's some masterful writing and direction here. Rappaport is also brilliant. Along with the rest of the cast he chimes perfectly with the feel of a movie that's inventive, touching and unpredictable.

Specials ★★★★

2000, USA
Director: Craig Mazin
Cast: Rob Lowe, Thomas Haden Church, Paget Brewster

Spider-Man: Into the Spider-Verse

Members of America's least distinguished superhero team struggle with everyday challenges, jealousies and insecurities.

Although not directed by him, *Specials* was conceived, written and produced by James Gunn, the filmmaker behind the *Guardians of the Galaxy* series. It's an uncompromising satire on the genre and strips away all the mythos and dignity usually inherent to the superhero archetype. The famous *Guardians* wit seems even sharper here thanks to the more mature (and sweary) avenues opened up by the movie's R rating, and with Judy Greer, Thomas Hayden Church, Rob Lowe and others there are some very talented comedic actors on hand.

The Spider Returns ★★★

1941, USA
Director: James W. Horne
Cast: Warren Hull, Mary Ainslee, Dave O'Brien

When a ruthless crime lord known only as The Gargoyle begins sabotaging The USA's industrial facilities, police seek help from amateur criminologist Richard Wentworth (Hull), who adopts alter ego The Spider for his investigation.

For some reason much of this sequel to *The Spider's Web* serial seems to be played for laughs, with the villain's henchmen and Wentworth's second alter ego (the street hustler Blinky McQuade) full on comedy characters. Like its predecessor it has good pace, a suitably diabolic antagonist and a strong lead performance.

The Spider Returns

1943, USA
Director: James W. Horne
Cast: Warren Hull, Mary Ainslee, Dave O'Brien

Feature-length edit of the serial of the same name. Made for international distribution and long since lost.

Spider-Man ★★★★★

2002, USA
Director: Sam Raimi
Cast: Tobey Maguire, Kirsten Dunst,
Willem Dafoe

Student Peter Parker (Maguire) is bitten by a radioactive spider, develops superpowers, and battles a crazed industrialist.

Eyebrows were raised when Sam Raimi was appointed to shepherd Spider-Man to the big screen. This was the most significant comic book property never to have received the Hollywood treatment, and it was finally going to be administered by the *Evil Dead* guy? As it happens the director's mix of both playful and commercial instincts proved ideal for the character, who's rendered with a pleasing twist of the camp absurdity most superhero movies were then avoiding. The CG web-slinging is incredible; pumped up and extended, its improbable choreography has become standard, but such dizzyingly implausible acrobatics were the reserve of cartoons until Raimi demonstrated what filmmakers could get away with (the climax of Burton's *Batman* is essentially a fistfight between a stiff comedian and an old man). And action isn't the focus, the movie's more interested in character. Intriguiningly Peter Parker is no faux goon like Clark Kent, or supercool icon like Logan. He's a legitimate clutz and believable loser, which makes him powerfully relatable.

Spider-Man 2 ★★★★★

2004, USA
Director: Sam Raimi
Cast: Tobey Maguire, Kirsten Dunst,
Alfred Molina

An insane scientist with metal tentacles causes trouble for Spider-Man (Parker).

Raimi ideosyncracies abound in a movie that successfully juggles several emotionally weighty strands, and is brave enough to let the action take a back seat at times. Like the first film it's not afraid of a little camp, either, and Raimi has particular fun with the tentacles, imbuing them with personality and using them as he might in a horror film.

Spider-Man 3 ★★★

2007, USA
Director: Sam Raimi
Cast: Tobey Maguire, Kirsten Dunst,
James Franco

Some alien gunge and a man made of sand conspire to ruin Peter Parker's (Maguire) newly idyllic life.

Maguire's relentless wide-eyed innocence has run its course, rendering him slightly irritating in the role, and the screenplay featues too many lazy clichés. Backstories are rewritten to allow for new contrivances, and characters routinely behave illogically. It feels like all involved are out of ideas and enthusiasm. All apart from the visual effects artists, that is. *Spider-Man 3* delivers the most dynamic and exciting web-slinging jaunts of any Spidey movie so far.

Spider-Man Strikes Back ★★★

1978, USA
Director: Ron Satlof
Cast: Nicholas Hammond, Robert F. Simon,
Chip Fields

Lecturer Dr. Baylor (Simon Scott) decides to build a nuclear reactor in class for no reason. Spider-Man gets the blame when the plutonium is stolen.

Second of three TV movies for Hammond's Spider-Man. It's less hokey than the first but Hammond himself remains weak. At least there's strong support from guest star JoAnna Cameron as a reporter looking for a scoop. Parker's surly editor J. Jonah Jameson (Simon) rides a tricycle.

Spider-Man: Far From Home ★★★★

2019, USA
Director: Jon Watts
Stars: Tom Holland, Samuel L. Jackson,
Jake Gyllenhaal

Peter Parker (Holland) takes a school trip to Europe, where he meets a new superhero, a fiery Elemental and an angry Nick Fury.

The script is brilliant when dealing with the teen character stuff – Parker's struggle with responsibility and his bond with misguided would-be superhero Mysterio (Gyllenhaal) – but lets us down around the middle of the movie with some lousy exposition and plot development. There's also an over-reliance on Iron Man tech. Things pick up again as Mysterio develops in unexpected directions, and the humour somehow grows even sharper. A particularly light and enjoyable way to follow *Avengers: Endgame*.

Spider-Man: Homecoming ★★★★

2017, USA
Director: Jon Watts
Cast: Tom Holland, Michael Keaton,
Robert Downey Jr.

As Peter Parker 's (Holland) crimefighting gets more ambitious, disgruntled contractor turned avian arms dealer Adrian Toomes (Keaton) crosses his radar.

Great writing and a superb performance from Holland make this the most believable and entertaining version of Spider-Man to date. He actually talks and behaves broadly like a high school kid for once, and doesn't spend half the movie moping about MJ. Keaton is a morally interesting villain with a low stakes agenda that ties in nicely with the wider MCU narrative. The one thing missing is the origin story. Normally that should be applauded, but in Spider-Man's case its events are crucial to his motivation. Remember how "with great power comes great responsibility"? We learn that from Uncle Ben's death in a key scene that isn't featured in the movie. (Followed by *Spider-Man: Far From Home*.)

Spider-Man: Into the Spider-Verse ★★★★★

2018, USA
Directors: Bob Persichetti, Peter Ramsey,
Rodney Rothman
Cast: Shameik Moore, Jake Johnson,
Hailee Steinfeld

Spider-Man fan Miles Morales (Moore) is bitten by a radioactive arachnid shortly before seeing his hero killed in an event that transports a variety of other Spider-People into our dimension.

The standard formula for animated comic book movies demands lots of action scenes interspersed with hugely exaggerated and unconvincing melodrama. The developed characters and detailed plots of mainstream fare such as *The Incredibles* (and to a much lesser extent *Henchmen, Ivan the Incredible, Americano* et al) represent a different kind of filmmaking. *Into the Spider-Verse* tries to bridge the gap between the two approaches in every conceivable way; with even the animation blending 2D (favoured by Marvel and DC straight-to-video adventures) and 3D (favoured by mainstream studio fare). For comic book aficionados there's a high concept plot that makes no sense, and lots of fan service, while multiplexers get good production values and characters written to sound like Deadpool and Tony Stark. There's also a lot going on with a script full of emotionally potent relationships, some of which ring true and some of which don't. As long as you aren't planning to think too hard about whether it makes sense, *Into the Spider-Verse* is an absolute blast.

Spider-Man: The Animated Series (cut-and-shuts): see Grouped Franchises

Spider-Man: The Dragon's Challenge ★★★

1979, USA
Director: Don McDougall
Cast: Nicholas Hammond, Robert F. Simon, Chip Fields

Peter Parker (Hammond) and boss J. Jonah Jameson (Simon) become embroiled in the defection of a Chinese politician accused of crimes he didn't commit. Together they must find a way to prove his innocence.

The Hong Kong setting is well exploited (as if to prove the production really went there) and provides a more epic feel than might be expected from a TV series. Seeing Spider-Man scaling skyscrapers with Kowloon in the background is probably the closest this show got to being impressive. There's less Peter Parker than usual, which is a huge boon, and the plot isn't bad either.

The Spider's Web ★★★

1938, USA
Directors: James W. Horne, Ray Taylor
Cast: Warren Hull, Iris Meredith, Richard Fiske

A crime boss known only as The Octopus tries to take over the USA. Can The Spider (Hull) stop him?

The first of two serials based on The Spider, a once popular pulp masked hero created as competition for the Shadow. On paper it's pretty standard: the wealthy playboy protagonist works with police to catch a villain whose identity is revealed only thirty seconds (literally) before the final fade-out. It's better than most serials, though, thanks to a strong lead performance from Hull, who also played Mandrake the Magician and the Green Hornet around the same time. Features edgy-for-the-era violence and surprisingly vigorous direction allied to a sinister pre-war sabotage plot reminiscent of something Hitchcock might have tackled.

The Spirit ★★★

1987, USA
Director: Michael Schultz
Cast: Sam J. Jones, Nana Visitor, Bumper Robinson

Believed to have been killed in the line of duty, detective Denny Colt (Jones) adopts the persona of masked vigilante The Spirit and secretly pursues the criminals who murdered his best friend.

Flash Gordon himself, Sam J. Jones, returns to his superhero roots and, when not trying to be serious, he's not bad. The writing, courtesy of *Die Hard* scribe Steven E. de Souza, is even better. One-liners land very well, the investigation makes sense and a handful of directorial touches elevate the drily amusing script well above the average. It's an odd concept though, and it's easy to see why ABC buried it. The mix of severe, comical and childish tones won't be to everyone's taste.

The Spirit ★★

2008, USA
Director: Frank Miller
Cast: Gabriel Macht, Samuel L. Jackson, Scarlett Johansson

After cop Denny Colt (Macht) is killed in the line of duty, he's resurrected as The Spirit. In no time at all he finds a nemesis in The Octopus (Jackson), who plans to create an immortality serum.

As with the *Sin City* movies (the stylistic brethren of this take on *The Spirit*), the plot is revealed via numerous tightly scripted character moments. Although few of those moments conjure much in the way of magic there's still some good stuff, mostly by way of random explosions and empty style. But there's more bad than good. Macht doesn't have the presence to carry the movie and there's a stifling sense of density brought on by both visual peculiarities and Miller's inability to stage even the simplest scenes with any fluidity.

Split ★★★★

2016, USA
Director: M. Night Shyamalan
Cast: James McAvoy, Anya Taylor-Joy, Haley Lu Richardson

A trio of girls kidnapped by a man with 23 diagnosed personalities (all of which jostle for dominance), must escape before the monstrous 24th takes over.

The girls are good. They're 'types' but not excessively so, and behave like real people. However, this is unquestionably McAvoy's film. He's magnificent as Kevin Wendell Crumb, the DID-suffering zoo worker who's in turns terrifying, sympathetic and utterly unreadable. Although he has what must be called supernatural qualities, *Split* is not a superhero movie. But sandwiched as it is between *Unbreakable* and *Glass* in M. Night Shyamalan's 'Eastrail 177 Trilogy' it seems wrong to omit it.

The SpongeBob Movie: Sponge Out of Water ★★★

2015, USA
Directors: Paul Tibbitt, Mike Mitchell
Cast: Tom Kenny, Antonio Banderas, Bill Fagerbakke

Spongebob and friends transform into superheroes to battle a crooked pirate with a magic book.

This second Spongebob movie isn't quite as successful as the first, but does stick like a limpet to the frantic, psychedelic vibe of the TV show, even when taking an ill-advised lurch into live-action. The superhero stuff is confined to the last act and isn't the movie's strongest element, that honour goes to the outright insanity of it all.

Spy Smasher ★★★★

1942, USA
Director: William Witney
Cast: Kane Richmond, Marguerite Chapman, Sam Flint

Spy Smasher (Richmond) battles with Nazi saboteurs trying to turn the tide of the war.

Frequently described as the best action serial ever made, *Spy Smasher* is the only legitimate and original screen outing for Fawcett Comics' Batmanesque eponymous masked detective, leading scientist and genius inventor. It's extremely fast-paced and innovative, boasts a very strong dual performance from Richmond (playing twin brothers), and features some of the best stuntwork and effects of the era.

Spy Smasher ★★★★

aka *Casus Kiran*, 1968, Turkey
Director: Yilmaz Atadeniz
Cast: Sevda Ferdag, Irfan Atasoy, Yildirim Gencer

A masked criminal is attempting to take over the world, luckily Casus Kiran (Atasoy, going by Spy Smasher's Turkish name) and his beautiful girlfriend Sevda (Ferdag) are on the case.

One of a handful of foreign language films to blend James Bond with Batman (1966 Pinoy offering *James Batman* being the most literal example), this Turkish B-movie also takes cues from hardboiled US thrillers of the 1930s and 1940s, while adding a pinch of European New Wave style to what is essentially an unauthorised remake of the 1942 serial of the same name. There's not much plot, it's really just a long string of action scenes, but this is one of the most entertaining films of its kind.

Spy Smasher Returns

1966, USA

Director: William Witney
Cast: Kane Richmond, Marguerite Chapman, Sam Flint

Feature-length edit of the 1942 serial *Spy Smasher*. Sold for TV syndication as part of a package with other Republic serials.

Spy Smasher: Man of 7 Lives ★★★

aka *Casus Kiran - 7 canli adam*, 1970, Turkey
Director: Yilmaz Atadeniz
Cast: Irfan Atasoy, Feri Cansel, Süleyman Turan

Casus Kiran (Atasoy) tries to stop bad guys doing bad stuff.

In keeping with the traditions of proper Turksploitation, scant thought is given to matters of copyright and in the first four minutes alone we get scraps of music lifted from two James Bond theme tunes. Much of the rest of the film is spent watching Atasoy being cool, which he's remarkably good at. First he's cool on a motorcycle, then he's cool in a nightclub before being cool while beating bad people up. Both the tone of the movie and Kiran's character are a little different this time around, with the swinging 60s and Eurotastic superheroes like Argoman proving more of an inspiration here than on the previous movie (1968's *Spy Smasher*. There's also a dollop of *Danger: Diabolik* in the mix, with the previous goofy Batman cape and mask dropped in favour of a more lithe look.

Squid Man ★★★

2013, USA
Director: Charlie Cline
Cast: Andrew Roth, Laurel Schroeder, Eric Bryant

Reduced to living on a buddy's couch after being fired from the Superhero Society, Squid Man (Roth) finds himself the subject of a book being written by a local reporter, and is encouraged to look back on his life.

Low-key indie comedy with imaginative elements and a sombre tone. It doesn't really go anywhere, being more a series of moments and ideas, but they're quite funny moments and ideas (a sequence in which an anonymous temp goes feral and starts living wild in a company's expansive file room is particularly successful).

Stan Lee's Mighty 7 ★★

2014, USA
Director: Allyson Bosch
Cast: Stan Lee, Armie Hammer, Christian Slater

Stan Lee (himself) stumbles on a crashed spaceship in the desert and teaches its alien occupants to be superheroes.

I'm not sure whether this is self-indulgence or lazy fan service, but either way it isn't very good. There's a sense these characters and scenarios have been knocking around in Lee's back pocket for years, and I picture a succession of editors politely convincing him to leave them there (a superhero with the power to turn into a ball... reeeeeally?). Lee's self-deprecating humour is sometimes funny, though.

Star Kid ★★

1997, USA
Director: Manny Coto
Cast: Joseph Mazzello, Joey Simmrin, Alex Daniels

Warring aliens send a cybernetic exosuit to Earth in order to prevent it falling into the hands of the enemy. It's found by bullied seventh grader Spencer Griffith (Mazzello).

This patchy attempt to recreate 1980s-style Spielbergian family fun gets the basics right but can't manage the magic, and it forgets to have a plot until the final act. Highlights include a strong performance from Griffith's teacher Janet Holloway (Corinne Bohrer), and some lovely special effects, particularly in the opening scene. Lowlights include the boy and the talking 'Cyborsuit.'

Star Warrior: see *Locke the Superman*

Steel ★

1997, USA
Director: Kenneth Johnson
Cast: Shaquille O'Neal, Annabeth Gish, Judd Nelson

Arms developing pacifist (erm...) John Henry Irons (O'Neal) returns to civvy street and discovers a criminal gang is using the high-tech weapons he designed for the military. After teaming up with a former colleague he uses some of his advanced tech to clean up the neighbourhood.

This could have been an important movie. In O'Neil it boasts a star who's clean-cut and inspirational, an icon for disaffected kids. With the likes of Judd Nelson's screwball villain, Charles Napier's crusty commander and Richard Roundtree's eccentric uncle, the support is a blast. And by more seriously addressing the proliferation of firearms on America's urban streets it could have been relevant to communities who have hitherto been underrepresented in superhero films. Unfortunately, nobody saw it because it's so terrible.

The Subjects ★★★★

2015, Australia
Director: Robert Mond
Cast: Paul O'Brien, Charlotte Nicdao, Emily Wheaton

Eight strangers are locked in a sound studio to take part in a clinical drug trial. One by one they start to develop superpowers.

High-concept claustrophobic sci-fi thriller in the vein of *Cube* (1997), *Identity* (2003) and *Exam* (2009). The improbably stereotypical stereotypes are well drawn and the actors do a good job, while the script is extremely tight and cleverly conceived, striking the right balance when it comes to keeping us engaged without dishing out too many clues. This isn't going to change the world, but it's a great little film and deserves to be more widely seen.

Suicide Squad ★★

2016, USA
Director: David Ayer
Cast: Will Smith, Jared Leto, Margot Robbie

With the arrival, and sudden departure, of Superman, secretive government official Amanda Waller (Davis) recruits a handful of criminal meta-humans to battle extra-terrestrial threats. Their first challenge comes in the form of an ancient witch bent on mankind's destruction.

Suicide Squad is a confused, desperate film. Confused because the screenplay bounces about between undercooked strands, and desperate because it snatches at any idea with a chance of ingratiating it to audiences. There's no coherent through line and the threat is never really established, rendering the movie a series of fuzzy, disappointing set pieces. On the plus side, Margot Robbie is fun as Harley Quinn (even though her presence makes no sense) and Will Smith pulls off Deadshot's internal conflict well enough to suggest a narrower focus with him at the centre would have been a better way to go.

Suicide Squad: Hell to Pay ★★★

2018, USA,
Director: Sam Liu
Cast: Christian Slater, Vanessa Williams, Billy Brown

The Suicide Squad, aka Task Force X, are sent to retrieve a card allowing its holder to escape hell.

Gory and extremely brutal R rated entry in the DC Animated Movie Universe. At times it feels like it's so violent simply because it can be, not because it needs to be, and this team remains pretty nonsensical. But there's a winning plot and some quite good character stuff.

Super ★★★★
2010 USA
Director: James Gunn
Cast: Rainn Wilson, Ellen Page, Liv Tyler

When his wife leaves him for a drug dealer, Frank Darbo (Wilson) decides becoming a superhero is the best way to deal with it. Eventually allied with comic book store clerk and unwelcome sidekick Libby (Page), Frank sets out to win back his wife.

What sounds dangerously like a 'quirky' romcom avoids PG-13 banality thanks to the sort of tone we might expect from the wry, edgy character study of an oddball suffering a breakdown. In fact, once we lift its mask and stare it in the face, it becomes clear that's basically what James Gunn's movie is. Although it never quite reaches its full potential, Darbo remains pleasingly unsympathetic, and there's brilliantly dark humour on display throughout. If you're already a fan, consider checking out the thematically similar (and just as good) *Special* and *Defendor*.

Süper adam Istanbul'da ★★
1972, Turkey
Director: Yavuz Yalinkiliç
Cast: Erdo Vatan, Safiye Yanki, Hayati Hamzaoglu

Superman (unidentified) takes a commercial airliner to Istanbul in order to help out a crime gang (he's a baddie for some reason) consisting entirely of men with moustaches.

I didn't know there was such a thing as stock footage shot on video, but there you go. This Turkish ripoff is just standard issue fight scenes intercut with men talking in rooms. The score is full of particularly obnoxious drumming and blasts of brass, while the comedy relief 'clumsy Clark' stuff grates horribly with the gangster scenes.

Super Badass ★★
1999, USA
Director: Charles E. Cullen
Cast: Charles E. Cullen, Lucy Coronado, Grant Plaskon

There isn't really a plot – it's just a series of grotesquely bloody killings.

Lo-fi, low-brow, low-budget rogue filmmaker Charles E. Cullen (*Killer Klowns from Kansas on Krack*, among other gems) turns his uniquely creative hand to the superhero genre in this surreal (and sick) comedy. One day it will be presented as evidence in his trial. I want to hate it but can't.

Super Batman & Mazinger V ★
aka *Star Jjangga II: Super Betaman, Majingga V,*

The universally moustachioed villains of
Süper adam Istanbul'da

1990, South Korea
Director: Yeong-han Kim
Cast: Hyeon-gon Kim, Hie-ju Lee, Yu-seong Jeon

Batman (Kim) prevents a space witch from acquiring a giant robot that will help her take over the universe.

If you've ever wondered whether a movie can mix live-action, cel animation, stolen footage from US cartoons, stolen footage from Japanese anime, and photographs cut out and glued to cardboard; the answer is yes, but not successfully. At least not on the evidence of this ridiculous thing. It's hard to accept it's a real movie and not a YouTube mashup made for a laugh (the giveaway is the live-action footage, which is of a lower quality than the typical YouTuber would be content with). You may be surprised to learn it isn't entirely official.

Super Bobrovs ★★★

aka *SuperBobrovy*, 2016, Russia
Director: Dmitriy Dyachenko
Cast: Oksana Akinshina, Pavel Derevyanko, Aleksandr Karpilovskiy

A working-class Russian family develop superpowers when a meteorite lands on them, so they cook up a plan to rob a bank.

Lightweight comedy with good effects and an absurdist streak. Much of the humour stems from a single surprisingly useful idea: family members' powers are dependent on their proximity to each other, and when too far apart their abilities are lost. It's a well exploited conceit. Perhaps too much effort is made to introduce conflict within the family and tick as many commercial boxes as possible, but there are worse crimes.

Super Boy ★★

1986 or 1988, India
Director: Ravikanth Nagaiah
Cast: Srinath, Sujatha, Hari

A wizard from the sea bestows an array of superpowers on a young boy who, after messing about for a bit, uses them to defeat a supercriminal who has an experimental mind-control device.

Aimed at a young audience, *Super Boy's* simple plot and one-dimensional characters are barely functional in cinematic terms, but might be welcomed by those viewers who don't speak the Southern Indian Dravidian language of Kannada (if you don't know the language it's a lot easier to follow a simple plot). Note the director's consideration for his audience in opening the movie with the following hand-written announcement: "This film is specially photographed to enhance the 4th dimension for a better and comfortable viewing. I have tried my best that viewers will not get strained."

Super Boy

1998, Israel
Director: Hanoch Rosen
Cast: Tom Avni, Alon Dahan, Zofit Eliashiv

Tom (Avni), a shy schoolboy who dreams of becoming a superhero, sees his wish come true. Unavailable on home formats at the time of writing.

Super Capers: The Origins of Ed and the Missing Bullion ★★

2009, USA
Director: Ray Griggs
Cast: Justin Whalin, Ray Griggs, Danielle Harris

An ordinary loser is accidentally enrolled into a superhero team.

Another indie superhero comedy stuffed with cameos and in-jokes. The characters are shallow, inconsistent and forgettable, while the script is devoid of real laughs and feels like a first draft. It is at least produced professionally, and Michael Rooker's baddie, Dark Winged Vesper, makes it tolerable.

Súper Cóndor

2016, Peru
Director: Alejandro Nieto-Polo
Cast: Gerardo Zamora, Jose Luis Ruiz,
Reynaldo Arenas

Unavailable at the time of writing.

Super Demetrios ★★

2011, Greece
Director: Georgios Papaioannou
Cast: Dimitrios Vainas, Paris Papadopoulos,
Olga Sfetsa

Crime lord Captain F.ROM (Papadopoulos)
wants to blow up buildings with a satellite
or something (apparently there are English
subtitles but they didn't work for me). Super
Demetrios (Vainas) is on hand to stop him.

Super Demetrios perhaps shouldn't qualify
on the grounds it's technically a fan film,
but with such a significant cult following in
its native Greece it can't be ignored. There
is heart, but the quality of the production
is atrocious and the acting hugely irritating.
As a comedy, the movie's appeal may be
clearer to Greek audiences, who should be
familiar with the humour and the tropes
being spoofed.

Super Detention ★★★

2016, Canada
Director: Justin G. Dyck
Cast: Nina Kiri, Jessica Vano, Aaron Chartrand

Kaeluss (Brian Cook), Earth's outstanding
superhero, visits his old superschool on
the pretext of choosing his supersuccessor.
Instead he steals the students' powers,
leaving five young misfits to save the day.

This Canadian comedy is more Saturday
morning kids' show than movie, and it hits
every conceivable cliché on the way to the
predictable climax. But the script is sharper

than you'd expect from something so low-
budget, and the direction more assured.
According to the IMDb synopsis it's '*X-Men*
meets *The Breakfast Club*', an appraisal
that's difficult to improve upon.

Super Force ★★

1990, USA
Director: Richard Compton
Cast: Ken Olandt, Larry B. Scott, Lisa Niemi

When astronaut Zach Stone (Olandt) finds
his detective brother has been murdered,
he becomes a motorcycling, mecha-suited
crimefighter extraordinaire.

Feature-length pilot for the TV series of
the same name. If you've ever wondered
whether quasi-vigilante law enforcement
shows such as *Airwolf* and *Knight Rider* are
representive of some kind of right wing

Super Fuzz aka *Poliziotto superpiù*

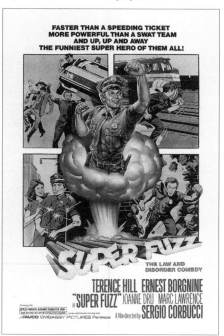

fantasy for their makers, look no further than the actor chosen to portray recurring antagonist Teo Satori. You might think a Japanese thespian would be best for the role, but instead, producers went with the man who organised the Watergate break-in. Seriously; G. Gordon Liddy, Nixon's former fixer, head of the White House Plumbers Unit and radical right poster boy stars in this thing. And he attempts a Japanese accent. I'm on about it not only because it seems incredible, but also because there's nothing else to say. *Super Force* edges into superhero territory where similar properties (most obviously *Street Hawk*) do not, thanks largely to our hero's supernatural space armour and other structural elements. It's enjoyable up to a point, assuming you like this sort of thing, but Olandt is a dull lead and it takes itself too seriously. G. Gordon Liddy, though. *Doing a Japanese accent!*

Super Fuzz ★★★

aka *Poliziotto superpiù*, 1980, Italy
Director: Sergio Corbucci
Cast: Terence Hill, Ernest Borgnine, Joanne Dru

Cop Dave Speed (Hill) gains superpowers from a NASA rocket, but winds up neck-deep in trouble when a former Hollywood starlet frames him for murder.

Kooky US-set Italian comedy. Like Terence Hill's biggest hit, *They Call Me Trinity*, *Super Fuzz* relies on the double act he forms with a burly co-star, in this case Ernest Borgnine. Their chemistry is good, the script is quite funny, and Hill is as likeable as ever as an enthusiastic but half-witted patrolman.

Super Gee

1973, Philippines
Director: Armando Garces
Cast: Nora Aunor, Celia Rodriguez, Eddie Garcia

Nora Aunor stars as a black-clad female superhero. This movie is believed lost.

Super Giant (1960s Japanese series): see *Atomic Rulers, Attack from Space, Evil Brain from Outer Space* and *Invaders from Space*

Super Hero Central ★

2004, USA
Director: Scott Shaw
Cast: Scott Shaw, Hae Won Shin, Linnea Quigley

Two members of a rock band moonlight as a superhero team.

Lo-fi genre filmmaker Scott Shaw brings his uniquely dire 'Zen' filmmaking philosophy (which entails having no plan, no objective and no idea - I'm not joking) to the superhero genre. The results are unspeakable.

Super Inday and the Golden Bibe ★★★

1988, Philippines
Director: Luciano B. Carlos
Cast: Maricel Soriano, Aiza Seguerra, Eric Quizon

Space children send a magic duck to Earth, where it gives a young woman named Inday (Soriano) superpowers. She uses them to defend her community from demons intent on something.

Predictably this little seen (at least in the West) female-centric adventure lacks any English subtitles but, even so, there's no concealing its charm. Essentially a comedy version of Darna (Inday eats special duck eggs to become her alter ego), the movie spends most of its time setting the scene, developing character dynamics and having fun with the duck, leaving what little action there is to the final act.

Super Inday and the Golden Bibe ★★

2010, Philippines

Director: Michael Tuviera
Cast: Marian Rivera, Jake Cuenca, John Lapus

As a means of gaining them admission to heaven, a vampire child and a fallen angel give an adopted girl superpowers.

Shinier, more expansive and ambitious sort-of remake of the previous. This time Inday (Rivera) learns she was adopted and moves to Manilla, where she becomes embroiled in her new boss's penchant for demonism. The tone is sillier and it feels like each gag, emotional moment and plot device is nailed with a sledge hammer. That lack of subtlety is to the film's detriment, and despite being better made and more coherent it isn't as entertaining as the earlier version.

Super Islaw and the Flying Kids ★★★

1986, Philippines
Director: J. Erastheo Navoa
Cast: Richard Gomez, Janice de Belen, Nadia Montenegro

Islaw (Gomez), a good-natured boy with a limp, is (eventually) granted superpowers by a dirty hobo, who then charges the child with defending his home town from a malevolent devil who keeps turning people into zombies.

Generally well made (relative to slightly earlier equivalents) and coherent feel-good family fantasy. *Super Islaw* spends more time on character and story than action, and Gomez is an appealing lead. Without English subtitles it's hard to understand how Islaw's girlfriend has supernatural powers she only uses for cleaning, but the conceit does lead to a fun song and dance number in which various fruit, vegetables and kitchen items come to life.

Super K: see *Kiara the Brave*

Super Mouse and the Roborats ★★

1989, Philippines
Director: Tony Y. Reyes
Cast: Joey de Leon, Rene Requiestas, Manilyn Reynes

Circus performer Mickey (de Leon) learns he was adopted and that his biological father was an alien rodent.

From the director of the bonkers *Alyas Batman en Robin* (and a dozen other Pinoy superhero movies), *Super Mouse and the Roborats* isn't quite as much fun but could be worth a punt. Highlights include a race of aliens in Darth Vader costumes and Joey de Leon singing Raindrops Keep Fallin' On My Head (in Tagalog) to animated mice. And with so many circus performers knocking about there's plenty of colour. Sadly there's not much Super Mouse.

Super Noypi ★★★

2006, Philippines
Director: Quark Henares
Cast: Jennylyn Mercado, Mark Herras, John Prats

The various offspring of legendary superhero team the Super Noypi, each of whom has inherited their parents' powers, must come together to rescue them from evil dictator Diego Azaren (Monsour del Rosario).

With our time split between a colourful present and depressing future, *Super Noypi* bounces between two equally derivative settings. Here and now things feel a lot like an X-Men movie, while scenes set in 2075 have the bleak, cyber-punk air of a tech thriller. Some of the CGI is predictably dodgy, but the visual style and action set pieces are interesting.

The Super Rider: see Grouped Franchises and Kamen Rider

Superargo and the Faceless Giants

Super Sentai (series): see Grouped Franchises

Super Singh ★★

2017, India
Director: Anurag Singh
Cast: Diljit Dosanjh, Sonam Bajwa, Pavan Malhotra

A magic turban gives Sajjan Singh (Dosanjh) superpowers, which he uses to find out about himself.

Comedy with a tendency to vociferously extol the virtues of Sikhism. Nothing truly original happens (unless we count the magic turban, that's pretty original), Dosanjh is irksome and much of the humour fails. The songs, though, are great, while the digital grade and cinematography make the movie's vibrant colour scheme pop.

Super Soul Brother ★

aka *The Six Thousand Dollar Nigger*, 1978, USA
Director: Rene Martinez Jr.
Cast: Steve Gallon, Joycelyn Norris, Benny Latimore

A scientist creates a superpower elixir for his criminal cronies, but when it proves unstable they decide to test it on local bum, Wildman Steve (Gallon). Things don't go according to plan.

Awful sub-Rudy Ray Moore blaxploitation non-comedy. Most of the movie consists of amateur actors sitting on a couch tripping over their crass dialogue. Looks like it was knocked up over a weekend, which is about how long it takes to shake the feeling you've let yourself down by watching it to the end.

Super Stooges vs the Wonder Women ★★★

aka *Superuomini, superdonne, superbotte*, 1974, Italy
Director: Alfonso Brescia
Cast: Aldo Canti, Marc Hannibal, Hua Yueh

A trio of wandering superheroes defend simple village folk from Amazon women in search of 'the sacred fire'.

Presumably inspired by the success of the Three Supermen series (original member Aldo Canti stars), this slapdash and frankly bizarre action-comedy also draws heavily on the Phantom's mythology, folk hero tropes and kung fu cinema. The result is confused, to say the least, but fun if you like your movies full of cartoon sound effects. If you don't, you're likely to take away little more than a headache. Unusually for a superhero film of the era (and uniquely for an Italian superhero film of any era), the Super Stooge trio includes non-white members Chung, aka 'Asian Superhero' (Yueh), and Moog, aka 'African Superhero' (Hannibal). That's really how they're credited.

Super Task Force One ★

2013, USA,
Director: Steve Rudzinski
Cast: Steve Rudzinski, Bill Murphy,
Seth Gontkovic

Unassuming author Jason Oliver (Rudzinski) finds himself in possession of a henshin hero power suit and must use it to defeat the evil Emperor Zagel (Murphy), who has constructed a superweapon.

American tokusatsu spoof/hommage with some admirable enthusiasm and a clear affection for the genre. Nevertheless it's surprising this thing found distribution. There's no proper lighting or audio recording, the cast is apparently made up of writer/producer/editor/star (always a good sign) Rudzinski's buddies, and the camerawork is slapdash at best. Some attention to detail might have elevated *Super Task Force One* beyond the bottom wrung of the ladder, but it seems there wasn't time.

Super wan-tu-tri ★★

aka *Super 1, 2, 3*, 1985, Philippines
Director: Luciano B. Carlos
Cast: Tito Sotto, Vic Sotto, Joey de Leon

Three perpetually unfortunate and endlessly moronic street food vendors hatch a giant egg containing an alien baby who grants them superpowers.

Although it's tempting to say this 'Tito, Vic & Joey' (as the troupe is known) sci-fi comedy is worth seeing just for the theme tune, it's probably not true. Built on the broadest of broad humour, *Super wan-tu-tri* presumably loses much in translation (or at least it would if it had been translated) and not all of the humour lands, in spite of the leads being among the Philippines' most popular comic stars. The camp mugging grates, while the timing of the physical humour is all over the place.

Super-B ★★★

2002, Philippines
Director: Joyce Bernal
Cast: Rufa Mae Quinto, Marvin Agustin,
Melanie Marquez

Aliens who want to steal all our flowers must first get past Bilma (Rufa Mae Quinto), a street-food vendor who possesses a magic that gives her superpowers.

Deeply strange exercise in camp posturing full of musical interludes, extended comedy routines and ridiculous diversions. Quinta commits fully, which was probably the only sensible course of action, and delivers one of the oddest performances you're likely to see. Some of her footage feels like B-roll, and when she breaks the fourth wall it brings to mind DVD special features. Think of it as a spiritual cousin to the equally bizarre *ZsaZsa Zaturnah, ze Mooveeh*.

Superandy, il fratello brutto di Superman ★★

1979, Italy
Director: Paolo Bianchini
Cast: Andy Luotto, Gino Santercole,
Eurilla del Bono

A fully grown (and fully bearded) baby is despatched from his alien homeworld to the safety of Earth, where he grows up to have superpowers.

Surprisingly faithful (for a time) and very silly Superman spoof. The plot pokes its head round the corner every now and then but isn't inclined to interfere with Andy Luotto's schtick. At the time of production he was enjoying a spell of popularity thanks to a role on successful Italian variety show *L'altra domenica*, and it feels like *Superandy* was an attempt to establish him as a leading comedy star of the movies. It soon gets tired but some of the gags are so joyously idiotic they'll raise a smile regardless.

Superargo Against Diabolicus ★★★

aka *Superargo contro Diabolikus, Superargo vs. Diabolicus*, 1966, Italy
Director: Nick Nostro
Cast: Giovanni Cianfriglia, Gérard Tichy, Loredana Nusciak

Champion wrestler Superargo (Cianfriglia) is recruited into the secret service by old friend Colonel Alex Kenton (Josep Castillo Escalona). His first mission involves solving the robbery of components used in the manufacture of nuclear bombs.

The inaugural entry in a series of stylised 1960s Italian superhero movies that seem to have been inspired more by James Bond and fumetti neri comics than the recent *Batman* TV series. Largely typical of what would follow, *Superargo vs Diabolikus* features an abundance of great jazz, bad wrestling and Jaguar E-Types. Where it differs is in our protagonist's nature. He's not a cat burglar or a smug aristocrat, and he's not one for cracking wise, which lends this movie a credibility most of those that followed lack. It's actually possible to enjoy it sincerely rather than ironically.

Superargo and the Faceless Giants ★★★

aka *L'invincibile Superman*, 1968, Italy/Spain
Director: Paolo Bianchini
Cast: Giovanni Cianfriglia, Guy Madison, Luisa Baratto

A villain does crime with robots. Superargo (Cianfriglia), a wrestler who's also a magical shaman who's also a superhero who's also a 'freelance police officer' won't stand for it.

Superargo returns in a slightly sillier Euro-romp. He still drives an E-Type (obviously) and wrestles hairy men (obviously), but has gained the ability to levitate in order to escape deadly gas (less obviously). There's a fast pace and fantastic score to keep it

moving, and the hokey robots and dubbing make it reasonably funny.

Superbabies: Baby Geniuses 2 ★

2004, USA
Director: Bob Clark
Cast: Jon Voight, Scott Baio, Vanessa Angel

Various superbabies and a superchild tackle media mogul Bill Biscane's (Voight) scheme to decipher baby talk.

Jon Voight as a Nazi in a bad wig counts for something, but this is horrifying. There are no circumstances under which any human being would benefit from exposure to it.

Superbob ★★★★★

2015, UK
Director: Jon Drever
Cast: Brett Goldstein, Catherine Tate, Natalia Tena

A very ordinary man gains superpowers and goes to work for the British government.

Mockumentary style comedy with a lovely lead performance and an excellent script. Driver and Goldstein (who co-write with William Bridges) speculatively mine the mundanity of a superhero's everyday life, unearthing comedy gold in the process. The humour is reminiscent of the sort of dry, absurdist satire popularised by English writer/performers such as Chris Morris and Steve Coogan. Exceptional.

SuperBrother ★★★

aka *Superbror*, 2009, Denmark
Director: Birger Larsen
Cast: Lucas Odin Clorius, Viktor Kruse Palshøj, Andrea Reimer

A young boy desperate to improve the lot of his autistic brother faces many challenges when his sibling gains superpowers.

Almost Spielbergian coming-of-age drama. There's much childhood anguish to contend with, but we don't get too bogged down in it thanks to a considered approach to the material. Good writing and performances mean the relationships and emotions are authentic and involving.

Superdragon vs. Supermen: see *Bruce Lee Against Superman*

Supergirl

1973, Philippines
Director: Howard Petersen
Cast: Pinky Montilla, Walter Navarro, Barbara Perez

"5 MONTHS IN THE MAKING WITH A HALF-A-MILLION BUDGET!! THE BEST OF ALL SUPER-SUPER PICTURES!!" At least according to the poster. This unlicensed movie is lost.

Supergirl ★

1984, USA
Director: Jeannot Szwarc
Cast: Helen Slater, Faye Dunaway, Peter O'Toole

Kal-El's cousin Kara Zor-El (Slater) comes to Earth somehow and for some reason.

Supergirl opens with lots of talk: Zoltar (O'Toole) might leave, Alura (Mia Farrow) doesn't want him to, Nigel (Peter Cook) is interested in invisibility, Selina (Dunaway) wants power and so on. Who the hell are these people? Then suddenly, and without any explanation: Supergirl! She just bursts out of a lake on Earth. It's the stupidest of first acts. Then she starts at a boarding school where we spend 40 minutes killing time. There's no tension, no objective, no payoff and no story. It's the stupidest of second acts. When Supergirl finally comes into conflict with her antagonist (for want

of a better word), their clash stems from the latter's jealousy of the former. Rather than being plot-related, the film's central conflict results from the gardener on whom both characters have a crush preferring Supergirl. It's the stupidest of... etc.

Superguy: Behind the Cape ★★★★

2000, USA
Directors: Bill Lae, Mark Teague
Cast: Mark Teague, Charles Dierkop, Katherine Victor

A documentary on Superguy (Teague), a possibly, but probably not, alien superhero.

What differentiates *Superguy* from other faux documentaries is its commitment to the concept. Nobody winks at the camera and nothing is exaggerated for comic effect. It's completely sincere and must have called for incredible discipline. The documentary approach negates budget issues and the

Superbob

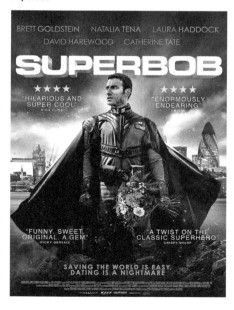

humour grows naturally from the situation. It's a slow burner, perhaps a little dry for some, but ever so good and replete with the twists and arcs of a narrative film.

Superhelde ★★

2011, South Africa
Director: Stefan Nieuwoudt
Cast: Ivan Botha, Neil Sharim, Andrew Tompson

Two friends become superheroes, sort of, in order to stop dodgy property developers bulldozing their favourite comic book store.

Steeped in superherodom rather than a superhero movie per se, *Superhelde* never amounts to more than a nice idea with a couple of half decent jokes. The central duo are appealing enough but the shady father and son developers are cringeworthy, and there's some very dodgy acting among the supporting characters. Ultimately, it's just not funny enough.

The Superhero ★

2007, UK
Director: Adam Simcox
Cast: Damien Hannaway, David Platt, Anarosa De Eizaguirre Butler

Bare knuckle boxer Luke Lang (Hannaway) becomes a vigilante.

Horribly made, comprehensively miserable realist melodrama that wallows in the woe of characters living in a community ravaged by drugs and crime.

Superhero Man ★★★

aka *The Movie Extra*, 2015, USA
Director: F.C. Rabbath
Cast: Chris Martin, Sergio Soltero, Michael Varde

After losing both his car and fiancée to Hero Man (Salter), timid loser Bob (Martin) decides to get his own back.

An ambitious concept (the movie relies on ironic self-awareness and familiarity with numeorus cinematic conventions) is well executed by writer/director Fred Rabbath and his crew. Micro-budget comedies are generally pretty miserable, what with the filmmakers being unable to afford the time and talent that's usually essential for this most challenging of genres, but *Superhero Man* is a well written, well made and perfectly amusing movie.

Superhero Movie ★★

2008, USA
Director: Craig Mazin
Cast: Drake Bell, Leslie Nielsen, Sara Paxton

On being bitten by a genetically modified dragonfly, high school student Rick Riker (Bell) develops superpowers.

Less freewheeling and schizophrenic than similar stuff such as *Scary Movie*, *Disaster Movie*, etc., *Superhero Movie* prefers to draw most of its inspiration from just one source (Sam Raimi's 2002 take on *Spider-Man*) and follows its structure surprisingly closely. With a proper framework from which to hang the bad jokes, the overall experience is slightly less harrowing than expected, but that's not an endorsement. Stephen Hawking revealing his nurse to be a lesbian, "but not the hot kind" is fairly typical of the comedy on offer.

Superjuffie ★★★

2018, Netherlands
Director: Martijn Smits
Cast: Diewertje Dir, Hassan Slaby, Harry Piekema

A teacher uses her superpowers to help animals, but when a whole Zoo needs rescuing she finds she's out of her depth.

This pleasant Dutch family comedy strikes a tone similar to that of 1995's *Babe* and should somewhat appeal to that movie's audience. While nothing like as clever as Chris Noonan's Antipodean porcine parable, it boasts a solid lead performance from Diewrtje Dir and kids who aren't annoying, which is more than we might reasonably expect from a movie like this.

Superlopez ★★★★

aka *Superlópez*, 2018, Spain
Director: Javier Ruiz Caldera
Cast: Dani Rovira, Alexandra Jiménez, Julián López

On the planet Chiton, desperate parents face annihilation. After packing their baby son off to the hoped for safety of Earth, the child grows up with incredible powers, which he decides to keep secret.

What if Kal-El's little space pod landed in Spain instead of the USA? And what if he was a bit of an idiot? *Superlopez* sets out to answer those important questions, and on the whole does so quite well. It's fun watching our Superman stand-in grow up in a different environment, his adoptive parents struggling with the realities of raising an infinitely powerful infant (of course he's going to snap any adult finger he gets hold of!). Even after the transition to adulthood things hold together nicely, with character moments taking the lead over an alien threat our hero himself has inadvertantly attracted.

Superman ★★★★

1948, USA
Directors: Spencer Gordon Bennet, Thomas Carr
Cast: Kirk Alyn, Noel Neill, Tommy Bond

With the planet Krypton on the brink of destruction, leading scientist Jor-El (Nelson Leigh) despatches his baby son to Earth. There, or rather here, the boy is taken in by simple farming folk, christened Clark Kent, and grows up to possess incredible powers.

As alter ego Superman, the adult Kent (Alyn) sets about rescuing all and sundry from danger, but soon faces a malevolence that even he will struggle to overcome.

One of the most popular and successful serials ever shown, Superman's first live-action appearance is as good an example as any for this undeniably antiquated form of storytelling. After ploughing through the origin story in the first episode, we're soon into a rhythm that sees each new chapter's 15-minute runtime (excluding credits and recap) conclude with a cliffhanger; usually involving Lois Lane (an entertainingly broad Neill) and peril. There's a lot of peril. But isn't that what we want from Superman? He typically rescues more people from danger in each instalment than he has so far managed in the entire DCEU franchise. The time and financial pressures are more apparent here than in the sequel, *Atom Man vs Superman*, but the odd fluffed line and wonky set only add to the charm, and the pace means the four hours relatively fly by.

Supperjuffie

Margot Kidder as Lois Lane and Christopher Reeve as Superman in *Superman* (1978 version)

Superman

1953, USA
Directors: Spencer Gordon Bennet, Thomas Carr
Cast: Kirk Alyn, Noel Neill, Tommy Bond

Feature-length edit of the 1948 serial, *Superman*. Made for foreign markets.

Superman

1960, India
Directors: Mohammed Hussain, Anant Thakur
Cast: Helen, Paidi Jairaj, Nirupa Roy

A faithful take on Kal-El's origin story, and one of two unlicensed Indian Superman films released in 1960. Bafflingly the other one, *Return of Superman*, also stars Paidi Jairaj despite being unrelated. This one is either lost or unavailable.

Superman ★★

1973, USA
Directors: George Blair, Lew Landers, Harry Gerstad
Stars: George Reeves, Noel Neill, Jack Larson

Superman (Reeves) faces various generic underworld figures.

Having debuted as Superman in 1951's *Superman and the Mole-Men*, George Reeves fills the red boots again in this cut-and-shut assembled from 1952 TV series *Adventures of Superman*. Noel Neill also returns as Lois Lane (replacing Phyllis Coates, who played the part in the *Mole-Men* movie and the show's first season before departing), and provides a nice through-line from the Kirk Alyn starring serials all the way up to 2006's *Superman Returns*, in which she cameos. Truth be told Reeves isn't the most enigmatic Superman and the plot is a complete mess (the separate episodes don't tie together). Fans who were there at the time seem to get it, though. (Five shorter cut-and-shuts were released in 1954.)

Superman ★★★★★

1978, USA
Director: Richard Donner
Cast: Christopher Reeve, Margot Kidder, Gene Hackman

An alien child is despatched to Earth so he might escape his dying planet. He grows up to be a reporter.

When *Superman* went into pre-production in 1974, there was no such thing as the mainstream Hollywood superhero movie. There had been B-movie outings for radio characters like the Shadow, and Zorro had acquitted himself well on several occasions. But, as kids' entertainment, superheroes proper were pretty much confined to serials and TV. So when *Superman* proved such an extraordinary success in 1978, it's strange a wider trend didn't develop. We got more Superman (three sequels and a spinoff in 1984's *Supergirl*, which were aimed at increasingly younger audiences), but Hollywood just didn't seem interested in anyone else. For an explanation we might look to *Star Wars'* influence on the era's popular culture, something that makes this film's continued reputation as a seminal linchpin even more impressive (to have carved out such a niche in the midst of the *Star Wars* boom is quite something). Over 40 years since its release, it could be time to acknowledge its immense popularity is almost entirely down to the score and the star. It's a wonderfully executed film and nothing should be taken away from anyone involved. But those two elements have simply never been bettered.

Superman ★★

aka *Indian Superman*, 1980, India
Director: V. Madhusudan Rao
Cast: Taraka Rama Rao Nandamuri, Jaya Prada, Jayamalini

When eight-year-old Raja's (uncredited) parents are murdered, Hindu god Hanuman gifts him supernatural powers. Years later he sets out for revenge.

South Asia alone produced at least three *Superman* ripoffs in the decade following Richard Donner's 1978 classic (and more before): one from Bangladesh, one from India's Bengal region, and this Bollywood curiosity (all are called *Superman*). This is the least like the original, as the synopsis suggests, and probably the most amusing: Superman (Nandamuri) boasts a pot belly, pencil moustache and Elvis hairstyle. He sings, dances and jumps on the heads of possessed elephant assassins (there are also cowboy assassins and a killer dwarf). A lot of time is spent on romance and dull subplots, but the facial expressions they demand never get boring.

Superman ★★

aka *Bangla Superman*, Unknown year, Bangladesh
Director: Iftekhar Jahan
Cast: Danny Sidak, Nuton, Antora

A child from a dying world is sent to Earth, where his alien physiology renders him a superhuman. Following much singing and dancing, three criminals from his home planet arrive to spoil the fun.

Very little is known about this unlicensed Bengali remake of the 1978 Christopher Reeve movie and its first sequel. It steals numerous effects shots from the original (and the theme music, which needs to be played twice over the opening credits because it doesn't run long enough), and duplicates most of the key scenes, albeit with a profoundly Bangla twist. There are some enormously funny spikes of nonsense but overall it's slow and prone to lengthy musical interludes. Needless to say, there are no subtitles.

Superman ★

aka *The Indian Superman*, 1987, India
Director: B. Gupta
Cast: Puneet Issar, Sonia Sahni, Shakti Kapoor

Faithful remake of the 1978 film. I think we can skip another plot outline.

There are some minor deviations, mostly involving singing, but otherwise this is a meticulous ripoff. Sadly, it's all quite flat, with comparatively little of the silliness that can sometimes make these things enjoyable. Issar is an uncharismatic Superman and a humourless Clark Kent, while the movie itself can't make up its mind whether to be a comedy or not.

Superman II ★★★★★

1980, USA

Directors: Richard Lester, Richard Donner
Cast: Gene Hackman, Christopher Reeve, Margot Kidder

Unaware three Kryptonian supervillains have arrived on Earth, Superman (Reeve) surrenders his powers in order to make a new life with Lois Lane (Kidder).

Smaller scale than the previous film and less mythic in its presentation of the Man of Steel, *Superman II* is a bit ropey if we're honest. It feels cheap for a blockbuster and the screenplay is full of inconsistencies. But there's an agreeable quality that seems to override objectivity. The three villains, led by Terence Stamp's Zod, are fantastic, and Reeve shares some great character scenes with Kidder. Somehow it works in spite of itself. This theatrical cut of the movie is just one of two options, though. With the shoot nearly complete, original director Richard Donner left the project after falling out with the producers, Alexander and Ilya Salkind. His replacement, Richard Lester, all but started from scratch and would deliver a film vastly different to Donner's vision. In 2006 the ousted auteur finally realised that vision with a reconstruction based on his original material (including a number of Marlon Brando scenes Lester had omitted for financial reasons) with gaps filled by rehearsal footage and Lester's later work. The result is a fairly different movie with a serious and grandiose tone, but it's debatable whether it's any better.

Superman III ★★

1983, USA
Director: Richard Lester
Cast: Christopher Reeve, Richard Pryor, Robert Vaughan

Computer wiz Gus Gorman (Pryor) teams up with industrialist Ross Webster (Vaughan) to both corner the oil market and develop a synthetic kryptonite. Superman (Reeve) is split into good and bad versions of himself.

This is a terrible, terrible movie. We can enjoy the majesty of Christopher Reeve without having to deny that fundamental fact. Everything hangs on three conceits: One, that a lesson in computer programming makes a moron the world's greatest hacker and programmer; 2, that being good at computers means knowing how to make kryptonite; 3, that weather satellites create, rather than monitor and predict, the weather. Most of the new ideas seem to be based on doing the opposite of what worked in the previous movies. Audiences loved Margot Kidder's Lois Lane and her chemistry with Clark, so she's written out. Audiences loved the more serious tone than previous superhero adventures had offered, so it's an all-out comedy. Audiences loved watching Superman flying around Metropolis, so most of the movie is spent watching Clark trip over things in Smallville. If you're of a certain age then none of this will matter, but it still needs saying: this is a terrible film.

Superman IV: The Quest for Peace
★★

1987, UK/USA
Director: Sidney J. Furie
Cast: Christopher Reeve, Gene Hackman, Margot Kidder

Superman (Reeve) must face Lex Luthor's (Hackman) latest creation: a superhuman made from the sun.

With Cannon taking over the Superman rights after the disastrous one-two punch of *Superman III* and *Supergirl* obliterated their value, Reeve agreed to return to the franchise only if he could dictate the story, which is rubbish. A lack of money is more crippling, though. The financing secured by a struggling Cannon ended up being shared among several different projects, leaving the visual effects roughly on a par with 1951's *Superman and the Mole-Men*, and shooting limited to Milton Keynes in the

UK. Whatever appeal *Superman IV* might have for some audiences is of the so-bad-it's-good variety.

Superman Against the Will ★

aka *Supermen ponevole ili eroticheskiy mutant*, 1993, Russia
Directors: Nikita Dzhigurda, Stanislav Gajduk
Cast: Sonya Belkina, Alla Budnitskaya, Nikita Dzhigurda

If there's a plot I couldn't tell.

Strange, tense sounds hammer at our heads as the shaky camera urgently tries to escape some unseen peril. Emotionless men chase each other about and we see the same footage over and over again. A stressful and deeply unpleasant experience.

Superman and the Mole-Men ★★

1951, USA
Director: Lee Sholem
Cast: George Reeves, Phyllis Coates, Jeff Corey

Workers boring a well disturb a subterranean race who come to the surface to be shot at by yokels. Fortunately, Clark Kent (Reeves) is on hand doing a story on the hole.

This is an underwhelming feature debut for Superman. There's no villain, we hardly see our hero suited and booted, and the makers seem more interested in political allegory than storytelling. Superman's objective is to protect the odd-looking (they're children in bald caps) Mole-Men from an angry mob trying to lynch them, and we're issued with several polemics on the need for a society to welcome outsiders. It's a bit like *Star Trek* only with wonky science (apparently Earth has a hollow centre).

Superman Returns ★★★

2006, USA
Director: Bryan Singer
Cast: Brandon Routh, Kevin Spacey, Kate Bosworth

Some years after the discovery of Krypton's remains heralded the disappearance of Superman (Routh), he returns as suddenly as he departed, and just in time to stop Lex Luthor (Spacey) destroying the world as we know it.

With hindsight this may as well have been called *Superman V: Superman Returns*. It uses the same titles and score as the Christopher Reeve iteration, goes for the same tone, features three-decade-old footage of Marlon Brando as poppa Soops, and most of the performances are based on Reeve's cannon. Especially Routh's. In an age in which our superheroes are seldom allowed to be simple boy scouts (and are rebooted as often as studio executives), it's nice to see a modern movie with an old heart. But it's certainly not without its problems. It's too long, the script is clumsy, the key twist is beyond stupid and Kate Bosworth is badly miscast as Lois Lane.

Superman the Invincible ★

aka *Ssuperzam el invencible*, 1971, Mexico/Guatemala
Directors: Federico Curiel, Ángel Rodríguez
Cast: Raúl Martínez Solares, Superzan, Federico Curiel

Three aliens visit Mexico. Then they leave. Ssuperzam (Superman) watches on.

A marketing department might spin the synopsis into a superhero protecting Earth from alien invasion, but the truth is nothing happens in *Superman the Invincible*. The aliens are pretty benign; they just want to see the sights and get a feel for us. To fill the time we watch them walk about, enjoy a musical interlude with a singing luchador, walk about again, respectfully appreciate a church, walk about a bit, then visit farms, caves and a few other free shooting locations. Ssuperzam hangs about looking impressive and keeping an eye on things, but offers nothing in the way of action. It's odd, really. Luchador movies don't tend to ascribe overtly supernatural characteristics to their protagonists, but this one does. To then do nothing with him seems a waste.

Superman vs. Fantômas

aka *Süpermen Fantoma'ya karsi*, 1969, Turkey
Director: Kayahan Arikan
Cast: Yasar Güçlü, Fazli Balkan, Faruk Panter

This dual assault on two different copyrights seems to be unreleased on home formats.

Superman vs. The Elite ★★

2012, USA
Director: Michael Chang
Cast: George Newbern, Pauley Perrette, Robin Atkin Downes

Superman's (Newbern) boy scout morality is called into question when a morally flexible superhero team begin to gain popularity.

Punk-inspired opening credits and talk of media manipulation do little to conceal the fact this is just a rudimentary rumination on the superhero's responsibility to be whiter than white. A little more research could have gone into the colloquial pejoratives used by villain Manchester Black (Downes), because one in particular is significantly more offensive in his native UK than the US writers seem to realise.

Superman: Brainiac Attacks ★★

2006, USA
Director: Curt Geda
Cast: Tim Daly, Powers Boothe, Dana Delany

A jealous Lex Luthor (Boothe), begins mining kryptonite in space and unleashes an updated Brainiac (Lance Henriksen) on Superman (Daly).

Basic and strangely dated (the early 1990s style animation is rendered in an aspect ratio of 1.33:1), *Brainiac Attacks* boasts winning voice work from both Boothe and Henriksen, and a few old-school charms, but it isn't enough. The plot is thin and there's nothing new to get excited about – how many times can we watch Luthor try to obtain kryptonite or Clark run out on Lois (Delany) to attend to superhero business?

Superman: The Last Son of Krypton ★★★

1996, USA
Directors: Curt Geda, Scott Jeralds, Dan Riba
Cast: Tim Daly, Dana Delany, Clancy Brown

When his warnings of impending doom are ignored, Kryptonian scientist Jor-El (Christopher McDonald) sends his only son to the relative safety of Earth, where young Kal grows to become the metaphysical miracle Superman (Daly).

Culled from episodes of the TV series, this debut animated Superman feature begins the story from scratch with lengthy scenes on Krypton, and then skips through Clark Kent's childhood before getting to the good stuff around the halfway mark. It has a cool, retro look and low-key vibe that leave it pleasingly unpretentious.

Superman: Unbound ★★★

2013, USA
Director: James Tucker
Cast: Matt Bomer, Stana Katic, Molly C. Quinn

Superman (Bomer) and Supergirl (Quinn) battle Brainiac.

The animated Batman's habit of nagging subordinate superheroes into being less violent seems to be catching. Must be a DC thing. Aside from the tedious moralising this isn't a bad effort. The dialogue is better than usual, there's a decent story and it's kind of fun to see Superman and Supergirl working together.

Superman/Batman: Apocalypse ★★★

2010, USA
Director: Lauren Montgomery
Cast: Andre Braugher, Kevin Conroy, Tim Daly

Superman's (Daly) Kryptonian cousin Kara (Summer Glau) arrives on Earth ahead of an attack by Darkseid (Braugher), who has an unhealthy interest in the young woman.

Sequel to *Superman/Batman: Public Enemies* but, despite the title, essentially a Supergirl origin movie. The presence of Wonder Woman (Susan Eisenberg), Big Barda (Julianne Grossman) and several other female characters should lend the movie a uniquely feminine outlook, but in reality it just means the people fighting each other wear fewer clothes.

Superman/Batman: Public Enemies ★★★

2009, USA
Director: Sam Liu
Cast: Clancy Brown, Kevin Conroy, Tim Daly

In a dizzyingly improbable turn of events, truculent, narcissistic businessman Lex Luthor (Brown) is elected US president only to exploit the office in pursuit of his petty, selfish and divisive agenda.

Although just as formulaic and relentlessly focused on superfighting as any of DC's animated output, *Superman/Batman: Public Enemies* does at least present an intriguing take on the relationship between these legendary heroes. But a lack of attention to plot detail and the failure to fully commit to the more adult themes hold back what could have been a standout DC Universe Animated Original. (Followed by *Superman/ Batman Apocalypse*.)

Superman/Doomsday ★★

2007, USA
Directors: Lauren Montgomery, Bruce Timm, Brandon Vietti
Cast: Adam Baldwin, Anne Heche, James Marsters

Superman (Baldwin), who is busy having a relationship with Lois Lane (Heche), must stop a doomsday machine destroying Earth.

Grandiose adaptation of the seminal *Death of Superman* comic crossover. It's the first instalment in the catchily titled (direct-to-video) DC Universe Animated Original Movies series, and as such was released amidst much hype. Too great a deviation from its source left fans underwhelmed, but is not its real problem – that would be the endless scenes involving a particularly lousy Lois Lane chiding Superman for being a commitment-phobe.

Supersonic Man, **aka** *El supersónico*

Superpowerless

2016, USA

Duane Andersen

Josiah Polhemus, Amy Prosser, Natalie Lander

A superhero must come to terms with a new life after losing his powers. Unavailable at the time of writing.

Superseven Is Still My Name ★★★

2015, USA

Director: Scott Rhodes

Cast: Jerry Kokich, Olivia Dunkley, Anne Leighton

Another collection of episodes from web series *The Adventures of Superseven*.

The imitation Argoman is back (his feature debut, *They Call Me Superseven*, came earlier in the year). This time there's a sliver more in the way of recycled footage from the classic Eurospy movies the series spoofs,

The SuperVips

including an amusingly re-dubbed scene or two. The music and Rhodes' commited performance as the eponymous hero are the standout elements. (Followed by the below.)

Superseven Unchained ★★★

2015, USA

Director: Scott Rhodes

Cast: Jerry Kokich, Olivia Dunkley, Anne Leighton

Superseven (Rhodes) returns for a final roundup of webisodes.

To Burbank, California one last time, where Superseven is staying cool, Sandra West (Dunkley) has gone even more rogue and Sparky (Leighton) is still mugging too much. This is a fun series and essential viewing for fans of the 1960s Italian genre movies that inspired it. Some of the performances are too broad and the technical aspects are weak (at least when compared to a proper film), but a lot of thought and care has gone into *Superseven* and it pays off handsomely.

Supersonic Man ★★★★

aka *El supersónico*, 1979, Spain

Director: Juan Piquer Simón

Cast: Antonio Cantafora, Cameron Mitchell, José Luis Ayestarán

Humanoid alien, Kronos (Richard Yesteran), is sent to Earth in the hope of preventing the evil Dr. Gulik (Mitchell) taking over.

The term 'so bad it's good' will inevitably mean different things to different people, each of whom will apply it to different movies for different reasons. But if there is such a thing as a good bad superhero movie singularity, this is it: the point at which all usually divergent interpretations, perspectives and opinions can meet in agreement. Seek out this masterpiece and enjoy. Then watch *The Pumaman* because it's almost as good. Or bad.

SüperTürk ★

2012, Turkey
Director: Tamer Karadagli
Cast: Tamer Karadagli, Arzu Balkan, Cem Emüler

Arriving alone on Earth, a superpowered alien child is adopted by an apparently kindly couple and christened Ekber. As an adult, Ekber (Karadagli) broods over his lost love Zeynap (Balkan).

Oh my god it's a comedy. The only thing funny about *SüperTürk* is how similar it is to *Fateful Findings*, the best known work of notoriously inept amateur filmmaker and professional egotist Neil Breen. Both are low-budget and exist solely to provide their delusional director/star with an opportunity to live out his fantasy; both begin with flashbacks to a childhood romance before showing us our adult protagonist yearning for his lost love; both of those protagonists possess metaphysical abilities; and both are ultimately reunited with their suitors, who are clearly played by much younger actresses despite supposedly being the exact same age. On paper they're almost identical. In reality *Fateful Findings* is inadvertently hilarious while *SüperTürk* is an irredeemable disaster.

The SuperVips ★★★★

aka *Vip, mio fratello superuomo*, 1968, Italy
Director: Bruno Bozzetto
Cast: Oreste Lionello, Pino Locchi, Carlo D'Angelo

The diminutive Mini VIP (Lionello), the last in a long line of superhero protectors, must conquer his insecurities in order to prevent ambitious industrialist Happy Betty (Lydia Simoneschi) taking over the world.

Barbed satire on the injustice of (what was then) modern life. Thank goodness it's all ok now. The elemental animation does the job just fine and the voice work, from an array of Italian industry veterans, fits perfectly. The director's uncompromising ideology is front and centre, and likely to prompt some tricky questions from kids, not to mention irritation from viewers of opposing political persuasions.

Surge of Power: Revenge of the Sequel ★

2016, USA
Directors: Antonio Lexerot, Vincent J. Roth
Cast: Vincent J. Roth, John T. Venturini, Many Celebz

Surge (Roth) pursues the villainous Metal Master (Venturini) to Las Vegas, where he has teamed up with Augur (Eric Roberts), an even greater threat to world safety.

Presumably pleased with how the celebrity cameos went in the first *Surge of Power* movie, Roth isn't keen to offer much else in this sequel. So we get Eric Roberts (out of focus), Bruce Vilanch (reading from cue cards), Reb Brown (looking embarrassed), Gil Gerrard (looking lost) and dozens more (generally filmed next to their tables at comic conventions). I have no idea what the point to any of it is. It seems a web series followed in 2017.

Surge of Power: The Stuff of Heroes ★★

2004, USA
Director: Mike Donahue
Cast: Vincent J. Roth, John T. Venturini, Joey Bourgeois

Corporate Attorney Gavin Lucas (Roth) and mad scientist Hector Harris (Venturini) each gain superpowers in a laboratory explosion. The former decides to become a superhero, the latter a supervillain.

Cameo-laden passion project for Roth, who writes, produces and even designed the costumes in addition to starring as Gavin, aka Surge. There's a strange tone and it's hard to get a handle on the intention, but whether it's meant to be a spoof, a homage or light comedy with serious elements, it doesn't work. There's the inescapable sense *Surge of Power* only exists because Roth wanted to dress up like a superhero and act opposite the cameoing celebs (Nichelle Nichols, Lou Ferrigno, various comic book authors...). (Followed by *Surge of Power: Revenge of the Sequel*.)

Swamp Thing ★★★★

1982, USA
Director: Wes Craven
Cast: Louis Jourdan, Adrienne Barbeau, Ray Wise

Doctor Alec Holland (Wise), a scientist working on a bioengineering experiment, mistakenly turns himself into a plant-beast. A paramilitary group show up and try to steal his work, leaving Alice Cable (Barbeau) to help Hollandmonster save the day.

Seldom has a superhero movie's setting been so crucial to its flavour. You can feel the sticky sweat of South Carolina (standing in for the Louisiana bayou) and even start to develop the cabin fever exhibited by some of the characters. Barbeau's earnest performance is in sharp contrast to the corny rubber monster suit and Jourdan's ham. (Followed by *Return of Swamp Thing*.)

Taigâ masuku: see *The Tiger Mask*

Tank Girl ★★
1995, USA
Director: Rachel Talalay
Cast: Lori Petty, Ice-T, Naomi Watts

Twelve years after a comet strike wiped out civilisation, a handful of survivors live among the rubble of society. Upon falling foul of Water & Power, an evil corporation contolling most of the planet's remaining resources, ferociously impulsive survivor Rebecca Buck (Petty) steals a tank and fights back.

There's plenty of the graphic novel's energy and imagery thanks to a liberal sprinkling of artwork among live-action material that mixes up conventional and radical styles (it was the style at the time), but *Tank Girl* isn't about visuals, it's about Lori Petty. Her performance will make or break the movie depending on how you feel about relentlessly shrill sociopaths.

Tarzan: see Grouped Franchises

Teen Titans Go! To the Movies ★★★★
2018, USA
Directors: Aaron Horvath, Peter Rida Michail
Cast: Greg Cipes, Scott Menville, Khary Payton

Jealous they don't have their own movie deal, the Teen Titans set out to find a nemesis in the hope of progressing to the big league.

Every line of dialogue is some kind of gag and the humour is all over the place, but at least this incarnation of the Teen Titans is treated with levity. A *Lion King* reference is bizarre and brilliant, there's hipster irony that fails horribly, the best cameo Stan Lee ever made, far too many self-aware in-

STAY COOL THIS SUMMER
WITH AMERICA'S NEW WAVE HEROES.

HEY DUDES
HANG THREE!

TEENAGE MUTANT
NINJA TURTLES

Newspaper ad for *Teenage Mutant Ninja Turtles*
(1990 version)

jokes, and a *Batman v Superman* spoof that's
better than anything in *Batman v Superman*.
It's inconceivable any one individual could
enjoy all of it, but there's bound to be
something to float your boat.

Teen Titans: The Judas Contract ★★

2017, USA
Director: Sam Liu
Cast: Stuart Allan, Jake T. Austin, Taissa Farmiga

Nightwing (Sean Maher) rejoins the Teen
Titans in order to help them hunt down cult
leader Brother Blood (Gregg Henry).

Are no characters safe from DC's obsessive
befouling? Of all the properties to reboot
as part of the adult-oriented DC Universe
Animated Original Movies, this is the most
baffling. The Teen Titans should be plucky
kids learning a trade, not nihilistic avengers
cracking jokes about sex in the face of

existential quandaries. The contradictions
are insurmountable.

Teen Titans: Trouble in Tokyo ★★

2006, USA
Directors: Michael Chang, Ben Jones,
Matt Youngberg
Cast: Greg Cipes, Scott Menville, Khary Payton

After being attacked on home ground by a
mysterious ninja, the Teen Titans head to
Japan in search of answers.

Follow-up/conclusion to the 2003 *Teen
Titans* TV series, and the first feature-length
outing for Robin (Menville), Starfire (Hynden
Walch) and co. Fans of the show will likely
find this a fitting denouement and hopefully
appreciate the old-school innocence. The
rest of us might struggle with a movie that
offers little to adult audiences. The lazy
clichés don't help (Godzilla attacks within
minutes of us landing in Tokyo).

Teenage Alien Avengers: see *Alien Arsenal*

Teenage Mutant Ninja Turtles ★★★

1990, USA
Director: Steve Barron
Cast: Judith Hoag, Elias Koteas, Josh Pais

New York is experiencing a crimewave
perpetrated by the ninja Foot Clan and its
leader The Shredder (James Saito). Luckily
for New York: Toitles!

The first Teenage Mutant Ninja Turtles
movie draws at least a little on the early
comics for inspiration, covering their
origin story, debut as crimefighters and
introductions to April O'Neil (Hoag), Casey
Jones (Koteas) and Shredder. The relatively
meagre budget limits its scale and leaves
everything feeling unpolished, but such
characteristics only serve the amiable
B-movie aesthetic. Somehow it feels like it

was made by kids while their parents were out, with all the advantages and drawbacks that implies. As rough as it is, somehow you want to like this excitable little movie.

Teenage Mutant Ninja Turtles ★★
2014, USA
Director: Jonathan Liebesman
Cast: Megan Fox, Will Arnett, William Fichtner

The Turtles emerge from the sewers to challenge Shredder's (Tohoru Masamune) grip on New York.

This confused and deeply unsatisfactory reboot from Hollywood mega-producer Michael Bay features none of the charm and lightness inherent to earlier Turtles incarnations. The 1990s movies aren't very good, but at least they raise the odd smile and don't give you eye strain. Too much gloom, too much shouting and too much Megan Fox.

Teenage Mutant Ninja Turtles II: The Secret of the Ooze ★★
1991, USA
Director: Michael Pressman
Cast: Paige Turco, David Warner, Michelan Sisti

Shredder (François Chau) learns about the radioactive ooze responsible for mutating the Turtles, and determines to steal it for his own nefarious purposes.

Hitting screens just 12 months after the first movie, *Secret of the Ooze* tones down the violence and amps up the silliness, with largely negative consequences. If the first movie felt like children had been entrusted to make it all on their own, this one feels like horrified parents vetted every frame. There are some surprising changes among the cast with Shredder, two of the Turtles and April O'Neil played by different actors (rumour has it Judith Hoag was a struggle to work with and wasn't invited back), while

Casey Jones is dropped altogether. But don't worry, Vanilla Ice is on hand instead.

Teenage Mutant Ninja Turtles III ★
1993, USA
Director: Stuart Gillard
Cast: Elias Koteas, Paige Turco, Stuart Wilson

When a magic sceptre transports April (Turco) 300 years back in time to feudal Japan, the Turtles follow.

There's less dumb humour (and less Vanilla Ice) than in the first sequel, but this is a boring, lazy and poorly conceived finale to the original Turtles film series. It's as if production company Golden Harvest knew it had run its course and didn't want to risk time and money on doing a proper job.

Teenage Mutant Ninja Turtles: Coming Out of Their Shells Tour ★
1990, USA
Directors: Lorenzo Jordan, Thomas White
Cast: Gregory Garrison, Roger Kachel, David Shatraw

Filmed stage production featuring music and comedy skits.

This is a real thing. Dressed like Guns 'N' Roses and armed with 90 minutes of soft rock, the Turtles play 'live' for their adoring fans. The dreadful songs are interspersed with dire 'he's behind you' pantomimery featuring boo-hiss villain Shredder (Beau Allen), ballad-warbling April (Sherie Rene Scott) and ninja rat Splinter (Mark Eris), who's clearly wearing a mouse costume. It's so much worse than it sounds.

Teenage Mutant Ninja Turtles: Out of the Shadows ★★
2016, USA
Director: Dave Green
Cast: Megan Fox, Will Arnett, Tyler Perry

Shredder (Brian Tee) and the sinister Krang (Brad Garrett) team up to conquer the world and so on.

Second of producer Michael Bay's almost live-action Turtles movies. The visual style employed is bewildering, particularly when the Turtles are on screen. They emit a green glow as the camera constantly pans, zooms and swirls around them, which leads to a strong association with nausea. I have to give it two stars because it's in focus and the dialogue is audible. But I'm not happy about it.

Terror Toons ★
2002, USA
Director: Joe Castro
Cast: Beverly Lynne, Lizzy Borden, Brandon Ellison

The Devil (Jack Roberts) of the cartoon dimension tries to corrupt human children with unholy animation, until a kidnapped bimbo realises she can be a superhero and sets out to stop him.

This gleefully inept shot-on-video shambles blends gratuitous gore with dumb humour, then sprays it straight through the screen into our faces. It's one of those movies that seems only to exist because a misguided amateur filmmaker wanted to demonstrate his depraved psyche to the world. For most it will seem like a literal nightmare, what with all the gore, freaky masks and weird animation. For others it might seem like a work of avant garde genius.

Thelma ★★★★
2017, Norway
Director: Joachim Trier
Cast: Eili Harboe, Kaya Wilkins, Henrik Rafaelsen

After leaving home for university, Thelma (Harboe) realises she has psychokinetic powers and soon finds herself spiralling into emotional turmoil.

Moody arthouse drama that draws a link between the maturing of our protagonist's psychic abilities and the realisation of her homosexuality. It's a nice way of illustrating Thelma's existential turmoil, but challenging for an actor. Fortunately Harboe is excellent and delivers a subtle, moving performance. Her superhero credentials are questionable, but she ultimately uses her power for good.

They Call Me Jeeg ★★★★
aka Lo chiamavano Jeeg Robot, 2015, Italy
Director: Gabriele Mainetti
Cast: Claudio Santamaria, Luca Marinelli, Ilenia Pastorelli

Enzo Ceccoti (Santamaria), a petty thief pursued by the police, falls into a drum of radioactive oil and emerges with all sorts of superpowers. Desperate to know the secret behind Ceccoti's incredible abilities, an unhinged crime lord kidnaps his girlfriend to force a confrontation.

Cheerless crime thriller-cum-character study inspired by the Steel Jeeg manga. It's as if a cloud of doom follows Ceccoti and his girlfriend Alessia (Pastorelli) everywhere they go, the grubbily authentic staging and sober cinematography only adding to the impression things won't end well. The short bursts of violence are palpably brutal, the acting excellent and the conclusion surprisingly powerful.

They Call Me Superseven ★★★
2015, USA
Director: Scott Rhodes
Cast: Jerry Kokich, Olivia Dunkley, Anne Leighton

The various adventures of superhero secret agent Superseven (Kokich) and his on-off love interest Sandra West (Dunkley).

Created in 2011 by Andy Palmer, Jerry Kokich and Scott Rhodes, award-winning web series *The Adventures of Superseven* is a comedic homage to Eurospy and fumetti neri superhero movies of the 1960s. This feature-length collection of episodes (the first of three; *Superseven is Still My Name* and *Superseven Unchained* would follow) is a good introduction to the character. Kokich and most of the cast play it straight, and there's a clear passion for the cinema they're spoofing. Unfortunately, a handful of performances wink at us too much and the episodic structure is frustrating.

Thelma

Thor ★★★★

2011, USA 115m
Director: Kenneth Branagh
Cast: Chris Hemsworth, Anthony Hopkins, Natalie Portman

Banished from Asgard after falling prey to Loki's (Tom Hiddleston) manipulations, Thor (Hemsworth) goes on an Earthbound journey of discovery.

This early entry in the MCU is a tale of two movies, both of which might leave action fans feeling short-changed. The scenes on Asgard are Shakespeare-for-kids scheming, while the stuff on Earth is typical fish-out-of-water dramedy that, until the finale, remains free of CGI. Both work very well, with the latter having Hemsworth's self-deprecating charm to thank. (Followed by *Thor: The Dark World*.)

Thor the Conqueror ★

aka *Thor il conquistatore*, 1983, Italy
Director: Tonino Ricci
Cast: Bruno Minniti, Maria Romano, Malisa Longo

Thor (Minniti) quests.

Obnoxious throwback to Italy's peplum craze with none of the original movement's spirit. Laughably bewigged, interminably oiled and appallingly rapey, Minniti's 'Thor' (presumably he was someone else in the original Italian but is re-branded as Thor in the English dub) wanders around the countryside starting fights and being dull. There's a mean streak to this movie that would make it a miserable way to spend 90 minutes even if it wasn't so monotonous and crudely made.

Thor: Ragnarok ★★★★

2017, USA
Director: Taika Waititi
Cast: Chris Hemsworth, Tom Hiddleston, Cate Blanchett

Lost on the planet Sakaar thanks due to his psychotic sister Hela's (Blanchett) thirst for vengeance, Thor (Hemsworth) must find a way home to Asgard in time to prevent its violent destruction.

After a brace of fairly generic solo outings for Thor, Marvel handed *Ragnarok's* reigns to Taika Waititi, a filmmaker with distinct vision and a dominant sense of humour. The New Zealander turned out to be a perfect fit for the franchise. By exploiting Hemsworth's gift for comedy, doubling down on the fisticuffs and focusing our hero's motivation on his responsibility to his people, there's a sense Thor's potential has been fully exploited for the first time. Blanchett positions her pantomime villain perfectly between Disney's Maleficent and the Wicked Witch of the West, while Hiddleston has never looked so comfy in Loki's shapeshifting shoes. As ever, an alternative to the de riguer CGI finale might have been welcome, but this is good stuff and a return to form after the first sequel.

Thor: Tales of Asgard ★★
2011, USA
Director: Sam Liu
Cast: Matthew Wolf, Rick Gomez, Tara Strong

A teen Thor (Wolf) seeks to prove himself in battle.

Animated movie aimed at young audiences, and all the more unremarkable for it. There's nothing worth commenting on apart from the comedy English accents. It sounds like auditions were limited to a stage school in Surrey (that means they all talk dead posh).

Thor: The Dark World ★★
2013, USA
Director: Alan Taylor
Cast: Chris Hemsworth, Natalie Portman, Tom Hiddleston

The Dark Elves, a race dating from before the birth of the universe, finally make their move against Asgard. On Earth, Jane Foster (Portman) becomes the host for a terrible power that threatens to destroy all of the nine realms.

Every now and again we get a glimpse behind the curtain of the Marvel Cinematic Universe. Just for a moment we might see through a CGI alien warrior to the hooded, headphoned VFX artists who conjured the pixels. Or perhaps one too many perfectly timed witicisms bring to mind the writing committee and army of executives who signed them off. *Thor: The Dark World* is a bit like a whole movie of those moments. You can see the cogs turning. The MCU has an extraordinary strike rate, but I guess they can't all be home runs. (Followed by *Thor: Ragnarok.*)

Thou Gild'st the Even ★★★★
aka Sen Aydinlatirsin Geceyi
2013, Turkey
Director: Onur Ünlü
Cast: Ali Atay, Tansu Biçer, Cengiz Bozkurt

In a town in which everyone possesses superpowers an unhappy everyman (who is able to see through walls) dreams of running away with the woman he loves (who can move objects via telekinesis).

Existential contemplation on identity and our place in things. At times the overtly arty aesthetic threatens to devolve into student film caricature, but it's engrossing and lends itself to moments of true beauty. Poetic leanings and a surreal air maintain a sense anything might happen.

3 Dev Adam ★
aka *Three Giant Men*, 1973, Turkey
Director: T. Fikret Uçak
Starring: Aytekin Akkaya, Deniz Erkanat, Yavuz Selekman

Lead by an evil (and unlicensed, obviously) Spider-Man (Tevfik Sen), the Spider gang is up to no good in Istanbul. Luckily, an equally unlicensed Captain America (Akkaya) is on hand, and he teams up with an unlicensed El Santo (Selekman) to defeat them.

There's none of the style or dynamism of superficially similar ripoffs like *Spy Smasher* or *Iron Claw the Pirate*, just plenty of poorly staged fight scenes, nonsensical editing and some of the worst cinematography you'll ever see (crash zooms invariably miss their targets and the constant wobbling induces motion sickness). For some reason this is a cult classic.

Three Inches ★★

2011, USA
Director: Jace Alexander
Cast: Noah Reid, Stephany Jacobsen, James Marsters

After being struck by lightning, everyday loser Walter Spackman (Reid) discovers he can move objects telekinetically... but only three inches at a time. He's soon recruited into a superhero team.

As can be the case with TV movies designed as pilots, too much time is spent setting up future storylines. On this occasion storylines that draw on the hero's personal problems. That means watching a forgettable nobody fret over the sort of insipid irrelevancies usually reserved for high school melodramas. With the series format apparently designed around trivial bouts of introspection on a clifftop sofa, I don't think we've missed much with it being rejected.

The Three Stooges Meet Hercules ★★★

1962, USA
Director: Edward Bernds
Cast: Larry Fine, Moe Howard, Joe DeRita

Larry (Fine), Moe (Howard) and Curly (DeRita) accidentally go back in time, where they run into Hercules (Samson Burke) and change the course of history.

The most successful Three Stooges movie and a reflection on how popular the Italian peplum genre was in the early 1960s, even in the USA. Some of the humour hasn't dated well (the boys, in disguise, getting hot and bothered having to massage pretty women is cringe-inducing) but the anarchic stuff is timeless, and any movie with the nerve to hold a pie fight in ancient Greece deserves our adulation.

Three Supermen (series): see Grouped Franchises

Thundercats Ho! The Movie ★★★

1987, USA
Director: Katsuhito Akiyama
Cast: Bob McFadden, Earl Hammond, Larry Kenney

Lion-O (Kenney) and the gang attempt to rescue three fellow Thunderians who have been living on Earth in secret.

Conceived as a theatrical release before being downgraded to TV status and then ignominiously split into five episodes before being recombined for home-video, this thing still manages to do what is says on the tin: you want a Thundercats movie, you get a Thundercats movie. Much like the He-Man and Bravestarr equivalents it sticks to the formula and ends up being pretty good. The plot zips along, everyone gets stuff to do and the action scenes are surprisingly exciting after all these years.

Thunderstorm: The Return of Thor ★

2011, Canada
Director: Brett Kelly
Cast: Ray Besharah, Celine Filion, Jody Haucke

A cult is attempting to piece together the mythic Dragon's Cross in order to summon Ragnarok. Grant Farrel (Besharah), a scientist working on a supersuit for the government, is contacted by Thor (director Brett Kelly) and told he needs to sort it all out.

Another Tom Cat mockbuster. This one is lighter than most thanks to the dynamic between Farrel and his colleague Earl (who is played by a Randy Kimmett... why do the actors in these movies invariably have more interesting names than their characters?), but that doesn't make it any better. A grand finale involving a CGI dragon must have drained the production's coffers, but it's well worth it for the comedy provided. At 75 minutes (excluding the interminable title sequences), this is a veritable epic by Tom Cat standards.

Tie chao ren: see *Iron Superman*

Tiger & Bunny: The Beginning ★★★

aka *Gekijouban Tiger & Bunny: The Beginning*, 2012, Japan
Director: Yoshitomo Yonetani
Cast: Hiroaki Hirata, Masakazu Morita, Minako Kotobuki

In the futuristic Stern Build City numerous superheroes keep the peace while gaudy live TV broadcasts rate their every exploit. The unfashionable Wild Tiger (Hirata) is forced to collaborate with young gun Barnaby 'Bunny' Brooks (Morita) to catch a dangerous supercriminal.

Based on the anime TV series *Tiger & Bunny*, this seems to be the inevitable result of a world obsessed by superheroes and reality television. The central dynamic, defined by the mutual animosity between Tiger and Bunny, is unoriginal but functional. There's a lot of satire (the superheroes each have sponsors and supplement their income via product endorsements, etc. It's all well thought out), which can be tricky in a movie aimed at younglings, but it comes off fine. (Followed by the below.)

Tiger & Bunny: The Rising ★★★

2014, Japan

Director: Yoshitomo Yonetani
Cast: Hiroaki Hirata, Masakazu Morita, Yûichi Nakamura

Tiger (Hirata) and Bunny (Morita) are split up when their sponsor re-jigs the lineup.

More of the same. Which means we've seen these narcissistic superheroes, ambitious villains and sinister corporations do all this stuff before. The unique and detailed world gives us something to enjoy.

The Tiger Mask ★★

aka *Taigâ masuku*, 2013, Japan
Director: Ken Ochiai
Cast: Eiji Wentz, Natsuna, Shô Aikawa

Orphan Naote Date (Went) is tricked into joining the Tiger's Den, a kind of academy for evil wrestlers. After years of brutal training, he goes against the wishes of his criminal masters.

The Tiger Mask starts well with a lengthy origin story depicting young Date suffering through the brutality of the Tiger's Den, and then graduating to become a fearsome costumed 'heel wrestler' (the bad guy in the scenario). It's fairly interesting at first, but once Date reconnects with the orphanage he'd somehow forgotten about we descend into a melodramatic funk that derails the whole movie. A particularly unsatisfying conclusion seals a bad deal in spite of some interesting visuals and design work.

TMNT ★★

2007, USA
Director: Kevin Munroe
Cast: Patrick Stewart, Mako, Chris Evans

Years after defeating Shredder, the Turtles have disbanded and are working in various improbable capacities. When an industrialist teams up with ancient monsters, they're forced to reunite.

Although *TMNT* frequently threatens to throw in the towel and descend into total awfulness, it just about maintains a steady level of bland irrelevance. This is one for fans only. The CG animation is generally good (in fact a neon-lit rainy rooftop fight is stunning) but it leaves us at a distance just when we need to be fully engaged for all the domestic strife. And it's that strife that's the big problem. If you aren't already invested in these characters then their endless bickering won't be of interest. If you are invested it seems likely you'll be more interested in them working together to crack Foot Clan skulls than in them complaining about each other.

The Toxic Avenger

Todd McFarlane's Spawn ★★★★

1997, USA
Director: Eric Radomski
Cast: Keith David, Richard Dysart,
Michael Nicolosi

Burned to death during his tour of Vietnam, former commando Al Simmons (David) is resurrected as a decomposing cadaver. On returning to Earth as Spawn, he attempts to protect his former wife, tackle a murderer and dodge both his demonic responsibilities and the henchmen of Jason Wynn (John Rafter Lee), a businessman inconvenienced by his recent vigilantism.

Overseen by Spawn's creator, comic book titan Todd McFarlane, this animated movie based on the HBO series sticks close to the character's original concept. That means it's a sweary and bloody affair full of sleaze and violence. The long runtime allows for plenty of detail and the assumed maturity of the target audience allows for a steady pace that lets us soak it all up. A nebulous voiceover gradually fills in the mythology while we're left to work out how characters like the Violator (Jamie Hanes), a monstrous clown apparently sent to steer our hero towards evil, fit in. The writing is as good as that of any animated superhero movie.

Todd McFarlane's Spawn 2 ★★★★

1998, USA
Directors: Jennifer Yuh Nelson, Tom Nelson,
Mike Vosburg
Cast: Keith David, Richard Dysart,
Dominique Jennings

Spawn (David) discovers an old friend was responsible for his death.

Seamless extension of the first movie/show.

Todd McFarlane's Spawn 3: The Ultimate Battle ★★★★

1999, USA
Directors: Jennifer Yuh Nelson, Mike Vosburg
Cast: Keith David, Richard Dysart,
Dominique Jennings

Spawn (David) battles Wynn as the forces of heaven and hell step up their assault.

The plot is a bit looser in this third instalment in what amounts to a seven hour narrative arc across three movies (or TV series, if you prefer to watch it that way). Ultimately all that was said about the first film still stands. If anything the cumulative effect makes this final chapter even more impressive. It's expansive, compelling, detailed and great to look at.

De tøffeste gutta: see *The Tough Guys*

Tômei ningen to hae otoko: see *The Invisible Human and the Fly Man*

Tomei Ningen: see *Invisible Avenger* (1954)

Tomica Hero: Rescue Force Explosive Movie ★★

aka *Tomika Hīrō Resukyū Fōsu Bakuretsu Mūbī Mahha Torein o Resukyū seyo!*, 2008, Japan
Director: Masato Tsujino
Cast: Kenta Izuka, Seigo Noguchi, Haruno

Neo Terror, an organisation dedicated to causing 'super disasters', attempts to hijack a new high speed train. Teen defence team Rescue Force use enthusiasm and cars to stop them.

A creation of Japanese toy company Tomy, this henshin hero hooey is spun off from a TV series designed to promote their cars. Cheaply produced live-action is enhanced by over-the-top CGI to willfully cartoonish effect. The cast is adequate and the general levels of lunacy most impressive.

Tonyong Bayawak ★★

1979, Philippines
Director: Jose Yandoc
Cast: Ramon Revilla, Boots Anson-Roa, Julie Ann Fortich

Granted superpowers by a mad fairy, kind-hearted hunter Tonyong Bayawak (Revilla) angers a witch and is attacked by deadly oompa loompas.

Full disclosure: I didn't always know what was going on in this bizarre, subtitle-free apparent morality tale. Bayawak seems to anger the fairy by killing a boar, so perhaps the amulet she gives him is as much curse as blessing (he does turn into a half animal monster for a while). The important thing is the thugs who killed his wife (I think) get their comeuppance (I think). It's an intriguing cultural oddity along vaguely similar lines to better known fantastical foreign B-movies such as 1981's *Mystics in Bali*, but is less accessible, entertaining and crazy.

Toofan ★★

1975, India
Director: Kedar Kapoor
Cast: Vikram, Priyadarshinee, Jagdeep

Kidnapped in early childhood by a knight disillusioned with his king's failure to reign in a tyrannical vizier, Prince Baldi (Vikram) grows up in anonymity before eventually becoming masked avenger Toofan.

This 1975 take on an oft told (and infinitely variable) tale adopts Zorro's costume and ethos for its eponymous protagonist, while delivering all the colour, melodrama and dancing we'd expect from a Bollywood film. Something doesn't quite click, though, and it's missing the screen presence of an actor such as Dara Singh, who may not be the most nuanced of thespians but can be relied upon to swing a sword with vigour.

Toofan ★★

1989, India
Director: Ketan Desai
Cast: Amitabh Bachchan, Meenakshi Sheshadri, Amrita Singh

Twin boys separated at birth grow up to become a magician and a superhero. Both have cause to seek vengeance for injustices visited upon their fathers and, when their paths eventually cross, an alliance seems to be inevitable.

Industrial strength charm machine Amitabh Bachchan plays both brothers in this Indian blockbuster that revisits the Toofan myth. Aimed largely at children, it's a periodically entertaining movie with a gloriously over-the-top villain, but at nearly three hours is too long. Not one of Bachchan's best, and a Hindi version of Bobby McFerrin's 'Don't Worry Be Happy' is quite discombobulating.

Toonpur Ka Superrhero ★★
2010, India
Director: Kireet Khurana
Cast: Ajay Devgn, Kajol, Ameya Pandya

In Toonpur, the homeland of cartoons, the Devtoons kidnap human action star Aditya (Devgn) to help in their war against the malevolent Toonasurs.

There's something unsettling about this. The character designs are bizarre, at least to a European like me, with some Toonasurs likely to scare the hell out of children. The poor blocking, lighting and compositing also make it unlikely audiences will be able to suspend their disbelief, particularly when CG and live-action characters interact. It's as if everyone was so pleased with the idea they didn't think to execute it properly.

The Tough Guys ★★★
aka De tøffeste gutta, 2013, Norway
Director: Christian Lo
Cast: Sondre Blakstad Henriksen, Regine Stokkevåg Eide, Martin Røsjorde Linstad

By sacrificing himself to bullies in the stead of other kids, schoolbuy Modulf (Henriksen) sees himself as a superhero.

There's no Earth-shattering insight to be found in The Tough Guys, but it does offer a tightly written, well considered examination of how childhood bullying can work and, crucially, be combatted. Whether that's enough to attract kids to a subtitled movie, or their parents to a largely 11-year-old cast, is another matter.

The Toxic Avenger ★★★★
1984, USA
Directors: Michael Herz, Lloyd Kaufman
Cast: Andree Maranda, Mitch Cohen, Jennife

A health club janitor is bullied into a vat of toxic waste, develops superstrength, and sets out to clean up his home town.

In a way, this is the archetypal superhero movie. The protagonist starts as a bullied weakling before being superised through radioactivity, at which point he works out his personal demons and dedicates himself to good causes. There are surprisingly few examples of that stereotypical narrative arc, so for Troma (of all production companies) to pretty much define it is at least amusing. Being a Troma movie the jokes are childish, the technical elements embarassing and the acting atrocious. But that's what Troma fans want, right?

The Toxic Avenger Part II ★★
1989, USA
Directors: Michael Herz, Lloyd Kaufman
Cast: Ron Fazio, John Altamura, Phoebe Legere

The executives of Apocalypse Inc. hatch a scheme to rid Tromaville of the Toxic Avenger (Fazio & Altamura).

There's at least as much gore, violence and general nonsense on display as in the first movie, and even more dumb comedy, but once we get to Tokyo (where Toxie searches for his father) it turns into a travelogue. It's as if producer/director Kaufman didn't want to waste his free trip to Japan having to shoot a movie.

The Toxic Avenger Part III: The Last Temptation of Toxie ★★

1989, USA
Directors: Michael Herz, Lloyd Kaufman
Cast: Ron Fazio, Phoebe Legere, John Altamura

Toxie (Fazio) goes to work for Apocalypse Inc. in an attempt to raise money for blind girlfriend Claire's (Legere) eye operation.

OK, this was funny to begin with (sort of) but the joke has run its course now. Not that it really matters with a series like this, but the mythology has begun falling apart, too (Toxie goes to work for the previous movie's villains, somehow unaware they're evil). Probably of greater concern to fans is the fact it's not as gory or imaginative as the previous movies.

The Toxic Avenger Part IV: Citizen Toxie ★★★

aka Citizen Toxie: The Toxic Avenger IV, 2000, USA
Director: Lloyd Kaufman
Cast: David Mattey, Clyde Lewis, Heidi Sjursen

When Toxie (Mattey) is sucked through a dimensional tear, malignant imposter the Noxious Offender (also Mattey) takes his place in Tromaville.

Considered a return to form by fans of the series, this fourth and so far final Toxic Avenger is certainly an improvement on the second and third. It opens in a school for the developmentally disabled, which offers Kaufman an unparalleled opportunity to be outrageous, and he certainly doesn't waste it. Probably the funniest and most extreme movie of the franchise (although the musical is ultimately its high water mark). I have to say I mentally checked out when a nurse tried to perform an abortion on a woman already in labour.

The Toxic Avenger: The Musical ★★★★

2018, USA
Director: Nick Morris
Cast: Emma Salvo, Ben Irish, Natalie Hope

Stage musical adaptation of the 1984 movie The Toxic Avenger. You read that right.

Who thought these silly things would get better? Funnier, cleverer and more accessible than any of the proper movies, this musical was first performed in New Jersey in 2008 before spawning international versions and winning numerous awards. More visual variety would be appreciated (it's confined to a single set: Toxie's home/dump), but that's splitting hairs. The performances are great, the music's even better, and there's a real joie de vivre to everything.

Toxic Crusaders: The Movie ★★★

1997, USA
Directors: Bill Hutten, Tony Love
Cast: Gregg Berger, Susan Blu, Rodger Bumpass

The Toxic Avenger (Bumpass) battles the supervillain Dr. Killemoff (also Bumpass) in an attempt to keep home town Tromaville free of pollution.

Episodes of the short-lived Toxic Avenger cartoon series are nailed together until they reach feature-length. We get Melvin's origin story over again, only this time he meets a couple of similarly superstrong, similarly hideous, similarly ecologically themed monsters, and begins putting a superhero team together. No effort is made to re-edit the episodes into a single narrative (the material is so weird it probably wouldn't have made much difference anyway) but it's surprisingly well made nonetheless, and with the Troma humour toned down and fit for children there's a chance of it finding some new fans.

The Trial of the Incredible Hulk ★★

1989, USA
Director: Bill Bixby
Cast: Bill Bixby, Lou Ferrigno, Marta DuBois

Having returned to his wandering ways, Dr. David Bruce Banner (Bixby) finds himself in a city under the thumb of brutal crime boss Wilson Fisk (John Rhys-Davies), and teams up with blind superhero Daredevil (Rex Smith) to take him down.

Despite the previous movie ending with a happy Banner in a good job and stable relationship, this one starts with him at his lowest ebb; closed off from society, living in a miserable hovel and digging ditches for a living. It all marks an attempt to get back to the (relatively) grittier tone originally envisaged for the series. It half works and this is slightly better than its predecessor, but perhaps only because the plot is more interesting. (Followed by *The Death of the Incredible Hulk*.)

The True Story of Barman and Droguin ★★★

aka *La verdadera historia de Barman y Droguin*, 1991, Mexico
Director: Gilberto de Anda
Cast: Ausencio Cruz, Víctor Trujillo, Valentín Trujillo

Inspired by Batman, dozy bar owner Bruno (Trujillo) and his hapless buddy Ricardo (Cruz) decide to become superheroes.

There isn't much plot to worry about in this unofficial Mexican Batman spoof. Although apparently inspired by Tim Burton's 1989 film (just for a change) the references seem to relate more to the 1966 TV series (just for a change) and even include fight scene freeze frames accompanied by captions like 'PUM!' and 'PAS!' (presumably the Spanish equivalent of 'POW!' and 'BOFF!'). It's daft as hell and even funny at times.

Turbo Kid ★★★★★

2015, USA
Director: François Simard, Anouk Whissell, Yoann-Karl Whissell
Cast: Munro Chambers, Laurence Leboeuf, Michael Ironside

A teenager clinging to the margins of his reality in a post-apocalyptic hell becomes embroiled in a feud with the pre-eminent murderous warlord, and falls in love with a lunatic.

What do you get if you cross *The BMX Bandits* with *Mad Max*? This achingly post-modern, and mightily entertaining, slice of twisted nostalgia, apparently. It's violent, perhaps excessively so at times, but that's a warning more than a criticism. The synth-based soundtrack is exquisite and overall this is easily the most successful of various recent attempts to sentimentally invoke 1980s cheese.

Turbo: A Power Rangers Movie ★★

1997, USA
Directors: Shuki Levy, David Winning
Cast: Jason David Frank, Catherine Sutherland, Hilary Shepard

An incomprehensible villain releases an unfathomable MacGuffin with unintelligible results. Power Rangers show up.

While it could be worse, this sequel to *Mighty Morphin Power Rangers: The Movie* (1995) is further evidence that children should never be allowed to choose what they watch.

'Turkish Batman': see *Yarasa adam – Bedmen*

Turok: Son of Stone ★★★★

2008, USA

Directors: Curt Geda, Dan Riba, Frank Squillace
Cast: Iyari Limon, Rick Mora, Adam Gifford

A Native American warrior fights dinosaurs, avenges the murder of his father, and fights more dinosaurs.

Uniquely for a comic book character, Turok is probably best known as the protagonist of a series of video games (starting with 1997's Nintendo 64 hit, *Turok: Dinosaur Hunter*). This animated feature arrived over half a century after he was created, and is his only film or TV appearance thus far. It's a straightforward avenging muscleman fantasy in the shape of *Conan the Barbarian*, and despite looking like a typical 90s kids cartoon it's almost as bloody and violent. That, and a sense those behind it really cared, makes *Turok* more absorbing than might be expected.

Turtles Forever ★★★★

2009, USA
Directors: Roy Burdine, Lloyd Goldfine
Cast: Michael Sinterniklaas, Wayne Grayson, Sam Riegel

A teleporter mishap transports the Turtles of the 1987 animated series into the world of the 2003 animated series, where they team up with their millennial counterparts to confuse the hell out of us.

Produced to mark the 25th anniversary of the Turtles, someone deserves an award for this idea. Rather than do the obvious and put on a cringeworthy celebratory show (been there), or reboot the franchise with repellently high contrast CGI (that came later), imagination and creativity won out! *Turtles Forever* is unashamedly an all out comedy, its humour derived chiefly from contrasting the breezily anarchic 1987 Turtles with their more severe 2003 counterparts. The result is way funnier than we have any right to expect, which makes this easily the best Turtles movie.

Twisted Pair ★ or ★★★★★

2018, USA
Director: Neil Breen
Cast: Neil Breen, Sara Meritt, Siohbon Chevy Ebrahimi

Twins raised to be artificial intelligence (I don't know either) take divergent paths. One remains good, the other turns evil.

Cult filmmaker Neil Breen delivered his most ambitious work to date in this fifth film in a series of anti-corporate, anti-government, anti-coherence diatribes. In nebulous alter ego Cade Altair, the infamously egomaniacal writer/director/producer/star/etc. finds his ideal avatar: a superhuman avenger with a motivation and objective so vague it's as if Breen just projected a paranoid hallucination directly onto the screen and left us to figure out what it means. Insane, inept and utterly brilliant. If you like this sort of thing. Avoid it like the plague if you don't.

Uchu Kaisoku-sen: see *Invasion of the Neptune Men*

Ultimate Avengers ★★★

2006, USA
Directors: Curt Geda, Steven E. Gordon,
Bob Richardson
Cast: Justin Gross, Grey Griffin, Marc Worden

Nick Fury (Andre Ware) assembles a team of elite scientists and warriors to defend Earth from alien invaders, the Chitauri.

The first release in the Marvel Animated Features series is a Captain America-centric take on the Avengers' origin story. What could easily seem like just another obsolete dress rehearsal for an incoming live-action Marvel blockbuster becomes its own thing thanks to a handful of different perspectives and ingredients. Cap' (Gross) makes for a great lead and with Iron Man/Tony Stark (Worden) relegated to bit player the tone becomes more mythic and less snarky. It's nice to see soem room made for characters such as Giant-Man (Nolan North) and the Wasp (Griffin).

Ultimate Avengers II ★★★

2006, USA
Directors: Will Meugniot, Dick Sebast,
Bob Richardson
Cast: Justin Gross, Grey Griffin, Jeffrey D. Sams

The Ultimate Avengers continue their battle against the Chitauri, now with the aid of Black Panther (Sams).

More of the same, only with an African theme courtesy of the Wakandan setting. Sams is no Chadwick Boseman and doesn't create the necessary gravitas, but I doubt anyone will care. There's a low-tech *Lord of the Rings* vibe to some of the battle scenes and the previous film's accessibility and old-school animation remain.

Ultrachrist! ★

2003, USA
Director: Kerry Douglas Dye
Cast: Jonathan C. Green, Celia A. Montgomery, Samuel Bruce Campbell

Jesus second comes only to find the world and its inhabitants have changed since his day. In an attempt to become more relevant to modern youth, he adopts the guise of a caped superhero.

There are a handful of smiles to be drawn like blood from the stone that is *Ultrachrist!*, but production quality and filmmaking expertise is pretty much non-existent, and the script opts for easy crudity over the satire seemingly demanded by the setup.

Ultraman: see Grouped Franchises

Untama Giru

Ultraviolet ★★★

2006, USA
Director: Kurt Wimmer
Cast: Milla Jovovich, Cameron Bright, Nick Chinlund

In a war between humans and hemophages (genetically enhanced victims of a vampiric plague), an infected superagent protects a human child whose blood could be crucial to both sides.

The whole movie is basically just exposition, repetitive melodrama and action scenes. Lots of action scenes. Like everything else they're overblown, ultra-stylised, make no sense, but work strangely well regardless. The perspective-bending visuals and physics-defying dynamism are reminiscent of anime and legitimately thrilling. It's emptier even than its reputation suggests, but also more engrossing.

Unbreakable ★★★★

2000, USA
Director: M. Night Shyamalan
Cast: Bruce Willis, Samuel L. Jackson, Robin Wright

Elijah Price (Jackson), an eccentric comic book collector searching for a human with supernatural abilities, believes he has found such a person in disillusioned security guard David Dunn (Willis).

Some superhero movies hold clearly defined positions on the genre's landscape. *The Dark Knight* is the critical darling, *The Incredibles* the family favourite, Richard Donner's *Superman* the nostalgic choice (for all ages, somehow), etc. *Unbreakable* is the movie for cinema snobs who think they don't like superheroes. It's compellingly iconoclastic in its treatment of the genre and related tropes, but at times perhaps too self-conscious and not as clever as it wants to be. (Followed by *Split*, kind of, and *Glass*.)

Untama Giru ★★★★

1989, Japan
Director: Go Takamine
Cast: Chikako Aoyama, Kaoru Kobayashi, John Sayles

Allegorical tale of the USA's occupation of Okinawa during WWII.

There's a surreal, melancholic air to this satirical examination of Okinawan folk hero Untama Giru (Kobayashi) that, combined with an absence of traditional superhero business, might confine its appeal to arthouse audiences. If you're in the mood to invest the returns are handsome.

Up, Up, and Away! ★★

2000, Canada/USA
Director: Robert Townsend
Cast: Robert Townsend, Michael J. Pagan, Alex Datcher

A family of superheroes battle a gang of phoney environmentalists who are using a computer program to hypnotise the public.

There are all sorts of fun details, like the grandfather's bitter rivalry with Superman and the challenge of being a soccer mom while preventing bank robberies. Such frippery is probably enough to make *Up, Up and Away* worthwhile (at least for audiences who know what to expect from a Disney Channel Original Movie), which is a good thing because there's nothing else to it.

Upgrade ★★★★

2018, Australia
Director: Leigh Whannell
Cast: Logan Marshall-Green, Melanie Vallejo, Steve Danielsen

An A.I. computer widget is installed in the spine of recent widower and quadriplegic Grey Trace (Marshall-Green), enabling him to perform incredible physical acts. However, pursuing his wife's killers brings Trace into conflict with Stem (Simon Maiden), the A.I. able to control his body, and Eron Keen (Harrison Gilbertson), its mad genius creator.

Upgrade has a good peer into many of the philosophical avenues opened up by a concept this high, but it isn't concerned with strolling too far down any of them. There's just enough meat to underpin the action, which is unique and impressive but sparser than ideal. Although this is a better movie it's strikingly similar to *Venom*. Logan Marshall-Green's Trace is the spit of Tom Hardy's Eddie Brock, and has precisely the same relationship with the omnipotent voice in his head.

Urufu gai: Moero ôkami-otoko: see *Wolf Guy*

Urutoraman: see Grouped Franchises and Ultraman

US Catman: see *Catman*

V for Vendetta ★★★★

2005, USA/UK/Germany
Director: James McTeigue
Cast: Hugo Weaving, Natalie Portman,
Stephen Rea

In a totalitarian future United Kingdom, the masked anarchist V (Weaving) orchestrates a bloody revolution.

Imagine George Orwell's *1984* if the author was reacting against Donald Trump rather than Joseph Stalin. That's essentially the world depicted in this contradictory but intriguing primal scream of a movie. Both conventional and subversive, silly and earnest, it's difficult to get a handle on *V for Vendetta's* intended tone and objectives, particularly when it comes to Weaving's performance. Ultimately, a bit of chaos suits the theme, and while it may be flawed and trite, it's still quite something to see a studio blockbuster encourage its audience to question the status quo like this.

Valentine ★★★

2017, Indonesia,
Directors: Ubay Fox, Agus Pestol
Cast: Estelle Linden, Matthew Settle,
Arie Dagienkz

Talented martial artist, dissatisfied waitress and wannabe actress Srimaya (Linden) is chosen to star in a new superhero epic when prospective filmmaker Bono (Settle) witnesses her defending herself from rowdy customers. Little does she know the movie doesn't yet have funding, and Bono plans to acquire it by having Srimaya demonstrate her abilities in real-life situations.

An interesting and original idea is handled well by first time directors Fox and Pestol. The Western aesthetic includes a US actor starring as Bono (Settle is from Hickory, North Carolina, which sounds about as US as you can get) and points to hopes of international success. But his scenes are stolen by radio star Arie Dagienkz as his sidekick Wawan, who provides some well judged comedic balance.

Vampire Assassin ★

2005, USA
Director: Ron Hall
Cast: Ron Hall, Mel Novak, Gerald Okamura

Cop Derek Washington (Hall) must become part vampire to defeat a counterfeiting ring.

Like watching rehearsals for an amateur production of *Blade* while the school rock band practice in the next room.

Vampirella ★★★

1996, USA
Director: Jim Wynorski
Cast: Talisa Soto, Roger Daltrey, Richard Joseph Paul

Vlad (Daltrey), a rogue vampire from the otherwise enlightened planet Drakulon, is pursued to Earth by Ella (Soto), the daughter of a man he once murdered. 3,000 years later Ella, now Vampirella, teams up with Adam Van Helsing (Paul), leader of a militarised holy task force pursuing Vlad.

Although *Vampirella* is blessed with a larger budget than the typical Jim Wynorski and Roger Corman production, they don't let it get in the way of their usual nonsense; the plot's crazy, the filming slapdash and the women keep taking their tops off for no reason. The additional money is only really evident in the casting, with Roger Daltrey belonging to the premium range of terrible actors who will appear in anything. Fast, daft and easy-going enough if you're looking for something silly.

Van Helsing ★★

2004, USA

Director: Stephen Sommers
Cast: Hugh Jackman, Kate Beckinsale, Richard Roxburgh

Having spent centuries secretly protecting us from Universal's classic monsters, the Catholic Church faces its greatest ever challenge in Dracula (Roxburgh). Vatican types dispatch Van Helsing (Jackman), an immortal amnesiac evangelist with the ability to sense evil.

Van Helsing opens with a lengthy black-and-white sequence homaging the 1930s horror movies that allegedly inspired it – which, ironically, only serves to remind us what we could be watching instead. With 30 minutes of cuts and 10 percent of the CGI, this could have been a dumb but fun B-movie, but instead it's an overblown boor. Clichéd presentation renders Van Helsing himself little more than a cool-looking silhouette, and Kate Beckinsale's feisty love interest nothing more than a generic unit of feisty love interest.

Velayudham ★★★★

2011, India
Director: Mohan Raja
Cast: Joseph Vijay, Genelia D'Souza, Santhanam

After inadvertently thwarting a number of terrorist attacks, humble milkman Velu (Vijay) is persuaded to adopt the persona of hitherto fictional superhero Velayudham.

Strap yourself in for some wild tonal shifts as gratuitous mutilations sit side-by-side with light comedy. It's a disconcerting mix at first but once you slip into the right, or wrong, frame of mind it's wonderful fun. Although hardly unappealing to look at, Velu isn't the typical chiselled superhero and his love interest Vaidehi (Motwani) not an archetypal beauty. It makes them more relatable than the typically pristine Bollywood protagonists and really draws us into the performances.

Hugo Weaving as V in *V for Vendetta*

The Vengeance of the Red Mask

aka *Kizil maske'nin intikami*, *Revenge of the Red Mask*, 1971, Turkey
Director: Cavit Yürüklü
Cast: Levent Çakir, Fatma Belgen, Oktar Durukan

At least the third Turkish movie to 'borrow' the Phantom. Although released just three years after the previous two (both titled *The Red Mask/Kizil Mask*) there are no direct connections: different star, director, writer, producer and production company. This movie is considered lost.

Venom ★★

2018, USA
Director: Ruben Fleischer
Cast: Tom Hardy, Michelle Williams, Riz Ahmed

Disgraced Investigative reporter Eddie Brock (Hardy) becomes inadvertent host to an alien monster as he feuds with an evil techno-industrialist.

Venom is an odd movie for this superhero-savvy day and age. We get nothing new and the normal stuff is spoon-fed to us as if we've never seen one of these things before. It might not matter if the screenplay wasn't so full of inconsistent characters with clichéd dialogue. What's meant to be serious is funny, and what's meant to be funny is just weird. Even Tom Hardy lets us down with a performance that never gets beyond the stock Disgraced Drunk Man. Other characters include Grumpy Woman (Williams), Dr. Nice Man (Reid Scott) and Bond Villain (Ahmed).

Veritas, Prince of Truth ★

aka *Veritas - El príncipe de la verdad*, 2007, Mexico/USA
Director: Arturo Ruiz-Esparza
Cast: Sean Patrick Flanery, Amy Jo Johnson, Bret Loehr

Fictional superhero Veritas (Flanery) comes to life and, along with thirteen-year-old Kern (Loehr), must save Earth from the evil Nemesii (Kate Walsh).

Comprehensively predictable and drenched in terrible visual effects, hideous animated sequences and pomposity. Nobody cares about a superhero whose special powers include "knowing who you really are" (least of all Flanery, who phones in a particularly stale performance). There are kids who will like it, but their age range is so narrow that parents will have about a month to pull off a successful screening.

The Vigilantes are Coming ★★

aka *The Eagle in The Vigilante's Are Coming*
1936, USA
Directors: Ray Taylor, Mack V. Wright
Cast: Robert Livingston, Kay Hughes, Guinn 'Big Boy' Williams

A Russian attempt to invade America is prevented by church organist Chuck Norris, I mean Don Loring, aka masked hero The Eagle (Livingston).

Early Republic serial supposedly based on Valentino's 1925 silent film *The Eagle*, but apparently more inspired by Zorro and the Lone Ranger. It's as basic as they come with a cast of stereotypical ranchers thundering about on horses fretting about "Roo-shuns". The cliffhangers are hackneyed and the performances stodgy.

Vincent ★★

aka *Vincent n'a pas d'écailles*, 2014, France
Director: Thomas Salvador
Cast: Thomas Salvador, Vimala Pons, Youssef Hajdi

A man has superpowers when wet. After his superpowers are discovered, he moves away. The end.

Almost completely dialogue-free French mumblecore movie riven with affectation and pretension (the director also stars you say? Quelle surprise). It could have worked as a short, but the only way to give this thing the depth it strives for is to project meaning onto it. Some might say that's the point. I say it would be just as enriching and considerably more entertaining to project that meaning onto a Jason Statham film.

Vivian Volta

1974, Philippines
Director: Bobby P. Santiago
Cast: Vilma Santos, Edgar Mortiz, Eddie Garcia

One of many female-lead superhero films produced in The Philippines and believed to be lost.

Vixen: The Movie ★★★

2017, USA
Directors: Curt Geda, James Tucker
Cast: Megalyn Echikunwoke, Stephen Amell, Katie Cassidy

Mari McCabe, aka Vixen, (Echikunwoke), an African orphan with a magical necklace that allows her to call on the powers of wild animals, becomes a crimefighter in Detroit.

Movie adaptation of DC's web series. Vixen is a pretty humourless character and there's little originality to the mythology. But a stab at proper character arcs is welcome and there's a real plot, too (rather than a series of loosely connected fight scenes).

Volcano High ★★★

aka *Hwasango*
2001, Japan
Director: Tae-gyun Kim
Cast: Hyuk Jang, Min-a Shin, Su-ro Kim

After falling into a tank of electric eels, Kim Kyeong-su (Jang) finds he has superpowers. Years later, and after being kicked out of eight different schools, he's enrolled at the rather unusual Volcano High.

If Harry Potter was reimagined in manga form and then adapted as a very R-rated tokusatsu, it might look something like this. It's hard to judge how funny *Hwasango* was originally supposed to be, because by the time it became *Volcano High* an army of rappers (Snoop Dogg, Andre 3000, Big Boi, etc.) had been drafted in to re-dub it. The result is bizarre but amusing. The movie itself is predictably excessive with plenty of stylised violence and wacky mythology. If you're a serious fan of such things it's worthwhile, but track down the original

Japanese version. If you just want a laugh and to enjoy Michael Winslow's (the funny sounds guy from *Police Academy*) badly dubbed kung fu movie schtick, then check out the US version.

Volta ★★★

2004, Philippines
Director: Wenn V. Deramas
Cast: Ai-Ai de las Alas, Diether Ocampo, Jean Garcia

After being struck by lightning (on at least three occasions), dowdy dressmaker Perla Magtoto (de las Alas) becomes Volta, an electricity-powered superhero.

Volta is built around the surprisingly rare conceit of superpowering a genuinely ordinary woman (i.e. not a supermodel in glasses and a baggy sweater). Perla isn't funny, sexy or cool even as her alter ego, but she does have spirit and she ultimately prevails. With the villain a female corporate executive, the movie could be accused of archaic gender role propaganda (career woman = bad; homely woman = good), but it seems more likely the message is one of universality: superheroes and supervillains can spring from anywhere. Either way, there's a scene in which Volta literally fries an evil child with her lightsaber.

Walet Merah ★★★

1993, Indonesia
Director: S.A. Karim
Cast: Devi Permatasari, Barry Prima, Yunita
Sarah Boom

Stranded on a pirate island, Walet Merah (Permatasari) hunts for treasure and her missing love, fellow Indonesian superhero Panji Tengkorak (Prima).

At least I think that's what's going on. With an abundance of breakneck action scenes and a lack of subtitles, it's not always easy to tell. The fight scenes position *Walet Merah* as a Silat story (fantasy themed kung fu) and are generally quite exceptional. Fast, fierce and fun, they bring to mind Hong Kong classics such as *Zu Warriors*. There's also a lot of melodrama, but I'd recommend fast-forwarding through that.

Wander Woman si ako!

1980, Philippines
Director: Pablo Santiago
Cast: Maria Teresa Carlson, Bembol Roco,
Julie Ann Fortich

This unlicensed Wonder Woman knock-off is thought to be lost.

Wanted ★★★★

2008, USA
Director: Timur Bekmambetov
Cast: Angelina Jolie, James McAvoy,
Morgan Freeman

Wesley Gibson (McAvoy), a disillusioned account managing office drone, learns he is the son of an assassin and has inherited his father's supernatural abilities.

A heavy-handed mixed bag of monomyth constantly teetering on the edge of inanity. Much of the visual ingenuity now comes as standard on this kind of movie, and the pedestrian script isn't always worthy of its energetic execution. But this is a hugely exciting and original movie, and McAvoy an atypical lead who delivers a refreshingly unselfconscious performance.

Wapakman ★★

2009, Phillipines
Director: Topel Lee
Cast: Manny Pacquiao, Angelique Velez, Arvin Sadsad

Commando plumber and unappreciated husband Magno Meneses (Pacquiao) is exposed to a serum that leaves him with superpowers. Helped by an American spy investigating the death of her father, he faces an evil scientist as Wapakman.

Family-friendly nuttiness in which Filipino boxing great Manny Pacquiao fights a host of superpowered villains including giant CGI crabs, robots, a fire monster, a Wonder

Wanted

Woman clone with scream power and the Borg. Much hyped on release, it was a colossal box office failure and isn't much improved with age.

War of the Infras ★★

aka *Shan Dian Qi Shi Da Zhan Di Yu Jun Tuan, Superriders Against the Devils,* 1976, Taiwan
Director: Lin Chong-Guang
Cast: Wen Chiang-Long, Li Yi-Min, Chang Feng

Two students are kitted out for superhero duty by a disillusioned scientist.

Incomprehensible Taiwanese Kamen Rider ripoff. The costumes and fight scenes are far superior to those featured in *Hanuman and the Five Riders*, the Thai Kamen clone from 1974, but there's still no reason to bother with it. Whether the whole stunt team survived filming is not documented but seems doubtful.

Watchmen ★★★★★

2009, USA
Director: Zack Snyder
Cast: Jackie Earle Haley, Patrick Wilson, Malin Akerman

In an alternate 1985, cold war tensions escalate as retired superheroes investigate the murder of one of their own.

Watchmen's obsession with character and the passage of time means it works like an epic saga rather than a superhero movie, particularly if you watch the extended cut. Although the plot is well developed it's a relatively small part of the equation, with the lengthy runtime largely dedicated to meaty character development. It's an ambitious approach that creates a richness almost unique within the genre. Although far from flawless and extremely unpopular in some fan circles, it's among the most determined and least compromised of superhero films.

The Whip ★★★

aka *El Latigo*, 1978, Mexico
Director: Alfredo B. Crevenna
Cast: Juan Miranda, Gustavo Rojo,
Yolanda Ochoa

The corrupt officials of a Mexican town meet their righteous match in El Latigo, aka The Whip (Miranda).

Fun little Zorro knock-off with oater DNA. The action is precise and simple, almost like it was handled by a TV crew, and the overall effect of the movie is perfectly pleasant. (Followed by the below.)

The Whip vs. Satan ★★★

aka *El látigo contra Satanás, The Whip Against Satan*, 1979, Mexico
Director: Alfredo B. Crevenna
Cast: Juan Miranda, Noé Murayama,
Rubén Rojo

Zorro, I mean the Whip (Miranda), rides into town just in time to save everyone from devil worshippers.

More action, not to mention volcanoes and satanism, than we might expect going on the first movie, but it's all welcome. As is the striking cinematography and lighting. There's a likeability to this series. It takes itself completely seriously without ever getting heavy or pretentious, and somehow it feels as if those behind the camera cared about what they were doing. (Followed by the below.)

The Whip vs. the Killer Mummies ★★★

aka *El latigo contra las momias asesinas, The Whip Against Murderous Mummies*, 1980, Mexico
Director: Ángel Rodríguez Vázquez
Cast: Juan Miranda, Rosa Gloria Chagoyán, Marco de Carlo

Our hero investigates a Guatemalan mummy cult who prefer unitards painted with bandages to the real thing.

The opening credit sequence used in this series is magnificent. In the space of 60 seconds we're treated to 23 whip-cracks and 11 thunder-claps – it's as if El Latigo's (Miranda) whip is arguing with a storm. This is the third and last of his adventures and part of the fun this time around is watching for the mummies slipping on tiled floors in their 'bandaged' feet.

Who Wants to Kill Jessie? ★★★★

aka *Kdo chce zabít Jessii?*, 1966, Czechoslovakia
Director: Václav Vorlícek
Cast: Dana Medrická, Jirí Sovák,
Olga Schoberová

Top scientist Doctor Ruzenka Beránková (Medrická) invents a serum guaranteeing pleasant dreams, but when she gives it to her husband his female superhero fantasy figure comes to life.

Surreal comedy from Czech auteur Václav Vorlícek. It works on numerous levels with wonderful visual gags, humour derived from the relationship between the central couple, some solid spoofing of comic book clichés (all of which are easily accessible to English speaking audiences) and razor sharp satire of mid-60s Czechoslovakian politics. (Or so I'm told.)

The Wild World of Batwoman ★

1966, USA
Director: Jerry Warren
Cast: Katherine Victor, George Mitchell,
Steve Brodie

A female vampire club overseen by masked oddball Batwoman (Victor) must prevent Rat Fink (Richard Banks) acquiring an atomic hearing aid.

Reprehensible trash clearly desperate to show us more skin than it was allowed to. The plot is nonexistent, the acting useless and the constant breaks for inexplicable dance scenes beyond tedious.

Witchblade ★★★★

2000, USA
Director: Ralph Hemecker
Cast: Yancy Butler, Anthony Cistaro, Conrad Dunn

NYPD cop Sara Pezzini (Butler) comes into possession of a magical gauntlet, which she uses to help her topple a master criminal responsible for the death of her father and best friend.

Sombre TV movie that lead to a short-lived series. The tone feels appropriate and earned; this is a gritty cop drama that just happens to feature a supernatural element. Pezzini is an atypical female superhero in that she's allowed to out-macho the men without having to sacrifice femininity, and, amazingly, is never sexualised (you watch a thousand superhero movies and something like that stands out). There are plenty of dud notes and a dearth of action set pieces (it's all about the investigation and Pezzini's struggle to stave off a nervous breakdown), but there are great little explosions of weird music and editing, and if you can buy into the central performances it's kind of an underrated gem.

Wolf Guy ★★★★★

aka *Urufu gai: Moero ôkami-otoko*, *Wolf Guy: Enraged Lycanthrope*, 1975, Japan
Director: Kazuhiko Yamaguchi
Cast: Shin'ichi Chiba, Kyôsuke Machida, Yuriko Azuma

A werewolf cop in human form (we assume) uses his metaphysical powers to investigate a series of deaths apparently caused by an invisible tiger.

Stunning supernatural thriller bursting with style, sleaze and funky music. Chiba is at his taciturn best as lychanthropic loose canon Akira Inugami, the lone scion of an ancient werewolf clan. Few faces look better when half-lit among murky shadows. There's an immediate, vérité style to the camerawork and editing that begins with the first shot and doesn't let up. And a seedy, sexually charged atmosphere emphasises Inugami's animalistic lubricity. He seems dangerous, but Yamaguchi makes us wait to find out, teasing us with shots of an ever waxing moon and leaving us to wonder what Inugami will be capable of once it's full.

WolfCop ★★★★

2014, Canada
Director: Lowell Dean
Cast: Leo Fafard, Amy Matysio, Sarah Lind

Drunken deputy sheriff Lou Garou (Fafard) is subjected to a Satanic ritual that turns him into a werewolf. With a strange gang apparently trying to kidnap him, Garou investigates a string of murders.

While *WolfCop* doesn't conjure much of the retro vibe its promotional artwork suggests it's going for, it is a thoroughly enjoyable little movie. Depending on your perspective it either gets dumber or funnier as it progresses, but is extremely well acted and shot throughout: this is not the slapdash nostalgia-fest it might appear to be, and is laced with the kind of subtle humour you probably wouldn't expect (as well as plenty of the less subtle stuff you would). Everything points to director Lowell Dean knowing up from down. (Followed by *Another Wolfcop*.)

The Wolverine ★★★

2013, USA
Director: James Mangold
Cast: Hugh Jackman, Tao Okamoto, Rila Fukushima

Logan (Jackman) travels to Japan at the invitation of wealthy industrialist Yashida (Hal Yamanouchi), whom he saved from the atomic blast that destroyed Nagasaki nearly 70 years previous. Once there, our man is reluctantly drawn into a highly dangerous power struggle.

Taking place between *The Last Stand* and *Days of Future Past* X-Men movies, *The Wolverine* finds our hero at rock bottom living rough in the Yukon mountains and battling the demons of his past. Tipping him into a thriller full of sinister businessmen, deadly assassins and yakuza is an idea with potential and it works well while they stick with it. The change in style (and setting) is a breath of fresh air and there is good action, an unusual cast and an absorbing plot. Unfortunately, everything goes off the rails towards the end when it becomes the 'Giant Robot & Snake Woman Show'.

Wolverine and the X-Men: see Grouped Franchises

Wonder Woman

aka *Wonder Vi*, 1973, Philippines
Director: Arsenio Bautista
Cast: Vilma Santos, George Estregan, Marissa Delgado

This movie is considered lost.

Wonder Woman ★★

1974, USA
Director: Vincent McEveety
Cast: Cathy Lee Crosby, Kaz Garas, Andrew Prine

Compelled to protect mankind, an Amazon goddess leaves her celestial home and becomes a secretary.

Stilted, poorly written ("Let me make love to you." "Why?") and distractingly edited

TV movie. Ricardo Montalban chews the scenery from behind various large pieces of furniture (his face is glimpsed so rarely I assume the production only had him for a day and generally relied on stand-ins) and Crosby is just awful. It's mostly talking, but at least we learn the world's most deadly blackmailer comes from Wales.

Wonder Woman ★★★★

aka *The New Original Wonder Woman*, 1975, USA
Director: Leonard J. Horn
Cast: Lynda Carter, Lyle Waggoner, John Randolph

An Amazon leaves her supernatural home to do good in the world.

Pilot for the popular TV series and secret comedy masterpiece. If you tuned in part way through and Wonder Woman herself wasn't on screen you'd be sure it was a Mel Brooks movie. Sometimes it gets broader, as with the sitcom Nazis (Wonder Woman's

Jackie Earle Haley as Rorschach in *Watchmen*

Nazis are sillier than *The Producers'*), but on the whole it's mainly concerned with being amiably absurd. The acting is heightened and the script so clichéd the writers must have been in on the joke. Stella Stevens gives one of the 1970's funniest performances as a Nazi sympathiser, all that's missing is a laugh track.

Wonder Woman ★★★

2009, USA
Director: Lauren Montgomery
Cast: Keri Russell, Nathan Fillion, Alfred Molina

Ares, the god of war (Molina), escapes from prison on the island of Themyscira, which leads to Wonder Woman (Russell) and US fighter pilot Steve Trevor (Fillion) embarking on a journey to find and destroy him.

DC's animated take on the Wonder Woman origin story is a more fantastical affair than the live-action movie of 2017, and delves a little deeper into the character's mythology. So we see the events that lead up to the founding of Themyscira, and spend a lot more time there. It works for an animated movie aimed at comic book devotees (as opposed to the later blockbuster's broader target audience), and there's plenty of fan service. A tone-deaf ear for dialogue leads to lines like "my sword is thirsty, I intend she gets her fill".

Wonder Woman ★★★★

2017, USA
Director: Patty Jenkins
Cast: Gal Gadot, Chris Pine, Robin Wright

Partnered with American spy Steve Trevor (Pine), Amazonian demigod Diana Prince (Gadot) tackles Ares, the God of War, whose string-pulling is behind World War I.

This isn't a particularly convivial movie, it has that in common with the rest of the DCEU. The war isn't just there to provide a convenient conflict from which to hang the story; it's used to demonstrate how complicated and contradictory mankind can be, and we don't get the Marvel funnies to cut the mood. This is a movie that deals with big themes directly, sincerely and, on the whole, well. There's some cheese and wonky CGI, and the finale is a letdown, but we buy into everything thanks to an intelligent script and great performances from Gadot and Pine. There are also some excellent action sequences that make good use of the beautiful score.

The Wraith ★★★

1986, USA
Director: Mike Marvin
Cast: Charlie Sheen, Nick Cassavetes, Sherilyn Fenn

A gang of murderous car thieves get their comeuppence when one of their victims returns from the dead with a sportscar, a shotgun and a grudge.

They don't come much more 80s than this, or more haphazard in concept. There's no explanation for the means by which the resurrection occurs or how the mythology works, and no consistency to the wraith's powers. We don't find out why he seems to have come back in a different body, why he rides an old Honda when he has a magical regenerating supercar, or how the entire population of an Arizona town, bar the sheriff, can be teenagers. It seems like the script was finished within half an hour of writer/director Mike Marvin having the idea. Cheesy and painfully predictable, but that seems to be why some love it.

X-Men ★★★★★

2000, USA
Director: Bryan Singer
Cast: Patrick Stewart, Hugh Jackman,
Ian McKellen

With superpowered mutants living among us, vanilla humans are manipulated into a state of fear by opportunist politicians. Two mutant groups – one dedicated to peace, the other to the obliteration of mankind – battle over our future.

Although a big talking point at the time of release, it's easy to forget how impressively Singer weaves themes of social justice and civil rights into the DNA of this first X-Men film. Like everything else, it's judged just right: not exactly subtle, but never preachy or cringeworthy. Presenting costumed freaks as viable avatars for Martin Luther King and Malcolm X is kind of impressive, and strong performances are vital. Stewart and McKellen each nail their allegorical figurehead, and Paquin's fragility as the lonely Rogue finds the perfect foil in the brusque savagery of Jackman's Wolverine, her unlikely but dedicated protector. Superhero movies don't get much better.

X-Men 2 ★★★★★

aka *X2: X-Men United*, 2003, USA
Director: Bryan Singer
Cast: Patrick Stewart, Hugh Jackman,
Halle Berry

Embittered colonel William Stryker (Brian Cox) kidnaps Professor X (Stewart) in order to turn his psychic abilities on humankind. The X-Men team up with Magneto (Ian McKellen) to stop him. At the same time, Wolverine (Jackman) searches for clues to his past.

Picking up a couple of years after the first film's conclusion, *X2* uses the widespread public paranoia resulting from an apparent attempt on the US president's life to keep exploring issues of minority oppression and 'fear of the other'. Additional threads woven into the tapestry involve dramas surrounding various X-teens struggling to come to terms with what they are. Although fairly light on action compared to what would follow, set pieces like the raid on the White House and Wolverine's uncompromising defence of the Xavier School are breathtaking. (Followed by *X-Men: The Last Stand*.)

Without a focal point among the ensemble cast it can be harder to engage with *X-Men Apocalypse* than with previous films in the series. Matters aren't helped by a tired script, anemic villain and shift away from character drama towards action. But none of that is terminal, and with a cast like this there's still plenty to enjoy. Fassbender in particular gets to do some heavy lifting in a subplot that brings depth to Magneto and calm to the hectic narrative. (Followed by *X-Men: Dark Phoenix*.)

X-Men Origins: Wolverine ★★

2009, USA
Director: Gavin Hood
Cast: Hugh Jackman, Liev Schreiber, Danny Huston

The life of James Howlett/Wolverine/Logan (Jackman), from childhood through to his rebirth as adamantium-enhanced avenger.

Via the opening titles we watch Wolverine flagrantly contravene haircut regulations during military service in a succession of wars. This tells us that his early life was one of perpetual violence (and possibly that Marvel wouldn't let 20th Century Fox shave off that iconic head of hair). Pondering such lapses in credibility would not have been an option during earlier films in the franchise, they're all too exciting. This one isn't a disaster but it is the weakest. Highlights include Will.i.am doing acting and a pre-*Deadpool* Deadpool (Ryan Reynolds).

X-Men: Apocalypse ★★★

2016, USA
Director: Bryan Singer
Cast: James McAvoy, Michael Fassbender, Jennifer Lawrence

In the early 1980s a powerful and ancient mutant awakes in a bad mood and, aided by Magneto (Fassbender), sets out to destroy the world.

X-Men: Dark Phoenix ★★★

aka Dark Phoenix, 2019, USA
Director: Simon Kinberg
Stars: Sophie Turner, James McAvoy, Michael Fassbender

In 1992 Jean Grey (Turner) is bitten by the cosmic force that gave life to the universe.

After the disappointingly generic *X-Men: Apocalypse*, *Dark Phoenix* at least attempts a return to the series' more contemplative themes. Instead of following a CG Big Bad's attempt to destroy Earth, it's all about manipulation and acceptance. Much of this ground has been covered before, though, and nothing new is said about Xavier's (McAvoy) arrogance or mankind's innate paranoia. Turner is ok, if exhausting, as the overwrought Grey. However, the movie's dreadful box office suggests it's unlikely we'll see her, or the rest of the gang, again in a hurry.

X-Men: Days of Future Past ★★★★★

2014, USA
Director: Bryan Singer
Cast: Hugh Jackman, James McAvoy. Michael Fassbender

Wolverine (Jackman) conscious-shifts 50 years into the past in order to prevent an assassination that will lead to anti-mutant robo-mutants decimating Earth.

Although bookended by scenes of cheesy fan service, *Days of Future Past* is among the most interesting modern superhero extravaganzas. The ultimate objective may be to save the world, but the plot is driven by a need to prevent Mystique (Jennifer Lawrence) assassinating scientist Dr. Trask (Peter Dinklage), thereby triggering a series of events that will lead to the creation of the sentinel army responsible for mankind's doom. Magneto (Fassbender), Professor X (McAvoy) and Mystique (Jennifer Lawrence) each hold different and subtly shifting views on how to handle human/mutant relations, and they're debated with intelligence and wit. With Wolverine along to provide the energy, and a great new character in Evan Peters' Quicksilver, this is a well balanced exercise in character-driven blockbusting. (Followed by *X-Men Apocalypse*.)

X-Men: First Class ★★★★

2011, USA
Director: Matthew Vaughn
Cast: James McAvoy, Michael Fassbender, Jennifer Lawrence

During the Cuban missile crisis, mutants Charles Xavier (McAvoy) and Erik Lensherr (Fassbender) team up to create The X-Men.

The bold decision to reboot a still popular and successful franchise pays off thanks to a good script and superb casting. By getting to know the younger versions of Xavier and Magneto it fleshes out the previous films. (Followed by *X-Men: Days of Future Past*.)

X-Men: The Last Stand ★★★

2006, USA
Director: Breet Ratner
Cast: Hugh Jackman, Patrick Stewart, Famke Janssen

With the discovery of a controversial 'cure' for the mutant gene, tensions between mutants and humans rise. Magneto (Ian McKellen) readies for war.

The third movie in the series combines an increase in ambition with a decrease in sophistication. The timing is unfortunate – this would have been a great story for previous director Bryan Singer to tell. Having said that, *The Last Stand* has aged quite well. Some heavy-duty character stuff is handled well and the various narratives tie together nicely. (Followed by *X-Men: First Class*.)

Xing ying bu li: see *Inseperable*

The impressive cast of *X-Men: Days of Future Past*

Yarasa adam – Bedmen ★

aka *Turkish Batman, Turkish Batman & Robin,*
1973, Turkey
Director: Günay Kosova
Cast: Levent Çakir, Emel Özden, Hüseyin Sayan

Bad guys keep murdering Bedmen's (Çakir) favourite strippers, so he and Bedrobin (Sayan) fight them. I'm not making this up.

Horrendously exploitative and incoherent mess. The unofficial caped crusaders differ from their legitimate counterparts with a fondness for strip joints and unlicensed James Bond music, while Bedmen has a disconcerting habit of copping off with the women he rescues, leaving Bedrobin to hang around awkwardly.

Yatterman ★★★★

aka *Yattâman,* 2009, Japan
Director: Takashi Miike
Cast: Shô Sakurai, Saki Fukuda, Kyoko Fukada

In a surreal alternative world, superhero duo Yatterman (Sakurai) and the nefarious Doronbo gang each seek the four pieces of the Skull Stone, a mystical artefact capable of destroying time.

Takashi Miike, one of Japan's most original and outlandish filmmakers, subjects the Yatterman franchise to his barmy creative impulses. Imagine Terry Gilliam was spiked with LSD and made a Power Rangers film. With singing. *Yatterman* is an extraordinary thing to behold, mixing as it does surreal technicolor cityscapes, Sentai costumes, cel animation, unique mecha designs and bags of unconventional CGI.

Yeom-lyeok: see *Psychokinesis*

Yilmayan seytan: see *Deathless Devil*

Yin doi hou hap zyun: see *Heroic Trio 2: Executioners*

You gui zi: see *The Oily Maniac*

Young Hercules ★★

1998, USA
Director: T.J. Scott
Cast: Ian Bohen, Dean O'Gorman, Chris Conrad

Hercules skips god school to search for the Golden Fleece.

Prequel movie to TV series *Young Hercules*, which in turn was a prequel to *Hercules: The Legendary Adventures*. While the series would give a young Ryan Gosling his big break in the lead role, this pilot stars one Ian Bohen, who favoured a return to his native US over sticking around on the New Zealand set. Oops. He's no worse than Gosling would prove to be, in fact if anything he's better, but this is a cheap and silly franchise of interest only for its nostalgic value.

Yûsei ôji: see *Prince of Space*

Yatterman

Zagor

1970, Turkey
Director: Mehmet Aslan
Cast: Cihangir Gaffari, Yilmaz Köksal,
Nükhet Egeli

The first of three Turkish movies based
on the eponymous Italian comic book
character. Zagor (Gaffari) roams the old
West righting wrongs as he searches for his
parent's killers. This movie is assumed lost.

Zagor kara bela ★★

1971, Turkey
Director: Nisan Hançer
Cast: Levent Çakir, Ece Cansel, Nevzat Açikgöz

Zagor (Cenir) is back, and this time he's on
the trail of an enigmatic cloaked murderer.

This second Zagor movie is unrelated to
the first and feels almost subversive for its
sympathetic depiction of Native Americans.
Our hero (a maskless cross between the
Lone Ranger and Batman) is appealing
enough, but a lack of action stymies
the entertainment value. Even so, it's
interesting to see such a uniquely American
genre as the Western through Turkish eyes.

Zagor kara korsan'in hazineleri ★★

1971, Turkey
Director: Nisan Hançer
Cast: Levent Çakir, Kazim Kartal,
Nevzat Açikgöz

This time Zagor (Cakir) faces off against
pirates in a hunt for missing treasure.

From the same team who brought us *Zagor
kara bela* comes this remarkably similar
sequel. It's perhaps a little more confident
but you could still swap numerous scenes
between the two without causing many
narrative issues. Zagor's sidekick Chico
(Açikgöz) returns, and once again he's a

lazy, stupid, greedy Mexican played by a Turk, which might raise some greasepaint eyebrows today.

Zatôichi (Shintarô Katsu series): see Grouped Franchises

Zatôichi ★★★★★

aka *The Blind Swordsman: Zatoichi*, 2003, Japan
Director: Takeshi Kitano
Cast: Takeshi Kitano, Tadanobu Asano, Yui Natsukawa

The blind masseur and blademaster comes across a town under the cosh of a violent gang. Feathers are ruffled.

Sublime modern(ish) take on the amourotic samurai and roaming folk hero. Compared to the original Shintarô Katsu film series, Kitano's direction is more precise and poetic, his Ichi more nuanced and layered. An ambitious plot jumps back and forth in time weaving together the stories of a ronin forced to sell his soul, vengeful geishas seeking their parents' murderers and the eponymous hero's meander in the general direction of redemption. It comes together perfectly with a wry sense of humour and hypnotic beauty.

Zatôichi: The Last ★★

2010, Japan
Director: Junji Sakamoto
Cast: Shingo Katori, Takashi Sorimachi, Satomi Ishihara

Seeking a quiet life after his wife's murder, Zatôichi (Katori) is instead drawn into a feud with the yakuza, and betrayed by the people of his home town.

If you're going to stray this far from the format, then commercial considerations must be the only reason for retaining the name Zatôichi. Pretentiously styled, crudely

choreographed and just plain tedious, there are few reasons for *Zatôichi: The Last* to exist, and even fewer to watch it.

Zebraman ★★★

aka *Zeburâman*, 2004, Japan
Director: Takashi Miike
Cast: Shô Aikawa, Kyôka Suzuki, Atsuro Watabe

Shin'ichi Ichikawa (Aikawa), a put-upon husband, father and teacher, escapes into a fantasy world each night by dressing up as Zebraman, the title character of his favourite childhood TV show. Meanwhile, a series of strange crimes have the locals on edge.

Wonderfully absurd deadpan comedy from prolific provocateur Takashi Miike. It works as both homage to and revision of tokusatsu series of the 1970s, and takes some pretty bizarre turns, particularly in the final act. Although suitable for all ages, Miike's patented weirdness bubbles away just beneath the surface and not all audiences will appreciate his sense of humour.

Zebraman 2: Attack on Zebra City ★★★

aka *Zeburâman: Zebura Shiti no gyakushû*, 2010, Japan
Director: Takashi Miike
Cast: Shô Aikawa, Riisa Naka, Tsuyoshi Abe

Fifteen years after the events of the first movie, Zebraman (Aikawa) is considered the world's greatest superhero and Tokyo has been renamed in his honour. Inclined to step back from his alter ego, Shin'ichi Ichikawa must face one last challenge in the Zebra Queen (Naka), who plans to destroy law and order.

Without the grounding of Ichikawa's home and work life, this *Zebraman* sequel, again directed by Takashi Miike, is even more surreal than its predecessor. If the first movie was a character study with fantastic elements, this one is all out sci-fi. The visual effects are better, which is lucky because there are a lot of them, as are the costumes and character designs. It's also faster paced.

Zenitram ★★

2010, Argentina
Director: Luis Barone
Cast: Juan Minujín, Verónica Sánchez, Jordi Mollà

After being given superpowers by a weirdo in a toilet, refuse collector Rubén Martínez (Minujin) becomes Zenitram... and struggles to decide what to do next.

Satire on politics disguised as a superhero movie. Or maybe it's the other way around. The comedy sits uneasily alongside glum characters occupying a grubby aesthetic, and we never get a handle on Zenitram himself. There are some interesting visuals and half-explored ideas, but it never quite pulls together.

Zhong guo chao ren: see *Infra-Man*

Zokkomon ★★★★

2011, India
Director: Satyajit Bhatkal
Cast: Darsheel Safary, Anupam Kher, Manjari Fadnnis

After being abandoned by his uncle, who claims the boy is dead, orphan Kunal (Safary) eventually finds his way home, only to be greeted as a ghost by townsfolk. He decides to become a superhero in order to right local wrongs.

Disney India's first live-action movie is, predictably, aimed at families and produced to a high standard. It looks gorgeous, with excellent camerawork and bright primary colours popping all over the place. There's darkness in the story, though, and Western kids might not expect some of the more significant emotional bumps in the road. But the well-defined characters, mature themes and a worthy reluctance to dish up easy answers to difficult questions (for a while, at least) makes *Zokkomon* that rarest of things: a superhero movie from which thoughtful children might get something of value.

Zombies of the Stratosphere ★★

1952, USA
Director: Fred C. Brannon
Cast: Judd Holdren, Aline Towne, Wilson Wood

With Mars drifting too far from the sun, its leader Marex (Lane Bradford) concocts a scheme to swap orbits with Earth. Larry Martin (Holdren) of the Inter-Planetary Patrol takes it upon himself to save the day.

The third of Republic's four 'Rocket Man' serials has nothing to do with zombies or the stratosphere, and doesn't feature any Rocket Man, but let's not worry about that. It's remarkably similar to its predecessor, *Radar Men from the Moon*, in the 'aliens scheme with gangsters in hats' plot. The most remarkable aspect is perhaps Leonard Nimoy's presence as a Martian henchman.

Zombies of the Stratosphere

1995, USA
Director: Fred C. Brannon
Cast: Judd Holdren, Aline Towne, Wilson Wood

Colourised feature-length edit of the serial of the same name (see above). It gained cult status when released on VHS.

Zoom ★

2006, USA
Director: Peter Hewitt
Cast: Tim Allen, Courteney Cox, Chevy Chase

Retired superhero Jack Shepard, aka Captain Zoom (Allen), trains young meta-humans.

In January 1978, the popular South Korean actress Choi Eun-hee disappeared from a Hong Kong hotel. Months later, her former husband and frequent collaborator, leading filmmaker Shin Sang-ok, vanished in similar circumstances. It was some time before the astonishing truth behind these abductions came to light, but we now know Choi and Shin were kidnapped by agents of the North Korean government, taken against their will to Pyongyang, and forced to make movies at figurative gunpoint. It seems former dictator Kim Jong-il was a film fan and, embarrassed by the low standard of North Korean productions, decided to abduct some talent and have them make the movies he wanted. I've seen one of them; a *Godzilla* ripoff titled *Pulgasari*. What's that got to do with Zoom? Nothing, really. It just struck me that even Shin and Choi seemed more committed to *Pulgasari* than anyone did to *Zoom*.

Zoom, Zoom, Superman!
1973, Philippines
Directors: Elwood Perez, Ishmael Bernal, Joey Gosiengfiao
Cast: Ariel Ureta, Rita Gomez, Boots Anson-Roa

Ariel Ureta stars as an unofficial Superman in this lost Pinoy parody.

Zorro (Italian series): see Grouped Franchises and Peplum Movies

---

Zorro ★★★
1975, India
Director: Shibu Mitra
Cast: Navin Nischol, Rekha, Urmila Bhatt

After fathering an illegitimate offspring, the Maharaj Bahadur Singh (Om Shivpuri) weds and starts a family. While new son Vikram (Sudhir) grows up to usurp him, Gunawar, (Nischol), the one born out of wedlock, grows up to be Zorro.

Don't be fooled by the title, this is a classic Indian folk superhero movie (rival brothers in a game of thrones is the genre's bread and butter). It's vivid and exciting, and the crash zooms onto stern faces are a glory to behold. If it had been condensed into 75 minutes the songs, random bursts of action and comedic tendencies would have made this a camp classic. At twice that length it's occasionally a chore (mainly due to the lack of English subtitles on my copy) but still worthwhile.

Zebraman 2: Attack on Zebra City

Zorro and Scarlet Whip Revealed! ★★

2010, USA
Director: Chris Evans
Cast: Ben Small, Jules de Jongh, Janet Brown

Zorro (Small), teams up with Scarlet Whip (de Jongh) in a series of confrontations.

Like its predecessor *Zorro: Return to the Future*, this animated movie is derived from episodes of 2006 TV series *Zorro: Generation Z*. Unfortunately, without the origin story as a framework it's even less coherent. There are more Batman similarities (like Batgirl, Scarlet Whip is the daughter of the show's leading official, Morgan Deare's Mayor Martinez). Although I'm probably imagining it, the animation seems even worse.

Zorro Rides Again ★★

1937, USA
Directors: John English, William Witney
Cast: John Carroll, Helen Christian,
Reed Howes

Zorro's great-grandson James Vega (Carroll) thwarts a criminal organisation trying to gain control of the still under construction California-Yucatan railroad.

Reed Hadley as Zorro in *Zorro's Fighting Legion*

Twelve chapter serial placing Zorro in a 'modern' context. His distracting habit of bursting into song can be put down to the cinematic trends of the day, which prove rather more of an influence than might be ideal. John Carroll is fine as de la Vega but lacks charisma as Zorro, and slow pacing makes everything a struggle. (Followed by *Zorro's Fighting Legion*.)

Zorro Rides Again

1959, USA
Directors: John English, William Witney
Cast: Helen Christian, Reed Howes,
Duncan Renaldo

Feature-length edit of the 1937 serial of the same name.

Zorro, the Avenger ★★★

1959, USA
Director: Charles Barton
Cast: Guy Williams, Charles Korvin, Henry Calvin

Zorro (Williams) must prevent a dictator known as the Eagle (Korvin) taking over all Southern California.

Second feature-length cut-and-shut edited from the 1957 Disney TV series (the first being 1958's *The Sign of Zorro*). This one uses the Eagle storyline from season one. It's predictably stage-bound and talky but the characters are likeable and share great chemistry. There's plenty of light humour, but the funniest element is accidental. The score was composed by William Lava, who was responsible for hundreds of early Disney cartoons and seems to have had just one style. If you close your eyes you can almost see Mickey Mouse up to his shenanigans.

Zorro: Return to the Future ★★

2007, USA
Director: Stuart Evans
Cast: Ben Small, Jules de Jongh, Morgan Deare

In near future Pueblo Grande, California, the teenage descendent of Don Diego de la Vega, aka Zorro, takes on the mantle of the legendary caballero in order to rescue his kidnapped father.

Pulled from the first few episodes of the short-lived TV series *Zorro: Generation Z*. The show reboots our hero as a motorcycle-riding, gadget-wielding urban crimefighter, but, as the only thing separating Zorro from Batman are the realities of their respective eras, it ends up feeling like *Bruce Wayne: The Teen Years*. It's a humdrum story with poor animation and ultimately disappoints. (A sequel of sorts, *Zorro and Scarlet Whip Revealed!*, was released four years later.)

Zorro: the Gay Blade ★★
1981, Peter Medak
Director: Peter Medak
Cast: George Hamilton, Lauren Hutton, Brenda Vaccaro

Wealthy Mexican landowner Don Diego Vega (Hamilton) inherits the Zorro persona from his dying father and shakes things up in his corrupt home town. After breaking his foot in the line of duty, Vega must persuade his effete twin brother to take his place behind Zorro's mask.

Although dated in its social attitudes, the film's absurdist tone softens the relentless stereotyping of homosexuals (not to mention Mexicans and women, who both come off worse) just enough for it to remain almost inoffensive. It feels like a showcase for Hamilton, whose outrageous accent will either be the main source of amusement or a profound annoyance to viewers.

Zorro's Black Whip ★★
1944, USA
Directors: Spencer G. Bennet, Wallace Grissell
Cast: Linda Stirling, George J. Lewis, Lucien Littlefield

A Zorro-like vigilante known as The Black Whip (Stirling) tries to prevent a dishonest stagecoach operator scuppering Idaho's imminent statehood.

The five-year gap between the second Zorro serial (1939's *Zorro's Fighting Legion*) and this third in the series is down to the film rights being taken over by 20th Century Fox. As a result we have a bizarre situation in which Zorro doesn't appear in a serial bearing his name. Instead, we get The Black Whip, a stand-in played by a woman, no less, in possibly the first case of a female-lead American superhero film. Sadly there's little else remarkable about it. Men in fancy suits sit at fancy tables discussing stuff, then men (plus a woman) in dusty cowboy gear ride horses about shooting at people. It's a shame more wasn't made of a good opportunity to put an interesting slant on things. (Followed by *Son of Zorro*.)

Zorro's Fighting Legion ★★★★
1939, USA
Directors: John English, William Witney
Cast: Reed Hadley, Sheila Darcy, William Corson

The recently formed Republic of Mexico is threatened by the nefarious Don Del Oro (C. Montague Shaw), who intends to install himself as Emperor. Don Diego Vega, aka Zorro (Hadley), leads the fight against him.

The second Zorro serial (after his debut in 1937's confusingly titled *Zorro Rides Again*) takes some liberties with the character's background but is nevertheless one of the better examples of the genre. Much is fairly standard: a cliffhanger is worked into each episode and a main character is revealed as the masked criminal mastermind in the finale. But the cinematography and editing are excellent, the setting well used and the plot nicely paced. There are some inventive touches, like Zorro using a wasp's nest as a weapon. (Followed by *Zorro's Black Whip*.)

Zsa Zsa Zaturnnah Ze Moveeh ★★★

2006, Philippines
Director: Joel Lamangan
Cast: Zsa Zsa Padilla, Bb Gandanghari,
Pops Fernandez

When his/her/their heart is broken, Ada
(Gandanghari) leaves the big city and opens
a beauty parlour in a rural province. An alien
invasion follows.

(Ada, Zsa Zsa's public persona, appears
to be a homosexual male but is played by
a transgender homosexual actress. Upon
transforming into their female alter ego Zsa
Zsa, a different actress, who is not trans or
gay, takes over. It's proved a mite tricky
to find a consensus on which pronoun or
pronouns are appropriate in this scenario.)
What initially seems like a Bollywood
musical directed by Stephen Chou suddenly
develops into a Bollywood musical directed
by Takashi Miike when our protagonist eats
a meteorite and a giant space-frog attacks.
Eventually, aliens with a gender-changing
weapon arrive on Earth and Ada goes into
superhero mode. Sexuality and gender
themed shenanigans ensue in a joyously
bonkers explosion of style, affirmation and
brightly coloured wigs.

GROUPED FRANCHISES

Home to the marginal, the missing and the unchanging mega-series. English titles are given first when their use is common, original titles follow with year of release and country of origin.

Ajin

Gamon Sakurai's acclaimed manga series *Ajin: Demi-Human*, about warring immortals whose 'black ghosts' can manifest physical forms in order to do battle, launched in 2012 and soon saw a flurry of adaptations.

An anime trilogy shares material with the 2016 TV series which also spawned three short OVA spinoffs. A live-action film, *Ajin: Demi-Human*, followed in 2017. The series features controversial CG animation but, for my money, looks great. And though the stand-alone film is good, the anime takes a deeper dive into the material.

Ajin movies:
Ajin Part 1: Shoudou (2015, JP)
Ajin Part 3: Shougeki (2016, JP)
Ajin Part 2: Shoutotsu (2016, JP)
Ajin: Demi-Human (2017, JP)

Asterix & Obelix

Created by René Goscinny (author) and Albert Uderzo (illustrator) in 1959, Asterix the plucky Gaul and his dim-witted friend Obelix have starred in over 30 volumes of their hugely popular comic book series. Aided by druid potion master Getafix (Panoramix in the original French), whose magical elixir is the source of their powers, the two defend their corner of France from Roman invasion around the year 50 BC.

Their first screen adaptation was the largely forgotten 1967 black-and-white TV movie *Deux romains en Gaule*, while in recent years a series of live action films starring French megastar Gerard Depardieu have impressed at the box office. But it's the classic animated series which is best loved. Beginning with 1967's *Asterix the Gaul*, eight traditionally animated features were released, with the first few in particular being exceptional.

Asterix movies:

Deux romains en Gaule (1967, FR)
Asterix the Gaul (1967, FR)
Asterix and Cleopatra (1968, FR)
The Twelve Tasks of Asterix (1976, FR)
Asterix and Caesar (1985, FR)
Asterix in Britain (1986, FR)
Asterix and the Big Fight (1989, FR)
Asterix in America (1994, FR)
Asterix and Obelix vs. Caesar (1999, FR)
Asterix and Obelix Meet Cleopatra (2002, FR)
Asterix and the Vikings (2006, FR)
Asterix and Obelix Meet Cleopatra (2002, FR)
Asterix at the Olympic Games (2008, FR)
Astérix and Obélix: God Save Britannia (2012, FR)
Asterix and Obelix: Mansion of the Gods (2014, FR)
Asterix: The Secret of the Magic Potion (2018, FR)

Captain Barbell

From the pen of Mars Ravelo (the 'Pinoy Stan Lee'), Captain Barbell, aka agreeable asthmatic Tenteng Mumolingot, debuted in 1963 and went on to become the most popular (male) Pinoy superhero. Mumolingot, a bullied wimp who dreams of becoming a strongman, gains powers from an enchanted barbell that would go on to bestow abilities on other put-upon misfits.

The first movie was released in 1964 with Mumolingot played by comic star Dolphy (the character's original inspiration) and Barbell himself by Bob Soler. Other big names have subsequently taken on the roles, notably 'Bong' Revilla in 2003. While the early films are, unsurprisingly, thought lost, *Captain Barbell Boom!* and the later examples still exist, with 1986's comedic take still popular with Filipino audiences.

Captain Barbell movies:

Captain Barbell (1964, PH)
Captain Phillipines at Boy Pinoy (1965, PH)
Captain Barbell kontra Captain Bakal (1965, PH)
Captain Barbell Boom! (1973, PH)
Captain Barbell (1986, PH)
Captain Barbell (2003, PH)

Chakra: The Invincible

Indian series of animated kids' TV movies revolving around a boy named Raju Rai and his scientist friend Dr. Singh, who builds a special suit in order to weaponise Rai's chakras (the body's spiritual focal points).

This is an emminently disposable series despite Stan Lee's totemic involvement.

Chakra: The Invincible movies:
Chakra the Invincible (2013, IN)
Chakra the Invincible: The Rise of Infinitus (2016, IN)
Chakra the Invincible: The Revenge of Magnus Flux (2017, IN)

The Coyote
aka El coyote

The protagonist of nearly 200 Spanish pulp novels, all of which appeared between 1944

Captain Barbell kontra Captain Bakal

and 1953, the Coyote is Zorro's informal successor. Like the caballero, he's a Spanish nobleman who plied his heroic trade in California. His tenure covered the period following Zorro's (after US incorporation).

Four films have documented the Coyote's exploits: a matching pair of entertaining 1950s B-movies, and two random offerings that are more of a struggle.

The Coyote movies:
Coyote (El coyote, 1955, ES/MX)
The Coyote's Justice (La justicia del Coyote, 1956, ES)
The Sign of the Coyote (Il segno del coyote, 1963, IT/ES)
The Return of El Coyote (La vuelta del Coyote, 1998, ES)

The Crimson Bat
aka Mekura no Oichi

With the success of the Zatôichi series starring Shintarô Katsu, Shochiku Studios began casting around for similar ideas, and soon landed on Teruo Tanashita's manga about blind swordswoman Oichi. She's basically a female Zatôichi, although there's no official connection (there would eventually be a licensed female Zatôichi film in 2008's *Ichi*).

Four movies were made, each starring the superb Yoko Matsuyama. The first is a little slow, setting up as it does Oichi's backstory (abandoned by mother, father murdered), but the rest move quickly and with immense style. There are some imaginative and powerfully evocative touches (such as a villain with a whip woven from the hair of heartbroken women).

Crimson Bat movies:
Crimson Bat, the Blind Swordswoman (Mekura no Oichi Monogatari: Makkana Nagaradori, 1969, JP)
Trapped, the Crimson Bat (Mekura no Oichi: Jigokuhada, 1969, JP)
Watch Out, Crimson Bat! (Mekura no Oichi: Midaregasa, 1969, JP)
Crimson Bat - Oichi: Wanted, Dead or Alive (Mekura no Oichi: Inochi Moraimasu, 1970, JP)

Darna

Another creation of Mars Ravelo, Darna is probably the best known, best loved and most prolific of all Filipino superheroes. As the spirit of an alien warrior transferred into the body of typical Pinoy girl Narda, Darna is essentially invulnerable, possesses superhuman speed and strength, and can fly. In appearance she's vaguely similar to Wonder Woman, usually sporting a red and gold bikini, and is frequently backed up by sidekick/younger brother Ding.

The first Darna movies starred Rosa Del Rosario and appeared not long after the character's creation, proving successful at the box office. In 1963 Liza Moreno took over for a couple of more faithful movies, before the actress frequently cited as the definitive Darna, Vilma Santos, made the first of four appearances in 1973. Since the mid 1960s stand-alone Darna TV series and movies have generally been lucrative, with even (male) comedian Dolphy tackling the Pinoy queen in 1979's *Darna, Kuno...?* Darna has also made numerous cameos, most notably in the 1986 and 2003 Captain Barbell movies. Unsurprisingly, many of the films are considered lost.

Darna star vehicles:
Darna (1951, PH)
Darna at ang Babaeng Lawin (1952, PH)
Isputnik vs. Darna (1963, PH)
Si Darna at ang Impakta (1963, PH)
Darna at ang Babaing Tuod (1965, PH)
Si Darna at ang Planetman (1969, PH)
Lipad, Darna, lipad! (1973, PH)
Darna and the Giants (1973, PH)
Darna vs. the Planet Women (1975, PH)
Bira! Darna! Bira! (1979, PH)
Darna, Kuno...? (1979, PH)
Darna at Ding (1980, PH)
Darna ajaib (1980, IDN)
Darna (1991, PH)
Darna! Ang pagbabalik (1994, PH)
Darna (2019, PH)

DC Super Hero Girls

The DC Super Hero Girls series is formed from a series of animated movies spun off from the 2015 US TV show of the same name. The premise sees teenage (largely) female DC characters attending Super Hero High School while occasionally breaking off to battle cosmic threats.

Although primarily written and directed by women, these films' feminist credentials remain questionable. Negative stereotypes (such as Wonder Woman interrupting a crucial fight to answer her cell phone, and Katana's obsession with appearances and fashion) prevail, regardless of the creative forces at work behind the scenes. They're also dreadful. In addition to a triptych of 2D films is a pair of 3D Lego animations.

DC Super Hero Girls movies:
DC Super Hero Girls: Hero of the Year (2016, US)
DC Super Hero Girls: Intergalactic Games (2017, US)
Lego DC Super Hero Girls: Brain Drain (2017, US)
Lego DC Super Hero Girls: Supervillain High (2018, US)
DC Super Hero Girls: Legends of Atlantis (2018, US)

Diabolik Super-Kriminals

What to do with the handful of Italian and Turkish supervillains who have traditionally been presented as superheroes? Lump them all together under a handy umbrella term (coined by publisher and Diabolik Super-Expert Mort Todd), that's what.

Fantômas was the first supervillain on film (in 1913, prior to anyone we'd recognise as a superhero) and proved to be a crucial influence on those who followed. But the Diabolik Super-Kriminal sprang primarilly from Italian fumetti neri (black comics) of the 1960s. Characterised by themes of violence, sex, crime and sadomasochism, the first fumetti neri starred Diabolik – a master thief dreamt up by sisters Angela

Darna Ajaib

and Luciana Giussani in 1962 – who was equipped with extensive gadgetry and quasi-supernatural resources such as life-like masks. But while he may be the best known of the Diabolik Super-Kriminals (in the mainstream at least, thanks to the success of Mario Bava's 1968 film *Danger: Diabolik*), it was Kriminal who made it to screens first.

As the Catholic Church's stranglehold on Italian censorship loosened during the 1960s, authors began probing the limits in an attempt to judge what they could get away with, and what the public wanted; complete bastards, apparently. Created in 1964 by another pair of siblings, Magnus and Max Bunker, Kriminal's eponymous 1966 movie debut marks the start of the genre proper on screen. The character is basically a nastier Diabolik in a jumpsuit adorned with a skeleton motif. It was a look that proved popular and was adapted for Killing, who was probably cinema's most prolific fumetti neri character. The star of a popular fotoromanzo (photo comic) started in 1966, Killing shares many of Kriminal's characteristics. The photography, however, gave his exploits a sleazy immediacy which proved very popular outside Italy, and his magazine format stories were translated for audiences in France (where he was known as Satanik), South America (Kiling), the US (Sadistik) and, most importantly, Turkey, where KiLiNK, as he's known, would go on to star in around a dozen B-movies.

These usually low-budget B-movies cover the gamut from visceral demonstrations of style to purely cynical exploitation. *Danger: Diabolik* is probably the slickest and most easily digesible example of the genre (too much so to be considered typical), with late-1960s Italian superheroes such as Argoman also offering a taster of it.

Diabolik Super-Kriminal movies:
Kriminal (1966, IT)
Avenger X (Mister X, 1967, IT)
How to Kill 400 Duponts (Arriva Dorellik, 1967, IT)
Kilink in Istanbul (Kilink Istanbul'da, 1967, TR)

Kilink vs the Flying Man (Kilink uçan adama karsi, 1967, TR)
Kilink: Strip and Kill (Kilink Soy ve Öldür, 1967, TR)
Fantômas: Appointment in Istanbul (Fantoma Istanbul'da bulusalim, 1967, TR)
Django the Cavalier Killer (Cango - korkusuz adam, 1967, TR)
Mandrake vs Kilink (Sihirbazlar Krali Mandrake Killing'in pesinde, 1967, TR)
Kilink v Frankenstein (Kilink Frankestayns karsi, 1967, TR)
Kilink: Corpses Can't Talk! (Killing Oluler Konusmaz, 1967, TR)
The Baffled Detective vs Kilink (Saskin Hafiye Kilink'e karsi, 1967, TR)
Female Kilink (Disi Killing, 1967, TR)
Killing caniler krali (1967, TR)
Danger: Diabolik (1968, IT)
The Mark of Kriminal (Il marchio di Kriminal, 1968, IT)
Satanik (1968, IT)
Superman vs. Fantômas (Süpermen Fantoma'ya karsi, 1969, TR)
Kiling Murder Spree (Kiling Olum Saciyor, 1971, TR)
Kilink vs the Armless Hero (Killing Kolsuz Kahraman'a Karsi, 1975, TR)
Mr. Kilink in Istanbul (Bay Kilink Istanbul'da, 2011, TR)

Dick Tracy

Plainclothes Tracy debuted in the Detroit Mirror in 1931, the creation of writer and artist Chester Gould. Familiar for his bright yellow jacket, intercom wristwatch and relentless pursuit of criminals, Dick Tracy, as he became, has moved with the times (and the mediums) throughout his nearly 90 years on duty as an urban supercop. He falls into a difficult category and I'm disinclined to consider him a superhero, despite his heritage, but for much of his early life I would have been in the minority.

Tracy's first four screen outings were serials that effectively saw him seconded to the FBI in California. They were successful at the time and still hold up pretty well, as do the four noir B-movies that followed. A 1950 TV show produced two cut-and-shuts, and there was an animated series on the way to the notorious 1990 reboot starring Warren Beatty and Madonna.

Kilink Istanbul'da, a Diabolik Super-Kriminal movie

Dick Tracy movies:

Dick Tracy (1937, USA, serial)
Dick Tracy Returns (1938, USA, serial)
Dick Tracy's G-Men (1939, USA, serial)
Dick Tracy vs. Crime, Inc. (1941, USA, serial)
Dick Tracy (Dick Tracy, Detective, 1945, US)
Dick Tracy vs. Cueball (1946, US)
Dick Tracy's Dilemma (1947, US)
Dick Tracy Meets Gruesome (1947, US)
Dick Tracy: The Mole (1950, USA, cut-and-shut)
Dick Tracy: The Brain (1950, USA, cut-and-shut)
Dick Tracy (1990, US)

Doctor Who

The Gallifreyan Time Lord first appeared on British TV screens in November 1963 after a brief conception supervised by BBC Head of Drama, Sydney Newham. The show sees the eponymous immortal alien use his time-travelling spaceship, the TARDIS, to roam history saving mankind from supernatural and alien threats. First played by William Hartnell as a crotchety old man, the Doctor, as he tends to be known, has since passed through a dozen eccentric iterations and, as of 2019, is played by Yorkshirewoman Jodie Whittaker. The series occupies a unique position within the British cultural landscape. Not only is it one of the most recognisable and influential shows in the nation's history, a combination of longevity and accessibility have made it popular with all ages, rendering it mainstream programming despite niche sensibilities and a distinctly child-friendly tone.

During its original run, from 1963-1989, the series tended to focus on multi-episode narrative arcs rather than one-off weekly adventures (typical stories might take up between four and six 25-minute episodes, but there is much variation). Obviously this is a format that lends itself well to cut-and-shut home media releases, and most story arcs (a surprising number are considered lost) have appeared on VHS and DVD packaged in such a manner. They make up the bulk of the character's 'filmography' (missing episodes have occasionally been recreated via animation in order to complete a particular story arc). Falling ratings lead to the series being cancelled in 1989, but a 2005 relaunch saw it quickly regaining its early popularity. This 'Revived Era' still features occasional multi-episode arcs, but is more likely to throw up an extended single episode.

In addition to the cut-and-shuts there are two theatrical spinoff movies dating from the mid 1960s (starring Peter Cushing as a slightly less exotic version of the Doctor), and an era-spanning feature-length TV movie from 1996 (these receive individual entries but are included here in the interests of punctiliousness).

Doctor Who theatrical movies:

Dr. Who and the Daleks (1965, UK)
Daleks' Invasion Earth 2150 A.D. (1966, UK)
Doctor Who: The Movie (1996, UK/USA)

For a complete list of Doctor Who cut-and shuts see appendix A.

Dragon Ball (Z)
aka Doragon Bōru

Created by Akira Toriyama with inspiration from Wu Cheng en's 16th-century novel *Journey to the West*, Dragon Ball (also styled Dragonball) relates the adventures of Son Goku, an alien warrior questing for the seven dragon balls, mythical MacGuffins that wield enormous power. Blessed with superhuman strength and an abnormal prowess in the martial arts (something he needs minimal provocation to demonstrate), Goku is able to concentrate his chi into magical energy for use in combat. The franchise broke America in the 1990s when the *Dragon Ball Z* TV series began airing internationally, and has gone on to become one of the most successful pop culture properties in the world.

As normal for these enormous Japanese franchises, a plethora of cheaply produced direct-to-video animated movies supplement offerings from other media, and develop every conceivable aspect of the mythology well beyond the point at which it stops making sense to 'amateur' fans.

Dragon Ball (Z) movies:

Dragon Ball: Curse of the Blood Rubies (Doragon Bōru Shenron no Densetsu, 1986, JP)

Dragon Ball: Sleeping Princess in Devil's Castle (Doragon Bōru Majin-jō no nemuri hime, 1987, JP)

Dragon Ball: Mystical Adventure (Doragon Bōru: Makafushigi Dai-Bōken, 1988, JP)

Dragon Ball Z: Dead Zone (Doragon Bōru Zetto, 1989, JP)

Dragon Ball Z: The World's Strongest (Doragon Bōru Zetto: Kono Yo de Ichiban Tsuyoi Yatsu, 1990, JP)

Dragon Ball Z: The Tree of Might (Doragon Bōru Zetto: Chikyū Marugoto Chōkessen, 1990, JP)

Dragon Ball Z: Lord Slug (Doragon Bōru Zetto Sūpā Saiyajin da Son Gokū, 1991, JP)

Dragon Ball Z: Cooler's Revenge (Doragon Bōru Zetto: Tobikkiri no Saikyō tai Saikyō, 1991, JP)

Dragon Ball Z: The Return of Cooler (Doragon Bōru Zetto Gekitotsu!! Hyaku-Oku Pawā no Senshi-tachi, 1992, JP)

Dragon Ball Z: Super Android 13! (Doragon Bōru Zetto Kyokugen Batoru!! San Dai Sūpā Saiyajin, 1992, JP)

Dragon Ball Z: Broly – The Legendary Super Saiyan (Doragon Bōru Zetto Moetsukiro!! Nessen Ressen Chō-Gekisen, 1993, JP)

Dragon Ball Z: Bojack Unbound (Doragon Bōru Zetto: Ginga Giri-Giri!! Butchigiri no Sugoi Yatsu, 1993, JP)

Dragon Ball Z: Broly – Second Coming (Doragon Bōru Zetto Kiken na Futari! Sūpā Senshi wa Nemurenai, 1994, JP)

Dragon Ball Z: Bio-Broly (Doragon Bōru Zetto Sūpā Senshi Gekiha!! Katsu No wa Ore da, 1994, JP)

Dragon Ball Z: Fusion Reborn (Dragon Ball Z Fukkatsu no Fusion!! Goku to Vegeta, 1995, JP)

Dragon Ball Z: Wrath of the Dragon (Dragon Ball Z Ryū-Ken Bakuhatsu!! Gokū ga Yaraneba Dare ga Yaru, 1995, JP)

Dragon Ball: The Path to Power (Doragon Bōru Saikyō e no Michi, 1996, JP)

Dragonball Evolution (2009, USA, live action)

Dragon Ball Z: Battle of Gods (Doragon Bōru Zetto: Kami to Kami, 2013, JP)

Dragon Ball Z: Resurrection 'F' (Doragon Bōru Zetto: Fukkatsu no 'Efu', 2015, JP)

Dragon Ball Super: Broly (Doragon Bōru Sūpā: Burorī, 2018, JP)

Fantômas

A masked criminal genius and, according to the original stories, alter ego of Archduke Juan North, Fantômas was created in 1911 by French authors Marcel Allain and Pierre Souvestre for a series of pulp thrillers. He shares characteristics with Arthur Conan Doyle's Professor Moriarty and Maurice Leblanc's Arsène Lupin, but his mythic air, extraordinary abilities, distinct costume, secret identity and status as the story's protagonist identifies him as the first film supervillain. In addition to beating even the earliest Zorro and Judex adaptations to the screen, he would have a hefty influence on Italian fumetti neri characters such as Diabolik (see Diabolik Super-Kriminals).

The following list covers several formats. The first five silents starring René Navarre were something of a phenomenon and lead to less well received remakes both in France and abroad. In 1964 Fantômas was rebooted for three successful adventures starring the excellent Jean Marais. A less popular mini-series (that can also be seen as a tetrad of TV movies) with Helmut Berger followed in 1980.

Fantômas movies:

Fantômas: In the Shadow of the Guillotine (Fantômas - À l'ombre de la guillotine, 1913, FR)

Fantomas: The Man in Black (Fantômas: Juve versus Fantômas, 1913, FR)

Fantomas: The Dead Man Who Killed (Le mort qui tue, 1913, FR)

Fantômas: The Mysterious Finger Print (Fantômas contre Fantômas, 1914, FR)

Fantômas: The False Magistrate (Le faux magistrat, 1914, FR)

Fantomas (1920, US)

Fantomas (1932, FR)

Fantomas (1947, FR)

Fantomas Against Fantomas (Fantômas contre Fantômas, 1949, FR)

Fantomas (1964, FR)

Fantomas Unleashed (Fantômas se déchaîne, 1965, FR)

Fantomas vs. Scotland Yard (Fantômas contre Scotland Yard, 1967, FR)

Fantômas: Appointment in Istanbul (Fantoma Istanbul'da bulusalim, 1967, TR)

The Golden Claws of the Cat Girl (La louve solitaire, 1968, FR/IT)

L'échafaud magique (1980, FR)

L'étreinte du diable (1980, FR)

Le mort qui tue (1980, FR)

Le tramway fantôme (1980, FR)

Fist of the North Star
aka Hokuto no Ken

Perhaps not a property that immediately suggests 'superhero', FotNS's protagonist Kenshiro is nevertheless a supernaturally gifted Hokuo Shinken martial artist, and he spends most of his time defending the weak from marauding post-apocalyptic gangs. Created in 1983 by Buronson and Tetsuo Hara, the original manga tells the story of Ken's search for fiancée Yulia, and various clashes with adversaries Shin and Raoh. Influenced by *Mad Max*, Kenshiro is among the most popular of all manga characters.

There have been three theatrical releases, one of which is an unofficial Korean effort (don't even think about it), in addition to a brace of series comprising feature-length instalments. The first, 'Legend', reimagines the events of the original manga from the perspective of different characters. The animation is great and it was received reasonably well by fans. The second, 'Saga', repackages episodes of the TV show as feature-length movies.

Fist of the North Star movies:
Fist of the North Star (1986, JP)

Legend of Fist of the North Star (1993, KR)

Fist of the North Star (1995, US)

Fist of the North Star: New Saviour Legend (Shin kyûseishu densetsu Hokuto no Ken: Raô den - Jun'ai no shô, 2006, JP)

Legend of Raoh: Chapter of Death in Love (Raô Den: Jun'ai no Shô, 2006, JP)

Legend of Raoh: Chapter of Fierce Fight (Raô Den Gekitô no Shô, 2007, JP)

Legend of Yuria (Yuria Den, 2007, JP)

Legend of Toki (Zero Kenshirô Den, 2008, JP)

Zero: Legend of Kenshiro (Zero Kenshirô Den, 2008, JP)

Fist of the North Star: The Kaioh Saga (2011, JP)

Fist of the North Star: The Shin Saga (2009, JP)

Fist of the North Star: The Ray Saga (2011, JP)

Fist of the North Star: The Raul Saga (2011, JP)

Fist of the North Star: The Souther Saga (2011, JP)

Fist of the North Star: The Toki Saga (2011, JP)

G.I. Joe

The first G.I. Joe cartoon was published in the debut issue of *Yank* magazine in 1942, but the property has since gone through so many updates and changes of ownership that the recent live-action movies (which represent the only take we're really interested in here, and even then just barely) are all but unrecognisable.

The original 1985 TV series spawned an animated movie in 1987, followed by a 2004 CG reboot and a 2006 spinoff from the 2D series *G.I. Joe Sigma Six*. The much derided but defiantly entertaining live-action films followed, and there are allegedly more in the works. Each version is quite different, but the transition from military procedural to hi-tech superheroics is reasonably linear.

G.I. Joe movies:
G.I. Joe: The Movie (1986, US)

G.I. Joe - Valor Vs. Venom (2004, US)

G.I. Joe: Sigma Six - First Strike (2006, US)

G.I. Joe: The Rise of Cobra (2009, US)

G.I. Joe: Retaliation (2013, US)

Gagamba

Gagamba (literally 'Spider') was adapted for the big screen within a few months of his debut in *Tagalog Klasiks* komik. Created by Virgilio and Nestor Redondo, he pre-dates Spider-Man by a year but shares little in common with Marvel's teen web slinger.

Four movies were made before he fell out of fashion, including a crossover with the better known Palos (played, like Gagamba, by Bernard Bonnin in what must have been quite a feat). They all appear to be lost.

Gagamba movies:
Bakas ng gagamba (1962, PH)
Palos kontra gagamba (1963, PH)
Ang lihim ni gagamba (1964, PH)
Gagamba at si Scorpio (1969, PH)

Garo

The original Garo tokusatsu TV show was created in 2005 by Keita Amemiya and has so far lead to around a dozen series and this fistful of movies. Most trace the fortunes of the Makai Knight (mankind's defenders against demons) Kouga Saezima, his ally Rei Suzumura and a young girl named Kaoru.

Garo movies:
Garo Special: Beast of the Demon Night (GARO Supesharu Byakuya no Majū, 2006, JP)
Garo: Red Requiem (2010, JP)
Garo: Soukoku no Maryu (2013, JP)
Garo: Gold Storm Sho (2015, JP)
Bikuu: The Movie (2015, JP, spinoff)
Garo: Kami no Kiba (Garo Kami no Kiba, 2017, JP)

The Golden Bat
aka Ōgon batto

Created in Japan in 1931 by Suzuki Ichiro and Takeo Nagamatsu, Ōgon batto is a time-travelling Atlantean thwarter of evil often cited as the world's first superhero. Whether that claim stands up to scrutiny will, as ever, depend on how you define a superhero's characteristics. Interestingly he wasn't introduced in pulp novels or newspaper comic strips but via the art of Kamishibai, a form of Japanese street theatre utilising paper cut-outs.

The Golden Bat first found his way to the big screen in a lost film from 1950, *Ōgon bat: Matenrô no kaijin*, but a 1966 reboot

starring Sonny Chiba, *Ōgon batto*, proved more popular. That movie's appeal is similar to the Toho Godzilla/kaiju outings of the era, with an alien invasion leading scientists on a trip to Atlantis, where a splash of water revives our supposed hero (Chiba's skeletal appearance and odd manner combine to create a surprisingly unnerving character). A 1972 spoof, *Ōgon batto ga yattekuru* (aka *The Golden Bat Shows Up*), followed but remains unavailable.

Then things get complicated. 1967 saw an animated Golden Bat TV series launched in Japan which, according to accepted wisdom, was adapted into 1979's *Black Star and the Golden Bat*, an unlicensed cut-and-shut from South Korea. However, the two Golden Bat's don't look alike. As mentioned, the Japanese version is reminiscent of the Phantom of the Opera; a cross between Mandrake the Magician and Skeletor. The South Korean version is a Batman clone (albeit with a mainly yellow costume). This bootleg Batman crops up in at least one other movie; 1990 live-action obscurity *Star Jjangga II: Super Betaman, Majingga V*. To add to the confusion, in 1992 South Korea's Du Wul Productions released a sci-fi adventure featuring a Golden Bat aligned with the Japanese version (*Young-guwa hwanggeum bakjwi*). The 'yellow Batman' movies are so rare perhaps those commenting on them don't realise they're a jumble of borrowed concepts rather than Ōgon batto ripoffs.

Golden Bat movies:
Ôgon bat: Matenrô no kaijin (1950, JP)
Ôgon batto (1966, JP)
Ôgon batto ga yattekuru (1972, JP)
Black Star and the Golden Bat (1979, KR)
Star Jjangga II: Super Betaman, Majingga V (1990, KR)
Young-guwa hwanggeum bakjwi (1992, KR)

Hercules: The Legendary Journeys

Preceding the syndicated TV series that launched in 1995, five Hercules TLJ movies introduced audiences to the show's primary characters and themes. As such, we get lots of absent father melodrama, pseudo-Greek mythology, comely wenches, terrible CGI monsters, and fighting.

Signs of Sam Raimi's stewardship (he was exec producer) show particularly strongly in the humour, pacing and occasional bursts of frenetic action, while Kevin Sorbo made his name playing the amiable demigod struggling with tricky familial relationships and bouts of minor smugness. The first four movies stand alone and are largely interchangeable in terms of entertainment value. The last, *Hercules in the Maze of the Minotaur*, is a clip show.

Hercules: The Legendary Journeys TV movies:
Hercules and the Amazon Women (1994, US)
Hercules and the Lost Kingdom (1994, US)
Hercules and the Circle of Fire (1994, US)
Hercules in the Underworld (1994, US)
Hercules in the Maze of the Minotaur (1994, US)

Italian poster for *Ôgon batto*, or *Il ritorno di Diavolik* as it was titled domestically

Jungle Jim

Beginning in 1934 as a newspaper strip for King Features Syndicated (who were also responsible for Popeye, Flash Gordon and the Phantom, among others) before progressing to radio in 1935, Jim Bradley, better known as Jungle Jim, is an American adventurer created by author Don Moore as a rival to Tarzan.

After a generic 1937 serial starring Grant Withers, Columbia began a series of highly forgettable B-movies with former Tarzan Johnny Weissmuller in the lead. While he may not seem like much of a superhero today, he rubbed shoulders with the kings back in his own time and certainly has royal blood in his veins.

Jungle Jim movies:
Jungle Jim (1948, US)
The Lost Tribe (1949, US)

Mark of the Gorilla (1950, US)
Captive Girl (1950, US)
Pygmy Island (1950, US)
Fury of the Congo (1951, US)
Jungle Manhunt (1951, US)
Jungle Jim in the Forbidden Land (1952, US)
Voodoo Tiger (1952, US)
Savage Mutiny (1953, US)
Valley of the Head Hunters (1953, US)
Killer Ape (1953, US)
Jungle Man-Eaters (1954, US)
Cannibal Attack (1955, US)
Jungle Moon Men (1955, US)
Devil Goddess (1956, US)

Kamen Rider

This enormous, marauding franchise began life in 1971 as a tokusatsu TV show simply titled *Kamen Rider* (*Masked Rider* in English), and has continued through approaching 30 spinoff, continuation and reboot series in addition to numerous movies, manga and other media. The show's original setup was conceived by Shotaro Ishinomori and built around motorcycling biochemistry prodigy Takeshi Hongo (Hiroshi Fujioka), a bionic survivor of the villainous Shocker group's attempt to turn him into a brainwashed cyborg footsoldier. The series sparked an explosion in similarly themed tokusatsu known as the Henshin Boom. The franshise continued through the 1980s with a 1990s lull proving to be the calm before the storm. The Heisei Period (named for Japan's then reigning Emperor) launched in 2000 with *Kamen Rider Kuuga*, featuring another morally upstanding and incredibly energetic young motorcyclist, Yusuke Godai (Joe Odagiri), as protagonist. The rate of reinvention picked up and a new TV series has been introduced every year since.

At first, feature-length movies were largely shunned in favour of expanded TV episodes and clipshows. The majority of early Kamen Rider movies are TV adventures on steroids, and at the start of the 1980s there were more semi or unofficial feature-length films than legitimate ones, with *Hanuman and the Five Riders* (1974, Thailand) and *The Super Rider* (1975, Taiwan) still cult favourites today. Feature-length releases have ramped up over the last decade, with each new show receiving a variety of theatrical adaptations including cut-and-shuts and alternate reality adventures. Kamen Riders also team up with tokusatsu heroes from franchises such as Super Sentai and Space Sheriff.

For a list of Kamen Rider movies see Appendix B.

LEGO DC

After dipping their toe in the spinoff movie market with the Bionicle franchise (the *Star Wars* rights were deemed too expensive at the time), LEGO signed up with Warner Bros., DC's parent company, to produce movies based on their properties.

The first to include superheroes was *Lego Batman: The Movie – DC Super Heroes Unite* in 2013, which portrays Batman as a grump undermined by Superman's superiority. The following year *The Lego Movie* became a hit, its depiction of Batman (voiced amusingly by Will Arnett) deemed a particular highlight. As a result *The Lego Batman Movie* went straight into production, followed by *The Lego Movie 2: The Second Part*. In addition to such banner releases, LEGO has produced several direct-to-video DC adventures. They lack the polished scripts and scope of their blockbuster cousins but share their sense of humour.

LEGO DC movies:

Lego Batman: The Movie – DC Super Heroes Unite (2013, US)

The Lego Movie (2014, US)

Lego DC Comics Super Heroes: Justice League vs. Bizarro League (2015, US)

Lego DC Comics Super Heroes: Justice League – Attack of the Legion of Doom (2015, US)

Lego DC Comics Super Heroes: Justice League – Cosmic Clash (2016, US)

Lego DC Comics Super Heroes: Justice League – Gotham City Breakout (2016, US)

The Lego Batman Movie (2017, US)

Lego DC Super Hero Girls: Brain Drain (2017, US)

Lego DC Comics Super Heroes: The Flash (2018, US)

Lego DC Super Hero Girls: Super-Villain High (2018, US)

Lego DC Comics Super Heroes: Aquaman: Rage of Atlantis (2018, US)

The Lego Movie 2: The Second Part (2019)

Luchador Movies

Although the luchador genre is considered to have begun with 1952's *Huracán Ramírez*, it wasn't until a decade or so later that these low-budget peculiarities found their raison d'être as Mexico's answer to the superhero movie. Defined by their stars (masked Latin American lucha libre wrestlers) and simple plots (burly man defeats supervillain/alien/monster, usually via the art of wrestling), they're instantly identifiable. The heyday for the luchador movie ran from the mid 1960s to the late 1970s, when stars such as Mil Máscaras, Blue Demon and the inimitable El Santo ruled screens. These enigmatic figures generally played themselves (or at least their pre-existing wrestling alter egos) as heroic secret agents. Over 200 movies were produced (around a quarter starring El Santo), although not all feature what we might call a superhero, and only a handful were ever dubbed into English.

As an outsider, there are effectively two ways to appreciate luchador movies. In the modern English speaking world it tends to be ironically, thanks to a couple of badly dubbed Santo films being dominant in our experience. But watching any of the best in the original Spanish with English subtitles is a different experience. With the dub you lose the sincerity of the performances, of course, but you also lose all cultural identity to re-writing. Locations are unidentified, Santo the Luchador becomes Samson the Wrestler (or similar), nationalities are altered and colloquial idiosyncrasies squashed. All the little world-building details that create a sense of grounded cohesion are destroyed by generic whitewashing.

See Appendix C for a list of Mexican luchador movies.

Mega Mindy

Flemish language Belgian movie series spun off from the TV show of the same name. Mindy is the crimefighting superhero alter ego of policewoman Mieke Fonkel, a kids TV presenter sort who lives with her aunt and uncle and is desperately in love with her colleague, Toby.

The target audience is decidedly young (we get a lot of cartoon sound effects and some hardcore mugging) and there's nothing to the series that will interest adults, with 'cheap and cheerful' definitely being the order of the day.

Mega Mindy movies:

The secret of Mega Mindy (Het geheim van Mega Mindy, 2009, BE)

Mega Mindy and the Black Crystal (Mega Mindy en het zwarte kristal, 2010, BE)

Mega Mindy and the Candy Baron (Mega Mindy en de Snoepbaron, 2011, BE)

Mega Mindy Versus ROX (2015, BE)

Metal Hero Series & Space Sheriff
aka Metaru Hīrō Series & Uchū Keiji

Metal Hero Series is a tokusatsu franchise best known for launching the Space Sheriff metaseries. It deals with various cyborg and human henshin heroes, and has its roots in 1980s TV, beginning with 1982's *Space Sheriff Gavan*, aka *Space Cop Gabin*, a show in which the eponymous hero, an agent of the Galactic Union Police, must protect Earth from evil despot Don Horror.

Despite making around 50 film appearances El Santo never removed his mask

A string of completely impenetrable direct-to-video feature-length releases are popular with fans.

MHS & Space Sheriff movies:

Space Sheriff Shaider (Uchū Keiji Shaider, 1984, JP)

Pursuit! The Strange Kidnappers! (Uchū Keiji Shaidā: Shikisiki! Shingi-Shingi Yukaidan, 1984, JP)

Superhuman-Machine Metalder (Chōjinki Metarudā, 1987, JP)

Mobile Cop Jiban: The Movie (Kidou Keiji Jiban, 1989, JP)

Tokusou Robo Janperson (Tokusô Robo Janpâson, 1993, JP)

Blue SWAT (Burû suwatto, 1994, JP)

Toei Hero Big Gathering (Tōei Hīrō Daishugō, 1994, JP)

Juukou B-Fighter (Jūkō Bî-Faitâ, 1995, JP)

B-Robo Kabutack: The Epic Christmas Battle (Bī Robo Kabutakku: Kurisumasu Daikessen, 1998, JP)

Tetsuwan Tantei Robotack and Kabutack: The Great Strange Country Adventure (Tetsuwan Tantei Robotakku to Kabutakku: Fushigi no Kuni no Daibōken, 1999, JP)

Space Sheriff Gavan: The Movie (Uchū Keiji Gyaban Za Mūbī, 2012, JP)

Kaizoku Sentai Gokaiger vs. Space Sheriff Gavan: The Movie (Kaizoku Sentai Gōkaijā Tai Uchū Keiji Gyaban Za Mūbī, 2012, JP)

Kamen Rider × Super Sentai × Space Sheriff: Super Hero Taisen Z (Kamen Raidā × Sūpā Sentai × Uchū Keiji Supā Hīrō Taisen Zetto, 2013, JP)

Space Sheriff Sharivan: The Next Generation (Uchuu Keiji Sharivan Next Generation, 2014, JP)

Space Sheriff Shaider: The Next Generation (Uchuu Keiji Shaider Next Generation, 2014, JP)

Space Squad (Supēsu Sukuwaddo, 2017, JP)

Space Sheriff Gavan vs. Tokusou Sentai Dekaranger (Uchû Keiji Gyaban vs Tokusô Sentai Dekarenjā, 2017, JP)

Space Squad: Space Sheriff Gavan vs. Tokusou Sentai Dekaranger (Space Squad: Uchuu Keiji Gavan vs. Tokusou Sentai Dekaranger, 2017, JP)

Uchu Sentai Kyuranger vs. Space Squad (Uchū Sentai Kyūrenjā Bāsasu Supēsu Sukuwaddo, 2018, JP)

Moonlight Mask
aka Gekko Kamen

Japan's first TV superhero brings together a nutty blend of elements. Armed with six-shooters, boomerangs and ninja throwing stars, the turban-wearing motorcyclist's (who is also known as the Moonbeam

Man) costume makes him look like some sort of Arabian Evel Knievel, but he was a phenomenon in late-1950s Japan.

Six movies were made to accompany the 1958 TV series. A much derided big budget reboot came along in 1981.

Moonlight Mask movies:

Moonlight Mask (Gekkō Kamen, 1958, JP)

Moonlight Mask: Duel to the Death in Dangerous Waters (Gekkō Kamen: Zekkai no Shitō, 1958, JP)

Moonlight Mask: The Claws of Satan (Gekkō Kamen: Satan no Tsume, 1958, JP)

Moonlight Mask: The Monster Kong (Gekkō Kamen: Kaijū Kongu, 1959, JP)

Moonlight Mask: The Ghost Party Strikes Back (Gekkō Kamen: Yureitō no Gyakushū, 1959, JP)

Moonlight Mask: The Last of the Devil (Gekkō Kamen: Akuma no Saigo, 1959, JP)

Moon Mask Rider (Gekkō Kamen, 1981 reboot, JP)

Palos

Alyas Palos (**Alias the Eel** in English), was a breakout hit for bi-weekly Filipino comic *Tagalog Klasiks* when introduced in 1961. Its hero, a sort of acrobatic master thief-cum-folk hero preoccupied with helping the needy, struck a chord with audiences and found himself fast-tracked to the big screen with rising star Bernard Bonnin in a role he would make his own. It seems likely that seven Palos movies were made although accounts vary and, either way, almost all of them are considered lost. Unusually for the ephemeral world of superhero movies, Bonnin starred in each film and remained the only actor to portray the character until his reboot for TV in 2008.

Palos movies:

Alyas Palos (1961, PH)

Palos kontra gagamba (1963, PH)

Palos: Counterspy (1966, PH)

Palos Strikes Again (1968, PH)

Palos Fights Back! (1969, PH)

Ang pagbabalik ni palos (1977, PH)

Alyas Palos II (1982, PH)

Peplum Movies

(Classic Italian series)

Peplum movies or 'pepla' are essentially Italian sword-and-sandal B-movies. Usually featuring a hulking hero and a supernatural twist, the genre dates back to the silent era (1914's *Maciste* was probably the first) but it's the craze that began with 1958's *Hercules* (*Le fatiche di Ercole*) that best fits our superhero bill. The magical elements and protagonists featured in these films differ greatly from analogous Hollywood offerings such as 1960's *Spartacus*, which tend to focus on historical or biblical figures in apparently factual scenarios. Pepla prefer mythic heroes in fantastic scenarios. Their physical similarity (each is a loin-clothed muscleman) proved useful for American distributors, who would rename characters such as Maciste, perhaps the most popular peplum protagonist in Italy but unknown in the US, as Hercules or Samson in order to improve marketability. That only a handful of actors shared all the roles must have aided the subterfuge.

There are occasional peaks, often resulting from an interesting director managing to smuggle some style past producers (horror icon Mario Bava helmed one of the genre's better examples; *Hercules in the Haunted World*), but sixty years removed from the start of the craze it's not that easy to see what its appeal was. Although the muscled men were short-lived (by 1965 audiences had lost interest), Zorro plodded on into the 1970s).

See Appendix D for a list of peplum movies.

Power Rangers

aka Mighty Morphin' Power Rangers

The first Power Rangers television series was launched by US production company Saban Entertainment in 1993, and soon became the centrepiece of the Fox Kids Saturday morning programming block. The show follows a team of high school henshin heroes responsible for protecting Earth from all manner of evil aliens, monsters and alien monsters. The odd aesthetic results from the show combining action scenes from the Japanese Super Sentai franchise with sequences featuring young American actors as the Rangers' public personae.

There have been three theatrical feature films and a string of cut-and-shut. They're all awful.

Power Rangers theatrical movies:

Mighty Morphin Power Rangers: The Movie (1995, US/JP)
Turbo: A Power Rangers Movie (1997, US/JP) .
Power Rangers Time Force - Quantum Ranger: Clash for Control (2001, US/JP)
Power Rangers Ninja Storm: Samurai's Journey (2003, US/JP)
Power Rangers Mystic Force: Dark Wish (2006, US/JP)
Power Rangers: Jungle Fury: Way of the Master (2008, US/JP)
Power Rangers Samurai: Clash of the Red Rangers – The Movie (2011, US/JP)
Power Rangers Samurai: Monster Bash (2012, US/JP)
Power Rangers Samurai: A New Enemy (2012, US/JP)
Power Rangers Samurai: The Team Unites (2012, US/JP)
Power Rangers SS: A Christmas Wish (2013, US/JP)
Power Rangers Super Samurai: Rise Of The Bullzooka (2013, US/JP)
Power Rangers Megaforce: Ultimate Team Power (2013, US/JP)
Power Rangers Super Megaforce: The Silver Warrior (2014, US/JP)
Power Rangers Super Megaforce: The Legendary Battle (2015, US/JP)
Power Rangers (2017, US/HK/JP)

Pretty Cure

aka PreCure, Glitter Force

Izumi Todo's magical girl anime franchise launched in 2004 and has been reinvented every year since. Each new series spawns a spinoff movie and, more often than not, an additional crossover movie teaming current

Steve Reeves as peplum favourite Hercules in
Le fatiche di Ercole

Golden Eagle, which marked the character's final appearance).

That tragic 1970 movie is the only one of Chaibancha's readily available with English subtitles and most others are lost. Originally screened without dialogue (actors would give live performances), the version available today features an odd soundtrack lurching between cast commentary and amateur dub. In 2010 acclaimed Thai filmmaker Wisit Sasanatieng rebooted the franchise with big budget actioner *The Red Eagle* (see main section), but it underwhelmed audiences and failed at the box office.

Red Eagle movies starring Mitr Chaibancha:
Gangster (Chao Nakleng, Gangster Lord, Jao Nak-leng, 1959, TH)
Thap Sa Ming Kla (1962, TH)
The Red Eagle (Chao Insee (The Eagle, Insee Daeng, Jao Insee, 1963, TH)
Pisat Dam (1966, TH)
Eagle (1968, TH)
The Golden Eagle (Insee Thong, 1970, TH)

'Cures' with earlier characters (usually under the 'Pretty Cure All Stars' banner). Each follows a group of schoolgirls who derive superpowers from magical items, and use them to defend Earth from monsters.

See Appendix E for a full list of Pretty Cure movies.

The Red Eagle
aka Insee Daeng (Mitr Chaibancha series)

Created by popular Thai novelist Sek Dusit in 1954, Red Eagle (or, by day, drunken oaf Rome Rittikrai) is a superhero in the Batman mould; a wealthy playboy who dons a mask for his crepuscular vigilantism. First brought to the screen in 1959's *Chao Nakleng*, actor Mitr Chaibancha played the role in six feature outings before the star's untimely death on the set of 1970's *Insee Thong* (*The

Rocky Jones, Space Ranger

This syndicated TV series about clean-cut space cop Rocky Jones (think Flash Gordon with a badge) emerged dazed from its own merchandising blitz in 1954, shone briefly, then trailed off into obscurity. As with early *Doctor Who*, each story arc spanned several episodes and was, sooner or later, released as a TV movie.

Rocky Jones, Space Ranger cut-and-shuts:
Beyond the Curtain of Space (aka Beyond the Moon, 1954, US)
Rocky's Odyssey (Gypsy Moon, 1954, US)
Bobby's Comet (Menace from Outer Space, 1954, US)
Escape Into Space (1954, US)
The Pirates of Prah (Manhunt in Space, 1954, US)
Silver Needle in the Sky (Duel in Space, 1954, US)
The Forbidden Moon (1954, US)
Crash of Moons (1954, US)
Kip's Private War (1954, US)
Blast-Off (1954, US)

The Cold Sun (1954, US)
Inferno in Space (The Magnetic Moon, 1954, US)
Vena and the Darnamo (1954, US)
Out of This World (Robot of Regalio, 1954, US)
The Trial of Rocky Jones (1954, US)

Sailor Moon
aka Bishōjo Senshi Sērā Mūn

Serialised in the Nakayoshi shōjo manga from 1991, Naoko Takeuchi's *Sailor Moon* follows the exploits of Usagi Tsukino, who transforms into her eponymous alter ego if and when the universe needs defending from oddballs determined to steal a crystal MacGuffin. She's been adapted into anime and tokusatsu TV shows, not to mention dozens of ghastly stage musicals.

The movies are bewildering, oversaturated nightmares (imagine being trapped with an army of excited schoolgirls in a room made of fireworks). Dreamy boys, crazy witches and talking cats feature prominently.

Sailor Moon movies:
Sailor Moon R: The Movie: The Promise of the Rose (Gekijô-ban - Bishôjo senshi Sêrâ Mûn R, 1993, JP)
Sailor Moon S: The Movie - Hearts in Ice (Gekijô-ban - Bishôjo senshi Sêrâ Mûn S, 1994, JP)
Sailor Moon SuperS: The Movie: Black Dream Hole (Bishôjo senshi Sêrâ Mûn super S: Sêrâ 9 senshi shûketsu! Burakku dorîmu hôru no kiseki, 1995, JP)

Spider-Man: The Animated Series

Developed by Bob Richardson, the 1994 animated Spider-Man TV series is still one of the most popular takes on any of Marvel's characters, despite running for just three years.

It's bursting with action, electric guitars, earnest performances and breakneck plots involving classic villains. Story arcs were often spread over multiple episodes, which better lends the show to the cut-and-shut adaptations listed here.

Spider-Man TAS cut-and-shuts:
The Venom Saga aka The Alien Costume (1996, US)
Revenge of the Goblins (1997, US)
Spider Slayer (1997, US)
Insidious Six (1997, US)
Mutant Agenda (1997, US)
Tablet of Time (1997, US)
Neogenic Nightmare (1998, US)
Forgotten Warriors (1998, US)
The Sins of the Fathers (1999, US)
Secret Wars (1999, US)
Spider-Man: The Ultimate Villain Showdown (2002, US)
Spider-Man: The Return of the Green Goblin (2002, US)
Daredevil vs. Spider-Man (2003)
Spider-Man vs. Doc Ock (2004)
Spider-Man: The Venom Saga (2005, US, longer edit of the 1996 release)

(Super) Sentai

Like Kamen Rider, the original Super Sentai series was created by Shotaro Ishinomori for Japanese film and TV corporation Toei Company, and went on to spawn numerous variants. These contribute to one of the most bewildering etymologies in modern pop culture. Starting in 1975 with *Himitsu Sentai Gorenger*, a new show has been added to the Sentai universe almost every year.

Typical movies see a team of colour-coded teens defending the earth by jumping about, usually in a quarry. Again like Kamen Rider, early theatrical releases are padded cut-and-shuts running to about half an hour. The various Power Rangers TV series are based on footage taken from this franchise.

(Super) Sentai movies:
Choushinsei Flashman: Big Rally! Titan Boy!! (1987, JP)
Hyakujuu Sentai Gaoranger vs. Super Sentai (2001, JP)
Samurai Sentai Shinkenger vs. Go-onger: GinmakuBang!! (2010, JP)
Tensou Sentai Goseiger vs. Shinkenger: Epic on Ginmaku (2011, JP)
Gokaiger Goseiger Super Sentai 199 Hero Great Battle (2011, JP)
Kaizoku Sentai Gokaiger vs. Space Sheriff Gavan: The Movie (2012, JP)

Kamen Rider × Super Sentai: Super Hero Taisen (2012, JP)

Tokumei Sentai Go-Busters vs. Kaizoku Sentai Gokaiger: The Movie (2013, JP)

Kamen Rider × Super Sentai × Space Sheriff: Super Hero Taisen Z (2013, JP)

Zyuden Sentai Kyoryuger vs. Go-Busters: The Great Dinosaur Battle! Farewell Our Eternal Friends (2014, JP)

Heisei Riders vs. Shōwa Riders: Kamen Rider Taisen feat. Super Sentai (2014, JP)

Ressha Sentai ToQger vs. Kyoryuger: The Movie (2015, JP)

Super Hero Taisen GP: Kamen Rider 3 (2015, JP)

Shuriken Sentai Ninninger vs. ToQger the Movie: Ninja in Wonderland (2016, JP)

Doubutsu Sentai Zyuohger vs. Ninninger the Movie: Super Sentai's Message from the Future (2017, JP)

Kamen Rider × Super Sentai: Ultra Super Hero Taisen (2017, JP)

Space Squad: Uchuu Keiji Gavan vs. Tokusou Sentai Dekaranger (2017, JP)

Uchu Sentai Kyuranger vs. Space Squad (2018, JP)

Kaitou Sentai Lupinranger VS Keisatsu Sentai Patranger en Film (2018, JP)

Tarzan

John Clayton, Viscount Greystoke, better known as Tarzan, first appeared in Edgar Rice Burroughs' novel *Tarzan of the Apes*. Initially published as a magazine series in 1912, it lead to a sizeable franchise covering 25 official sequels (more were unauthorised), dozens of movies and numerous video games, stage plays, TV shows, radio series, newspaper strips and comics. While the movie version of Tarzan (as personified by Johnny Weissmuller in the 1930s and 40s) bares little resemblance to Burroughs' original character, he does work a lot like a superhero and is generally accepted as such. I'm not convinced, but he certainly belongs in the conversation.

The first screen Tarzan was played by US actor Elmo Lincoln, who starred in a few early silents, but with the advent of sound a new series was developed with Austro-Hungarian-born champion swimmer Johnny Weissmuller in the role. These movies

established numerous tropes that were not part of Burroughs' original concept, most notably Tarzan's monosyllabic illiteracy and chimp sidekick Cheetah. With Weismuller retiring from the role after 1948's *Tarzan and the Mermaids* (he would later star in a series of similar movies as Jungle Jim), Lex Barker began his stint as a lower-budget Tarzan, before bodybuilder Gordon Scott took over. Under producer Sy Weintraub, a succession of forgettable faces donned the loincloth throughout the 1960s.

Many stand-alone films have appeared alongside entries in these series. As early as 1920 *The Revenge of Tarzan*, an almost forgotten silent based on Burroughs' own sequel, offered Elmo Lincoln competiton, and in 1933 a pre-*Flash Gordon* Buster Crabbe graduated from clones such as *King of the Jungle* to star in *Tarzan the Fearless*. The character has possibly featured in more bootleg adventures than any other.

Elmo Lincoln Tarzan series:
Tarzan of the Apes (1918, US)
The Romance of Tarzan (1918, US)
Adventures of Tarzan (1921, US)

Johnny Weissmuller Tarzan series:
Tarzan the Ape Man (1932, US)
Tarzan and His Mate (1934, US)
Tarzan Escapes (1936, US)
Tarzan Finds a Son! (1939, US)
Tarzan's Secret Treasure (1941, US)
Tarzan's New York Adventure (1942, US)
Tarzan Triumphs (1943, US)
Tarzan's Desert Mystery (1943, US)
Tarzan and the Amazons (1945, US)
Tarzan and the Leopard Woman (1946, US)
Tarzan and the Huntress (1947, US)
Tarzan and the Mermaids (1948, US)

Lex Barker Tarzan series:
Tarzan's Magic Fountain (1949, US)
Tarzan and the Slave Girl (1950, US)
Tarzan's Peril (1951, US)
Tarzan's Savage Fury (1952, US)
Tarzan and the She-Devil (1953, US)

Gordon Scott Tarzan series:

Tarzan's Hidden Jungle (1955, US)
Tarzan and the Lost Safari (1957, US)
Tarzan's Fight for Life (1958, US)
Tarzan's Greatest Adventure (1959, US)
Tarzan and the Trappers (1960, TV movie, US)
Tarzan the Magnificent (1960, US)

Other Tarzan movies:

The Revenge of Tarzan (1920, US)
The Son of Tarzan (1920, US)
Tarzan and the Golden Lion (1927, US)
Tarzan the Mighty (1928, US)
Tarzan the Tiger (1929, US)
Tarzan the Fearless (1933, US)
The New Adventures of Tarzan (1935, US)
Toofani Tarzan (1937, IN)
Tarzan's Revenge (1938, US)
Vanaraja Karzan (1938, IN)
Tarzan and the Green Goddess (1938, US, serial edit)
Tarzan in Istanbul (Tarzan Istanbulda, 1952, TR)
Sengottai Singam (1958, IN)
Tarzan, the Ape Man (1959, US)
Tarzan Goes to IN (1962, US)
Tarzan's Three Challenges (1963, US)
Tarzan the Fearless (1964, edit of the 1933 serial, US)
Tarzan and Jane Regained... Sort of (1964, US)
Tarzan and the Valley of Gold (1966, US)
Tarzan and Hercules (1966, IN)
Tarzan and the Great River (1967, US)
Tarzan's Jungle Rebellion (1967, US)
Tarzan and the Jungle Boy (1968, US)
Tarzan in the Golden Grotto (Tarzán en la gruta del oro, 1969, ES/IT)
Tarzan's Deadly Silence (1970, US)
Tarzan and the Brown Prince (Tarzán y el arco iris, 1972, ES/IT)
Karzan, il favoloso uomo della jungla (1972, IT)
Green Inferno (Tarzán y el misterio de la selva, 1973, ES)
Tarzan Mighty Man (Tarzan korkusuz adam, 1974, TR)
Tarzan in King Solomon's Mines (Tarzán en las minas del rey Salomón, 1974, ES)
Tarzan in the City (Tarsan kota, 1974, ID)
Tarzan the Ape Man (1981, US)
Lady Tarzan (Tarzan Sundari, 1983, IN)
Greystoke: The Legend of Tarzan (1984, US)
Adventures of Tarzan (1985, IN)
Tarzan in Manhattan (1989, US)
Lady Tarzan (1990, IN)
Tarzan: the Epic Adventures (1996, TV movie, US)

Tarzan and the Lost City (1998, US)
Tarzan of the Apes (1998, US)
Tarzan (1999, US)
Junglee Tarzan (2001, IN)
Tarzan & Jane (2002, US)
Daughter of Tarzan (Tarzan Ki Beti, 2002, IN)
Tarzan II (2005, US)
Tarzan (2013, DE)
The Legend of Tarzan (2016, US)

Three Supermen

aka The Three Fantastic Supermen

This slightly crazy but thoroughly enjoyable series of budget European capers features an evolving triptych of performers adept in acrobatics and looking good in red spandex. Although primarily an Italian series (it was overseen by Roman production company Cinesecolo), funding came from all over the world and some productions followed the money to Turkey and Hong Kong.

The Red Eagle aka **Chao Insee** (1963 version)

317

The first of the series boasts a particularly good cast with likeable American muscleman Brad Harris, Italian charmer Luciano Stella (credited as Tony Kendall) and alleged mob enforcer Aldo Canti as protagonists (former stuntman Canti's 1990 death is generally thought to be the result of a mafia hit). The most notable superman was perhaps Lion Man himself, Turkish action star Cüneyt Arkin (best known for 'Turkish Star Wars') who appeared in the sixth film, *Süpermenler*. Sal Borgese is as close to a series stalwart as we get, having featured in most entries.

These are particularly fun movies if you can keep your expectations in check. Plots are generally simple James Bond yarns featuring bags of top stunt work and action, while the music and style is pure swinging 60s (the opening theme used in *Supermen Against the Orient* is particularly fantastic).

Three Supermen movies:

The Three Fantastic Supermen (I fantastici 3 $upermen, 1967, IT)

Three Supermen in Tokyo (Supermen a Tokio, 1968, IT)

Three Supermen in the Jungle (Che fanno i nostri supermen tra le vergini della jungla?, 1970, IT)

Supermen Against the Orient (Crash! Che botte... strippo strappo stroppio, 1973, IT/HK)

Three Supermen of the West (...e così divennero i 3 supermen del West, 1973, IT)

Three Supermen and Mad Girl (Çilgin kiz ve üç süper adam, 1973, TR)

Süpermenler (1979, IT/TR)

Three Supermen at the Olympic Games (Üç süpermen olimpiyatlarda, 1984, TR)

Three Supermen in Santo Domingo (3 Supermen in S. Domingo, 1986, IT)

Ultraman
aka Urutoraman

Among the first of his kind, Ultraman did more to spawn the kyodai hero subgenre than any other character. Conceived by Eiji Tsuburaya (the man responsible for special effects in the original Godzilla series) for the eponymous 1966 TV show, the solar powered alien/human hybrid has seen action in a variety of versions and has been reimagined for numerous media properties (collectively known as the Ultra Series). Without wishing to denigrate the erstwhile Ultra, he (or she, they, it... there have been a lot of them) is probably not for adults who didn't grow up with him (it's almost always a him). Adventures generally see Ultra prevail over the antagonist by growing to immense size and beating it up.

Oddities such as *Space Warriors 2000*, a mysterious dubbed bootleg of *The Six Ultra Brothers vs. the Monster Army*, have regular entries. See Appendix F for a full list of Ultraman movies.

Wolverine and the X-Men

The fourth animated TV outing for Marvel's X-Men franchise appeared in Autumn 2008 and places the spotlight, unsurprisingly, on Wolverine. It shares a universe with *Hulk vs Wolverine, Hulk vs Thor, Thor: Tales of Asgard* and *The Avengers: Earth's Mightiest Heroes*.

Although short-lived (there were only 26 episodes), it's generally superior to those made-for-video feature-length relatives, tackling as it does some quite adult themes that generate real depth.

Wolverine and the X-Men cut-and-shuts:

Heroes Return Trilogy (2009, US)

Deadly Enemies (2009, US)

Beginning of the End (2009, US)

Fate of the Future (2010, US)

Revelation (2010, US)

Final Crisis Trilogy (2010, US)

Zatôichi
(Shintarô Katsu series)

Created by Kan Shimozawa, Zatôichi is a highly skilled Kenjutsu master of the 19th century Edo period. Blind since childhood, his extraordinary skills lead him down a path of violence he would ultimately regret. To atone for his sins he patrols Japan aiding the needy.

Actor Shintarô Katsu made the character his own across the series' original 25 film run (which was followed by a popular TV show in the late 1970s and a theatrical denouement in 1989). The films are largely excellent: stylish, nuanced and well made. It's fair to say few franchises of this size have maintained such a high standard across all entries.

The series inspired a remake (1989's *Blind Fury* starring Rutger Hauer), a gender-swapping spinoff (2008's *Ichi*) and at least two re-imaginings (2003's superb *Zatoichi* and 2010's forgettable *Zatoichi: The Last*).

Zatôichi movies starring Shintarô Katsu:

The Tale of Zatoichi (Zatōichi monogatari, 1962, JP)

The Tale of Zatoichi Continues (Zoku Zatōichi monogatari, 1962, JP)

New Tale of Zatoichi (Shin Zatōichi monogatari, 1963, JP)

Zatoichi The Fugitive (Zatōichi kyōjō-tabi, 1963, JP)

Zatoichi on the Road (Zatōichi kenka-tabi, 1963, JP)

Zatoichi and the Chest of Gold (Zatōichi senryō-kubi, 1964, JP)

Zatoichi's Flashing Sword (Zatōichi abare tako, 1964, JP)

Fight, Zatoichi, Fight (Zatōichi kesshō-tabi, 1964, JP)

Adventures of Zatoichi (Zatōichi sekisho-yaburi, 1964, JP)

Zatoichi's Revenge (Zatōichi nidan-giri, 1965, JP)

Zatoichi and the Doomed Man (Zatōichi sakate-giri, 1965, JP)

Zatoichi and the Chess Expert (Zatōichi jigoku-tabi, 1965, JP)

Zatoichi's Vengeance (Zatōichi no uta ga kikoeru, 1966, JP)

Zatoichi's Pilgrimage (Zatōichi umi o wataru, 1966, JP)

Zatoichi's Cane Sword (Zatōichi tekka-tabi, 1967, JP)

Zatoichi the Outlaw (Zatōichi rōyaburi, 1967, JP)

Zatoichi Challenged (Zatōichi chikemurikaidō, 1967, JP)

Zatoichi and the Fugitives (Zatōichi hatashijō, 1968, JP)

Samaritan Zatoichi (Zatōichi kenka-daiko, 1968, JP)

Zatoichi Meets Yojimbo (Zatōichi to Yōjinbō, 1970, JP)

Zatoichi Goes to the Fire Festival (Zatōichi abare-himatsuri, 1970, JP)

Zatoichi Meets the One-Armed Swordsman (Shin Zatōichi: Yabure! Tōjin-ken, 1971, JP)

Zatoichi at Large (Zatōichi goyō-tabi, 1972, JP)

Zatoichi in Desperation (Shin Zatōichi monogatari: Oreta tsue, 1972, JP)

Zatoichi's Conspiracy (Shin Zatōichi monogatari: Kasama no chimatsuri, 1973, JP)

Zatoichi: Darkness Is His Ally (Zatōichi, 1989, JP)

Shintarô Katsu in classic Zatōichi pose. *The Tale of Zatoichi Continues* aka *Zoku Zatōichi monogatari*

TEN OF THE BEST

Superhero movies deserving of a little more attention, for one reason or another.

Obscurities

Movies with fewer than 100 ratings on the IMDb, or no IMDb entry at all.

American Rescue Squad
2015, USA
Heavy-handed but intriguing and bizarre surrealist satire.

Descendant of the Sun
aka *Ri Jie*, 1983, Hong Kong
The Shaw Brothers put their spin on the classic superhero origin story.

Esupai
aka *Espy*, 1974, Japan
Imaginative sci-fi thriler.

Hero Tomorrow
2007, USA
Zero budget navel-gazing comedy.

Ophelia Learns to Swim
2000, USA
Zero budget female-lead comedy. As with the previous, this is seriously lo-fi.

Panji Tengkorak vs Jaka Umbaran
1983, Indonesia
Insane (I can't emphasise that enough) martial arts adventure.

Real Heroes
2014, USA
Superheroes do *Big Brother*.

Sign Gene
2017, USA
Intriguing deaf-themed thriller.

Spy Smasher
1968, Turkey
Violent and stylish Turkish B-movie.

Superguy: Behind the Cape
2000, USA
Extremely dry, and funny, mockumentary.

Foreign Essentials

Don't expect high production values or a familiar take on the superhero concept.

Death Note
aka *Death Note: Desu nôto*, 2006, Japan
The ultimate in stripped down revisionism.

Deathless Devil
aka *Yilmayan seytan*, 1972, Turkey
Nonsensical, absurd and fantastic.

Fullmetal Alchemist the Movie: Conqueror of Shamballa
aka *Gekijô-ban hagane no renkinjutsushi: Shanbara wo yuki mono*, 2005, Japan
Stunning, original anime.

The Heroic Trio
aka *Dung fong sam hap*, 1993, Hong Kong
Hong Kong Kung Fu at its finest.

Judex
1963, France
Haunting mood piece.

Krrish
2006, India
Lavish Bollywood spectacle.

Mr. India
1987, India
Touching and amusing Indian favourite.

They Call Me Jeeg
aka *Lo chiamavano Jeeg Robot*, 2015, Italy
Well acted and gritty thriller.

Wolf Guy
aka *Urufu gai: Moero ôkami-otoko*, 1975, Japan
Tense supernatural mystery with an electric Sonny Chiba in one of his best roles.

Zatôichi
aka *The Blind Swordsman: Zatoichi*, 2003, Japan
Simply sublime reboot for the blind swordsman.

Underrated Gems

They're not masterpieces, but online ratings and/or general reputation do these movies an injustice.

Abar
1977, USA
Uncompromising blaxploitation.

American Hero
2015, USA
Among the best of (what I'm calling) the 'sun-bleached concrete revisionist indies'.

Comic Book: The Movie
2004, USA
Mark Hamill's very funny mockumentary.

Electra Woman and Dyna Girl
2016, USA
I'm going with Grace Helbig's Electra Woman as the best female American superhero on film.

Machete Kills
2013, USA
More action, more comedy, more stupid.

Officer Downe
2016, USA
Hugely violent exploitation.

The Specials
2000, USA
Early James Gunn-penned team comedy.

The Subjects
2015, Australia
Intense, blackly comic thriller.

Witchblade
2000, USA
Moody TV movie with an interesting lead.

WolfCop
2014, Canada
Extremely enjoyable comedy schlock.

For Non-Fans

Because there's always one.

The Adventures of Buckaroo Banzai Across the 8th Dimension
1984, USA
Uniquely left-field.

Black Mask
Hak hap, 1996, Hong Kong
Jet Li in a festival of Kung fu.

Chronicle
2012, USA
Ideal for those who think they're too clever for superheroes, but probably aren't.

The Darkest Minds
2018, USA
High concept YA sci-fi thriller that's ideal for young folks seeking something different.

Dr Syn Alias the Scarecrow
1963, UK
Folk horror in the vein of Hammer.

Hardcore Henry
2015, Russia/USA
Find superhero movies too calm and coherent? Try this.

Locke the Superman
Chôjin Locke, 1984, Japan
Thoughtful old-school anime.

Scott Pilgrim vs The World
2010, USA
Twisted and spectacular romantic comedy.

Unbreakable
2000, USA
Mentioning *Unbreakable* in this context is actually enshrined in law.

Who Wants to Kill Jessie?
1966, Czechoslovakia
Arthouse satire.

For Families

Movies to enjoy as a family. Disclaimer: I can't judge your child's ability to process peril, dramatic intensity or Adam West.

Batman: The Movie
1966, USA
Not just powered by nostalgia.

Big Hero Six
2014, USA
Satisfying emotional rollercoaster.

Flash Gordon
1980, USA
Big characters and striking visuals.

Hercules
1997, USA
Traditionally animated Disney adventure.

The Incredibles
2004, USA
Testing demonstrates all human beings adore *The Incredibles*.

The Lego Movie
2014, USA
Post-modern mayhem.

Mr. India
1987, India
The lack of an English dub will limit its audience, but this is a wonderful family film.

The Rocketeer
1991, USA
A Spielbergian spin on Commando Cody.

Shazam!
2019, USA
Surprisingly old-school formulaic fun.

Superman
1978, USA
You can never be too old or too young for Christopher Reeve and that score.

For Enthusiasts of Crazy

The weirdest of the weird.

Attack of the Super Monsters
1982, Japan
Cyborgs battle suitmation dinosaurs.

Faust: Love of the Damned
2000, Spain
Avant-garde metaphysical horror.

Gothic Lolita Battle Bear
aka *Nuigurumâ Z*, 2013, Japan
Mad woman and alien teddy fight zombies.

James Batman
1966, Philippines
Dolphy plays both roles in an unlicensed simultaneous spoof of Bond *and* Batman.

Jumborg Ace and Giant
1974, Thailand
The entire movie is one long fight scene.

Mutant Girls Squad
aka *Sentô shôjo: Chi no tekkamen densetsu*, 2010, Japan
One of the team has a chainsaw for a butt.

Shoktir Lorai
aka *Bangla RoboCop*, Bangladesh
Cardboard RoboCop dances on the beach.

Super-B
2002, Philippines
Aliens want to steal all our flowers, but it's ok, they're susceptible to magic farts.

Super Batman & Mazinger V
Star Jjangga II: Super Betaman, Majingga V, 1990, South Korea
Less said the better.

Twisted Pair
2018, USA
If you happen to see this and are able to figure it out, please tell the internet.

For Masochists

The absolute worst superhero movies ever made. (These are *not* so bad they're good.)

Barbie in Princess Power
2015, USA
Dead eyes. Such cold, dead eyes.

The Black Knight Returns
2009, USA
I'm limiting mockbuster merchants Tom Cat to one entry, and this is as bad as any.

Bratz: Super Babyz
2007, USA
Nausea-inducing kaleidoscope of horror.

Captain Z & the Terror of Leviathan
2014, USA
Kitsch failure.

Cosplay Fetish Battle Drones
Struggled Reasons, 2013, USA
It's a comedy.

Electra
1996, USA
Just... no.

Inspector Gadget's Biggest Caper Ever
2005, Canada/USA
CG abomination that makes the live-action Gadget movies look good.

Missy and the Maxinator
2009, USA
The least a movie should be is in focus.

The Superhero
2007, UK
Miserablist melodrama.

Superman Against the Will
Supermen ponevole ili eroticheskiy mutant, 1993, Russia
A stressful and unpleasant experience.

WORLDWIDE BOX OFFICE
INFLATION ADJUSTED

Box office figures are a sensible means of gauging commercial success week to week, but inflation makes comparisons across different eras meaningless, that is unless the figures take into account changes in a currency's value. 'Adjusting for inflation' is common practice for US grosses, but the number of different economies contributing to international figures make applying the process worldwide time-consuming.

I have excluded entries not fitting entirely within the superhero sphere, the two most notable examples of which being Disney animations *Frozen* and *Tarzan*.

This is not an exact science. Figures for older movies are often incomplete, and different inflation calculation services use different equations. Ultimately, this is just a bit of fun and these figures should not be relied upon in life and death circumstances.

The cutoff point is July 2019 and figures in millions.

1. Avengers: Endgame ($2,744)
2019, USA

2. Avengers: Infinity War ($2,048)
2018, USA

3. The Avengers ($1,858)
2012, USA

4. Avengers: Age of Ultron ($1,497)
2015, USA

5. Iron Man 3 ($1,358)
2013, USA

6. Black Panther ($1,347)
2018, USA

7. The Dark Knight ($1,335)
2008, USA

8. The Dark Knight Rises ($1,276)
2012, USA

9. Incredibles 2 ($1,266)
2018, USA

10. Spider-Man ($1,250)
2002, USA

11. Captain America: Civil War ($1,218)
2016, USA

12. Spider-Man 3 ($1,157m)
2007, USA

13. Aquaman ($1,148)
2018, USA

14. Captain Marvel ($1,125)
2019, USA

15. Superman ($1,098)
1978, USA

16. Spider-Man 2 ($1,038)
2004, USA

17. The Matrix Reloaded ($1,019)
2003, USA

18. Men in Black ($1,000)
1997, USA

19. Batman ($918)
1989, USA

20. Batman v Superman: Dawn of Justice ($912)
2016, USA

21. Spider-Man: Homecoming ($898)
2017, USA

22. The Incredibles ($881)
2004, USA

23. The Amazing Spider-Man ($880)
2012, USA

24. Thor: Ragnarok ($872)
2017, USA

25. Guardians of the Galaxy 2 ($869)
2017, USA

26. Venom ($855)
2018, USA

27. Guardians of the Galaxy ($849)
2014, USA

28. Wonder Woman ($837)
2017, USA

29. Superman II ($830)
1981, USA

30. Deadpool ($819)
2016, USA

31. X-Men: Days of Future Past ($812)
2014, USA

32. Hancock ($788)
2008, USA

33. Deadpool 2 ($785)
2018, USA

34. The Amazing Spider-Man 2 ($771)
2014, USA

35. Captain America: The Winter Soldier ($752)
2014, USA

36. The Matrix ($747)
1999, USA

37. Iron Man ($740)
2008, USA

38. Iron Man 2 ($739)
2010, USA

39. Man of Steel ($731)
2013, USA

40. Big Hero Six ($715)
2014, USA

41. Doctor Strange ($708)
2016, USA

42. Suicide Squad ($687)
2016, USA

43. Batman Forever ($675)
1995, USA

44. Justice League ($671)
2017, USA

45. Logan ($626)
2017, USA

46. Ant-Man and the Wasp ($623)
2018, USA

47. X-Men: The Last Stand ($616)
2006, USA

48. Men in Black II ($601)
2002, USA

49. X-Men 2 ($597)
2003, USA

50. X-Men: Apocalypse ($570)
2016, USA

MOST PROLIFIC SUPERHEROES

Based on appearances made in feature-length theatrical movies, animated movies (hence all the Justice Leaguers), TV movies, serials, cut-and-shuts (hence Doctor Who) and direct-to-video releases.

For public domain characters (e.g. Hercules) all versions count towards a single tally, as long as they meet the superhero criteria. Due to the ubiquity of Marvel's Thor he is the exception to that rule. Teams such as the Power Rangers count, but only for one entry (not one per member). Tokusatsu superheroes can be portrayed by different characters/public personae as long as that superhero's identity remains fundamentally unchanged. Unlicensed appearances do not count, although with older characters such as Zorro and Tarzan it isn't always possible to ascertain a movie's legal status. Randomly virtuous villains such as Loki and Harley Quinn are excluded. Figures are derived from research carried out for this book and pay no heed to existing tallys. While they're as accurate as possible, different eligibility criteria will result in different figures.

Character key:
(A) primarily in anime
(L) primarily in luchador movies
(P) primarily in peplum movies
(T) primarily in tokusatsu

1. Doctor Who (171)
From 1963, UK

2. Tarzan (73)
From 1918, USA, India and Italy

3. Batman (70)
From 1943, USA

4. Zorro (63)
From 1920, USA

5. Kamen Rider (54)
From 1980, Japan, (T)

6. El Santo (52)
From 1958, Mexico, (L)

7. Superman (44)
From 1948, USA

8. Hercules (42)
From 1953, Italy, USA, (P)

9. Spider-Man (34)
From 1977, USA

10. Wonder Woman (32)
From 1974, USA

11. Zatōichi (30)
From 1962, Japan

=12. Blue Demon (28)
From 1965, Mexico, (L)

=12. Ultraman (28)
From 1967, Japan, (T)

14. Maciste (25)
From 1960, Italy, (P)

=15. The Hulk (24)
From 1977, USA

=15. The Flash (24)
From 1979, USA

=17. Green Lantern (21)
From 1979, USA

=17. Son Goku (21)
From 1986, Japan, (A)

=19. Mil Máscaras (20)
From 1966, Mexico, (L)

=19. Cyborg (20)
From 2006, USA

=21. Darna (19)
From 1951, Philippines

=21. (Super) Sentai (19)
From 1987, Japan, (T)

=23. Iron Man (18)
From 2006, USA

=23. Kenshiro (18)
From 1986, Japan (A - Fist of the North Star)

=25. Jungle Jim (16)
From 1948, USA

=25. Asterix & Obelix (16)
From 1967, France

=25. Power Rangers (16)
From 1995, USA/Japan

=25. Black Widow (16)
From 2006, USA,

=29. Captain America (15)
From 1944, USA

=29. Robin (15)
From 1949, USA

=29. Rocky Jones (15)
From 1954, USA

=29. Thor (15)
From 1988, USA

=29. Nick Fury (15)
From 1998, USA

=29. Wolverine (15)
From 2001, USA

=35. Flash Gordon (14)
From 1936, USA

=35. Batgirl (14)
From 1997, USA

=37. Dick Tracy (11)
From 1937, USA

=37. The Lone Ranger & Tonto (11)
From 1938, USA

=37. Samson (11)
1961, Italy, (P)

=37. Aquaman (11)
From 2008, USA

=41. The Green Hornet/Kato (10)
From 1940, USA

=41. Neutron (10)
From 1960, Mexico, (L)

=41. Frankenstein (10)
From 1961, Mexico, (L)

=41. Teenage Mutant Ninja Turtles (10)
From 1990, USA

=41. Professor X (10)
From 2000, USA

=46. Ursus (9)
From 1960, Italy, (P)

=46. Huracán Ramirez (9)
From 1962, Mexico (P)

=46. The Three Supermen (9)
From 1967, Italy, Turkey

=49. The Shadow (8)
From 1937, USA

=49. Supergirl (8)
1984, USA

MOST PROLIFIC COUNTRIES

Movies from 50 countries appear in this book, with these 15 the most prolific.

Three tallies have been notably skewed by marginal subgenres. Peplum movies account for 79 of Italy's total, luchador movies 151 of Mexico's, and Doctor Who cut-and-shuts 168 of the UK's. Ignore them for a more relevant appraisal.

1. USA (768)
From 1920

2. Japan (303)
From 1950

3. UK (182)
From 1963

4. Mexico (163)
From 1954

=5. Philippines (109)
From 1953

=5. Italy (109)
From 1958

7. India (65)
From 1935

8. Turkey (30)
From 1967

9. France (25)
From 1916

10. Hong Kong (20)
From 1973

11. Canada (15)
From 1994

12. Indonesia (13)
From 1971

=13. Spain (12)
From 1955

=13. Thailand (12)
From 1959

15. South Korea (9)
From 1977

Countries you may be surprised to learn have produced at least one superhero movie include Finland, Guatemala, Peru and The Marshall Islands.

SUPERHERO DEMOGRAPHICS

While this isn't the place to get into the masses of character data collected from 3,000 individual superhero appearances in just under 2,000 movies, I want to at least touch on it.

Figures are derived from the character, not the actor playing them, and apply worldwide (where possible the US number follows in brackets). Not all totals add up to 100% due to some characters being hard to classify. Although these figures are derived from all movies, some dating back over 100 years, it's worth pointing out the massive recent increase in production significantly reduces the impact of historically different attitudes to gender and race. Figures such as the US's drastically lower proportion of, for example, superheroes appearing to have East Asian heritage, need to be seen in context. The vast majority of the 23.38% of East Asian superheroes appear in East Asian movies.

As ever, figures are derived for research carried out exclusively for this book, and are not presented as infallible.

Please be aware there is a requirement to categorise characters in problematic ways, make assumptions based on appearance and mix demonyms and races, etc. It's unavoidable when collecting data like this and I hope it causes no offence.

Movie superheroes established as:

Male – 78.03% (76.76% in the US)
Female – 21.91% (23.24%)
Gay – 0.43% (0.50%)
Trans – 0.33% (0%)

Movie superheroes appear to be:

White – 56.66% (78%)
East Asian – 23.38% (2.52%)
White Latinx – 5.90% (1.34%)
Black – 5.35% (9.46%)
South Asian – 1.9% (0.17%)

Movie superheroes originate from:

North America – 47.97%
East Asia – 22.96%
Space – 8.42%
Fantasy Realms – 6.39%
Europe – 5.72%
Asian Subcontinent – 1.92%
The Middle East – 0.97%
Oceania – 0.33%
South and Central America – 0.30%

Movie superheroes debuted via:

US Comic Books – 31.45%
TV – 19.74%
Film – 19.46%
Books (largely pulp novels) – 6.02%
Wrestling – 5.32%
Manga – 4.01%
Greek Myth – 3.13%
Radio – 1.43%
Comic Strips – 1.19%

US films are the most racially diverse with 97% of the world's black superheroes. But minorities are still less likely to be cast in the lead than in a team, and Asian women far more likely to appear than Asian men.

Asia in general, and the Philippines in particular, offers the most gender diversity, with 55% of all trans superheroes and women twice as likely to play the lead in a Pinoy film than a US one.

APPENDIX

A: Doctor Who cut-and-shuts

Filmographies too extensive to feature in
Grouped Franchises.

An Unearthly Child (1963, UK)
The Daleks (1963, UK)
Marco Polo (1964, UK)
The Keys of Marinus (1964, UK)
The Aztecs (1964, UK)
The Sensorites (1964, UK)
The Reign of Terror (1964, UK)
Planet of Giants (1964, UK)
The Dalek Invasion of Earth (1964, UK)
The Romans (1965, UK)
The Web Planet (1965, UK)
The Crusade (1965, UK)
The Space Museum (1965, UK)
The Chase (1965, UK)
The Time Meddler (1965, UK)
Galaxy 4 (1965, UK)
The Myth Makers (1965, UK)
The Daleks' Master Plan (1965, UK)
The Massacre of St Bartholomew's Eve (1966, UK)
The Ark (1966, UK)
The Celestial Toymaker (1966, UK)
The Gunfighters (1966, UK)
The Savages (1966, considered lost, UK)
The War Machines (1966, UK)
The Smugglers (1966, UK, considered lost)
The Tenth Planet (1966, UK)
The Highlanders (1966, UK, considered lost)
The Power of the Daleks (1966, UK)
The Macra Terror (1967, UK)
The Underwater Menace (1967, UK)
The Moonbase (1967, UK)
The Faceless Ones (1967, UK)
The Evil of the Daleks (1967, UK)
The Tomb of the Cybermen (1967, UK)
The Abominable Snowmen (1967, UK)
The Ice Warriors (1967, UK)
The Enemy of the World (1967, UK)
The Web of Fear (1968, UK)
Fury from the Deep (1968, UK, considered lost)
The Wheel in Space (1968, UK)
The Dominators (1968, UK)
The Mind Robber (1968, UK)
The Invasion (1968, UK)
The Krotons (1969, UK)
The Seeds of Death (1969, UK)
The Space Pirates (1969, UK)
The War Games (1969, UK)
Spearhead from Space (1970, UK)
Doctor Who and the Silurians (1970, UK)
The Ambassadors of Death (1970, UK)

Inferno (1970, UK)
Terror of the Autons (1971, UK)
The Mind of Evil (1971, UK)
The Claws of Axos (1971, UK)
Colony in Space (1971, UK)
The Dæmons (1971, UK)
Day of the Daleks (1972, UK)
The Curse of Peladon (1972, UK)
The Sea Devils (1972, UK)
The Mutants (1972, UK)
The Time Monster (1972, UK)
The Three Doctors (1973, UK)
Carnival of Monsters (1973, UK)
Frontier in Space (1973, UK)
Planet of the Daleks (1973, UK)
The Green Death (1973, UK)
The Time Warrior (1973, UK)
Invasion of the Dinosaurs (1974, UK)
Death to the Daleks (1974, UK)
The Monster of Peladon (1974, UK)
Planet of the Spiders (1974, UK)
Robot (1975, UK)
The Ark in Space (1975, UK)
The Sontaran Experiment (1975, UK)
Genesis of the Daleks (1975, UK)
Revenge of the Cybermen (1975, UK)
Terror of the Zygons (1975, UK)
Planet of Evil (1975, UK)
Pyramids of Mars (1975, UK)
The Android Invasion (1975, UK)
The Brain of Morbius (1976, UK)
The Seeds of Doom (1976, UK)
The Masque of Mandragora (1976, UK)
The Hand of Fear (1976, UK)
The Deadly Assassin (1976, UK)
The Face of Evil (1977, UK)
The Robots of Death (1977, UK)
The Talons of Weng-Chiang (1977, UK)
Horror of Fang Rock (1977, UK)
The Invisible Enemy (1977, UK)
Image of the Fendahl (1977, UK)
The Sun Makers (1977, UK)
Underworld (1978, UK)
The Invasion of Time (1978, UK)
The Ribos Operation (1978, UK)
The Pirate Planet (1978, UK)
The Stones of Blood (1978, UK)
The Androids of Tara (1978, UK)
The Power of Kroll (1978, UK)
The Armageddon Factor (1979, UK)
Destiny of the Daleks (1979, UK)
City of Death (1979, UK)

The Creature from the Pit (1979, UK)
Nightmare of Eden (1979, UK)
The Horns of Nimon (1979, UK)
Shada (shot in 1979 and released 2017, UK)
The Leisure Hive (1980, UK)
Meglos (1980, UK)
Full Circle (1980, UK)
State of Decay (1980, UK)
Warriors' Gate (1981, UK)
The Keeper of Traken (1981, UK)
Logopolis (1981, UK)
Castrovalva (1982, UK)
Four To Doomsday (1982, UK)
Kinda (1982, UK)
The Visitation (1982, UK)
Earthshock (1982, UK)
Time-Flight (1982, UK)
Arc of Infinity (1983, UK)
Snakedance (1983, UK)
Mawdryn Undead (1983, UK)
Terminus (1983, UK)
Enlightenment (1983, UK)
The Five Doctors (1983, UK)
Warriors of the Deep (1984, UK)
Frontios (1984, UK)
Planet of Fire (1984, UK)
The Caves of Androzani (1984, UK)
The Twin Dilemma (1984, UK)
The Two Doctors (1987, UK)
The Mysterious Planet (1986, UK)
Mindwarp (1986, UK)
Terror of the Vervoids (1986, UK)
Time And the Rani (1987, UK)
Paradise Towers (1987, UK)
Delta And the Bannermen (1987, UK)
Dragonfire (1987, UK)
Remembrance of the Daleks (1988, UK)
The Happiness Patrol (1988, UK)
Silver Nemesis (1988, UK)
The Greatest Show In the Galaxy (1988, UK)
Battlefield (1989, UK)
Ghost Light (1989, UK)
The Curse of Fenric (1989, UK)
Survival (1989, UK)
The Christmas Invasion (2005, UK)
The Runaway Bride (2006, UK)
Voyage of the Damned (2007, UK)
The Stolen Earth/Journey's End (2008, UK)
The End of Time (2009, UK)
The Eleventh Hour (2010, UK)
A Christmas Carol (2011, UK)
The Snowmen (2012, UK)

The Doctor, the Widow and the Wardrobe (2012, UK)

The Day of the Doctor (2013, UK)

The Time of the Doctor (2013, UK)

Deep Breath (2014, UK)

Dark Water/Death in Heaven (2014, UK)

Last Christmas (2014, UK)

The Magician's Apprentice/Witch's Familiar (2015, UK)

Under the Lake/Before the Flood (2015, UK)

The Husbands of River Song (2015, UK)

The Return Of Doctor Mysterio (2016, UK)

World Enough and Time/The Doctor Falls (2017, UK)

Twice Upon a Time (2017, UK)

The Woman Who Fell to Earth (2018, UK)

Resolution (2019, UK)

B: Kamen Rider movies

Eight Riders vs. Gingaoh (Kamen Raidā: Hachi'nin Raidā Tai Gingaō, 1980, JP)

Shin Kamen Rider: Prologue (Shin Kamen Raidā: Purorōgu, 1992, JP)

Ultraman vs. Kamen Rider (Urutoraman tai Kamen Raidā, 1993, JP)

Kamen Rider Ryuki The Movie: Episode Final (Gekijōban Kamen Raidā Ryūki Episōdo Fainaru, 2002, JP)

Kamen Rider 555: Paradise Lost (Gekijōban Kamen Raidā Faizu Paradaisu Rosuto, 2003, JP)

Kamen Rider Blade the Movie: Missing Ace (Gekijouban Kamen raidâ Bureido: Missing Ace, 2004, JP)

Kamen Rider Hibiki & the Seven Fighting Demons (2005, JP)

Kamen Rider: The First (Kamen Raidâ: The First, 2005, JP)

Kamen Rider Hibiki & The Seven Senki Movie (Gekijōban Kamen Raidā Hibiki to Shichinin no Senki, Masked Rider Hibiki & The Seven War Ogres Movie, 2005, JP)

Kamen Rider Kabuto the Movie: God Speed Love (Gekijōban Kamen Raidā Kabuto Goddo Supīdo Rabu, 2006, JP)

Kamen Rider: The Next (Kamen raidā: The next, 2007, JP)

Kamen Rider Den-O the Movie: I'm Born! (Gekijōban Kamen Raidā Den'ō Ore, Tanjō!, 2007, JP)

Kamen Rider Den-O & Kiva the Movie: Climax Deka (Gekijōban Kamen Raidā Den'ō Ando Kiba Kuraimakkusu Deka, 2008, JP)

Kamen Rider Kiva the Movie: King of the Castle in the Demon World (Gekijōban Kamen Raidā Kiba Makaijō no Ō, 2008, JP)

Saraba Kamen Rider Den-O the Movie: Final Countdown (Gekijōban Saraba Kamen Raidā Den'ō Fainaru Kauntodaun, Farewell, Masked Rider Den-O The Movie: Final Countdown, 2008, JP)

Saraba Kamen Rider Den-O: Final Countdown (Gekijōban Saraba Kamen Raidâ Den'ô Fainaru Kauntodaun, 2008, JP)

Cho Kamen Rider Den-O & Decade NEO Generations: The Onigashima Battleship (Gekijô ban Chô Kamen raidâ den'ô & Dikeido Neo generêshonzu onigashima no senkan, 2009, JP)

Kamen Rider Decade: All Riders vs. Dai-Shocker (Gekijōban Kamen Raidā Dikeido Ōru Raidā Tai Daishokkā, 2009, JP)

Kamen Rider × Kamen Rider Double & Decade: Movie War 2010 (Kamen raidâ x Kamen raidâ W & Dikeido Movie taisen 2010, 2009, JP)

Kamen Rider × Kamen Rider W & Decade: Movie War (Kamen Raidā × Kamen Raidā Daburu Ando Dikeido Mūbī Taisen Nisenjū, 2010, JP)

Kamen Rider × Kamen Rider × Kamen Rider The Movie: Cho-Den-O Trilogy - Episode Red - Zero no Star Twinkle (Episōdo Reddo Zero no Sutā Towinkuru, 2010, JP)

Kamen Rider × Kamen Rider × Kamen Rider the Movie: Cho-Den-O Trilogy - Episode Blue - The Dispatched Imagin is Newtral (Episōdo Burū Haken Imajin wa Nyūtoraru, 2010)

Kamen Rider × Kamen Rider × Kamen Rider The Movie: Cho-Den-O Trilogy - Episode Yellow - Treasure de End Pirates (Episōdo Ierō Otakara DE Endo Pairētsu, 2010, JP)

Kamen Rider W Forever: A to Z/The Gaia Memories of Fate (Kamen Raidā Daburu Fōebā Ē tu Zetto/Unmei no Gaia Memori, 2010, JP)

Kamen Rider × Kamen Rider OOO & W Featuring Skull: Movie War Core (Gekijōban Kamen Raidā × Kamen Raidā Ōzu Ando Daburu Fīcharingu Sukaru Mūbī Taisen Koa, 2010, JP)

OOO, Den-O, All Riders: Let's Go Kamen Riders (Ōzu Den'ō Ōru Raidā: Rettsu Gō Kamen Raidā, 2011, JP)

Gekijouban Kamen raidâ Ôzu Wonderful: Shougun to 21 no koa medaru (Gekijōban Kamen Raidā × Kamen Raidā Ōzu Ando Daburu Fīcharingu Sukaru Mūbī Taisen Koa, 2011, JP)

Kamen Rider x Kamen Rider Fourze & OOO Movie War Mega Max (Kamen Raidā × Kamen Raidā Fōze Ando Ōzu Mūbī Taisen Mega Makkusu, 2011, JP)

Kamen Rider OOO Wonderful the Movie: The Shogun and the 21 Core Medals (Gekijōban Kamen Raidā Ōzu Wandafuru Shōgun to Nijū-ichi no Koa Medaru, 2011, JP)

Kamen Rider W Returns: Kamen Rider Eternal (2011, JP)

Kamen Rider × Super Sentai: Super Hero Taisen (Kamen Raidâ × Supâ Sentai Supâ Hīrô Taisen, 2012, JP)

Kamen Rider Fourze the Movie: Everyone, Space Is Here! (Kamen Raidā Fōze Za Mūbī Minna de Uchū Kitā!, 2012, JP)

Kamen Rider × Kamen Rider Wizard & Fourze: Movie War Ultimatum (Kamen Raidā × Kamen Raidā Wizādo Ando Fōze Mūbī Taisen Arutimeitamu, 2012, JP)

Kamen Rider × Super Sentai × Space Sheriff: Super Hero Taisen Z (Kamen Raidā × Sūpā Sentai × Uchū Keiji Supā Hīrō Taisen Zetto, 2013, JP)

Kamen Rider Wizard in Magic Land (Gekijōban Kamen Raidā Wizādo In Majikku Rando, 2013, JP)

Kamen Rider × Kamen Rider Gaim & Wizard: The Fateful Sengoku Movie Battle (Kamen Raidā × Kamen Raidā Gaimu Ando Wizādo Tenkawakeme no Sengoku Mūbī Daigassen, 2013, JP)

Heisei Rider vs. Shōwa Rider: Kamen Rider Taisen feat. Super Sentai (Heisei Raidā Tai Shōwa Raidā Kamen Raidā Taisen feat. Sūpā Sentai, 2014, JP)

Kamen Rider Gaim the Movie: Great Soccer Battle! Golden Fruits Cup! (ekijōban Kamen Raidā Gaimu Sakkā Daikessen! Ōgon no Kajitsu Sōdatsu Kappu!, 2014, JP)

Kamen Rider × Kamen Rider Drive & Gaim: Movie War Full Throttle (Kamen Raidā × Kamen Raidā Doraibu Ando Gaimu Mūbī Taisen Furu Surottoru, 2014, JP)

Super Hero Taisen GP: Kamen Rider 3 (Supā Hīrō Taisen Guranpuri Kamen Raidā Sangō, 2015, JP)

Kamen Rider Drive the Movie: Surprise Future (Gekijōban Kamen Raidā Doraibu Sapuraizu Fyūchā, 2015, JP)

Kamen Rider × Kamen Rider Ghost & Drive: Super Movie War Genesis (Kamen Raidā × Kamen Raidā Gōsuto Ando Doraibu Chō Mūbī Taisen Jeneshisu, 2015, JP)

Kamen Rider Ghost the Movie: The 100 Eyecons and Ghost's Fated Moment (Gekijōban Kamen Raidā Gōsuto Hyaku no Aikon to Gōsuto Unmei no Toki, 2015, JP)

Kamen Rider 1 (Kamen Raidā Ichigō, 2016, JP)

Kamen Rider Drive Saga: Kamen Rider Chaser (Kamen Raidâ Doraibu Sâga: Kamen Raidā Cheisâ, 2016, JP)

Kamen Rider Heisei Generations: Dr. Pac-Man vs. Ex-Aid & Ghost with Legend Rider (Kamen raidā Heisei jenerêshonzu: Dr. Pakkuman tai Eguzeido & Gôsuto with Rejendo raidâ, 2016, JP)

Kamen Rider × Super Sentai: Ultra Super Hero Taisen (Kamen Raidā × Supâ Sentai Chô Supâ Hîrô Taisen, 2017, JP)

Kamen Rider Heisei Generations Final: Build & Ex-Aid with Legend Riders (Kamen Raidā Heisei Jenerêshonzu Fainaru Birudo Ando Eguzeido Wizu Rejendo Raidā, 2017, JP)

Kamen Rider Ex-Aid the Movie: True Ending (Gekijōban Kamen Raidā Eguzeido Turū Endingu, 2017, JP)

Kamen Rider Ghost RE:BIRTH: Kamen Rider Specter (Kamen Raidâ Gôsuto Ribâsu Kamen Raidâ Supekutâ, 2017, JP)

Kamen Rider Build the Movie: Be the One (Gekijōban Kamen Raidā Birudo Bī Za Wan, 2018, JP)

Kamen Rider Amazons the Movie: The Last Judgement (Kamen Raidā Amazonzu Za Mūbī Saigo no Shinpan, 2018, JP)

Kamen Rider Ex-Aid Trilogy: Another Ending (Kamen Raidā Eguzeido Torirojī Anazā Endingu, 2018, JP)

C: Luchador movies

El enmascarado de plata (The Silver Masked Man, 1954, MX)

La sombra vengadora (The Avenging Shadow, 1956, MX)

La sombra vengadora vs. La mano negra (The Avenging Shadow vs. The Black Hand, 1956, MX)

El tesoro de Pancho Villa (The Treasure of Pancho Villa, 1957, MX)

Ladrón de cadáveres (The Body Snatcher, 1957, MX)

La maldición de la momia azteca (The Curse of the Aztec Mummy, 1957, MX)

Secuestro diabolico (1957, MX)

Furias desatadas (1957, MX)

Santo contra el cerebro del mal (Santo vs. the Evil Brain, 1958, MX)

Santo contra hombres infernales (Santo vs. the Infernal Men, 1958 or 1961, MX)

El superflaco (1959, MX)

La última lucha (1959, MX)

El torneo de la muerte (1960, MX)

Los tigres del ring (Tigers of the Ring, 1960, MX)

El correo del norte (Northern Coruier, 1960, MX)

Neutrón, el enmascarado negro (Neutron, the Man in the Black Mask, 1960, MX)

Santo contra los zombis (Santo vs the Zombies, 1961, MX)

Santo contra el rey del crimen (Santo vs. The King of Crime, 1961, MX)

Santo en el hotel de la muerte (Santo in the Hotel of Death, 1961 or 1963, MX)

El buena suerte (1961, MX)

La máscara de la muerte (The Mask of Death, 1961, MX)

La furia del ring (1961, MX)

Santo contra las mujeres vampiro (Santo vs. The Vampire Women, 1962, MX)

Asesinos de la lucha libre (1962, MX)

La venganza de la sombra (1962, MX)

Los autómatas de la muerte (Robots of Death, 1962, MX)

El misterio de Huracán Ramírez (The Mystery of Huracan Ramirez, 1962, MX)

Sangre en el ring (1962, MX)

Neutrón contra el Dr. Caronte (Neutron vs. the Amazing Dr. Caronte, 1963, MX)

Santo en el museo de cera (Santo in the Wax Museum, 1963, MX)

Santo contra el estrangulador (Santo vs. the Strangler, 1963, MX)

Santo contra el espectro del estrangulador (Santo vs.

the Ghost of the Strangler, 1963, MX)

El señor Tormenta (1963, MX)

Las luchadoras contra el médico asesino (Sex Monster, 1963, MX)

Tormenta en el ring (1963, MX)

La sombra blanca (The White Shadow, 1963, MX)

Santo en Atacan las brujas (The Witches Attack, 1964, MX)

Santo en el hacha diabólica (The Diabolical Axe, 1964, MX)

El ciclón de Jalisco (1964, MX)

Las luchadoras contra la momia (Wrestling Women vs. the Aztec Mummy, 1964, MX)

Neutrón contra el criminal sádico (Neutron vs. the Maniac, 1964, MX)

Santo en los profanadores de tumbas (The Grave Robbers, 1965, MX)

Santo en el Barón Brakola (Baron Brakola, 1965, MX)

El asesino invisible (Neutron Traps the Invisible Killers, 1965, MX)

Las lobas del ring (She-Wolves of the Ring, 1965, MX)

Blue Demon: El Demonio Azul (Blue Demon, 1965, MX)

Los asesinos del karate (Neutron Battles the Karate Assassins, 1965, MX)

La mano que aprieta (The Clutching Hand, 1966, MX)

Blue Demon vs. el poder satánico (Blue Demon vs. the Satanic Power, 1966, MX)

Los endemoniados del ring (1966, MX)

Superargo contra Diabolikus (Superargo vs. Diabolikus, 1966, IT/ES)

Santo contra la invasión de los marcianos (Santo vs. the Martian Invasion, 1966, MX)

Santo contra los villanos del ring (Santo vs. the Villains of the Ring, 1966, MX)

Santo en Operación 67 (Operation 67, 1966, MX)

Goldface il fantastico Superman (Goldface, the Fantastic Superman, 1967, IT/ES)

Cada quién su lucha (1966, MX)

El hijo de Huracán Ramírez (1966, MX)

Santo en el tesoro de Moctezuma (The Treasure of Montezuma, 1967, MX)

Las mujeres panteras (The Panther Women, 1967, MX)

La mujer murcielago (The Batwoman, 1968, MX)

Los canallas (Infernal Angels, 1968, MX)

Arañas infernales (Hellish Spiders, 1968, MX)

Blue Demon destructor de espias (Blue Demon: Destructor of Spies, 1968, MX)

La sombra del murciélago (The Shadow of the Bat, 1968, MX)

Santo en el tesoro de Drácula (The Treasure of Dracula, 1968, MX)

Blue Demon contra cerebros infernales (1968, MX)

Blue Demon contra las diabólicas (Blue Demon vs. The Diabolical Women, 1968, MX)

Pasaporte a la muerte (1968, MX)

L'invincibile Superman (Superargo and the Faceless Giants, 1968m IT/ES)

Santo contra Capulina (Santo vs. Capulina, 1968, MX)

Las luchadoras vs el robot asesino (Wrestling Women versus the Murderous Robot, 1969, MX)

Santo contra Blue Demon en la Atlántida (Santo vs. Blue Demon in Atlantis, 1969, MX)

Santo y Blue Demon contra los monstruos (Santo and Blue Demon vs. the Monsters, 1969, MX)

Santo y Blue Demon en el mundo de los muertos (Santo and Blue Demon in the World of the Dead, 1969, MX)

Santo contra los cazadores de cabezas (Santo vs. the Headhunters, 1969, MX)

Santo frente la muerte (Santo Faces Death, 1969, MX)

La venganza de Huracán Ramírez (1969, MX)

Mil máscaras (1969, MX)

Las vampiras (The Vampires, 1969, MX)

Enigma de muerte (1969, MX)

Cazadores de espías (1969, MX)

Blue Demon y las invasoras (1969, MX)

Santo contra los jinetes del terror (Santo vs. the Terror Riders, 1970, MX)

Las momias de Guanajuato (The Mummies of Guanajuato, 1970, MX)

Santo en la venganza de las mujeres vampiro (The Revenge of the Vampire Women, 1970, MX)

Santo contra los jinetes del terror (Santo vs. the Terror Riders, 1970, MX)

Santo contra la mafia del vicio (Santo vs. the Mafia of Vice, 1970, MX)

Santo en la venganza de la momia (The Mummy's Revenge, 1970, MX)

Los campeones justicieros (The Champions of Justice, 1971, MX)

Santo en el misterio de la perla negra (The Mystery of the Black Pearl, 1971, MX)

Santo contra la hija de Frankenstein (Santo vs. Frankenstein's Daughter, 1971, MX)

Santo en misión suicida (Suicide Mission, 1971, MX)

Santo contra los asesinos de otros mundos (Santo vs. the Killers from Other Worlds, 1971, MX)

Santo y el tigresa en el aguila real (The Royal Eagle, 1971, MX)

Ssuperzam el invencible (Superzan the Invincible, 1971, MX)

El robo de las momias de Guanajuato (Robbery of the Mummies of Guanajuato, 1972, MX)

Vuelven los campeones justicieros (The Champions Five Supermen, 1972, MX)

Santo y Blue Demon contra Drácula y el Hombre Lobo (Santo and Blue Demon vs. Dracula and the Wolf Man, 1972, MX)

Santo contra los secuestradores (Santo vs. the Kidnappers, 1972, MX)

Santo contra la magia negra (Santo vs. Black Magic, 1972, MX)

Santo y Blue Demon en las bestias del terror (The Beasts of Terror, 1972, MX)

Santo contra las lobas (Santo vs. the She-Wolves, 1972, MX)

Santo en Anónimo mortal (Anonymous Death Threat, 1972, MX)

Huracán Ramírez y la monjita negra (Huracan Ramirez and the Black Nun, 1973, MX)

3 Dev Adam (Three Giant Men, 1973, TR)

Santo y Blue Demon contra el doctor Frankenstein (Santo and Blue Demon vs. Dr. Frankenstein, 1973, MX)

Santo contra el doctor Muerte (Santo vs. Dr. Death, 1973, MX)

Titanes en el ring (1973, AR)

Una rosa sobre el ring (1973, MX)

El castillo de las momias de Guanajuato (The Castle of Mummies of Guanajuato, 1973, MX)

Superzan y el niño del espacio (Superzan and the Space Boy, 1973, MX)

Leyendas macabras de la colonia (Macabre Legends of the Colony, 1974, MX)

El triunfo de los campeones justicieros (The Triumph of the Champions of Justice, 1974, MX)

Los vampiros de Coyoacán (The Vampires of Coyoacan, 1974, MX)

Los leones del ring (Lions of the Ring, 1974, MX)

Los leones del ring contra la Cosa Nostra (1974, MX)

De sangre chicana (Of Chicana Blood, 1974, MX)

Santo en la venganza de la llorona (The Revenge of the Crying Woman, 1974, MX)

Karla contra los jaguares (Karla vs. The Jaguars, 1974, MX)

Las momias de San Ángel (The Mummies of San Angel, 1975, MX)

Santo en Oro negro (Santo in the Mystery of the Black Pearl, 1975, MX)

El investigador Capulina (Capulina the Detective, 1975, MX)

La mafia amarilla (1975, MX)

Noche de muerte (Night of Death, 1975, MX)

Los jaguares contra el invasor misterioso (The Jaguars vs. The Mysterious Invaders, 1975, MX)

El hijo de Alma Grande (The Son of Alma Grande, 1976, MX)

La mansion de las 7 momias, (The Mansion of the 7 Mummies, 1977, MX)

Santo en el Misterio en las Bermudas (The Bermuda Mystery, 1977, MX)

Ángel del silencio (1979, MX)

El torito puños de oro (1979, MX)

Santo en la frontera del terror (The Border of Terror, 1979, MX)

Chanoc y el hijo del Santo contra los vampiros asesinos (Chanoc and the Son of Santo vs. The Killer Vampires, 1981, MX)

Santo contra el asesino de televisión (Santo vs. the TV Killer, 1981, MX)

El torito de Tepito (1982, MX)

Santo en el puño de la muerte (The Fist of Death, 1982, MX)

Santo en la furia de los karatekas (The Fury of the Karate Experts, 1982, MX)

El hijo de Santo en frontera sin ley (1983, MX)

Huracán Ramírez contra los terroristas (1989, MX)

La verdad de la lucha (1990, MX)

La llave mortal (1990, MX)

Mágico, el enviado de los dioses (Magico, 1990, MX)

La revancha (The Revenge, 1992, MX)

Luchadores de las estrellas (Starfighters, 1992, MX)

Lucha a muerte (Octagon and Mascara Sagrada in Fight to the Death, 1992, MX)

Vampiro, guerrero de la noche (1993, MX)

Atomic Blue Mexican Wrestler (1999, US)

616 DF: El diablo español vs. Las luchadoras del este (Wrestle with the Devil, 2004, ES)

Santo: Infraterrestre (2001, MX)

Polvo de ángel (2007, MX)

Súper héroes galácticos: Al rescate del planeta azul (2007, MX)

Súper héroes galácticos vs. el imperio del mal (2007, MX)

Máscara Sagrada vs. la mafia del ring (2007, MX)

El fantasma vs. la aldea de los zombies (2007, MX)

Mil Mascaras vs. the Aztec Mummy (2007, US)

Academy of Doom (2008, US)

El gato salvaje (2008, MX)

Kato Kung Lee vs. la mafia oriental (2008, MX)

AAA, la película: Sin límite en el tiempo (2010, MX)

El Santos vs la Tetona Mendoza (2012, animation, MX)

Aztec Revenge (2015, US)

D: Peplum movies

Hercules (Le fatiche di Ercole, 1958, IT)

Goliath and the Barbarians (Il terrore dei barbari, 1959, IT)

Hercules Unchained (Ercole e la regina di Lidia, 1959, IT)

Goliath Against the Giants (Goliath contro i giganti, 1960, IT)

Goliath and the Dragon (La vendetta di Ercole, 1960, IT)

The Loves of Hercules (Gli amori di Ercole, 1960, IT)

Son of Samson (Maciste nella valle dei re, 1960, IT)

Ursus, Son of Hercules (Mighty Ursus, 1960, IT)

Atlas in the Land of the Cyclops (Maciste nella terra dei ciclopi, 1961, IT)

Goliath and the Vampires (Maciste contro il vampiro, 1961, IT)

Hercules Conquers Atlantis aka Hercules and the Captive Women (Ercole alla conquista di Atlantide, 1961, IT)

Hercules in the Haunted World (Ercole al centro della Terra, 1961, IT)

Hercules in the Vale of Woe (Maciste contro Ercole nella valle dei guai, 1961, IT)

Mole Men vs the Son of Hercules (Maciste, l'uomo più forte del mondo, 1961, IT)

Samson (Sansone, 1961, IT)

Samson and the Seven Miracles of the World (Maciste alla corte del gran khan, 1961, IT)

Triumph of the Son of Hercules (Il trionfo di Maciste, 1961, IT)

Ursus and the Tartar Princess (Ursus e la Ragazza Tartara, 1961, IT)

The Vengeance of Ursus (La Vendetta di Ursus, 1961, IT)

Colossus and the Headhunters (Maciste contro i cacciatori di teste, 1962, IT)

Colossus of the Arena (Maciste, il gladiatore piu forte del mondo, 1962, IT)

Fire Monsters Against the Son of Hercules (Maciste contro i mostri, 1962, IT)

The Fury of Hercules (La furia di Ercole, 1962, IT)

The Rebel Gladiators (Ursus gladiatore ribelle, 1962, IT)

Samson Against the Sheik (Maciste contro lo sceicco, 1962, IT)

Totò contro Maciste (peplum spoof unreleased in the US, 1962, IT)

Ulysses Against Hercules aka Ulysses Against the Son of Hercules (Ulisse contro Ercole, 1962, IT)

Valley of the Lions (Ursus Nella Valle dei Leoni, 1962, IT)

The Witch's Curse (Maciste all'inferno, 1962, IT)

Zorro the Avenger (La venganza del Zorro, 1962, IT)

The Masked Conqueror aka Zorro at the Court of Spain (Zorro alla corte di Spagna, 1962, IT)

Shades of Zorro (L'ombra di Zorro, 1962, IT)

Vulcan, Son of Giove (Vulcano, figlio di Giove, 1962, IT)

Conquest of Mycene aka Hercules Attacks (Ercole contro Moloch, 1963, IT)

Goliath and the Rebel Slave (Goliath e la schiava ribelle, 1963, IT)

Goliath and the Sins of Babylon (Maciste, l'eroe piu grande del mondo, 1963, IT)

Hercules Against the Barbarians (Maciste nell'inferno di Gengis Khan, 1963, IT)

Hercules Against the Mongols (Maciste contro i Mongoli, 1963, IT)

Hercules and the Black Pirate (Sansone contro il corsaro nero, 1963, IT)

Hercules and the Masked Rider (Golia e il cavaliere mascherato, 1963, IT)

Hercules, Samson & Ulysses aka (Ercole sfida Sansone, 1963, IT)

Samson and the Sea Beast (Sansone contro i pirati, 1963, IT)

Samson and the Slave Queen (Zorro contro Maciste, 1963, IT)

Son of Hercules in the Land of Fire aka Son of Atlas in the Land of Fire (Ursus Nella Terra di Fuoco, 1963, IT)

Sign of Zorro aka Duel at the Rio Grande (Il segno di Zorro, 1963, IT)

Sword of Zorro aka The Three Swords of Zorro (Le tre spade di Zorro, 1963, IT)

Zorro Against Maciste aka Samson and the Slave Queen (Zorro contro Maciste, 1963, IT)

Zorro and the Three Musketeers (Zorro e i tre moschettieri, 1963, IT)

Atlas Against The Czar (Maciste alla corte dello zar, 1964, IT)

Goliath at the Conquest of Damascus (Golia alla conquista di Bagdad, 1964, IT)

Hercules Against Rome (Ercole contro Roma, 1964, IT)

Hercules Against the Moon Men (Maciste e la regina de Samar, 1964, IT)

Hercules Against the Sons of the Sun (Ercole l'invincibile, 1964, IT)

Hercules and the Black Pirates (Sansone contro il corsaro nero, 1964, IT)

Hercules and the Treasure of the Incas (Sansone e il tesoro degli Incas, 1964, IT)

Hercules and the Tyrants of Babylon (Ercole contro i tiranni di Babilonia, 1964, IT)

Hercules of the Desert (La valle dell'eco tonante, 1964, IT)

Hercules, Prisoner of Evil (Ursus, il terrore dei kirghisi, 1964, IT)

Hercules the Invincible (Ercole l'invincibile, 1964, IT)

Hercules vs. the Giant Warriors aka Hercules and the Ten Avengers (Il trionfo di Ercole, 1964, IT)

The Invincible Brothers Maciste (Maciste il Vendicatore dei Mayas, 1964, IT)

Messalina vs. the Son of Hercules (L'ultimo gladiatore, 1964, IT)

Samson and His Mighty Challenge (Ercole, Sansone, Maciste e Ursus: gli invincibili, 1964, IT)

Samson in King Solomon's Mines (Maciste nelle miniere de re salomone, 1964, IT)

The Slave Merchants aka Devil of the Desert (Anthar l'invincibile, 1964, IT)

Terror of Rome Against the Son of Hercules (Maciste, gladiatore di Sparta, 1964, IT)

Three Avengers (Gli Invincibili Tre, 1964, IT)

Hercules and the Princess of Troy aka Hercules vs. the Sea Monster (1965, IT)

Hercules the Avenger (La sfida dei giganti, 1965, IT)

Zorro the Rebel (Zorro il ribelle, 1966, IT)

Nephews of Zorro (I nipoti di Zorro, 1968, IT)

Zorro the Fox (el Zorro, 1968, IT)

Zorro in the Court of England (Zorro alla corte d'Inghilterra, 1969, IT)

Zorro's Latest Adventure (La última aventura del Zorro, 1969, IT)

Zorro the Avenger (El Zorro justiciero, 1969, IT)

Zorro, the Navarra Marquis (Zorro marchese di Navarra, 1969, IT)

Zorro's Last Adventure (La última aventura del Zorro, 1970, IT)

Zorro, Rider of Vengeance (Zorro il cavaliere della vendetta, 1971, IT)

Zorro the Invincible (El Zorro de Monterrey, 1971, IT)

Zorro of Monterrey (El Zorro de Monterrey, 1971, IT)

Son of Zorro aka Man with the Golden Winchester (Il figlio di Zorro, 1973, IT)

Mark of Zorro (Ah si? E io lo dico a Zzzzorro!, 1975, IT

E: Pretty Cure movies

Futari wa Pretty Cure Max Heart the Movie (Eiga Futari wa Purikyua Makkusu Hāto, 2005, JP)

Futari wa Pretty Cure Max Heart the Movie 2: Friends of the Snow-Laden Sky (Eiga Futari wa Purikyua Makkusu Hāto 2: Yukizora no Tomodachi, 2005, JP)

Futari wa Pretty Cure Splash Star: Tick-Tock Crisis Hanging by a Thin Thread! (Eiga Futari wa Purikyua Supurashu Sutā Tiku Taku Kiki Ippatsu!, 2006, JP)

Yes! PreCure 5 the Movie: Great Miraculous Adventure in the Mirror Kingdom! (Eiga Iesu! Purikyua Faibu: Kagami no Kuni no Mirakuru Daibōken!, 2007, JP)

Yes! Precure 5 GoGo! the Movie: Happy Birthday in the Sweets Kingdom (Eiga Iesu! Purikyua Faibu GōGō! Okashi no Kuni no Happī Bāsudi, 2008, JP)

Fresh Pretty Cure! the Movie: The Toy Kingdom has Lots of Secrets!? (Eiga Furesshu Purikyua! Omocha no Kuni wa Himitsu ga Ippai!?, 2009, JP)

Pretty Cure All Stars DX: Everyone's Friends*the Collection of Miracles! (PuriKyua Ōru Sutāzu Dirakkusu: Minna Tomodachi*Kiseki no Zenin Daishūgō, 2009, JP)

Pretty Cure All Stars DX2: Light of Hope*Protect the Rainbow Jewel! (PuriKyua Ōru Sutāzu Dirakkusu Tsū: Kibō no Hikari*Reinbō Jueru wo Mamore!, 2010, JP)

HeartCatch PreCure! the Movie: Fashion Show in the Flower Capital... Really?! (Eiga HātoKyatchi Purikyua! Hana no Miyako de Fasshon Shō...Desu ka!?, 2010, JP)

Suite PreCure the Movie: Take it back! The Miraculous Melody that Connects Hearts (Eiga Suīto Purikyua: Torimodose! Kokoro ga Tsunagu Kiseki no Merodi!, 2011, JP)

Pretty Cure All Stars DX3: Deliver the Future! The Rainbow-Colored Flower That Connects the World (Ōru Sutāzu Dirakkusu Surī: Mirai ni Todoke! Sekai o Tsunagu Niji-Iro no Hana, 2011, JP)

Pretty Cure All Stars New Stage: Friends of the Future (PuriKyua Ōru Sutāzu Nyū Sutēji: Mirai no Tomodachi, 2012, JP)

Smile Precure! the Movie: Big Mismatch in a Picture Book! (Eiga Sumairu Purikyua!: Ehon no Naka wa Minna Chiguhagu!, 2012, JP)

DokiDoki! Precure the Movie: Mana's Getting Married!!? The Dress of Hope that Connects to the Future (Eiga Dokidoki! Purikyua: Mana Kekkon!!? Mirai ni Tsunagu Kibō no Doresu, 2013, JP)

Pretty Cure All Stars New Stage 2: Friends of the Heart (PuriKyua Ōru Sutāzu Nyū Sutēji Tsū: Kokoro no Tomodachi, 2013, JP)

Pretty Cure All Stars New Stage 3: Eternal Friends (Eiga Purikyua Ōru Sutāzu Nyū Sutēji Surī: Eien no Tomodachi, 2014, JP)

HappinessCharge PreCure! the Movie: The Ballerina of the Land of Dolls (Eiga HapinesuChāji Purikyua! Ningyō no Kuni no Barerīna, 2014, JP)

Go! Princess Precure the Movie: Go! Go!! Splendid Triple Feature!!! (Eiga Gō! Purinsesu Purikyua: Gō! Gō!! Gōka San-bon Date!!!, 2015, portmanteau, JP)

Pretty Cure All Stars: Carnival of Spring (Eiga Purikyua Ōru Sutāzu: Haru no Kānibaru, 2015, JP)

Pretty Cure All Stars: Singing with Everyone Miraculous Magic! (Eiga Purikyua Ōru Sutāzu: Minna de Utau Kiseki no Mahō!, 2016, JP)

Maho Girls PreCure! the Movie: The Miraculous Transformation! Cure Mofurun! (Eiga Mahōtsukai Purikyua!: Kiseki no Henshin! Kyua Mofurun!, 2015, JP)

Kirakira PreCure a la Mode the Movie: Crisply! The Memory of Mille-feuille! (Eiga Kirakira * Purikyua Ara Mōdo: Paritto! Omoide no Mirufiyu!, 2017, JP)

Pretty Cure Dream Stars! (Eiga Purikyua Dorīmu Sutāzu!, 2017, JP)

Pretty Cure Super Stars! (Eiga Purikyua Sūpā Sutāzu!, 2018, JP)

Hugtto! PreCure Futari wa Pretty Cure: All Stars Memories (Eiga Hagutto! Purikyua Futari wa Puri Kyua Ōru Sutāzu Memorīzu, 2018, JP)

F: Ultraman movies

Ultraman: Monster Movie Feature (Chōhen Kaijū Eiga Urutoraman, 1967, JP)

The Six Ultra Brothers vs. the Monster Army (Urutora Roku Kyōdai tai Kaijū Gundan, 1974, TH/JP)

GLOSSARY

Know your henshin heroes from your
fumetti neri.

*Ultraman (Jissouji Akio Kantoku Sakuhin Urutoraman,
1979, JP)*

*Ultraman: Great Monster Decisive Battle (Urutoraman
Kaijū Daikessen, 1979, JP)*

*Ultraman Zoffy: Ultra Warriors vs. the Giant Monster
Army (1984, JP)*

Ultraman Story (Urutoraman Sutōrī, 1984, JP)

Ultraman: The Adventure Begins (Yū Esu Ē, 1987, JP)

*Ultra Q The Movie: Legend of the Stars (Urutora Q Za
Mūbi: Hoshi no Densetsu, 1990, JP)*

Ultraman Zearth (Urutoraman Zeasu, 1996, JP)

*Ultraman Zearth 2: Superhuman Big Battle - Light and
Shadow (Urutoraman Zeasu Tsū: Chōjin Taisen Hikari
to Kage, 1997, JP)*

*Ultra Nyan: Extraordinary Cat who Descended from
the Starry Sky (1997, anime, JP)*

*Ultraman Tiga & Ultraman Dyna: Warriors of the Star
of Light (Urutoraman Tiga & Urutoraman Daina: Hikari
no Hoshi no Senshi-tachi, 1998, JP)*

*Ultraman Tiga & Ultraman Dyna & Ultraman Gaia:
Battle in Hyperspace (Urutoraman Tiga, Urutoraman
Daina & Urutoraman Gaia Chō Jikū no Daisakusen,
1999, JP)*

*Ultraman Tiga: The Final Odyssey (Urutoraman Tiga Za
Fainaru Odesei, 2000, JP)*

*Ultraman Cosmos: The First Contact (Urutoraman
Kosumosu: Za Fāsuto Kontakuto, 2001, JP)*

*Ultraman Cosmos 2: The Blue Planet (Urutoraman
Kosumosu Tsū: Za Burū Puranetto, 2002, JP)*

*Ultraman Cosmos vs. Ultraman Justice: The Final
Battle (Urutoraman Kosumosu Vs Urutoraman Jasutisu
Za Fainaru Batoru, 2003, JP)*

ULTRAMAN (URUTORAMAN, 2004, JP)

*Ultraman Mebius & The Ultra Brothers (Urutoraman
Mebiusu ando Urutora Kyōdai, 2006, JP)*

*Superior Ultraman 8 Brothers (Daikessen! Chō Urutora
Hachi Kyōdai, 2008, JP)*

*Mega Monster Battle: Ultra Galaxy Legends The Movie
(Daikaijū Batoru: Urutora Ginga Densetsu Za Mūbī,
2009, JP)*

*Ultraman Zero The Movie: Super Deciding Fight! The
Belial Galactic Empire (Urutoraman Zero THE MOVIE:
Chōkessen! Beriaru Ginga Teikoku, 2010, JP)*

Ultraman Saga (Urutoraman Sāga, 2012, JP)

*Ultraman Ginga S Movie Showdown! The 10 Ultra
Warriors! (Gekijōban Urutoraman Ginga S Kessen!
Urutora 10 Yūshi!, 2015, JP)*

*Ultraman X The Movie: Here Comes! Our Ultraman
(Gekijōban Urutoraman Ōbu Kizuna no chikara,
okarishimasu!, 2016, JP)*

*Ultraman Orb The Movie: Lend Me The Power of
Bonds! (Gekijōban Urutoraman Ōbu Kizuna no chikara,
okarishimasu!, 2017, JP)*

*Ultraman Geed The Movie: Connect The Wishes!
(Gekijōban Urutoraman Jīdo Tsunagu Negai, 2018, JP)*

alter ego
A character's superhero persona.

anting-anting (aka agimat movies)
A subgenre of Filipino cinema in which superpowers are derived from magical amulets.

cut-and-shut
The practice of editing multiple episodes of a TV series into one feature-length movie.

DCAU
DC Animated Universe; a related series of animated movies based on DC characters.

DCEU
DC Extended Universe; a related series of live-action movies based on DC characters.

direct-to-video
A (usually lower budget) movie made for home consumption.

fumetti neri
Literally 'black comics'. European subgenre in which the hero is of questionable virtue.

henshin hero
A Japanese superhero who transforms via a series of verbal commands and gestures.

kaiju
A giant monster in Japanese pop culture.

kyodai hero
A Japanese superhero whose primary power is the ability to grow to enormous size.

luchador
A (usually Mexican) 'lucha libre' wrestler who (in this context) moonlights as a superhero.

MacGuffin
An object or piece of information sought by characters as a means of driving the plot.

MCU
Marvel Cinematic Universe; a related series of movies based on Marvel characters.

mockbuster
A low-budget imitation of a particular blockbuster.

origin story
The part of the narrative dealing with how the protagonist came to be.

OVA
Original Video Animation; a Japanese animation made for home video.

shōjo
Manga (and in practice other Japanese media) aimed at teenage girls.

shōnen
Manga (and in practice other Japanese media) aimed at teenage boys.

silat story (aka cersil)
An Indonesian fantasy martial arts movie (in this context).

suitmation
The technique of filming actors (usually in kaiju costumes) on miniature sets in order to achieve a sense of enormous scale.

supermarionation
A technique utilising puppets/marionettes and miniatures.

tokusatsu
A Japanese special effects driven live-action TV show or movie.

Turksploitation
Low-budget and usually unlicensed Turkish adaptations of popular foreign movies.

NOT AN INDEX

A complete list of every superhero movie covered or cited in this book, including as many alternate titles as seem sensible. Movies followed by bracketed information, e.g. '[GF/Peplum]', belong to a Grouped Franchise (in this case the section dealing with peplum movies) and do not have individual entries. Those not followed by bracketed information can be found in the main section.

American Rescue Squad, 2015, USA
Americano, 2016, USA/MEX
An Unearthly Child, 1963, UK [GF/Dr Who]
Anak ng kidlat, 1959, PH
Android Invasion, The, 1975, UK [GF/Dr Who]
Androids of Tara, The, 1978, UK [GF/Dr Who]
Ángel del silencio, 1979, MEX [GF/Luchadors]
Angel Wars: The Messengers, 2009, USA
Anonymous Death Threat, 1972, MEX [GF/Luchadors]
Another WolfCop, 2017, Canada
Ant-Man and the Wasp, 2018, USA
Ant-Man, 2015, USA
Antboy, 2013, Denmark
Antboy 3, 2016, Denmark
Antboy: Den Røde Furies hævn: see Antboy: Revenge of Red Fury
Antboy: Revenge of the Red Fury, 2014, Denmark
Anthar l'invincibile, 1964, ITL [GF/Peplum]
Aquaman, 2018, USA
Arahan, 2004, South Korea
Arañas infernales, 1968, MEX [GF/Luchadors]
Arc of Infinity, 1983, UK [GF/Dr Who]
Argoman the Fantastic Superman, 1967, ITL
Ark, The, 1966, UK [GF/Dr Who]
Ark in Space, The, 1975, UK [GF/Dr Who]
Armageddon Factor, The, 1979, UK [GF/Dr Who]
Armstrong, 2017, USA
Arriva Dorellik, 1967, ITL [GF/Diabolik S-Ks]
asesino invisible, El, 1965, MEX [GF/Luchadors]
Asesinos de la lucha libre, 1962, MEX [GF/Luchadors]
Asesinos de la lucha libre, 1962, MEX [GF/Luchadors]
asesinos del karate, Los, 1965, MEX [GF/Luchadors]
Ashes of CHIKARA, The, 2014, USA
Asterix (SERIES) [GF/Asterix]
Asterix and Caesar, 1985, FR [GF/Asterix]
Asterix and Cleopatra, 1968, FR [GF/Asterix]
Asterix and Obelix Meet Cleopatra, 2002, FR [GF/Asterix]
Asterix and Obelix Meet Cleopatra, 2002, FR [GF/Asterix]
Asterix and Obelix vs. Caesar, 1999, FR [GF/Asterix]
Astérix and Obélix: God Save Britannia, 2012, FR [GF/Asterix]
Asterix and Obelix: Mansion of the Gods, 2014, FR [GF/Asterix]
Asterix and the Big Fight, 1989, FR [GF/Asterix]
Asterix and the Vikings, 2006, FR [GF/Asterix]
Asterix at the Olympic Games, 2008, FR [GF/Asterix]
Asterix in America, 1994, FR [GF/Asterix]
Asterix in Britain, 1986, FR [GF/Asterix]
Asterix the Gaul, 1967, FR [GF/Asterix]
Asterix: The Secret of the Magic Potion, 2018, FR [GF/Asterix]
Astro Boy, 1962, JAP
Astro Boy, 1964, JAP
Astro Boy, 2009, HK/USA/JAP
Athisayan, 2007, IN
Atlas Against The Czar, 1964, ITL [GF/Peplum]

Atlas in the Land of the Cyclops, 1961, ITL [GF/Peplum]
Atlas, 1961, USA
Atom Man vs. Superman, 1950, USA
Atom Nine Adventures, 2007, USA
Atomic Blue Mexican Wrestler, 1999, USA [GF/Luchadors]
Atomic Rulers, 1965, JAP
Attack from Space, 1965, JAP
Attack of the Flying Saucers: see Atomic Rulers
Attack of the Super Monsters, 1982, JAP
August in the Water, 1995, JAP
Autâman: see Outer Man
autómatas de la muerte, Los, 1962, MEX [GF/Luchadors]
Avenger X, 1967, ITL/ES
Avengers Assemble: see The Avengers
Avengers Confidential: Black Widow & Punisher, 2014, USA
Avengers Grimm, 2015, USA
Avengers Grimm: Time Wars, 2018, USA
Avengers of Justice: Farce Wars, 2018, USA
Avengers, 2012, USA
Avengers: Age of Ultron, 2015, USA
Avengers: Infinity War, 2018, USA
Avenging Force: The Scarab, 2010, Canada
Avenging Shadow, The, 1956, MEX [GF/Luchadors]
Avenging Shadow vs. The Black Hand, 1956, MEX [GF/Luchadors]
Awara Abdulla, 1963, IN
Aztec Revenge, 2015, USA [GF/Luchadors]
Aztecs, The, 1964, UK [GF/Dr Who]
B-Robo Kabutack... 1998, JAP [GF/Metal Hero Series]
babaeng isputnik Ang babaeng Isputnik, 1963, PH
Babaing kidlat, 1964, PH
Baffled Detective vs Kilink, 1967, Turkey [GF/Diabolik S-Ks]
Baji, 2015, IN
Bajrang Bali, 1956, IN
Bajrangbali, 1976, IN
Bak bin sing gwan: see Sixty Million Dollar Man
Bakas ng gagamba, 1962, PH [GF/Gagamba]
Bangla RoboCop: see Shoktir Lorai
Bangla Superman: see Superman (year unknown, Bengal)
Barb Wire, 1996, USA
Barbie in Princess Power, 2015, USA
Baron Brakola, 1965 or 1967, MEX [GF/Luchadors]
Bat-man contra los...: see Black Star and the Golden Bat
Batman & Mr. Freeze: SubZero, 1998, USA
Batman & Robin, 1997, USA
Batman and Harley Quinn, 2017, USA
Batman and Robin, 1949, USA
Batman Begins, 2005, USA
Batman Beyond: Return of the Joker, 2000, USA
Batman Beyond: The Movie, 1999, USA
Batman Dracula, 1964, USA
Batman Fights Dracula, 1967, PH
Batman Forever, 1995, USA

Batman Ninja, 2018, USA

Batman Returns, 1992, USA

Batman Superman Movie: World's Finest, The, 1997, USA

Batman Unlimited: Animal Instincts, 2015, USA

Batman Unlimited: Mechs vs. Mutants, 2016, USA

Batman Unlimited: Monster Mayhem, 2015, USA

Batman v Superman: Dawn of Justice, 2016, USA

Batman vs Dracula, The, 2005, USA

Batman vs. Robin, 2015, USA

Batman vs. Teenage Mutant Ninja Turtles, 2019, USA

Batman vs. Two-Face, 2017, USA

Batman, 1943, USA

Batman, 1989, USA

Batman: Assault on Arkham, 2014, USA

Batman: Bad Blood, 2016, USA

Batman: Gotham by Gaslight, 2018, USA

Batman: Gotham Knight, 2008, USA

Batman: Mask of the Phantasm, 1993, USA

Batman: Mystery of the Batwoman, 2003, USA

Batman: Return of the Caped Crusaders, 2016, USA

Batman: The Dark Knight Returns, 2012, USA

Batman: The Killing Joke, 2016, USA

Batman: The Movie, 1966, USA

Batman: Under the Red Hood, 2010, USA

Batman: Year One, 2011, USA

BATMoN vs MAJURo, 2016, Marshall Islands

Battle of the Planets: The Movie, 2002, USA/JAP

Battlefield, 1989, UK [GF/Dr Who]

Batwoman, The, 1968, MEX

Batwoman & Robin Meet the Queen of the Vampires, 1972, PH

Batwoman and Robin, 1972, PH

Bay Kilink Istanbul'da, 2011, Turkey [GF/Diabolik S-Ks]

Beastmaster, The, 1982, USA/Germany

Beastmaster 2: Through the Portal of Time, 1991, USA/FR

Beastmaster III: The Eye of Braxus, 1996, USA

Beasts of Terror, The, 1972, MEX [GF/Luchadors]

Beginning of the End, 2009, USA [GF/Wolverine and the X-Men]

Behind the Mask of Zorro, 1965, ES/ITL

Behind the Mask, 1946, USA

Behold the Raven, 2004, USA

Ben 10: Alien Swarm, 2009, USA

Ben 10: Destroy All Aliens, 2012, USA

Ben 10: Race Against Time, 2007, USA

Ben 10: Secret of the Omnitrix, 2007, USA

Bermuda Mystery, The, 1977, MEX [GF/Luchadors]

Bertong Ipu-Ipo, 1969, PH

Beyond the Curtain of Space, 1954, USA, [GF/Rocky Jones]

Beyond the Moon, 1954, USA, [GF/Rocky Jones]

Bhavesh Joshi Superhero, 2018, IN

Bī Robo Kabutakku... 1998, JAP [GF/Metal Hero Series]

Bianong Bulag, 1977, PH

Big Hero 6, 2014, USA

Big Man JAP, 2007, JAP

Bikuu: The Movie, 2015, JAP [GF/Garo]

Bikuu: The Movie, 2015, JAP [GF/Garo]

Binibining Tsuper-Man, 1987, PH

Biokids, 1990, PH

Bionic Boy, The, 1977, PH

Bionic Boy II The Return of the Bionic Boy, 1979, HK/PH

Bionic Ever After?, 1994, USA

Bionic Showdown: The Six Million Dollar Man &... 1989, USA

Bira! Darna! Bira!, 1979, PH [GF/Darna]

Bishôjo senshi Sêrâ Mûn... 1995, JAP, [GF/Sailor Moon]

Black Cougar, 2002, USA

Black Knight Returns, The, 2009, USA

Black Lightning, 2009, Russia

Black Mask 2: City of Masks, 2002, HK/USA

Black Mask, 1996, HK

Black Ninja, 2003, USA

Black Panther, 2018, USA

Black Scorpion, 1995, USA

Black Scorpion II: Aftershock, 1996, USA

Black Scorpion Returns, 2001, USA

Black Scorpion: Sting of the Black Scorpion, 2002, USA

Black Star and the Golden Bat, 1979, South Korea

Blackbelt Avengers, 1969, PH

Blade, 1998, USA

Blade II, 2002, USA

Blade of the Phantom Master, 2004, JAP

Blade: The Series (pilot), 2007, USA

Blade: Trinity, 2004, USA

Blankman, 1994, USA

Blast-Off, 1954, USA, [GF/Rocky Jones]

Blind Fury, 1989, USA

Blood: The Last Vampire, 2009, HK

BloodRayne, 2005, USA

BloodRayne: Deliverance, 2007, USA

BloodRayne: The Third Reich, 2011, USA

Bloody Mallory, 2002, FR

Blubberella, 2011, Germany

Blue Demon contra cerebros... 1968, MEX [GF/Luchadors]

Blue Demon contra las diabólicas, 1968, MEX [GF/Luchadors]

Blue Demon destructor de espias, 1968, MEX [GF/Luchadors]

Blue Demon vs. el poder satánico, 1966, MEX [GF/Luchadors]

Blue Demon vs. The Diabolical... 1968, MEX [GF/Luchadors]

Blue Demon vs. the Satanic Power, 1966, MEX [GF/Luchadors]

Blue Demon y las invasoras, 1969, MEX [GF/Luchadors]

Blue Demon, 1965, MEX [GF/Luchadors]

Blue Demon: Destructor of Spies, 1968, MEX [GF/Luchadors]

Blue Demon: El Demonio Azul, 1965, MEX [GF/Luchadors]

Blue SWAT, 1994, JAP [GF/Metal Hero Series]

Bobby's Comet, 1954, USA, [GF/Rocky Jones]

BoBoiBoy: The Movie, 2016, Malaysia

Body Snatcher, The, 1957, MEX [GF/Luchadors]

Boku no Hero Academia: see My Hero Academia: Two Heroes
Bold Caballero, The, 1936, USA
Bomb Squad, 2011, USA
Border of Terror, The, 1979, MEX [GF/Luchadors]
Boy putik, 1979, PH
Boy Wonder, 2010, USA
Brain of Morbius, The, 1976, UK [GF/Dr Who]
Bratz: Super Babyz, 2007, USA
BraveStarr: The Legend, 1988, USA
Bride of the Incredible Hulk, 1978, USA
Brijes 3D: see Guardians of the Lost Code 3D
Brittle Glory, 1997, USA
Bruce Lee Against Superman, 1975, HK
Buck Rogers in the 25th Century, 1979, USA
Buck Rogers, 1939, USA
Buck Rogers, 1977, USA
buena suerte, El, 1961, MEX [GF/Luchadors]
Buffy the Vampire Slayer, 1992, USA
Buffy the Vampire Slayer: Welcome to Hellmouth, 1996, USA
Bulletproof Monk, 2003, USA
Bunny Whipped, 2007, USA
Burû suwatto, 1994, JAP [GF/Metal Hero Series]
Cada quién su lucha, 1966, MEX [GF/Luchadors]
campeones justicieros, Los 1971, MEX [GF/Luchadors]
canallas, Los, 1968, MEX [GF/Luchadors]
Cango - korkusuz adam, 1967, Turkey [GF/Diabolik S-Ks]
Cannibal Attack, 1955, USA, [GF/Jungle Jim]
Capitan Basilico 2 - I Fantastici 4+4, 2011, ITL
Capitan Basilico, 2008, ITL
Captain America, 1944, USA
Captain America, 1979, USA
Captain America, 1990, USA
Captain America II: Death Too Soon, 1979, USA
Captain America: Civil War, 2016, USA
Captain America: The First Avenger, 2011, USA
Captain America: The Winter Soldier, 2014, USA
Captain Barbell (SERIES) [GF]
Captain Barbell (Boom!), 1973, PH [GF/Captain Barbell]
Captain Barbell kontra... 1965, PH [GF/Captain Barbell]
Captain Barbell, 1964, PH [GF/Captain Barbell]
Captain Barbell, 1986, PH [GF/Captain Barbell]
Captain Barbell, 2003, PH [GF/Captain Barbell]
Captain Battle: Legacy War, 2013, USA
Captain Berlin versus Hitler, 2009, Germany
Captain Eager and the Mark of Voth, 2008, USA
Captain Karate: Katulong Ng Batas, 1965, PH
Captain Pinoy at Boy Pinoy, 1965, PH [GF/Captain Barbell]
Captain Underpants: The First Epic Movie, 2017, USA
Captain Video, Master of the Stratosphere, 1951, USA
Captain Z & the Terror of Leviathan, 2014, USA
Captive Girl, 1950, USA, [GF/Jungle Jim]
Capulina the Detective, 1975, MEX [GF/Luchadors]

Carnival of Monsters, 1973, UK [GF/Dr Who]
Casshern, 2004, JAP
castillo de las momias... El, 1973, MEX [GF/Luchadors]
Castrovalva, 1982, UK [GF/Dr Who]
Casus Kiran: see Spy Smasher
Catalina: A New Kind of Superhero, 2009, UK
Catman in Boxer's Blow, 1993, HK
Catman in Lethal Track, 1990, HK
Catwoman, 2004, USA
Caves of Androzani, The, 1984, UK [GF/Dr Who]
Cazadores de espías, 1969, MEX [GF/Luchadors]
Celestial Toymaker, The, 1966, UK [GF/Dr Who]
Chakra: The Invincible (SERIES) [GF]
Chakra the Invincible, 2013, IN, [GF/Chakra]
Chakra the Invincible: The Revenge... 2017, IN, [GF/Chakra]
Chakra the Invincible: The Rise... 2016, IN, [GF/Chakra]
Chameleons, 1989, USA
Champions Five Supermen, The, 1972, MEX [GF/Luchadors]
Champions of Justice, The, 1971, MEX [GF/Luchadors]
Chandu on the Magic Island, 1935, USA
Chandu the Magician, 1932, USA
Chanoc y el hijo del Santo contra... 1981, MEX [GF/Luchadors]
Chao Insee, 1963, Thailand [GF/The Red Eagle]
Chao Nakleng, 1959, Thailand [GF/The Red Eagle]
Chase, The, 1965, UK [GF/Dr Who]
Che fanno i nostri super... 1970, ITL, [GF/Three Supermen]
Cheng fung hap: see Dragon and the Green Hornet
Chinese Superman: see Infra-Man
Cho Kamen Rider Den-O... 2009, JAP [GF/Kamen Rider]
Chōhen Kaijū Eiga Urutoraman, 1967, JAP [GF/Ultraman]
Chôjin Locke: see Locke the Superman
Chōjinki Metarudā, 1987, JAP [GF/Metal Hero Series]
Chosen One The Chosen One: Legend of the Raven, 1998, USA
Choushinsei Flashman... 1987, JAP [GF/Super Sentai]
Christmas Invasion, 2005, UK [GF/Dr Who]
Chronicle, 2012, USA
Cicak-man, 2006, Malaysia
Cicak-Man 2: Planet Hitam, 2008, Malaysia
Cicak Man 3, 2015, Malaysia
ciclón de Jalisco, El, 1964, MEX [GF/Luchadors]
Çilgin kiz ve üç süper... 1973, Turkey, [GF/Three Supermen]
Citizen Toxie: The Toxic Avenger IV, 2000, USA
City of Death, 1979, UK [GF/Dr Who]
Claws of Axos, The, 1971, UK [GF/Dr Who]
Clutching Hand, The, 1966, MEX [GF/Luchadors]
Code Name: Dynastud, 2018, USA
Cold Sun, The, 1954, USA, [GF/Rocky Jones]
Colony in Space, 1971, UK [GF/Dr Who]
Colossus (Italian SERIES) [GF/Peplum]
Colossus and the Headhunters, 1962, ITL [GF/Peplum]
Colossus of the Arena , 1962, ITL [GF/Peplum]
Come rubare la corona...: see Argoman the Fantastic Superman

Comic Book: The Movie, 2004, USA

Commando Cody: Sky Marshal of the Universe, 1953, USA

Computer Superman, 1977, Thailand

Conan the Barbarian, 1982, USA

Conan the Barbarian, 2011, USA

Conan the Destroyer, 1984, USA

Conan: The Heart of the Elephant, 1997, USA

Condor The Condor, 2007, USA

Condorman, 1981, USA

Conquest of Mycene, 1963, ITL [GF/Peplum]

Constantine City of Demons: The Movie, 2018, USA

Constantine, 2005, USA

Cornman: American Vegetable Hero, 2001, USA

correo del norte, El, 1960, MEX [GF/Luchadors]

Cosplay Fetish Battle Drones, 2013, USA

Coyote, El, (SERIES) [GF]

Coyote's Justice, The, 1956, ES/MEX [GF/The Coyote]

Crash of Moons, 1954, USA, [GF/Rocky Jones]

Crash! Che botte, 1973, ITL/HK, [GF/Three Supermen]

Creature from the Pit, The, 1979, UK [GF/Dr Who]

Crimson Bat (SERIES) [GF]

Cross Wars, 2017, USA

Cross, 2011, USA

Crow, The, 1994, USA

Crow: City of Angels, The, 1996, USA

Crow: Salvation, The, 2000, USA

Crow: Wicked Prayer, The, 2005, USA

Crusade, The, 1965, UK [GF/Dr Who]

Cucuo's Big Adventure: see Americano

Curse of Fenric, The, 1989, UK [GF/Dr Who]

Curse of Peladon, The, 1972, UK [GF/Dr Who]

Curse of the Aztec Mummy, The, 1957, MEX [GF/Luchadors]

Cutie Honey: Live Action, 2004, JAP

Cutie Honey: Tears, 2016, JAP

Cyber Desesperado: see 8 Man After

Cyber-C.H.I.C., 1990, USA

Dæmons, The, 1971, UK [GF/Dr Who]

Dai-Nihonjin: see Big Man JAP

Daikaijū Batoru: Urutora... 2009, JAP [GF/Ultraman]

Daikessen! Chō Urutora Hachi Kyōdai, 2008, JAP [GF/Ultraman]

Dalek Invasion of Earth, The, 1964, UK [GF/Dr Who]

Daleks, The, 1963, UK [GF/Dr Who]

Daleks' Invasion Earth 2150 A.D., 1966, UK

Daleks' Master Plan, The, 1965, UK [GF/Dr Who]

Danger: Diabolik, 1968, ITL [GF/Diabolik S-Ks]

Daredevil vs. Spider-Man, 2003, USA, [GF/Spider-Man: TAS]

Daredevil, 2003, USA

Dark Avenger, 1990, USA

Dark Knight, The, 2008, USA

Dark Knight Rises, The, 2012, USA

Dark Water/Death in Heaven, 2014, UK [GF/Dr Who]

Darkest Minds, The, 2018, USA

Darkman, 1990, USA

Darkman II: The Return of Durant, 1995, USA

Darkman III: Die Darkman Die, 1996, USA

Darna (SERIES) [GF]

Darna ajaib, 1980, ID [GF/Darna]

Darna and the Giants, 1973, PH [GF/Darna]

Darna at ang Babaeng Lawin, 1952, PH [GF/Darna]

Darna at ang Babaing Tuod, 1965, PH [GF/Darna]

Darna at Ding, 1980, PH [GF/Darna]

Darna vs. the Planet Women, 1975, PH [GF/Darna]

Darna, 1951, PH [GF/Darna]

Darna, 1991, PH [GF/Darna]

Darna, 2019, PH [GF/Darna]

Darna, Kuno...?, 1979, PH [GF/Darna]

Darna! Ang pagbabalik, 1994, PH [GF/Darna]

Daughter of Tarzan, 2002, IN, [GF/Tarzan]

Day of the Daleks, 1972, UK [GF/Dr Who]

Day of the Doctor, 2013, UK [GF/Dr Who]

DC Superhero Girls (SERIES) [GF]

DC S.H.G.: Hero of the Year, 2016, USA [GF/DC S.H.G.]

DC S.H.G.: Intergalactic Games, 2017, USA [GF/DC S.H.G.]

DC S.H.G.: Legends of Atlantis, 2018, USA [GF/DC S.H.G.]

De sangre chicana, 1974, MEX [GF/Luchadors]

De tøffeste gutta: see The Tough Guys

Dead One, The, 2007, USA

Deadly Assassin, The, 1976, UK [GF/Dr Who]

Deadly Enemies, 2009, USA [GF/Wolverine and the X-Men]

Deadly Ray from Mars, 1966, USA

Deadpool, 2016, USA

Deadpool 2, 2018, USA

Deadwood Dick, 1940, USA

Death Note, 2006, JAP

Death Note, 2017, USA

Death Note: Light Up the New World, 2016, JAP

Death Note: The Last Name, 2006, JAP

Death of Superman, The, 2018, USA

Death of the Incredible Hulk, The, 1990, USA

Death to the Daleks, 1974, UK [GF/Dr Who]

Deathless Devil, The, 1973, Turkey

Deathless Man: see Deathless Devil

Deep Breath, 2014, UK [GF/Dr Who]

Defendor, 2009, USA

Delta And the Bannermen, 1987, UK [GF/Dr Who]

Demir Yumruk...: see Iron Fist: The Giants Are Coming

Democrazy, 2005, USA

Demolition Man, 1993, USA

Demolitionist, The, 1995, USA

Denjin Zabôgâ: see Karate-Robo Zaborgar

Descendant of the Sun, 1983, HK

Destination Saturn, 1966, USA

Eiga HapinesuChāji Purikyua!... 2014, JAP [GF/PreCure]

Eiga HātoKyatchi Purikyua! Hana... 2010, JAP [GF/PreCure]

Eiga Iesu! Purikyua Faibu GōGō!... 2008, JAP [GF/PreCure]

Eiga Iesu! Purikyua Faibu: Kagami... 2007, JAP [GF/PreCure]

Eiga Kirakira * Purikyua... 2017, JAP [GF/PreCure]

Eiga Mahōtsukai Purikyua!: Kiseki... 2015, JAP [GF/PreCure]

Eiga Purikyua Dorīmu Sutāzu!, 2017, JAP [GF/PreCure]

Eiga Purikyua Ōru Sutāzu Nyū... 2014, JAP [GF/PreCure]

Eiga Purikyua Ōru Sutāzu: Haru... 2015, JAP [GF/PreCure]

Eiga Purikyua Ōru Sutāzu: Minna... 2016, JAP [GF/PreCure]

Eiga Purikyua Sūpā Sutāzu!, 2018, JAP [GF/PreCure]

Eiga Suīto Purikyua... 2011, JAP [GF/PreCure]

Eiga Sumairu Purikyua!: Ehon... 2012, JAP [GF/PreCure]

Eiga: minna! Esupâ da yo!: see Everyone is Psychic

Eight Man (1992), 1992, JAP

Eight Man After, 1993, JAP

Eight Ranger 2, 2014, JAP

Eight Rangers, The, 2012, JAP

Eight Riders vs. Gingaoh, 1980, JAP [GF/Kamen Rider]

Eito renjâ 2: see Eight Ranger 2

Eito renjâ: see The Eight Rangers

Eitoman - Subete no sabishii yoru no tame ni : see Eight Man

Electra, 1996, USA

Electra Woman and Dyna Girl, 2016, USA

Electrika kasi, eh!, 1977, PH

Elektra, 2005, USA

Eleventh Hour, 2010, UK [GF/Dr Who]

Elf-Man, 2012, USA

Elias Paniki: see The Mysterious World of Elias Paniki

End of Time, 2009, UK [GF/Dr Who]

Enemy of the World, The, 1967, UK [GF/Dr Who]

Enigma de muerte, 1969, MEX [GF/Luchadors]

Enlightenment, 1983, UK [GF/Dr Who]

enmascarado de plata, El, 1954, MEX [GF/Luchadors]

Enteng Kabisote 10 and the Abangers, 2016, PH

Episōdo Burū Haken Imajin... 2010, JAP [GF/Kamen Rider]

Episōdo Ierō Otakara... 2010, JAP [GF/Kamen Rider]

Episōdo Reddo Zero... 2010, JAP [GF/Kamen Rider]

Ercole al centro della Terra, 1961, ITL [GF/Peplum]

Ercole alla conquista di Atlantide, 1961, ITL [GF/Peplum]

Ercole contro i tiranni di Babilonia, 1964, ITL [GF/Peplum]

Ercole contro Moloch, 1963, ITL [GF/Peplum]

Ercole contro Roma, 1964, ITL [GF/Peplum]

Ercole e la regina di Lidia, 1959, ITL [GF/Peplum]

Ercole l'invincibile, 1964, ITL [GF/Peplum]

Ercole sfida Sansone, 1963, ITL [GF/Peplum]

Ercole, Sansone, Maciste e Ursus... 1964, ITL [GF/Peplum]

Escape Into Space, 1954, USA, [GF/Rocky Jones]

Everyone Is Psychic!, the Movie, 2015, JAP

Evil Brain from Outer Space, 1965, JAP

Evil of the Daleks, The, 1967, UK, incomplete [GF/Dr Who]

Executioners: see Heroic Trio 2: Executioners

Exo-Man, 1977, USA

Extranghero, 1997, PH

Face of Evil, The, 1977, UK [GF/Dr Who]

Faceless Ones, The, 1967, UK, incomplete [GF/Dr Who]

Fantabulous Inc., 1967, ITL

Fantasma vs. aldea de los zombies, 2007, MEX [GF/Luchadors]

Fantastic 4: Rise of the Silver Surfer, 2007, USA

Fantastic Four The Fantastic Four, 1994, USA

Fantastic Four, 2005, USA

Fantastic Four, 2015, USA

Fantastic Man, 2003, PH

fantastici 3 $upermen, I, 1967, ITL, [GF/Three Supermen]

Fantoma Istanbul'da bulusalim, 1967, Turkey [GF/Fantômas]

Fantômas (French SERIES) [GF]

Fantômas - l'ombre de la guillotine, 1913, FR [GF/Fantômas]

Fantomas Against Fantomas, 1949, FR [GF/Fantômas]

Fantômas contre Fantômas, 1914, FR [GF/Fantômas]

Fantômas contre Fantômas, 1949, FR [GF/Fantômas]

Fantômas contre Scotland Yard, 1967, FR [GF/Fantômas]

Fantômas se déchaîne, 1965, FR [GF/Fantômas]

Fantomas Unleashed, 1965, FR [GF/Fantômas]

Fantomas vs. Scotland Yard, 1967, FR [GF/Fantômas]

Fantomas, 1920, FR [GF/Fantômas]

Fantômas, 1932, FR [GF/Fantômas]

Fantômas, 1947, FR [GF/Fantômas]

Fantômas, 1964, FR [GF/Fantômas]

Fantômas: Appointment in Ist... 1967, Turkey [GF/Fantômas]

Fantômas: In the Shadow of the... 1913, FR [GF/Fantômas]

Fantômas: Juve versus Fantômas, 1913, FR [GF/Fantômas]

Fantômas: The Dead Man Who Killed, 1913, FR [GF/Fantômas]

Fantômas: The False Magistrate, 1914, FR [GF/Fantômas]

Fantomas: Mysterious Finger Print, 1914, FR [GF/Fantômas]

Farewell, Masked Rider... 2008, JAP [GF/Kamen Rider]

Fate of the Future, 2010, USA [GF/Wolverine and the X-Men]

fatiche di Ercole, Le,1958, ITL [GF/Peplum]

Faust (2000), 2000, ES

faux magistrat, Le 1914, FR [GF/Fantômas]

Fearless Frank, 1967, USA

Fehérlófia: see Son of the White Mare

Fei Ying: see Silver Hawk

Female Kilink, 1967, Turkey [GF/Diabolik S-Ks]

Fenomenal and the Treasure of Tutankamen, 1968, ITL

Fight, Zatoichi, Fight, 1964, JAP [GF/Zatōichi]

Fight! Batman, Fight!, 1973, PH

figlio di Zorro, Il, 1973, ITL [GF/Peplum]

Final Crisis Trilogy, 2010, USA [GF/Wolverine and the X-Men]

Fire Monsters Against Son of Hercules, 1962, ITL [GF/Peplum]

Firebreather, 2010, USA

Firestarter, 1984, USA

Fist of Death, The, 1982, MEX [GF/Luchadors]

Fist of the North Star, 1986, JAP

Fist of the North Star, 1995, USA

Fist of the North Star: New Saviour Legend, 2006, JAP [GF/FotNS]
Fist of the North Star: The Kaioh Saga, 2011 [GF/FotNS]
Fist of the North Star: The Raul Saga, 2011 [GF/FotNS]
Fist of the North Star: The Ray Saga, 2011 [GF/FotNS]
Fist of the North Star: The Shin Saga, 2009 [GF/FotNS]
Fist of the North Star: The Souther Saga, 2011 [GF/FotNS]
Fist of the North Star: The Toki Saga, 2011 [GF/FotNS]
Five Doctors, The, 1983, UK [GF/Dr Who]
Flash, The, 1990, USA
Flash II: Revenge of the Trickster, The, 1991, USA
Flash III: Deadly Nightshade, 1991, USA
Flash Gordon Conquers the Universe, 1940, USA
Flash Gordon, 1936, USA
Flash Gordon, 1980, USA
Flash Gordon: The Greatest Adventure of All, 1982, USA
Flash Gordon's Battle in Space, 1967, Turkey
Flash Gordon's Trip to Mars, 1938, USA
Flashman, 1967, ITL
Fly Me to the Moon, 1988, PH
Flying Jatt A Flying Jatt, 2016, IN
Flying Mr. B, The, 1985, HK
Forbidden Moon, The, 1954, USA, [GF/Rocky Jones]
Forgotten Warriors, 1998, USA, [GF/Spider-Man: TAS]
Four To Doomsday, 1982, UK [GF/Dr Who]
Franklyn, 2008, UK
Fresh Pretty Cure! the Movie... 2009, JAP [GF/PreCure]
Frontier in Space, 1973, UK [GF/Dr Who]
Frontios, 1984, UK [GF/Dr Who]
Frozen, 2013, USA
Full Circle, 1980, UK [GF/Dr Who]
Full Eclipse, 1993, USA
Full Metal gokudô: see Full Metal Yakuza
Full Metal Yakuza, 1997, JAP
Fullmetal Alc. the Movie: Conqueror of Shamballa, 2005, JAP
Fullmetal Alchemist, 2017, JAP
Fullmetal Alchemist: The Sacred Star of Milos, 2011, JAP
furia del ring, La, 1961, MEX [GF/Luchadors]
furia di Ercole, La, 1962, ITL [GF/Peplum]
Furias desatadas, 1957, MEX [GF/Luchadors]
Fury from the Deep, 1968, UK, considered lost [GF/Dr Who]
Fury of Hercules, The, 1962, ITL [GF/Peplum]
Fury of the Congo, 1951, USA, [GF/Jungle Jim]
Fury of the Dragon, 1976, USA
Fury of the Karate Experts, The, 1982, MEX [GF/Luchadors]
Futari wa PC Max Heart the Movie 2... 2005, JAP [GF/PreCure]
Futari wa PC Max Heart the Movie, 2005, JAP [GF/PreCure]
Futari wa PC Splash Star... 2006, JAP [GF/PreCure]
G.I. Joe: The Movie, 1986, USA [GF/G.I. Joe]
G.I. Joe - Valor Vs. Venom, 2004, USA [GF/G.I. Joe]
G.I. Joe: Sigma Six - First Strike, 2006, USA [GF/G.I. Joe]
G.I. Joe: The Rise of Cobra, 2009, USA [GF/G.I. Joe]
G.I. Joe: Retaliation, 2013, USA [GF/G.I. Joe]

Gacchaman: see Gatchaman
Gadis bionik, 1982, ID
Gagamba (SERIES) [GF]
Gagamba at si Scorpio, 1969, PH [GF/Gagamba]
Gagamboy, 2004, PH
Galaxy 4, 1965, UK [GF/Dr Who]
Gandarrapiddo! The Revenger Squad, 2017, PH
Gangster, The, 1959, Thailand [GF/The Red Eagle]
Gangster Lord, 1959, Thailand [GF/The Red Eagle]
Garo (SERIES) [GF]
Garo ~Sōkoku no Maryū~, 2013, JAP [GF/Garo]
Garo Kami no Kiba, 2017, JAP [GF/Garo]
Garo Special: Beast of the Demon Night, 2006, JAP [GF/Garo]
GARO Supesharu Byakuya no Majū, 2006, JAP [GF/Garo]
Garo: Gold Storm Sho, 2015, JAP [GF/Garo]
Garo: Gold Storm Sho, 2015, JAP [GF/Garo]
Garo: Kami no Kiba, 2017, JAP [GF/Garo]
Garo: Red Requiem, 2010, JAP [GF/Garo]
Garo: Soukoku no Maryu, 2013, JAP [GF/Garo]
Garuda Superhero, 2015, ID
Gatchaman The Movie, 1978, JAP
Gatchaman, 2013, JAP
gato salvaje, El, 2008, MEX [GF/Luchadors]
Gegege no Kitarô: see Kitaro
geheim van Mega Mindy, Het, 2009, BE [GF/Mega Mindy]
Gekijô ban Chô Kamen raidâ den'ô... 2009, JAP [GF/Kamen
Rider]
Gekijô-ban - Bishôjo senshi... 1993, JAP, [GF/Sailor Moon]
Gekijô-ban hagane no... see Fullmetal Alchemist the Movie
Gekijōban Kamen R × K. Raidā... 2010, JAP [GF/Kamen Rider]
Gekijōban Kamen R Birudo Bī... 2018, JAP [GF/Kamen Rider]
Gekijōban Kamen R Den'ō Ando... 2008, JAP [GF/Kamen Rider]
Gekijōban Kamen R Den'ō Ore... 2007, JAP [GF/Kamen Rider]
Gekijōban Kamen Raidā Dikeido... 2009, JAP [GF/Kamen Rider]
Gekijōban Kamen Raidā Doraibu... 2015, JAP [GF/Kamen Rider]
Gekijōban Kamen Raidā Eguzeido... 2017, JAP [GF/Kamen Rider]
Gekijōban Kamen Raidā Faizu... 2003, JAP [GF/Kamen Rider]
Gekijōban Kamen Raidā Gaimu... 2014, JAP [GF/Kamen Rider]
Gekijōban Kamen Raidā Gōsuto... 2015, JAP [GF/Kamen Rider]
Gekijōban Kamen Raidā Hibiki... 2005, JAP [GF/Kamen Rider]
Gekijōban Kamen Raidā Kabuto... 2006, JAP [GF/Kamen Rider]
Gekijōban Kamen Raidā Kiba... 2008, JAP [GF/Kamen Rider]
Gekijōban Kamen Raidā Ōzu... 2011, JAP [GF/Kamen Rider]
Gekijōban Kamen Raidā Ryūki... 2002, JAP [GF/Kamen Rider]
Gekijōban Kamen Raidā Wizādo... 2013, JAP [GF/Kamen Rider]
Gekijōban Saraba Kamen Raidâ... 2008, JAP [GF/Kamen Rider]
Gekijōban Urutoraman Ginga... 2015, JAP [GF/Ultraman]
Gekijōban Urutoraman Jīdo... 2018, JAP [GF/Ultraman]
Gekijōban Urutoraman Ōbu... 2016, JAP [GF/Ultraman]
Gekijouban Kamen raidâ Bureido... 2004, JAP [GF/Kamen Rider]
Gekijouban Kamen raidâ Ōzu... 2011, JAP [GF/Kamen Rider]
Gekijouban Tiger & Bunny: see Tiger & Bunny

Gekko Kamen (SERIES) [GF/Moonlight Mask]
Gekkō Kamen, 1958, JAP [GF/Moonlight Mask]
Gekkō Kamen, 1981, JAP [GF/Moonlight Mask]
Gekkō Kamen: Akuma no Saigo, 1959, JAP [GF/Moonlight Mask]
Gekkō Kamen: Kaijū Kongu, 1959, JAP [GF/Moonlight Mask]
Gekkō Kamen: Satan no Tsume, 1958, JAP [GF/Moonlight Mask]
Gekkō Kamen: Yureitō no... 1959, JAP [GF/Moonlight Mask]
Gekkō Kamen: Zekkai no Shitō, 1958, JAP [GF/Moonlight Mask]
Gemma: Babaing Kidlat, 1974, PH
Gen 13, 2000, USA
Generation X, 1996, USA
Genesis of the Daleks, 1975, UK [GF/Dr Who]
Ghost Light, 1989, UK [GF/Dr Who]
Ghost of Zorro, 1949, USA
Ghost of Zorro, 1959, USA
Ghost Rider, 2007, USA
Ghost Rider: Spirit of Vengeance, 2011, USA
Giant and Jumborg Ace: see Jumborg Ace & Giant
Glass, 2019, USA
Gli amori di Ercole, 1960, ITL [GF/Peplum]
Gli Invincibili Tre, 1964, ITL [GF/Peplum]
Glitter Force (SERIES) [GF/PreCure]
Go! Princess Precure the Movie... 2015, JAP [GF/PreCure]
God of Thunder, 2015, USA
Godzilla vs. Megalon, 1973, JAP
Gojira tai Megaro: see Godzilla vs. Megalon
Gokaiger Goseiger Super Sentai... 2011, JAP [GF/Super Sentai]
Golden Bat (SERIES) [GF]
Golden Bat, The, 1966, JAP
Golden Batman: see Black Star and the Golden Bat
Golden Blaze, The, 2004, USA
Golden Claws of the Cat Girl, The, 1968, FR [GF/Fantômas]
Golden Eagle, The, 1970, Thailand [GF/The Red Eagle]
Goldface, the Fantastic Superman, 1967, ITL
Golia alla conquista di Bagdad, 1964, ITL [GF/Peplum]
Golia e il cavaliere mascherato, 1963, ITL [GF/Peplum]
Goliath (Italian SERIES) [GF/Peplum]
Goliath Against the Giants, 1960, ITL [GF/Peplum]
Goliath and the Barbarians, 1959, ITL [GF/Peplum]
Goliath and the Dragon, 1960, ITL [GF/Peplum]
Goliath and the Rebel Slave, 1963, ITL [GF/Peplum]
Goliath and the Sins of Babylon, 1963, ITL [GF/Peplum]
Goliath and the Vampires, 1961, ITL [GF/Peplum]
Goliath at the Conquest of Damascus, 1964, ITL [GF/Peplum]
Goliath contro i giganti, 1960, ITL [GF/Peplum]
Goliath e la schiava ribelle, 1963, ITL [GF/Peplum]
Gothic Lolita Battle Bear Nuigulumar Z, 2013, JAP
gran aventura del Zorro, La: see The Great Adventure of Zorro
Grave Robbers, The, 1965, MEX [GF/Luchadors]
Great Adventure of Zorro, The, 1976, MEX
Great Shu Ra Ra Boom Idainaru, Shurarabon, 2014, JAP
Greatest Show In the Galaxy, The, 1988, UK [GF/Dr Who]

Green Death, The, 1973, UK [GF/Dr Who]
Green Hornet, The, 1940, USA
Green Hornet, The, 1974, USA
Green Hornet, The, 1990, USA
Green Hornet, The, 2011, USA
Green Hornet (1994): see Dragon and the Green Hornet
Green Hornet Movie Edition, The, 2011, USA
Green Hornet Strikes Again, The, 1941, USA
Green Inferno, 1973, ES, [GF/Tarzan]
Green Lantern, 2011, USA
Green Lantern: Emerald Knights, 2011, USA
Green Lantern: First Flight, 2009, USA
Greystoke: The Legend of Tarzan, 1984, USA, [GF/Tarzan]
Griff the Invisible, 2010, USA
Groove Squad, 2002, USA
Guardians, The, 2017, Russia
Guardians of the Galaxy, 2014, USA
Guardians of the Galaxy Vol. 2, 2017, USA
Guardians of the Lost Code 3D, 2010, MEX
Gui ma fei ren: see The Flying Mr. B
Gummi T: see Ivan the Incredible
Gundala putra petir, 1981, ID
Gunfighters, The, 1966, UK [GF/Dr Who]
Guyver, The, 1991, USA/JAP
Guyver: Dark Hero, 1994, USA
Gypsy Moon, 1954, USA, [GF/Rocky Jones]
Hagane no renkinjutsushi: see Fullmetal Alchemist
Hak hap (2): see Black Mask (2)
Hamara Hero Shaktimaan, 2013, IN
Hancock, 2008, USA
Hand of Fear, The, 1976, UK [GF/Dr Who]
Hanuman and the Five Riders, 1974, JAP [GF/Kamen Rider]
Hanuman pob Har Aimoddaeng, 1974, JAP [GF/Kamen Rider]
Happiness Patrol, The, 1988, UK [GF/Dr Who]
Happiness Charge PreCure! Movie... 2014, JAP [GF/PreCure]
Hardcore Henry, 2015, Russia/USA
Hariken Porimâ: see Hurricane Polymar
Haunted World of El Superbeasto, The, 2009, USA
He-Man and She-Ra: The Secret of the Sword, 1985, USA/JAP
He-Man & the Masters of the 'verse: Beginning, 2002, USA
HeartCatch PreCure! the Movie... 2010, JAP [GF/PreCure]
Hectic Knife, 2016, USA
Heisei Rider vs. Shōwa Rider... 2014, JAP [GF/Kamen Rider]
Hellboy, 2004, USA
Hellboy II: The Golden Army, 2008, USA
Hellboy Animated: Blood and Iron, 2007, USA
Hellboy Animated: Sword of Storms, 2006, USA
Hellish Spiders, 1968, MEX [GF/Luchadors]
Henchmen, 2018, Canada
Hercules (mondo), 1997, ITL
Hercules (Italian SERIES) [GF/Peplum]
Hercules Against Rome, 1964, ITL [GF/Peplum]

Hercules Against the Barbarians, 1963, ITL [GF/Peplum]

Hercules Against the Mongols, 1963, ITL [GF/Peplum]

Hercules Against the Moon Men, 1964, ITL [GF/Peplum]

Hercules Against the Sons of the Sun, 1964, ITL [GF/Peplum]

Hercules & the Amazon Women, 1994, USA [GF/Hercules: TLJ]

Hercules and the Black Pirate, 1963, ITL [GF/Peplum]

Hercules and the Black Pirates, 1964, ITL [GF/Peplum]

Hercules and the Circle of Fire, 1994, USA [GF/Hercules: TLJ]

Hercules and the Lost Kingdom, 1994, USA [GF/Hercules: TLJ]

Hercules and the Masked Rider, 1963, ITL [GF/Peplum]

Hercules and the Princess of Troy, 1965, ITL [GF/Peplum]

Hercules and the Treasure of the Incas, 1964, ITL [GF/Peplum]

Hercules and the Tyrants of Babylon, 1964, ITL [GF/Peplum]

Hercules and Xena - The Animated Movie... 1998, USA

Hercules Conquers Atlantis, 1961, ITL [GF/Peplum]

Hercules in New York, 1969, USA

Hercules in the Haunted World, 1961, ITL [GF/Peplum]

Hercules in the Maze of the... 1994, USA [GF/Hercules: TLJ]

Hercules in the Underworld, 1994, USA [GF/Hercules: TLJ]

Hercules in the Vale of Woe, 1961, ITL [GF/Peplum]

Hercules of the Desert, 1964, ITL [GF/Peplum]

Hercules Reborn, 2014, USA

Hercules Recycled 2.0, 2014, USA

Hercules Recycled, 1994, USA

Hercules the Avenger, 1965, ITL [GF/Peplum]

Hercules the Invincible, 1964, ITL [GF/Peplum]

Hercules Unchained, 1959, ITL [GF/Peplum]

Hercules vs. the Giant Warriors, 1964, ITL [GF/Peplum]

Hercules vs. the Sea Monster, 1965, ITL [GF/Peplum]

Hercules, 1953, PH

Hercules, 1958, ITL [GF/Peplum]

Hercules, 1964, IN

Hercules, 1983, ITL/USA

Hercules, 1997, USA

Hercules, 1997, USA

Hercules, 1998, ITL

Hercules, 2014, USA

Hercules, Prisoner of Evil, 1964, ITL [GF/Peplum]

Hercules, Samson & Ulysses aka, 1963, ITL [GF/Peplum]

Hercules: TLJ (SERIES) [GF]

Hercules: Zero to Hero, 1999, USA

Hero at Large, 1980, USA

Hero Tomorrow

Heroes Return Trilogy, 2009, USA [GF/Wolverine and the X-Men]

Heroic Trio, The, 1993, HK

Heroic Trio 2: Executioners, 1993, HK

Hi-Yo Silver, 1940, USA

Highlanders, The, 1966, UK [GF/Dr Who]

hijo de Alma Grande, El, 1976, MEX [GF/Luchadors]

hijo de Huracán Ramírez, El, 1966, MEX [GF/Luchadors]

hijo de Santo en frontera sin ley, 1983, MEX [GF/Luchadors]

Hokuto no Ken: see Fist of the North Star

Holy Musical B@man!, 2012, USA

Honeymoon Travels Pvt. Ltd., 2007, IN

Horns of Nimon, The, 1979, UK [GF/Dr Who]

Horror of Fang Rock, 1977, UK [GF/Dr Who]

Hound, 2017, UK

How to Kill 400 Duponts, 1967, ITL [GF/Diabolik S-Ks]

Howard the Duck, 1986, USA

Hugtto! PreCure Futari wa... 2018, JAP [GF/PreCure]

Hulihin si Tiagong Akyat, 1973, PH

Hulk Vs., 2009, USA

Hulk, 2003, USA

Hulk: Where Monsters Dwell, 2016, USA

Hunterwali Ki Beti, 1943, IN

Hunterwali, 1935, IN

Huracan Ramirez and the Black Nun, 1973, MEX [GF/Luchadors]

Huracán Ramírez contra los... 1989, MEX [GF/Luchadors]

Huracán Ramírez y la monjita negra, 1973, MEX [GF/Luchadors]

Hurricane Hansa, 1937, IN

Hurricane Polymar, 2017, JAP

Husbands of River Song, 2015, UK [GF/Dr Who]

Hwasan Highschool: see Volcano High

Hwasango: see Volcano High

Hyakujuu Sentai Gaoranger vs... 2001, JAP [GF/Super Sentai]

Hydrozagadka, 1971, Poland

I Was a Teenage Superhero Sidekick, 2013, USA

I-Man, 1986, USA

iBoy, 2017, UK

Ice Warriors, The, 1967, UK [GF/Dr Who]

Ichi, 2008, JAP

Idainaru, Shurarabon: see The Great Shu Ra Ra Boom

Illusionauts, The, 2012, Peru

Image of the Fendahl, 1977, UK [GF/Dr Who]

In Your Face: see Abar, the First Black Superman

Incredible Hulk, The, 1977, USA

Incredible Hulk, The, 2008, USA

Incredible Hulk Returns, The, 1988, USA

Incredible H.: Death in the Family: see Return of the Inc...

Incredibles, The, 2004, USA

Incredibles 2, 2018, USA

Infernal Angels, 1968, MEX [GF/Luchadors]

Inferno in Space, 1954, USA, [GF/Rocky Jones]

Inferno, 1970, UK [GF/Dr Who]

Infra Superman, The: see Infra-Man

Infra-Man, 1975, HK

Inhumans, 2017, USA

Insae Daeng (Mitr Chaibancha series) [GF/The Red Eagle]

Inseparable, 2011, China

Insidious Six, 1997, USA, [GF/Spider-Man: TAS]

Inspector Gadget, 1999, USA

Inspector Gadget 2, 2003, USA

Inspector Gadget's Biggest Caper Ever, 2005, USA

Inspector Gadget's Last Case: Claw's Revenge, 2002, USA

Kamen Rider... Cho-Den-O Red... 2010, JAP [GF/Kamen Rider]
Kamen Rider... Cho-Den-O Yellow... 2010, JAP [GF/Kamen Rider]
Kamen Rider × KR Double... 2009, JAP [GF/Kamen Rider]
Kamen Rider × KR Drive... 2014, JAP [GF/Kamen Rider]
Kamen Rider × KR Gaim... 2013, JAP [GF/Kamen Rider]
Kamen Rider × KR Ghost... 2015, JAP [GF/Kamen Rider]
Kamen Rider × KR OOO... 2010, JAP [GF/Kamen Rider]
Kamen Rider × KR W... 2010, JAP [GF/Kamen Rider]
Kamen Rider × KR Wiz... 2012, JAP [GF/Kamen Rider]
Kamen Rider... Super Hero Taisen, 2013, JAP [GF/Kamen Rider]
Kamen Rider... Taisen, 2012, JAP [GF/Kamen Rider]
Kamen Rider... Super Hero Taisen, 2017, JAP [GF/Kamen Rider]
Kamen Rider 1, 2016, JAP [GF/Kamen Rider]
Kamen Rider 555: Paradise Lost, 2003, JAP [GF/Kamen Rider]
Kamen Rider Amazons the Movie... 2018, JAP [GF/Kamen Rider]
Kamen Rider Blade the Movie... 2004, JAP [GF/Kamen Rider]
Kamen Rider Build the Movie... 2018, JAP [GF/Kamen Rider]
Kamen Rider Decade: All Riders... 2009, JAP [GF/Kamen Rider]
Kamen Rider Den-O & Kiva... 2008, JAP [GF/Kamen Rider]
Kamen Rider Den-O the Movie... 2007, JAP [GF/Kamen Rider]
Kamen Rider Drive Saga... 2016, JAP [GF/Kamen Rider]
Kamen Rider Drive the Movie... 2015, JAP [GF/Kamen Rider]
Kamen Rider Ex-Aid the Movie... 2017, JAP [GF/Kamen Rider]
Kamen Rider Ex-Aid Trilogy... 2018, JAP [GF/Kamen Rider]
Kamen Rider Fourze the Movie... 2012, JAP [GF/Kamen Rider]
Kamen Rider Gaim the Movie... 2014, JAP [GF/Kamen Rider]
Kamen Rider Ghost RE:BIRTH... 2017, JAP [GF/Kamen Rider]
Kamen Rider Ghost the Movie:... 2015, JAP [GF/Kamen Rider]
Kamen Rider Heisei Gen. Final... 2017, JAP [GF/Kamen Rider]
Kamen Rider H. Gen. Dr. Pac... 2016, JAP [GF/Kamen Rider]
Kamen Rider Hibiki & The 7 Senki, 2005, JAP [GF/Kamen Rider]
Kamen Rider Kabuto... 2006, JAP [GF/Kamen Rider]
Kamen Rider Kiva... 2008, JAP [GF/Kamen Rider]
Kamen Rider OOO... 2011, JAP [GF/Kamen Rider]
Kamen Rider Ryuki... 2002, JAP [GF/Kamen Rider]
Kamen Rider W Forever... 2010, JAP [GF/Kamen Rider]
Kamen Rider W Returns... 2011, JAP [GF/Kamen Rider]
Kamen Rider Wizard in Magic Land, 2013, JAP [GF/Kamen Rider]
Kamen Rider x Kamen Rider... 2011, JAP [GF/Kamen Rider]
Kamen Rider: The First, 2005, JAP [GF/Kamen Rider]
Kamen Rider: The Next, 2007, JAP [GF/Kamen Rider]
Kanthaswamy, 2009, IN
Kapitan Inggo, 1984, PH
Kapitan Kidlat, 1981, PH
Kapoww!!, 2010, Malaysia
Karate-Robo Zaborgar, 2011, JAP
Karla contra los jaguares, 1974, MEX [GF/Luchadors]
Karla vs. The Jaguars, 1974, MEX [GF/Luchadors]
Karzan, il favoloso uomo della jungla, 1972, ITL, [GF/Tarzan]
Kataude mashin gâru: see The Machine Girl
Kato Kung Lee vs. la mafia oriental, 2008, MEX [GF/Luchadors]

Kaze no tani Naushika: See Nausicaa of the Valley of the Wind
Kdo chce zabít Jessii?: see Who Wants to Kill Jessie?
Keeper of Traken, The, 1981, UK [GF/Dr Who]
Kenny Begins, 2009, Sweden
Keys of Marinus, The, 1964, UK [GF/Dr Who]
Kiara the Brave, 2011, IN
Kibakichi, 2004, JAP
Kibakichi: Bakko-yokaiden 2, 2004, JAP
Kick-Ass, 2010, USA
Kick-Ass 2, 2013, USA
Kid Krrish 2 - Mission Bhutan, 2014, IN
Kid Krrish 3 - Mystery in Mongolia, 2014, IN
Kid Krrish 4 - Shakalaka Africa, 2015, IN
Kid Krrish, 2013, IN
Kidlat... ngayon!, 1953, PH
Kidou Keiji Jiban, 1989, JAP [GF/Metal Hero Series]
Kikaider: The Ultimate Human Robot, 2014, JAP
Kiliç Aslan: see Lion Man
Kiling Murder Spree, 1971, Turkey [GF/Diabolik S-Ks]
Kilink/Killing (SERIES) [GF/Diabolik S-Ks]
Kilink Frankestayn's karsi, 1967, Turkey [GF/Diabolik S-Ks]
Kilink in Istanbul, 1967, Turkey [GF/Diabolik S-Ks]
Kilink Istanbul'da, 1967, Turkey [GF/Diabolik S-Ks]
Kilink Soy ve Öldür, 1967, Turkey [GF/Diabolik S-Ks]
Kilink uçan adama karsi, 1967, Turkey [GF/Diabolik S-Ks]
Kilink vs Frankenstein, 1967, Turkey [GF/Diabolik S-Ks]
Kilink vs the Armless Hero, 1975, Turkey [GF/Diabolik S-Ks]
Kilink vs the Flying Man, 1967, Turkey [GF/Diabolik S-Ks]
Kilink: Corpses Can't Talk!, 1967, Turkey [GF/Diabolik S-Ks]
Kilink: Strip and Kill, 1967, Turkey [GF/Diabolik S-Ks]
Kill Order, 2017, Canada
Killer Ape, 1953, USA, [GF/Jungle Jim]
Killing caniler krali, 1967, Turkey [GF/Diabolik S-Ks]
Killing Kolsuz Kahraman Karsi, 1975, Turkey [GF/Diabolik S-Ks]
Killing Oluler Konusmaz, 1967, Turkey [GF/Diabolik S-Ks]
Killing vs. Mandrake: see Mandrake vs. Killing
Kinda, 1982, UK [GF/Dr Who]
King of the Rocket Men, 1949, USA
Kingsman: The Golden Circle, 2017, USA
Kingsman: The Secret Service, 2014, USA
Kip's Private War, 1954, USA, [GF/Rocky Jones]
Kirakira PreCure a la Mode... 2017, JAP [GF/PreCure]
Kiss Meets the Phantom of the Park, 1978, USA
Kitaro and the Millennium Curse, 2008, JAP
Kitaro, 2007, JAP
Kitaro's Graveyard Gang, 2009, USA/JAP
Kizil Maske: see The Red Mask
Koi... Mil Gaya (Krrish series), 2003, IN
Kriminal (SERIES) [GF/Diabolik S-Ks]
Kriminal, 1966, ITL [GF/Diabolik S-Ks]
Krotons, The, 1969, UK [GF/Dr Who]

Krrish 2: see Krrish 3 (there is no Krrish 2)

Krrish 3, 2013, IN

Krrish, 2006, IN

Kryptonita: see Kryptonite

Kryptonite, 2015, Argentina

Kyûtî Hanî: see Cutie Honey

Ladrón de cadáveres, 1957, MEX [GF/Luchadors]

Lady Tarzan, 1983, IN, [GF/Tarzan]

Lady Tarzan, 1990, IN, [GF/Tarzan]

Last Airbender, The, 2010, USA

Last Christmas, 2014, UK [GF/Dr Who]

Last Superhero, The: see All Superheroes Must Die 2

Lastik Man, 1965, PH

Lastikman, 2003, PH

Lastikman, 2004, PH

Latigo, El: see The Whip

Lazer Team, 2015, USA

Lazer Team 2, 2018, USA

League of Extraordinary Gentlemen, The, 2003, USA

League of Superheroes, 2015, Germany

Legend of Drona, The, 2008, IN

Legend Of Fist Of The North Star, 1993, South Korea

Legend of Hercules, The, 2014, USA

Legend of Raoh: Chapter of Death... 2006, JAP [GF/FotNS]

Legend of Raoh: Chapter of Fierce Fight, 2007, JAP [GF/FotNS]

Legend of Tarzan, 2016, USA, [GF/Tarzan]

Legend of the Fist: The Return of Chen Zhen, 2010, HK

Legend of the Lone Ranger, The, 1952, USA

Legend of the Lone Ranger, The, 1981, USA

Legend of the Lone Ranger (1952): see The Lone Ranger (1949)

Legend of Toki, 2008, JAP [GF/FotNS]

Legend of Yuria, 2007, JAP [GF/FotNS]

Legend of Zorro, The, 2005, USA

Legends of the Superheroes, 1979, USA

Lego Batman Movie, The, 2017, USA

Lego Batman: The Movie, 2013, USA [GF/Lego DC]

LEGO DC (SERIES) [GF]

Lego DC-CSH Aquaman: Rage of Atlantis, 2018, USA [GF/Lego DC]

Lego DC-CSH JL-Attack of the Legion... 2015, USA [GF/Lego]

Lego DC-CSH JL-Cosmic Clash, 2016, USA [GF/Lego DC]

Lego DC-CSH JL-Gotham City Breakout, 2016, USA [GF/Lego DC]

Lego DC-CSH JL vs. Bizarro League, 2015, USA [GF/Lego DC]

Lego DC-CSH The Flash, 2018, USA [GF/Lego DC]

Lego DC S.H.G.: Brain Drain, 2017, USA [GF/Lego DC]

Lego DC S.H.G.: Super-Villain High, 2018, USA [GF/Lego DC]

Lego Movie, The, 2014, USA

Lego Movie 2: The Second Brick, 2019, USA

Lego Ninjago Movie, The, 2017, USA

Leisure Hive, The, 1980, UK [GF/Dr Who]

Leonard Part 6, 1984, USA

leones del ring, Los, 1974, MEX [GF/Luchadors]

LeSeurdmin, 2017, USA

Leyendas macabras de la colonia, 1974, MEX [GF/Luchadors]

Lightspeed, 2006, USA

lihim ni gagamba, Ang 1964, PH [GF/Gagamba]

Lik wong: see Riki-Oh: The Story of Ricky

Limitless, 2011, USA

Lion Man Kiliç Aslan, 1975, Turkey

Lionman II: The Witchqueen, 1979, Turkey

Lions of the Ring, 1974, MEX [GF/Luchadors]

Lipad, Darna, lipad!, 1973, PH [GF/Darna]

Little Hercules in 3-D, 2009, USA

Little Superman, 2014, IN

llave mortal, La, 1990, MEX [GF/Luchadors]

lobas del ring, Las, 1965, MEX [GF/Luchadors]

Locke the Superman, 1984, JAP

Logan, 2017, USA

Logopolis, 1981, UK [GF/Dr Who]

Lone Ranger, The, 1938, USA

Lone Ranger, The, 1949, USA

Lone Ranger, The, 1956, USA

Lone Ranger, The, 2003, USA

Lone Ranger, The, 2013, USA

Lone Ranger and the Lost City of Gold, The, 1958, USA

Lone Ranger Rides Again, The, 1939, USA

Lord Hanuman: see Bajrangbali (1976)

Los endemoniados del ring, 1966, MEX [GF/Luchadors]

Lost Planet, The, 1953, USA

Lost Planet Airmen, 1951, USA

Lost Tribe, The, 1949, USA, [GF/Jungle Jim]

louve solitaire, La 1968, FR [GF/Fantômas]

Loves of Hercules, The, 1960, ITL [GF/Peplum]

Lucha a muerte, 1992, MEX [GF/Luchadors]

Luchador Movies [GF]

Luchadoras contra el médico asesino 1963, MEX [GF/Luchadors]

luchadoras contra la momia, Las, 1964, MEX [GF/Luchadors]

luchadoras vs el robot asesino, Las 1969, MEX [GF/Luchadors]

Luchadores de las estrellas, 1992, MEX [GF/Luchadors]

Lucy, 2014, FR

M.A.N.T.I.S., 1994, USA

Macabre Legends of the Colony, 1974, MEX [GF/Luchadors]

Machete Kills, 2013, USA

Machete, 2010, USA

Machine Girl, The, 2008, JAP

Maciste (Italian SERIES) [GF/Peplum]

Maciste all'inferno, 1962, ITL [GF/Peplum]

Maciste alla corte del gran khan, 1961, ITL [GF/Peplum]

Maciste alla corte dello zar, 1964, ITL [GF/Peplum]

Maciste contro Ercole nella... 1961, ITL [GF/Peplum]

Maciste contro i cacciatori di teste, 1962, ITL [GF/Peplum]

Maciste contro i Mongoli, 1963, ITL [GF/Peplum]

Maciste contro i mostri, 1962, ITL [GF/Peplum]

Maciste contro il vampiro, 1961, ITL [GF/Peplum]

Maciste contro lo sceicco, 1962, ITL [GF/Peplum]

Maciste e la regina de Samar, 1964, ITL [GF/Peplum]

Maciste il Vendicatore dei Mayas, ITL [GF/Peplum]

Maciste nell'inferno di Gengis Khan, 1963, ITL [GF/Peplum]

Maciste nella terra dei ciclopi, 1961, ITL [GF/Peplum]

Maciste nella valle dei re, 1960, ITL [GF/Peplum]

Maciste nelle miniere de re salomone, 1964, ITL [GF/Peplum]

Maciste, gladiatore di Sparta, 1964, ITL [GF/Peplum]

Maciste, il gladiatore piu forte... 1962, ITL [GF/Peplum]

Maciste, l'eroe piu grande del mondo, 1963, ITL [GF/Peplum]

Maciste, l'uomo più forte del mondo, 1961, ITL [GF/Peplum]

Macra Terror, The, 1967, UK [GF/Dr Who]

mafia amarilla, La, 1975, MEX [GF/Luchadors]

Magician's Apprentice/Witch's Familiar, 2015, UK [GF/Dr Who]

Magico, 1990, MEX [GF/Luchadors]

Mágico, el enviado...: see Magico: The Messenger of the Gods

Magico: The Messenger of the Gods, 1990, MEX

Magnetic Moon, The, 1954, USA, [GF/Rocky Jones]

Maho Girls PreCure! the Movie:... 2015, JAP [GF/PreCure]

Major Tayfun, 1968, Turkey

maldición de la momia azteca, La, 1957, MEX [GF/Luchadors]

Mallanna: see Kanthaswamy

Man with the Golden Winchester, 1973, ITL [GF/Peplum]

Man With the Power, 1977, USA

Man-Thing, 2005, Australia

man, el superhéroe nacional, El, 2009, Colombia

Manborg, 2011, Canada

Mandrake vs. Killing, 1967, Turkey

Mandrake, 1979, USA

Mandrake, the Magician, 1939, USA

Mandroid, 1993, USA

Manhunt in Space, 1954, USA, [GF/Rocky Jones]

mano que aprieta, La, 1966, MEX [GF/Luchadors]

mansion de las 7 momias, La, 1977, MEX [GF/Luchadors]

Mansion of the 7 Mummies, The, 1977, MEX [GF/Luchadors]

Mantera, 2012, Malaysia

Manusia 6.000.000 dollar: see Manusia enam juta dollar

Manusia enam juta dollar, 1981, ID

marchio di Kriminal, Il, 1968, ITL [GF/Diabolik S-Ks]

Marco Polo, 1964, UK [GF/Dr Who]

Mark of Kriminal, The, 1968, ITL [GF/Diabolik S-Ks]

Mark of the Gorilla, 1950, USA, [GF/Jungle Jim]

Mark of Zorro, The, 1920, USA

Mark of Zorro, The, 1940, USA

Mark of Zorro, The, 1974, USA

Mark of Zorro, The, 1975, FR

Mark of Zorro, 1975, ITL [GF/Peplum]

Mark of Zorro, 1975, ITL/ES

Mars Attacks the World, 1938, USA

Marvel Rising: Secret Warriors, 2018, USA

Marvel Super Hero Adventures: Frost Fight!, 2015, USA

máscara de la muerte, La, 1961, MEX [GF/Luchadors]

Máscara Sagrada vs. mafia del ring, 2007, MEX [GF/Luchadors]

Mask Man, 2017, IN

Mask of Death, The, 1961, MEX [GF/Luchadors]

Mask of Zorro, The, 1998, USA

Mask The Mask, 1994, USA

Masked Conqueror, The, 1962, ITL [GF/Peplum]

Masked Marvel, The, 1943, USA

Masked Rider Hibiki & The Seven... 2005, JAP [GF/Kamen Rider]

Maskeli Seytan, 1970, Turkey

Masque of Mandragora, The, 1976, UK [GF/Dr Who]

Massacre of St Bartholomew's Eve, The, 1966, UK [GF/Dr Who]

Masters of the Universe, 1987, USA

Matrix, The, 1999, USA

Matrix Reloaded, The, 2003, USA

Matrix Revolutions, The, 2003, USA

Mawdryn Undead, 1983, UK [GF/Dr Who]

Max Steel, 2016, USA

Mega Mindy (SERIES) [GF]

Mega Mindy and the Black... 2010, BE [GF/Mega Mindy]

Mega Mindy and the Candy... 2011, BE [GF/Mega Mindy]

Mega Mindy en de Snoepbaron, 2011, BE [GF/Mega Mindy]

Mega Mindy en het zwarte... 2010, BE [GF/Mega Mindy]

Mega Mindy Versus ROX, 2015, BE [GF/Mega Mindy]

Mega Monster Battle: Ultra... 2009, JAP [GF/Ultraman]

Megamind, 2010, USA

Meglos, 1980, UK [GF/Dr Who]

Mekura no Oichi (SERIES) [GF/The Crimson Bat]

Mekura no Oichi Mono... 1969, Japan [GF/The Crimson Bat]

Mekura no Oichi: Jigokuhaa, 1969, Japan [GF/The Crimson Bat]

Mekura no Oichi: Mida..., 1969, Japan [GF/The Crimson Bat]

Mekura no Oichi: Inochi... 1970, Japan [GF/The Crimson Bat]

Men in Black, 1997, USA

Men in Black II, 2002, USA

Men in Black 3, 2012, USA

Men of Action Meet Women of Dracula, 1969, PH

Menace from Outer Space, 1954, USA, [GF/Rocky Jones]

Meng long zheng dong: see Bruce Lee Against Superman

Mercury Man, 2006, Thailand

Messalina vs. the Son of Hercules, 1964, ITL [GF/Peplum]

Metal Hero Series (SERIES) [GF]

Metal Man, 2008, USA

Meteor Man, The, 1993, USA

Mga lawin Ang Mga lawin, 1963, PH

Middle Finger, The, 2016, Ireland

Mighty Man, 1978, South Africa

Mighty Morphin' Power Rangers (SERIES) [GF/Power Rangers]

Mighty Morphin' Power Rangers: The Movie, 1995, USA

Mighty Mouse in the Great Space Chase, 1982, USA

Mighty Rock, 1969, PH
Mighty Ursus, 1960, ITL [GF/Peplum]
Mil Mascaras vs. the Aztec Mummy, 2007, USA [GF/Luchadors]
Mil máscaras, 1969, MEX [GF/Luchadors]
Mind of Evil, The, 1971, UK [GF/Dr Who]
Mind Robber, The, 1968, UK [GF/Dr Who]
Mindwarp, 1986, UK [GF/Dr Who]
Minerva, 1960, PH
Minty: The Assassin, 2009, USA
Mirageman, 2007, Chile
Mirrorman Reflex, 2006, JAP
Misfits of Science (pilot: Deep Freeze), 1985, USA
Missing Lady, The, 1946, USA
Missy and the Maxinator, 2009, USA
Mister Freedom: see Mr. Freedom
Mister X: see Avenger X
misterio de Huracán Ramírez, El, 1962, MEX [GF/Luchadors]
Mizu no naka no hachigatsu: see August in the Water
Mobile Cop Jiban: The Movie, 1989, JAP [GF/Metal Hero Series]
Model by Day, 1994, USA/Canada
Mole Men vs the Son of Hercules, 1961, ITL [GF/Peplum]
momias de Guanajuato, Las, 1970, MEX [GF/Luchadors]
momias de San Ángel, Las 1975, MEX [GF/Luchadors]
Monarch of the Moon, 2006, USA
Monster of Peladon, The, 1974, UK [GF/Dr Who]
Moonbase, The, 1967, UK [GF/Dr Who]
Moonlight Mask (SERIES) [GF]
Moonlight Mask, 1958, JAP [GF/Moonlight Mask]
Moonlight Mask, 1981, JAP [GF/Moonlight Mask]
Moonlight Mask: Duel to... 1958, JAP [GF/Moonlight Mask]
Moonlight Mask: The Claws... 1958, JAP [GF/Moonlight Mask]
Moonlight Mask: The Ghost... 1959, JAP [GF/Moonlight Mask]
Moonlight Mask: The Last... 1959, JAP [GF/Moonlight Mask]
Moonlight Mask: The Monster... 1959, JAP [GF/Moonlight Mask]
Moron 5.2: The Transformation, 2015, PH
mort qui tue, Le, 1913, FR [GF/Fantômas]
Mosaic, 2006, USA
Mosquito-Man A Mosquito-Man, 2016, USA
Mounties Are Coming, The: see The Vigilante's Are Coming
Movie Extra, The: see Superhero Man
Mr. and Mrs. Incredible, 2011, China
Mr. Freedom, 1968, FR
Mr. IN, 1987, IN
Mr. Kilink in Istanbul, 2011, Turkey [GF/Diabolik S-Ks]
Mr. Superinvisible, 1970, ITL/Monaco/Germany
Mr. X, 2015, IN
Mugamoodi, 2012, IN
Mujeok 600manbul: see The Invincible Six-Million Dollar Man
mujer murcielago, La, 1968, MEX [GF/Luchadors]
mujeres panteras, Las, 1967, MEX [GF/Luchadors]
Mummies of Guanajuato, The, 1970, MEX [GF/Luchadors]

Mummies of San Angel, The, 1975, MEX [GF/Luchadors]
Mummy's Revenge, The, 1970, MEX [GF/Luchadors]
Mutant Agenda, 1997, USA, [GF/Spider-Man: TAS]
Mutant Girls Squad, 2010, JAP
Mutants, The, 1972, UK [GF/Dr Who]
My Hero Academia, 2018, JAP
My Super Ex-Girlfriend, 2006, USA
Mysterious Doctor Satan, 1940, USA
Mysterious Planet, The, 1986, UK [GF/Dr Who]
Mysterious World of Elias Paniki, The, 1989, PH
Mystery Men, 1999, USA
Mystery of Huracan Ramirez, The, 1962, MEX [GF/Luchadors]
Mystery of the Black Pearl, The, 1971, MEX [GF/Luchadors]
Myth Makers, The, 1965, UK [GF/Dr Who]
Nardong Putik, 1972, PH
Nardong Putik Version II, 1984, PH
Nauicaa of the Valley of the Wind, 1984, JP
Naya Ajooba - The Power of Child: see Athisayan
Neogenic Nightmare, 1998, USA, [GF/Spider-Man: TAS]
Nephews of Zorro, 1968, ITL [GF/Peplum]
Neutron Battles the Karate Assassins, 1965, MEX [GF/Luchadors]
Neutrón contra el criminal sádico, 1964, MEX [GF/Luchadors]
Neutrón contra el Dr. Caronte, 1963, MEX [GF/Luchadors]
Neutron Traps the Invisible Killers, 1965, MEX [GF/Luchadors]
Neutron vs. the Amazing Dr. Caronte, 1963, MEX [GF/Luchadors]
Neutron vs. the Maniac, 1964, MEX [GF/Luchadors]
Neutrón, el enmascarado negro, 1960, MEX [GF/Luchadors]
Neutron, the Man in the Black Mask, 1960, MEX [GF/Luchadors]
New Adventures of Tarzan, The, 1935, USA, [GF/Tarzan]
New Mission of Judex, The: see Judex's New Mission
New Original Wonder Woman, The, 1975, USA
New Original Wonder Woman, The: see Wonder Woman (1975)
New Tale of Zatoichi, 1963, JAP [GF/Zatōichi]
Next Avengers: Heroes of Tomorrow, 2008, USA
Nick Fury: Agent of Shield, 1998, USA
Night Is Day: The Movie, 2018, UK
Night of Death, 1975, MEX [GF/Luchadors]
NightMan, 1997, USA/Canada
Nightmare of Eden, 1979, UK [GF/Dr Who]
nipoti di Zorro, I, 1968, ITL [GF/Peplum]
Noche de muerte, 1975, MEX [GF/Luchadors]
Northern Coruier, 1960, MEX [GF/Luchadors]
Northstar, 1986, USA
nouvelle, mission de Judex, La: see Judex's New Mission
Oath of Zorro: see Behind the Mask of Zorro
Octagon and Mascara Sagrada... 1992, MEX [GF/Luchadors]
Of Chicana Blood, 1974, MEX [GF/Luchadors]
Officer Downe, 2016, USA
Ōgon batto (SERIES) [GF/The Golden Bat]
Ôgon bat: Matenrô no kaijin, 1950, JAP [GF/Golden Bat]
Ôgon batto ga yattekuru, 1972, JAP [GF/Golden Bat]

Ōgon batto, 1966, JAP [GF/Golden Bat]
Oily Maniac, The, 1976, HK
ombra di Zorro, L', 1962, ITL [GF/Peplum]
OOO, Den-O, All Riders:... 2011, JAP [GF/Kamen Rider]
Operation 67, 1966, MEX [GF/Luchadors]
Ophelia Learns to Swim, 2000, USA
Orgazmo, 1997, USA
Orishas: The Hidden Pantheon, 2016, Canada
Ōru Sutāzu Dirakkusu Surī:... 2011, JAP [GF/PreCure]
Out of This World, 1954, USA, [GF/Rocky Jones]
Outer Man, 2015, JAP
Ōzu Den'ō Ōru Raidā:... 2011, JAP [GF/Kamen Rider]
P.U.N.K.S., 1999, USA
pagbabalik ni palos, Ang, 1977, PH [GF/Palos]
Painkiller Jane, 2005, USA
Palos (Alyas Palos) (SERIES) [GF]
Palos Fights Back!, 1969, PH [GF/Palos]
Palos kontra gagamba, 1963, PH [GF/Gagamba]
Palos kontra gagamba, 1963, PH [GF/Palos]
Palos Strikes Again, 1968, PH [GF/Palos]
Palos: Counterspy, 1966, PH [GF/Palos]
Panji tengkorak vs Jaka Umbaran, 1983, ID
Panji tengkorak, 1971, ID
Panther Women, The, 1967, MEX [GF/Luchadors]
Paper Man, 2009, USA
Paradise Towers, 1987, UK [GF/Dr Who]
Paradox, 2010, Canada
Pasaporte a la muerte, 1968, MEX [GF/Luchadors]
Pepeng Agimat, 1973, PH
Pepeng Agimat, 1999, PH
Pepeng Kuryente, 1988, PH
Peril from the Planet Mongo, 1966, USA
Phantom, The, 1943, USA
Phantom, The, 1996, USA
Phantom 2040, 1994, USA
Phantom Boy, 2015, FR/BE
Phantom Lady, 1974, PH
Phantom Rancher, 1940, USA
Photon Effect, The, 2010, USA
Pirate Planet, The, 1978, UK [GF/Dr Who]
Pirates of Prah, The, 1954, USA, [GF/Rocky Jones]
Pizza Man, 2011, USA
Planet Hulk, 2010, USA
Planet of Evil, 1975, UK [GF/Dr Who]
Planet of Fire, 1984, UK [GF/Dr Who]
Planet of Giants, 1964, UK [GF/Dr Who]
Planet of the Daleks, 1973, UK [GF/Dr Who]
Planet of the Spiders, 1974, UK [GF/Dr Who]
Planet Outlaws, 1953, USA
Poliziotto superpiù: see Super Fuzz
Polvo de ángel, 2007, MEX [GF/Luchadors]

Popeye, 1980, USA
Portuguese Falcon The Portuguese Falcon, 2015, Portugal
Posthuman Project The Posthuman Project, 2014, USA
Power of Kroll, The, 1978, UK [GF/Dr Who]
Power of the Daleks, The, 1966, UK [GF/Dr Who]
Power Rangers (SERIES) [GF]
Power Rangers, 2017, USA
PR Megaforce... 2013, USA/JAP [GF/Power Rangers]
PR Mystic Force... 2006, USA/JAP [GF/Power Rangers]
PR NS: Samurai's... 2003, USA/JAP [GF/Power Rangers]
PR Sam.: A New Enemy, 2012, USA/JAP [GF/Power Rangers]
PR Sam.: Clash of... 2011, USA/JAP [GF/Power Rangers]
PR Sam.: Monster Bash, 2012, USA/JAP [GF/Power Rangers]
PR Sam.: The Team... 2012, USA/JAP [GF/Power Rangers]
PR SMF: Legendary... 2015, USA/JAP [GF/Power Rangers]
PR SMF: Silver... 2014, USA/JAP [GF/Power Rangers]
PR SS: Christmas... 2013, USA/JAP [GF/Power Rangers]
Power Rangers SS: Rise... 2013, USA/JAP [GF/Power Rangers]
PR TF - Quantum... 2001, USA/JAP [GF/Power Rangers]
PR: JF: Way of... 2008, USA/JAP [GF/Power Rangers]
Power, 1920, Germany
Powerpuff Girls Movie, The, 2002, USA
Pretty Cure (SERIES) [GF]
PreCure DX: Everyone's Friends... 2009, JAP [GF/PreCure]
PreCure DX2: Light of Hope... 2010, JAP [GF/PreCure]
PreCure DX3: Deliver the Future!... 2011, JAP [GF/PreCure]
PreCure New Stage 2: Friends of... 2013, JAP [GF/PreCure]
PreCure New Stage 3: Eternal... 2014, JAP [GF/PreCure]
PreCure New Stage: Friends... 2012, JAP [GF/PreCure]
PreCure All Stars: Carnival... 2015, JAP [GF/PreCure]
PreCure All Stars: Singing... 2016, JAP [GF/PreCure]
PreCure Dream Stars!, 2017, JAP [GF/PreCure]
Pretty Cure Super Stars!, 2018, JAP [GF/PreCure]
Prey of the Jaguar, 1996, USA
Prince of Space, 1959, JAP
Princess and the Hunter: see Hunterwali
Princess of Mars, 2009, USA
Psychic Kusuo, 2017, JAP
Psychokinesis, 2018, South Korea
Puella Magi Madoka Magica Part 1: Beginnings, 2012, JAP
Puella Magi Madoka Magica Part 2: Eternal, 2012, JAP
Puella Magi Madoka Magica Part III: Rebellion, 2013, JAP
Pumaman, The, 1980, ITL
Punisher, The, 1989, USA
Punisher, The, 2004, USA
Punisher: War Zone, 2008, USA
Punjab Mail, 1936 or 1939, IN
PuriKyua ŌSD Tsū: Kibō no Hikari... 2010, JAP [GF/PreCure]
PuriKyua ŌSD: Minna Tomodachi... 2009, JAP [GF/PreCure]
PuriKyua ŌSNS Tsū: Kokoro no..., 2013, JAP [GF/PreCure]
PuriKyua ŌSNS: Mirai no Tomodachi, 2012, JAP [GF/PreCure]

Purple Death from Outer Space, 1966, USA

Pursuit! The Strange Kidnappers!, 1984, JAP [GF/Metal Hero]

Push, 2009, USA

Pussy Cat, 1969, PH

Pygmy Island, 1950, USA, [GF/Jungle Jim]

Pyramids of Mars, 1975, UK [GF/Dr Who]

Ra.One, 2011, IN

Radar Men from the Moon, 1952, USA

Rafathar, 2017, ID

ragazzo invisibile, Il: see The Invisible Boy

Rama Superman ID, 1974, ID

Raō Den Gekitō no Shō, 2007, JAP [GF/FotNS]

Raō Den: Jun'ai no Shō, 2006, JAP [GF/FotNS]

Rat Pfink a Boo Boo, 1966, USA

Rat-Man - Il segreto del supereroe, 2007, ITL

Real Heroes, 2014, USA

Rebel Gladiators, The, 1962, ITL [GF/Peplum]

Red Eagle, The, 1963, Thailand [GF/The Red Eagle]

Red Eagle (Mitr Chaibancha series) [GF]

Red Eagle, 1966, Thailand [GF/The Red Eagle]

Red Eagle, 2010, Thailand

Red Mask, The, (Kizil Maske), 1968, Turkey (I)

Red Mask, The, (Kizil Maske), 1968, Turkey (II)

Red Sonja, 1985, USA

Reign of Terror, The, 1964, UK [GF/Dr Who]

Remembrance of the Daleks, 1988, UK [GF/Dr Who]

Rendel, 2017, Finland

Rendel: Dark Vengeance: see Rendel

Resident Evil, 2002, USA

Resident Evil: Afterlife, 2010, USA

Resident Evil: Apocalypse, 2004, USA

Resident Evil: Extinction, 2007, USA

Resident Evil: Retribution, 2012, USA

Resident Evil: The Final Chapter, 2016, USA

Resolution, 2019, UK [GF/Dr Who]

Ressha Sentai ToQger... 2015, JAP [GF/Super Sentai]

Retik, the Moon Menace, 1966, USA

Return of Captain Invincible, The, 1983, USA

Return of Chandu, The, (edit), 1934, USA

Return of Chandu, The, 1934, USA

Return Of Doctor Mysterio, 2016, UK [GF/Dr Who]

Return of El Coyote, The, 1998, ES [GF/The Coyote]

Return of Mr. Superman, 1960, IN

Return of Superman, The, 1979, Turkey

Return of Swamp Thing, The, 1989, USA

Return of the Incredible Hulk, The, 1977, USA

Return of the Six-Million-Dollar Man and the... 1987, USA

Return to the Batcave: The Misadventures of... 2003, USA

revancha, La, 1992, MEX [GF/Luchadors]

Revelation, 2010, USA [GF/Wolverine and the X-Men]

Revenge, The, 1992, MEX [GF/Luchadors]

Revenge of Tarzan, The, 1920, USA, [GF/Tarzan]

Revenge of the Crying Woman, The, 1974, MEX [GF/Luchadors]

Revenge of the Cybermen, 1975, UK [GF/Dr Who]

Revenge of the Goblins, 1997, USA, [GF/Spider-Man: TAS]

Revenge of the Red Mask: see Vengeance of the Red Mask

Revenge of the Vampire Women, 1970, MEX [GF/Luchadors]

Ri jie: see Descendant of the Sun

Ribos Operation, The, 1978, UK [GF/Dr Who]

Riki-Oh: The Story of Ricky, 1991, HK

Rise of the Black Bat, 2012, USA

Rise of the Guardians, 2012, USA

Robbery of Mummies of Guan..., 1972, MEX [GF/Luchadors]

RoboCop, 1987, USA

RoboCop, 2014, USA

RoboCop 2, 1990, USA

RoboCop 3, 1993, USA

RoboCop 4, 1994, USA

Roboman Hakaider Mechanical Violator, 1995, JAP

Robot Ninja, 1989, USA

Robot of Regalio, 1954, USA, [GF/Rocky Jones]

Robot, 1975, UK [GF/Dr Who]

Robots of Death, The, 1977, UK [GF/Dr Who]

Robots of Death, 1962, MEX [GF/Luchadors]

Rocco, ang batang bato, 1982, PH

Rocket Ship, 1936, USA

Rocketeer The Rocketeer, 1991, USA

Rocky Jones, Space Ranger (SERIES) [GF]

Rocky's Odyssey, 1954, USA, [GF/Rocky Jones]

Romance of Tarzan, The, 1918, USA, [GF/Tarzan]

Romans, The, 1965, UK [GF/Dr Who]

Royal Eagle, The, 1971, MEX [GF/Luchadors]

Rudraksh, 2004, IN

Runaway Bride, 2006, UK [GF/Dr Who]

Running Delilah, 1993, USA

Saiki Kusuo no sai-nan: see Psychic Kusuo

Sailor Moon (SERIES) [GF]

Sailor Moon R: The Movie... 1993, JAP, [GF/Sailor Moon]

Sailor Moon S: The Movie... 1994, JAP, [GF/Sailor Moon]

Sailor Moon SuperS: The Movie... 1995, JAP, [GF/Sailor Moon]

Sakima and the Masked Marvel, 1966, USA

Salvage Mice, 2011, JP

Samaritan Zatoichi, 1968, JAP [GF/Zatōichi]

Samson (Italian SERIES) [GF/Peplum]

Samson Against the Sheik, 1962, ITL [GF/Peplum]

Samson and His Mighty Challenge, 1964, ITL [GF/Peplum]

Samson and the Sea Beast, 1963, ITL [GF/Peplum]

Samson & the Seven Miracles of World, 1961, ITL [GF/Peplum]

Samson and the Slave Queen, 1963, ITL [GF/Peplum]

Samson in King Solomon's Mines, 1964, ITL [GF/Peplum]

Samson, 1961, ITL [GF/Peplum]

Samson, 1964, IN

Samson, 2018, South Africa/USA
Samurai Sentai Shinkenger vs.... 2010, JAP [GF/Super Sentai]
San kei hap lui: see Mr. and Mrs. Incredible
Sangre en el ring, 1962, MEX [GF/Luchadors]
Sansone contro i pirati, 1963, ITL [GF/Peplum]
Sansone contro il corsaro nero, 1963, ITL [GF/Peplum]
Sansone e il tesoro degli Incas, 1964, ITL [GF/Peplum]
Sansone, 1961, ITL [GF/Peplum]
Santo & Blue Demon in World of... 1969, MEX [GF/Luchadors]
Santo & Blue Demon vs. Franky... 1973, MEX [GF/Luchadors]
Santo & Blue Demon vs. Dracula... 1972, MEX [GF/Luchadors]
Santo & Blue Demon vs. the Monsters, 1969 [GF/Luchadors]
Santo contra Blue Demon en... 1969, MEX [GF/Luchadors]
Santo contra Capulina, 1968, MEX [GF/Luchadors]
Santo contra el asesino de TV, 1981, MEX [GF/Luchadors]
Santo contra el cerebro del mal, 1958, MEX [GF/Luchadors]
Santo contra el cerebro diabolico, 1962, MEX [GF/Luchadors]
Santo contra el doctor Muerte, 1973, MEX [GF/Luchadors]
Santo contra el espectro del... 1963, MEX [GF/Luchadors]
Santo contra el estrangulador, 1963, MEX [GF/Luchadors]
Santo contra el rey del... 1961 or 1962, MEX [GF/Luchadors]
Santo contra hombres infernales, 1958, MEX [GF/Luchadors]
Santo contra la hija de Franky, 1971, MEX [GF/Luchadors]
Santo contra la invasión de los... 1966, MEX [GF/Luchadors]
Santo contra la mafia del vicio, 1970, MEX [GF/Luchadors]
Santo contra la magia negra, 1972, MEX [GF/Luchadors]
Santo contra las lobas, 1972, MEX [GF/Luchadors]
Santo contra las mujeres vampiro, 1962, MEX [GF/Luchadors]
Santo contra los asesinos de... 1971, MEX [GF/Luchadors]
Santo contra los cazadores de... 1969, MEX [GF/Luchadors]
Santo contra los jinetes del terror, 1970, MEX [GF/Luchadors]
Santo contra los secuestradores, 1972, MEX [GF/Luchadors]
Santo contra los villanos del ring, 1966, MEX [GF/Luchadors]
Santo contra los zombis, 1961 or 1962, MEX [GF/Luchadors]
Santo en Anónimo mortal, 1972, MEX [GF/Luchadors]
Santo en Atacan las brujas, 1964, MEX [GF/Luchadors]
Santo en el Barón Brakola, 1965 or 1967, MEX [GF/Luchadors]
Santo en el hacha diabólica, 1964 or 1965, MEX [GF/Luchadors]
Santo en el hotel muerte, 1961 or 1963, MEX [GF/Luchadors]
Santo en el misterio de la perla... 1971, MEX [GF/Luchadors]
Santo en el Misterio Bermudas, 1977, MEX [GF/Luchadors]
Santo en el museo de cera, 1963, MEX [GF/Luchadors]
Santo en el puño de la muerte, 1982, MEX [GF/Luchadors]
Santo en el tesoro de Drácula, 1968, MEX [GF/Luchadors]
Santo en el tesoro de Moctezuma, 1967, MEX [GF/Luchadors]
Santo en la frontera del terror, 1979, MEX [GF/Luchadors]
Santo en la furia de los karatekas, 1982, MEX [GF/Luchadors]
Santo en la venganza de la llorona, 1974, MEX [GF/Luchadors]
Santo en la venganza de la momia, 1970, MEX [GF/Luchadors]
Santo en la veng... de las mujeres.., 1970, MEX [GF/Luchadors]
Santo en los profanadores tumbas, 1965, MEX [GF/Luchadors]

Santo en misión suicida, 1971, MEX [GF/Luchadors]
Santo en Operación 67, 1966, MEX [GF/Luchadors]
Santo en Oro negro, 1975, MEX [GF/Luchadors]
Santo Faces Death, 1969, MEX [GF/Luchadors]
Santo in the Hotel of Death, 1961 or 1963, MEX [GF/Luchadors]
Santo in the Mystery of the Black... 1975, MEX [GF/Luchadors]
Santo in the Wax Museum, 1963, MEX [GF/Luchadors]
Santo vs. Black Magic, 1972, MEX [GF/Luchadors]
Santo vs. Blue Demon in Atlantis, 1969, MEX [GF/Luchadors]
Santo vs. Capulina, 1968, MEX [GF/Luchadors]
Santo vs. Dr. Death, 1973, MEX [GF/Luchadors]
Santo vs. Frankenstein's Daughter, 1971, MEX [GF/Luchadors]
Santo vs. the Evil Brain, 1962, MEX [GF/Luchadors]
Santo vs. the Ghost of the Strangler, 1963, MEX [GF/Luchadors]
Santo vs. the Headhunters, 1969, MEX [GF/Luchadors]
Santo vs. the Kidnappers, 1972, MEX [GF/Luchadors]
Santo vs. the Killers from Other... 1971, MEX [GF/Luchadors]
Santo vs. The King of Crime, 1961 or 1962, MEX [GF/Luchadors]
Santo vs. the Mafia of Vice, 1970, MEX [GF/Luchadors]
Santo vs. the Martian Invasion, 1966, MEX [GF/Luchadors]
Santo vs. the She-Wolves, 1972, MEX [GF/Luchadors]
Santo vs. the Strangler, 1963, MEX [GF/Luchadors]
Santo vs. the Terror Riders, 1970, MEX [GF/Luchadors]
Santo vs. the Terror Riders, 1970, MEX [GF/Luchadors]
Santo vs. the TV Killer, 1981, MEX [GF/Luchadors]
Santo vs. The Vampire Women, 1962, MEX [GF/Luchadors]
Santo vs. the Villains of the Ring, 1966, MEX [GF/Luchadors]
Santo vs. the Zombies, 1961 or 1962, MEX [GF/Luchadors]
Santo y Blue Demon Drácula... 1972, MEX [GF/Luchadors]
Santo y Blue Demon el Franky, 1973, MEX [GF/Luchadors]
Santo y Blue Demon contra los... 1969, MEX [GF/Luchadors]
Santo y Blue Demon en el mundo... 1969, MEX [GF/Luchadors]
Santo y Blue... bestias del terror, 1972, MEX [GF/Luchadors]
Santo y el tigresa en el aguila real, 1971, MEX [GF/Luchadors]
Santo: Infraterrestre, 2001, MEX [GF/Luchadors]
Santos vs la Tetona Mendoza, El, 2012, MEX [GF/Luchadors]
Saraba Kamen Rider DenO Final... 2008, JAP [GF/Kamen Rider]
Sarubaeju maisu: see Salvage Mice
Saskin Hafiye Kilink'e karsi, 1967, Turkey [GF/Diabolik S-Ks]
Satan's Satellites, 1958, USA
Satanik (SERIES) [GF/Diabolik S-Ks]
Satanik, 1968, ITL [GF/Diabolik S-Ks]
Savage Mutiny, 1953, USA, [GF/Jungle Jim]
Savages, The, 1966, considered lost, UK [GF/Dr Who]
Scooby-Doo & Batman: The Brave and the Bold, 2018, USA
Scooby-Doo! Mask of the Blue Falcon, 2012, USA
Scott Pilgrim vs. the World, 2010, USA
Sea Devils, The, 1972, UK [GF/Dr Who]
Secret of Mega Mindy, The, 2009, BE [GF/Mega Mindy]
Secret Wars, 1999, USA, [GF/Spider-Man: TAS]
Secuestro diabolico, 1957, MEX [GF/Luchadors]

Seeds of Death, The, 1969, UK [GF/Dr Who]
Seeds of Doom, The, 1976, UK [GF/Dr Who]
segno del coyote, Il, 1963, ITL/ES [GF/The Coyote]
segno di Zorro, Il, 1963, ITL [GF/Peplum]
Sen Aydinlatirsin Geceyi: see Thou Gild'st the Even
Sengottai Singam, 1958, IN, [GF/Tarzan]
señor Tormenta, El, 1963, MEX [GF/Luchadors]
Sensorites, The, 1964, UK [GF/Dr Who]
Sentai (SERIES) [GF/Super Sentai]
Sentô shôjo: Chi no tekkamen...: see Mutant Girls Squad
Sex Monster, 1963, MEX [GF/Luchadors]
sfida dei giganti, La, 1965, ITL [GF/Peplum]
Sgt. Kabukiman N.Y.P.D. (1990), 1990, USA
Shada, 1979/2017, UK [GF/Dr Who]
Shades of Zorro, 1962, ITL [GF/Peplum]
Shadow, The, 1940, USA
Shadow, The, 1994, USA
Shadow of the Bat, The, 1968, MEX [GF/Luchadors]
Shadow Returns, The, 1946, USA
Shadow Strikes, The, 1937, USA
Shadowman, 1974, FR [GF/Fantômas]
Shahenshah, 1988, IN
Shapeshifter, 1999, USA
Shazam!, 2019, USA
She-Wolves of the Ring, 1965, MEX [GF/Luchadors]
Sheena, 1984, USA
Sheman: Mistress of the Universe, 1988, PH
Shin angyo onshi: see Blade of the Phantom Master
Shin Kamen Rider: Prologue, 1992, JAP [GF/Kamen Rider]
Shin kyûseishu densetsu Hokuto... 2006, JAP [GF/FotNS]
Shin Zatōichi monogatari, 1963, JAP [GF/Zatōichi]
Shin Zatōichi monogatari: Kasama... 1973, JAP [GF/Zatōichi]
Shin Zatōichi monogatari: Oreta tsue, 1972, JAP [GF/Zatōichi]
Shin Zatōichi: Yabure! Tōjin-ken, 1971, JAP [GF/Zatōichi]
Shiva Ka Insaaf, 1985, IN
Shoktir Lorai, Unknown Year, Bengal
Shuriken Sentai Ninninger vs... 2016, JAP [GF/Super Sentai]
Si Darna at ang Impakta, 1963, PH [GF/Darna]
Si Darna at ang Planetman, 1969, PH [GF/Darna]
Sidekick, 2005, Canada
SideKicked, 2016, USA
Sign Gene, 2017, ITL
Sign of the Coyote, The, 1963, ITL/ES [GF/The Coyote]
Sign of Zorro, The, 1958, USA
Sign of Zorro, 1963, ITL [GF/Peplum]
Sihirbazlar Krali Mandrake...: see Mandrake vs. Killing
Silver Hawk, 2004, HK
Silver Masked Man, The, 1954, MEX [GF/Luchadors]
Silver Needle in the Sky, 1954, USA, [GF/Rocky Jones]
Silver Nemesis, 1988, UK [GF/Dr Who]
Sin City, 2005, USA

Sin City: A Dame to Kill For, 2014, USA
Sinister Squad, 2016, USA
Sins of the Fathers, The, 1999, USA, [GF/Spider-Man: TAS]
Six Million Dollar Man, The, 1973, USA
Six Million Dollar Man: The Solid Gold Kidnapping, 1973, USA
Six Million Dollar Man: Wine, Women and War, 1973, USA
Six Thousand Dollar Nigger, The,: see Super Soul Brother
Six Ultra Brothers vs. the... 1974, Thailand [GF/Ultraman]
Sixty Million Dollar Man, 1995, JAP
Sky High, 2005, USA
Slave Merchants, 1964, ITL [GF/Peplum]
Sleight, 2016, USA
Smile Precure! the Movie... 2012, JAP [GF/PreCure]
Smugglers, The, 1966, UK [GF/Dr Who]
Snakedance, 1983, UK [GF/Dr Who]
Snowmen, 2012, UK [GF/Dr Who]
Sogni mostruosamente proibiti, 1982, ITL
sombra blanca, La, 1963, MEX [GF/Luchadors]
sombra del murciélago, La, 1968, MEX [GF/Luchadors]
sombra vengadora v La mano negra, 1956, MEX [GF/Luchadors]
sombra vengadora, La, 1956, MEX [GF/Luchadors]
Somebody's Hero, 2011, USA
Son of Alma Grande, The, 1976, MEX [GF/Luchadors]
Son of Atlas in the Land of Fire, 1963, ITL [GF/Peplum]
Son of Batman, 2014, USA
Son of Hercules in the Land of Fire, 1963, ITL [GF/Peplum]
Son of Hercules, 1964, IN
Son of Samson, 1960, ITL [GF/Peplum]
Son of Tarzan, The, 1920, USA, [GF/Tarzan]
Son of the Mask, 2005, USA
Son of the White Mare, 1981, Hungary
Son of Zorro, 1947, USA
Son of Zorro, 1973, ITL [GF/Peplum]
Sontaran Experiment, The, 1975, UK [GF/Dr Who]
Source, The, 2002, USA
Space Museum, The, 1965, UK [GF/Dr Who]
Space Pirates, The, 1969, UK, incomplete [GF/Dr Who]
Space Sheriff (SERIES) [GF/Metal Hero Series]
Space Sheriff G. vs. Tokusou... 2017, JAP [GF/Metal Hero]
Space Sheriff G.: The Movie, 2012, JAP [GF/Metal Hero Series]
Space Sheriff Shaider, 1984, JAP [GF/Metal Hero Series]
Space Sheriff Shaider... 2014, JAP [GF/Metal Hero Series]
Space Sheriff Sharivan... 2014, JAP [GF/Metal Hero Series]
Space Soldiers Conquer the Universe, 1972, USA
Space Squad, 2017, JAP [GF/Metal Hero Series]
Space Squad: Space Sheriff... 2017, JAP [GF/Metal Hero]
Space Warriors 2000, 1985, USA
Spaceship to the Unknown, 1966, USA
Spaghettiman, 2016, USA
Sparks, 2013, USA
Spawn (animated trilogy): see Todd McFarlane's Spawn

Spawn, 1997, USA
Spearhead from Space, 1970, UK [GF/Dr Who]
Special, 2006, USA
Specials, The, 2000, USA
Spider Returns, The, 1941, USA
Spider Returns, The, 1943, USA
Spider Slayer, 1997, USA, [GF/Spider-Man: TAS]
Spider-Man: The Animated Series (SERIES) [GF]
Spider-Man, 2002, USA
Spider-Man 2, 2004, USA
Spider-Man 3, 2007, USA
Spider-Man Strikes Back, 1978, USA
Spider-Man vs. Doc Ock, 2004, USA, [GF/Spider-Man: TAS]
Spider-Man: Homecoming, 2017, USA
Spider-Man: Into the Spider-Verse, 2018, USA
Spider-Man: The Dragon's Challenge, 1979, USA
Spider-Man: Return of... 2002, USA, [GF/Spider-Man: TAS]
Spider-Man: Ultimate... 2002, USA, [GF/Spider-Man: TAS]
Spider-Man: The Venom Saga, 2005 [GF/Spider-Man: TAS]
Spider's Web The Spider's Web, 1938, USA
Spirit, The, 1987, USA
Spirit, The, 2008, USA
Split, 2016, USA
Spongebob 2: Sponge Out of Water, 2015, USA
Spy Smasher Returns, 1966, USA
Spy Smasher, 1942, USA
Spy Smasher, 1968, Turkey
Spy Smasher: Man of 7 Lives, 1970, Turkey
Squid Man, 2013, USA
Ssuperzam el invencible: see Superman the Invincible
Stan Lee's Mighty 7, 2014, USA
Star Jjangga II... 1990, South Korea [GF/Golden Bat]
Star Kid, 1997, USA
Star Warrior (2: The Final Battle): see Locke the Superman
Starfighters, 1992, MEX [GF/Luchadors]
State of Decay, 1980, UK [GF/Dr Who]
Steel, 1997, USA
Stolen Earth/Journey's End, 2008, UK [GF/Dr Who]
Stones of Blood, The, 1978, UK [GF/Dr Who]
Subjects, The, 2015, Australia
Suicide Mission, 1971, MEX [GF/Luchadors]
Suicide Squad, 2016, USA
Suicide Squad: Hell to Pay, 2018, USA
Suite PreCure the Movie: Take it... 2011, JAP [GF/PreCure]
Sun Makers, The, 1977, UK [GF/Dr Who]
Supā Hīrō Taisen Guranpuri... 2015, JAP [GF/Kamen Rider]
Süper adam Istanbul'da, 1972, Turkey
Super Badass, 1999, USA
Super Batman & Mazinger V Star Jjangga II... 1990, JAP
Super Bobrovs 2016, Russia
Super Boy, 1988, IN

Super Boy, 1998, Israel
Super Capers: The Origins of Ed and the... 2009, USA
Súper Cóndor, 2016, Peru
Super Demetrios, 2011, Greece
Super Detention, 2016, Canada
Super Force, 1990, USA
Super Fuzz, 1980, ITL
Super Gee, 1973, PH
Super Giant Vs the Satellites: see Attack from Space
Super Hero Central, 2004, USA
Super Hero Taisen GP... 2015, JAP [GF/Super Sentai]
Súper héroes galácticos... 2007, MEX [GF/Luchadors]
Super Inday and the Golden Bibe, 1988, PH
Super Inday and the Golden Bibe, 2010, PH
Super Inframan, The: see Infra-Man
Super Islaw and the Flying Kids, 1986, PH
Super K: see Kiara the Brave
Super Mouse and the Roborats, 1989, PH
Super Noypi, 2006, PH
Super Rider, The, 1975, TW [GF/Kamen Rider]
Super Sentai (SERIES) [GF]
Super Singh, 2017, IN
Super Soul Brother, 1978, USA
Super Stooges vs the Wonder Women, 1974, ITL
Super Task Force One, 2013, USA
Super wan-tu-tri, 1985, PH
Super-B, 2002, PH
Super, 2010, USA
SuperAndy, 1979, ITL
Superargo and the Faceless Giants, 1968, ITL
Superargo contro Diabolikus, 1966, ITL
Superbabies: Baby Geniuses 2, 2004, USA
SuperBob, 2015, UK
SuperBrother, 2009, Denmark
Superdragon vs. Supermen: see Bruce Lee Against Superman
superflaco, El, 1959, MEX [GF/Luchadors]
Supergirl, 1973, PH
Supergirl, 1984, USA
Superguy: Behind the Cape, 2000, USA
Superhelde, 2011, South Africa
Superhero, The, 2007, UK
Superhero Man, 2015, USA
Superhero Movie, 2008, USA
Superhuman-Machine... 1987, JAP [GF/Metal Hero Series]
Superior Ultraman 8 Brothers, 2008, JAP [GF/Ultraman]
Superjuffie, 2018, Netherlands
Superlopez, 2018, ES
Superman (Bangla), Unknown Year, Bengal
Superman Against the Will, 1993, Russia
Superman and the Mole-Men, 1951, USA
Superman, 1948, USA

Tarzan's New York Adventure, 1942, USA, [GF/Tarzan]
Tarzan's Peril, 1951, USA, [GF/Tarzan]
Tarzan's Revenge, 1938, USA, [GF/Tarzan]
Tarzan's Savage Fury, 1952, USA, [GF/Tarzan]
Tarzan's Secret Treasure, 1941, USA, [GF/Tarzan]
Tarzan's Three Challenges, 1963, USA, [GF/Tarzan]
Teen Titans Go! To the Movies, 2018, USA
Teen Titans: The Judas Contract, 2017, USA
Teen Titans: Trouble in Tokyo, 2006, USA
Teenage Alien Avengers: see Alien Arsenal
Teenage Mutant Ninja Turtles, 1990, USA
Teenage Mutant Ninja Turtles, 2014, USA
Teenage Mutant Ninja Turtles II: Secret of the Ooze, 1991, USA
Teenage Mutant Ninja Turtles III, 1993, USA
Teenage Mutant Ninja Turtles: Coming Out... Tour, 1990, USA
Teenage Mutant Ninja Turtles: Out of the Shadows, 2016, USA
Tensou Sentai Goseiger... 2011, JAP [GF/Super Sentai]
Tenth Planet, The, 1966, UK [GF/Dr Who]
Teribol dobol, 1975, PH [GF/Darna]
Terminus, 1983, UK [GF/Dr Who]
Terror of Rome Against Son of Hercules, 1964, ITL [GF/Peplum]
Terror of the Autons, 1971, UK [GF/Dr Who]
Terror of the Vervoids, 1986, UK [GF/Dr Who]
Terror of the Zygons, 1975, UK [GF/Dr Who]
Terror Toons, 2002, USA
terrore dei barbari, Il, 1959, ITL [GF/Peplum]
tesoro de Pancho Villa, El, 1957, MEX [GF/Luchadors]
Tetsuwan Tantei Robotack... 1999, JAP [GF/Metal Hero Series]
Thap Sa Ming Kla, 1962, Thailand [GF/The Red Eagle]
Thelma, 2017, Norway
They Call Me Jeeg, 2015, ITL
They Call Me Superseven, 2015, USA
Thor the Conqueror, 1983, ITL
Thor, 2011, USA
Thor: Ragnarok, 2017, USA
Thor: Tales of Asgard, 2011, USA
Thor: The Dark World, 2013, USA
Thou Gild'st the Even, 2013, Turkey
Three Avengers, 1964, ITL [GF/Peplum]
Three Dev Adam, 1973, Turkey
Three Doctors, The, 1973, UK [GF/Dr Who]
Three Fantastic Supermen, The, 1967, ITL, [GF/Three Supermen]
Three Inches, 2011, USA
Three Stooges Meet Hercules, The, 1962, USA
Three Supermen (aka 3 Fantastic Supermen, etc.) (SERIES) [GF]
Three S.men and Mad Girl, 1973, Turkey, [GF/Three Supermen]
Three S.men at Olympics, 1984, Turkey, [GF/Three Supermen]
Three S.men in Santo Domingo, 1986, ITL [GF/Three Supermen]
Three Supermen in the Jungle, 1970, ITL [GF/Three Supermen]
Three Supermen in Tokyo, 1968, ITL [GF/Three Supermen]
Three Supermen of the West, 1973, ITL [GF/Three Supermen]

Thundercats Ho! The Movie, 1987, USA
Thunderstorm: The Return of Thor, 2011, Canada
Tie chao ren: see Iron Superman
Tiger & Bunny: The Beginning Gekijouban, 2012, JAP
Tiger & Bunny: The Rising, 2014, JAP
Tiger Mask The Tiger Mask, 2013, JAP
Tigers of the Ring, 1960, MEX [GF/Luchadors]
tigres del ring, Los, 1960, MEX [GF/Luchadors]
Time And the Rani, 1987, UK [GF/Dr Who]
Time Meddler, The, 1965, UK [GF/Dr Who]
Time Monster, The, 1972, UK [GF/Dr Who]
Time of the Doctor, 2013, UK [GF/Dr Who]
Time Warrior, The, 1973, UK [GF/Dr Who]
Time-Flight, 1982, UK [GF/Dr Who]
Titanes en el ring, 1973, Argentina [GF/Luchadors]
TMNT, 2007, USA
Todd McFarlane's Spawn, 1997, USA
Todd McFarlane's Spawn 2, 1998, USA
Todd McFarlane's Spawn 3: The Ultimate Battle, 1999, USA
Toei Hero Big Gathering, 1994, JAP [GF/Metal Hero Series]
Tokumei Sentai Go-Busters... 2013, JAP [GF/Super Sentai]
Tokusô Robo Janpâson, 1993, JAP [GF/Metal Hero Series]
Tomb of the Cybermen, The, 1967, UK [GF/Dr Who]
Tômei ningen to hae otoko: see Invisible Human and Fly Man
Tomei Ningen: see Invisible Avenger (1954)
Tomica Hero: Rescue Force Explosive Movie, 2008, JP
Tonyong Bayawak, 1979, PH
Toofan (I), 1989, IN
Toofan, 1975, IN
Toofani Tarzan, 1937, IN, [GF/Tarzan]
Toonpur Ka Superrhero, 2010, IN
torito de Tepito, El, 1982, MEX [GF/Luchadors]
torito puños de oro, El, 1979, MEX [GF/Luchadors]
Tormenta en el ring, 1963, MEX [GF/Luchadors]
torneo de la muerte, El, 1960, MEX [GF/Luchadors]
Totò contro Maciste, 1962, ITL [GF/Peplum]
Tough Guys The Tough Guys, 2013, Norway
Toxic Avenger, The, 1984, USA
Toxic Avenger Part II, The, 1989, USA
Toxic Avenger Part III: Last Temptation of Toxie, 1989, USA
Toxic Avenger: The Musical, The, 2018, USA
Toxic Crusaders: The Movie, 1997, USA
tre spade di Zorro, Le, 1963, ITL [GF/Peplum]
Treasure of Dracula, The, 1968, MEX [GF/Luchadors]
Treasure of Montezuma, The, 1967, MEX [GF/Luchadors]
Treasure of Pancho Villa, The, 1957, MEX [GF/Luchadors]
Trial of Rocky Jones, The, 1954, USA, [GF/Rocky Jones]
Trial of the Incredible Hulk, The, 1989, USA
trionfo di Ercole, Il 1964, ITL [GF/Peplum]
trionfo di Maciste, Il, 1961, ITL [GF/Peplum]
Triumph of the Son of Hercules, 1961, ITL [GF/Peplum]

triunfo de los campeones justicieros, 1974, MEX [GF/Luchadors]

True Story of Barman and Droguin, The, 1991, MEX

Turbo Kid, 2015, Canada/NZ

Turbo: A Power Rangers Movie, 1997, USA

Turkish Batman (and Robin): see Yarasa adam-Bedmen

Turok: Son of Stone, 2008, USA

Turtles Forever, 2009, USA

Twelve Tasks of Asterix, The 1976, FR [GF/Asterix]

Twice Upon a Time, 2017, UK [GF/Dr Who]

Twin Dilemma, The, 1984, UK [GF/Dr Who]

Twisted Pair, 2018, USA

Two Doctors, The, 1987, UK [GF/Dr Who]

Üç süpermen olimpiyatl..., 1984, Turkey, [GF/Three Supermen]

Uchu Kaisoku-sen: see Invasion of the Neptune Men

Uchû Keiji Gyaban VS Tokusô... 2017, JAP [GF/Metal Hero]

Uchū Keiji Gyaban Za Mūbī, 2012, JAP [GF/Metal Hero Series]

Uchū Keiji Shaidā:... 1984, JAP [GF/Metal Hero Series]

Uchu Sentai Kyuranger... 2018, JAP [GF/Super Sentai]

Uchū Sentai Kyūrenjā Bāsasu... 2018, JAP [GF/Metal Hero]

Uchuu Keiji Shaider Next Gen., 2014, JAP [GF/Metal Hero]

Uchuu Keiji Sharivan Next Gen., 2014, JAP [GF/Metal Hero]

Ulisse contro Ercole, 1962, ITL [GF/Peplum]

última aventura del Zorro, La, 1969, ITL [GF/Peplum]

última lucha, La, 1959, MEX [GF/Luchadors]

Ultimate Avengers, 2006, USA

Ultimate Avengers II, 2006, USA

ultimo gladiatore, L', 1964, ITL [GF/Peplum]

Ultra Nyan: Extraordinary Cat... 1997, JAP [GF/Ultraman]

Ultra Q The Movie: Legend... 1990, JAP [GF/Ultraman]

Ultrachrist, 2003, USA

Ultraman (SERIES) [GF]

Ultraman Cosmos 2: The Blue Planet, 2002, JAP [GF/Ultraman]

Ultraman Cosmos vs. Ultraman... 2003, JAP [GF/Ultraman]

Ultraman Cosmos: The First Contact, 2001, JAP [GF/Ultraman]

Ultraman Geed The Movie... 2018, JAP [GF/Ultraman]

Ultraman Ginga S Movie Showdown... 2015, JAP [GF/Ultraman]

Ultraman Mebius & The Ultra Bros, 2006, JAP [GF/Ultraman]

Ultraman Orb The Movie... 2017, JAP [GF/Ultraman]

Ultraman Saga, 2012, JAP [GF/Ultraman]

Ultraman Story, 1984, JAP [GF/Ultraman]

Ultraman Tiga & UD & Ultraman... 1999, JAP [GF/Ultraman]

Ultraman Tiga & UD: Warriors... 1998, JAP [GF/Ultraman]

Ultraman Tiga: The Final Odyssey, 2000, JAP [GF/Ultraman]

Ultraman vs. Kamen Rider, 1993, JAP [GF/Kamen Rider]

Ultraman X The Movie:... 2016, JAP [GF/Ultraman]

Ultraman Zearth 2: Superhuman... 1997, JAP [GF/Ultraman]

Ultraman Zearth, 1996, JAP [GF/Ultraman]

Ultraman Zero The Movie: Super... 2010, JAP [GF/Ultraman]

Ultraman Zoffy: Ultra Warriors... 1984, JAP [GF/Ultraman]

Ultraman, 1979, JAP [GF/Ultraman]

ULTRAMAN, 2004, JAP [GF/Ultraman]

Ultraman: Great Monster Decisive... 1979, JAP [GF/Ultraman]

Ultraman: Monster Movie Feature, 1967, JAP [GF/Ultraman]

Ultraman: The Adventure Begins, 1987, JAP [GF/Ultraman]

Ultraviolet, 2006, USA

Ulysses Against Hercules, 1962, ITL [GF/Peplum]

Una rosa sobre el ring, 1973, MEX [GF/Luchadors]

Unbreakable, 2000, USA

Under the Lake/Before the Flood, 2015, UK [GF/Dr Who]

Underwater Menace, The, 1967, UK [GF/Dr Who]

Underworld, 1978, UK [GF/Dr Who]

Untama giru, 1989, JAP

Up, Up, and Away!, 2000, USA/Canada

Ursus and the Tartar Princess, 1961, ITL [GF/Peplum]

Ursus e la Ragazza Tartara, 1961, ITL [GF/Peplum]

Ursus il gladiatore ribelle, 1962, ITL [GF/Peplum]

Ursus Nella Terra di Fuoco, 1963, ITL [GF/Peplum]

Ursus Nella Valle dei Leoni, 1962, ITL [GF/Peplum]

Ursus, 1960, ITL [GF/Peplum]

Ursus, il terrore dei kirghisi, 1964, ITL [GF/Peplum]

Ursus, Son of Hercules, 1960, ITL [GF/Peplum]

Urufu gai: Moero ôkami-otoko: see Wolf Guy

Urutoraman (SERIES) [GF/Ultraman]

Urutora Q Za Mûbi... 1990, JAP [GF/Ultraman]

Urutora Roku Kyōdai... 1974, Thailand [GF/Ultraman]

Urutoraman Kaijū Daikessen, 1979, JAP [GF/Ultraman]

Urutoraman Kosumosu Tsū... 2002, JAP [GF/Ultraman]

Urutoraman Kosumosu V Urutoraman... 2003, JAP [GF/Ultraman]

Urutoraman Kosumosu: Za Fāsuto... 2001, JAP [GF/Ultraman]

Urutoraman Mebiusu ando Urutora... 2006, JAP [GF/Ultraman]

Urutoraman Sāga, 2012, JAP [GF/Ultraman]

Urutoraman Sutōrī, 1984, JAP [GF/Ultraman]

Urutoraman tai Kamen Raidā, 1993, JAP [GF/Kamen Rider]

Urutoraman Tiga & UD & Urutoraman... 1999, JAP [GF/Ultraman]

Urutoraman Tiga & UD: Hikari no... 1998, JAP [GF/Ultraman]

Urutoraman Tiga Za Fainaru Odesei, 2000, JAP [GF/Ultraman]

Urutoraman Yū Esu Ē, 1987, JAP [GF/Ultraman]

Urutoraman Zeasu Tsū: Chōjin... 1997, JAP [GF/Ultraman]

Urutoraman Zeasu, 1996, JAP [GF/Ultraman]

Urutoraman Zero THE MOVIE... 2010, JAP [GF/Ultraman]

URUTORAMAN, 2004, JAP [GF/Ultraman]

US Catman 2: Boxer Blow: see Catman in Boxer's Blow

US Catman: Lethal Track: see Catman in Lethal Track

V for Vendetta, 2005, USA

Valentine, 2016, ID

valle dell'eco tonante, La, 1964, ITL [GF/Peplum]

Valley of the Head Hunters, 1953, USA, [GF/Jungle Jim]

Valley of the Lions, 1962, ITL [GF/Peplum]

vampiras, Las, 1969, MEX [GF/Luchadors]

Vampire Assassin, 2005, USA

Vampirella, 1996, USA

Vampires, The, 1969, MEX [GF/Luchadors]

Vampires of Coyoacan, The, 1974, MEX [GF/Luchadors]

Vampiro, guerrero de la noche, 1993, MEX [GF/Luchadors]

vampiros de Coyoacán, Los, 1974, MEX [GF/Luchadors]
Van Helsing, 2004, USA
Vanaraja Karzan, 1938, IN, [GF/Tarzan]
Veer Abhimanyu, 2012, IN
Velayudham, 2011, IN
Vena and the Darnamo, 1954, USA, [GF/Rocky Jones]
vendetta di Ercole, La, 1960, ITL [GF/Peplum]
venganza de Huracán Ramirez, La, 1969, MEX [GF/Luchadors]
venganza de la sombra, 1962, MEX [GF/Luchadors]
venganza del Zorro, La, 1962, ITL [GF/Peplum]
Vengeance of the Red Mask, 1971, Turkey
Vengeance of Ursus, The, 1961, ITL [GF/Peplum]
Venom Saga, The, 1996, USA, [GF/Spider-Man: TAS]
Venom, 2018, USA
verdad de la lucha, La, 1990, MEX [GF/Luchadors]
verdadera... Barman y Droguin: see The True Story of Barmen
Veritas, Prince of Truth, 2007, MEX
Vigilante's Are Coming, The, 1936, USA
Vincent, 2014, FR
Visitation, The, 1982, UK [GF/Dr Who]
Vivian Volta, 1974, PH
Vixen: The Movie, 2017, USA
Volcano High School, 2001, South Korea
Volta, 2004, PH
Voodoo Tiger, 1952, USA, [GF/Jungle Jim]
Voyage of the Damned, 2007, UK [GF/Dr Who]
vuelta del Coyote, La, 1998, ES [GF/The Coyote]
Vuelven los campeones justicieros, 1972, MEX [GF/Luchadors]
Vulcan, Son of Giove, 1962, ITL [GF/Peplum]
Vulcano, figlio di Giove, 1962, ITL [GF/Peplum]
Walet merah, 1993, ID
Wander Woman si ako!, 1980, PH
Wanted, 2008, USA
Wapakman, 2009, PH
War Games, The, 1969, UK [GF/Dr Who]
War Machines, The, The, 1966, UK [GF/Dr Who]
War of the Infras, 1976, Taiwan
Warriors of the Deep, 1984, UK [GF/Dr Who]
Warriors of the Wind: see Nausicaa of the Valley of the Wind
Warriors' Gate, 1981, UK [GF/Dr Who]
WaSanGo: see Volcano High
Watchmen, 2009, USA
Web of Fear, The, 1968, UK [GF/Dr Who]
Web Planet, The, 1965, UK [GF/Dr Who]
Wheel in Space, The, 1968, UK [GF/Dr Who]
Whip, The, 1978, MEX
Whip Against Murderous Mummies, The, 1980, MEX
Whip Against Satan, The, 1979, MEX
White Shadow, The, 1963, MEX [GF/Luchadors]
Who Wants to Kill Jessie?, 1966, Czechoslovakia
Wild World of Batwoman, The, 1966, USA
Witch's Curse, The, 1962, ITL [GF/Peplum]

Witchblade, 2000, USA
Witches Attack, The, 1964, MEX [GF/Luchadors]
Wolf Guy, 1975, JAP
WolfCop (2014), 2014, Canada
Wolverine, The, 2013, USA
Wolverine and the X-Men (SERIES) [GF]
Woman Who Fell to Earth, 2018, UK [GF/Dr Who]
Wonder Vi, 1973, PH
Wonder Woman, 1974, USA
Wonder Woman, 2009, USA
Wonder Woman, 2017, USA
World Enough and Time... 2017, UK [GF/Dr Who]
Wraith, The, 1986, USA
Wrestle with the Devil, 2004, ES [GF/Luchadors]
Wrestling Women vs the Murder... 1969, MEX [GF/Luchadors]
Wrestling Women v Aztec Mummy, 1964, MEX [GF/Luchadors]
X-Men, 2000, USA
X-Men 2, 2003, USA
X-Men Origins: Wolverine, 2009, USA
X-Men: Apocalypse, 2016, USA
X-Men: Days of Future Past, 2014, USA
X-Men: First Class, 2011, USA
X-Men: The Last Stand, 2006, USA
Xing ying bu li: see Inseparable
Yarasa adam - Bedmen, 1973, Turkey
Yatterman, 2009, JAP
Yeom-lyeok: see Psychokinesis
Yes! Precure 5 GoGo! the Movie:... 2008, JAP [GF/PreCure]
Yes! PreCure 5 the Movie:... 2007, JAP [GF/PreCure]
Yilmayan seytan: see Deathless Devil
Yin doi hou hap zyun: see Heroic Trio 2: Executioners
You gui zi: see The Oily Maniac
Young Hercules, 1998, USA
Young-guwa hwang... 1992, South Korea [GF/Golden Bat]
Yuria Den, 2007, JAP [GF/FotNS]
Yûsei ôji: see Prince of Space
Zagor kara bela, 1971, Turkey
Zagor kara korsan'in hazineleri, 1971, Turkey
Zagor, 1970, Turkey
Zatōichi (Shintarô Katsu series) [GF]
Zatōichi abare tako, 1964, JAP [GF/Zatōichi]
Zatōichi abare-himatsuri, 1970, JAP [GF/Zatōichi]
Zatoichi, 2003, JAP
Zatoichi and the Chess Expert, 1965, JAP [GF/Zatōichi]
Zatoichi and the Chest of Gold, 1964, JAP [GF/Zatōichi]
Zatoichi and the Doomed Man, 1965, JAP [GF/Zatōichi]
Zatoichi and the Fugitives, 1968, JAP [GF/Zatōichi]
Zatoichi at Large, 1972, JAP [GF/Zatōichi]
Zatoichi Challenged, 1967, JAP [GF/Zatōichi]
Zatōichi chikemurikaidō, 1967, JAP [GF/Zatōichi]
Zatoichi Goes to the Fire Festival, 1970, JAP [GF/Zatōichi]
Zatōichi goyō-tabi, 1972, JAP [GF/Zatōichi]

Zatōichi hatashijō, 1968, JAP [GF/Zatōichi]

Zatoichi in Desperation, 1972, JAP [GF/Zatōichi]

Zatōichi jigoku-tabi, 1965, JAP [GF/Zatōichi]

Zatōichi kenka-daiko, 1968, JAP [GF/Zatōichi]

Zatōichi kenka-tabi, 1963, JAP [GF/Zatōichi]

Zatōichi kesshō-tabi, 1964, JAP [GF/Zatōichi]

Zatōichi kyōjō-tabi, 1963, JAP [GF/Zatōichi]

Zatoichi Meets One-Armed Swordsman, 1971, JAP [GF/Zatōichi]

Zatoichi Meets Yojimbo, 1970, JAP [GF/Zatōichi]

Zatōichi monogatari, 1962, JAP [GF/Zatōichi]

Zatōichi nidan-giri, 1965, JAP [GF/Zatōichi]

Zatōichi no uta ga kikoeru, 1966, JAP [GF/Zatōichi]

Zatoichi on the Road, 1963, JAP [GF/Zatōichi]

Zatōichi rōyaburi, 1967, JAP [GF/Zatōichi]

Zatōichi sakate-giri, 1965, JAP [GF/Zatōichi]

Zatōichi sekisho-yaburi, 1964, JAP [GF/Zatōichi]

Zatōichi senryō-kubi, 1964, JAP [GF/Zatōichi]

Zatōichi tekka-tabi, 1967, JAP [GF/Zatōichi]

Zatoichi The Fugitive, 1963, JAP [GF/Zatōichi]

Zatoichi the Outlaw, 1967, JAP [GF/Zatōichi]

Zatōichi to Yōjinbō, 1970, JAP [GF/Zatōichi]

Zatōichi umi o wataru, 1966, JAP [GF/Zatōichi]

Zatōichi, 1989, JAP [GF/Zatōichi]

Zatoichi: Darkness Is His Ally, 1989, JAP [GF/Zatōichi]

Zatoichi: The Last, 2010, JAP

Zatoichi's Cane Sword, 1967, JAP [GF/Zatōichi]

Zatoichi's Conspiracy, 1973, JAP [GF/Zatōichi]

Zatoichi's Flashing Sword, 1964, JAP [GF/Zatōichi]

Zatoichi's Pilgrimage, 1966, JAP [GF/Zatōichi]

Zatoichi's Revenge, 1965, JAP [GF/Zatōichi]

Zatoichi's Vengeance, 1966, JAP [GF/Zatōichi]

Zebraman 2: Attack on Zebra City, 2010, JAP

Zebraman, 2004, JAP

Zenitram, 2010, Argentina

Zero Kenshirō Den, 2008, JAP [GF/FotNS]

Zero: Legend of Kenshiro, 2008, JAP [GF/FotNS]

Zhong guo chao ren: see Infra-Man

Zokkomon, 2011, IN

Zoku Zatōichi monogatari, 1962, JAP [GF/Zatōichi]

Zombies of the Stratosphere, 1952, USA

Zombies of the Stratosphere, 1995, USA

Zoom, 2006, USA

Zoom, Zoom, Superman!, 1973, PH

Zorro (II), 1975, IN

Zorro (Italian series)[GF/Peplum]

Zorro Against Maciste, 1963, ITL [GF/Peplum]

Zorro alla corte d'Inghilterra, 1969, ITL [GF/Peplum]

Zorro alla corte di Spagna, 1962, ITL [GF/Peplum]

Zorro and Scarlet Whip Revealed!, 2010, USA/UK

Zorro and the Three Musketeers, 1963, ITL [GF/Peplum]

Zorro at the Court of ES, 1962, ITL [GF/Peplum]

Zorro cabalga otra vez, El: see Behind the Mask of Zorro

Zorro contro Maciste, 1963, ITL [GF/Peplum]

Zorro de Monterrey, El 1971, ITL [GF/Peplum]

Zorro e i tre moschettieri, 1963, ITL [GF/Peplum]

Zorro il cavaliere della vendetta, 1971, ITL [GF/Peplum]

Zorro il ribelle, 1966, ITL [GF/Peplum]

Zorro in the Court of England, 1969, ITL [GF/Peplum]

Zorro justiciero, El, 1969, ITL [GF/Peplum]

Zorro marchese di Navarra, 1969, ITL [GF/Peplum]

Zorro of Monterrey, 1971, ITL [GF/Peplum]

Zorro Rides Again, 1937, USA

Zorro Rides Again, 1959, USA

Zorro the Avenger, 1962, ITL [GF/Peplum]

Zorro the Avenger, 1969, ITL [GF/Peplum]

Zorro the Fox, 1968, ITL [GF/Peplum]

Zorro the Invincible, 1971, ITL [GF/Peplum]

Zorro the Rebel, 1966, ITL [GF/Peplum]

Zorro, el, 1968, ITL [GF/Peplum]

Zorro, Rider of Vengeance, 1971, ITL [GF/Peplum]

Zorro, the Avenger, 1959, USA

Zorro, the Navarra Marquis, 1969, ITL [GF/Peplum]

Zorro: Return to the Future, 2007, USA/UK

Zorro: The Gay Blade, 1981, USA

Zorro's Black Whip, 1944, USA

Zorro's Fighting Legion, 1939, USA

Zorro's Last Adventure, 1970, ITL [GF/Peplum]

Zorro's Latest Adventure, 1969, ITL [GF/Peplum]

ZsaZsa Zaturnnah Ze Moveeh, 2006, PH

Zyuden Sentai Kyoryuger... 2014, JAP [GF/Super Sentai]

PICTURE CREDITS

We have made our best efforts to identify and credit the owners of copyrights in and sources of the images used in this book. We apologise in advance for any unintentional omission, error or neglect, and if you consider that we have failed to give an appropriate acknowledgement or credit that was due, please get in touch with us and we will be pleased to put this right in the next edition.

10 *Abar:* Jos-To Productions/Mirror Releasing/Xenon Pictures/Frank Packard

12 *Ajooba:* Aasia Films Pvt. Ltd./Kinostudiya imeni M. Gorkogo/Shashi Kapoor/Gennadiy Vasilev

16 *Alyas Batman en Robin:* Regal Films/Tony Y. Reyes

20 *Astro Boy* (1964): Mushi/Rintaro/Yositake Suzuki/ Eiichi Yamamoto

25 *Avenger X* aka *Mister X*: Copercines, Cooperativa Cinematográfica/Terra Film/Sánchez Ramade/Piero Vivarelli

27 *Avengers: Endgame:* Marvel Studios/Walt Disney Pictures/Walt Disney Studios Motion Pictures/Anthony Russo/Joe Russo

30 *Batman* (1943): Columbia Pictures/Mill Creek Entertainment/Lambert Hillyer

32 *Batman Ninja:* DC Comics/DC Entertainment/ Warner Bros. Animation/Warner Home Video/Junpei Mizusaki

41 *Batman: The Movie:* William Dozier Productions/ Twentieth Century Fox/20th Century Fox Home Entertainment Japan/Warner Home Video/Leslie H. Martinson

44 *Big Man Japan:* Realproducts/Yoshimoto Kogyo Company/Magnet Releasing/Revolver Entertainment/ Hitoshi Matsumoto

47 *The Bionic Boy II* aka *Dynamite Johnson*: BAS Film Productions Inc./Bobby A. Suarez

50 *Black Scorpion:* Concorde-New Horizons/Concorde Pictures/Showtime Networks/Jonathan Winfrey

53 *Bobo Cop:* Regal Films/Tony Y. Reyes

57 *Bravestarr: The Movie*: Filmation Associates/BCI Eclipse/ Tom Tataranowicz

64 *Casshern*: Tatsunoko Production/Shochiku/ Progressive Pictures/Kazuaki Kiriya

69 *Chronicle*: Twentieth Century Fox/Davis Entertainment/20th Century Fox/Josh Trank

72 *The Crow*: Crowvision Inc./Edward R. Pressman Film/Entertainment Media Investment Corporation/ Jeff Most Productions/Miramax/Alex Proyas

78 *The Dark Knight*: Warner Bros./Legendary Entertainment/Syncopy/DC Comics/Christopher Nolan

83 *The Death of the Incredible Hulk*: B & B Productions/New World Television/NBC/20th Century Fox Home Entertainment/Bill Bixby

86 *Doc Savage*: The Man of Bronze: George Pal Productions/Warner Bros./Warner Home Video/ Michael Anderson

92 *Esupai* aka *Espy*: Toho Eizo Co./United Productions of America/Toho Company/Jun Fukuda

97 *Fantastic Man*: OctoArts Films/M-Zet Productions/

Tony Y. Reyes

100 *Flashman*: Zenith Cinematografica/Mino Loy

107 *Gatchaman*: Nippon Television Network/Nikkatsu/Toho Company/Tôya Satô

110 *The Golden Blaze*: 120dB Films/Aurum Digital Entertainment/DH Institute of Media Arts/Urban Entertainment Group/Bryon E. Carson

114 *The Guyver*: New Line Cinema/Moonstone Entertainment/Screaming Mad George/Steve Wang

119 *He-Man and She-Ra: The Secret fo the Sword*: Filmation Associates/Mattel/Atlantic Releasing Corporation/Arthur H. Nadel/Lou Scheimer

121 *Hercules in New York*: Filmpartners/Trimark/Arthur A. Seidelman

123 *The Heroic Trio*: China Entertainment Films Production/Paka Hill Productions/Echo Bridge Home Entertainment/Johnnie To

126 *Hunterwali*: Bombay Talkies Studio/Wada Movietone/Homi Wadia

131 *Infra-Man*: Shaw Brothers/Shan Hua

135 *Isputnik vs Darna*: Tagalog Ilang-Ilang Productions/Natoy B. Catindig

142 *James Batman*: Sampaguita Pictures/Kabayan Central Net Works/Artemio Marquez

145 *Judex* (1963): Comptoir Français du Film Production (CFFP)/Filmes Cinematografica/The Criterion Collection/Georges Franju

148 *Jumborg Ace & Giant* aka *Mars Men*: Sompote Sands

151 *Kick-Ass*: Marv Films/Plan B Entertainment/Lionsgate Home Entertainment/Universal/Matthew Vaughn

154 *Krrish 3*: Film Kraft/Redchillies.VFX/Rakesh Roshan

161 *Legend of the Fist: The Return of Chen Zhen* aka *Jing wu feng yun: Chen Zhen*: Media Asia Films/Enlight Pictures/Shanghai Film Media Asia/Basic Pictures/Andrew Lau

162 *Legends of the Superheroes*: Hanna-Barbera Productions/NBC/Warner Home Video

166 *Locke the Superman* aka *Chôjin Locke*: Nippon Animation Co./Shochiku/Hiroshi Fukutomi

168 *Logan*: Twentieth Century Fox/Marvel Entertainment/TSG Entertainment/Kinberg Genre/Hutch Parker Entertainment/Donners' Company/James Mangold

172 *The Machine Girl* aka *Kataude mashin gâru*: Fever Dreams/Nikkatsu/Noboru Iguchi

175 *The Mark of Zorro* (1940): Twentieth Century Fox/Rouben Mamoulian

178 *Maskeli Seytan*: Atadeniz Film

183 *Misfits of Science*: James D. Parriott Production/Universal Television/NBC

187 *Mysterious Doctor Satan* (1940): Republic Pictures Corporation/John English/William Witney

192 *Nick Fury: Agent of Shield*: Fury Productions Limited Partnership/National Studios Inc./20th Century Fox Television/Marvel Enterprises/Fox/Rod Hardy

197 *Paradox*: American World Pictures (AWP)/BRON Studios/Legacy Filmworks/Arcana Studio/Eagle Films/Brenton Spencer

199 *The Portuguese Falcon* aka *Capitão Falcão*: Individeos/NOS Audiovisuais/João Leitão

202 *The Pumaman*: ADM Films Department/La Deantir/ACE/Alberto De Martino

207 *Real Heroes*: Waltzing Penguin Productions/Keith Hartman

210 *The Return of the Six Million Dollar Man and the Bionic Woman*: Michael Sloan Productions/Universal Television/NBC/Ray Austin

214 *R iki-Oh: The Story of Riki/Ricky,* aka *Lik Wong*: Diagonal Pictures/Paragon Films Ltd./Media Asia Distribution/Ngai Choi Lam

218 *The Rocketeer*: Walt Disney Pictures/Touchstone Pictures/Silver Screen Partners IV/Gordon Company/Dark Horse Entertainment/Warner Bros./Joe Johnston

223 *Sin City*: Dimension Films/Troublemaker Studios/Dimension Films/Frank Miller/Robert Rodriguez

226 *Sleight*: Diablo Entertainment/WWE Studios/Sony/J.D. Dillard

229 *Spaghettiman*: Heckbender/Luminis Picturae/Uncork'd Entertainment/Mark Potts

232 *Spider-Man: Into the Spider-Verse*: Sony Pictures Entertainment/Columbia Pictures/Marvel Entertainment/Avi Arad Productions/Lord Miller/Pascal Pictures/Sony Pictures Animation/Columbia Pictures/Bob Persichetti/Peter Ramsey/Rodney Rothman

239 *Süper adam Istanbul'da*: Tual Film/Yavuz Yalinkiliç

241 *Super Fuzz* aka *Poliziotto superpiù*: El Pico S.A./TVI/Transcinema/Columbia-EMI-Warner/Sergio Corbucci

244 *Superargo and the Faceless Giants*: G.V. Cinematografica/Società Europea Cinematografica/Ízaro Films/Paolo Bianchini

247 *Superbob*: Grain Media/Jonescompany Productions/thefyzz/The Fyzz Facility Film Five/Dragon Root Securities/Goldcrest Films International/Signature Entertainment/Jon Drever

249 *Superjuffie*: PV Pictures/Entertainment One

250 *Superman* (1978): Warner Bros./Dovemead

Films/Film Export A.G./International Film Production/
Richard Donner

255 *Supersonic Man*: Almena Films/Filmayer/Juan
Piquer Simón

256 *The SuperVips* aka *Vip, mio fratello superuomo*:
EastWest Entertainment/Videogram/Bruno Bozzetto

260 *Teenage Mutant Ninja Turtles* (1990): 888
Productions/Golden Harvest Company/Limelight
Entertainment/Mirage Productions/New Line Cinema/
Northshore Investments Ltd./Steve Barron

263 *Thelma*: Motlys/Memento/Film i Väst/Le Pacte/
Filmpool Nord/Snowglobe Films/B-Reel Films/Don't
Look Now/Norwegian Film Institute/Det Danske
Filminstitut/SFI/Copenhagen Film Fund/Joachim Trier

267 *The Toxic Avenger*: Troma Entertainment/Michael
Herz/Lloyd Kaufman

274 *Untama Giru*: Parco Co. Ltd./Go Takamine

278 *V for Vendetta*: Warner Bros./Virtual Studios/Silver
Pictures/Anarchos Productions/Warner Bros./Studio
Babelsberg/Medienboard Berlin-Brandenburg/DC
Comics/James McTeigue

282 *Wanted*: Universal Pictures/Spyglass
Entertainment/Relativity Media/Marc Platt Productions/
Kickstart Productions/Top Cow Productions/Ringerike
Zweite Filmproduktion/Bazelevs Production/Timur
Bekmambetov

285 *Watchmen*: Warner Bros./Paramount Pictures/
Legendary Entertainment/Lawrence Gordon
Productions/DC Comics/Zack Snyder

289 *X-Men: Days of Future Past*: Twentieth Century
Fox/Marvel Entertainment/TSG Entertainment/Bad
Hat Harry/Donners' Company/Ingenious Media/Down
Productions/Bryan Singer

291 *Yatterman* aka *Yattâman*: Horipro/J Storm/
Nikkatsu/NTV/OLM/Shochiku/Tatsunoko Production/
VAP/YTV/Takashi Miike

295 *Zebraman 2: Attack on Zebra City* aka *Zeburâman:
Zebura Shiti no gyakushû*: Central Arts/Toei Company/
Tokyo Broadcasting System/Zebraman2 Film Partners/
Takashi Miike

296 *Zorro's Fighting Legion*: Republic Pictures
Corporation/John English, William Witney

301 *Captain Barbell kontra Captain Bakal*: Cirio H.
Santiago Film Organization/People's Pictures/Ruben
Rustia

303 *Darna Ajaib*: PT Cancer Mas Film/Liliek Sudjio

304 *Kilink Istanbul'da*: Atadeniz Film/Yilmaz Atadeniz

309 *Ôgon batto* aka *Il ritorno di Diavolik*: Toei Tokyo/
Hajime Satô

314 *Hercules* aka *Le fatiche di Ercole* (1958): Embassy
Pictures/Galatea Film/O.S.C.A.R./Urania Film/Pietro
Francisci

317 *The Red Eagle* aka *Chao Insee* (1963):
thaiworldview.com/Neramit

319 *The Tale of Zatoichi Continues* aka *Zoku Zatōichi
monogatari*: Daiei Motion Picture Company/Kazuo
Mori

AUTHOR'S NOTE

It's rare to have an opportunity to peel all the way to the core of a genre onion like this: past the skin of Hollywood blockbusters, through the outer layers of indie hits and right down into the soggy mush well beyond ancient serials and popular foreign oddities.

The big surprise has been to discover how diverse the movie superhero can be; what they look like to different communities, the evolving role they fulfilled throughout history, and how much they reflect the cultures and eras within which they were formed. I've talked about this in the introduction so will keep it brief here, but I urge audiences to investigate the diversity of this genre.

ACKNOWLEDGEMENTS

Thank you to my wife, Emma. Also Simon Hill, Ben Turner, Todd Stadtman, Matt Gibson, Professor William Fulford, Andrew Leavold, Jeff Banning, Mort Todd, Kevin Ward and all at Graphius, Justin at Stonewall, Kim Grace, Cary Moses, Gupta Singh, Jerome Ryan, Blag Money, Nic Adams, Judy and Terry Fellinghman, Gwen and Brian Beare, Blaze, Alison Bowery, Carlo Martinez, Justin Prince, Chris Wilson, Laura Hale and Michael Sopkiw. My sincere apologies to anyone I have forgotten.